THE JACOBEAN AND
CAROLINE STAGE

THE JACOBEAN
AND
CAROLINE STAGE

BY

GERALD EADES BENTLEY

VOLUME VII

APPENDIXES TO VOLUME VI

GENERAL INDEX

OXFORD
AT THE CLARENDON PRESS
1968

Oxford University Press, Ely House, London W. 1

GLASGOW NEW YORK TORONTO MELBOURNE WELLINGTON
CAPE TOWN SALISBURY IBADAN NAIROBI LUSAKA ADDIS ABABA
BOMBAY CALCUTTA MADRAS KARACHI LAHORE DACCA
KUALA LUMPUR HONG KONG TOKYO

PRINTED IN GREAT BRITAIN

CONTENTS

VOLUME VII

APPENDIXES TO VOLUME VI

76042

APPENDIX A

LENTEN PERFORMANCES IN THE JACOBEAN AND CAROLINE THEATRES

THE observation of Lent in the London theatres during the Jacobean and Caroline period was less strict than in Elizabethan times, but it is not easy to make out precisely what the practice was.

Even under Queen Elizabeth the restrictions seem to have varied from time to time. An order of the Privy Council on 13 March 1578/9 had forbidden all playing in Lent (*Acts of the Privy Council*, xi. 73–74), and Sir Edmund Chambers notes that Henslowe's records of performances of the Admiral's men show long intervals for Lent in 1595 and 1596. But in 1597 the company played a good part of the season before Easter (Chambers, *E.S.* ii. 141–2), and in 1592 Lord Strange's men scarcely observed Lent at all. (Ibid. i. 315–16.) In the years 1600, 1601, and 1604 Council orders seem to reflect a strict enforcement of Lenten closing. (Ibid.) But again there were wholesale violations of the prohibition in 1615, for on 29 March of that year representatives of all four of the leading London companies were called before the Privy Council for presuming to play despite the order of the Master of the Revels during 'this prohibited time of Lent'. (*M.S.C.* i. 372.)

After 1615 I find no example of a strictly enforced prohibition of playing during Lent.[1] Indeed, in January 1618/19 certain of the inhabitants of the district of Blackfriars, in a petition of complaint against the private theatre in their precinct, recited the nuisances caused by the theatre, and concluded: 'Theise inconveniences fallinge out almost everie daie in the winter tyme (not forbearinge the tyme of Lent) from one or twoe of the clock till sixe att night....' (*M.S.C.* i. 92.) Perhaps the fact that the first

---

[1] The annual Privy Council order about Lent, regularly issued from 1616 to 1627, makes no mention of theatres or players or any other restrictions except those concerning butchering and meat-eating. There are numerous records of actions concerning Lenten offenders, 1616 to 1625, but none involves violations other than those concerned with meat-eating. See *Acts of the Privy Council*, volumes for 1615/16 to 1627/8.

signature to this petition is that of William Gouge, the Puritan
minister of St. Anne's, Blackfriars, should prompt one to expect
exaggeration in the statements about the frequency of the inconveniences caused by the theatre. On the other hand, a number of
other statements of comparable date indicate that the theatres were
usually under some kind of Lenten restriction. Later allusions to
the Lenten dejection of the players are not unlike the statement
by Stephens in 1615, in his character of 'A common Player': '. . .
when aduersities come, they come together: For Lent and
Shrouetuesday be not farre asunder, then he is deiected daily and
weekely'. (*Essayes and Characters*, V$_7$v–V$_8$.) For example, one of
the poems on the death of the great actor, Richard Burbage,
13 March 1618/19 (i.e. during Lent) has the lines:

> And you, his sad companions, to whom Lent
> Becomes more lenten yn this accident,
> Henceforth your wavering flag no more hang out.
> Play now noe more at all . . .
>   (C. C. Stopes, *Burbage and Shakespeare's Stage* [1913], p. 119.)

Ten years later writers are still assuming that their readers will be
familiar with the Lenten troubles of the players, for John Earle
writes in one of his characters, ' "24. *A Player*", . . . Shrouetuesday hee feares as much as the Baudes, and Lent is more damage
to him then the Butcher.' (*Micro-cosmographie* [1628], E$_7$v–E$_8$.) In
the following year Francis Lenton noted the same deprivation
as it applied to the spectators in his observations on the frivolities
of the young Inns of Court man:

> Your Theaters hee daily doth frequent
> (Except the intermitted time of Lent)
>   (*The Young Gallants Whirligigg* [1629], B$_4$.)

William Prynne, in his *Histriomastix*, published in 1633 but
written, at least in part, several years earlier, spoke of a recent
change: 'Thirdly, there are none so much addicted to Stage-playes,
but when they goe unto places where they cannot have them, or
when as they are suppressed by publike authority, (as in *times of
pestilence*, and in Lent till now of late) can well subsist without
them. . . .' (Ggggg$_4$v.)

All these allusions to the unhappiness of the players and the
deprivation of the spectators during Lent show clearly that in
the time of James I and Charles I the London theatres were not
open for business as usual during the weeks before Easter, in
spite of the fact that there are no records of absolute prohibition

like those of 1579 and 1601. Prynne, however, indicates that
there had recently been a change, and he seems to imply some
liberalization of the regulations. A century and a half later
Edmond Malone, in his enlarged history of the stage, indicated
the probable form which the relaxation of the prohibition took:

> Plays in the time of King James the First, (and probably after-
> wards,) appear to have been performed every day at each theatre
> during the winter season, except in the time of Lent, when they were
> not permitted on the sermon days, as they were called, that is, on
> Wednesday and Friday; nor on the other days of the week, except by
> special license: which however was obtained by a fee paid to the
> Master of the Revels.
>
> .   .   .   .   .
>
> These dispensations [i.e. for playing in Lent] did not extend to the
> sermon-days, as they were then called; that is, Wednesday and
> Friday in each week.
>
> After Sir Henry Herbert became possessed of the office of Master
> of the Revels, fees for permission to perform in Lent appear to have
> been constantly paid by each of the theatres. (*Variorum*, iii. 151–3,
> 65 n. 7, 66.)

Malone did not, unfortunately, document his assertions; but
scattered quotations from Sir Henry Herbert's manuscripts
extracted by others, or used by Malone in other contexts, are
helpful. Several passages record dispensations to the players and
managers for Lent. For example:

> [Received] of the King's players for a *lenten dispensation*, the
> other companys promising to doe as muche, 44s. March 23 1616'
>
> Of John Hemminges, in the name of the four companys, for tolera-
> tion in the holy-dayes, 44s. January 29, 1618. *Extracts from the office-
> book of Sir George Buc*. MSS. Herbert. (*Variorum*, iii. 65 n. 7.)
>
> .   .   .   .   .
>
> For the Kings company.
> Mr Hemings brought mee for Lent this 1 Apr. 1624–2^{li}
>
> .   .   .   .   .
>
> For a daye in Lent from the Cockpitt companye when their tyme
> was out 10: Mr Biston sent mee for Lent by Mr Blagrave in the name of
> the company this 5 April 2^{li}'

---

[1] These two items are taken from an independent transcript of Sir Henry
Herbert's manuscript, probably made by Craven Ord, and now pasted into
various volumes of Halliwell-Phillipps's Scrap-Books at the Folger Library.
The first extract is from the volume labelled *Kemp*, p. 142, the second from
Appliances, p. 127.

From Mr. Blagrave, in the name of the Cockpit company, for this Lent, this 30th March, 1624. £2.0.0.

March 20, 1626. From Mr. Hemminges, for this Lent allowanse, £2.0.0. *MSS. Herbert.* (*Variorum*, iii. 66 n.)

After the Restoration, when Sir Henry was endeavouring to maintain himself in his old office with all the old rights and fees, he asserted in a petition to the Lord Chancellor and the Lord Chamberlain that among his regular fees was 'For Lent Fee . . . [£3.0.0.]'. (*Variorum*, iii. 266.) The inflation is characteristic of Herbert's Restoration petitions, but in other instances scattered records usually show that he did exercise before the wars the rights he claimed after the Restoration.

One final example bears on the problem of the allowance of acting during Lent in the Caroline period. We know from Malone's extracts from Herbert's Office Book that in the midst of the long plague-closing from May 1636 to October 1637 (see above, ii. 661–5) the theatres were opened for a week near the end of February 1636/7. But the relation of Lent to this short playing period is indicated only by the Earl of Strafford's London corre-spondent, George Garrard, who wrote the Earl as follows:

Upon a little Abatement of the Plague, even in the first Week of *Lent*, the Players set up their Bills, and began to play in the *Black-Fryars* and other Houses. But my Lord of *Canterbury* quickly reduced them to a better Order; for, at the next Meeting at Council his Grace complained of it to the King, declared the Solemnity of *Lent*, the Unfitness of that Liberty to be given, both in respect of the Time and the Sickness, . . . concluding that if his Majesty did not command him to the contrary, he would lay them by the Heels, if they played again . . . [The Lord Chamberlain thereupon objected to the Archbishop's interference] . . . So the King put an End to the Business by command-ing my Lord Chamberlain that they should play no more. (*Straf-forde's Letters*, ii. 56.)

These surviving records seem to me generally to confirm Malone's understanding that so long as the managers paid the proper fee to the Master of the Revels the theatres could remain open during Lent for four days each week except Holy Week.

There is further confirmation in Herbert's Office Book (though Malone did not note it in this connexion) in some of the records of the French troupe which visited London in 1635 during and after Lent (11 February to 29 March). The French players are first noted on 15 and 17 February 1634/5, when they performed before the Queen at Denmark House and then before both the King and Queen at the Cockpit in Whitehall. But of course these

performances at court would not have been governed by the Lenten restrictions applicable to the London theatres. Sir Henry Herbert records:

This day being Friday, and the 20 of the same monthe [February], the kinge tould mee his pleasure, and commanded mee to give order that this Frenche company should playe the too sermon daies in the weeke, during their time of playinge in Lent, and in the house of Drury-lane, where the queenes players usually playe.

The kings pleasure I signifyed to Mr. Beeston [manager of the Phoenix in Drury Lane], the same day who obeyd readily.

The house-keepers are to give them by promise the benefit of their interest for the two days of the first weeke.

They had the benefitt of playinge on the sermon daies, and gott two hundred pounds at least; besides many rich clothes were given them.

They had freely to themselves the whole weeke before the weeke before Easter, which I obtaynd of the king for them. (*Variorum,* iii. 121.)

These records of the French visitors of 1635 fit precisely the interpretation already made that the acting dispensations which the London companies bought gave them four days a week for playing, but not the two sermon days in any week of Lent and not Holy Week. Since these were the days given to the French players for their performances, it is not surprising that Christopher Beeston 'obeyd readily', for the days he was graciously granting were days on which Queen Henrietta's company could not have performed at the Phoenix in any case.

So far Malone's understanding of Lenten regulations in the Jacobean and Caroline period seems confirmed. On the other hand, his understanding that it was for *plays* that the theatres were open during Lent is not so well sustained by the surviving records. Malone himself noted exceptions to dramatic fare in the Office Book:

The managers however did not always perform plays during that season. Some of the theatres, particularly the Red Bull and the Fortune, were then let to prize-fighters, tumblers, and rope-dancers, who sometimes added a Masque to the other exhibitions. These facts are ascertained by the following entries:

1622. 21 Martii. For a prise at the Red-Bull, for the howse; the fencers would give nothing. 10s. *MSS. Astley.*

From Mr. Gunnel, [Manager of the Fortune,] in the name of the dancers of the ropes for Lent, this 15 March, 1624. £1.0.0. (*Variorum,* iii. 66 n.)

There were other Herbert records of a like nature and dated during Lent, which Malone found no occasion to copy, but which are known from the extracts of others who saw the manuscript of the Office Book. For example:

For the Kings company.

Shankes Ordinary written by Shankes himself this 16 March 1623. (Halliwell-Phillipps Scrap-Books, *Kemp*, p. 127.)

Reced of Mr Lowins for allowinge of a Dutch vaulter att their house 18 ffeb: 1630.[1]

From Vincent—For dancing on the Ropes this Lent at ye Fortune by Blagrave 7 March 1634—2li (Halliwell-Phillipps, *Fortune*, p. 46.)

It is clear from these records that the activities which took place in the specially licensed London theatres on their allowed days in Lent were not always performances of plays. Were they ever plays? Was Malone mistaken in his reading of the accounts in Sir Henry Herbert's Office Book? W. J. Lawrence contended that he was. In an essay entitled 'The Origin of the Substantive Theatre Masque' he declared that

playing had long been rigorously prohibited during the period of abstinence, but . . . a loophole of escape from an intolerable position had been found. Finding that exhibitions of fencing and acrobatics gave little offence in the close time, the Master of the Revels availed of the circumstance to extract an extra fee and make things a trifle less stringent for the players. Though the proceeds of Lenten letting were the prerogative of the theatre owners, they doubtless shared them, by arrangement, with the players. . . . The secret is out. After acting in Lent had been regularly prohibited for some years in James's time, the players got out of their difficulty by letting their theatres during Lent to foreign mountebanks. (*Pre-Restoration Stage Studies* [1927], pp. 329–30.)

Lawrence thought that a further step in the development of non-dramatic entertainment at the theatres during Lent was the evolution of what he called the 'substantive theatre masque', of which *The World Tossed at Tennis*, *The Sun's Darling*, and *Microcosmus* are examples. His argument is the familiar combination of winning exuberance, *non sequiturs*, careless mis-statements of fact, irrelevancies, sweeping generalizations from slight evidence, and triumphant conclusion. Nevertheless, the account includes, as usual with Lawrence, shrewd observations, and cannot be ignored. One may ask, therefore, what evidence not cited by Lawrence exists to show that the Jacobean and Caroline

[1] Halliwell-Phillipps Scrap-Books, *Lowin*, p. 19. See also above, vi. 194–5.

theatres, though allowed to remain open a good part of the time
during Lent, did not present plays then?

The various previously noted laments about the poor players
are inconclusive, for the acknowledged prohibition during Holy
Week and on Wednesdays and Fridays in the preceding five and
a half weeks would have involved nearly fifty per cent. reduction
in playing time, and a lamentable shrinking of income, even if
the companies had performed their usual plays on *all* the per-
mitted days. The licences for new or newly revived plays which
have come down from Herbert's records during his period of
activity, 1622–42, suggest restricted activities, but they do not
support the assumption of a complete absence of plays in Lent.

There are nearly 140 of Herbert's dated licensing records now
known, and it is notable, to be sure, that fewer of them fall in
Lent than in any other period of the year. It is perfectly clear
that Lent was not a usual time for the production of new plays, as
January, May, June, October, and November clearly were. (See
above, i. 101–3.) Yet we know of records of performance licences
for five pieces granted by the Master of the Revels during Lent:
Dekker and Ford's *The Sun's Darling*, for the Lady Elizabeth's
men at the Phoenix, 3 March 1623/4; John Shank's piece called
Shank's Ordinary, for the King's men, 16 March 1623/4; Massinger's
Emperor of the East, for the King's men at Blackfriars and the
Globe, 11 March 1630/1; William Heminges's *Coursing of a Hare,
or The Madcap*, for the company at the Fortune, some time in
March 1632/3; and Henry Glapthorne's *The Hollander, or Love's
Trial*, for Queen Henrietta's company at the Phoenix, on 12
March 1635/6. (See above, iii. 459–61; v. 1050–1; iv. 777–81;
542–3; 482–3.)

Of the five one might argue for Lawrence that *The Sun's
Darling* is not a play but one of his 'substantive theatre masques',
and therefore a proper Lenten theatre production. But though
The Sun's Darling is allegorical, so is *A Game at Chess*, and that
piece was produced with sensational success at the Globe six
months later. (See above, iv. 870–9.) *Shank's Ordinary* is more to
Lawrence's purpose, for the actor and jig-dancer John Shank is
known as a writer only for his songs and jigs, and *Shank's Ordinary* may have been some special sort of Lenten entertainment.
(See above, ii. 562–7 and v. 1049–51.) Even for Massinger's
Emperor of the East Lawrence might present a weak case by con-
tending that it was one of the author's plays written in the
plague year of 1630, during which we have no Herbert licences,
and was therefore part of an accumulation of unacted plays

prepared by the prompter, in an idle period, for production later. (See above, iv. 755 and 777–81.)

Though the cases I have made to reconcile the Lenten acting licences of *The Sun's Darling* and *The Emperor of the East* with Lawrence's hypothesis that no plays were acted in the London theatres during Lent do not strike me as very impressive, I can make none at all for William Heminges's *The Coursing of a Hare, or The Madcap*, licensed for the Fortune some time in March 1632/3 [all but the first five days of March fell in Lent], or for Glapthorne's *The Hollander*, licensed ten days after the beginning of Lent in 1635/6. Lawrence's entertaining reconstruction of the Lenten practices of the players must therefore be rejected.

I think one must say, then, that an examination of the extant entries from Sir Henry Herbert's Office Book seems to indicate that in the Jacobean and Caroline period the theatres were theoretically closed during Lent, but that upon the payment of a fee to the Master of the Revels the prohibition was enforced only on Wednesdays and Fridays and during Holy Week; and that even on those days an exception was made at least once—in the case of the French players at the Phoenix in 1635. On the days when the theatres were open in Lent the entertainment often consisted of fencing, rope dancing, and vaulting, at least at the Fortune, the Red Bull, and the Globe. Though there were performances of plays, such performances were far fewer than at other times in the spring and autumn, and accordingly the earnings of the players were sufficiently reduced to make Lent an unpopular season with them.

An analysis of the *Annals* for the period (see below, vii. 16 ff.) roughly confirms this impression. Notable is the diary of Sir Humphrey Mildmay, the most consistent theatre-goer among private men of the time of whom we have record. Sir Humphrey records in the period of his diary and accounts (January 1631/2 to December 1641) some fifty-four visits to plays, exclusive of court performances. Only two of the visits fell in the period of Lent, though it must be noted that Sir Humphrey was often out of town at this season. The two entries are:

1633/4 20 March	'To a base play att the Cocke pitt' 'this after noone J went to the Cocke pitt to a playe wth Bor An^th: a fooleishe one'
1634/5, 19 February	'To a play, & to Supper'. . . .

(See above, ii. 676–7.)

Other Lenten activities found in the *Annals* mostly pertain to court activities or to licences, but play performances outside the

court are indicated or suggested in March 1621/2, when John Gill was wounded by an actor on the stage of the Red Bull (see above, i. 166–7); on 16 February 1634/5, when Herbert committed Cromes to the Marshalsea for lending the Salisbury Court players the church robe they used in a production in their theatre, presumably within the previous three or four days (see above, i. 294); in February and March 1634/5, when John Greene saw six plays performed at the Blackfriars and the Phoenix (*English Historical Review*, xliii [1928], 386; no specific days are recorded, but all but ten days of these two months fell in Lent); and 24–28 February 1636/7, when the companies all acted for five days between plague-closings. (See above, ii. 662.)

These activities are not extensive, and some of them do not necessarily indicate Lenten performances, but together they seem to me to refute Lawrence's contention, and to corroborate the other evidence that in the Jacobean and Caroline period the London theatres did present a reduced number of plays, as well as variety turns, four days a week during the first five and a half weeks of Lent.

APPENDIX B

SUNDAY PERFORMANCES
IN THE LONDON THEATRES

THERE has been a certain amount of discussion of Sunday performances of plays—perhaps because some of the Puritans speak
rather violently on the subject and have sometimes been taken too
literally. It may be convenient if I state first my conclusions, and
then such relevant facts as I have found. I find no clear evidence
of Sunday performances in the London theatres in this period.
Sunday performances of masques and plays at court were common,
but not so invariable as the Puritans asserted, and there appear
to have been a few years of Sabbath observance even at court
after the statute of 1 Car. I, c. 1.

In the first place one would assume that King James's proclamation of 7 May 1603 continued in force unless the evidence or allega-
tions indicated the contrary. This proclamation was explicit:

And for that we are informed that there hath beene heretofore
great neglect in this kingdome of keeping the Sabbath-day: For
better observing of the same, and avoyding all impious prophanation,
we do straightly charge and commaund, that no Beare-bayting,
Bul-bayting, Enterludes, Common Playes, or other like disordered
or unlawful Exercises, or Pastimes, be frequented, kept, or used at
any time hereafter upon the Sabbath-day. (Chambers, *E.S.* iv. 335.)

Perhaps the most notable evidence that this proclamation was
enforced and that the theatres were closed on Sundays under the
first two Stuarts is the absence of statements to the contrary by
the sabbatarian Puritans who had attacked Sunday performances
in Elizabeth's time, and who, in the reign of Charles I, are articu-
late enough about Sabbath-breaking at court. Positive evidence
indeed is supplied in 1615 by J[ohn] G[reen] in his *Refutation of
the Apology for Actors*, when he challenges Heywood: *'If Plaies
do so much good, why are they not suffered on the Sabbath, a day
select wherein to doe good.'* (H₃ᵛ.) I do not find that even William Prynne asserts that the London theatres were open on
Sundays.

In the *Annals* of Jacobean and Caroline theatrical affairs (see
below) I have listed records of performances at the public and

private theatres in London. Only two of these performances might be thought to fall on Sundays,[1] and I think they probably did not. For a period of five years, 1628–33, the King's men turned over to Sir Henry Herbert their profits on the second day of one revival in the winter and one in the summer. (See above, i. 23–24.) Two of the eleven records fall on Sundays (22 November 1629 and 12 June 1631), and they might be thought to constitute evidence of Sunday performances in the theatres of the King's men. It seems to me more likely, however, that Herbert recorded the day he received payment, not the day of the performance from which the payment was derived. In these particular accounts it is the money received which is important for him, not the play, since they were all old plays that had been licensed before, but the amounts of payment fluctuated. In the 1629 records he twice said 'being brought me by Blagrave', and in 1630, 1631, 1632, and 1633, he says 'Received of . . .' or 'R. of . . .'. (*Herbert*, pp. 43–44.) Probably the performance itself was on the previous day, but we cannot be sure.

If these two records are allowed to indicate dates of payment and not dates of performance, then I have found no evidence that the London theatres were open on Sundays. Sir Edmund Chambers pointed out that 'It is probable that the proclamation against Sunday plays, issued by James I as one of the first acts of his reign, did no more, so far as London was concerned, than reaffirm an already accepted practice.'[2] (*E.S.* i. 315.) As evidence of the continuance of Sunday abstinence he notes that twelve years later, when the Baskerviles made their agreement with Queen Anne's players in June 1615, the actors agreed to pay 1*s*. 8*d*. per day 'for every of sixe daies in the weeke wherin they should play'. A six-day week was still taken as normal at the Red Bull theatre eight years later. In his Chancery Bill of 25 October 1623, concerned with shares in the Red Bull, Thomas Woodford says that among other profits due to his eighteenth share was 'Three pence profit a day amounting to Eighteene pence a weeke . . .'. (Hotson, pp. 327–8.) I have found no reason to think that there

---

[1] W. J. Lawrence asserted, *Englische Studien*, xlviii (1914–15), 227 n. 3, that the French players acted at the Red Bull on Sunday in 1629. He has mistaken Herbert's date of receipt for a date of performance, however.

[2] W. J. Lawrence's evidence (loc. cit.) for Sunday performances in the London theatres seems to me negligible. In some instances he has taken the references to court performances as references to public or private theatre performances. His evidence for Sunday performances from Henslowe's records denies Greg's analysis of Henslowe's dates (*Henslowe's Diary*, ii. 324–6). Greg, as usual, seems to me more reliable than Lawrence.

was any change in this six-day week in the London theatres[1] before the Civil War.

SUNDAY PERFORMANCES AT COURT

AT court, however, Sunday performances were common, though not so common as the Puritans said. In *Britain's Remembrancer*, 1628, George Wither complained of the court:

> Gods holy *Sabbaths*, most among them, there,
> Observe not much; except it be to weare
> Their finest clothes . . .
> On *Sundayes* far more Coaches rumble thither,
> Then doe in some three other dayes together:
> And, seldome have they leisure for a *Play*,
> Or *Maske*, except upon Gods *Holy-day*.

$$(R_6{}^{r-v}.)$$

In 1640 Mr. Peirce, chaplain to the Earl of Salisbury and lecturer at Covent Garden, wrote in a paper preserved by Archbishop Laud: 'I wish the Parliament would reform two things: 1. The sitting of the Council on Sunday afternoon. 2. The having plays on Sunday night.' (*C.S.P., Dom.*, 1640–1, p. 212.)

In his *History of the Parliament of England* Thomas May reviewed the conduct of King Charles and his ministers from 1628 to 1640, and commented loftily: 'The example of the Court, where Playes were usually presented on Sundaies, did not so much draw the Country to imitation, as reflect with disadvantage upon the Court it selfe . . .'. (1647 ed., $E_4{}^v$.) And more entertainingly a writer in a Parliamentary newsbook jibed: '. . . in time they [the Cavaliers] will go neere to put downe all *preaching* and *praying*, and have some *religious Masque* or play instead of Morning and Evening Prayer; it has been an old fashion at Court, amongst the Protestants there, to shut up the *Sabbath* with some

---

[1] Miss Sybil Rosenfeld has collected some interesting evidence that in provincial towns playing on Sundays and at night was not unknown. In the York Corporation Minute Books 'Willowbies players' were allowed to perform in November 1595, provided they did not play 'in the night tyme nor on the Sabbath daie'; in July 1601 'my Lord Shandoze players' were allowed to perform at 'Marmaduke gill howse till Sunday next', but not at night; in September 1607 the Queen's players were allowed to play, but not 'on the Sabaoth daies and on the nights'; and in June 1628 players were allowed in 'the day tyme but not on the night'. (*Theatre Notebook*, viii [1953–1954], 57–58.) The repeated prohibitions indicate that both Sunday playing and night playing were to be expected unless forbidden.

wholesome Piece of *Ben Johnson* or *Davenant*, a kinde of *Comicall Divinity'*. (*Mercurius Britanicus*, 9–16 November 1643, as quoted in Hotson, p. 9.) The accusation that the masques and plays of Jonson and Davenant were thought fit to shut up the Sabbath at court is amusingly accurate, for extant records show that masques and plays by both dramatists had Sunday presentations before the court—Jonson's in 1616/17, 1621, 1621/2, 1622/3, 1624/5, 1630/1, and 1634; and Davenant's in 1636/7 and 1637/8.

On the other hand, the assertion that at court 'Playes were usually presented on Sundaies' and 'seldome have they leisure for a *Play*, / Or *Maske*, except upon Gods *Holy-day*' is the familiar Puritan distortion of the facts. We have records of some forty Sunday dramatic performances at court during our twenty-seven years, but there are about two hundred on weekdays. Perhaps the best approximation of court practice is to be derived from the three extant bills presented by the King's company for plays performed at court during the reign, in which each occasion is dated, giving us the complete record of court performances by the company in the period indicated. (See above, i. 27–28, 51–52, and *Herbert*, pp. 76–77.) The three bills record sixty-six performances in the years 1630, 1636, and 1638 (all Old Style). Of these sixty-six performances only eight took place on Sundays. Indeed, in 1636 only one of the twenty-two plays and in 1638 only one of the twenty-four were performed by the King's men at court on the Sabbath. These figures might almost suggest that the court officials, or perhaps the King's men, were trying to avoid Sunday performances.

I suspect that for the first five years of the reign of Charles I the court did follow a policy of avoiding Sunday performances. In these years I have been able to find only three records of Sunday dramatic entertainment at court in London—a masque given by Buckingham at York House, 5 November 1626; an unknown Queen's masque, 14 January 1626/7; and a 'running masque' on 6 January 1627/8. This number is abnormally small, and only one of the three was given at royal expense and in the usual hall. Must one assume a disproportionate number of lacunas in Sunday records? Or was the young King Charles, or the Lord Chamberlain, impressed by the Parliamentary action of 1625? The statute is specific about plays and interludes.

An Act for punishing divers Abuses committed on the Lord's Day, called *Sunday*. Forasmuch as . . . the holy keeping of the Lord's Day is a principal Part of the true Service of God, which in very many Places of this Realm hath been and now is profaned and

neglected by a disorderly Sort of People, in exercising and frequenting Bear-baiting, Bull-baiting, Interludes, Common Plays and other unlawful Exercises and Pastimes upon the Lord's Day; and for that many Quarrels, Bloodsheds and other great inconveniences have grown up by the Resort and Concourse of People going out of their own Parishes to such disordered and unlawful Exercises and Pastimes, neglecting Divine Service both in their own Parishes and elsewhere; (2) Be it enacted . . . That from and after forty Days next after the End of this Session of Parliament, there shall be no Meetings, Assemblies, or Concourse of People out of their own Parishes on the Lord's Day . . . for any Sports and Pastimes whatsoever; (3) nor any Bear-baiting, Bull-baiting, Interludes, Common Plays or other un-lawful Exercises and Pastimes, used by any Person or Persons within their own Parishes; (4) and that every Person or Persons offending in any of the Premisses shall forfeit for every Offence three Shillings four-pence . . . and in Default of such Distress that the party offend-ing be set publickly in the Stocks by the Space of three Hours. . . . (*The Statutes at Large* . . ., iii [1763], 121–2.)

William Prynne in his compendious attack on all aspects of the theatre says that Sunday dancing was an offence particularly in the mind of the Commons at the time the law was passed.

Dancing therefore on the Lords-day . . . is . . . an unlawfull pastime punishable by the *Statute of I Caroli. cap.* 1. which intended to sup-presse dancing on the Lords-day, *as well as Beare-bayting, Bull-bayting, Enterludes, and Common Playes*; which were not so rife, so common as dancing, when this law was first inacted. (*Histriomastix* [1633], Ii$_2$.)

Since so few of the three court performances as noted above—and only one a standard court masque—are recorded between the date of the statute and 1630, I suspect some sort of deference to the Sabbatarianism of Parliament in the early years of Charles's reign.

The early practice of King Charles does not seem to have been the same as that of the late years of his father's reign. Such in-complete records as we have show a contrast in these two periods. Edmond Malone's extracts from the Office Book of Sir Henry Herbert were admittedly incomplete, but I can think of no reason why he should have copied a higher proportion of Sunday re-cords than of week-day ones. For the last three seasons of the reign of King James, Malone copied the records of 25 performances of plays and masques at court, eight of them on Sundays: 1622–3, seven performances, three on Sundays; 1623–4, ten performances, three on Sundays; and 1624–5, eight performances, two on

Sundays. (*Herbert*, pp. 49–52.) This contrast with a single extant record of a regular royal performance on Sunday in the first five seasons of the reign of King Charles seems to me a clear indication of some wariness at court of current Sabbatarianism, at least so far as conspicuous entertainments like masques and plays were concerned.

If such wariness ever existed, it wore off in the course of 1630–31, when the court had a new theatre for a plaything. (See above, vi. 270–1.) In this year we have records of fifteen court performances, seven of them on Sundays.

In summary, then, we can say that Sunday performances of masques and plays at court were fairly common, except for the period 1625 to 1630, when the Sabbath seems to have been kept at court. This restriction came to an end with the opening of the remodelled Cockpit-at-Court in 1630, and thereafter no avoidance of Sunday performances can be detected.

APPENDIX C

ANNALS OF JACOBEAN AND CAROLINE THEATRICAL AFFAIRS

THESE annals have been assembled in the hope that a day-by-day ordering of events might be helpful to scholars seeking the theatrical context of a play or an event. Whenever possible references have been made to earlier volumes in this work, and citation has been reduced to simple volume and page. Publication dates for plays and Stationers' Register entries have not been documented, since they all come from the *Bibliography of the English Printed Drama to the Restoration* of Sir Walter Greg, who originally suggested to me the usefulness of a compilation of annals.

Other works have been cited when they contain material not used in the preceding volumes or when they give fuller transcriptions than I have needed. A certain number of non-dramatic events have been listed when they may be expected to have affected plays and their production—royal movements, birthdays, weddings, deaths, processions, and other occasions of wide public interest.

1615/16

JANUARY

1 (M) An unnamed masque was performed in the Banqueting House at Whitehall (*Diary of Lady Anne Clifford*, p. 17; *M.S.C.* vi. 61).

5 (F) The anonymous *The Wisdom of Doctor Dodipoll* transferred S.R.

6 (Sa) Lady Anne Clifford saw the masque of 1 January repeated at court. (*Diary of Lady Anne Clifford*, p. 17.)

FEBRUARY

1 (Th) Ben Jonson was granted a pension of one hundred marks a year for life by the King. (iv. 609.)

2 (F) An unknown show was performed at Trinity College, Cambridge. (G. C. Moore Smith, *College Plays*, p. 67, from Senior Bursars' Accounts.)

13 Shrove Tuesday.

14 (W) Lady Anne Clifford wrote that 'my Lord supped at the

Globe' (*Diary of Lady Anne Clifford*, p. 18), but the reference may be to a tavern.

28 (W) William Peadle the father and William Peadle the son presented feats of activity upon ropes before the Queen at Greenwich. (*M.S.C.* vi. 144.)

FEBRUARY–MARCH

James Maxwell and nine assistants were paid for four days of work in preparing the Cockpit at Whitehall twice for plays; Zachary Bethell and five assistants were paid for making ready three times for three different plays; and Richard Lecavell was paid for attending in the Banqueting House for two masques, presumably about this time. (*M.S.C.* vi. 113.)

MARCH

4 (M) William Peadle the father William Peadle the son presented feats of activity upon ropes before the Queen at Greenwich. (*M.S.C.* vi. 144.)

12 (Tu) John Chappell's *Susenbrotus or Fortunia* was performed before the King at Royston. (iii. 159–60.)

19 (Tu) Beaumont and Fletcher's *The Scornful Lady* entered S.R.

20 (W) Ten members of Prince Charles's (I) company agreed to pay Edward Alleyn and Jacob Meade one-fourth of the receipts from the galleries of the Hope toward their indebtedness of £400 for loans and costumes. (i. 199.)

1616

25 (M) The customary tilting for Coronation Day (i.e. Accession Day) was apparently held on the day following, since the 24th was a Sunday. (*M.S.C.* vi. 61, 113.)

31 Easter Sunday.

APRIL

1 (M) The King's company performed fourteen unnamed and undated plays at court between 1 November 1615 (W) and 1 April 1616, presumably the last one on this day. (i. 94.)

2 (Tu) William Pedel danced on the ropes and showed other feats of activity at court. (*M.S.C.* vi. 61.)

9 (Tu) The anonymous *The Fair Maid of the Exchange* transferred S.R.

29 (M) The Prince's company was paid for four unnamed and undated plays performed at court before the Prince, apparently beginning some time in 1615. (*M.S.C.* vi. 61.)

MAY

20 (M) The Queen's company was paid for four unnamed and undated plays performed at court before the King, apparently beginning some time in 1615. (*M.S.C.* vi. 62.)

MAY–JULY

John Heborne and nine assistants were paid for two days work in making ready for bear-baiting at Greenwich in this period. (*M.S.C.* vi. 112.)

JULY

16 (Tu) The Lord Chamberlain wrote to provincial officials that certain London players were touring illegally with warrants or duplicate warrants of the Queen's, Children of the Revels, Prince's, and Palsgrave's players. The players were ordered to be apprehended, since they were not London companies, but mostly vagabonds. (i. 178–9.)

AUGUST

9 (F) Christopher Beeston leased from John Best the buildings from which the Phoenix theatre was remodelled. (i. 160.)

21 (W) The Lord Mayor wrote the Privy Council again concerning the continuing construction of the Puddle Wharf theatre. (vi. 84.)

31 (Sa) Sir William Alexander's additions to Sidney's *Arcadia*, which already contained Sidney's *The Entertainment at Wanstead* (*The Lady of May*), entered S.R.

SEPTEMBER

10 (Tu) Christopher Beeston was ordered to stop new building in Drury Lane. (ii. 365–6.)

29 (Su) Christopher Beeston's lease of the Phoenix buildings became effective. (ii. 365.)

OCTOBER

1 (Tu) ⟨ ⟩ 30 September 1617 (Th) The Banqueting House at Whitehall was made ready for barriers at the investiture of Prince Charles (4 November) and for a masque performed there in November, December, and January 1616/17.

Somerset House was set up for plays in the Presence Chamber and for a masque in the Hall. Greenwich was made ready for a play in the Queen's Great Chamber and for a masque in the Hall. At Woodstock a room was prepared with quarters and rafters for a masque. (Declared Accounts of the Office of Works, P.R.O. E 351/3251.)

4 (F) Process was begun against Christopher Beeston and the rest of the players of the Red Bull for arrears in highway repair. (ii. 366.)

15 (Tu) The Benchers of Lincoln's Inn agreed to protest to the Queen's Council against the building of the Phoenix theatre. (i. 160.)

21 (M) The Prince's company presented fourteen plays before the Prince at court between 21 October 1616 and 13 January 1616/17 (M), presumably the first and last on these two days, but the entire entry has been crossed out. (*M.S.C.* vi. 67, and also pp. 113, 147.) Payments to Peter Young for work done between November 1616 and February 1616/17 in making ready St. James's for nine plays performed before the Prince are also crossed through. (*M.S.C.* vi. 113.) A receipt dated November 1617, in which Young requested payment for himself and eight assistants for four days' work at St. James's in making ready for two plays before the Prince, should be considered together with the foregoing 'ghost' payments. (*M.S.C.* vi. 147.)

29 (Tu) The Lord Mayor's show for Sir John Leman, fishmonger: Munday's *Chrysanaleia*, or *The Golden Fishing*, was performed. (Chambers, *E.S.* iii. 449, and *M.S.C.* iii. 89–91.) It was entered S.R. the same day.

31 (Th) At the arrival of Prince Charles for his creation as Prince of Wales, Middleton's pageant, *Civitatis Amor*, was presented by the City. (Nichols, *Progresses of James I*, iii. 207–14.)

OCTOBER–NOVEMBER

James Maxwell and nine assistants were paid for two days work in making ready for a play at Whitehall. (*M.S.C.* vi. 115.)

OCTOBER or NOVEMBER

Jonson's *The Devil Is an Ass* was performed at Blackfriars. (iv. 616.)

NOVEMBER

1 (F) ⟨·⟩ 2 February 1616/17 (Su) The King's company performed thirteen unnamed and undated plays at Court (i. 94)
   before the King, Queen, and Prince. (*M.S.C.* vi. 68.) Presumably the first and last were on these two days.
4 (M) Charles was invested Prince of Wales at Whitehall. (Stow,
   Annales [1631], sig. 4L₂; *Chamberlain*, ii. 31–32.) There were
   supposed to be tilting, barriers, and a masque by the Inns of
   Court (*Chamberlain*, ii. 25). At night an honourable combat
   by ten gentlemen from each of the four Inns of Court took
   place. (Nichols, *Progresses of James I*, iii. 207–14.)
9 (Sa) The Lord Mayor, Sir John Leman, entertained the Knights
   of the Bath with a play and supper at Drapers' Hall; the
   Knights behaved badly and, after a scandal, left before the
   banquet. (*Chamberlain*, ii. 35.)

NOVEMBER

   John Tunstall and eight assistants were paid for work done
   in this month in making ready the Queen's court for a play
   before the Queen. (*M.S.C.* vi. 114.)

NOVEMBER–DECEMBER

   William Marsh and four assistants were paid for fifty days of
   work in riding, waiting, and attending upon the masquers
   during their time of practising at Newmarket. (*M.S.C.* vi.
   114.) Thomas Footes (i.e., Sackville) and nine assistants were
   paid for eight days work in making ready the Banqueting
   House four times for plays. (*M.S.C.* vi. 114.) Zachary Bethell
   and eight assistants were paid for preparing the Council
   Chamber at Greenwich for dancing on the ropes. (*M.S.C.*
   vi. 114.)

DECEMBER

25 (W) Jonson's *Christmas His Masque* was performed at court.
   (iv. 638–9.)

CHRISTMAS SEASON

   Sir Thomas Edmonds, newly appointed Controller, broke two
   staves in 'stickling at the playes this Christmas'. (*Chamberlain*, ii. 47.)
28 (Sa) The Prince's company performed an unnamed play
   before the Prince. (v. 1017; *M.S.C.* vi. 67.)

DECEMBER–JANUARY 1616/17

James Maxwell and nine assistants were paid for twelve days work in preparing the Banqueting House, along with two adjoining chambers, twice for masques. (*M.S.C.* vi. 113.) Thomas Footes (i.e. Sackville) and nine assistants were paid for eighteen days work in making ready the Cockpit, presumably at Whitehall, nine times for some unnamed entertainments. (*M.S.C.* vi. 114.)

DECEMBER–MARCH 1616/17

James Maxwell and nine assistants were paid for making ready the Hall at Whitehall four times for plays, and for four days work in preparing the Banqueting House twice for dancing. (*M.S.C.* vi. 115.)

Plays published in 1616

Sir William Alexander, *The Monarchic Tragedies* ('*The third Edition*') a collection of four plays: *Croesus, Darius, The Alexandrean Tragedy, Julius Caesar*;

Anonymous, *Jack Drum's Entertainment* (Q2);

Francis Beaumont and John Fletcher, *The Scornful Lady* (Q1);

Thomas Dekker, *The Honest Whore*, Pt. I (4th edn.);

William Haughton, *Englishmen for My Money, or A Woman Will Have Her Will* (Q1);

Ben Jonson, *The Works* (F1), containing *Every Man in His Humour, Every Man out of His Humour, Cynthia's Revels, Poetaster, Sejanus, Volpone, Epicoene, The Alchemist, Catiline*; five entertainments, eleven masques, two barriers, and non-dramatic matter;

Christopher Marlowe, *Doctor Faustus* (4th edn.);

John Marston, *The Insatiate Countess* (Q2);

Thomas Middleton, *Civitatis Amor; A Trick to Catch the Old One* (2nd edn.);

Anthony Munday, *Chrysanaleia: The Golden Fishing*;

S. S., *The Honest Lawyer*;

Edward Sharpham, *Cupid's Whirligig* (Q3).

1616/17

JANUARY

1 (W) An unknown play was performed at Whitehall. (*Diary of Lady Anne Clifford*, p. 46.)

5 (Su) Fletcher's *The Mad Lover* was performed at court by the King's company. (iii. 373–4.)

6 (M) Jonson's masque, *The Vision of Delight*, was performed at court. (iv. 676–7.)

13 (M) The Prince's company presented fourteen plays before the Prince at court between 21 October 1616 (M) and 13 January 1616/17, presumably the first and last on these two days. (*M.S.C.* vi. 67.)

17 (F) The gentlemen of the Middle Temple entertained the Earl of Buckingham with a supper and a masque. (*Chamberlain*, ii. 49.)

19 (Su) Jonson's masque, *The Vision of Delight*, was repeated at court. (iv. 676–7.)

27 (M) The Privy Council ordered the Lord Mayor to have the nearly completed Puddle Wharf theatre pulled down. (vi. 84.)

FEBRUARY

2 (Su) The King's company acted thirteen unnamed and undated plays at court before the King, Queen, and Prince, from 1 November 1616 (F) to 2 February 1616/17, presumably the first and last on these two dates. (i. 94; *M.S.C.* vi. 68.)

16 (Su) The following plays were transferred S.R.: Munday's *The Downfall* and *Death of Robert Earl of Huntingdon*, Marston's *Parasitaster, or the Fawn*, and the anonymous *Thomas Lord Cromwell*.

19 (W) The Queen's French musicians entertained her with 'a kind of maske or antique' at Somerset House. (*Chamberlain*, ii. 56.)

22 (Sa) Lord Hay entertained the French Ambassador with a supper and a masque, Jonson's *Lovers Made Men*. (iv. 650–1.)

23 (Su) ⟨ ⟩ 4 March (Tu) Queen Anne's players opened at the Phoenix theatre. (i. 161).

FEBRUARY–MARCH

Richard Lecavell was paid for watching in the Banqueting House for danger of fire. (*M.S.C.* vi. 115.)

MARCH

4 Shrove Tuesday rioters despoiled the Phoenix theatre. (i. 161–2.) Anthony Cossart and his French company performed an unnamed play at court before the King; the performance was apparently at Somerset (Denmark) House, where the Queen entertained the King at dinner. (*M.S.C.* vi. 63–64.)

?4 ⟨ ⟩ 11 (Tu) Anthony Cossart and his French company performed an unnamed and undated play at court before the King, probably in this week. (*M.S.C.* vi. 64.)

8 (Sa) Peter Heylyn's *Spurius* was performed privately in the President's lodgings at Magdalen College, Oxford. (iv. 552.)

9 (Su) Queen Anne's company was paid for three unnamed and undated plays performed at court before the Queen and Prince. (*M.S.C.* vi. 65.)

14 (F) King James left Whitehall *en route* to Scotland. (Stow, *Annales* [1631], 4L₃.)

15 (Sa) ⟨ ⟩ 16 May (F) Lady Elizabeth's company performed three unnamed and undated plays before the King on his journey toward Scotland. (i. 180.)

17 (M) The King left Theobalds *en route* to Scotland. (Stow, *Annales* [1631], 4L₃.)

20 (Th) Fifty persons were charged with rioting at the Phoenix theatre and damaging Christopher Beeston's house. (ii. 366.)

23 (Su) The King's company paid Herbert 44s. for a Lenten dispensation. (vii. 3.)

24 (M) The customary running at tilt on Coronation Day was apparently held. Ralph Smith was paid for making scaffolds for the gentlemen of the Venetian and Savoyan ambassadors. (*M.S.C.* vi. 64, and 113.)

MARCH–APRIL 1617

John Gosnold and nine assistants were paid for two days of work in making ready at Lincoln for a cock-fighting; for two days of work in preparing at Lincoln for a fencing; for four days of work in preparing at Lincoln for two plays; and for two days of work at an unnamed place in making a standing to see the horse race. (*M.S.C.* vi. 114.) John Heborne and nine assistants were paid for four days of work in making ready at York for two plays. (*M.S.C.* vi. 114.) Presumably all were part of the entertainment of the King in his journey to Scotland.

1617

APRIL

17 (Th) Marlowe's *Edward II* transferred S.R.
20 Easter Sunday.

MAY

4 (Su) Robert White's masque, *Cupid's Banishment*, was performed by young ladies before the Queen at Greenwich. (v. 1257–8.)

8 (Th) Beaumont and Fletcher's *The Scornful Lady* transferred S.R.

JUNE

3 (Tu) Christopher Beeston and seven other fellows and sharers
of Queen Anne's company signed a new debt-funding agreement with the Baskerviles. (ii. 366.) About this time Queen
Anne's players returned from the Red Bull to the repaired
Cockpit theatre. (i. 163.)

22 (Su) In a letter to the Master of the Revels, the Privy Council
ordered the suppression of a play 'concerning the late Marquesse d'Ancre'. (v. 1371.)

AUGUST

6 (W) Francis Clifford, 4th Earl of Cumberland, provided an
entertainment with music (masque?) at Brougham Castle in
Westmorland when the King and Court stayed there. (Nichols,
Progresses of James I, iii. 389–92.)

17 (Su) The King was entertained by a masque of noblemen,
knights, gentlemen, and courtiers in the garden at Houghton
Tower in Lancashire. (*The Journal of Nicholas Assheton*, ed.
F. R. Raines, pp. 42–45.) Thomas Footes (i.e. Sackville) and
nine assistants were paid for two days of work in August
1617 in making ready a place at Houghton Tower for the
King to see dancing (*M.S.C.* vi. 114), and Richard Harris and
nine assistants were paid for two days of work in July–August
1617 in making ready a room at Houghton Tower for the
King to see the dancing. (*M.S.C.* vi. 115.)

SEPTEMBER

15 (M) On his return from Scotland, the King was met at Hyde
Park by the Lord Mayor, aldermen, and four hundred citizens.
(Stow, *Annales* [1631], sig. 4L₃; *C.S.P., Ven.*, 1617–19,
p. 15; *Chamberlain*, ii. 100.)

29 (M) An unknown masque was performed at Hampton Court
in celebration of the wedding of Sir John Villiers to Lady
Frances Coke. (John Campbell, *Lives of the Chief Justices of
England*, 1874, i. 311.)

OCTOBER

2 (Th) Christopher Beeston, with five other players of Queen
Anne's company, petitioned the Sessions of the Peace for
relief from charges for highway repairs at the Red Bull
theatre. (ii. 367.)

18 (Sa) Two anonymous plays, *The Maid's Metamorphosis* and
The Weakest Goeth to the Wall, transferred S.R.

29 (W) The Lord Mayor's Show for Sir George Bowles, grocer:
Middleton's *The Triumphs of Honour and Industry* was performed (iv. 897, and *M.S.C.* iii. 91–93); the ceremonies are
described at length by Horatio Busino. (*C.S.P., Ven.,*
1617–19, pp. 58–63.)

James Maxwell and ten assistants were paid for six days of
work in this month in making ready the Banqueting House at
Whitehall for three plays; for two days of work in making
ready the Great Chamber for a play; for eight days of work
in preparing the Great Hall at Whitehall for four different
plays; and for four days of work in preparing the Cockpit at
Whitehall for two plays. (*M.S.C.* vi. 115–16.)

DECEMBER CHRISTMAS SEASON

Queen Anne's company performed two unnamed and undated plays at court. (*M.S.C.* vi. 68.)

James Maxwell and nine assistants were paid for six days
of work in December–January 1617/18 in making ready the
Banqueting House at Whitehall for three different masques,
and again for six days of work in the same period in making
ready the Banqueting House, the Cockpit, and the Hall for
three different plays. (*M.S.C.* vi. 116.)

Plays published in 1617

Anonymous, *The Famous Victories of Henry V* (Q2—two
issues);

Anonymous, *The Merry Devil of Edmonton* (Q3);

Thomas Heywood, *A Woman Killed with Kindness* (Q2);

Ben Jonson, *Lovers Made Men*;

Thomas Lodge and Robert Greene, *A Looking Glass for London
and England* (Q5);

Thomas Middleton, *The Triumphs of Honour and Industry*;

Thomas Middleton and William Rowley, *A Fair Quarrel* (two
issues);

Thomas Tomkis, *Lingua* (Q3).

1617/18

JANUARY

1 (Th) The lost, anonymous *Masque of Amazons*, or *Amazon's
Masque*, planned by Lady Hay and others for this date, was
cancelled because of the disapproval of the King and Queen.
(v. 1288–90.)

6 (Tu) Jonson and Jones's masque, *Pleasure Reconciled to Virtue*, was performed by the Prince and others in the Banqueting House at Whitehall. (iv. 669–72.)

9 (F) Gentlemen of the court performed the anonymous *Tom of Bedlam* at Theobalds for the King. (v. 1422.)

FEBRUARY

2 (M) The anonymous *Masque at Coleoverton* was performed by the Earl of Essex and others. (v. 1311.) Students performed the anonymous *First Antimasque of Mountebanks* at Gray's Inn. (v. 1376–7.)

6 (F) Tobie Mathew expected to see a play at Blackfriars. (*Chamberlain*, ii. 137.)

12 (Th) London apprentices were planning to meet at the Fortune theatre and then to pull down the Red Bull and the Cockpit theatres. (i. 163.)

13 (F) Barton Holyday's *Technogamia, or The Marriages of the Arts*, was performed in Christ Church hall, Oxford. (iv. 590.)

17 Shrove Tuesday. Jonson's *For the Honour of Wales* was performed by the Prince and courtiers in the Banqueting House. (iv. 641.)

19 (Th) Gentlemen of Gray's Inn performed *The First Antimasque of Mountebanks* in the Banqueting House. (v. 1377.)

24 (Tu) The King's company was paid for fifteen unnamed and undated plays performed before the King and Prince at court, presumably beginning in 1617. (i. 94; *M.S.C.* vi. 69.)

MARCH

2 (M) The following plays transferred S.R.: the anonymous *George a Greene*, Greene's *Orlando Furioso*, the anonymous *Edward III*, Marlowe's *Doctor Faustus*, Nashe's *Summer's Last Will and Testament*, and Jonson's *Every Man in His Humour*.

20 (F) A new licence was granted to the Lady Elizabeth's company. (i. 181.)

24 (Tu) The French Ambassador and his family departed for France, and the customary running at tilt was held in Whitehall to celebrate the King's accession day. (*Chamberlain*, ii. 152.)

1618

APRIL

5 Easter Sunday.

6 (M) The King's company performed *Twelfth Night* at court (i. 94) before the King. (*M.S.C.* vi. 69.)

7 (Tu) The King's company performed *The Winter's Tale* at court (i. 94) before the King. (*M.S.C.* vi. 69.)

8 (W) A footmen's race from St. Albans to Clerkenwell was attended by the court. (*Chamberlain*, ii. 155.)

20 (M) Barton Holyday's *Technogamia, or The Marriages of the Arts* entered S.R.

24 (F) Buckingham gave a supper and a play at the Mitre in Fleet Street for his gentlemen. (*Chamberlain*, ii. 159.)

MAY

3 (Su) The King's company performed *The Merry Devil of Edmonton* at court (i. 94) before the King. (*M.S.C.* vi. 69.) James Maxwell and nine assistants were paid for two days of work in March–May, making ready the Cockpit in Whitehall for a play. (*M.S.C.* vi. 116.) The only known performances in this period are those for 6 April, 7 April, and 3 May. Other payments to Maxwell and his nine assistants at this time are for two days of work in making ready the Cockpit in Whitehall for a cocking; for four days of work in making ready for two different plays; and for four days of work in making ready the Cockpit for one or more unnamed entertainments. (*M.S.C.* vi. 116.)

26 Whitsun Tuesday. Bear-baiting and bull-baiting were presented before the King at Greenwich. (*M.S.C.* vi. 69.) John Heborne and ten assistants were paid for two days of work in May–June, making ready the tiltyard at Greenwich for bear-baiting. (*M.S.C.* vi. 116.)

JUNE

3 (W) Daubridgcourt Belchier's *Hans Beer-Pot, His Invisible Comedy of See Me and See Me Not* entered S.R.

JULY–AUGUST

Thomas Footes and ten assistants were paid for two days of work, apparently about this time, in making ready the hall at Hampton Court for a play; and Footes and seven assistants were paid for two days of work in August, making ready at Beaulieu for the King to see the bear-baiting. (*M.S.C.* vi. 116.)

AUGUST

7 (F) Beaumont and Fletcher's *A King and No King* entered S.R.

SEPTEMBER

17 (Th) The anonymous *Mucedorus* transferred S.R.
   Sir Richard Conningsby and eight assistants were paid for
   six days of work this month in making ready the Great
   Chamber three times for plays. (*M.S.C.* vi. 117.)
29 (Tu) ⟨ ⟩ 7 November (Sa) Three members of the Privy
   Council were seen at an ordinary play at Blackfriars. (*Chamberlain*, ii. 181.)

OCTOBER

14 (W) John Taylor saw the Earl of Derby's company perform
   Dekker and Day's *The Life and Death of Guy of Warwick*. (iii.
   251.)
29 (Th) The Lord Mayor's show for Sir Sebastian Harvey, ironmonger: Munday's *Siderothriambos, or Steel and Iron Triumphing*, was performed. (iv. 925; *M.S.C.* iii. 93–98.) Sir Walter
   Raleigh was beheaded on the same day. Aubrey notes that
   the time of execution was planned to coincide with Lord
   Mayor's Day, so that the pageants and shows would draw
   people away from witnessing Raleigh's tragedy. (Nichols,
   Progresses of James I, iii. 493.)
31 (Sa) Edward Alleyn leased the Fortune theatre to ten
   members of the Palsgrave's company for thirty-one years at
   £200 per year. (i. 138.)

NOVEMBER

1 (Su) The King's company performed eight unnamed and undated plays before the King at court at Allhallowtide and
   Christmas, presumably the first play about this time. (i. 94;
   M.S.C. vi. 70.) James Maxwell and eight assistants were
   paid for an unstated amount of work in September–November,
   making ready the Cockpit at Whitehall three different times
   for plays. (*M.S.C.* vi. 116.) In the same period Sir Richard
   Conningsby and seven assistants were paid for eight days
   of work in making ready the Hall at Whitehall four different
   times for plays; and for eight days of work in preparing the
   Banqueting House and the Lord Chancellor's Chamber for
   a masque. (*M.S.C.* vi. 117.) The Prince's company appear to
   have performed a play before the King. (*M.S.C.* vi. 71.)
16 (M) Sir George Buc licensed Fletcher's *The Loyal Subject* for
   performance. (iii. 370.)
30 (M) ⟨ ⟩ 5 December (Sa) Sir John Digby, who had been
   created Baron Digby of Sherborne, county Dorset, on

25 November (W), gave a great supper and a play at White-hall. (*Chamberlain*, ii. 193.)

DECEMBER

11 (F) The Countess of Salisbury provided a great feast and a play. (*Chamberlain*, ii. 195.)
21 (M) King James went to London from Newmarket, where Chamberlain had thought the court would probably stay over Christmas because of the smallpox in London. (*Chamberlain*, ii. 193, 196.)
23 (W) An actor killed Lord Doncaster's barber. (*Chamberlain*, ii. 198.)

CHRISTMAS SEASON

The King's company presented eight unnamed and undated plays before the King at court at Allhallowtide and Christmas. (See 1 November.) *Stoicus Vapulans* performed at St. John's College, Cambridge. (v. 1413–14.)
28 (M) ⟨ ⟩ 2 January 1618/19 (Sa) Lady Hatton made a great supper with a play. (*Chamberlain*, ii. 199–200.)

Plays published in 1618

Anonymous, *Jack Drum's Entertainment* (Q2—2nd issue);
Anonymous, *Mucedorus* (7th edn.);
Anonymous, *The Weakest Goeth to the Wall* (Q2);
Daubridgcourt Belchier, *Hans Beer-Pot, His Invisible Comedy of See Me and See Me Not*;
Thomas Dekker, *The Shoemakers' Holiday* (Q3);
Nathan Field, *Amends for Ladies* (Q1—two issues);
Barton Holyday, *Technogamia, or The Marriages of the Arts*;
Thomas Kyd, *The Spanish Tragedy* (8th edn.);
Anthony Munday, *Siderothriambos, or Steel and Iron Triumphing.*

1618/19

JANUARY

1 (F) The Prince's company performed a play before the King. (*M.S.C.* vi. 71.)
3 (Su) The Palsgrave's company presented an unnamed play before the King. (*M.S.C.* vi. 70.)
6 (W) An unidentified masque, in which Prince Charles danced, was presented in the Banqueting House. (*Chamberlain*, ii. 200.) Antonio Donato, the Venetian Ambassador, attended and wrote about it. (*C.S.P.*, *Ven.*, 1617–19, pp. 432–3.) The

Queen was ill at Hampton Court at this time. (*Diary of Lady Anne Clifford*, p. 84.)

6 (W) ⟨ ⟩ 2 February (Tu) Prince Charles's (I) company performed Middleton's *The Inner Temple Masque, or Masque of Heroes* at the Inner Temple. (iv. 881.)

12 (Tu) The Banqueting House at Whitehall burned at eleven o'clock in the morning. (*Chamberlain*, ii. 201–2.)

⟩21 (Th) Officers and inhabitants of Blackfriars petitioned the City authorities about the playhouse there. (i. 4.) On this date the London Common Council ordered the King's company to cease playing at the Blackfriars. (i. 5.)

29 (F) The four London acting companies paid the Master of the Revels, through John Heminges, £2. 4s. od. for an allowance to play during Lent. (vii. 3.)

FEBRUARY

2 (Tu) The masque which had been performed in the Banqueting House on Twelfth Night was intended to be repeated at Candlemas, but the Banqueting House had burned on 12 January. (*Chamberlain*, ii. 202.) James Maxwell and eight assistants were paid for six days of work in February–March, making ready at Whitehall for three different plays to be performed at Candlemas, and for four days of work in February–March, preparing at Whitehall for a masque, probably the one which finally took place on Shrove Monday, 8 February. (*M.S.C.* vi. 116–17.)

8 (M) The unknown masque of the previous Twelfth Night was repeated in the Hall at Whitehall. (*Chamberlain*, ii. 204, 212, 213.) James Maxwell and eight assistants were paid for four days of work in February–March, preparing at Whitehall for a masque, probably this one. (*M.S.C.* vi. 116–17.)

9 Shrove Tuesday.

10 (W) Stubbe's *Fraus Honesta* was performed at Trinity College, Cambridge. (v. 1196–7.)

24 (W) Goffe's *The Courageous Turk, or Amurath the First* was acted by the students of Christ Church College, Oxford. (iv. 506.)

MARCH

2 (Tu) Queen Anne died at Hampton Court at four o'clock in the morning, and all the theatres were probably closed in mourning until her funeral on 13 May (Th). (i. 164.)

12 (F) Richard Burbage, player, made his nuncupative will. (ii. 638.)

13 (Sa) Richard Burbage died. (i. 6.)

16 (Tu) Richard Burbage was buried at St. Leonard's, Shoreditch. (ii. 396.)

22 (M) Sir William Alexander's additions to Sidney's *Arcadia*, which already contained Sidney's *The Entertainment at Wanstead* (*The Lady of May*), transferred S.R.

24 (W) The customary Coronation Day tilting was apparently not held, since Queen Anne was still unburied and the King was at Royston. (*Chamberlain*, ii. 225.)

1619

27 (Sa) A new licence was issued to the King's company to play at the Globe and Blackfriars theatres. (i. 5.)

28 Easter Sunday.

APRIL

15 (Th) Beaumont and Fletcher's *Cupid's Revenge* and W. Smith's *Hector of Germany, or The Palsgrave* transferred S.R.

20 (Tu) A supper and a warlike dance or masque of twelve men in complete armour at Merchant Tailors' Hall. (*Chamberlain*, ii. 233.) John Heminges and Henry Condell, leaders of the King's company, were sued by John Witter for a one-sixth share of the actors' moiety in the Globe theatre. (Wallace, *Shakespeare and his London Associates*, pp. 47–76.)

28 (W) Beaumont and Fletcher's *The Maid's Tragedy* entered S.R.

MAY

13 (Th) The funeral procession of Queen Anne, for which seventeen players of her London and provincial companies were allowed black cloth for liveries. (i. 164–5.)

13 (Th) *or* 14 (F) The Earl of Dorset gave a supper, a play, and a banquet for certain members of the train of the French Ambassador. (*Diary of Lady Anne Clifford*, p. 101.)

19 (W) Royal liveries were granted to twelve members of the King's company. (i. 90.)

20 (Th) The Duke of Lennox had *Pericles* performed in the King's Great Chamber after supper for the departing French Ambassador. (i. 94; Chambers, *Shakespeare*, ii. 346.)

JUNE

1 (Tu) The Aldermen and citizens met the King behind Gray's
Inn on his return to London after his illness. (*Chamberlain*,
ii. 242.)

JULY

8 (Th) Shakespeare's *The Merchant of Venice* transferred
S.R.
10 (Sa) Middleton's *The Inner Temple Masque, or Masque of
Heroes* entered S.R.

JULY–AUGUST

John Gosnold and seven assistants were paid for two days of
work in making ready for the bull-baiting at an unnamed
place; and Thomas Footes (i.e., Sackville) and seven assistants were paid for two days of work in making ready a
standing for the King for the hunting of the bull. (*M.S.C.* vi.
117.)

AUGUST

⟩ 14 The King's company was prevented by the Bishop of
London from acting Fletcher's *Sir John van Olden Barnavelt*.
(iii. 415.)
⟩ 27 (F) The King's company presented Fletcher's *Sir John van
Olden Barnavelt* at the Globe. (iii. 415.)

SEPTEMBER

Charles le Noyer and his French company presented
two unnamed plays before the King during September.
(*M.S.C.* vi. 71.)

OCTOBER

17 (Su) The anonymous *Swetnam the Woman-Hater Arraigned by
Women* entered S.R.
29 (F) The Lord Mayor's Show for Sir William Cockayne,
skinner: Middleton's *The Triumphs of Love and Antiquity*
was performed. (iv. 899 and *M.S.C.* iii. 99.)

NOVEMBER

1 (M) ⟨ ⟩ 5 (F) Marioni wrote that the King was in London this week, witnessing the performances of comedies at court almost every evening. (*C.S.P.*, *Ven.*, 1619–21, p. 47.)

DECEMBER

20 (M) Sidney's *Arcadia*, which contained Sidney's *The Entertainment at Wanstead* (*The Lady of May*), entered S.R. to provide for the sale in England of copies of the Irish publication.

23 (Th) ⟨ ⟩ 31 (F) There were apparently several plays and revels at court. (*Chamberlain*, ii. 278.)

c. 25 (Sa) ⟨ ⟩ 30 (Th) An unknown play performed before the King by the Prince's company was said to have displeased the King. The play was one 'in which a king with his two sons has one of them put to death, simply upon suspicion that he wished to deprive him of the crown, and the other son actually did deprive him of it afterwards'. (*C.S.P.*, *Ven.*, 1619–21, p. 111.)

I.C.'s *The Two Merry Milkmaids* was probably acted at court during the Christmas season. (iii. 101.) The King's company performed ten unnamed and undated plays at court before 23 March 1619/20 (Th), some of them presumably in 1619. (i. 94; *M.S.C.* vi. 73.) The Prince's company performed four plays before the King before 8 March 1619/20, perhaps some of them in 1619. (*M.S.C.* vi. 72.)

Plays published in 1619

Anonymous, *Edward IV*, Pts. I and II (5th edn.);

Anonymous, *Mucedorus* (8th edn.);

Anonymous, *Two Wise Men and All the Rest Fools*;

Beaumont and Fletcher, *A King and No King* (Q1); *The Maid's Tragedy* (Q1);

Christopher Marlowe, *Doctor Faustus* (5th edn.);

Thomas Middleton, *The Inner Temple Masque, or Masque of Heroes*; *The Triumphs of Love and Antiquity*;

William Shakespeare, the so-called *Collection of 1619*, containing *The First Part of the Contention of York and Lancaster* (*2 Henry VI*); *The True Tragedy of Richard Duke of York* (*3 Henry VI*); *Pericles*; *A Yorkshire Tragedy* (ascribed); *The Merchant of Venice*; *The Merry Wives of Windsor*; *King*

Lear; *Henry V*; *Sir John Oldcastle*, Pt. I (ascribed); and *A Midsummer Night's Dream.*

1619/20

JANUARY–FEBRUARY

John Heborne and seven assistants were paid for twenty-four days of work in January–February in making ready the Great Chamber on the Queen's side at Whitehall for the King for nine different plays and three rehearsals of plays to be performed between the Christmas holidays and Easter. (*M.S.C.* vi. 118.)

JANUARY

2 (Su) Robert Lee and his company, formerly Queen Anne's men, presented an unnamed play at court before the King; the play was presumably *The Two Merry Milkmaids*, by I. C. (iii. 101–4, and *M.S.C.* vi. 72–73.)

3 (M) The 'Running Masque' was performed at the French Ambassador's house by Lennox, Buckingham, Hamilton, and other courtiers. (*Chamberlain*, ii. 279, 282; *C.S.P., Ven.*, 1619–21, p. 128.)

4 (Tu) The 'Running Masque' of 3 January was performed at Lady Hatton's house before the King and Prince. (*Chamberlain*, ii. 282.)

5 (W) The 'Running Masque' of 3 and 4 January was performed at the Earl of Exeter's house. (*Chamberlain*, ii. 282.)

6 (Th) Jonson's *News from the New World Discovered in the Moon* was performed before the King in the Banqueting House by the Prince, Buckingham, and others. (iv. 663–4; *C.S.P., Ven.*, 1619–21, pp. 128, 135, 138; *Chamberlain*, ii. 282.)

7 (F) The 'Running Masque' of 3, 4, and 5 January was apparently performed at the Earl of Warwick's house. (*Chamberlain*, ii. 282.)

8 (Sa) The 'Running Masque' of 3, 4, 5, and 7 January was to be performed at Viscount Doncaster's house. (*Chamberlain*, ii. 282.) Sir Francis Nethersole wrote that the King was to be present (*C.S.P., Dom.*, 1619–23, p. 112), and Girolamo Lando noted that both the King and Prince were present (*C.S.P., Ven.*, 1619–21, p. 155.)

10 (M) The 'Running Masque' of 3, 4, 5, 7, and 8 January was to be performed at Denmark House. (*Chamberlain*, ii. 282.) Beaumont and Fletcher's *Philaster* entered S.R.

11 (Tu) Jacob Tyn and George Hawkenborough were paid in a
    warrant of this date for sport [bear-baiting?] presented by
    them before the King. (*M.S.C.* vi. 72.)

15 (Sa) Dekker and Day's *The Life and Death of Guy of Warwick*
    entered S.R.

⟩ 20 (Th) An unusual number of masques had been performed
    this season by this date; Girolamo Lando noted that the
    Prince had been slightly indisposed recently, being tired from
    dancing in the masques. (*C.S.P.*, *Ven.*, 1619–21, p. 151.)
    During this month on an unspecified date Ben Jonson and the
    King's company were commanded to attend the King at
    court. (i. 7–8.) Peter Heylyn's *Doublet, Breeches, and Shirt* was
    performed in January at Magdalen College, Oxford. (iv.
    551.)

FEBRUARY

⟩12 (Sa) The 'Running Masque' was ranging over all the country
    in the vicinity of Newmarket, including Sir John Crofts's
    house at Saxham Parva, near Bury St. Edmunds. (*Chamber-
    lain*, ii. 288.) John Chamberlain noted that not later than
    12 February an anti-feminist campaign, originating in the
    pulpits, had been carried forward on the stage and in ballads.
    (*Chamberlain*, ii. 289.)

17 (Th) A masque was planned for the court by the daughters
    of Sir John Crofts at his house at Saxham Parva, Suffolk, near
    Bury St. Edmunds. (*Chamberlain*, ii. 288.) Thomas Sackville
    and seven assistants were paid for an unstated amount of
    work in January–February, making ready Sir John Crofts's
    house at Saxham for a masque for the King. (*M.S.C.* vi. 117.)

29 Shrove Tuesday. Jonson's masque, *News from the New World
    Discovered in the Moon*, was performed again. (iv. 663–5.)
    During February a messenger was sent from the court at
    Whitehall to the Prince's company in Shoreditch to com-
    mand them to attend the Prince. (*M.S.C.* vi. 148.)

MARCH

8 (W) The Prince's company was paid for four unnamed and un-
    dated plays performed before the King at court, perhaps some
    of them in 1619. (*M.S.C.* vi. 72.) Munday's *The Downfall* and
    Death of Robert Earl of Huntingdon transferred S.R.

23 (Th) The King's company was paid for ten unnamed and un-
    dated plays performed before the King, perhaps some of
    them in 1619. (i. 94; *M.S.C.* vi. 73.)

24 (F) The tilting for the King's Day was especially elaborate, since it was the first tilt of Prince Charles. (*Chamberlain*, ii. 294, 298; Stow, *Annales* [1631], sig. 4L₆; *C.S.P.*, *Ven.*, 1619–21, p. 225; and *M.S.C.* vi. 118.) In February–March, John Gosnold and seven assistants were paid for four days of work in making ready the tiltyard and the Prince's pavilion; for two days of work in preparing Sir Thomas Walsingham's house at Whitehall for the King of Bohemia's Ambassador and other Ambassadors for the tilting day; and for three days of work in preparing the Cockpit at Whitehall three different times for the King, perhaps for plays, or possibly for cock-fights. (*M.S.C.* vi. 117.)

1620

26 (Su) The King made his first procession to St. Paul's to hear the preaching, accompanied by the Bishops and Peers of the Realm, Lord Mayor and Aldermen. (*Chamberlain*, ii. 299.)

APRIL

14 (F) The King feasted Count Swartsenbuk, Ambassador from the Emperor, and his train in the Upper parliament House. (Stow, *Annales* [1631], sig. 4L₆.)

16 Easter Sunday.

18 (Tu) The tilting of 24 March was repeated. (*Chamberlain*, ii. 298; and *M.S.C.* vi. 117.)

30 (Su) The King's company performed an unnamed play at court (i. 94) before the King. (*M.S.C.* vi. 73.)

MAY

20 (Sa) Jonson's *Entertainment at Blackfriars* was performed. (iv. 639–40.)

22 (M) I. C.'s *The Two Merry Milkmaids* entered S.R.

JUNE

6 (Tu) A bear-baiting was presented before the King. (*M.S.C.* vi. 74.) Thomas Sackville and eight assistants were paid for two days of work in April–June, making ready for the bull-baiting and bear-baiting. (*M.S.C.* vi. 118.)

19 (M) Jonson and Jones's masque, *Pan's Anniversary, or The Shepherd's Holiday*, was performed at court by the Prince, Buckingham, and others. (iv. 665–9.)

JULY

4 (Tu) Middleton and Rowley's masque, *The World Tossed at Tennis*, entered S.R.

30 (Su) John Cotton, John Williams, and Thomas Dixon licensed to build a large amphitheatre in London. (vi. 292–3.)
Thomas Sackville and seven assistants were paid for 28 days of work in July–August, making ready at Bromham and Beaulieu for the King for five sermons and bull-baiting. (*M.S.C.* vi. 118.)

AUGUST

5 (Sa) At Salisbury the King was given a show or play of twelve parts in which prominent noblemen performed. (*C.S.P., Ven.,* 1619–21, p. 390.) Sir Richard Calverley and seven assistants were paid for four days of work in July–August, making ready twice at Salisbury for a masque [*sic*]. (*M.S.C.* vi. 118.)

28 (M) ⟨ ⟩ 16 September (Sa) On 28 August Sir Edward Zouch wrote his brother that he expected to give the King and Prince masques each night at Woking. (*C.S.P., Dom.,* 1619–23, p. 175.) Chamberlain's letter of 16 September indicates that the masques must have taken place. (*Chamberlain,* ii. 318.)

SEPTEMBER

6 (W) Middleton was appointed City Chronologer. (iv. 857–8.)

29 (F) The King wrote to the Privy Council to revoke a licence previously granted to John Cotton, John Williams, and Thomas Dixon, to build an amphitheatre. (vi. 296–7.) John Gosnold and eight assistants were paid for two days of work in September–October, making ready for a play on Michaelmas Night. (*M.S.C.* vi. 119.)

OCTOBER

6 (F) Sir George Buc censored Dekker and Massinger's *The Virgin Martyr* for the Red Bull. (iii. 263–6.)

30 (M) The Lord Mayor's Show for Sir Francis Jones, haberdasher: John Squire's *Tes Irenes Trophæa, or The Triumphs of Peace*, was performed on this day, apparently because the 29th fell on a Sunday. (v. 1185; *M.S.C.* iii. 100.)

NOVEMBER

29 (W) The suit of Witter against Heminges and Condell for shares in the Globe (see 20 April 1620) was finally dismissed. (ii. 411.)

DECEMBER

13 (W) Dekker and Day's *The Life and Death of Guy of Warwick* transferred S.R.

Thomas May's *The Heir* was acted by the Revels company some time this year. (iv. 836.) The King's company performed nine unnamed and undated plays at court before 17 March 1620/1, and the Prince's men two before 20 March, presumably some of them in 1620 (i. 94; *M.S.C.* vi. 74). In October–December John Heborne (deceased) and eight assistants performed work for which they received payment: for twelve days of work in making ready the Great Chamber on the Queen's side, and the Great Chamber and Hall on the King's side for six different plays; for two days of work in preparing the Great Chamber on the Queen's side for the Prince for his dancing; for four days of work in preparing the Privy Chamber on the Queen's side twice for the Prince for his practising; and for ten days of work in preparing the Hall twice for the Prince for his masques. (*M.S.C.* vi. 118–19.) John Gosnold and seven assistants were paid for two days of work done in December–March 1621, making ready the Great Chamber for dancing. (*M.S.C.* vi. 119.)

Plays published in 1620

Anonymous, *Swetnam the Woman-Hater Arraigned by Women*;
Francis Beaumont and John Fletcher, *Philaster* (Q1);
I. C., *The Two Merry Milkmaids*;
Ben Jonson, *Epicoene* (presumably the 3rd edn.—two issues);
Christopher Marlowe, *Doctor Faustus* (6th edn.);
Thomas Middleton and William Rowley, *The World Tossed at Tennis*;
John Squire, *Tes Irenes Trophœa, or The Triumphs of Peace*.

1620/21

JANUARY

6 (Sa) An unknown masque was performed at Whitehall in which a Puritan was ridiculed; it was not Jonson's *News from the New World Discovered in the Moon*, as has often been stated. (iv. 663–5; *Chamberlain*, ii. 333; *Finetti Philoxenis*, p. 71.) On 22 December 1620 (F) Chamberlain had written of preparations for the masque (*Chamberlain*, ii. 332).

8 (M) In the afternoon the Prince ran at tilt before the French

Ambassadors, along with six or seven noblemen. (*Chamberlain*, ii. 333.) In the evening Viscount Doncaster entertained the French Ambassadors and the King and Prince with an elaborate banquet and a masque presented by nine young gentlemen. (*Chamberlain*, ii. 333–4; *Finetti Philoxenis*, p. 72.)

20 (Sa) ⟨ ⟩ 12 February (M) Since the Thames was frozen over, ice fairs were held. (Stow, *Annales* [1631], sig. 4L₆ᵛ.)

30 (Tu) The King and Prince rode in great state to the Parliament House, accompanied by the Bishops and Nobility. (Stow, *Annales* [1631], sig. 4L₆ᵛ; *Chamberlain*, ii. 338; *C.S.P.*, *Ven.*, 1619–21, p. 562.)

FEBRUARY

Messages were sent from the Prince at St. James's to his players at the Curtain ordering them to attend the Prince. (vi. 134–5.)

10 (Sa) The Attorney-General was ordered to prepare a new licence for the proposed amphitheatre. (vi. 298.)

11 Shrove Sunday. The unknown masque of the previous Twelfth Night was repeated at court. (*Finetti Philoxenis*, p. 73.) It was presented by the Prince to the King and the Spanish and Flemish Ambassadors. (*C.S.P.*, *Ven.*, 1619–21, p. 579.)

13 Shrove Tuesday. An unnamed masque of the gentlemen of the Middle Temple was performed in the Great Hall at Whitehall for the six commissioners from the Netherlands. (*Finetti Philoxenis*, pp. 73–74; *C.S.P.*, *Ven.*, 1619–21, p. 579.) John Gosnold and seven assistants were paid for four days of work done in December–March, preparing for the masque from the Temple to be performed on Shrove Sunday, apparently an error for Shrove Tuesday. (*M.S.C.* vi. 119.)

MARCH

⟩20 (Tu) The Prince's company presented two unnamed and undated plays before the King at court, perhaps one or both of them in 1620. (*M.S.C.* vi. 74.)

24 (Sa) The Prince and thirteen lords tilted at Whitehall in celebration of King's Day. (*Chamberlain*, ii. 356, 359; *M.S.C.* vi. 119–20.)

1621

APRIL

1 Easter Sunday.

7 (Sa) Royal liveries were granted to twelve members of the King's company. (i. 90.)

9 (M) The Overseers of the Poor in Paris Garden recorded the receipt of £5. 3s. 6d. from a group of players, apparently an unknown company at the Swan theatre. (vi. 250.)
In April–May, John Gosnold and seven assistants performed two days of work at the Cockpit in Whitehall, and four days of work at the Banqueting House for the King to see the 'History of Abraham'. (M.S.C. vi. 119.)

MAY

22 (Tu) Bear-baiting was presented before the King. (M.S.C. vi. 75.) Sir Richard Calverley and eight assistants were paid for two days of work in April–June, making ready the Prince's side for the bear-baiting. (M.S.C. vi. 119.)

JULY

16 (M) The Spanish Ambassador and his train went to a play at the Fortune; afterwards the players made him a banquet in the garden adjoining the theatre. (Chamberlain, ii. 391.)

AUGUST

3 (F) Jonson's masque, The Gypsies Metamorphosed, was performed at Burley-on-the-Hill. (iv. 645; Chamberlain, ii. 395–6.)
5 (Su) Jonson's The Gypsies Metamorphosed, with slight alterations, was performed at Belvoir. (iv. 645–6.) Richard Harris and seven assistants were paid for two days of work in July, making ready at Belvoir for a masque. (M.S.C. vi. 120.)
26 (Su) Barton Holyday's Technogamia, or The Marriages of the Arts, with revisions, was performed before the King at Woodstock. (iv. 590–1.) Sir Richard Calverley and eight assistants were paid for two days of work done in July–August, making ready at Woodstock for the King to see a play that the scholars made. (M.S.C. vi. 119.) The Declared Accounts of the Office of Works for 1 October 1620 (Su) ⟨ ⟩ 30 September 1621 (Su) record payments for the construction of two partitions in the Hall at Woodstock to keep the people from pressing into the middle aisle of the Hall, because the scholars were to act a play before the King. (P.R.O. E 351/3254.)
Richard Harris and seven assistants were paid for two days of work done in August, making ready a room at Warwick for the wrestling. (M.S.C. vi. 120.)

SEPTEMBER

2 (Su) Middleton and Rowley's *A Fair Quarrel* and Cooke's
Greenes Tu Quoque transferred S.R.
Jonson's *The Gypsies Metamorphosed* was performed, with
substantial alterations, at Windsor. (iv. 645–7.) John
Gosnold and seven assistants were paid for work in September,
making ready at Wignor-bridge for a bull-baiting. (*M.S.C.*
vi. 119.)

OCTOBER

5 (F) The King granted Ben Jonson the reversion of the Mastership of the Revels. (iv. 610; *Chamberlain*, ii. 404.)
6 (Sa) Shakespeare's *Othello* entered S.R.
29 (M) The Lord Mayor's Show for Sir Edward Barkham, draper:
Middleton's *The Sun in Aries* was performed. (iv. 895–6;
M.S.C. iii. 100–3.)
31 (W) The King returned to London from his progress. (*Chamberlain*, ii. 406.)

NOVEMBER

5 (M) Massinger's *The Woman's Plot* was performed at court
by the King's company. (iv. 829.)
6 (Tu) The King departed about noon for Newmarket. (*Chamberlain*, ii. 406.)
26 (M) The anonymous *The Woman Is Too Hard for Him* was
performed at court by the King's company (v. 1444), probably before the Prince, since the King was still at Newmarket. (*Chamberlain*, ii. 409, 411, 413.)

DECEMBER

7 (F) Dekker and Massinger's *The Virgin Martyr* entered S.R.
9 (Su) At midnight the Fortune was completely burned down.
(vi. 153.)
) 22 (Sa) The daughters of Sir John Crofts entertained the King
with a masque at Saxham Parva, Suffolk. (*Chamberlain*, ii.
417.)
26 (W) Fletcher's *The Island Princess* was performed by the King's
men at court. (iii. 347.)
27 (Th) The anonymous *The Man in the Moon Drinks Claret* was
performed at court by Prince Charles's (I) company (v.
1370.)
29 (Sa) Dekker, Ford, and Rowley's *The Witch of Edmonton* was
performed at court by the Prince's men. (iii. 270.)

76042

30 (Su) The anonymous *Grammercy Wit* was performed at court
by the Revels company. (v. 1344.)

Six named plays are known to have been performed at
court in November and December: those for 5 and 26 November, and for 26, 27, 29, and 30 December. Sir Thomas Sackville and eight assistants were paid for twelve days of work
done in October–December, making ready the Great Chamber
on the Queen's side and the Hall at Whitehall for six plays.
(*M.S.C.* vi. 120.) Sir Richard Calverley and eight assistants
were paid for twelve days of work done in December–
February 1621/2, making ready the Great Chamber on the
Queen's side and the Banqueting House for six plays. (*M.S.C.*
vi. 121.)

Plays published in 1621

Anonymous, *Mucedorus* (9th edn.) ;

John Fletcher (and Francis Beaumont and Philip Massinger ?),
Thierry and Theodoret (Q1) ;

Thomas Middleton, *The Sun in Aries;*

Thomas Middleton, *Honorable Entertainments*, including *The
Cock, The Archer, The Water Nymph, Pallas, The Year's
Funeral, Comus the Great Sir of Feasts, The Triumph of
Temperance, The Seasons, Flora's Welcome, Flora's Servants;*

Samuel Rowley, *When You See Me, You Know Me* (Q3) ;

Philip Sidney, *Arcadia*, including *The Entertainment at Wanstead* (*The Lady of May*).

1621/22

JANUARY

1 (Tu) Fletcher's *The Pilgrim* was performed at court by the
King's company. (iii. 391.)

6 (Su) The Prince's masque, Jonson's *The Masque of Augurs*, was
danced in Inigo Jones's new Banqueting House. (iv. 655–8;
Ben Jonson, x. 635–40; *Chamberlain*, ii. 420; *M.S.C.* vi. 121.)

24 (Th) Fletcher's *The Wild Goose Chase* was performed at court
by the King's company. (iii. 425.)

FEBRUARY

16 (Sa) Chamberlain reported the King to be at Newmarket, but
expected in London in ten or twelve days (i.e., 26–28 February) ; the week of 18–23 February the King would at some
time be at Sir John Crofts's at Saxham Parva, Suffolk.
(*Chamberlain*, ii. 424.)

22 (F) Markham and Sampson's *Herod and Antipater* entered S.R.

MARCH

2 (Sa) The late Queen Anne's company were paid for presenting a play at court before the King, presumably the
anonymous *Grammercy Wit* on 30 December 1621. (*M.S.C.*
vi. 75.)

4 (M) The Prince arrived in London from Theobalds, where the
King was reported to be residing with an infection. (*Chamberlain*, ii. 426.)

5 Shrove Tuesday. The King's company performed *The Coxcomb* at court. (i. 94.)

6 (W) The Prince's company was paid for presenting two plays
before the King at court, presumably the anonymous *The
Man in the Moon Drinks Claret* on 27 December 1621, and
Dekker, Ford, and Rowley's *The Witch of Edmonton* on 29
December 1621. (*M.S.C.* vi. 76.)

16 (Sa) ⟨ ⟩ 30 (Sa) The King was in London and at Hampton
Court, but he had not attended sermons in the chapel so far
this Lent. (*Chamberlain*, ii. 428.)

20 (W) A new patent was granted for a Lady Elizabeth's
company of uncertain status. (i. 182; *M.S.C.* vi. 76–77.)
John Gill, a felt-maker's apprentice, was wounded on the
stage of the Red Bull theatre by Richard Baxter. (i. 167.)
Sir Thomas Sackville and eight assistants were paid for two
days of work done in March–May, making ready the Banqueting House at Whitehall for the bear-baiting. (*M.S.C.* vi.
120.)

1622

25 (M) The annual Coronation Day tilting was planned for this
day (*Chamberlain*, ii. 428), apparently because the 24th fell
on a Sunday, but bad weather caused it to be postponed until
30 March, 23 April, 25 April, and finally 18 May. (*Chamberlain*, ii. 428, 433.)

27 (W) The King's company was paid for presenting six plays at
court before the King (*M.S.C.* vi. 76): *The Woman's Plot* (5
November 1621), *The Woman Is Too Hard for Him* (26 November 1621), *The Island Princess* (26 December 1621), *The Pilgrim*
(1 January 1621/2), *The Wild Goose Chase* (24 January 1621/2),
and *The Coxcomb* (5 March 1621/2). (i. 94.)

30 (Sa) Sir George Buc was reported to have fallen stark mad in
his old age; his office as Master of the Revels was executed
by Sir John Astley. (*Chamberlain*, ii. 430.)

APRIL

21 Easter Sunday.

22 (M) Middleton's *Invention*, a musical allegory, was performed at a Lord Mayor's entertainment. (iv. 882.)

MAY

6 (M) Jonson and Jones's *The Masque of Augurs* was repeated at the Banqueting House, after postponement. (iv. 655–7; *Chamberlain*, ii. 436.)

7 (Tu) Herbert licensed Middleton and Rowley's *The Changeling* for performance by the Lady Elizabeth's company at the Phoenix. (iv. 862.)

10 (F) Herbert licensed the anonymous *The Welsh Traveller* for performance by the company of the Revels. (v. 1435.) Herbert also licensed the anonymous *The Black Lady* for performance by the Lady Elizabeth's company. (v. 1294.)

14 (Tu) Herbert licensed Fletcher's *The Prophetess* for performance. (iii. 395.)

?18 (Sa) The Coronation Day tilting, postponed from 25 March, 30 March, 23 April, and 25 April, apparently took place on this day. (*Chamberlain*, ii. 428, 433; *M.S.C.* vi. 120, 121. Chamberlain does not record when the tilting actually took place.)

20 (M) Edward Alleyn sold shares for the building of the new Fortune theatre. (i. 143–4.)

JUNE

3 (M) Herbert licensed the anonymous *The Valiant Scholar* for performance by the Lady Elizabeth's company. (v. 1430.)

10 (M) Herbert licensed the anonymous *The Dutch Painter and the French Branke* for performance by the Prince's company at the Curtain. (v. 1324.)

11 (Tu) Bear-baiting was performed before the King. (William Young, *The History of Dulwich College*, ii. 238.) Sir Richard Calverley and eight assistants were paid for four days of work done in April–June, preparing the Cockpit at Whitehall twice, and for two days of work done in April–June, preparing for the bear-baiting. (*M.S.C.* vi. 121.)

22 (Sa) Herbert licensed Fletcher's *The Sea Voyage* for performance at the Globe. (iii. 412.)

JULY

8 (M) Seven players of Queen Anne's or the Revels company were authorized to make up a children's company to be called the Children of the Revels. (i. 167–8.)

Sir Richard Calverley and eight assistants were paid for two days of work done in August–September, making ready for the bull-baiting. (*M.S.C.* vi. 121.)

SEPTEMBER

6 (F) Carlell's (?) *Osmond, the Great Turk* was licensed by Herbert for performance by the King's company. (iii. 119.)

OCTOBER

3 (Th) Christopher Beeston and five other Red Bull actors were named in an Order for repair of the highways at the theatre. (i. 169 n. 2.)

5 (Sa) The King left Hampton Court for Theobalds, intending to go on to Royston till Hallowtide, when he would return to Theobalds and thence to Newmarket, so that he would not be in London again till Christmas. (*Chamberlain*, ii. 455.)

24 (Th) Herbert licensed Fletcher's *The Spanish Curate* for performance at the Blackfriars. (iii. 418.)

29 (Tu) The Lord Mayor's Show for Sir Peter Proby, grocer: Middleton's *The Triumphs of Honour and Virtue* was performed. (iv. 897–8, and *M.S.C.* iii. 103–4.)

DECEMBER

26 (Th) The King's company performed *The Spanish Curate* at court. (i. 94; iii. 418.) Richard Harris and eight assistants were paid for eight days of work done in October–January 1622/3, preparing the Great Chamber on the Queen's side for four plays before [*sic*] Christmas (*M.S.C.* vi. 121), and for eight days of work done in the same period for preparing the Hall for four different plays at Christmas. (*M.S.C.* vi. 122.) During this Christmas season the King's company performed four plays at court (on 26 December, 27 December, 29 December, and 1 January); Prince Charles's (I) company one (on Twelfth Night).

27 (F) Fletcher's *Beggars' Bush* was performed by the King's men at Whitehall. (iii. 313.)

29 (Su) Fletcher's *The Pilgrim* was performed by the King's men at court. (iii. 392.)

Plays published in 1622

Anonymous, *The Troublesome Reign of King John*, Parts I and II (Q3);

Francis Beaumont and John Fletcher, *The Maid's Tragedy* (Q2);
   Philaster (Q2);
Jo. Cooke, *Greenes Tu Quoque* (Q2);
Thomas Dekker and Philip Massinger, *The Virgin Martyr* (Q1);
Ben Jonson, *The Masque of Augurs* (1st edn.—dated 1621);
Gervase Markham and William Sampson, *Herod and Antipater*;
Christopher Marlowe, *Edward II* (4th edn.);
Thomas May, *The Heir* (Q1);
Thomas Middleton, *The Triumphs of Honour and Virtue*;
Thomas Middleton and William Rowley, *A Fair Quarrel* (Q2);
William Shakespeare, *Henry IV*, Part I (Q7); *Othello* (Q1);
   Richard III (Q6);
Philip Sidney, *Arcadia*, containing *The Entertainment at Wan-
   stead* (*The Lady of May*) (reissue of 1621 edn.);
Thomas Tomkis, *Lingua* (Q4).

1622/23

JANUARY

1 (W) The King's company performed Jonson's *The Alchemist*
   at court. (i. 94.)
6 (M) The anonymous *A Vow and a Good One* was performed at
   court by Prince Charles's (I) company. (v. 1432–3.)
11 (Sa) S. S.'s *The Honest Lawyer* transferred S.R.
19 (Su) Jonson and Jones's masque, *Time Vindicated to Himself
   and to His Honours*, was performed at court by the Prince and
   others. (iv. 672–6; *M.S.C.* vi. 121.) Chamberlain indicates
   that the masque was intended for Twelfth Night, but was
   delayed until this date. (*Chamberlain*, ii. 472–3.)
20 (M) Massinger's *The Duke of Milan* entered S.R.
21 (Tu) The Lady Elizabeth's men were paid for presenting two
   unnamed and undated plays before the King at court.
   (*M.S.C.* vi. 77.)

FEBRUARY

2 (Su) The King's company performed Shakespeare's *Twelfth
   Night* at court. (i. 94.) John Gosnold and seven assistants
   were paid for two days of work done in January–March,
   making ready the Banqueting House for a play at Candlemas
   (*M.S.C.* vi. 121), which could of course refer to the season
   rather than the day itself.
17 (M) Jonson's *Epicoene* and Chapman's *The Revenge of Bussy
   D'Ambois* transferred S.R.

25 Shrove Tuesday. No plays or other entertainments were performed at court during Shrovetide. (*Herbert*, p. 50.)

28 (F) John Hacket's *Loyola* was performed at Trinity College, Cambridge. (iv. 528–9.)

MARCH

12 (W) John Hacket's *Loyola* was performed before the King at Trinity College, Cambridge. (iv. 528–9.)

14 (F) The King's company was paid for performing four unnamed and undated plays at court, in addition to the five on 26 December, 27 December, 29 December, 1 January, and 2 February. (i. 94.) A warrant of 14 March for all nine plays indicates that the King was present. (*M.S.C.* vi. 77.)

21 (F) Herbert was paid 10s. for allowing the Red Bull to be used for a fencing exhibition during Lent. (*Herbert*, p. 48.)

24 (M) There was apparently no tilting in honour of King's Day. The Prince was in Spain, and the King was apparently not in town. Chamberlain records only the sermon at Paul's Cross. (*Chamberlain*, ii. 487.)

1623

The new Fortune theatre opened in the spring. (vi. 157.) Probably in April or May royal livery was granted to twelve members of the King's company (i. 90).

APRIL

13 Easter Sunday.

MAY

5 (M) Massinger's *The Duke of Milan* transferred S.R.

JUNE

2 Whitsun Monday. Inigo Jones and Edward Alleyn accompanied a group of lords to prepare for the reception of the Infanta with shows and pageants. (*Chamberlain*, ii. 501.)

3 (Tu) Nicholas Tooley, player, made his will, with legacies to players. (ii. 649–51.)

16 (M) William Browne and his mother, Susan Baskervile, answered the complaint of former Queen Anne's players about payment of Thomas Greene's share. (ii. 392.)

30 June (M) ⟨ ⟩ ?5 July (Sa) The Spanish Ambassador saw bear-baiting at Paris Garden. (*Chamberlain*, ii. 507.) Richard

Harris and eight assistants were paid for two days of work done in April–June, making ready the Prince's lodging in the tiltyard for a bear-baiting. (*M.S.C.* vi. 122.)

JULY

5 (Sa) Five camels and an elephant, the gift of the King of Spain, passed through the streets of London. (*Chamberlain*, ii. 507.)

9 (W) Herbert licensed Middleton and Rowley's *The Spanish Gypsy* for performance by the Lady Elizabeth's company at the Phoenix. (iv. 893–4.)

20 (Su) Sir John Astley sold the Mastership of the Revels to Sir Henry Herbert for £150 a year. (*Herbert*, p. 8.)

27 (Su) Herbert licensed Samuel Rowley's *Richard III, or the English Profit* for the Palsgrave's men at the Fortune. (v. 1013.)

30 (W) Herbert licensed Dekker and Day's *The Bellman of Paris* for performance at the Red Bull. (iii. 246.)

AUGUST

Herbert licensed *A Tragedy of the Plantation of Virginia*, barring the profaneness, for performance by the company at the Curtain. (v. 1395–6.) Sackville and assistants paid for two days of work done in August, making ready a room at Cranborne House, the seat of William Cecil, 2nd Earl of Salisbury, for the King to see the bull-baiting (*M.S.C.* vi. 122); the King was at Cranborne House 10 (Su) ⟨ ⟩ 19 (Tu) August. (Nichols, iv. 888, 902–3.)

19 (Tu) Herbert licensed an old play previously allowed by Buc, *The Peaceable King or the Lord Mendall*, for performance by the Prince's company at the Red Bull. (v. 1393.) He also allowed Shakespeare's *The Winter's Tale*, as an old play, for the King's company, although the allowed book was missing. (i. 103.)

20 (W) Herbert licensed John Williams and four others to make a show of an elephant for one year. (*Herbert*, p. 46.)

21 (Th) Dekker's *Match Me in London*, formerly allowed by Buc, was allowed for performance by Herbert. (iii. 256.)

27 (W) Herbert licensed Bartholomew Cloys with three assistants to make a show of a musical organ. (*Herbert*, p. 47.)

28 (Th) Brewer's *A Knot of Fools* entered S.R.

29 (F) Herbert licensed Fletcher and Rowley's *The Maid in the Mill* for performance by the King's company. (iii. 377.)

SEPTEMBER

3 (W) A book of jigs entered S.R.

5 (F) Herbert granted a licence to make a show of a live beaver. (*Herbert*, p. 46.)

12 (F) Herbert licensed William Bonen's *The Cra . . . Marchant, or Come to My Country House* for the Lady Elizabeth's company. (iii. 30.)

13 (Sa) *The Two Merry Milkmaids* by I.C. was transferred S.R.

18 (Th) Herbert licensed John Day's *Come See a Wonder* for performance by a company of strangers at the Red Bull. (iii. 240.)

20 (Sa) Sir George Buc died. (*Herbert*, p. 67.)

29 (M) Fletcher and Rowley's *The Maid in the Mill* was performed by the King's men at Hampton Court. (iii. 377.) Sir Richard Calverley and eight assistants were paid for two days of work done in August–September, making ready the Presence Chamber for a play. (*M.S.C.* vi. 122.)

OCTOBER

2 (Th) Herbert licensed for the Prince's company *A Fault in Friendship*, written by young Johnson and Brome. (iii. 69.)

6 (M) Violent outbursts of joy prevailed when the Prince reached London on his return from Spain. (*Chamberlain*, ii. 515–16.)

17 (F) Herbert allowed Middleton's old play, *More Dissemblers besides Women*, previously allowed by Buc. (iv. 888.) He also licensed Fletcher's *The Devil of Dowgate, or Usury Put to Use* for performance by the King's men. (iii. 328.)

26 (Su) About four o'clock in the afternoon, the upper chamber in Hunsdon House in Blackfriars collapsed during a sermon by a Roman Catholic priest. (Stow, *Annales* [1631], sig. 4M$_1$.) Chamberlain wrote at great length about it. (*Chamberlain*, ii. 520–1.)

29 (W) The Lord Mayor's Show for Sir Martin Lumley, draper: Munday's *The Triumphs of the Golden Fleece* was performed on the water, and Middleton's *The Triumphs of Integrity* was performed on land. (iv. 898–9, 926, and *M.S.C.* iii. 104–6.) Herbert licensed Samuel Rowley's *Hardshift for Husbands, or Bilboe's the Best Blade* for the Palsgrave's men. (v. 1011.)

30 (Th) Lady Elizabeth's company paid a gratuity to the Master of the Revels. (vi. 59.)

NOVEMBER

1 (Sa) Fletcher and Rowley's *The Maid in the Mill* was performed by the King's men at St. James's. (iii. 377.)

5 (W) Middleton and Rowley's *The Spanish Gypsy* was performed at Whitehall by the Lady Elizabeth's company. (iv.
893.)

8 (Sa) Sixteen Shakespeare plays entered S.R.: *The Tempest,
The Two Gentlemen of Verona, Measure for Measure, The
Comedy of Errors, As You Like It, All's Well That Ends Well,
Twelfth Night, The Winter's Tale, Henry VI*, Part. III,
*Henry VIII, Coriolanus, Timon of Athens, Julius Caesar,
Macbeth, Antony and Cleopatra*, and *Cymbeline*. The Shake-
speare First Folio was probably published in November or
December. (i. 8; W. W. Greg, *The Shakespeare First Folio*,
pp. 452–4.)

18 (Tu) A great feast was given by Buckingham for the Spanish
embassy and attended by the King and Prince. An unknown
masque by John Maynard followed. (iv. 842–3.)

19 (W) Herbert licensed Bonen's *Two Kings in a Cottage* for the
Palsgrave's men. (iii. 32.)

28 (F) Herbert licensed Smith's *The Fair Foul One, or The
Baiting of the Jealous Knight* for performance by a company
of strangers at the Red Bull. (v. 1177.)

DECEMBER

3 (W) Herbert licensed Massinger's *The Bondman* for performance
by the Queen of Bohemia's company. (iv. 766.)

4 (Th) Herbert licensed Richard Gunnell's *The Hungarian Lion*
for performance by the Palsgrave's company. (iv. 518.)

6 (Sa) Herbert licensed Fletcher's *The Lovers' Progress* for performance by the King's men. (iii. 360.)

26 (F) Fletcher and Rowley's *The Maid in the Mill* was performed
at Whitehall by the King's men. (iii. 377.)

27 (Sa) Massinger's *The Bondman* was performed by the Queen
of Bohemia's company at Whitehall. (iv. 766.)

28 (Su) The anonymous *The Buck Is a Thief* was performed by
the King's company before the King and the Prince at
Whitehall. (v. 1297.)

In this year Christopher Beeston made a contribution of
£10. 7s. 0d. to St. Giles Cripplegate in the name of the Cockpit
theatre. (ii. 368.) The Lady Elizabeth's company was paid on
a warrant of 9 April 1624 for three plays presented before the
King in December 1623 and January 1623/4 (*M.S.C.* vi. 78);
but Herbert notes that the performances of 5 November, 27
December, and 4 January were before the Prince. (*Herbert*,
p. 51.) The King's company was paid for ten plays performed

before the King, in a warrant of 17 February 1623/4 (*M.S.C.* vi. 78); but the performances of 1 November, 1 January, 6 January, and ?18 January were before the Prince. The King's company was paid on another warrant, dated 22 March [1623/4?] for presenting five plays before the King, but the warrant may really belong to 1624/5. (*M.S.C.* vi. 79.)

Plays published in 1623

Anonymous, *Wily Beguiled* (Q3);

Samuel Daniel, *The Works*, containing *Philotas*, *Hymen's Triumph*, *The Queen's Arcadia*, *The Vision of the Twelve Goddesses*, and *Cleopatra*;

Thomas Heywood, *If You Know Not Me, You Know Nobody*, Parts I (Q6) and II (Q3);

Ben Jonson, *Time Vindicated to Himself and to His Honours* (dated 1622);

Thomas Kyd, *The Spanish Tragedy* (9th edn.);

Philip Massinger, *The Duke of Milan* (Q1);

Thomas Middleton, *The Triumphs of Integrity*;

Anthony Munday, *The Triumphs of the Golden Fleece* (non-dramatic);

William Shakespeare, the First Folio;

Philip Sidney, *Arcadia*, containing *The Entertainment at Wanstead* (*The Lady of May*) (reissue of 1621 edn.);

John Webster, *The Devil's Law-Case*; *The Duchess of Malfi* (Q1).

1623/24

JANUARY

1 (Th) Fletcher's *The Lovers' Progress* was performed at court by the King's company. (iii. 360.)

2 (F) Herbert licensed, after heavy censoring, Thomas Drue's *The Duchess of Suffolk*, for performance by the Palsgrave's company. (iii. 284.)

4 (Su) Middleton and Rowley's *The Changeling* was performed at Whitehall by the Lady Elizabeth's company. (iv. 862.) The Lady Elizabeth's company was paid on a warrant of 9 April 1624 for three plays presented before the King in December 1623 and January 1623/4 (*M.S.C.* vi. 78); but Herbert notes that the performances of 5 November, 27 December, and 4 January were before the Prince. (*Herbert*, p. 51.)

6 (Tu) Herbert licensed, as an old play, the anonymous *The Four Sons of Amon* for performance by the Prince's company. (v. 1337.) Middleton's *More Dissemblers besides Women* was performed by the King's company at Whitehall. (iv. 888.) The masque planned for Twelfth Night, Jonson's *Neptune's Triumph*, was postponed after much practice, apparently because of diplomatic difficulties, and was never given (iv. 660–3); the Declared Accounts of the Office of Works for 1 October 1623 (W) ⟨ ⟩ 30 September 1624 (Th) record payment for setting up degrees and making ready the Banqueting House at Whitehall for the masque and to give audience to the Spanish Ambassadors. (P.R.O. E 351/3257.)

18 (Su) The King's company performed Shakespeare's *The Winter's Tale* at court. (i. 95.)

26 (M) Herbert licensed the anonymous *The Whore in Grain* for performance by the Palsgrave's company. (v. 1440.)

FEBRUARY

10 Shrove Tuesday.

17 (Tu) The King's company was paid for performing three unnamed and undated plays before the King at court (i. 95), apparently in addition to the seven recorded performances of 29 September, 1 November, 26 December, 28 December, 1 January, 6 January, and 18 January. But the performances of 1 November, 1 January, and 6 January were before the Prince; and that of 18 January was in the absence of the King. (*M.S.C.* vi. 78.)

19 (Th) The King opened Parliament with great show and pomp. (*Chamberlain*, ii. 546.)

MARCH

3 (W) Herbert licensed Ford and Dekker's *The Sun's Darling* for performance at the Cockpit. (iii. 459.)

12 (F) Herbert licensed Massinger's *The Bondman* for the press. (iv. 766.) Massinger's *The Bondman* entered S.R.

16 (Tu) Herbert licensed *Shank's Ordinary* for performance by the King's company. (v. 1050.)
The King's company apparently presented fifteen plays before the King at court this season; they received payment for ten plays on a warrant of 17 February 1623/4 (*M.S.C.* vi. 78), and for five plays on a warrant of 22 March 1624 [i.e., 1623/4?]. (*M.S.C.* vi. 79.)

1624

28 Easter Sunday.

30 (Tu) Herbert received a £2 gratuity from the Cockpit company for a Lenten allowance. (vi. 59.)

APRIL

6 (Tu) Herbert licensed Samuel Rowley's *A Match and No Match* for performance at the Fortune theatre. (v. 1012.)

10 (Sa) Herbert licensed Davenport's *The History of Henry I* for performance by the King's company. (iii. 230.)

17 (Sa) Herbert licensed Massinger's *The Renegado, or The Gentleman of Venice* for performance by the Lady Elizabeth's company at the Phoenix. (iv. 812.) Herbert licensed Gunnell's *The Way to Content All Women, or How a Man May Please His Wife* for performance at the Fortune. (iv. 519.)

19 (M) There was great pomp and display at the funeral of the Duke of Richmond. (*Chamberlain*, ii. 554.)

27 (Tu) King James was present at the installation of the Duke of Lennox as a Knight of the Garter at Windsor. (*Chamberlain*, ii. 555.)

30 (F) Six members of the Palsgrave's company bound themselves to Richard Gunnell to continue to play together at the Fortune. (i. 148–9.)

MAY

3 (M) Herbert licensed Barnes's *The Madcap* for performance by the Prince's company. (iii. 9.) Herbert relicensed *Jugurth, King of Numidia*, by Boyle (?). (iii. 36.)

15 (Sa) Herbert licensed the anonymous *The Tragedy of Nero* (*Piso's Conspiracy*) for the press. (v. 1380.)

21 (F) Herbert licensed the anonymous *Honour in the End* for performance by the Palsgrave's company. (v. 1351.)

27 (Th) Herbert licensed Fletcher's *A Wife for a Month* for performance by the King's company. (iii. 422.) Herbert licensed the anonymous *The Parricide* for performance by the Prince's company. (v. 1387.)

JUNE

11 (F) Herbert licensed Dekker and Ford's *The Fairy Knight* for performance. (iii. 249.)

12 (Sa) Herbert licensed Middleton's *A Game at Chess* for performance by the King's men. (iv. 871.)

⟩ 19 (Sa) The Apollo Room at the Devil and St. Dunstan Tavern near Temple Bar finished with Jonson's *Legales convivales* for the Sons of Ben. (*Chamberlain*, ii. 566.)

21 (M) The anonymous *The Merry Devil of Edmonton* transferred S.R.

28 (M) Middleton and Rowley's *The Spanish Gypsy* entered S.R.

29 (Tu) The following plays transferred S.R.: the anonymous *Arden of Feversham*, and *Solomon and Bersheba*, the anonymous *King Leir*, Greene's *Friar Bacon and Friar Bungay*, the anonymous *Robin Hood and Little John* (lost), and Robert Daborne's (?) *The Owl* (a lost play?).

30 (W) Sir John Astley was granted £50 per year to provide himself with a house and office, as was granted his predecessor as Master of the Revels, Sir George Buc; payment was allowed for two years past as well as for the future. (*Herbert*, p. 71.)

JULY

1 (Th) Criers with drums began recruiting soldiers for service against Spain in the Low Countries. (*Chamberlain*, ii. 567.)

7 (W) Herbert allowed the addition of a new scene to Dekker and Massinger's *The Virgin Martyr*. (iii. 264.)

AUGUST

5 (Th) An unknown 'sylvan masque' written by John Maynard was performed at Burley-on-the-Hill as part of Buckingham's entertainment of the King, the Prince, and the French Ambassador. This was possibly a repetition of Maynard's masque of the previous 18 November. (iv. 842–3; *C.S.P., Ven.*, 1623–25, p. 420.)

6 (F) ⟨ ⟩ 17 (Tu) Nine consecutive performances of Middleton's *A Game at Chess* by the King's men took place at the Globe. (iv. 871–8.)

12 (Th) The King, upon hearing from the Spanish Ambassador that Middleton's *A Game at Chess* was offensive, ordered that the author and the actors be brought before the Privy Council. (iv. 872–3.)

14 (Sa) Herbert licensed Edward James to set forth a Showing Glass, called the World's Wonder. (*Herbert*, p. 47.)

18 (W) A warrant was issued to have Thomas Middleton brought before the Privy Council because of *A Game at Chess*. (iv. 874.)

Also because of *A Game at Chess* the King's company was forbidden to perform until licensed by the King, and bonds were required of them. (iv. 874.)

19 (Th) Jonson's *The Masque of Owls* was performed before the Prince at Kenilworth. (iv. 658–9.)

27 (F) King James wrote to the Privy Council to allow the King's company to perform again. (iv. 875.)

30 (M) A warrant was issued to bring Middleton's son before the Privy Council concerning *A Game at Chess*. (iv. 876.)

SEPTEMBER

3 (F) Herbert licensed Heywood's *The Captives, or The Lost Recovered* for performance by the Cockpit company. (iv. 560.)

⟩15 (W) Benjamin Garfield paid 20s. to William Blagrave to forbid the playing of *The Late Murder of the Son upon the Mother*. (iii. 253.)

3 (F) ⟨ ⟩ 15 (W) Herbert licensed for performance Dekker, Rowley, Ford, and Webster's *The Late Murder of the Son upon the Mother, or Keep the Widow Waking*. (iii. 253.)

15 (W) Herbert licensed the anonymous *The Fair Star of Antwerp* for performance by the Palsgrave's company. (v. 1327.)
In September, Herbert licensed for performance an unknown tragedy by Thomas Drue on the same subject as Dekker, Rowley, Ford, and Webster's *The Late Murder of the Son upon the Mother*. (iii. 286.)

OCTOBER

4 (M) John Underwood, player, made his will, with theatrical legacies. (ii. 651.)

14 (Th) Herbert licensed Robert Davenport's *The City Nightcap* for performance at the Cockpit. (iii. 227.)

15 (F) Herbert licensed the anonymous *The Angel King* for performance by the Palsgrave's company. (v. 1290.)

19 (Tu) Herbert licensed Fletcher's *Rule a Wife and Have a Wife* for performance by the King's men. (iii. 408.)

22 (F) Herbert licensed Dekker and Ford's *The Bristow Merchant* for performance by the Palsgrave's company. (iii. 247.)

29 (F) The Lord Mayor's show for Sir John Gore, merchant-taylor: Webster's *Monuments of Honour* was performed. (v. 1254–5, and *M.S.C.* iii. 106–8.)

NOVEMBER

2 (Tu) The Lord Chamberlain had the King's company perform
Fletcher's *Rule a Wife and Have a Wife* at court for the ladies.
(iii. 408.)

3 (W) Herbert licensed Massinger's *The Parliament of Love* for
performance by the Lady Elizabeth's men. (iv. 806.)

3 (W) *or* 11 (Th) Herbert licensed Richard Gunnell's *The
Masque* for performance by the Palsgrave's company. (iv.
518–19.)

7 (Su) Public rejoicing was ordered in London for the good for-
wardness of the French match. (*Chamberlain*, ii. 588.)

26 (F) There is a Bill of Information in the Star Chamber of
this date against dramatists Dekker and Rowley, actors, and
others, for their part in producing *The Late Murder of the
Son upon the Mother* at the Red Bull. (*The Library*, viii
[1927–8], pp. 233–7.)

DECEMBER

9 (Th) A comedy was planned for the entertainment of the King,
Prince, and French Ambassadors, but it was cancelled be-
cause of the King's indisposition and the shortness of the time.
(*Chamberlain*, ii. 591.)

20 (M) The patented members of the King's company, except
Heminges and Condell, signed a letter of submission to
Herbert after production of a play not licensed by him, the
anonymous *The Spanish Viceroy*. (v. 1412–13.)

26 (Su) Fletcher's *Rule a Wife and Have a Wife* was performed
at court by the King's men. (iii. 408.) Chamberlain indicates
that the King kept his chamber all this Christmas, not
coming once to the chapel or to any of the plays. (*Chamberlain*, ii. 594.)

27 (M) Herbert issued a protection for 21 attendants of the
King's players. (i. 15–16.) Jonson's *Volpone, or The Fox* was
performed at Whitehall by the King's company. (i. 95.)

27 (M) ⟨ ⟩ 31 (F) The Duke of Brunswick on one or more occasions attended the theatre at Blackfriars. (*Chamberlain*, ii.
594.)

28 (Tu) The Lady Elizabeth's company performed Beaumont
and Fletcher's *Cupid's Revenge* at Whitehall. (i. 186 n.)

29 (W) Herbert licensed Jonson's masque, *The Fortunate Isles
and Their Union*, for the press. (iv. 642.) Richard Sharpe, a
player of the King's company, was granted immunity from
arrest during the time of the Revels. (ii. 570.)

Plays published in 1624

Anonymous, *The Tragedy of Nero* (*Piso's Conspiracy*) (Q1) ;
Anthony Brewer, *A Knot of Fools* (semi-dramatic) ;
Thomas Dekker, *The Shoemakers' Holiday* (Q4) ;
Ben Jonson, *Neptune's Triumph for the Return of Albion*
(dated 1623 as having been performed, but it was not) ;
Christopher Marlowe, *Doctor Faustus* (7th edn.) ;
Philip Massinger, *The Bondman* (Q1) ;
Thomas Middleton, *A Game at Chess* (1624 or 1625; Q1 un-
dated; Q2, two issues, the 2nd dated 1625; Q3 undated and
printed at Leyden) ;
John Webster, *Monuments of Honour.*

1624/25

JANUARY

1 (Sa) The King's company performed *Sir John Falstaff*, Part I,
presumably 1 Henry IV at court. (i. 95.)
6 (Th) The Lady Elizabeth's company performed Cooke's *Greenes
Tu Quoque* at Whitehall. (i. 186 n.)
9 (Su) Jonson's masque, *The Fortunate Isles and Their Union*,
was performed at court, postponed from Twelfth Night.
(iv. 642–4.) The Declared Accounts of the Office of Works
for 1 October 1624 (F) ⟨ ⟩ 30 September 1625 (F) provide
payment for repairing the Banqueting House for a masque
at Whitehall. (P.R.O. E 351/3258.)
12 (W) The King's company performed an unnamed play at
court (i. 96) before the King (*M.S.C.* vi. 80); but on 8 January (Sa) Chamberlain wrote that the King was to go to
Theobalds or Hampton Court on 10 January (M). (*Chamberlain*, ii. 596.)
25 (Tu) Herbert licensed Sampson's *The Widow's Prize, or The
Woman Captain*, as revised by him. (v. 1046.)

FEBRUARY

4 (F) George Wilson was sworn a Groom of His Majesty's Revels,
in ordinary. (*Herbert*, p. 68.)
8 (Tu) Herbert reallowed an old play, *The Honest Man's Fortune*,
the original being lost. (i. 104.)
11 (F) Herbert licensed James Shirley's *Love Tricks with Compliments* (*The School of Compliment, or Love Tricks*) for performance at the Cockpit. (v. 1144.)
14 (M) ⟨ ⟩ 25 (F) John Chamberlain noted that the Privy

Council had recently ordered a play on the Amboyna massacre, ready to be acted, to be forbidden. (*Chamberlain*, ii. 602.)

26 (Sa) After a quarrel at a play, Will Murray of the Prince's Bedchamber and Sir Humphry Tufton went to fight in St. George's Fields, where Murray killed James Gibson, his second. (*Chamberlain*, ii. 604; Godfrey Goodman, *The Court of James the First*, London [1839], ii. 404–5.)

MARCH

1 Shrove Tuesday.

9 (W) William Perry and his troupe allowed to act at the Curtain. (vi. 137–8.)

⟩ 12 (Sa) A play was presented before the King at Newmarket by the students of Queens' College, Cambridge. (*Chamberlain*, ii. 606.) The King was at Newmarket on 8 (Tu), 15 (Tu), 20 (Su) and 24 (Th) February. (Nichols, *Progresses of James I*, iv. 1027.)

15 (Tu) Richard Gunnell of the Fortune theatre paid the Master of the Revels £1 for a Lenten allowance for the rope dancers. (vii. 5.)

19 (Sa) Richard Gunnell of the Fortune theatre paid Herbert £2 for allowing a Lenten masque by the rope dancers. (ii. 456.)

22 (Tu) The King's company was paid for performing an unnamed and undated play at court, in addition to the performances of 2 November, 26 December, 27 December, and 1 January (i. 95), provided the warrant of 22 March '1624' is actually 1624/5, rather than 1623/4. (*M.S.C.* vi. 79.)

1625

27 (Su) James I died, at which the theatres were almost certainly closed; they continued closed because of the plague. (ii. 654–6.) The same afternoon Charles I was proclaimed from Whitehall, High Cross in Cheapside, and elsewhere. (Stow, *Annales* [1631], sig. 4M$_1$^{v}.)

APRIL

Royal livery was granted to thirteen members of the King's company during this month. (i. 90.)

17 Easter Sunday.

MAY

1 (Su) The marriage of King Charles and Princess Henrietta Maria was performed by proxy in Paris. (Gardiner, *History of England*, v. 325–6.)

7 (Sa) The funeral procession of James I took place, for which fifteen players of King James's company and eight players of Prince Charles's (I) company were granted black cloth for livery. (i. 90, 209.)

12 (Th) Two notes of this date provide for John Lowen, a King's player, to be sworn as porter for the new King, and for the King's players to be sworn in again. (ii. 502.)

23 (M) Thomas Hobbes petitioned to be sworn in as a King's player. (i. 18.)

JUNE

21 (Tu) The publication and confirmation of the marriage articles of Charles and Henrietta Maria were solemnized in the Great Room at Whitehall, where all the Ambassadors were feasted; the King and Queen were not present. (Stow, *Annales* [1631], sig. 4M₄; *Chamberlain*, ii. 624–5.)

22 (W) Buckingham entertained at York House with a prodigal feast for the King and the new Queen. (*Chamberlain*, ii. 624–5.)

24 (F) A new patent was issued for the King's players. (i. 17–18.)

JULY

1 (F) A confirmation was granted of the King's company's patent to travel for a year. (i. 19.)

AUGUST

5 (F) Thomas Downton, player, made his will. (ii. 642–3.)

SEPTEMBER

10 (Sa) A group of players addressed *The Runaways' Answer to a Book Called, A Rod for Runaways* to Condell in thanks for a farewell entertainment. (ii. 412.)

OCTOBER

29 (Sa) Lord Mayor's Show cancelled because of the plague.

NOVEMBER

27 (Su) Ralph Crane completed his transcript of Fletcher's *Demetrius and Enanthe* (*The Humorous Lieutenant*). (iii. 343.)

DECEMBER

c. 1 (Th) The theatres reopened. (ii. 656–7.)

6 (Tu) An order was issued to prohibit playing at the Cockpit because of the plague. (ii. 656.)

30 (F) The King granted the King's company a gift of one hundred marks. (i. 20.)

A warrant of 30 May 1626 provided for payment to the King's company for ten unnamed and undated plays acted at court before the King, some of them presumably in 1625. (i. 96; *M.S.C.* vi. 80.)

Plays published in 1625

Anonymous, *The Fair Maid of the Exchange* (Q2);

Francis Beaumont and John Fletcher, *A King and No King* (Q2); *The Scornful Lady* (Q2);

George Chapman, *Charles, Duke of Byron*, Parts I and II (Q2);

Ben Jonson, *The Fortunate Isles and Their Union* (dated 1624);

Thomas Middleton, *A Game at Chess* (1624 or 1625; Q1 undated; Q2, two issues, the 2nd dated 1625; Q3 undated and printed at Leyden).

1625/26

JANUARY

22 (Su) Herbert licensed Fletcher's *The Fair Maid of the Inn* for performance at Blackfriars. (iii. 337.)

FEBRUARY

2 (Th) Candlemas. King Charles was crowned at Westminster Abbey. (Stow, *Annales* [1631], sig. 4M₄ᵛ.)

3 (F) Herbert licensed Fletcher's *The Noble Gentleman* for performance at Blackfriars. (iii. 387.)

9 (Th) Herbert licensed James Shirley's *The Maid's Revenge* for performance. (v. 1132.)

Jonson's *The Staple of News* was performed by the King's company at Blackfriars during February. (iv. 629–30.)

21 Shrove Tuesday. Queen Henrietta Maria and her women performed in Racan's *L'Artenice* at Somerset House before a restricted audience. (iv. 548–50; *Chamberlain*, ii. 630; *Harvard Library Bulletin*, xiv [1960], pp. 183–90.) The Declared Accounts of the Office of Works for 1 October 1625 (Sa) ⟨ ⟩ 30 September 1626 (Sa) provide payment for making a large theatre at the upper end of the Hall at Denmark House and performing sundry other works for the scene of a pastoral there, along with soap for the engines of the pastoral. (P.R.O. E 351/3259.)

23 (Th) The following plays transferred S.R.: the anonymous *George a Greene*, Greene's *Orlando Furioso*, Nashe's *Summer's Last Will and Testament*, Jonson's *Every Man in His Humour*, the anonymous *Edward III*, Marlowe's *Doctor Faustus*.

28 (Tu) Petition against Blackfriars theatre renewed. (vi. 21.)

1626

APRIL

3 (M) Marston's *Parasitaster, or the Fawn* and the anonymous *Thomas Lord Cromwell* transferred S.R.

9 Easter Sunday.

14 (F) Jonson's *The Staple of News* entered S.R.

MAY

c. 15 (M) In a riot at the Fortune theatre, a headborough, a constable, and others were beaten, and sailors threatened to tear down the theatre. (i. 264–6.)

16 (Tu) Two men were charged with rioting at the Fortune theatre. (ii. 432–3.)

17 (W) The Privy Council issued an order to stop a play by the King's company at the Globe the following Thursday because of a proposed riot there. (i. 21.)

30 (Tu) The King's company was paid for performing ten unnamed and undated plays at court before the King. (i. 96; *M.S.C.* vi. 80.)

31 (W) James Shirley's *The Wedding* probably opened at the Phoenix. (v. 1164.)

JULY

7 (F) Licence to build the amphitheatre in Lincoln's Inn Fields renewed, but later stayed. (vi. 299–300.)

17 (M) Sir Henry Herbert received a gratuity of £3 from Heminges for a courtesy done him about Blackfriars. (ii. 469.)

AUGUST

4 (F) The following plays were transferred in the S.R.: Shakespeare's *Henry V*, Pavier's rights to Shakespeare's plays, the anonymous *Sir John Oldcastle*, Part I, Kyd's *The Spanish Tragedy*, Shakespeare's *Titus Andronicus*.

12 (Sa) The Lord Keeper wrote Secretary Conway expressing doubts about the licence for the amphitheatre. (vi. 300.)

SEPTEMBER

4 (M) The anonymous *The Tragedy of Nero* (*Piso's Conspiracy*) and Field's *A Woman is a Weathercock* transferred S.R.

?10 (Su) A certificate of privilege was issued to the King and Queen of Bohemia's company. (i. 260.)

28 (Th) The licence to build the new amphitheatre cancelled. (vi. 300–1.)

OCTOBER

11 (W) Herbert licensed Massinger's *The Roman Actor* for the King's company. (iv. 815.)

29 (Su) The Lord Mayor's Show for Sir Cuthbert Hacket, draper: Middleton's *The Triumphs of Health and Prosperity* was performed. Since the 29th fell on a Sunday, the performance may have been on the 30th instead. (iv. 896–7, and *M.S.C.* iii. 108–11.)

NOVEMBER

4 (Sa) Herbert licensed James Shirley's *The Brothers* for performance. (v. 1082.)

5 (Su) The Duke of Buckingham entertained the King, Queen, and French Ambassador with a banquet and an unnamed masque at York House. (*Finetti Philoxenis*, p. 191; Birch, *The Court and Times of Charles I*, i. 166, 169; J. P. Feil, *Shakespeare Survey*, xi [1958], p. 116, n. 50.)

6 (M) An unnamed play, referred to as 'The Duke's Play', was performed at court. (J. P. Feil, *Shakespeare Survey*, xi [1958], p. 116, n. 50.)

16 (Th) The Queen gave an unknown masque at Somerset House in honour of the departing French Ambassador. (*Finetti Philoxenis*, p. 190 [i.e., 192]; *C.S.P., Ven.*, 1626–8, pp. 21, 32; Birch, *The Court and Times of Charles I*, i. 180; J. P. Feil, *Shakespeare Survey*, xi [1958], p. 116, n. 50.) Sir John Tunstall and six assistants were paid £12. 18s. 0d. for eighteen days of work done in November, making ready the Presence Chamber and other rooms at Denmark House for the Queen for a masque on her birthday (*M.S.C.* vi. 123), supposedly the 15th of November.

19 (Su) An unnamed play, referred to as 'The Queen's Play', was performed at court (J. P. Feil, *Shakespeare Survey*, xi [1958], p. 116, n. 50.)

Thomas May's *The Tragedy of Cleopatra Queen of Egypt* was acted during 1626. (iv. 834.) The King's company was paid on

a warrant of 26 February 1626/7 for acting twelve plays at court before the King, presumably some of them in 1626. (*M.S.C.* vi. 80.) Richard Harris and eight assistants were paid for 26 days of work done in October–March 1627, making ready the Hall and the Great Chamber for thirteen plays. (*M.S.C.* vi. 122.)

Plays published in 1626

Anonymous, *Edward IV*, Parts I and II (6th edn.);
Anonymous, *The Merry Devil of Edmonton* (Q4);
Anonymous, *Mucedorus* (10th edn.); also 11th edn. ?(1626 ⟨ ⟩ 1631);
William Haughton, *Englishmen for My Money, or A Woman Will Have Her Will* (Q2);
Thomas Middleton, *The Triumphs of Health and Prosperity.*

1626/27

JANUARY

12 (F) Herbert licensed Davenant's *The Cruel Brother* for performance at Blackfriars. (iii. 201.)
14 (Su) The unknown Queen's masque was performed at Denmark House (?); the King and Queen danced. (*Finetti Philoxenis*, pp. 198–9; *C.S.P., Ven.*, 1626–8, p. 107; Birch, *The Court and Times of Charles I*, i. 185; *M.S.C.* ii. 332–4.) The Declared Accounts of the Office of Works for 1 October 1626 (Su) ⟨ ⟩ 30 September 1627 (Su) indicate work and preparations done in the Banqueting House at Whitehall for a masque for the Queen. (P.R.O. E 351/3260.) Also, Richard Harris and eight assistants were paid for six days of work done in October–March 1627, making ready the Banqueting House for the Queen's masque, apparently this one rather than the one at Denmark House on 16 November 1626. (*M.S.C.* vi. 122.)

FEBRUARY

6 Shrove Tuesday. William Hawkins's *Apollo Shroving* was performed by the boys of the Free School of Hadleigh in Suffolk. (iv. 539.)
26 (M) The King's men were paid for acting twelve unnamed and undated plays at court. (*M.S.C.* vi. 80.) Richard Harris and eight assistants were paid for 26 days of work done in

October–March 1627, making ready the Hall and the Great Chamber for thirteen plays. (*M.S.C.* vi. 122.)

MARCH

20 (Tu) On behalf of the King's men, Heminges paid Herbert £2 for a Lenten allowance. (vii. 4.)

1627

25 Easter Sunday.

APRIL

8 (Su) William Hawkins's *Apollo Shroving* entered S.R.

9 (M) Herbert issued a warrant to the musicians of the King's company. (*Herbert*, p. 46.)

10 (Tu) Jonson's *Poetaster* and Marston's *Antonio and Mellida* transferred S.R. Sir William Alexander's additions to, along with the former owner's part of, Sidney's *Arcadia*, which already contained *The Entertainment at Wanstead* (*The Lady of May*), transferred S.R.

11 (W) Heminges paid Herbert £5 for forbidding the Red Bull company to play Shakespeare's plays. (ii. 469.)

26 (Th) Thomas Newman's translations of two comedies by Terence, *The Andrian Woman* and *The Eunuch*, entered S.R. Probably in April or May royal livery was granted to fourteen members of the King's company. (i. 90.)

MAY

15 (Tu) Buckingham gave a farewell supper and a masque at York House for the King and Queen. (Birch, *The Court and Times of Charles I*, i. 224, 226; *C.S.P., Ven.*, 1626–8, p. 239.)

30 (W) Jonson's *Poetaster* and Marston's *Antonio and Mellida* transferred S.R. The anonymous *Edward IV*, Parts I and II, transferred S.R. The rights to previous owner's part, including Alexander's additions, in Sidney's *Arcadia*, which contained *The Entertainment at Wanstead* (*The Lady of May*), transferred S.R.

JUNE

6 (W) Herbert licensed Massinger's *The Judge* for the King's company. (iv. 793.)

19 (Tu) *or* 19 (Tu) ⟨ ⟩ 7 July (Sa) Bills for players and Dorothy Jaggard's rights to Shakespeare's plays transferred S.R.

Walter Alexander and eight assistants were paid for four days of work done in April–June, making ready the Great Hall for two plays, and for two days of work done in April–June, making ready the Banqueting House for the King and Queen to see the bear-baiting. (*M.S.C.* vi. 122.)

JULY

5 (Th) Herbert licensed Massinger's *The Great Duke of Florence* for the Queen's company. (iv. 786.)

17 (Tu) Herbert was granted £52 for lodging out of court for one year. (*Herbert*, p. 72.)

SEPTEMBER

29 (Sa) The King's company performed ten unnamed and undated plays at court between Michaelmas and 31 January 1627/8, presumably the first and last on these days. (i. 96; *M.S.C.* vi. 80.)
Walter Alexander and eight assistants were paid for two days of work done in August–September, making ready at Nonesuch for a play. (*M.S.C.* vi. 122.) In the autumn Thomas Randolph's *Salting* was probably acted at Trinity College, Cambridge. (v. 991–3.)

OCTOBER

29 (M) The Lord Mayor's Show for Sir Hugh Hammersley, haberdasher: a lost pageant by Thomas Dekker, was performed. (*M.S.C.* iii. 111–12.)

NOVEMBER

7 (W) Henry (John?) Reynolds's translation of Tasso's *Aminta* entered S.R.
On unspecified days in November two plays were performed in the Banqueting House, for which Clement Kinnersley and his men were paid for making ready. (*M.S.C.* ii. 348.)

DECEMBER

3 (M) Middleton's *The Family of Love*, Day's *Humour out of Breath*, Middleton and Rowley's *A Fair Quarrel*, and Jo. Cooke's *Greenes Tu Quoque* transferred S.R.

13 (Th) Henry Condell, player, made his will, with theatrical legacies. (ii. 640–2.) William Vincent and company were granted a licence to exhibit legerdemain and acrobatics. (ii. 613.)

29 (Sa) Henry Condell was buried at St. Mary, Aldermanbury. (ii. 412.)

Clement Kinnersley and his men were paid for work done in December and January 1627/8, taking down stuff and laying it up five different times for plays during the Christmas holidays. (*M.S.C.* ii. 348.)

Plays published in 1627

William Hawkins, *Apollo Shroving*;

Thomas Newman, *The Two First Comedies of Terence*, including *The Andrian Woman* and *The Eunuch*;

Philip Sidney, *Arcadia*, containing *The Entertainment at Wanstead* (*The Lady of May*) (also 1628).

1627/28

JANUARY

6 (Su) A 'running masque which is not of above six days' conception' was planned for performance at court on this day (*C.S.P., Dom.*, 1627–8, p. 502), but it was apparently not presented. (Reyher, *Les Masques Anglais*, p. 529.)

9 (W) Six plays by John Lyly entered S.R. by Stationers' Court order: *Campaspe, Sappho and Phao, Galathea, Endymion, Midas*, and *Mother Bombie*.

31 (Th) One of the ten unnamed plays performed by the King's men at court between Michaelmas and 31 January was presumably acted on this day. (*M.S.C.* ii. 346; vi. 80.)

FEBRUARY

2 (Sa) An unknown play was acted at court on Candlemas night. (*M.S.C.* ii. 348.)

24 (Su) ⟨ ⟩ 26 (Tu) There is no record of any masque during Shrovetide, but on 12 January (Sa) Mead wrote Stuteville about a proposed Shrovetide masque at the Temple and a King's great masque by a hundred actors in the Banqueting House. (Birch, *The Court and Times of Charles I*, i. 312.) A warrant of 11 February (M) provided for payment of £600 to Edmund Taverner for the expense of a masque to be presented shortly before the King at Whitehall. (*C.S.P., Dom.*, 1627–8, p. 556.) The King was apparently at Newmarket during Shrovetide. (Steele, *Plays and Masques at Court*, pp. 236–7.) The Declared Accounts of the Office of Works for 1 October 1627 (M) ⟨ ⟩ 30 September 1628 (Tu) provide

for extensive expenditures for the new masque intended to have been performed at Whitehall. (P.R.O. E 351/3261.)

26 Shrove Tuesday.

27 (W) Robert Gomersall's *The Tragedy of Lodovick Sforza, Duke of Milan* entered S.R.

MARCH

1 (Sa) Beaumont and Fletcher's *A King and No King* and *Philaster*, along with Shakespeare's *Othello*, transferred S.R.

3 (M) Thomas Vincent's *Paria* was performed before King Charles at Trinity College, Cambridge. (v. 1232–3.)

17 (M) The King, with the Nobility and Clergy, rode in great state from Whitehall to Parliament House to open Parliament. (Stow, *Annales* [1631], sig. 4M$_5$.)

18 (Tu) Book VI of Sidney's *Arcadia*, which already contained *The Entertainment at Wanstead* (*The Lady of May*), entered S.R.

1628

APRIL

13 Easter Sunday.

15 (Tu) Henry Shirley's lost play, *The Dumb Bawd of Venice*, was performed before the King by the King's company. (v. 1059; *M.S.C.* vi. 80–81.)

MAY

6 (Tu) Herbert licensed Massinger's *The Honour of Women.* (iv. 790.)

21 (W) Day's *Humour out of Breath*, Middleton and Rowley's *A Fair Quarrel*, and Cooke's *Greenes Tu Quoque* transferred S.R.

25 (Su) Herbert made an agreement with the King's company that they should give him the benefit of two days each year—one in summer, the other in winter—to be taken out of the second day of a revival, at his choice; the housekeepers to give their shares also, their daily charge only deducted. (i. 23.) This day he recorded his first payment. The play is unnamed. (i. 24.)

JUNE

A bear-baiting was watched by the King and Queen from the Banqueting House on an unspecified day in June. (*M.S.C.* ii. 349.)

13 (F) On leaving a play at the Fortune theatre Dr. Lambe was assaulted by a mob and later beaten and stoned to death. (i. 266–8.)

30 (M) A warrant was issued to swear ten Queen of Bohemia's players as Grooms of the King's Chamber. (i. 188.)

JULY

17 (Th) A warrant was issued to prepare a King's bill for the Lady Elizabeth's players to play in London and elsewhere. (i. 189.)

AUGUST

5 (Tu) The Duke of Buckingham saw a performance of *Henry VIII* at the Globe. (i. 22–23.)

6 (W) The Duke of Buckingham saw *The Rape of Lucrece* at the Cockpit. (i. 253.)

23 (Sa) The Duke of Buckingham was assassinated at Portsmouth. (Stow, *Annales* [1631], sig. $4M_5^v$.)

SEPTEMBER

Jonson was appointed Chronologer to the City of London during this month. (iv. 611.)

29 (M) The King's men performed sixteen unnamed and undated plays at court between Michaelmas and 10 January 1628/9, presumably the first and last on these dates. (*M.S.C.* vi. 81.) But L.C. 5/132, p. 99, gives the period as Christmas to Candlemas.

OCTOBER

3 (F) Herbert licensed James Shirley's *The Witty Fair One* for performance. (v. 1166.)

29 (W) The Lord Mayor's Show for Sir Richard Deane, skinner: Dekker's *Britannia's Honour* was performed. (iii. 248, and *M.S.C.* iii. 112–14.)

NOVEMBER

6 (Th) Jonson's *Poetaster*, Marston's *Antonio and Mellida*, and the anonymous *Edward IV*, Parts I and II, transferred S.R. Also, part of Sidney's *Arcadia*, including Alexander's additions, transferred S.R.

22 (Sa) Herbert recorded the second day of a revival of Fletcher's *The Custom of the Country* at Blackfriars. (i. 23–24.)

24 (M) Herbert licensed Ford's *The Lover's Melancholy* for performance at Blackfriars. (iii. 449.) The Lord Chamberlain
ordered Heminges to garnishee the dividends of Richard
Sharpe. (i. 22.)

29 (Sa) John Felton was hanged at Tyburn for the murder of
Buckingham. (Stow, *Annales* [1631], sig. 4M₅ᵛ.)

DECEMBER

8 (M) Fletcher's *The Faithful Shepherdess* transferred S.R.

14 (Su) On the complaint of John Heminges, business manager of
the King's company, the Lord Chamberlain issued a warrant
for the arrest of Ambrose Beeland and Henry Wilson, musicians and attendants of the King's company. (*M.S.C.* ii.
348.)
The King's company performed sixteen unnamed and undated plays at court between Christmas and Candlemas
1628/9 (i. 96) ; another warrant gives the period as Michaelmas
to 10 January. (*M.S.C.* vi. 81.) The Declared Accounts of the
Office of Works for 1 October 1628 (W) ⟨ ⟩ 30 September
1629 (W) provide payment for making ready the Banqueting House, Great Chamber, and the Hall at Whitehall, with
setting up degrees, and making a great footpace there.
(P.R.O. E 351/3262.) Thomas May's *The Tragedy of Julia
Agrippina* was acted during 1628. (iv. 838.)

Plays published in 1628

Francis Beaumont and John Fletcher, *Philaster* (Q3) ;
Thomas Dekker, *Britannia's Honour* ;
Robert Gomersall, *The Tragedy of Lodovick Sforza, Duke of
Milan* (1st edn.) ;
Christopher Marlowe, *Doctor Faustus* (8th edn.) ;
Henry (John ?) Reynolds, translation of Tasso's *Aminta;*
Philip Sidney, *Arcadia*, containing *The Entertainment at
Wanstead (The Lady of May)* (also in 1627).

1628/29

JANUARY

10 (Sa) John Bugge was sworn a Groom of the Chamber as one of
the Queen of Bohemia's players. (i. 190.) The King's company
performed sixteen unnamed and undated plays at court between Michaelmas and 10 January, presumably the last on

this day (*M.S.C.* vi. 81) ; but another warrant gives the period as Christmas to Candlemas. (i. 96.)

19 (M) Jonson's *The New Inn* was licensed by Herbert for performance at Blackfriars. (iv. 622.)

FEBRUARY

9 (M) Herbert licensed Brome's *The Lovesick Maid* for the King's company, acted with extraordinary success at the Blackfriars. (iii. 77–78.)

17 Shrove Tuesday.

1629

APRIL

5 Easter Sunday.

6 (M) Richard Brome's *The Lovesick Maid* was acted at court by the King's company. (iii. 78.)

26 (Su) Eleven Knights of the Garter, each with fifty men in livery, were honourably entertained and feasted by the Lord Mayor. (Stow, *Annales* [1631], sig. 4M$_5$v.)

MAY

6 (W) Royal livery was granted to fourteen members of the King's company. (i. 90.)

13 (W) Herbert licensed a new act in an unnamed old play. (*Herbert*, p. 32.)

24 (Su) ⟨ ⟩ 30 (Sa) Bear-baiting and bull-baiting were presented before the King and Queen at Whitehall. (*M.S.C.* vi. 84.)

JUNE

2 (Tu) Ford's *The Lover's Melancholy* entered S.R.

8 (M) Herbert licensed Massinger's *The Picture* for the King's company. (iv. 809.)

19 (F) Livery allowances were made to Christopher Beeston for fourteen members of the Queen Henrietta's company. (i. 223.)

JULY

2 (Th) Thomas Seabrooke, John Daunce, and Thomas Barnes were sworn Grooms of the Chamber as Queen of Bohemia's players. (i. 190.)

6 (M) William Blagrave and Richard Gunnell leased ground at Salisbury Court from the Earl of Dorset for a playhouse. (vi. 87–89.)

21 (Tu) Herbert recorded receipts from the second day of a revival of Fletcher's *The Prophetess* at the Globe. (i. 23–24.)

22 (W) Herbert licensed Davenant's *The Colonel* (*The Siege*?) for performance. (iii. 215.)

29 (W) Herbert licensed Brome's *The Northern Lass* as acted by the King's company. (iii. 81.)

SEPTEMBER

18 (F) William Perry was granted a commission to assemble an acting company to be called 'His Majesty's servants' for the city of York. (i. 271.)

24 (Th) Stubbe's *Fraus Honesta* was performed again at Trinity College, Cambridge, before Lord Holland and the French Ambassador. (v. 1197.)

27 (Su) *or* 25 September 1631 (Su) A play, perhaps *A Midsummer Night's Dream*, was performed before John Williams, Bishop of Lincoln, and his guests, probably at Buckden Palace, near Huntingdon. (Chambers, *Shakespeare*, ii. 348–9.)

29 (Tu) An unknown comedy was expected to be acted before the King at Hampton Court. (*M.S.C.* ii. 351.)

OCTOBER

Ten plays were presented at court before the King and Queen by Queen Henrietta's company 'between October 1629 and February following', for which Anthony Turner was payee. (i. 249; *M.S.C.* vi. 81.) The Declared Accounts of the Office of Works for 1 October 1629 (Th) ⟨ ⟩ 30 September 1630 (Th) provide payment for considerable work on the Cockpit at Whitehall. (P.R.O. E 351/3263; vi. 271–2.)

2 (F) Herbert licensed Davenant's *The Just Italian* for performance at Blackfriars. (iii. 204.)

12 (M) The anonymous *Wily Beguiled* transferred S.R.

20 (Tu) A French company with actresses is said to have been received with hostility by an audience at Blackfriars (i. 25; Birch, *The Court and Times of Charles I*, i. 418); but the performance may have been 7 November (Sa). (See also vi. 225–7.)

27 (Tu) Beaumont and Fletcher's *The Maid's Tragedy* transferred S.R.

29 (Th) The Lord Mayor's Show for Sir James Campbell, ironmonger: Dekker's *London's Tempe, or the Field of Happiness*,
was performed. (iii. 256, and *M.S.C.* iii. 114–19.)

NOVEMBER

3 (Tu) Herbert licensed Massinger's *Minerva's Sacrifice* for the
King's company. (iv. 799.) He also licensed James Shirley's
The Faithful Servant (*The Grateful Servant*) for performance.
(v. 1114.)

4 (W) Herbert licensed a French company to play a farce at the
Blackfriars. (i. 25.)

7 (Sa) A French company with actresses is said to have been received with hostility by an audience at Blackfriars. (i. 25.)
A letter from Mead to Stuteville would appear to date the performance 20 October (Tu). (Birch, *The Court and Times of
Charles I*, i. 418.) (See also vi. 225–7.)

13 (F) Drue's *The Duchess of Suffolk* entered S.R.

22 (Su) Herbert allowed a French company at the Red Bull. (i.
272.) He recorded his receipts from the second day of a
revival of *Othello* at Blackfriars. (i. 23–24.)

DECEMBER

14 (M) Herbert licensed the French company to play one afternoon at the Fortune. (*Herbert*, p. 59.)

20 (Su) Book VI of Sidney's *Arcadia* entered S.R.

Christmas. The King's company performed twelve unnamed
and undated plays at court before the King, according to
a warrant of 22 March 1629/30 naming Ellyardt Swanston as
payee. (i. 96; *M.S.C.* vi. 81.) Another warrant, dated 3 April
1630, names John Heminges as payee. (*M.S.C.* ii. 352.) Presumably one of the twelve was at Somerset House, where the
Surveyor was ordered to erect a stage and scene, according to
a warrant of 8 December. (*M.S.C.* ii. 351.)

An unknown masque of uncertain date was supposed to be
performed at court in 1629–30. (Reyher, *Les Masques Anglais*,
p. 529.)

Plays published in 1629

Anonymous, *Wine, Beer, and Ale* (Q1);
Lodowick Carlell, *The Deserving Favourite* (1st edn.);
William Davenant, *Albovine, King of the Lombards*;
Thomas Dekker, *London's Tempe, or The Field of Happiness* (?);
John Fletcher, *The Faithful Shepherdess* (Q2);

John Ford, *The Lover's Melancholy*;
Philip Massinger, *The Roman Actor*;
William Shakespeare, *Richard III* (Q7—8th edn.);
James Shirley, *The Wedding* (Q1);
Philip Sidney, *Arcadia*, containing *The Entertainment at Wanstead* (*The Lady of May*) (reissue of 1627–1628 edn.);
George Wilkins, *The Miseries of Enforced Marriage* (Q3).

1629/30

JANUARY

1 (F) Davenant's *The Colonel* (*The Siege*?) entered S.R.
10 (Su) Davenant's *The Cruel Brother* and *The Just Italian* entered S.R.
29 (F) Edward Sharpham's *Cupid's Whirligig*, Middleton's *Michaelmas Term*, Shakespeare's *The Merry Wives of Windsor*, and Middleton's *The Phoenix* transferred S.R.

FEBRUARY

9 Shrove Tuesday.
26 (F) James Shirley's *The Grateful Servant* and Chettle's *Hoffman* entered S.R.
27 (Sa) James Mabbe's translation of de Rojas's *The Spanish Bawd* entered S.R.
) 28 (Su) The Queen's company performed ten plays at court before the King and Queen between October 1629 and February 1629/30; Anthony Turner was named payee on a warrant of 4 July 1630. (*M.S.C.* vi. 81.) Another warrant, dated 5 July, gives neither the payee nor the fact that the King and Queen were present. (*M.S.C.* ii. 352.)

MARCH

22 (M) Massinger's *The Renegado, or The Gentleman of Venice* entered S.R.

1630

26 (F) Randolph's *Aristippus, or The Jovial Philosopher* and *The Conceited Pedlar* entered S.R.
28 Easter Sunday.

APRIL

8 (Th) Middleton's *A Chaste Maid in Cheapside* entered S.R., and Davenport's *The Pedlar* (lost?) transferred S.R.

16 (F) The anonymous *Pathomachia, or The Battle of the Affections, or Love's Loadstone* entered S.R.

17 (Sa) Herbert closed the theatres because of the plague. (ii. 657–8.)

MAY

29 (Sa) Prince Charles was born at St. James's. (Stow, *Annales* [1631], sig. 4M₆.)

JUNE

27 (Su) Prince Charles was christened with all state, the Lord Mayor, etc., attending. (Stow, *Annales* [1631], sig. 4M₆.)

29 (Tu) Dekker's *The Honest Whore*, Part II, entered S.R.

JULY

3 (Sa) Jonson's *Cynthia's Revels*, Middleton's *A Mad World, My Masters*, Jonson's *The Alchemist*, Jonson's *Epicoene*, and George Ruggle's *Ignoramus* transferred S.R.

20 (Tu) George Ruggle's *Ignoramus* transferred S.R.

AUGUST

2 (M) Thomas Tomkis's *Albumazar* and Heywood's *The Four Prentices of London*, *The Silver Age*, *The Golden Age*, and *The Iron Age* transferred S.R.

SEPTEMBER

13 (M) John Hacket's *Loyola* entered S.R.

20 (M) Because of the plague restraint, the King gave £100 to the King's players. (i. 26–27.)

30 (Th) Wilson's *The Inconstant Lady, or Better Late than Never* was performed by the King's company at Hampton Court. (v. 1271–2.) This was apparently the first of twenty-one plays acted by the King's company at court before the King and Queen in the period 30 September ⟨ ⟩ 21 February 1630/1 (M); it must be one of the four plays acted at Hampton Court during this period. (*M.S.C.* vi. 82 and ii. 354–5.)

OCTOBER

1 (F) ⟨ ⟩ 30 September 1631 (F) The Declared Accounts of the Office of Works for this period provide payment for sundry extraordinary works about the Cockpit and playhouse at Whitehall, as well as for work done in the summer of 1630 at the Cockpit and Whitehall. (P.R.O. E 351/3264.) (See vi. 272–3.)

3 (Su) The anonymous *Alphonsus, Emperor of Germany* was performed at court by the King's company. (v. 1286.)

9 (Sa) John Heminges, player, made his will, with theatrical legacies. (ii. 643–5.) A proclamation of 15 September (W) had provided for adjournment of the term in the period 9 October (Sa) ⟨ ⟩ 27 October (W), because of the plague. (Stow, *Annales* [1631], sig. 4M₆ᵛ.)

10 (Su) ⟨ ⟩ 20 February 1630/1 (Su)   Sixteen plays were presented at court by Queen Henrietta's company, presumably on the days mentioned and fourteen others; three were at Hampton Court. (i. 249.) One warrant is dated 25 May 1631 (*M.S.C.* ii. 355), while another is dated 28 November 1631, and adds the information that the plays were presented before the King and Queen. (*M.S.C.* vi. 82.)

17 (Su) The King's company performed *A Midsummer Night's Dream* at Hampton Court. (i. 27.)

24 (Su) The King's company performed Fletcher's *The Custom of the Country* at Hampton Court. (iii. 324.)

29 (F) The Lord Mayor's Show for Sir Robert Ducy, merchant tailor, was supposed to be performed; Dekker had proposed a pageant to the company, but none was given. (*M.S.C.* iii. 120.)

NOVEMBER

5 (F) The anonymous *An Induction for the House* and Fletcher's *The Mad Lover* were performed by the King's men at the new Cockpit-in-Court, probably for the opening of that theatre. (v. 1353–4; iii. 374.)

7 (Su) Fletcher's *Rollo, or The Bloody Brother* was performed by the King's men at court. (iii. 401–2.)

8 (M) The anonymous *Sir John Oldcastle*, Part I; Shakespeare's *Titus Andronicus, Henry VI*, Part II, *Henry V*, and *Pericles*; and the anonymous *A Yorkshire Tragedy* transferred S.R. Dekker's *Match Me in London* entered S.R.

12 (F) The theatres reopened. (ii. 657–8.) Sometime later, 18 February 1630/31 (F) ⟨ ⟩ 10 June 1631 (F), the theatres were closed, owing to a renewal of the plague. (ii. 658–9.)

16 (Tu) The following Shakespeare plays transferred S.R.: *The Tempest, The Two Gentlemen of Verona, Measure for Measure, A Comedy of Errors, As You Like It, All's Well That Ends Well, Twelfth Night, The Winter's Tale, Henry VI*, Part III, *Henry VIII, Coriolanus, Timon of Athens, Julius Caesar, Macbeth, Antony and Cleopatra*, and *Cymbeline*.

19 (F) The King's company performed Jonson's *Volpone* at the Cockpit-in-Court. (i. 28.)

20 (Sa) An order was issued to William Allen for liveries for fourteen Queen Henrietta's men. (i. 226.)

25 (Th) Herbert licensed Randolph's *The Muses' Looking Glass, or The Entertainment*; the play seems to have been acted in the summer of 1630. (v. 986.)

26 (F) Herbert licensed Randolph's *Amyntas, or The Impossible Dowry* for the Children of the Revels. (v. 969.)

28 (Su) Ford's *Beauty in a Trance* was performed at Whitehall by the King's men. (iii. 438.)

30 (Tu) Fletcher's *Beggars' Bush* was performed at court by the King's men. (iii. 313.)

Randolph's *Praeludium* was performed at the reopening of the Salisbury Court theatre after the plague, probably in November 1630. (v. 989–90.)

DECEMBER

6 (M) Jonson's *Poetaster*, Marston's *Antonio and Mellida*, and the anonymous *Edward IV*, Parts I and II, transferred S.R. Sidney's *Arcadia*, containing *The Entertainment at Wanstead* (*The Lady of May*) and Alexander's additions, transferred S.R.

9 (Th) The King's company performed Beaumont and Fletcher's *The Maid's Tragedy* at the Cockpit-in-Court. (i. 28.)

13 (M) The King and Queen of Bohemia's players, restrained by the justices, were granted leave to play. (i. 260.)

14 (Tu) The King's company performed Beaumont and Fletcher's *Philaster* at the Cockpit-in-Court. (i. 28.)

26 (Su) The King's company performed Webster's *The Duchess of Malfi* at the Cockpit-in-Court. (i. 28.)

27 (M) The King's company performed Beaumont and Fletcher's *The Scornful Lady* at the Cockpit-in-Court. (i. 28.)

30 (Th) The King's company performed Fletcher's *The Chances* at the Cockpit-in-Court. (iii. 319.)

Plays published in 1630

Anonymous, *How a Man May Choose a Good Wife from a Bad* (Q6);

Anonymous, *Pathomachia, or The Battle of the Affections, or Love's Loadstone*;

Anonymous, *Wily Beguiled* (Q4);

Anonymous, *Wine, Beer, Ale, and Tobacco* (Q2);

Francis Beaumont and John Fletcher, *Cupid's Revenge* (Q2); *The Maid's Tragedy* (Q3); *The Scornful Lady* (Q3);

William Davenant, *The Cruel Brother*; *The Just Italian*;

Thomas Dekker, *The Honest Whore*, Part II ;

Robert Greene, *Friar Bacon and Friar Bungay* (Q2) ;

Thomas Heywood, *The Rape of Lucrece* (Q4) ;

Barton Holyday, *Technogamia, or The Marriages of the Arts* (Q2) ;

Philip Massinger, *The Picture* ; *The Renegado, or The Gentleman of Venice* ;

Thomas Middleton, *A Chaste Maid in Cheapside* ; *Michaelmas Term* (Q2) ; *The Phoenix* (Q2) ;

Thomas Randolph, *Aristippus, or The Jovial Philosopher* (Q1, Q2, Q3, and possibly the Dublin Q4) ; *The Conceited Pedlar* (Q1, Q2, Q3, and possibly the Dublin Q4) ;

George Ruggle, *Ignoramus* (two edns.) ;

William Shakespeare, *The Merry Wives of Windsor* (Q3—4th edn.) ; *Othello* (Q2—3rd edn.) ; *Pericles* (Q5) ;

Edward Sharpham, *Cupid's Whirligig* (Q4) ;

James Shirley, *The Grateful Servant* (Q1).

1630/31

JANUARY

6 (Th) The King's company presented *Sir John Oldcastle*, Part I, at the Cockpit-in-Court. (i. 28.)

9 (Su) Jonson and Jones's masque, *Love's Triumph through Callipolis*, was performed by the King and others for the court. (iv. 652.) The preparations for the masques at Whitehall, as well as other items concerning building the Cockpit in the Declared Accounts of the Office of Works for the period 1 October 1630 (F) ⟨ ⟩ 30 September 1631 (F), apparently include the masques of 9 January and 22 February (Tu). (P.R.O. E 351/3264.)

11 (Tu) Herbert refused to license Massinger's play, later titled *Believe as You List*. (iv. 762.)

FEBRUARY

3 (Th) Massinger and Field's *The Fatal Dowry* was performed at court by the King's company. (iv. 783.)

9 (W) Edward Forsett's (?) Latin comedy, *Pedantius*, entered S.R.

?10 (Th) Middleton and Dekker's *The Roaring Girl*, Webster's *The White Devil*, and Marston and Barkstead's *The Insatiate Countess* transferred S.R. The King's company presented Beaumont and Fletcher's *A King and No King* at the Cockpit-in-Court. (i. 28.)

15 (Tu) The King's company presented *The Merry Devil of Edmonton* at the Cockpit-in-Court. (i. 28.)

17 (Th) The King's company performed *Every Man in his Humour* at the Cockpit-in-Court. (i. 28.)

18 (F) Herbert granted John Lowin a licence for a Dutch vaulter to perform at their 'house[s?]'. Probably only Globe intended. (vi. 194 n. 4.) On the same day he recorded his receipts at the second day of a revival of *Every Man in His Humour* at Blackfriars. (i. 24.)

20 (Su) One of the sixteen unknown plays acted by Queen Henrietta's players at court in the period 10 October 1630 (Su) ⟨ ⟩ 20 February 1630/1 was presumably performed on this day. (*M.S.C.* ii. 355 and vi. 82.)

21 (M) The King's men presented Fletcher's *Rollo, or The Bloody Brother* at the Cockpit-in-Court during the daytime. (i. 28; iii. 402; *M.S.C.* ii. 354–5.) This was apparently the last of twenty-one plays acted before the King and Queen at court by the King's company in the period 30 September 1630 (Th) ⟨ ⟩ 21 February 1630/1 (*M.S.C.* vi. 82); the names and dates of performance of all twenty-one plays are known. (i. 96.)

22 Shrove Tuesday. Jonson's masque *Chloridia* was performed at court by the Queen and her ladies. (iv. 636–8.) The preparations for the masque on 9 January would appear to apply to this performance as well.

25 (F) James Shirley's *The School of Compliment, or Love Tricks* entered S.R.

MARCH

11 (F) Herbert licensed Massinger's *The Emperor of the East* for the King's company. (iv. 778.)

1631

APRIL

2 (Sa) George Ruggle's *Ignoramus* transferred S.R.

10 Easter Sunday.

17 (Su) Jonson's *The New Inn* entered S.R.

25 (M) Phineas Fletcher's *Sicelides*, which had been acted at King's College, Cambridge, in 1615, entered S.R.

27 (W) Royal livery was granted to fourteen members of the King's company. (i. 90.)

MAY

3 (Tu) Knevet's *Rhodon and Iris* was performed at the Florists' Feast in Norwich. (iv. 715.) (See 12 November.)

4 (W) Herbert licensed James Shirley's *The Traitor* for performance. (v. 1150.)

6 (F) Herbert licensed Massinger's *Believe as You List* for performance. (iv. 762.)

16 (M) Dekker's *The Noble Soldier* and *The Wonder of a Kingdom* entered S.R.

17 (Tu) Herbert licensed James Shirley's *The Duke* (*The Humorous Courtier*) for performance. (v. 1120.)

18 (W) Chapman's *Caesar and Pompey* entered S.R.

30 (M) ⟨ ⟩ 4 June (Sa) Bear-baiting and bull-baiting were presented before the King and Queen at Greenwich in Whitsun week. (*M.S.C.* vi. 82.)

JUNE

⟩ 10 (F) The King's men performed *Pericles* at the Globe. (ii. 375.)

10 (F) Herbert received a gratuity from the King's men for allowing them to resume playing after plague-closing. (ii. 375.)

12 (Su) Herbert recorded his receipts at the second day of a revival of *Richard II* at the Globe. (i. 23–24.)

13 (M) Herbert licensed Massinger's *The Unfortunate Piety* for the King's company. (iv. 820.)

16 (Th) Heywood's *The Fair Maid of the West, or A Girl Worth Gold*, Parts I and II, entered S.R.

22 (W) John Mason's *The Turk* transferred S.R.

SEPTEMBER

7 (W) Thomas Goffe's *The Courageous Turk, or Amurath the First* and *The Raging Turk, or Bajazet the Second* entered S.R. Jonson's *The Staple of News* transferred S.R.

25 (Su) *or* 27 September 1629 (Su) A play, perhaps *A Midsummer Night's Dream*, was performed before John Williams, Bishop of Lincoln, and his guests, probably at Buckden Palace near Huntingdon. (Chambers, *Shakespeare*, ii. 348–9.)

28 (W) Stubbe's *Fraus Honesta* entered S.R.

OCTOBER

18 (Tu) A warrant was issued for the arrest of John Platt, a constable at Ware, for forbidding players to show there. (*M.S.C.* ii. 355.)

29 (Sa) The Lord Mayor's Show for Sir George Whitmore, haberdasher: Heywood's *London's Jus Honorarium* was performed. (iv. 578, and *M.S.C.* iii. 120–1.)

Nine plays were presented at court by Queen Henrietta's company, one at Hampton Court, in 'October &c.' (i. 249.)

NOVEMBER

12 (Sa) 'A Flora Show at Norwich', probably Knevet's *Rhodon and Iris* of 3 May, entered S.R. (iv. 715.)

14 (M) Herbert licensed James Shirley's *Love's Cruelty* for performance. (v. 1129.)

19 (Sa) Massinger's *The Emperor of the East* entered S.R.

24 (Th) William Rowley's *A New Wonder, A Woman Never Vext* entered S.R.

28 (M) John Atkins was granted permission to sue four members of the King and Queen of Bohemias company. (i. 261.)

DECEMBER

1 (Th) Herbert recorded his receipts at the second day of a revival of *The Alchemist* at Blackfriars. (i. 23–24.)

Andrew Cane and others were licensed as Prince Charles's (II) company, to perform at the Salisbury Court theatre, sometime in December. (i. 302.) In this month also Marmion's *Holland's Leaguer* was acted six successive days at Salisbury Court. (iv. 745–6.)

Christmas Season. The King's company performed eleven unnamed plays before the King, one of which was at Hampton Court. (i. 97; *M.S.C.* ii. 358.)

Sometime in 1631 the churchwardens and constables at Blackfriars petitioned the Bishop of London for suppression of the Blackfriars theatre. (vi. 24–25.) A warrant of 20 January 1634/5 provided for payment to the King's Revels' company for three unnamed and undated plays acted by them before the King at Whitehall in 1631. (i. 299; *M.S.C.* vi. 84.)

Plays published in 1631

Anonymous, *Fair Em* (Q2);
Anonymous, *The Merry Devil of Edmonton* (Q5);
Anonymous, *Mucedorus* (12th edn.);
Anonymous, *Pedantius* (by Edward Forsett?);
Francis Beaumont and John Fletcher, *A King and No King* (Q3);
George Chapman, *Caesar and Pompey* (Q1);
Henry Chettle, *Hoffman*;

Thomas Dekker, *Match Me in London*; *The Shoemakers' Holiday* (Q5);

Thomas Dekker and Philip Massinger, *The Virgin Martyr* (Q2);

Thomas Drue, *The Duchess of Suffolk*;

Phineas Fletcher, *Sicelides*;

Thomas Goffe, *The Raging Turk, or Bajazet the Second*;

William Haughton, *Englishmen for My Money, or A Woman Will Have Her Will* (Q3);

Thomas Heywood, *The Fair Maid of the West*, Parts I and II; *London's Jus Honorarium*;

Ben Jonson, *Chloridia* (dated 1630); *The New Inn*;

Ben Jonson, *The Works*, Vol. ii, containing *Bartholomew Fair*, *The Devil Is an Ass*, and *The Staple of News*;

Ben Jonson, *Love's Triumph through Callipolis* (dated 1630);

Ralph Knevet, *Rhodon and Iris*;

James Mabbe, *The Spanish Bawd*;

Christopher Marlowe, *Doctor Faustus* (9th edn.);

John Marston and William Barkstead, *The Insatiate Countess* (Q3—two issues);

Thomas May, *The Tragedy of Antigone, the Theban Princess*;

Thomas Randolph, *Aristippus* and *The Conceited Pedlar* (Q5);

William Shakespeare, *Love's Labour's Lost* (Q2—3rd edn.); *The Taming of the Shrew* (Q4—5th edn.);

Edward Sharpham, *The Fleir* (Q4);

James Shirley, *The School of Compliment, or Love Tricks* (Q1);

John Webster, *The White Devil* (Q2).

1631/32

JANUARY

8 (Su) Townshend's masque, *Albion's Triumph*, was performed at court. (v. 1227–8.) The Declared Accounts of the Office of Works for the period 1 October 1631 (Sa) ⟨ ⟩ 30 September 1632 (Su) provide payment for preparations in and about the Banqueting House at Whitehall in making a stage and fitting and preparing it for two masques by the King (8 January) and Queen (14 February). (P.R.O. E 351/3265.)

10 (Tu) Herbert licensed James Shirley's *The Changes, or Love in a Maze* for performance. (v. 1091.)

12 (Th) Lord Goring entertained the Queen with an unknown masque, perhaps by Davenant. (J. P. Feil, *Shakespeare Survey*, xi [1958], 108. Herbert, allowed an old play rewritten by Christopher Beeston. (iii. 17.)

16 (M) Massinger's *The Maid of Honour* entered S.R.
26 (Th) Marmion's *Holland's Leaguer* entered S.R.
26 (Th) *or* 27 (F) Sir Humphrey Mildmay saw a play. (ii. 674.)

FEBRUARY

9 (Th) James Shirley's *The Changes, or Love in a Maze* entered S.R.
14 Shrove Tuesday. Townshend's masque *Tempe Restored* was performed at Whitehall. (v. 1229.) (See 8 January for the preparations for the King's masque [8 January] and the Queen's masque [14 February].)

MARCH

19 (M) Peter Hausted's *The Rival Friends* was performed before the King and Queen at Trinity College, Cambridge. (iv. 534; J. P. Feil, *Shakespeare Survey*, xi [1958], 108.)
20 (Tu) Randolph's *The Jealous Lovers* was performed before the King and Queen at Trinity College, Cambridge. (v. 984; J. P. Feil, *Shakespeare Survey*, xi [1958], 108.)
24 (Sa) Brome's *The Northern Lass* entered S.R.

1632

30 (F) Massinger and Field's *The Fatal Dowry* entered S.R.

APRIL

1 Easter Sunday.
20 (F) Herbert licensed James Shirley's *Hyde Park* for performance. (v. 1122.)

MAY

3 (Th) The King's company acted twenty-three plays before the King at Hampton Court, Whitehall, and Denmark House in the period 3 May 1632 ⟨ ⟩ 3 March 1632/3 (Su). (*M.S.C.* ii. 360.) The first of these, apparently performed on this date, was probably the Lord Chamberlain's entertainment of the King and Queen at the Cockpit at Whitehall. (J. P. Feil, *Shakespeare Survey*, xi [1958], 109.)
9 (W) William Alabaster's Latin tragedy, *Roxana*, entered S.R.
10 (Th) ⟨ ⟩ 15 (Tu) Eleven members of Prince Charles's (II) company were sworn Grooms of the Chamber. (i. 303.)
25 (F) Herbert licensed Massinger's *The City Madam* for the King's company. (iv. 771.)

JUNE

1 (F) A warrant was issued to swear George Stutville a Groom of the Chamber as one of Prince Charles's (II) players. (ii. 581.)

13 (W) Peter Hausted's *The Rival Friends* entered S.R.

25 (M) Sir Humphrey Mildmay saw a play at an unnamed London theatre. (ii. 674.)

SEPTEMBER

15 (Sa) John Pory noted that Ben Jonson had written *The Magnetic Lady*. (J. P. Feil, *Shakespeare Survey*, xi [1958], 109.) Pory also noted that the Queen and some of her ladies were practising Walter Montagu's *The Shepherd's Paradise* and were being coached daily by Joseph Taylor, the prime actor at the Globe. (J. P. Feil, *Shakespeare Survey*, xi [1958], 109.)

27 (Th) William Rowley's *All's Lost by Lust* entered S.R.

28 (F) ⟨ ⟩ 5 October (F) The Queen danced in a masque in a country village not far from London. (*C.S.P., Ven.*, 1632–6, pp. 15–16.)

OCTOBER

12 (F) Herbert licensed Jonson's *The Magnetic Lady, or Humours Reconciled*. (iv. 619.)

?27 (Sa) John Pory remarked about the extreme length of Walter Montagu's *The Shepherd's Paradise*, intended for performance at Denmark House on the King's birthday on 19 November. (J. P. Feil, *Shakespeare Survey*, xi [1958], 109.)

29 (M) The Lord Mayor's Show for Sir Nicholas Raynton, haberdasher: Heywood's *Londini Artium et Scientiarum Scaturigo, or London's Fountain of Arts and Sciences*, was performed. (iv. 575–6; *M.S.C.* iii. 121–2.)

NOVEMBER

2 (F) The anonymous *The Costly Whore* entered S.R.

6 (Tu) Herbert records his receipts at the second day of a revival of Fletcher's *The Wild Goose Chase* at Blackfriars. (i. 23–24.)

9 (F) James Shirley's *A Contention for Honour and Riches* entered S.R.

10 (Sa) Massinger's *A New Way to Pay Old Debts* and Fulke Greville's *Works*, containing *Alaham* and *Mustapha*, entered S.R.

12 (M) Blagrave and Beeston petitioned the Lord Chamberlain for the return of a boy actor inveigled from them and employed at Blackfriars. (i. 35–36.)

15 (Th) The actors at Blackfriars were summoned before the Court of High Commission at Lambeth to answer charges of uttering the profanity contained in Jonson's new comedy, *The Magnetic Lady*. (J. P. Feil, *Shakespeare Survey*, xi [1958] 109.)

16 (F) Herbert licensed James Shirley's *The Ball* for performance by the Queen's company. (v. 1077.) A warrant was issued for the apprehension of John Jerome, gentleman; Roades, a stationer; and Booker, a sergeant-at-mace in London, upon the complaint of George Stutville, actor. (ii. 581.)

17 (Sa) Sir Humphrey Mildmay saw a play at an unnamed London theatre. (ii. 675.)

18 (Su) Herbert recorded objections to the impersonation of recognizable court figures in James Shirley's *The Ball*. (v. 1077.)

20 (Tu) Marlowe's *The Jew of Malta* entered S.R.

30 (F) Sir Humphrey Mildmay saw a play at an unnamed London theatre. (ii. 675.)

The Queen's company acted fourteen unnamed and undated plays at court between November 1632 and February 1632/3. (i. 249; *M.S.C.* ii. 361 and vi. 82.) James Clegorne and six assistants were paid £67. 10s. 0d. for ninety days of work done in November–April 1633, making ready the Cockpit for twenty-nine plays; in preparing the Great Hall for the practising; and in preparing the New Year's Gift Chamber and the Hall for the Maundy. (*M.S.C.* vi. 123.)

DECEMBER

5 (W) An order for liveries was made to fourteen members of Queen Henrietta's company. (i. 229.)

10 (M) William Crome petitioned the Lord Chamberlain against six members of Prince Charles's (II) company. (ii. 392.)

19 (W) ⟨ ⟩ 22 (Sa) Sir Humphrey Mildmay saw a play at an unnamed London theatre. (ii. 675.)

21 (F) William Crome's petition to sue six members of Prince Charles's (II) company was granted by the Lord Chamberlain. (ii. 392.)

Richard Brome's *Novella* was acted by the King's company at the Blackfriars sometime in 1632, according to the 1653 title-page. (iii. 84.) Also, his *Weeding of Covent Garden* was apparently acted in 1632. (iii. 89–91.)

Plays published in 1632

William Alabaster, *Roxana* (two edns.);

Richard Brome, *The Northern Lass* (Q1) ;
Thomas Goffe, *The Courageous Turk, or Amurath the First*;
Peter Hausted, *The Rival Friends*;
Thomas Heywood, *The Four Prentices of London* (Q2) ; *If You
  Know Not Me, You Know Nobody*, Part I (Q7) ; *The Iron
  Age*, Parts I (two issues) and II ; *Londini Artium et Scien-
  tiarum Scaturigo, or London's Fountain of Arts and Sciences*;
John Lyly, *Six Court Comedies*, including *Endymion, Campaspe,
  Sappho and Phao, Galathea, Midas,* and *Mother Bombie* (two
  issues) ;
Shakerley Marmion, *Holland's Leaguer*;
John Mason, *The Turk* (*Muleasses the Turk*) (Q2) ;
Philip Massinger, *The Emperor of the East*; *The Maid of
  Honour* (Q—two issues) ;
Philip Massinger and Nathan Field, *The Fatal Dowry*;
Thomas Randolph, *The Jealous Lovers* (Q1) ;
Samuel Rowley, *When You See Me, You Know Me* (Q4) ;
William Rowley, *A New Wonder, a Woman Never Vext*;
William Shakespeare, *Henry IV*, Part I (Q8—9th edn.) ;
William Shakespeare, the Second Folio ;
James Shirley, *The Changes, or Love in a Maze*;
Edmund Stubbe, *Fraus Honesta*;
Thomas Tomkis, *Lingua* (Q5) ;
Aurelian Townshend, *Albion's Triumph* (two issues—dated
  1631) ; *Tempe Restored* (dated 1631).

1632/33

JANUARY

9 (W) The Queen performed in Montagu's pastoral, *The Shepherd's Paradise*, at Somerset House. (iv. 917–18.)

14 (M) The King's company was paid £2 by the Earl of Essex's
  servants, apparently for permitting them to perform Wilson's
  The Corporal. (v. 1270–1.) Herbert licensed James Shirley's
  The Witty Fair One for the press. (v. 1166.)

15 (Tu) James Shirley's *The Witty Fair One* and William
  Rowley's *A Match at Midnight* entered S.R.

16 (W) Sir Humphrey Mildmay saw a play at an unnamed
  London theatre. (ii. 675.)

21 (M) Herbert licensed James Shirley's *The Bird in a Cage* (as
  The Beauties). (v. 1080.) Ford's *Love's Sacrifice* entered S.R.

22(Tu) Sir Humphrey Mildmay saw a play at Blackfriars. (ii. 675.)

FEBRUARY

2 (Sa) A second performance of the Queen in Montagu's pastoral, *The Shepherd's Paradise*, was planned for this date. (iv. 918.)

27 (W) A warrant was issued for a licence to William Perry and his associates to act in York and elsewhere. (i. 273.)

About this month Nabbes's *Covent Garden* was performed at the Phoenix by Queen Henrietta's men. (iv. 932–4.) Between November 1632 and February 1632/3 the Queen's company acted fourteen plays at court before the King and Queen (*M.S.C.* vi. 82); these should be considered along with the preparations by James Clegorne and six assistants for twenty-nine plays between November 1632 and April 1633. (*M.S.C.* vi. 123.)

MARCH

3 (Su) The last of the twenty-three plays performed by the King's men before the King in the period 3 May 1632 (Th) ⟨ ⟩ 3 March 1632/3 was presumably acted on this day (*M.S.C.* ii. 360); these should be considered along with the preparations by James Clegorne and six assistants for twenty-nine plays between November 1632 and April 1633. (*M.S.C.* vi. 123.)

Sometime in March, William Heminges's *The Coursing of a Hare, or The Madcap* was performed at the Fortune theatre. (iv. 542.)

5 Shrove Tuesday. An unknown Queen's masque was performed 'in the public hall' (*C.S.P., Ven.*, 1632–6, p. 86); John Flower wrote that it was to be at Denmark House, where it probably was, in which case it may have been the second performance of Montagu's *The Shepherd's Paradise*. (J. P. Feil, *Shakespeare Survey*, xi [1958], 110.)

19 (Tu) James Shirley's *The Bird in a Cage* entered S.R.

1633

28 (Th) Ford's *The Broken Heart* entered S.R.

APRIL

15 (M) Royal livery was granted to fourteen members of the King's company (i. 90); John Honyman and John Thompson sworn Grooms of the Chamber as King's men. (ii. 477; 600.)

21 Easter Sunday.

27 (Sa) ⟨ ⟩ 27 April 1634 (M) The King's company acted twenty-two plays at court before the King. (*M.S.C.* ii. 373 and vi. 84.) James Clegorne and six assistants were paid £67. 10s. 0d. for ninety days of work done between November 1632 and April 1633 in making ready the Cockpit for twenty-nine plays; in preparing the Great Hall for the practising; and in preparing the New Year's Gift Chamber and the Hall for the Maundy. (*M.S.C.* vi. 123.)

MAY

4 (Sa) Beeston secured an additional term of nine years to his lease of the Cockpit and adjacent property, to run until 28 September 1656 (Su). (ii. 368.)

6 (M) Lowin and Taylor were given a Lord Chamberlain's warrant to draft, for the King's company, players from any other London troupe. (i. 34.)

7 (Tu) Herbert licensed Jonson's *A Tale of a Tub*, with deletions. (iv. 632.)

9 (Th) Markham and Sampson's *Herod and Antipater* transferred S.R.

11 (Sa) Herbert licensed Fletcher's *The Night Walker*, as revised by Shirley, for performance by the Queen's company. (iii. 384.)

14 (Tu) Sir Humphrey Mildmay saw a play. (ii. 675.)

16 (Th) Sir Humphrey Mildmay saw a play at the Globe. (ii. 675.)

21 (Tu) Jonson's *The King's Entertainment at Welbeck* (Nottinghamshire) was performed. (iv. 648–9.)

23 (Th) Sir Humphrey Mildmay saw Fletcher's *Rollo, or The Bloody Brother* at the Globe. (ii. 675.)

JUNE

6 (Th) Herbert recorded his receipts at the second day of a revival of an unnamed play at the Globe. (i. 23–24.) Sir Humphrey Mildmay saw 'a pretty & Merry Comedy' at the Phoenix. (ii. 675.)

8 (Sa) ⟨ ⟩ 10 (M) Sir Humphrey Mildmay saw a play at the Globe. (ii. 675.)

10 (M) ⟨ ⟩ 15 (Sa) Bear-baiting and bull-baiting were presented before the King at Whitsuntide. (*M.S.C.* vi. 84.)

15 (Sa) Marmion's *A Fine Companion* entered S.R.

27 (Th) Herbert licensed, with deletions, Mountfort's *The Launching of the Mary, or The Seaman's Honest Wife*, for performance. (iv. 923–4.)

JULY

3 (W) Herbert licensed James Shirley's *The Young Admiral* for performance, with a special approbation. (v. 1168.)

15 (M) Heywood's *The English Traveller* entered S.R.

18 (Th) Sir Humphrey Mildmay saw a play at the Globe. (ii. 675.)

AUGUST

1 (Th) Jasper Fisher's *Fuimus Troes, or The True Trojans* entered S.R., as acted at Magdalen College, Oxford.

3 (Sa) Markham and Sampson's *Herod and Antipater* transferred S.R.

15 (Th) Beeston, for Queen Henrietta's men, paid Herbert for the latter's interest in, as well as for his allowing alterations to, an old play, William Rowley's *Hymen's Holiday, or Cupid's Vagaries*. (v. 1023.)

SEPTEMBER

6 (F) *Il Pastor Fido*, translated by 'Dymock', transferred S.R.

OCTOBER

⟩ 1 (Tu) The Prince's company acted three unnamed and undated plays before the King at court. (*M.S.C.* vi. 83.)

9 (W) The Privy Council appointed a committee to evaluate the Blackfriars theatre preparatory to abolition. (vi. 27.)

18 (F) Herbert ordered the King's company to suppress *The Tamer Tamed* at Blackfriars. (i. 37.) The King's company acted Beaumont and Fletcher's *The Scornful Lady* at Blackfriars. (i. 37.)

19 (Sa) Herbert purged the prompt copy of *The Tamer Tamed* of oaths, profaneness, and ribaldry. (i. 37.)

24 (Th) In a petition to the Court of High Commission the King's company admitted that Sir Henry Herbert was not responsible for the inclusion of offensive oaths in Jonson's *The Magnetic Lady*. (iv. 619.) The following plays transferred S.R.: the anonymous *The Tragedy of Nero (Piso's Conspiracy)*, Dekker and Massinger's *The Virgin Martyr*, May's *The Heir*, Beaumont and Fletcher's *Cupid's Revenge*, Beaumont and Fletcher's *The Scornful Lady*, and W. Smith's *The Hector of Germany, or The Palsgrave*.

29 (Tu) The Lord Mayor's Show for Sir Ralph Freeman, clothworker: Heywood's *Londini Emporia, or London's Mercatura*, was performed. (iv. 576.)

30 (W) The King's men agreed to pay the Master of the Revels gratuities of £10 every Christmas and £10 every midsummer; this agreement superseded the old one of 25 May 1628. (*Herbert*, p. 44.)

31 (Th) Herbert licensed Massinger's *The Guardian* for the King's company. (iv. 789.)
During October the Salisbury Court company was enjoined by Herbert from playing *The City Shuffler*, Part II. (v. 1309.)

NOVEMBER

11 (M) Herbert licensed James Shirley's *The Gamester* for performance. (v. 1110.)

16 (Sa) The King's company performed *Richard III* for the King and Queen at St. James's. (*Herbert*, p. 53.)

19 (Tu) James Shirley's *The Young Admiral* was performed by the Queen's company for the court at St. James's. (v. 1168.)

20 (W) The King's men evaluated Blackfriars at £21,000, while the commissioners evaluated it at £3,000. (vi. 27–28.) The Privy Council ordered coaches to park no nearer Blackfriars than St. Paul's churchyard or the Fleet Street Conduit. (vi. 29.)

23 (Sa) Herbert allowed, with some reformations, Fletcher's old play, *The Loyal Subject*. (iii. 370.)

26 (Tu) Shakespeare's *The Taming of the Shrew* was performed at St. James's. (*Herbert*, p. 53.)

28 (Th) Fletcher's *The Tamer Tamed* was performed at St. James's. (*Herbert*, p. 53.)

DECEMBER

9 (M) Dekker's *The Noble Soldier* re-entered S.R.

10 (Tu) The King's men performed Fletcher's *The Loyal Subject* at court. (iii. 370.)

16 (M) Queen Henrietta's men performed William Rowley's *Hymen's Holiday, or Cupid's Vagaries* at Whitehall. (v. 1023.)

29 (Su) The Privy Council ordered that coaches might park within Blackfriars gate. (vi. 30.)
Sometime in 1633 Sir Matthew Brend unsuccessfully attempted to cancel the extension of the lease on the Globe to the King's company. (i. 30.) Bulstrode Whitelocke's *Coranto* was frequently played by musicians at Blackfriars during 1633. (i. 40.) Nabbes's *Tottenham Court* was acted at Salisbury Court theatre sometime in 1633. (iv. 940–2.) Seven plays (five known and two unknown) were presented at court by Queen

Henrietta's company before 25 March 1634. (i. 249; *M.S.C.* vi. 84.)

Plays published in 1633

Anonymous, *Arden of Feversham* (Q3);
Anonymous, *The Costly Whore*;
Anonymous, *The Tragedy of Nero* (*Piso's Conspiracy*) (Q2);
John Day, *The Isle of Gulls* (Q2);
William Drummond, *The Entertainment of King Charles at Edinburgh*;
'Dymock', translation of *Il Pastor Fido* (2nd edn.);
Jasper Fisher, *Fuimus Troes, or The True Trojans*;
John Ford, *The Broken Heart*; *Love's Sacrifice*; *'Tis Pity She's a Whore* (two issues);
Thomas Goffe, *The Tragedy of Orestes*;
Robert Gomersall, *Poems*, including *The Tragedy of Lodovick Sforza, Duke of Milan* (2nd edn.);
Fulke Greville, *The Works*, including *Alaham* and *Mustapha*;
Peter Hausted, *Senile Odium*;
Thomas Heywood, *The English Traveller*; *If You Know Not Me, You Know Nobody*, Part II (Q4); *Londini Emporia, or London's Mercatura*;
Thomas Kyd, *The Spanish Tragedy* (10th edn.);
Gervase Markham, *The Dumb Knight* (Q2);
Christopher Marlowe, *The Jew of Malta*;
Shakerley Marmion, *A Fine Companion*;
John Marston, *The Works*, including *Antonio and Mellida, Antonio's Revenge, The Wonder of Women, What You Will, Parasitaster*, and *The Dutch Courtesan* (two issues);
Philip Massinger, *A New Way to Pay Old Debts*;
Thomas May, *The Heir* (Q2);
William Rowley, *All's Lost by Lust*; *A Match at Midnight*;
James Shirley, *The Bird in a Cage*; *A Contention for Honour and Riches*; *The Wedding* (Q2); *The Witty Fair One*;
Philip Sidney, *Arcadia*, including *The Entertainment at Wanstead* (*The Lady of May*).

1633/34

JANUARY

1 (W) The King's company performed Shakespeare's *Cymbeline* at court. (*Herbert*, p. 53.)

2 (Th) Markham and Sampson's *Herod and Antipater* reassigned S.R.

6 (M) The King's company performed Fletcher's *The Faithful Shepherdess* at Denmark House. (*Herbert*, p. 53.)

9 (Th) The King examined Herbert's deletions in *The Wits* and allowed minor oaths to stand, while he approved the greater part of Herbert's reformations. (iii. 222.)

10 (F) Herbert returned to Davenant the playbook of *The Wits* corrected by the King. (iii. 222.)

12 (Su) The King's company performed Massinger's *The Guardian* at court. (iv. 789.)

14 (Tu) The Queen's company performed Jonson's *A Tale of a Tub* at court. (iv. 633.) Sir Humphrey Mildmay saw a play at an unnamed London theatre. (ii. 675.)

16 (Th) The King's company performed Shakespeare's *The Winter's Tale* at court. (*Herbert*, p. 54.)

19 (Su) Herbert licensed Davenant's *The Wits* for performance at Blackfriars. (iii. 223.)

21 (Tu) Sir Humphrey Mildmay saw a play at Blackfriars. (ii. 675.)

22 (W) Sir Humphrey Mildmay saw Davenant's *The Wits* at Blackfriars. (ii. 675.)

24 (F) James Shirley's *The Triumph of Peace* entered S.R., as it was to be presented before the King at Whitehall on the following 3 February (M).

27 (M) Sir Humphrey Mildmay saw a new play at an unnamed London theatre. (ii. 675.)

28 (Tu) Davenant's *The Wits* was performed at court. (iii. 223.)

30 (Th) Fletcher's *The Night Walker*, revised by Shirley, was performed at court. (iii. 384.)

FEBRUARY

3 (M) Sir Humphrey Mildmay saw the procession of Shirley's masque, *The Triumph of Peace*, in the Strand. (ii. 675.) The gentlemen of the Inns of Court presented James Shirley's masque, *The Triumph of Peace*, at court before the King and Queen. (v. 1156–60.)

6 (Th) James Shirley's *The Gamester*, written from a plot by the King, was performed at court and well liked. (v. 1110.) Sir Humphrey Mildmay saw Shirley's *The Gamester* at Whitehall. (ii. 675.)

7 (F) Sir Humphrey Mildmay saw an unnamed play at Blackfriars. (ii. 675.)

13 (Th) James Shirley's masque, *The Triumph of Peace*, was per-
formed a second time before the King and Queen at the
Merchant Tailors' Hall in London. (v. 1158.) Sir Humphrey
Mildmay noted the performance. (ii. 676.)

18 Shrove Tuesday. Carew's *Coelum Britannicum* was acted at
court. (iii. 107–8.) Sir Humphrey Mildmay saw Carew's
masque performed at Whitehall and, apparently, he pur-
chased the text. (ii. 676.)

24 (M) Ford's *Perkin Warbeck* entered S.R.

MARCH

20 (Th) Sir Humphrey Mildmay went to 'a base play' at the
Phoenix. (ii. 676.)
In addition to the five named and dated plays given by Queen
Henrietta's men at court (i. 249), they gave two unnamed and
undated plays not later than 24 March 1633/4. (*M.S.C.* vi.
84.)

1634

APRIL

6 Easter Sunday.

7 (M) The King's company performed Chapman's *Bussy d'Ambois*
for the court. (*Herbert*, p. 55.)

8 (Tu) Shakespeare and Fletcher's *The Two Noble Kinsmen* entered S.R. The King's company performed 'The Pastoral',
probably Fletcher's *The Faithful Shepherdess*, at the Cockpit-
in-Court. (*Herbert*, p. 55.)

17 (Th) *Bellum Grammaticale*, a Latin play by 'Master Spense',
entered S.R.

⟩27 (Su) In addition to the eleven named and dated plays
(i. 97), the King's men performed eleven others before the
King and Queen at court between 27 April 1633 (Sa) and this
date. (*M.S.C.* ii. 373 and vi. 84.)

MAY

1 (Th) Sir Humphrey Mildmay saw a new play, Carlell's *The
Spartan Lady*. (iii. 124.)

7 (W) Herbert licensed Massinger's *Cleander*, revised from
Fletcher's *The Lovers' Progress* (?), for the King's company.
(iv. 774.)

8 (Th) Sir Humphrey Mildmay saw a play at an unnamed London
theatre. (ii. 676.)

13 (Tu) Massinger's *Cleander*, revised from Fletcher's *The Lovers'*

Progress (?), was performed before the Queen at Blackfriars. (iv. 774; *Herbert*, p. 65.) The King's men acted five unnamed and undated plays at Hampton Court and fifteen at Whitehall in the period 13 May 1634 (Tu) ⟨ ⟩ 30 March 1635 (M), presumably the first and the last on the days mentioned. (*M.S.C.* ii. 376 and vi. 86.)

21 (W) Sir Humphrey Mildmay saw *Lisander and Callista* (Fletcher and Massinger's *The Lovers' Progress*). (ii. 676.)

26 (M) ⟨ ⟩ 31 (Sa) Bear-baiting and bull-baiting were presented before the King on an unspecified day in Whitsuntide, apparently in addition to the baiting before the Prince on 29 May (Th). (*M.S.C.* vi. 83.)

29 (Th) Bear-baiting and bull-baiting were presented before the Prince at St. James's. (*M.S.C.* vi. 83.)

JUNE

6 (F) Herbert licensed Massinger's *A Very Woman, or The Prince of Tarent* for the King's company. (iv. 825.)
During the summer, the Lancashire witches were exhibited in London, and public plays about them were acted. (i. 41.)

24 (Tu) Herbert licensed James Shirley's *The Example* for performance. (v. 1108.)

25 (W) Heywood's *A Maidenhead Well Lost* entered S.R.

JULY

14 (M) ⟨ ⟩ 24 August (Su) The Prince's players attended the King and Queen on progress. (i. 310–11; *M.S.C.* vi. 83.)

18 (F) Richard Kendall, wardrobe keeper at the Salisbury Court theatre, told Thomas Crosfield at Oxford a good deal about the London dramatic companies. (ii. 688–9.)

20 (Su) Prince Charles's (II) company were provided with a tent for the King's progress. (i. 310.) The King's company petitioned against the insertion of witch scenes into a rival play, probably the anonymous *Doctor Lamb and the Witches*. (v. 1455.)

20 (Su) ⟨ ⟩ 28 October (Tu) Heywood and Brome's *The Late Lancashire Witches* opened at the Globe. (iii. 75.)

30 (W) Jonson's *Love's Welcome at Bolsover* (Derbyshire) was performed. (iv. 653.)

AUGUST

8 (F) Massinger's *The Picture* transferred S.R.

16 (Sa) Herbert licensed an old play, *Doctor Lamb and the*

Witches, with new scenes, for performance by the King's Revels company at Salisbury Court. (v. 1455.)

25 (M) Prince Charles's (II) company was paid for attending King Charles on progress. (i. 310.) In the period 14 July (M) ⟨ ⟩ 25 August (M) Prince Charles's (II) company presented not more than ten plays at court. (i. 322.)

SEPTEMBER

3 (W) Lord Goring entertained the Queen and the Marquis of San Germano with comedies, dancing, music, and other agreeable pastimes. (*C.S.P., Ven.*, 1632–6, p. 275.)

11 (Th) Thomas Basse, player, made his will. (ii. 631.)

15 (M) Marston and Barkstead's *The Insatiate Countess* and Webster's *The White Devil* transferred S.R.

29 (M) Milton's masque *Comus* was performed at Ludlow Castle. (iv. 913–14.)

In September and October, Prince Charles's (II) company presented three unnamed plays at Hampton Court. (i. 311; *M.S.C.* ii. 377 and vi. 86.)

OCTOBER

22 (W) ⟨ ⟩ 29 (W) Juan Navarro and his Spanish troupe apparently performed before the King and Queen at Hampton Court. (J. P. Feil, *Shakespeare Survey*, xi [1958], 110.)

23 (Th) William Browne, player, made his will. (ii. 636–7.)

28 (Tu) Brome and Heywood's *The Late Lancashire Witches* entered S.R. (iii. 73.) The play opened at the Globe sometime in the period 20 July (Su) ⟨ ⟩ 28 October. (iii. 75.)

29 (W) The Lord Mayor's Show for Sir Robert Parkhurst, clothworker: Taylor's *The Triumphs of Fame and Honour* was performed. (v. 1225.)

NOVEMBER

3 (M) James Shirley's *The Traitor* entered S.R.

9 (Su) Sir Humphrey Mildmay saw Jonson's *Catiline* at court. (ii. 676.)

13 (Th) ⟨ ⟩ 18 (Tu) Heywood's *Love's Mistress, or The Queen's Masque* was performed before the King and Queen at the Phoenix. (iv. 582.)

18 (Tu) Sir John Suckling attacked Mr. Digby as he came from the Blackfriars theatre. (i. 42.)

19 (W) Heywood's *Love's Mistress, or The Queen's Masque* was performed at court. (iv. 582.)

20 (Th) Herbert licensed Davenant's *Love and Honour* for performance at Blackfriars. (iii. 205.)
20 (Th) ⟨ ⟩ 26 (W) Heywood's *Love's Mistress, or The Queen's
   Masque* was performed at court. (iv. 582.)
24 (M) Herbert allowed the anonymous *The Proxy, or Love's
   Aftergame* to be produced at Salisbury Court. (v. 1399.)
29 (Sa) Herbert licensed James Shirley's *The Opportunity* for
   performance. (v. 1135.) Sir Humphrey Mildmay saw a play,
   'a fine one', at an unnamed London theatre. (ii. 676.)

DECEMBER

12 (F) Sir Humphrey Mildmay saw Davenant's *Love and Honour*,
   apparently at Blackfriars. (ii. 676.)
16 (Tu) Livery allowance was granted to fourteen members of
   Queen Henrietta's company. (i. 247.)
   Sometime in 1634 Benfield, Swanston, and Pollard petitioned the Lord Chamberlain to be admitted sharers in the
   Globe and Blackfriars. (i. 43–45.) The petition to build the
   amphitheatre was renewed. (vi. 301–3.)

Plays published in 1634

   Anonymous, *How a Man May Choose a Good Wife from a Bad*
      (Q7);
   Anonymous, *Mucedorus* (13th edn.);
   Francis Beaumont and John Fletcher, *Philaster* (Q4);
   Thomas Carew, *Coelum Britannicum*;
   Thomas Dekker, *The Noble Soldier*;
   John Fletcher, *The Faithful Shepherdess* (Q3);
   John Ford, *Perkin Warbeck*;
   Thomas Heywood, *A Maidenhead Well Lost*;
   Thomas Heywood and Richard Brome, *The Late Lancashire
      Witches*;
   James Mabbe, *The Spanish Bawd* (reissue of 1631 edn.);
   Thomas Randolph, *The Jealous Lovers* (Q2);
   William Shakespeare, *Richard II* (Q6—8th edn.); *Richard III*
      (Q8–10th edn.);
   William Shakespeare and John Fletcher, *The Two Noble
      Kinsmen*;
   James Shirley, *The Triumph of Peace* (Q1, Q2, and Q3—two
      issues of Q3—all dated 1633);
   John Taylor, *The Triumphs of Fame and Honour*;
   Thomas Tomkis, *Albumazar* (Q3).

1634/35

JANUARY

8 (Th) Henry Killigrew's *The Conspiracy* was apparently performed at York House in celebration of the marriage of
Lady Mary Villiers to Lord Charles Herbert. (iv. 691–2.)

10 (Sa) Herbert licensed Massinger's *The Orator* for the King's
company. (iv. 803.)

19 (M) Rutter's *The Shepherds' Holiday* entered S.R.
During the month plays were performed at the Temple and
Gray's Inn. (Symonds 'Diary', p. 386.) Also Prince
Charles's (II) company performed once or twice at St. James's
and/or the Cockpit-in-Court. (i. 311; *M.S.C.* ii. 377 and
vi. 86.)

FEBRUARY

5 (Th) George Wilde's *Eumorphus sive Cupido-Adultus* was performed at St. John's College, Oxford. (v. 1260.)

6 (F) Herbert licensed James Shirley's *The Coronation* for performance. (v. 1098.)

10 Shrove Tuesday. Davenant's *The Temple of Love* was performed at court. (iii. 216–18.) Not later than this date Queen
Henrietta's company performed seven unnamed and undated
plays before the Queen at Whitehall and one at Hampton
Court. (i. 249; *M.S.C.* vi. 85.)

11 (W) Davenant's *The Temple of Love* was repeated at court.
(iii. 216–18.)

12 (Th) Davenant's *The Temple of Love* was repeated at court.
(iii. 216–18.)

?14 (Sa) Davenant's *The Temple of Love* was repeated at court.
(iii. 216–18.) Sir Humphrey Mildmay saw a masque, probably
Davenant's *The Temple of Love*. (ii. 677.)

15 (Su) Queen Henrietta 'approved of' the French players 'at her
house', possibly in a performance at Denmark House. (i.
233–4.)

16 (M) Herbert imprisoned Cromes, a broker, for lending a church
robe to the King's Revels company. (vi. 101.)

17 (Tu) A company of French players presented du Rocher's
La Melise before the King and Queen at the Cockpit-in-
Court. (i. 234.) Josias Floridor and his French company were
paid for acting three plays before the court in the Cockpit-in-
Court in February; this performance must have been one
of them. (i. 235 n. 1; *M.S.C.* ii. 376 and vi. 85.)

19 (Th) Sir Humphrey Mildmay saw a play. (ii. 677.)

20 (F) Beeston agreed to allow the French players to use the Phoenix for performances on Wednesdays and Fridays during Lent. (vii. 4–5.)

During February, Prince Charles's (II) company performed once or twice at Whitehall and/or the Cockpit-in-Court. (i. 311; *M.S.C.* ii. 377 and vi. 86.) John Greene saw Fletcher's *The Elder Brother*, presumably at Blackfriars (iii. 332); Fletcher's *Rule a Wife and Have a Wife* at Blackfriars (iii. 408); *Truth's Triumph*, presumably at Blackfriars or the Phoenix (Symonds 'Diary', p. 386); and Marston's *The Malcontent*, presumably at Blackfriars. (i. 123.)

MARCH

During March John Greene saw Wilson's *The Inconstant Lady, or Better Late than Never* (v. 1272) and Middleton and Rowley's *The Changeling*. (iv. 862.)

23 (M) ⟨ ⟩ 28 (Sa) The French company played the whole week before Easter at the Phoenix. (vi. 65–66.)

1635

29 Easter Sunday.

30 (M) The last of the twenty King's company plays acted at court in the period 13 May 1634 (Tu) ⟨ ⟩ 30 March 1635 (M) was presumably acted on this day at Hampton Court or Whitehall. (i. 98; *M.S.C.* ii. 376 and vi. 86.)

APRIL

3 (F) Royal livery was granted to fourteen members of the King's company. (i. 90.)

?4 (Sa) The French company performed Scuderi's *Le Trompeur Puni, ou Histoire Septentrionale* at the Cockpit–in–Court. (*Herbert*, p. 61; *M.S.C.* ii. 376.)

?16 (Th) Floridor's French company performed Duryer's *Alcimedon* at the Cockpit-in-Court. (*Herbert*, p. 61; *M.S.C.* ii. 376.)

18 (Sa) A warrant was issued for the erection of a stage, scaffolds, and seats in M. Le Fevre's riding academy for the French company. (vi. 46.)

25 (Sa) Sir Humphrey Mildmay saw Fletcher's *The Elder Brother* at Blackfriars. (ii. 677.)

28 (Tu) Sir Humphrey Mildmay saw a play at Blackfriars. (ii. 677.)

29 (W) Herbert licensed Chapman and James Shirley's *Chabot, Admiral of France* for performance. (v. 1089.)

During April John Greene saw a performance of *Falstaff*. (Symonds 'Diary', p. 386.)

MAY

c. 1 (F)—15 (F) On 19 May Garrard wrote of a quarrel that lately broke out between Lord Digby and Will Crofts at a play at Blackfriars. (i. 47.)

5 (Tu) A warrant was issued to the French company, allowing them to act in M. Le Fevre's remodelled riding academy. (vi. 46.)

6 (W) Sir Humphrey Mildmay saw Shakespeare's *Othello* at Blackfriars. (ii. 677.)

10 (Su) The Lord Chamberlain issued a warrant for the payment of £30 to the French players for three plays acted by them at the Cockpit-in-Court. (ii. 437.)

During May, Prince Charles's (II) company performed once or twice at Whitehall and/or the Cockpit-in-Court. (i. 311; *M.S.C.* ii. 377 and vi. 86.)

JUNE

10 (W) John Greene saw Beaumont and Fletcher's *Wit without Money*, presumably at the Phoenix. (i. 250.)

JULY

4 (Sa) The following plays by Ben Jonson transferred S.R.: *Every Man in His Humour, Cynthia's Revels, Sejanus, Volpone, Epicoene, The Alchemist*, and *Catiline*.

12 (Su) The Lord Chamberlain ordered that Benfield, Pollard, and Swanston be allowed to buy shares in the Globe and Blackfriars from John Shank, Cuthbert Burbage, and the Robinsons. (i. 46.)

17 (F) Walter Hawkesworth's Latin comedy *Labyrinthus* entered S.R.

20 (M) Richard Brome signed a contract to write plays for the Salisbury Court theatre. (iii. 52–53.)

AUGUST

1 (Sa) Herbert licensed Davenant's *News from Plymouth* for performance at the Globe. (iii. 209.) After John Shank com-

plained that Benfield, Pollard, and Swanston had refused his offer of shares in the Globe and Blackfriars and had restrained him from the stage, the Lord Chamberlain appointed Sir Henry Herbert, Sir John Finett, and Daniel Bedingfield to set the price to be paid Shank for his shares. (*M.S.C.* ii. 372–3.)

19 (W) The following plays transferred S.R.: Daniel's *Cleopatra, Philotas*, and *The Queen's Arcadia*; Tomkis's *Lingua*; and part of Sidney's *Arcadia*, which contained *The Entertainment at Wanstead* (*The Lady of May*).

29 (Sa) Heywood's *Pleasant Dialogues and Dramas*, containing *Amphrisa* and *Apollo and Daphne*, entered S.R.

SEPTEMBER

1 (Tu) Elizabeth Condell, wife of Henry Condell, player, made her will, with theatrical legacies. (ii. 638–40.)

16 (W) Herbert renewed the performance licence of Fletcher's *Love's Pilgrimage* for the King's company. (iii. 367.)

30 (W) Heywood's *Love's Mistress, or The Queen's Masque* entered S.R.

OCTOBER

15 (Th) Henry Glapthorne's *The Lady Mother* was licensed by Blagrave, Herbert's deputy. (iv. 484.) Herbert licensed James Shirley's *The Lady of Pleasure* for performance. (v. 1125.)

29 (Th) The Lord Mayor's Show for Sir Christopher Clethrowe, ironmonger: Heywood's *Londini Sinus Salutis, or London's Harbour of Health and Happiness*, was presented by the Ironmongers' Company. (iv. 576–7, and *M.S.C.* iii. 122–5.) During October the King's Revels company presented one or two plays before the King and Queen at court. (i. 296; *M.S.C.* vi. 86.)

NOVEMBER

5 (Th) *or* 6 (F) John Greene and his friends saw Henry Killi-grew's *The Conspiracy* performed at Blackfriars (iv. 691) and James Shirley's *The Lady of Pleasure* performed at the Phoenix (v. 1125.)

16 (M) Herbert licensed Davenant's *The Platonic Lovers* for per-formance at Blackfriars. (iii. 211.)

19 (Th) Whitehall was prepared for the performance of 'the Pastorall' (*Florimene*?) on the King's birthday. (*M.S.C.* ii. 376.)

25 (W) Sir Humphrey Mildmay saw 'a fooleishe play' at Blackfriars. (ii. 677.)

27 (F) Sir Humphrey Mildmay saw a play at an unnamed London
theatre. (ii. 677.)

During November, Juan Navarro and his company of Spanish
players acted an unnamed and undated play at court before
the King. (*M.S.C.* vi. 88.) Between November 1635 and
12 May 1636 (Th) Carlell's *Arviragus and Philicia*, Part II,
was acted before the Queen at Blackfriars. (i. 98; iii. 113.)

DECEMBER

7 (M) Massinger's *The Great Duke of Florence* entered S.R.

8 (Tu) Sir Humphrey Mildmay saw James Shirley's *The Lady
of Pleasure*, presumably at the Phoenix. (v. 1125.)

11 (F) Sir Humphrey Mildmay saw 'the Newe playe' at an unnamed London theatre. (ii. 677.)

12 (Sa) Four members of Prince Charles's (II) company were
sworn as Grooms of the Chamber. (i. 311.)

14 (M) Herbert licensed the argument of the anonymous pastoral
Florimene for the press. (v. 1334.)

16 (W) Sir Humphrey Mildmay saw a play at Blackfriars. (ii.
678.)

21 (M) The anonymous pastoral *Florimene* was performed before the court by the French ladies of the Queen in the Great
Hall at Whitehall. (v. 1334.)

31 (Th) John Shank, player, made his will, with theatrical legacies.
(ii. 646–8.)

During December, Josias Floridor and his French company
acted an unnamed tragedy before the King at court. (i. 235;
M.S.C. ii. 378 and vi. 88.)

During 1635 Nabbes's *Hannibal and Scipio* was performed by
the Queen's company at the Phoenix. (iv. 935.) Brome's *The
Sparagus Garden* was acted at the Salisbury Court theatre by
the Company of the Revels, according to the 1640 title-page.
(iii. 87.) Nine plays were presented at court by Queen
Henrietta's company. (i. 249.) The King's company performed
four unnamed and undated plays at Hampton Court and ten
at Whitehall 'in Anno 1635'. (*M.S.C.* vi. 86 and ii. 378.)

Plays published in 1635

Anonymous, *The Argument of the Pastoral of Florimene* (non-
dramatic—an otherwise lost play);

Anonymous, *Bellum Grammaticale*;

Anonymous, *Wily Beguiled* (Q5);

Francis Beaumont and John Fletcher, *Cupid's Revenge* (Q3);
The Knight of the Burning Pestle (Q2), (Q3 dated 1635, but
probably printed several years later); *The Scornful Lady* (Q4);

?Samuel Daniel, *The Works* (a reissue of 1623 edn.—a unique
copy recorded only by Hazlitt, *Handbook*, p. 138);

William Davenant and Inigo Jones, *The Temple of Love* (Q—
dated 1634);

Thomas Dekker, *The Honest Whore*, Part I (5th edn.);

Thomas Heywood, *Londini Sinus Salutis, or London's Harbour
of Health and Happiness*;

John Jones, *Adrasta, or The Woman's Spleen and Love's Conquest*;

Ben Jonson, *Catiline* (3rd and 4th edns.);

Thomas Randolph, *Aristippus* and *The Conceited Pedlar* (Q6);

Joseph Rutter, *The Shepherds' Holiday*;

William Shakespeare, *Pericles* (6th edn.);

James Shirley, *The Traitor* (Q1).

1635/36

JANUARY

18 (M) Herbert licensed James Shirley's *The Duke's Mistress* for
performance. (v. 1107.)

19 (Tu) Herbert licensed Davenant's *The Wits* (iii. 223) and *The
Platonic Lovers* (iii. 211) for publication.

)25 (M) The Duke of Lennox and the Lord Chamberlain quar-
relled about a box at a new play at Blackfriars. (i. 48.)

FEBRUARY

4 (Th) Davenant's *The Wits* and *The Platonic Lovers* entered S.R.

16 (Tu) Carlell's *Arviragus and Philicia*, Part II, was acted at
court. (iii. 113.)

⟩ 17 (W) The King's Revels company presented one or two plays
at court before the King and Queen. (i. 296; *M.S.C.* vi. 86.)

18 (Th) The King's company performed Jonson's *Epicoene* at
court. (i. 98.)

19 (F) Davenant's *The Triumphs of the Prince D'Amour* entered S.R.

20 (Sa) Bear-baiting was presented before the Prince Elector
Palatine. (*M.S.C.* vi. 86.)

22 (M) *or* 25 (Th) James Shirley's *The Duke's Mistress* was performed at St. James's. (v. 1107.)

24 (W) Dekker's *The Wonder of a Kingdom* re-entered S.R.
Davenant's *The Triumphs of the Prince D'Amour* was performed at the Middle Temple. (iii. 218–20.) The anonymous
The Proxy, or Love's Aftergame was performed at St. James's
by the Salisbury Court company. (v. 1399.)

27 (Sa) The anonymous *The Fair Maid of the Exchange* transferred S.R. Kynaston's masque, *Corona Minervæ*, was performed before the royal children at the college, Museum
Minervæ. (iv. 717.)

28 (Su) Beaumont's *The Knight of the Burning Pestle* was performed at St. James's by the Queen's company. (*Herbert*, p. 56.)

MARCH

1 Shrove Tuesday. Lady Hatton presented a royal supper and
a brave masque to the King, the Queen, the Palsgrave, and
his brother. (Gawdy MSS., *Hist. MSS. Comm.*, 10th Report,
Part 2, p. 157.)

8 (Tu) The anonymous *Wily Beguiled* transferred S.R. Prince
Charles's (II) company was playing in Norwich by candlelight.
(i. 312.)

12 (Sa) Herbert licensed Henry Glapthorne's *The Hollander, or
Love's Trial* for the Queen's company. (iv. 482.)
The King's company acted four unnamed and undated plays
at Hampton Court and ten at Whitehall before 25 March
1636; two of them were probably those of 16 and 18 February 1635/6. (i. 98; *M.S.C.* ii. 378 and vi. 85–86.)

1636

APRIL

7 (Th) John Honyman, player, made his will. (ii. 645.)

17 Easter Sunday.

18 (M) Carlell's *Arviragus and Philicia*, Part I, was acted at
court. (iii. 113.)

19 (Tu) Carlell's *Arviragus and Philicia*, Part II, was acted at
court. (iii. 113.)

21 (Th) The King's men acted Jonson's *Epicoene* at the Cockpit-
in-Court. (i. 51.)

MAY

5 (Th) The King's company performed the anonymous *Alphonsus,
Emperor of Germany* before the Queen and the Prince
Elector at Blackfriars. (v. 1286.)

9 (M) Herbert licensed Massinger's *The Bashful Lover* for the King's company. (iv. 760.)

12 (Th) Herbert received £1 for allowing the Fortune company to add scenes to an old play and 'give it out for a new one'. (ii. 404.) Herbert closed the theatres because of the plague; this closure lasted for fifteen months. (ii. 661–5.)

17 (Tu) A pass was issued for eighteen members of the King's company to accompany King Charles on his summer progress. (i. 49–50.)

JUNE

17 (F) Heywood's *A Challenge for Beauty* entered S.R.

AUGUST

6 (Sa) Nabbes's *Hannibal and Scipio* and *Microcosmus* entered S.R.

23 (Tu) The Presentment of Bushell's Rock to Queen Henrietta took place. (Greg, *Bibliography*, ii. 655–6.)

29 (M) Strode's *The Floating Island* (*Passions Calmed, Prudentius*) was performed before the King at Christ Church, Oxford, with airs and songs by Henry Lawes. (v. 1189–91.)

30 (Tu) Wilde's *Love's Hospital* (*The Lovers' Hospital*) was performed before the King and Queen at St. John's, Oxford, before supper (v. 1260–4); Cartwright's *The Royal Slave* was performed before the King and Queen at Christ Church, Oxford, after supper. (iii. 135–7.)

SEPTEMBER

2 (F) Cartwright's *The Royal Slave* was acted again at Christ Church, Oxford, in the afternoon. (iii. 137.)

3 (Sa) Strode's *The Floating Island* (*Passions Calmed, Prudentius*) was performed again at Christ Church, Oxford, in the afternoon. (v. 1192.)

12 (M) An anonymous masque, *The King and Queen's Entertainment at Richmond*, was presented. (v. 1357.) Among the 'Payments to officers of the Wardrobe etc.' is a payment to Theobald Peirce for work done in March–October 1636, making ready the lodgings for the Prince's masque. (*M.S.C.* vi. 123.) The Declared Accounts of the Office of Works for the period 1 October 1635 (Th) ⟨ ⟩ 30 September 1636 (F) provide payment for painting a scene and making, painting, and gilding six shields with empresses for a masque presented before the Prince. (P.R.O. E 351/3269.)

OCTOBER

29 (Sa) Sir Edward Bromfield, fishmonger, took office as Lord Mayor, but there is no record of a pageant. In spite of preparations (*M.S.C.* iii. 125), the pageant was probably cancelled because of the plague. (ii. 669.)

NOVEMBER

17 (Th) The King's men acted *The Coxcomb* at Hampton Court. (i. 51.)

19 (Sa) Fletcher's *Beggars' Bush* was performed by the King's men at Hampton Court. (iii. 313.)

29 (Tu) The King's men performed Beaumont and Fletcher's *The Maid's Tragedy* at Hampton Court. (i. 51.)

DECEMBER

6 (Tu) Fletcher's *The Loyal Subject* was performed by the King's men at Hampton Court. (iii. 371.)

8 (Th) The King's men performed *Othello* at Hampton Court. (i. 51.)

13 (Tu) The King ordered his company to stay near the court and gave them an allowance of £20 per week, beginning 1 November (Tu). (i. 53.)

16 (F) The King's men performed Fletcher's *Love's Pilgrimage* at Hampton Court. (iii. 367.)

26 (M) Carlell's *Arviragus and Philicia*, Part I, was acted at Hampton Court. (iii. 114.)

27 (Tu) Carlell's *Arviragus and Philicia*, Part II, was acted at Hampton Court. (iii. 114.)

Sometime in 1636 Herbert licensed May's *The Old Couple* for performance. (iv. 839.)

Plays published in 1636

Anonymous, *The King and Queen's Entertainment at Richmond*;
Anonymous, *The Presentment of Bushell's Rock*;
Anonymous, *Sir Gyles Goosecap* (Q2);
David, Lord Barry, *Ram Alley* (3rd edn.);
William Davenant, *The Platonic Lovers*; *The Triumphs of the Prince D'Amour* (dated 1635); *The Wits*;
Thomas Dekker, *The Wonder of a Kingdom*;
Walter Hawkesworth, *Labyrinthus*;
Thomas Heywood, *A Challenge for Beauty*; *Love's Mistress, or The Queen's Masque* (Q1);

Francis Kynaston, *Corona Minervæ* (Q—two issues—dated 1635);

Philip Massinger, *The Great Duke of Florence*;

William Sampson, *The Vow-Breaker, or The Fair Maid of Clifton.*

1636/37

JANUARY

1 (Su) The King's men performed Davenant's *Love and Honour* at Hampton Court. (iii. 206.)

5 (Th) The King's men performed Fletcher's *The Elder Brother* at Hampton Court. (iii. 332.)

10 (Tu) The King's men performed Beaumont and Fletcher's *A King and No King* at Hampton Court. (i. 51.)

12 (Th) A ticket of privilege for freedom from arrest was granted to eleven minor actors and other employees of the King's company. (i. 49–50 n.) The King's men performed Cartwright's *The Royal Slave* at court. (iii. 135.)

17 (Tu) The King's men performed Fletcher's *Rollo, or The Bloody Brother* at Hampton Court. (iii. 402.)

24 (Tu) The King's men performed *Hamlet* at Hampton Court. (i. 51.)

30 (M) Sir William Alexander, Earl of Stirling's *Recreations with the Muses* (containing *Croesus, Darius, The Alexandrean Tragedy*, and *Julius Caesar*) entered S.R.

31 (Tu) The King's men performed Shakespeare's *Julius Caesar* at St. James's. (i. 51.)

FEBRUARY

2 (Th) Cowley's *Naufragium Joculare* was performed at Trinity College, Cambridge. (iii. 181.)

7 (Tu) Beeston's Boys performed Beaumont and Fletcher's *Cupid's Revenge* at St. James's. (i. 325.)

9 (Th) The King's men performed Fletcher's *A Wife for a Month* at St. James's. (iii. 422.)

14 (Tu) Beeston's Boys performed the anonymous *Wit without Money* at St. James's. (i. 325.)

16 (Th) *or* 17 (F) The King's men performed *The Governor*, by Sir Cornelius Formido (?), at St. James's. (iii. 465.)

21 Shrove Tuesday. Christopher Beeston was sworn governor of the King and Queen's young company at the Cockpit. (ii. 369.) The King's company performed Beaumont and Fletcher's *Philaster* at St. James's. (i. 52.)

24 (F) The theatres reopened for a week or so. (ii. 662.)

?24 (F) Christopher Beeston was commanded to make a company of boys, and he had them begin performances at the Phoenix the same day. (ii. 369.)

MARCH

24 (F) Fletcher's *The Elder Brother* entered S.R.

1637

25 (Sa) Heywood's *The Royal King and the Loyal Subject* entered S.R.

27 (M) Heywood and Brome's *The Late Lancashire Witches* transferred S.R.

APRIL

9 Easter Sunday.

13 (Th) James Shirley's *Hyde Park*, *The Lady of Pleasure*, and *The Young Admiral* entered S.R.

22 (Sa) Royal livery was granted to sixteen members of the King's company. (i. 90.)

26 (W) J. W.'s *The Valiant Scot* entered S.R.

28 (F) George Wilkins's *The Miseries of Enforced Marriage* transferred S.R.

MAY

12 (F) A warrant was issued to arrest Christopher Beeston and four other members of Beeston's Boys and to stop performances at the Cockpit. (i. 327.)

During May, Christopher Beeston craved pardon of the Privy Council for presenting a play at the Cockpit during plague-closing. (i. 327–8.)

JUNE

10 (Sa) The Lord Chamberlain ordered all London printers to refrain from publishing any play belonging to the King's company or to Beeston's Boys without consent of the company. (i. 54.)

JULY

1 (Sa) The following plays transferred S.R.: Matthew Gwinne's Latin tragedy *Nero*, Field's *A Woman Is a Weathercock*, Thomas Randolph's *Aristippus*, the former owners' part of

Shakespeare's works, Jonson's *The Staple of News* and *Bartholomew Fair*, Jasper Fisher's *Fuimus Troes, or The True Trojans*, and Massinger's *The Roman Actor*.

AUGUST

3 (Th) A comedy was performed at York House in honour of the marriage of the Duke of Lennox to Lady Mary Villiers. (*C.S.P., Dom.*, 1637, pp. 355–6.)

SEPTEMBER

3 (Su) The King's men petitioned the Privy Council to be allowed to resume playing. (ii. 663–4.)

17 (Su) Beeston petitioned permission for his company to rehearse at the Cockpit in spite of the plague-closing. (ii. 664.) King's men's petition granted. (ii. 664.)

24 (Su) Queen Henrietta's players petitioned to have the plague restriction removed so that they could play. (ii. 664.)

25 (M) Shirley's *The Wedding*, Chettle's *Hoffman*, Shirley's *The Grateful Servant*, and Marmion's *Holland's Leaguer* transferred S.R.

30 (Sa) The King's men presumably performed a play at court on this date. (i. 57, 99; *M.S.C.* ii. 387 and vi. 88.)

OCTOBER

c. 2 (M) Herbert joined Perkins, Sumner, Sherlock, and Turner with the best players at the Salisbury Court theatre. (ii. 608.)

2 (M) The theatres reopened after the plague-closing of 1636–7. (ii. 664–5.)

18 (W) James Shirley's *The Example* entered S.R.

30 (M) Since the 29th fell on a Sunday, the Lord Mayor's Show for Sir Richard Fenn, haberdasher: Heywood's *Londini Speculum, or London's Mirror*, was performed on the 30th. (iv. 577, and *M.S.C.* iii. 125.)

NOVEMBER

1 (W) Sir John Finett reported progress on a building at Whitehall to be used only for masques and dancing. (J. P. Feil, *Shakespeare Survey*, xi [1958], 111.)

3 (F) Sir Humphrey Mildmay saw a play at Blackfriars. (ii. 678.)

)9 (Th) Lady Newport attended a play at the Phoenix. (i. 329.)

15 (W) James Shirley's *The Gamester* entered S.R.

28 (Tu) William Rowley's *A Shoemaker a Gentleman* entered S.R. During November, Prince Charles's (II) company performed

one or two plays before the King at Richmond and/or St. James's. (*M.S.C.* vi. 88.)

DECEMBER

Christmas Season. The Gentlemen of Exeter College presented a comedy to the University. (E. S. de Beer, *The Diary of John Evelyn* [1955], ii. 20.)

During December, Prince Charles's (II) company performed one or two plays before the King at Richmond and/or St. James's. (*M.S.C.* vi. 88.)

Plays published in 1637

Sir William Alexander, *Recreations with the Muses*, containing *Croesus, Darius, The Alexandrean Tragedy*, and *Julius Caesar*;

Anonymous, *The Fair Maid of the Exchange* (3rd edn.);

John Fletcher, *The Elder Brother* (Q1; Q2, dated 1637, must be 1637 ⟨ ⟩ 1661, and perhaps even after the quarto of 1651);

Thomas Heywood, *Londini Speculum, or London's Mirror*; *The Royal King and the Loyal Subject*; *Pleasant Dialogues and Dramas*, containing *Jupiter and Io, Apollo and Daphne*, and *Amphrisa*;

John Milton, *Comus*;

Thomas Nabbes, *Hannibal and Scipio*; *Microcosmus*;

William Shakespeare, *Hamlet* (Q5—7th edn.); *The Merchant of Venice* (Q3—5th edn.); *Romeo and Juliet* (Q5—7th edn.);

James Shirley, *The Example*; *The Gamester*; *The Grateful Servant* (Q2); *Hyde Park*; *The Lady of Pleasure*; *The School of Compliment, or Love Tricks* (Q2); *The Young Admiral*;

J. W., *The Valiant Scot*;

George Wilkins, *The Miseries of Enforced Marriage* (Q4).

1637/38

JANUARY

7 (Su) Davenant's *Britannia Triumphans* was danced in the new Masquing House at Whitehall. (iii. 200; J. P. Feil, *Shakespeare Survey*, xi [1958], 111–13.) The Declared Accounts of the Office of Works for the period 1 October 1637 (Su) ⟨ ⟩ 30 September 1638 (Su) provide payment for building the new Masquing House at Whitehall. (P.R.O. E 351/3271.)

8 (M) Davenant's *Britannia Triumphans* was licensed for the press by Herbert. (iii. 200.)

12 (F) Herbert licensed Rutter's version of *The Cid*, Part I, for the press. (v. 1030.)

16 (Tu) Thomas Pinnocke was indicted for threatening to pull down the Red Bull playhouse. (i. 313–14.)

26 (F) Thomas Wykes licensed Rutter's version of *The Cid*, Part I, for the press. (v. 1030.)

29 (M) Rutter's version of *The Cid*, Part I, entered S.R.

FEBRUARY

3 (Sa) Ford's *The Fancies Chaste and Noble* entered S.R. In the period 30 September 1637 (Sa) ⟨ ⟩ 3 February 1637/8 (Sa) the King's company performed *Aglaura* and thirteen other plays, unnamed and undated, at court, presumably the first and the last on the days named. (i. 57, 99; *M.S.C.* ii. 387 and vi. 88.) Sir Humphrey Mildmay was unable to see the play at Whitehall because the house was full. (ii. 678.)

5 (M) Sir Humphrey Mildmay saw 'the fooleishe Newe play'. (ii. 678.)

6 Shrove Tuesday. William Johnson's *Valetudinarium* was performed at Queens' College, Cambridge. (iv. 601.) Davenant's *Luminalia* was danced in the new Masquing House at Whitehall. (iii. 207–8.)

7 (W) George Garrard wrote that plays by Suckling (*Aglaura*) and Berkeley (*The Lost Lady*) had been produced at court and at Blackfriars. (iii. 24.)

15 (Th) Henry Shirley's *The Martyred Soldier* entered S.R.

28 (W) John Ogilby was appointed Master of the Revels in Ireland. (iv. 949.)

MARCH

5 (M) Berkeley's *The Lost Lady* entered S.R.

12 (M) Heywood's *The Wise Woman of Hogsdon* entered S.R.

13 (Tu) Henry Killigrew's *The Conspiracy*, James Shirley's *The Duke's Mistress*, and *The Royal Master* entered S.R.

14 (W) Cowley's *Love's Riddle* and *Naufragium Joculare* entered S.R.

1638

25 Easter Sunday. A performance of the Queen's masque, Davenant's *Luminalia*, of 6 February was planned for Easter

for the entertainment of the Duchess of Chevreuse, but there is no evidence of performance; it was probably a false rumour, or the plan was not carried through. (J. P. Feil, *Shakespeare Survey*, xi [1958], 113.)

26 (M) Berkeley's *The Lost Lady* was acted at court by the King's company. (i. 99.)

27 (Tu) The King's company performed Chapman's *Bussy D'Ambois* at court. (i. 99.)

30 (F) *Cornelianum Dolium*, by 'T. R.', entered S.R.

APRIL

3 (Tu) Suckling's *Aglaura* was performed before the King and Queen at court by the King's company. (i. 99.)

5 (Th) Nabbes's *Tottenham Court* entered S.R.

16 (M) Herbert licensed Davenant's *The Unfortunate Lovers* for performance at Blackfriars. (iii. 220.)

18 (W) Suckling's *Aglaura* entered S.R.

23 (M) Herbert licensed James Shirley's *The Royal Master* for performance. (v. 1140.) Davenant's *The Unfortunate Lovers* was performed before the Queen at Blackfriars (iii. 220); payment for this performance was apparently included among those for Hampton Court, Richmond, and Whitehall this season. (*M.S.C.* vi. 89.)

28 (Sa) Jonson's *Every Man Out of His Humour* transferred S.R.

MAY

3 (Th) Herbert licensed Ford's *The Lady's Trial* for performance at the Cockpit. (iii. 446.)

15 Whitsun Tuesday. Bear-baiting and bull-baiting were presented before the King at Whitehall. (*M.S.C.* vi. 88.)

28 (M) Nabbes's *Covent Garden* entered S.R.

29 (Tu) The following plays transferred S.R.: Elizabeth, Lady Cary's *Mariam*, the anonymous *The Maid's Metamorphosis*, the anonymous *The Weakest Goeth to the Wall*, Beaumont and Fletcher's *A King and No King* and *Philaster*, Shakespeare's *Othello*, and Beaumont and Fletcher's *The Maid's Tragedy*. Thomas Nabbes's *Presentation Intended* was prepared for performance before the Prince on his birthday, but was not performed. (iv. 938–9.) The King's company performed *Oldcastle* at court. (i. 99; *M.S.C.* vi. 89.)

31 (Th) Davenant's *The Unfortunate Lovers* was performed at court. (i. 99.)

JUNE

4 (M) Herbert censored a specified passage in Massinger's *The King and the Subject*. (iv. 794–5.)

5 (Tu) Herbert licensed Massinger's *The King and the Subject*, provided that the title be changed and that a passage objectionable to the King be omitted. (iv. 794–5.)

9 (Sa) Herbert granted a licence to make a show of an opossum. (*Herbert*, p. 46.)

23 (Sa) Nabbes's masque, *The Spring's Glory*, and *A Presentation Intended for the Prince His Highness on His Birthday* entered S.R.

During the summer, Nabbes's *The Bride* was performed by Beeston's Boys at the Phoenix. (iv. 930.)

JULY

10 (Tu) The King's company performed Carlell's *The Passionate Lovers*, Part I, at Somerset House. (iii. 122; *M.S.C.* vi. 89.)

13 (F) Kirke's *The Seven Champions of Christendom* entered S.R.

28 (Sa) The Venetian Ambassador's lady attended the Queen's play at Somerset House; this may be one of the seven plays for which Queen Henrietta's men were paid on 6 March 1639/40 for acting in 1638 and 1639. (J. P. Feil, *Shakespeare Survey*, xi [1958], 114.)

AUGUST

23 (Th) Thomas Jacob was indicted for committing a great disorder at the Red Bull. (i. 314.)

During August, Richard Brome's contract with the Salisbury Court theatre was renewed for seven years. (iii. 53.)

SEPTEMBER

4 (Tu) The following plays transferred S.R.: Barton Holyday's *Technogamia, or The Marriages of the Arts*, Munday's *The Downfall* and *Death of Robert Earl of Huntingdon*, Marston's *Parasitaster, or The Fawn*, the anonymous *Thomas Lord Cromwell*, Marlowe's *Edward II*, and the anonymous *The Wisdom of Doctor Dodipoll*.

24 (M) Sir William Berkeley's *The Lost Lady* transferred S.R.

30 (Su) The King's men performed Davenant's *The Unfortunate Lovers* at Hampton Court (*Herbert*, p. 77); this was apparently one of the six Hampton Court performances this season. (*M.S.C.* vi. 89.)

OCTOBER

4 (Th) Christopher Beeston made his will, with theatrical legacies. (ii. 631–3.)

15 (M) Christopher Beeston, governor of the Cockpit theatre, was buried. (ii. 370.)

18 (Th) A military show and sham battle by the Gentlemen of the Artillery Garden was performed at the Merchant Tailors' Hall. (Withington, *English Pageantry*, i. 237–8.)

24 (W) James Shirley's *The Ball* and Chapman and Shirley's *Chabot, Admiral of France* entered S.R.

26 (F) Carlell's *Arviragus and Philicia*, Parts I and II, entered S.R. Matthew Clay licensed May's *The Tragedy of Julia Agrippina* (iv. 838); this play and his *The Tragedy of Cleopatra Queen of Egypt* entered S.R.

27 (Sa) Sir Humphrey Mildmay saw Jonson's *Volpone* at Blackfriars. (ii. 678.)

29 (M) The Lord Mayor's Show for Sir Maurice Abbott, draper: Heywood's *Porta Pietatis* was performed. (iv. 584; *M.S.C.* iii. 126–8.)

NOVEMBER

3 (Sa) Matthew Clay licensed Zouche's *The Sophister* for the press. (v. 1277.)

6 (Tu) Ford's *The Lady's Trial* entered S.R. The King's company performed *The Merry Devil of Edmonton* at court. (i. 99.)

7 (W) Zouche's *The Sophister* entered S.R.

8 (Th) The King's company performed Jonson's *Volpone* at court. (i. 99.)

13 (Tu) The King's company performed *Julius Caesar* at court. (i. 99.)

15 (Th) The King's company performed *The Merry Wives of Windsor* at court. (i. 99.)

17 (Sa) Herbert licensed Davenant's *The Fair Favourite* for performance at Blackfriars. (iii. 203.)

20 (Tu) Davenant's *The Fair Favourite* was presented at the Cockpit-in-Court by the King's company. (iii. 203; *M.S.C.* vi. 89.)

22 (Th) The King's men performed Fletcher's *The Chances* at the Cockpit-in-Court. (iii. 319; *M.S.C.* vi. 89.)

27 (Tu) The King's men performed Fletcher and Massinger's *The Custom of the Country* at the Cockpit-in-Court. (iii. 324; *M.S.C.* vi. 89.)

29 (Th) The King's company performed Richard Brome's *The Northern Lass* at the Cockpit-in-Court. (iii. 82; *M.S.C.* vi. 89.)

DECEMBER

6 (Th) Fletcher's *The Spanish Curate* was performed at the Cockpit-in-Court. (iii. 418; *M.S.C.* vi. 89.)

11 (Tu) The King's company performed Davenant's *The Fair Favourite* at the Cockpit-in-Court again. (iii. 203; *M.S.C.* vi. 89.)

18 (Tu) The King's company performed Carlell's *The Passionate Lovers*, Part I, at the Cockpit-in-Court. (iii. 122; *M.S.C.* vi. 89.)

20 (Th) A warrant was issued for liveries for fourteen members of Queen Henrietta's company. (i. 244.) The King's company performed Carlell's *The Passionate Lovers*, Part II, at the Cockpit-in-Court. (iii. 122; *M.S.C.* vi. 89.) The Declared Accounts of the Office of Works for the period 1 October 1638 (M) ⟨ ⟩ 30 September 1639 (M) provide payment for work done in preparing Somerset House for two plays acted there before the King and Queen in December 1638.

27 (Th) Carlell's *The Passionate Lovers*, Part II, was acted at the Cockpit-in-Court by the King's men. (iii. 122; *M.S.C.* vi. 89.)

28 (F) The King's company performed Richard Brome's *The Northern Lass* at Richmond. (iii. 82; *M.S.C.* vi. 89.)
During 1638 Richard Brome's *The Antipodes* was performed at the Salisbury Court theatre by Queen Henrietta's men. (iii. 56–57.)
Queen Henrietta's company presented seven plays at court in the 1638–9 season. (i. 249.) Twenty-two named and dated plays were performed at court by the King's men in 1638. (i. 99–100.)

Plays published in 1638

Anonymous, *Selimus*, Part I (reissue of 1594 edn.);
Anonymous, *Wily Beguiled* (Q6—two issues);
Francis Beaumont and John Fletcher, *The Maid's Tragedy* (Q4);
William Berkeley, *The Lost Lady* (F1; F2—1st issue);
Abraham Cowley, *Love's Riddle*; *Naufragium Joculare*;
William Davenant, *Britannia Triumphans* (dated 1637); *Luminalia* (dated 1637);
John Ford, *The Fancies Chaste and Noble*;

Matthew Gwinne, *Nero* (2nd edn.—1st issue);
Thomas Heywood, *Porta Pietatis*; *The Rape of Lucrece* (Q5);
  The Wise Woman of Hogsdon;
Henry Killigrew, *The Conspiracy*;
John Kirke, *The Seven Champions of Christendom*;
Philip Massinger, *The Bondman* (Q2); *The Duke of Milan* (Q2);
Thomas Nabbes, *Covent Garden* (Q—1st issue); *A Presentation
  Intended for the Prince His Highness on His Birthday* (Q—
  1st issue); *The Spring's Glory* (Q—1st issue); *Tottenham Court*
  (Q—1st issue);
'T. R.', *Cornelianum Dolium*;
Thomas Randolph, *Poems*, including *The Muses' Looking Glass*
  and *Amyntas*;
William Rowley, *A Shoemaker a Gentleman*;
Joseph Rutter, *The Cid*, Part I (dated 1637);
Henry Shirley, *The Martyred Soldier*;
James Shirley, *The Duke's Mistress*; *The Royal Master*;
Philip Sidney, *Arcadia*, containing *The Entertainment at
  Wanstead (The Lady of May)*;
John Suckling, *Aglaura*.

1638/39

JANUARY

1 (Tu) The King's company performed Fletcher's *Beggars' Bush*
  at Richmond (iii. 313–14); this was apparently one of the
  six plays performed at Hampton Court and Richmond this
  season. (*M.S.C.* vi. 89.)

7 (M) The King's company performed Fletcher's *The Spanish
  Curate* at Richmond. (iii. 418.)

11 (F) Henry Glapthorne's *Argalus and Parthenia* entered S.R.

21 (M) Thomas Wykes allowed Massinger's *The Unnatural
  Combat* for the press. (iv. 822.)

22 (Tu) Fletcher's *Monsieur Thomas, or The Father's Own Son*
  entered S.R.

25 (F) The following plays transferred S.R.: Elizabeth, Lady
  Cary's *Mariam*, the anonymous *The Maid's Metamorphosis*
  and *The Weakest Goeth to the Wall*, Beaumont and Fletcher's
  A King and No King and *Philaster*, Shakespeare's *Othello*, and
  Beaumont and Fletcher's *The Maid's Tragedy*.

FEBRUARY

12 (Tu) Sir Humphrey Mildmay saw a play at an unnamed
  London theatre. (ii. 678.)

13 (W) Sir Humphrey Mildmay saw a play at an unnamed London theatre. (ii. 678.)

14 (Th) Massinger's *The Unnatural Combat* entered S.R. Sir Humphrey Mildmay saw a play at an unnamed London theatre. (ii. 678.)

18 (M) Sir Humphrey Mildmay saw a play at an unnamed London theatre. (ii. 678.)

26 Shrove Tuesday.

MARCH

1 (F) Sir Ralph Freeman's *Imperiale* entered S.R.

4 (M) The anonymous *George a Greene*, Greene's *Orlando Furioso*, the anonymous *Edward III*, and the former owner's part of Jonson's works (see 4 July 1635) transferred S.R.

14 (Th) Royal livery was granted to sixteen members of the King's company. (i. 90.)

23 (Sa) The anonymous *Wily Beguiled* transferred S.R.

1639

26 (Tu) Davenant secured from King Charles a royal patent to erect a large theatre in Fleet Street. (vi. 305–6.)

28 (Th) Davenport's *A New Trick to Cheat the Devil* entered S.R.

APRIL

5 (F) William Beeston was sworn governor and instructor of the King and Queen's young company. (i. 330.)

6 (Sa) Matthew Clay allowed Nabbes's *The Bride* for the press. (iv. 931.) He also allowed Rutter's *The Cid*, Part II, for the press (v. 1031), and the play was entered S.R. the same day.

12 (F) James Shirley's *The Maid's Revenge* entered S.R.

14 Easter Sunday.

25 (Th) Fletcher's *Wit Without Money*, and *The Night Walker* (revised by Shirley); Shirley's *The Opportunity, Love's Cruelty*, and *The Coronation* entered S.R.

MAY

2 (Th) The company at the Fortune theatre was fined £1,000 for using properties in contempt of the ceremonies of the Church. (v. 1300.)

18 (Sa) Sir Humphrey Mildmay saw Jonson's *The Alchemist* at an unnamed London theatre. (ii. 678.)

21 (Tu) The following plays transferred S.R.: Samuel Rowley's *When You See Me, You Know Me*; Heywood's *If You Know Not Me, You Know Nobody*, Parts I and II; Shakespeare's *King Lear*; Heywood's *The Rape of Lucrece*; and Dekker's *The Honest Whore*, Part II. Sir Humphrey Mildmay saw Fletcher's *The Mad Lover* at an unnamed theatre. (ii. 678–9.)

JUNE

18 (Tu) J. D.'s *The Knave in Grain, New Vampt* entered S.R.
20 (Th) The French Ambassador and other gentlemen of quality were entertained with bear-baiting at the Beargarden. (*M.S.C.* vi. 89.)

JULY

8 (M) Nabbes's *The Bride* entered S.R.
27 (Sa) Davenant's *Albovine, King of the Lombards* entered S.R.
29 (M) James Shirley's *The Humorous Courtier* entered S.R.

AUGUST

6 (Tu) The King's men presented a play at court, presumably on this date. (i. 100; *M.S.C.* vi. 89.)
6 (Tu) ⟨ ⟩ 11 February 1639/40 The King's men presented nineteen plays at Whitehall and two at Richmond, the first and last presumably on these days. (i. 100; *M.S.C.* vi. 89.)
10 (Sa) The Lord Chamberlain issued an order forbidding any other London company to act any of a list of forty-five plays belonging to the King and Queen's young company. (i. 330–1.) A ticket of privilege was issued to twelve actors of the King and Queen's young company. (i. 331–2.)
26 (M) Richard Benfield, a friend of the players, made his will. (ii. 633–5.)

SEPTEMBER

22 (Su) Henry Glapthorne's *Albertus Wallenstein* entered S.R.
25 (W) Herbert licensed Massinger's *Alexius, or The Chaste Lover* for the King's company. (iv. 758.)
29 (Su) A warrant was issued to swear Joseph Taylor, the actor in the King's company, Yeoman of the Revels. (ii. 596.) The Privy Council ordered the arrest of the author, players, and licenser of the anonymous *The Whore New Vamped*, which had been performed by Prince Charles's (II) company at the Red Bull, because of slanders against aldermen and the proctors of the City. (v. 1441–2.)

OCTOBER

2 (W) Davenant's patent to build a new theatre severely restricted. (vi. 308.)

3 (Th) Richards's *The Tragedy of Messallina, the Roman Empress* entered S.R.

4 (F) Fletcher's *Rollo, or The Bloody Brother* entered S.R.

7 (M) Francis Beaumont's *Poems*, containing *The Masque of the Inner Temple and Gray's Inn*, prologues, epilogues, and songs to the plays, entered S.R.

9 (W) Sandys's *Christ's Passion*, translated from Hugo Grotius, entered S.R.

14 (M) A play was presented before Prince Charles at Richmond on the birthday of Prince James, the Duke of York. (*M.S.C.* vi. 152.)

22 (Tu) J. D.'s *The Knave in Grain, New Vampt* transferred S.R.

28 (M) A warrant was issued against John Rhodes of the Fortune theatre, on the complaint of the King's company that he was selling their plays. (i. 279.)

29 (Tu) The Lord Mayor's Show for Sir Henry Garway, draper: Heywood's *Londini Status Pacatus, or London's Peaceable Estate*, was performed. (iv. 577–8, and *M.S.C.* iii. 128–30.)

30 (W) Herbert licensed James Shirley's *The Gentleman of Venice* for performance. (v. 1112.)

NOVEMBER

4 (M) Nabbes's *The Unfortunate Mother* entered S.R.

8 (F) Sir Humphrey Mildmay saw a play at an unnamed London theatre. (ii. 679.)

11 (M) A patent was issued to Joseph Taylor, principal actor of the King's company, to succeed William Hunt, deceased, as Yeoman of the Revels. (*M.S.C.* ii. 343–6.)

14 (Th) Sir Humphrey Mildmay saw a play at an unnamed London theatre. (ii. 679.)

20 (W) Rawlins's *The Rebellion* entered S.R.

29 (F) James Shirley's *The Arcadia* entered S.R., and Shirley's *Love's Cruelty* re-entered S.R.

30 (Sa) Herbert licensed Davenant's *The Spanish Lovers* (*The Distresses*) for performance, possibly at Blackfriars. (iii. 202.) Henry Fay and eight assistants were paid for six days of work done in November–December, making ready at Richmond for two plays acted before Prince Charles (*M.S.C.* vi. 152), and John Aiton and eight assistants were paid for nine days

of work done in November–December, making ready at Richmond for three plays acted before Prince Charles. (*M.S.C.* vi. 152–3.) Prince Charles's (II) company gave three plays before the court at Richmond in November. (i. 315.) The King's company performed two plays at Richmond (as well as nineteen at Whitehall) in the period 6 August 1639 (Tu) ⟨ ⟩ 11 February 1639/40 (Tu). (i. 100; *M.S.C.* vi. 89.)

Plays published in 1639

Anonymous, *Mucedorus* (14th edn.) ;

Francis Beaumont and John Fletcher, *A King and No King* (Q4) ; *Philaster* (Q5—two issues) ; *The Scornful Lady* (Q5) ;

William Berkeley, *The Lost Lady* (F2—2nd issue) ;

Lodowick Carlell, *Arviragus and Philicia*, Parts I and II ;

William Cartwright, *The Royal Slave* (Q1) ;

Robert Davenport, *A New Trick to Cheat the Devil* (Q—two issues) ;

Thomas Drue, *The Bloody Banquet* ;

Nathan Field, *Amends for Ladies* (Q2) ;

John Fletcher, *Monsieur Thomas, or The Father's Own Son* (Q1—1st issue) ; *Rollo, or The Bloody Brother* (Q1) ; *Wit Without Money* (Q1) ;

John Ford, *The Lady's Trial* ;

Ralph Freeman, *Imperiale* (Q1) ;

Henry Glapthorne, *Albertus Wallenstein* (1st issue) ; *Argalus and Parthenia* ;

Matthew Gwinne, *Nero* (2nd edn.—2nd issue) ;

Thomas Heywood, *If You Know Not Me, You Know Nobody*, Part I (Q8) ; *Londini Status Pacatus, or London's Peaceable Estate* ;

William Lower, *The Phoenix in Her Flames* ;

Philip Massinger, *The Unnatural Combat* ;

Thomas May, *The Tragedy of Cleopatra Queen of Egypt* (1st edn.—1st issue) ; *The Tragedy of Julia Agrippina* (1st edn.—1st issue) ;

Jasper Mayne, *The City Match* ;

Thomas Nabbes, *Covent Garden* (Q—2nd issue) ; *The Presentation for the Prince* (*Time and the Almanac-Makers*) (Q—2nd issue) ; *The Spring's Glory* (Q—2nd issue) ; *Tottenham Court* (Q—2nd issue) ; *Plays, Masques, Epigrams, Elegies, and Epithalamiums*, containing *Hannibal and Scipio, Microcosmus, Tottenham Court, Covent Garden, The Spring's Glory, The Bride*, and *The Unfortunate Mother* ;

William Shakespeare, *Henry IV*, Part I (Q9—11th edn.);
James Shirley, *The Ball*; *The Maid's Revenge*;
James Shirley and George Chapman, *Chabot, Admiral of France*;
Richard Zouche, *The Sophister*.

1639/40

JANUARY

6 (M) Cokayne's masque was acted at Bretbie, Derbyshire. (iii. 168.)

?7 (Tu) ⟨ ⟩ 31 (F) Two plays were acted before Prince Charles at Richmond. (*M.S.C.* vi. 153.) The Declared Accounts of the Office of Works for the period 1 October 1639 (Tu) ⟨ ⟩ 30 September 1640 (W) provide payment for preparations for plays at Richmond. (A.O. 71/2429.)

21 (Tu) Davenant's *Salmacida Spolia* was performed at court. (iii. 213–14.) The Declared Accounts of the Office of Works for the period 1 October 1639 (Tu) ⟨ ⟩ 30 September 1640 (W) provide payment for preparations at the Masquing Room at Whitehall for a masque. (P.R.O. A.O. 1/71/2429.) (See also 9 April 1640.)

26 (Su) Herbert licensed Massinger's *The Fair Anchoress of Pausilippo* for the King's company. (iv. 781.)

31 (F) John Gough's *The Strange Discovery* entered S.R.

FEBRUARY

8 (Sa) Jonson's translation of Horace's *The Art of Poetry*, which was published with Jonson's *The Gypsies Metamorphosed* in 1640, entered S.R. (But see also 20 February.)

11 (Tu) The King's company presented a play at court, presumably on this date. (i. 100; *M.S.C.* vi. 89.)

14 (F) James Shirley's *The Tragedy of St. Albans* entered S.R.

16 (Su), 17 (M), or 18 (Tu) Davenant's *Salmacida Spolia* was repeated at court, and a play was apparently performed at Richmond on one of the other two days. (*M.S.C.* vi. 153.)

18 Shrove Tuesday.

20 (Th) Jonson's *The Gypsies Metamorphosed* entered S.R. (See also 8 February.)

MARCH

6 (F) Queen Henrietta's players were paid for seven plays acted at court in 1638 and 1639. (i. 249.)

11 (W) Marmion's *The Antiquary* and James Shirley's *Look to the Lady* entered S.R.

17 (Tu) Burnell's *Landgartha* was acted in Dublin. (iii. 97.)

18 (W) Massinger was buried in St. Saviour's, Southwark. (iv. 757.)

19 (Th) Richard Brome's *The Sparagus Garden, The Antipodes,* and *Wit in a Madness* entered S.R.

20 (F) The following masques by Jonson entered S.R.: *Pan's Anniversary, or The Shepherd's Holiday, The Masque of Augurs, Time Vindicated to Himself and to His Honours,* and *Neptune's Triumph for the Return of Albion.*

23 (M) Thomas Carew's *Works,* containing *Coelum Britannicum,* entered S.R.

1640

APRIL

2 (Th) T. Killigrew's *The Prisoners,* Chamberlain's *The Swaggering Damsel,* and William Habington's *The Queen of Aragon, or Cleodora* entered S.R.

4 (Sa) Henry Glapthorne's *The Lady's Privilege* entered S.R.

5 Easter Sunday. About this time Prince Charles's (II) company went to the Fortune, and the Fortune company to the Red Bull. (i. 279–80 and 315–16.)

9 (Th) Habington's *The Queen of Aragon, or Cleodora* was performed by the servants of the Lord Chamberlain before the court at Whitehall. (iv. 522.) The Declared Accounts of the Office of Works for the period 1 October 1639 (Tu) ⟨ ⟩ 30 September 1640 (W) provide payment for preparations at the Masquing Room at Whitehall for a masque (A.O. 1/71/ 2429). (See also 21 January 1639/40.)

10 (F) ⟨ Habington's *The Queen of Aragon, or Cleodora* was performed a second time for the court at Whitehall. (iv. 522.)

11 (Sa) ⟨ Habington's *The Queen of Aragon, or Cleodora* was performed at Blackfriars. (iv. 523.)

22 (W) The following plays transferred S.R.: Robert Daborne's (?) *The Owl* (a lost play?), the anonymous *Leir,* Greene's *Friar Bacon and Friar Bungay,* the anonymous *Robin Hood and Little John* (lost), and Ulpian Fulwell's *Like Will to Like.*

25 (Sa) A ticket of privilege was granted to four hired men of Prince Charles's (II) company. (i. 316.)

27 (M) Henry Glapthorne's *Wit in a Constable* entered S.R.

28 (Tu) James Shirley's *The Constant Maid* and *St. Patrick for Ireland* entered S.R.

MAY

3 (Su) The Lord Chamberlain prohibited acting at the Phoenix because the company had performed a new play without the licence of the Master of the Revels and then had defied his prohibition. (i. 332–3.) The leaders of Beeston's Boys were imprisoned for the offence. (i. 333.)

7 (Th) Herbert released Beeston and the other Cockpit players from the Marshalsea but confiscated their offending play. (i. 333.)

8 (F) Sir Humphrey Mildmay saw a play at an unnamed London theatre. (ii. 678.)

15 (F) Sir Humphrey Mildmay saw 'the Newe play' at Blackfriars. (ii. 679.)

22 (F) Henry Glapthorne's *The Hollander* and Heywood's *Love's Masterpiece* entered S.R.

In May or June, a play was presented before the Prince at Richmond. (*M.S.C.* vi. 153.)

JUNE

1 (M) Herbert licensed James Shirley's *The Doubtful Heir, or Rosania, or Love's Victory* for performance. (v. 1105.)

27 (Sa) William Davenant was appointed governor of the King and Queen's young company at the Phoenix in place of William Beeston. (i. 334–5.)

JULY

7 (Tu) Mrs. Beeston borrowed £150 from William Wilbraham, perhaps for the Cockpit theatre. (vi. 75.)

AUGUST

4 (Tu) Thomas Killigrew's *Claracilla* entered S.R. Also, Richard Brome's *Christianetta, The Jewish Gentleman, A New Academy, The Lovesick Court, The Weeding of the Covent Garden,* and *The English Moor* entered S.R.

SEPTEMBER

5 (Sa) William Berkeley's *The Lost Lady* transferred S.R.

11 (F) The Privy Council ordered the theatres to be closed because of the plague. (ii. 665.)

OCTOBER

15 (Th) John Tatham's *Fancies Theatre*, containing his pastoral play, *Love Crowns the End*, entered S.R.

29 (Th) The Lord Mayor's celebration for Sir Edmund Wright, grocer, consisted of a procession without pageants or shows. (*M.S.C.* iii. 131.)

Theobald Peirce and seven assistants were paid for fifty days of work done in October–March 1640/1, making ready at Richmond for diverse plays, dancing on the ropes, and other pastimes before Prince Charles and the rest of the royal children. (*M.S.C.* vi. 153–4.)

NOVEMBER

⟩ 6 (F) The theatres reopened after the plague of 1640. (ii. 665–6.)

6 (F) Sir Humphrey Mildmay saw a play at an unnamed London theatre. (ii. 679.)

9 (M) Sir Humphrey Mildmay saw a play at an unnamed London theatre. (ii. 679.)

10 (Tu) Herbert licensed James Shirley's *The Imposture* for performance. (v. 1124.) The King's company performed a play at court, presumably on this day. (i. 100.) (See 22 February 1640/1.)

16 (M) Sir Humphrey Mildmay saw a play at an unnamed London theatre. (ii. 679.)

18 (W) T. B.'s *The Country Girl* entered S.R.

24 (Tu) Herbert licensed Sadler's *Masquerade du Ciel* for the press, and the play entered S.R. the same day. (v. 1038.)

DECEMBER

17 (Th) John Shank, junior, was sworn a Groom as one of Prince Charles (II) players. (ii. 568.)

The King's company performed not more than sixteen plays at court in the period 10 November 1640 (Tu) to 22 February 1640/1 (M). (i. 100.) Robert Bent and nine assistants were paid for work done at Richmond in November to January 1640/1 in preparation for plays before Prince Charles during the Christmas holidays and at other times. (*M.S.C.* vi. 154.)

Plays published in 1640

Richard Brome, *The Antipodes*; *The Sparagus Garden*;
Thomas Carew, *Poems*, containing *Coelum Britannicum*;
William Cartwright, *The Royal Slave* (Q2);

Robert Chamberlain, *The Swaggering Damsel* (Q—two issues);
J. D., *The Knave in Grain, New Vampt*;
William Davenant, *Salmacida Spolia* (dated 1639);
John Fletcher, *The Night Walker* (Q1—revised by Shirley);
  Rollo, or The Bloody Brother (Q2); *Rule a Wife and Have a*
  Wife;
Ralph Freeman, *Imperiale* (2nd edn.);
Henry Glapthorne, *Albertus Wallenstein* (2nd issue); *The*
  Hollander; *The Lady's Privilege*; *Wit in a Constable*;
John Gough, *The Strange Discovery*;
William Habington, *The Queen of Aragon, or Cleodora* (F—two
  issues);
Samuel Harding, *Sicily and Naples, or The Fatal Union*;
Thomas Heywood, *Love's Mistress* (Q2);
Ben Jonson, *The Gypsies Metamorphosed* (1st edn.—two issues);
Ben Jonson, *The Works* (F2), 2 vols. (vol. I—the contents of
  the Folio of 1616; vol. II—re-issue of 1631 edn.);
Thomas Middleton, *A Mad World, My Masters* (Q2);
Thomas Nabbes, *The Bride*; *The Unfortunate Mother*;
Thomas Randolph, *The Jealous Lovers* (3rd edn.);
Thomas Randolph, *Poems*, including *The Muses' Looking*
  Glass and *Amyntas* (2nd edn.);
Thomas Rawlins, *The Rebellion* (Q—1st issue);
Nathanael Richards, *The Tragedy of Messallina, the Roman*
  Empress;
Joseph Rutter, *The Cid*, Part II;
John Sadler, *Masquerade du Ciel*;
George Sandys, *Christ's Passion* (1st edn.—three issues);
Lewis Sharpe, *The Noble Stranger*;
James Shirley, *The Arcadia*; *The Constant Maid* (Q1); *The*
  Coronation (as written by Fletcher); *The Humorous Courtier*;
  Love's Cruelty; *The Opportunity*; *St. Patrick for Ireland*;
Thomas Snelling, *Thibaldus sive Vindictæ Ingenium, or*
  Pharamus sive Libido Vindex, Hispanica Tragœdia (1st issue);
John Tatham, *Fancies Theatre* (1st issue), containing *Love*
  Crowns the End;
John Webster, *The Duchess of Malfi* (Q2—1st issue).

1640/41

JANUARY

6 (W) Salusbury's *A Masque at Knowsley* was performed at Lord
  Strange's house, Knowsley. (v. 1041.)

8 (F) The usual warrant for liveries for fourteen members of Queen Henrietta's company was issued. (i. 247.)

19 (Tu) A ticket of privilege was issued for Theophilus Bird as a King's player. (ii. 379.)

22 (F) Six men were sworn Grooms of the Chamber as King's players. (i. 64; *M.S.C.* ii. 397.)

FEBRUARY

15 (M) Sir Humphrey Mildmay saw a play. (ii. 679.)

22 (M) The King's company performed not more than sixteen unnamed and undated plays at court in the period 10 November 1640 (Tu) ⟨ ⟩ 22 February 1640/1 (M), presumably the first and the last on the days mentioned. (i. 100.)

25 (Th) William Beeston entered into a bond of £400 to Michael Bowyer, probably on a theatrical arrangement. (ii. 387.)

26 (F) Inhabitants of Blackfriars petitioned Parliament against the playhouse. (vi. 39.)

MARCH

9 Shrove Tuesday.

20 (Sa) Royal livery was granted to eighteen members of the King's company. (i. 90.)

23 (Tu) John Day's *The Parliament of Bees* (not a genuine play or masque, but a dialogue among twelve characters) entered S.R.

Theobald Peirce and seven assistants were paid for fifty days of work done in October–March 1640/1, making ready at Richmond for diverse plays, dancing on the ropes, and other pastimes before Prince Charles and the rest of the royal children. (*M.S.C.* vi. 153–4.)

1641

APRIL

15 (Th) Three lost plays entered S.R.: *Charles, Duke of Bourbon, The Parroiall of Princes,* and *England's First Happiness, or The Life of St. Augustine.*

25 Easter Sunday. About this date, Brome's *The Jovial Crew* opened at the Cockpit in Drury Lane. (iii. 71–72.)

MAY

6 (Th) Davenant was involved in the Army Plot with Suckling and Jermyn, and he fled with the others. (i. 335.)

18 (Tu) Sir Humphrey Mildmay saw a play at an unnamed London theatre. (ii. 679.)

?19 (W) Sir Humphrey Mildmay saw a play at Blackfriars. (ii. 679.)

24 (M) Sir Humphrey Mildmay saw a play at an unnamed London theatre. (ii. 679.)

26 (W) James Shirley's *The Politic Father* (*The Brothers*) was licensed by Herbert. (v. 1082–4.)

JUNE

23 (W) Herbert licensed the anonymous *The Doge and the Dragon* for performance by the Fortune company. (v. 1321.)
In June a satirical broadside made derogatory comments on the acting at the Fortune and the Red Bull. (i. 319.)

JULY

28 (W) The anonymous *The Tragedy of Nero* (*Piso's Conspiracy*), Dekker and Massinger's *The Virgin Martyr*, and Beaumont and Fletcher's *The Scornful Lady* and *Cupid's Revenge* transferred S.R.

AUGUST

2 (M) Thomas Jordan's *The Walks of Islington and Hogsdon* was licensed by Herbert for performance at the Red Bull; the title-page says that it was acted nineteen consecutive days. (iv. 688.)

5 (Th) The theatres were ordered closed because of the plague. (ii. 666–7.)

7 (Sa) The Lord Chamberlain sent the London printers a list of sixty-one plays constituting the repertory of the King's company which were not to be printed without their consent. (i. 65–66.)

OCTOBER

29 (F) There was no Lord Mayor's Pageant this year.

NOVEMBER

25 (Th) Herbert licensed James Shirley's *The Cardinal* for performance. (v. 1085.)

26 (F) *or* 27 (Sa) The theatres reopened. (ii. 666–7.)

DECEMBER

1 (W) Sir Humphrey Mildmay saw a play at an unnamed London theatre. (ii. 679–80.)

10 (F) Sir Humphrey Mildmay saw a play at an unnamed London theatre. (ii. 680.)

William Beeston was reinstated as governor of Beeston's Boys some time this year. (i. 335.)

Plays published in 1641

Anonymous, *Canterbury His Change of Diet*;

Francis Beaumont and John Fletcher, *The Maid's Tragedy* (Q5);

Richard Brathwaite, *Mercurius Britannicus* (1641 ⟨ Latin version—two issues); *Mercurius Britannicus, or The English Intelligencer* (Q1, Q2, and Q3);

Henry Burnell, *Landgartha* (Dublin);

George Chapman, *Bussy D'Ambois* (Q2—two issues);

John Day, *The Parliament of Bees*;

Ben Jonson, *The Works*, Vols. II (two reissues: the first containing *Bartholomew Fair*, *The Staple of News*, and a reprint of *The Devil Is an Ass*; the second containing *The Devil Is an Ass* alone) and III, containing twenty dramatic items: *Christmas His Masque*, *The Masque at Lord Hay's* (*Lovers Made Men*), *The Vision of Delight*, *Pleasure Reconciled to Virtue* (including *For the Honour of Wales*), *News from the New World Discovered in the Moon*, *The Gypsies Metamorphosed*, *The Masque of Augurs*, *Time Vindicated*, *Neptune's Triumph*, *Pan's Anniversary*, *The Masque of Owls*, *The Fortunate Isles*, *Love's Triumph through Callipolis*, *Chloridia*, *The Entertainment at Welbeck*, *Love's Welcome at Bolsover*, *Mortimer His Fall*, *The Magnetic Lady*, *A Tale of a Tub*, and *The Sad Shepherd*;

Thomas Killigrew, *The Prisoners* (dated 1640) and *Claracilla*, in a collected edition;

Shakerley Marmion, *The Antiquary*.

1641/42

JANUARY

6 (Th) The King's company performed Beaumont and Fletcher's *The Scornful Lady* before the Prince at the Cockpit-in-Court; this was the only play acted at court this Christmas season. (i. 67; *Herbert*, p. 58.)

FEBRUARY

4 (F) A newspaper recorded that there was a great complaint

made against the playhouses, and that a motion was made for suppressing them. (i. 67.)

22 Shrove Tuesday.

MARCH

12 (Sa) Cowley's *The Guardian* was acted before Prince Charles at Trinity College, Cambridge. (iii. 176.)

1642

APRIL

5 (Tu) Thomas Randolph's *Poems*, containing *The Muses' Looking Glass* and *Amyntas*, and Suckling's *Brennoralt, or The Discontented Colonel* entered S.R.

10 Easter Sunday.

26 (Tu) Herbert licensed James Shirley's *The Sisters* for performance. (v. 1147).

JUNE

8 (W) Herbert licensed the anonymous *The Irish Rebellion*, apparently for performance by Prince Charles's (II) company. (v. 1355.) Also, Herbert burned an unnamed play because of the ribaldry and offence in it. (iv. 714.)

14 (Tu) Heywood and Brome's *The Late Lancashire Witches* transferred S.R.

AUGUST

6 (Sa) Sir John Denham's *The Sophy* entered S.R.

24 (W) Four Shakespeare plays transferred S.R.: *Hamlet, The Taming of the Shrew, Romeo and Juliet*, and *Love's Labour's Lost.*

SEPTEMBER

2 (F) Parliament closed the theatres. (ii. 690.)

14 (W) Four Shakespeare plays transferred S.R.: *Hamlet, The Taming of the Shrew, Romeo and Juliet*, and *Love's Labour's Lost.*

OCTOBER

29 (Sa) There was no Lord Mayor's Pageant this year.

Plays published in 1642

Thomas Carew, *Poems* (2nd edn.), containing *Coelum Britan-nicum*;

John Denham, *The Sophy*;

John Suckling, *Brennoralt, or The Discontented Colonel* (Q1).

GENERAL INDEX FOR VOLUMES
I TO VII

A., G. E. P., 'Proposals for Building an Amphitheatre in London 1620', *N. & Q.*, Eleventh Series, x (1914), vi. 291, 293–6, 297.
A., M., iii. 1.
A., M., *Tereus with a Pastoral*, iii. 1.
A., M., iv. 866.
A., W., v. 1131.
Abbe, Monsieur L', ii. 694.
Abbot, Archbishop, iii. 455; iv. 878.
Abbot, Sir Maurice, iv. 584.
Abdy, Sir Chr., ii. 677.
Abell, E. T., 'A Note on Jasper Mayne', *Report and Transactions of the Devonshire Association for the Advancement of Science, Literature, and Art*, lvii (1925), 257–65, iv. 843, 844.
Abell, William, blacksmith in Holborn, i. 314; v. 1442; vi. 228.
Abercrombie, iv. 670.
Abergwelly, Carmarthenshire, iii. 29.
Abingdon, Berkshire, iv. 725.
Abington, *see* Habington, William.
Abington, Cambridgeshire, iv. 520.
Abridgements, iii. 430.
Abuses Stript and Whipt (1613), *see* Wither, George.
Academy, vi. 298, 299.
Academy, Kynaston's, iv. 716.
Academy of Eloquence, The, *see* Blount, Thomas.
Accession Day, *see also* King's Day; vii. 17, 26.
Account Book of the Overseers of the Poor of the Liberty of Paris Garden, 1608–1671 (MS.), vi. 250.
Account of the English Dramatick Poets, *see* Langbaine, Gerard.
Achilles Tatius, iii. 3.
Acrobatics, vii. 6, 65.
Act intervals, vi. 9–11.
'Act-Divisions in Shakespeare', *see* Greg, W. W.
Acteon and Diana, 1656, *see* Cox, Robert.
Acting monopoly, iii. 64, 196–7.
Acting, surreptitious, iii. 457.
Acting technique, v. 1317.
Actis . . . de Henrico 8o, *see* Carleton, Thomas.

Acton, Francis, ii. 343, 682.
Acton, Sir William, ii. 640.
Acton, Walter, ii. 640.
Actor-dramatists, ii. 357, 388–9, 389, 417, 427, 434–6, 454–8, 472, 476–8, 487–90, 492–3, 507, 555, 581; iii. 17, 35–38, 42, 44, 45, 65, 182, 271, 299–303, 378–9; iv. 516–20, 553–7, 607, 678–90, 711, 749, 752; v. 1009–14, 1015–18, 1049; vi. 10.
Actor-lists, iii. 449.
Actor-lists: of Beaum. and Fletch. Folio of 1679, iii. 316.
Actors, *see* Players.
Actors Remonstrance, The (1643), vi. 151 n.
Actors, Restoration, *see* Restoration players.
Actresses, *see* Women actors.
Acts of the Privy Council, xi. 73–74, vii. 1.
Acts, iii. 18, 304; iv. 703, 722, 871, 909; v. 1174, 1175, 1456; vi. 43, 53, 108–9, 110, 163, 172.
Acts, alternate versions, v. 1206.
Acts and scenes, iii. 14, 26, 29.
'"Act Time" in Elizabethan Theatres, The', *see* Graves, Thornton Shirley.
Adams, F., '"Aery" (in *The Maid of Honour*): Curious Misinterpretation', *N. & Q.*, Eighth Series, ii (1892), 64–65, iv. 796.
Adams, John Cranford, *Globe Playhouse, The: Its Design and Equipment*, Cambridge, Mass., 1942; New York, 1961 (rev. ed.), iii. 394; vi. 178, 185 n. 1, 187.
Adams, Joseph Quincy, i. 27 n. 2; iii. 253; iv. 853; v. 1013.
'Authorship of Two Seventeenth Century Plays, The', *M.L.N.* xxii (1907), iv. 923.
'Conventual Buildings of Blackfriars, London, and the Playhouses Constructed Therein, The', *Stud. in Phil.*, xiv (1917), vi. 3.
'*Cyprian Conqueror, or The Faithless Relict, The'*, *M.L.N.* xxiii (1908), v. 1316.

Adams, Joseph Quincy (*cont.*)
  *Dramatic Records of Sir Henry
    Herbert, The* (1917), *see* Herbert
    for entries in his records.
  '*Every Woman in Her Humor* and
    The Dumb Knight', *Mod. Phil.*
    x (1913), iv. 732, 733, 735.
  'Four Pictorial Representations
    of the Elizabethan Stage',
    JEGP, x (1911), v. 1004.
  ed., *Ghost, of Lucrece by Thomas
    Middleton, The* (1937), iv. 856,
    857.
  'Hill's List of Early Plays in
    Manuscript', *Library*, Fourth
    Series, xx (1939), iii. 1, 58–59,
    67, 69, 93, 94, 120, 122, 187,
    188–9, 249, 258, 268, 269, 271,
    272; iv. 488, 562, 563, 714, 718,
    864, 865; v. 1046, 1285, 1314,
    1325, 1331, 1332, 1340, 1368,
    1372, 1373, 1375, 1378–9,
    1385, 1386, 1404, 1410, 1422,
    1423, 1424, 1440, 1448, 1449.
  "Hitherto Unknown Actor" of
    Shakespeare's Troupe, An',
    M.L.N. xxxiv (1919), ii. 623.
  Jonson Allusion Book, The, see
    Bradley, Jesse Franklin.
  ed., *Macbeth* (1931), iv. 904.
  ed., *Oenone and Paris. By T. H.*
    (1943), iv. 553, 554.
  'Office-Book, 1622–42', of Sir
    Henry Herbert, Master of the
    Revels, The', in *To Doctor R.*
    (1946), iv. 644; vi. 250 n. 1.
  'Peter Hausted's *The Rival
    Friends* with Some Account of
    His Other Works', *J.E.G.P.* xi
    (1912), iv. 532, 534, 535, 536,
    537; v. 982, 985.
  Shakespearean Playhouses (1917),
    iii. 64, 195; iv. 502, 748, 910;
    v. 1093; vi. 3, 5, 47, 49, 77, 86,
    89, 115, 121, 122, 131, 132, 139,
    145, 152, 179, 185, 186, 200,
    214, 247, 249, 252, 267, 291, 304.
  'Some Notes on Henry Glap-
    thorne's *Wit in a Constable*',
    J.E.G.P. xiii (1914), iv. 483,
    494, 495, 497.
  'Sources of Ben Jonson's *News
    from the New World Discovered
    in the Moon*, The', *M.L.N.* xxi
    (1906), iv. 663, 665.
  To Doctor R. (1946), iv. 644.
  'William Heminge and Shake-
    speare', *M.P.* xii (1914), iv. 543,
    546.

Adams, Joseph Quincy, and
  Bradley, Jesse Franklin, *Jonson
  Allusion-Book* (1922), vi. 26 n. 1.
Adams, Thomas, ii. 649.
Addis, John, 'Massinger and Molière'
  (*The Emperor of the East* and
  Molière's *Malade imaginaire*),
  N. & Q., Third Series, viii
  (1865), iv. 777.
Address to Reader, iii. 45, 51, 101,
  103, 116, 131, 155, 168–9, 189,
  220, 226, 234–5, 258, 311, 363;
  iv. 426, 475, 499, 512, 555, 566,
  583, 632, 691, 693, 735, 740, 746,
  848, 849–50, 851, 852, 901, 909,
  910, 943, 944, 951, 952, 957; v.
  985, 987, 993, 998, 1011, 1017,
  1061, 1062, 1063, 1071, 1103, 1117,
  1119, 1214, 1243, 1265, 1287; vi.
  62.
Adkins, Mary Grace Muse, 'Puritanism in the Plays and Pamphlets of
  Thomas Dekker', *University of
  Texas Studies in English* (1939),
  iii. 241.
Adkinson, Will, ii. **343**.
Admiral's company, i. 1, 135, 322;
  ii. 486, 490, 507; iii. 239, 259;
  iv. 749, 808, 857; v. 1014; vii. 1.
Admiralty, High Court, Judge of,
  v. 1277.
Admission fees, iii. 23, 51, 59, 71,
  102, 107–8, 179, 192, 223, 264,
  315, 320, 333, 334, 344, 371, 374,
  385, 402, 403, 419, 462; iv. 706,
  767, 801, 812, 868, 900; v. 1091,
  1114, 1124, 1125, 1135, 1169,
  1211, 1342, 1453; vi. 36, 45, 110,
  166, 171, 243.
*Admission Registers of St. Paul's
  School, see*, Gardiner, Robert.
Adrasta, see Jones, John.
*Adrastus Parentans sive Vindicta
  Tragoedia, see* Mease, Peter.
Adson, F., *see* Adson, J.
Adson, John, ii. **343**; iii. 1–2.
  Courtly Masquing Ayres, ii. 343.
  Adson's Masque, iii. 2.
Advertisements, vi. 178, 213.
Adye, Mr., ii. 510.
Aeschylus, vi. 276.
Aesop, *Fables*, v. 1103.
Aethiopica, see Heliodorus.
'Affezionati' (Comedia dell' arte
  company), iii. 171.
African Catholics, v. 1062.
Afterpieces, v. 989.
Agamemnon, see Manuche, Cosmo.
Agas map, vi. 268.

Agathon, vi. 276 n. 2.
Aglaura, see Suckling, Sir John.
Ainsworth, George, iii. 2.
Ainsworth (Aynsworth), William, iii. 2–3.
  Clytophon, iii. 2, 3, 42.
  Medulla Bibliorum, the Marrow of the Bible, iii. 2.
  Triplex Memoriae, iii. 2.
Aitken collection, U. of Texas, v. 1094.
Aiton, John, vii. 117.
Alabaster, William, *Roxana,* iv. 854; v. 1453; vii. 82, 84.
Alaham, see Greville, Fulke.
'Alas! poor scholar, whither wilt thou go?', *see* Wild, Robert.
Alban, the first British martyr, v. 1142.
Albany, Duke of, i. 198.
Albemarle, Duke of, *see* Monck, George.
Albert of Belgium, v. 1292.
Albertus Wallenstein, see Glapthorne.
Albion's Triumph, see Townshend, Aurelian.
Albovine, King of the Lombards, see Davenant, William.
Albright, E. M., *Dramatic Publication in England, 1580–1640* (1927), iii. 285.
Albright, V. E., *The Shakesperian Stage* (1909), v. 1004.
Albumazar, see Tomkis, Thomas.
Alchemist, The, see Jonson, Ben.
Alchorne, Thomas, iv. 622.
Alcimedon, see Du Ryer, Pierre.
Aldee, Edward, v. 1385.
Aldee, Mrs., v. 1385.
Alderbury parish, Wiltshire, iii. 443.
Alderman No Conjurer, An, see Tate, Nahum, *Cuckold's Haven.*
Aldermanbury, *see* London, streets and districts.
Aldermen, i. 314; iv. 497; v. 1441, 1442; vi. 27, 83, 84, 166, 174, 175; vii. 24, 36.
Aldermen, Court of, iv. 911.
Alderson, Thomas, i. 265; ii. 432; vi. 160, 161.
Aldgate, *see* London, streets and districts.
Alehouses, vi. 147.
Alemán, Mateo, iv. 727.
  Guzman d'Alfarache, iii. 358.
Ale-sellers, vi. 291 n. 1.
Aleumista, see Anonymous.
Alexander, Daniel Ben, *The Converted Jew* (1621), iii. 280, 281.

Alexander et Aristobulus, see Anonymous.
Alexander, Sir Sigismund, iv. 736.
Alexander, Sir William, Earl of Stirling, vii. 18, 64.
  Alexandrean Tragedy, vii. 21, 105.
  Croesus, vii. 21.
  Darius, vii. 21.
  Julius Caesar, vii. 21, 105.
  Monarchic Tragedies, The, vii. 21.
  Recreations with the Muses, vii. 105, 108.
Alexander, Walter, iv. 664; vii. 65.
Alexandrean Tragedy, The, see Sir William Alexander, Earl of Stirling.
Alexius, see Massinger, Philip.
Aleyn, Charles, v. 1116.
Alfonso, see Anonymous, *Alphonsus, Emperor of Germany.*
Alfred the Great, iii. 290.
Alfrida and Edgar, Story of, iv. 788.
Alice and Alexis, see Anonymous.
Aliens, Registration of, iii. 21.
Alimony Lady, The, see Anonymous, *Lady Alimony.*
Alisbury, Mr., vi. 300.
All Fools, see Chapman, George.
All for the Better, see Manning, Francis.
All Hallows, London Wall, ii. 589, 592, 593, 615.
All Hallows the Less, ii. 626.
All Is Not Gold that Glisters, see Anonymous.
All is True, see Shakespeare, William, *Henry VIII.*
All Mistaken, or The Mad Couple, see Howard, James.
'All night I weepe' (song), iii. 320.
All Saints', Worcester, v. 1005, 1007.
All Souls College, Oxford, iv. 845.
Allegorical plays, *see* Plays.
Allegory, iv. 596; v. 1119.
Allen, Alice, ii. 345.
Allen, Ann, ii. 345.
Allen, Don Cameron, 'Ben Jonson and the Hieroglyphics', *P.Q.* xviii (1939), iv. 604.
  'Milton's "Comus" as a Failure in Artistic Compromise', *E.L.H.* xvi (1949), iv. 914.
Allen, Edward, *see* Alleyn, Edward.
Allen, Elizabeth, ii. 346.
Allen, Herbert F., *A Study of the Comedies of Richard Brome, Especially as Representative of Dramatic Decadence* (1912), iii. 49.

Allen, Hester, ii. 345.
Allen, Jeremy, ii. 344.
Allen, John, ii. 345.
Allen, Mary, ii. 345.
Allen, Michael, ii. 345.
Allen, Mr., a fencer, vi. 221 n. 1.
Allen, Percy, *Shakespeare, Jonson, and Wilkins as Borrowers* (1928), iv. 604.
Allen, Richard, ii. 344.
Allen, Robert, ii. 345; iv. 964.
Allen, Samuel, ii. 345.
Allen, Sheriff of London, iv. 881.
Allen, Thomas, i. 137.
Allen, Thomas (Lord Mayor), v. 1220.
Allen, William, i. 56, 57, 64, 69 n. 2, 73–89, 220, 221, 226, 231, 239, 246, 247; ii. 344–6; iii. 311; iv. 570, 813; v. 1131.
Alleyn, Edward, i. 6, 135, 136, 137, 138, 142, 143, 144, 146 and n. 1, 152, 153, 177, 198, 199 and n. 2, 200, 201 n. 2, 202, 209; ii. 346–9, 507, 528, 633, 694; iii. 190, 243, 274; iv. 516, 573, 606, 733, 749; v. 1446, 1448; vi. 79, 85, 123, 139, 140, 141–144, 145, 150, 151, 153, 154–8, 165, 202, 208, 209, 210, 219, 220; vii. 47.
Alleyn, Joan, vi. 123, 126.
Alleyn, Mathias, i. 144.
'Alleyn's Fortune in the Making', *see* Hotson, Leslie.
Allibond, John, schoolmaster, iii. 26.
Allington, John, i. 49 n. 2 cont., 73–89; ii. 349.
Allington, Sir Giles, iii. 463.
Allott, Kenneth, ed. *The Poems of William Habington* (1948), iv. 520, 521, 522; v. 1301.
Allott, Robert, stationer, iii. 235, 236; iv. 615, 629, 797, 798–9, 815; v. 971, 973, 974.
Allott, Mrs. Robert, iii. 304; iv. 629, 815; v. 972, 975.
Allott, Thomas, iii. 402; v. 1140.
All's Lost by Lust, see Rowley, William.
All's Well That Ends Well, see Shakespeare.
Allusions (to dramatists), iii. 310; *see also* the individual dramatists.
Almanacs, i. 243 n. 2; iii. 260.
Almeyda, Queen of Granada, see Lee, Sophia.
Almoners, vi. 256.
Alnwick Castle, ii. 363.

Alnwick Castle, MS. v. 1433.
Aloysius sive Saeculi Fuga, see Anonymous.
Alphonso, King of Naples, see Powell, George.
Alphonsus, Emperor of Germany, see Anonymous.
Alsace, v. 1006.
Alsop, Bernard, stationer, iii. 18.
Alston, Thomas, iv. 536.
Altars, i. 277–8; v. 1235, 1300; vi. 167, 169.
Altemira, see Boyle, Roger.
Alum, manufacture of, iii. 468.
Alumni Cantabrigienses, see Venn, John.
Alumni Oxonienses, see Foster, Joseph.
Alvredus sive Alfredus, see Drury, William.
Amanuensis, v. 1053.
Amateur dramatists, iii. 114; *see also* Dramatists.
Amazonians' Masque, The, see Anonymous.
Ambassador to Germany, iv. 526.
Ambassadors, vi. 257, 259, 261, 280, 292, 295, 301, 303; vi. 59; *see also* under the separate nations.
Ambitio Infelix sive Absalom tragoedia, see Anonymous.
Ambitious Brother, The, see Buc, George.
Ambitious Politique, The, see Brome, *The Lovesick Court.*
Ambitious Stepdame, The, see Anonymous, *Roxalana.*
Amboyna massacre, play about, iv. 924; vii. 58.
Amends for Ladies, see Field.
America, iii. 175.
  Colonies in, vi. 137.
  Sailing for, iii. 22.
  Proposed flight to, iii. 175.
  Artisans for, iii. 196.
American performances, iv. 817; v. 1152.
Aminta, see Tasso.
Amiott, Jaques, iii. 142.
Amorea, see Jenkyn, Pathericke.
Amorous Phantasm, The, see Lower, Sir William.
Amorous War, The, see Mayne, Jasper.
Amphitheatre, *see* Proposed amphitheatre.
Amphrisa, see Heywood, Thomas.
Amsterdam, i. 267; iv. 631; v. 1407; vi. 184, 202.

Burgomaster of, v. 1329, 1330.
English comedians in, v. 1337.
Amurath the First, see Goffe, Thomas, *The Courageous Turk.*
Amyntas, see Digby, Kenelm.
Amyntas, or The Impossible Dowry, see Randolph, Thomas.
Amyot, Thomas, F.R.S., vi. 116.
Anabaptists, iv. 599.
Anacreon, iii. 48.
Anagram, Ford's (*Fide Honor*), iii. 440.
Anastasius, v. 1175.
Ancre, Marechal d', murder of, v. 1252.
'Andrei Melvini Anti-Tami-Cunicategoria', *see* Atkinson, Thomas.
Andrewes, Lancelot, iv. 853.
Andrewes, William, ii. 483.
Andrews, Clarence Edward, *Richard Brome: A Study of His Life and Works* (1913), iii. 49, 50, 53, 55, 57, 70, 73, 74, 75, 89.
Andrews, C. E., 'The Authorship of *The Late Lancashire Witches*', *M.L.N.* xxviii (1913), iii. 73.
Andria, see Terence.
Andrian Woman, The, see Terence, *Andria.*
Andromana, or The Merchant's Wife, see S. J.
Andronicus Comnenus, see Bernard, Samuel.
Anecdotes, collections of, iii. 152.
Angel, Edward, iii. 377.
Angel in Cornhill, *see* Inns and Taverns.
Angel King, The, see Anonymous.
Angell, Thomas, ii. 510.
Angels Inn, ii. 348.
Anglesey, Isle of, vi. 4.
Anglo-Saxon, iv. 596.
Anhalt, Prince of, iv. 669.
Annales, 1615, 1631, *see* Stow, John.
Annals of England, see Stow, John.
Annals of the New York Stage, see Odell, G. C. D.
Annals of theatrical affairs, vii. 16–128.
Anne, Princess (later Queen Anne), vi. 270 n. 1.
Anne, Queen of England, iii. 26, 103; iv. 641, 908, 909; v. 1257, 1288, 1304, 1305; vi. 57, 220.
Anne, Queen, Company of, i. 37 n. 3, 158–75, 167–9, 177, 178, 183 n. 2, 185 n. 9, 200, 202 and n. 6, 208, 222, 237; iii. 74, 75, 101, 102, 192, 266, 280,

283, 284, 555, 556, 566; iv. 713, 735, 797, 836, 1015, 1017, 1020, 1061, 1062, 1241, 1247; v. 1250, 1251, 1344, 1416, 1427, 1453; vi. 12 n. 1, 48, 50, 56, 57, 58, 73, 122, 123, 130, 133, 216 n. 2, 217, 218, 219, 225; vii. 11, 12 n., 20.
Company of, Wardrobe, i. 204.
Council of, vi. 50.
Dancer in masques, iv. 549, 677.
Death of, i. 6, 139 n. 7, 164; vi. 20; vii. 30.
Funeral of, i. 6, 7.
Masques for, v. 1258.
Red Bull Revels Company, i. 164–5, 165–75, 200, 308, 309; iii. 101, 102, 103, 244; iv. 734, 735; v. 1435; vi. 12 n. 1, 78, 136, 138, 220–1.
ANONYMOUS, *Academy of Compliments,* v. 1277.
Actors Remonstrance, The (1643), vi. 151 n.
Advice from Parnassus (1681), iv. 719.
Airs Songs and Duettos from The Jovial Crew (1792), iii. 71.
Aleumista, iv. 866; v. 1283.
Alexander et Aristobulus, v. 1283.
Alice and Alexis, i. 123; v. 1283–4.
All Is Not Gold that Glisters, iv. 865, 866; v. 1285
Aloysius sive Saeculi Fuga, v. 1285.
Alphonsus, Emperor of Germany, i. 27, 48 n. 5, 51, 66, 96,98, 132–3; iii. 156; iv. 955; v. 1285; vi. 35.
'Amazons Masque, The', iii. 2.
Amazonians' Masque, The, v. 1289.
Ambitio Infelix sive Absalom tragoedia, v. 1290.
Amours tragiques d'Hypolite et Isabelle, Les (1610), iv. 907.
Angel King, The, i. 150, 157; iii. 265; v. 1290–1.
Annæ Funebria Sacra, v. 1188.
Antoninus Bassianus Caracalla, v. 1291.
Arden of Feversham, vii. 54, 90.
Astraea, v. 1292.
Baggs Seneca, v. 1292, 1293.
Ballet de la Foire St. Germain, iv. 677.
'Barton Holiday's *Marriages of the Arts*', *The Retrospective Review,* viii (1823), iv. 589.

ANONYMOUS (*cont.*)
Battle of Alcazar, The, see Peele.
Battle of the Vices against the Virtues, The, v. 1293.
Bays, v. 1293.
Beggars, The, i. 66, 133; v. 1293–4.
Bellum Grammaticale, see Spense, Master.
Black Batman of the North, v. 1045.
Black Lady, The, i. 185, 196–7, 205 n. 5; v. 1294, 1430; vi. 59.
Black Wedding, The, v. 1294, 1445.
Bloody Banquet, The, see Thomas Drue.
Bond Woman, The, v. 1294–5, 1445.
'Booke in Meeter of Robin Conscience, The', v. 1402.
Boot and Spur, v. 1295, 1306, 1350.
Bourbon, v. 1302.
Bridegroom and the Madman, The, i. 66, 95 n. c, 133; iii. 382; v. 1296.
Briefe Description of the notorious Life of Iohn Lambe, otherwise called Doctor Lambe, A. Together with his Ignominious Death, Amsterdam (1628), i. 267; vi. 161.
Britanniae Primitiae, sive S. Albanus protomartyr, v. 1297.
Buck Is a Thief, The, i. 95, 133; iii. 329; v. 1297.
Cabala, sive Scrinia Sacra: Mysteries of State, v. 1425.
Callidamus et Callanthia, v. 1297–8.
Cancer, iv. 527; v. 1232, 1298–9, 1413.
Canterbury His Change of Diet, v. 1299–1300.
Cardinal's Conspiracy, The, i. 278, 282; v. 1234, 1235, 1300–1; vi. 167, 168.
Cariclia, iii. 269.
'Cartwright's Poems and Plays', The Retrospective Review (1824), iii. 126.
Carwidgeon, The, v. 1301.
Castara, or Cruelty without Hate, v. 1301–2, 1445.
Catalogue of the Additions to the MSS. in the British Museum in the years MDCCCLIV–MDCCCLXXV, A (1877), v. 451.
Catalogue of the Additions to the

MSS. in the British Museum, A, 1882–7 (1889), v. 1304.
Catalogue of the Harleian Manuscripts in the British Museum, A, 4 vols. (1808–12), v. 1196.
Catilina Triumphans (lost), v. 1302.
Character of an Oxford Incendiary, The, n.d., iii. 143.
Charles, Duke of Bourbon (lost), v. 1302, 1326, 1387; vii. 124.
Chaste Woman against Her Will, The, v. 1303.
Cheater and the Clown, The, v. 1303.
'Christening, The; A Masque, By Ben Jonson; Not in his Works', The Monthly Magazine; or, British Register, xli (1816), iv. 639.
Christes Bloodie Sweat, Or the Sonne of God in His Agonie (1613), iii. 435.
Christmas Messe (1619), iv. 551; v. 1295, 1305–6, 1307, 1343, 1350.
Christmas Ordinary, iii. 263; v. 964, 1004–5, 1306, 1343.
Christmas Prince, The, v. 1308.
Chronicle History of Perkin Warbeck, The, A Tragedy. A Strange Truth (1714), iii. 454.
City, The, v. 1308–9.
'City Dog in a Saint's Doublet, A', v. 1244.
City Shuffler, The, i. 293 n. 2; v. 1309–10; vi. 99.
Claudius Tiberius Nero, v. 1381.
Cleopatra, v. 1310.
Cloudy Queen and the Singing Moor, The, iv. 865, v. 1310.
Collection of poems, written upon several occasions by several persons, A (1673; 2nd edition), iii. 134.
College Life in the Time of James the First as Illustrated by an Unpublished Diary of Sir Symonds D'Ewes (1851), iii. 11; v. 1414.
Conceited Duke, The, i. 331, 342; iii. 389; v. 1120, 1311–12.
Conceits, The, v. 1312, 1445.
Contention between Liberality and Prodigality, The, iv. 631.
Copy of Two Remonstrances, Brought Over the River Stix in Carons Ferry-boat, by the Ghost of Sir John Suckling, A (1643), v. 1200.

Costly Whore, The, i. 175, 301; iv. 500, 851; v. 1312–14.

'Countrie Girl, The', *The Retrospective Review*, Second Series, ii (1828), iii. 5.

Countryman, The (lost), v. 1314, 1360, 1397.

Court Purge, A, iv. 865; v. 1314.

Cruel War, The, v. 1315.

Cuckolds' Masque, The, v. 1315.

Cupid's Festival, v. 1315.

Cure of Pride, or Every One in Their Way, The, iv. 774.

Cyprian Conqueror, or The Faithless Relict, The, v. 1316–17.

De Probatis Sanctorum Historiis, iii. 266.

Death of the Black Prince, The, v. 1317.

Declaration of the Variance between the Pope and the Segniory of Venice, A (1606), iv. 878.

Deep Sigh Breath'd Through the Lodgings at White-Hall, Deploring the absence of the Court. And the Miseries of the Pallace, A (1642), vi. 284.

Demetrius and Marina (Marsina), or The Imperial Impostor and Unhappy Herione, v. 1317.

Der Herzog von Florentz, iv. 788.

Diana's Grove, or The Faithful Genius, v. 1317.

Dice, Wine, and Women, or the Unfortunate Gallant gull'd at London (Ballad), vi. 240.

Dick of Devonshire, iii. 283; v. 1318–20.

Dioclesian, iii. 266, 397.

Disguises, The, iii. 249.

Divine Tragedie Lately Acted, or A Collection of Sundry Memorable Example of Gods Judgements upon Sabbath-Breakers, A (1636), v. 1398.

Divorce, The (lost), v. 1321, 1445.

Doctor Lambe and the Witches, i. 41, 294 and n. 1, 301; iii. 75, 634; v. 1455; vi. 100–101.

Doge and the Dragon, The, iv. 635; v. 1321–2; vi. 173.

Don Pedro, v. 1322.

Dramatic Works of John Ford: with an Introduction and Notes Critical and Explanatory, The, 2 vols. (1831), iii. 438.

'Duchesse of Suffolke' (ballad), iii. 285.

Duke Humphrey, iii. 19; v. 1049, 1323, 1354, 1361.

'Duke Return'd Againe, The', v. 1353.

'Duke's Play, The', vii. 62.

Durance Masque, v. 1323–4.

Dutch Gazette, The, iv. 499.

Dutch Painter and the French Brawle, The, i. 205, 216; iii. 265; iv. 805, 865; v. 1324–5; vi. 136.

'Early London Theatres', *The Architect,* cvii, no. 2777 (10 March 1922), vi. 3.

Edmond Ironside, i. 323; ii. 388–9, 443, 450, 509, 510, 580, 581; iii. 43, 44.

Edward III, iv. 831; vii. 26, 115.

Edward IV, vii. 33, 61.

Edward IV, Parts I and II, vii. 63, 64, 68, 76.

Elegie upon the Death of the Renowned Sir John Suckling, An (1642), v. 1200, 1203.

England's First Happiness, or the Life of St. Augustine, v. 1326, 1387; vii. 124.

English Arcadia, The, v. 1326–7.

English Secretorie, The, iii. 437.

Entertainment at Chirke Castle (Entertainment at Sir Thomas Middleton's) (Masque of the Four Seasons), v. 1303–5.

Entertainment of the High and Mighty Monarch Charles, King of Great Britain, France, and Ireland into his Ancient and Royal City of Edinburgh, the fifteenth of June, 1633, iii. 288.

Epigrams, Theological, Philosophical and Romantic (1651), iii. 236.

Essay in Defence of the Female Sex (1696), iv. 681.

Essex Antic Masque, The, v. 1326.

Exchange Ware, or Band, Cuff and Ruff, v. 1443.

Fair Em, vii. 80.

Fair Maid of the Exchange, The, vii. 17, 60, 102, 108.

Fair Spanish Captive, The (lost), v. 1327.

Fair Star of Antwerp, The, i. 150, 157; iii. 265; v. 1327–8.

Fairy Knight, or Oberon the Second, The, v. 977, 978, 979, 170, 1328–30.

Fairy Masque, The, v. 1330–1.

Fairy Queen, The, v. 1331.

ANONYMOUS (cont.)

False Friend, The, i. 111; iv. 866; v. 1331-2.

Famous Tragedy of King Charles I Basely Butchered, The, iv. 499; v. 1360.

Famous Victories of Henry the Fifth, The, i. 133; vii. 25.

Fashionable Lover: Or Wit in Necessity, iv. 932.

Fatal Banquet, The, iv. 865; v. 1332.

Fatal Marriage, The, or a Modern Lucretia, v. 1332-3.

Father's Own Son, The, see Beaumont and Fletcher, *Monsieur Thomas*.

Fickle Shepherdess, The, v. 971.

First Antimasque of Mountebanks, The, v. 1376-8.

'First of the Ladyes after the Cuckolds, The', v. 1289.

'First of the Lords, The', v. 1289.

First Part of the Knaves, The, v. 1024.

'First witches dance, The', v. 1289.

Florentine Friend, The (lost), v. 1333, 1445.

Florentine Ladies, The, v. 1333.

Florimene, v. 1333-5; vi. 263, 264, 283.

Fool and Her Maidenhead Soon Parted, A, i. 331, 342; iii. 230; v. 1335-6, 1445.

Fool's Masque, The, v. 1336.

Fool's Preferment, or, The Three Dukes of Dunstable, A, iii. 391.

'Forc'd Vallour' (droll from *The Humorous Lieutenant*), iii. 344.

Fortunate Isles, The, v. 1336-7.

'Fortune my foe, why dost thou frown on me ?', v. 1300.

Fortune's Tennis, ii. 578.

Four Sons of Amon, The, i. 206 n. 3, 216; v. 1337.

Fratrum Discordia Felix sive Stanislaus Fuga Victor, v. 1337-8.

Fraus Pia, v. 1338.

Frederick and Basilea, ii. 481.

Free Parliament Quaeries, proposed to Tender Consciences, and published for the use of Members now elected (1660), iv. 500; v. 1313.

French Doctor, The, iii. 252.

French Schoolmaster, The, v. 1338.

Funebria Sacra (1619), iv. 499.

Furies' Masque, The, v. 1338.

Galiaso, v. 1333.

Geminus Alcides, v. 1339.

General, The, v. 1112, 1339.

Gentleman No Gentleman—A Metamorphosed Courtier, A, iv. 865; v. 1339-40.

George a Greene, i. 331, 342; v. 1340, 1356; vii. 26, 61, 115.

Gerardo, The Unfortunate Spaniard, iii. 379.

Gesta Grayorum, v. 1377.

Gesta Romanorum, iii. 400.

Ghismonda, or Tancred and Ghismonda, v. 1340-2.

Ghost, or the Woman Wears the Breeches, The, v. 1342, 1344.

Gigantomachia, or Work for Jupiter, v. 1343, 1350.

'Godley Warning for all Maidens, A', v. 1045.

Golden Meane, The, iii. 435.

Gonsalvus Sylveira, v. 1344.

Gossips' Brawl, or The Women Wear the Breeches, The, v. 1344, 1365.

Gramercy Wit, i. 166, 173, 175; v. 1344.

Great Cham, The, v. 1345.

Great Duke, The, see Massinger, *The Great Duke of Florence*.

Greek Slave; or, the School for Cowards, The, iii. 347.

Greeks and Trojans, The, ii. 690; v. 1345-6.

Guelphs and Ghibellines, The, ii. 690; v. 1346.

Guido Varvicensis, v. 1346-7.

Gull upon Gull, v. 1347.

Gypsy, The, v. 1343.

'Habington's Castara', *Retrospective Review*, xii (1825), iv. 520.

Haeresis Triumphata sive B. Ignatius Societatis Jesu Fundator, v. 1349.

Hannibal, v. 1349.

Haymakers' Masque, The, v. 1349.

Hengist, iv. 885, 887.

'Henry Glapthornes Plays', *Retrospective Review* (1824), iv. 473.

Henry the Una . . ., v. 1350.

Hermophus, v. 1350.

Heteroclitanomalonomia, v. 1350-1.

Historical and Miscellaneous Tracts of the Reverend and Learned Peter Heylyn D.D. . . . and an Account of the Life of the Author, The (1681), iv. 550, 552, 553.

History from 1276 to 1956 of the Site in Blackfriars Consisting of Printing House Square . . . Being the Freehold Property of the Times Publishing Company Limited, The (1956), vi. 3, 5.

History of Abraham, vii. 40.

History of Don Quixote, or the Knight of the Ill-Favoured Face, v. 1322–3.

History of King Stephen, The, iii. 19; v. 1049, 1323, 1354, 1361.

History of Lewis II, King of France, The, v. 1364.

History of Richard Whittington, iii. 44.

Histriomastix, v. 1238.

Honest Lawyer, The, i. 174; vi. 218.

Honour in the End, i. 150, 157; v. 1351–2.

Honour of Women, The, i. 134.

House Is Haunted, The, v. 1352.

How a Man May Choose a Good Wife from a Bad, vii. 76, 95.

Humour in the End, v. 1352.

Humours of Monsieur Galliard, The (droll), v. 1079.

'Hunt Is Up, The', v. 1374.

Huon of Bordeaux, iii. 250.

Hymen's Holiday, iv. 634.

Hypochondriac, or The Turmoil of Love, The, v. 1352.

Il Creduto Principe, iii. 171.

Impatient Grissell, v. 1353.

In Duc Reducem, or A Welcome from the Isle of Rhe, v. 1353.

Induction for the House, i. 28 and n. 1, 96, 97 n. 1†; iii. 374; v. 1353–4; vi. 271, 275.

Invisible Knight, The, v. 1354.

Iphis and Iantha, or A Marriage without a Man, iii. 19; v. 1049, 1323, 1354–5, 1361.

Irish Gentleman, The, iii. 97; v. 1112, 1355.

Irish Rebellion, The, ii. 493; iv. 635, 711, 712.

Italian Night Masque, The, *see* Massinger.

Italian Night-piece or the Unfortunate Piety, The, *see* Massinger.

Jack Drum's Entertainment, vii. 21, 29.

Jenkins Love-Course, and Perambulation, v. 1147.

John a Green, iii. 187; v. 1356.

Joseph's Afflictions, v. 1356.

Josephus, Jude von Venedig, iii. 252.

Jovis et Junonis Nuptiae, v. 1452.

Jugurth, King of Numidia, *see* William Boyle.

Julio und Hippolyta, iv. 808.

Juno in Arcadia, v. 1419–20.

Juno's Pastoral, or The Bonds of Peace, v. 1419–20.

Kermophus, v. 1357.

Key to the Cabinet of Parliament, A, ii. 549; iii. 347.

King and Queen's Entertainment at Richmond, The, v. 1037, 1357–60.

'King John and Matilda, a Tragedy . . . Written by Robert Davenport, Gent. . . . 1655', *The Retrospective Review*, iv (1821), iii. 232.

King Leir, vii. 54, 120.

King's Mistress, The, v. 1360–1, 1397.

Knack to Know a Knave, A, iv. 788.

'Knight and the Shepherd's Daughter, The' (ballad), iii. 61, 394.

Lacrymae Cantabrigiensis, ii. 444.

Ladies, A Second Time, Assembled in Parliament, The (1647), vi. 112, 175.

Lady Alimony, or The Alimony Lady, v. 1361–3.

Laelia, v. 1238.

'Lame Common-Wealth, The' (droll), iii. 314.

Landlady, The (droll from *Chances*), iii. 319, 323.

Last Will and Testament of the Doctors Commons, The (1641), vi. 173, 244.

Late (and the Last) Will and Testament of the Doctors Commons, The, i. 319.

'Latin Plays acted before the University of Cambridge, The', *The Retrospective Review* (1825), iii. 2.

Law Case, The, v. 1363–4, 1445.

Life and death of Iack Straw and Watt Tyler, The, iv. 712.

'Life and Writings of James Shirley, The', *Quarterly Review* (1833), v. 1064.

Like to Like, or a Match Well Made Up, v. 1149.

London Chanticleers, The, iv. 494; v. 1364–5.

ANONYMOUS (cont.)
London Prodigal, The, iv. 445,
631, 632.
Long Meg of Westminster, v. 1440.
Look about You, iii. 260.
Look on Me and Love Me, or
Marriage in the Dark, iv. 865;
v. 1365.
Look to the Lady, v. 1365–6.
Louis the Eleventh, King of
France, v. 1366.
Love Feigned and Unfeigned, iv.
599.
Love Lost in the Dark; or, The
Drunken Couple, iv. 761, 790,
828.
Love Tricks with Compliments, see
Shirley, The School of Com-
pliment.
Love Yields to Honour (lost?), v.
1369.
'Lovely Northern Lass, The'
(ballad), iii. 81.
Lover's Holiday, The, iv. 866.
Lover's Holiday, or the Bear, The,
iv. 865; v. 1366.
Lovers of Ludgate, The, v. 1366–7.
Love's Aftergame, see The Proxy.
Love's Changelings' Change, v.
1367.
Love's Infancy, iv. 866; v. 1367–8.
Love's Loadstone, v. 1279, 1280.
'Love's Solace, or Sweet is the
Lass that Loves me' (ballad),
iii. 82.
'Love's Victory: a Tragi-Comedy
by William Chamberlayne of
Shaftesbury in the County of
Dorset', Retrospective Review
(1820), iii. 154.
Love's Victory, v. 1368–9.
Loyola, v. 1298.
Lusiuncula, v. 1369.
Lysander and Calista, see Fletcher,
The Lovers' Progress.
Mad Couple Well Met, A, see
Brome, A Mad Couple Well
Matched.
Maid's Metamorphosis, The, v.
1222; vii. 24, 110, 114.
Male Courtesan, The, see Anon-
ymous, The Younger Brother.
Man in the Moon Drinks Claret,
The, i. 205, 213, 216; iii. 270;
v. 1370, 1453; vi. 58, 135, 136.
Manhood and Misrule, v. 1369–70.
Marcus Tullius Cicero, v. 1370.
Marquesse d'Ancre, The, v. 1371.
Marriage Night, The, v. 1371–2

Marriage of the Farmer's Son, The,
v. 1372, 1422.
Marrow of complements, The
(1655), iii. 134.
Masque, The, see Gunnell.
Masque at Coleoverton, v. 1311.
'Masque at Fryers, A' (music),
iii. 2.
Masque of Amazons, or The
Ladies' Masque, The, v. 1288–
90.
Masque of Disappointed Ladies,
The, v. 1289.
Masque of the Twelve Months, The,
v. 1041.
Masque of Vices, The, v. 988–9,
1430–2.
'Masques & other Tunes', iii. 2.
'Massinger and the Inns of Court
Mission', Spectator, cxxviii (18
February 1922), iv. 786.
Match without Money, or The
Wives' Prize, A (lost), iv. 865;
v. 1373.
'Matron of Ephesus', v. 1316.
Medea, v. 1373.
Melanthe, v. 1299.
Merchant's Sacrifice, The, v. 1373.
Mercurius Britanicus, iii. 144,
150; iv. 589.
Mercurius Fumigosus, iii. 188.
Mercurius Rusticans, v. 1373–4.
Merry Devil of Edmonton, The, i.
28, 94, 96, 99, 133; ii. 690; iii.
272; vi. 198, 239; vii. 25, 63, 80.
Merry Milkmaid of Islington, or
the Rambling Gallants defeated,
The, iv. 942.
Metamorphosed Courtier, A, see A
Gentleman No Gentleman.
Microcosmus, v. 1374.
Moor's Masque, The, v. 1375.
More than Nine Days' Wonder:
Two Constant Women, iv. 865;
v. 1375.
Mors Valentiniani Imperatoris,
v. 1375–6.
Mother Rumming, v. 1376.
'Mountebanks Dance at Grayes
Inne, The', v. 1378.
Mountebanks Masque, The, iii. 104.
'Mountebankes Receipts, The', v.
1378.
Mucedorus, vii. 28, 29, 33, 42, 63,
80, 95, 118.
Mull Sack, or The Looking Glass,
the Bachelor, or the Hawk, iii.
187, 188; iv. 865; v. 1356,
1378–9.

Musarum Deliciae, ii. 472.
Muse of New-Market, The: or Mirth and Drollery, Being Three Farces (1680), iii. 227; iv. 942.
Mustapha, v. 1379.
Natural History of Wiltshire, The (1847), iv. 757.
Nero, iii. 359.
New Book of Songs to the Jovial Crew, A (1731), iii. 71.
Newes from Rome: Spalato's Doom (1624), iv. 878.
Nineveh's Repentance, v. 1382.
Noble Friend, The, v. 1382.
Noble Ravishers, The, v. 1383, 1445.
Nobody and Somebody, iv. 584.
North Country Song, A, vi. 210.
'Northern Lass, or Sweet is the Lass that Loves me, The' (ballad), iii. 82.
'Note on the Swan Theatre Drawing, A', *Shakespeare Survey*, i (1948), vi. 249.
Nottola, v. 1383.
Ode to the Pretender, An, Humbly Inscrib'd to Mr. Lesley and Mr. Pope. To which is added Earl Mortimer's Fall (1713), iv. 621.
Odoardus Varvici Comes, v. 1383.
Oenone, a Pastoral (droll), iv. 481.
Old Ben's Light Heart Made Heavy by Young John's Melancholy Lover, iii. 450.
'On the Time Poets', *see* William Heminges, *Elegy on Randolph's Finger*.
Orpheus, v. 1384.
Ortenus or *Ortenas*, v. 1384.
Osman the Turk, or the Ottoman Custom, v. 1384-5.
Ovo Frisius, v. 1385.
Owl, The, v. 1385.
Pageant of David, The, v. 1415.
Pageant of Elias, The, v. 1415.
Pageant of Gideon, The, v. 1415.
Pageant of 'Iepthe', The, v. 1415.
Pageant of 'Iosue', The, v. 1415.
Pageant of Jacob, The, v. 1415.
Pageant of Joseph, The, v. 1415.
Pageant of 'Moyses', The, v. 1415.
Pageant of Naaman, The, v. 1415.
Pageant of Sampson, The, v. 1415.
Pageant of Saul, The, v. 1415.
Pageant of Solomon, The, v. 1415.
Painted Lady, The, iv. 865; v. 1386.

Painter, The, or Wandering Lovers, v. 1325.
Pandorae Pyxis, iv. 866; v. 1386.
'Paradoxes, as they were spoken in a Maske, and presented before his Maiesty at White-Hall', v. 1378.
Paria, v. 1232-3, 1298.
Parliament of Ladies, The (1647), vi. 112, 175.
Parliament of Love, The, iii. 263.
Parnassus plays, iv. 539.
Parricide, The, i. 216; v. 1387.
Parrioall of Princes, The, . . ., v. 1302, 1326, 1387; vii. 124.
Parthenia, iv. 854; v. 1387-8.
Partial Law, The, v. 1388-9.
Pastoral, The, i. 97, 133; ii. 675; v. 1389-90.
Pathomachia, or the Battle of Affections, or Love's Loadstone, iii. 297; iv. 921; v. 1225, 1390-2.
Paulus Japonensis, v. 1392.
Peaceable King, or the Lord Mendall, The, i. 206, 216; iii. 265; v. 1393; vi. 137.
Pedantius, vii. 80.
Pelopidarum Secunda, v. 1393.
Perfidus Hetruscus, v. 1394.
Philander, King of Thrace, v. 1395.
Philetis and Constantia (droll) iv. 481.
Philip of Macedon, iv. 865, 1395.
'Philip Massinger (1583-1640)', *T.L.S.*, 16 March 1940, iv. 749.
Philipo and Hippolito, iv. 808.
Pilgrim of Castile, The, iii. 392, 393.
Pilgrimage to Parnassus, iv. 539.
Pity the Maid, v. 1395, 1445.
Plantation of Virginia, see A Tragedy of the Plantation of Virginia.
Play of the Netherlands, The, v. 1382.
Plenum Reconciled to Kulum, v. 1396.
Poems on Affairs of State, from the time of Oliver Cromwell to the Abdication of King James the Second (1697), iii. 278.
Politic Bankrupt, The, or Which Is the Best Girl, v. 1360, 1397.
Politick Whore, The: or, The Conceited Cuckold, iii. 227, 228.
Poor Robin (1681), *An Almanack of the Old and New Fashion*, v. 1127.
Praeludium to Thomas Goffe's

ANONYMOUS (*cont.*)
The Careless Shepherdess, vi.
109–12, 166, 243.
Presentment of Bushell's Rock,
The, vii. 104.
Prince of Conceit, A (jig), v.
1137.
'Prince's Masque, The' (music),
iii. 2.
Priscianus Vapulans, v. 1397–8.
Projector Lately Dead, A, v.
1398.
'Prologue to his Majesty at the
first Play presented at the
Cock-pit in Whitehall, The', vi.
284.
'Prophesie of Mother Shipton,
The', v. 1365.
Proxy, or Love's Aftergame, The, i.
294 and n. 2, 296 ,299 and n. d,
301; v. 1399, 1445.
Publius Cornelius Scipio Sui
Victor, v. 1400.
Pygmalion, v. 1400.
Queen, or the Excellency of Her
Sex, The, see Ford.
Queen of Ethiopia, iii. 269.
'Queene's Masque the first, The'
(music), iii. 2.
'Queen's Play, The', vii. 62.
Querolus, iii. 404.
Rampant Alderman, The (1685),
iv. 744.
Relation of the Death of that Great
Generalissimo (of His Imperial
Maiestie) the Duke of Mecklen-
burg, Fridland, Sagan, and
Great Glogaw &c Together with
the Cause thereof, The (1634),
iv. 478.
Remarks upon E. Settle's Nar-
rative (1683), vi. 171.
Return from Parnassus, The, v.
1266.
Review, 'Diaries and Despatches
of the Venetian Embassy at
the Court of King James I, in
the Years 1617, 1618', by
Rawdon Brown, Quarterly Re-
view, cii (1857), vi. 152.
Review of performance of
Shirley's The Opportunity at
University of Illinois, Nation,
lxxxii (1906), v. 1134.
Ring, The, v. 1400.
Risus Anglicanus, v. 1401.
'Rival Friends, The', N. & Q.,
Third Series, ii (5 July 1862),
iv. 536.

Rival Nymphs, The, iii. 180.
Roaring Girl, or the Catchpole, The,
v. 1401–2.
Robin Conscience, v. 1402.
Robin Hood, Parts I and II, v.
1402–3.
Robin Hood and Little John, vii.
54, 120.
Romanus (fragment), iii. 166; v.
1403.
Roxalana, or the Ambitious Step-
dame, iv. 865; v. 1403–4.
Runaways' Answer to a Book
Called, A Rod for Runaways,
The (1625), i. 19, 20; ii. 410,
412.
Sailors' Masque, The, v. 1404–5.
Salisbury Plain, v. 1184, 1405,
1445.
Sanguis Sanguinem, siue Con-
stans, fratricida tragoedia, v.
1297, 1405–6.
S. Pelagius Martyr, tragoedia, v.
1405.
Scholar Turned to School Again,
The, v. 1406.
Scyros, v. 1299.
Second Discovery by the Northern
Scout, A (1642), v. 1235; vi.
168.
Second Maiden's Tragedy, The, ii.
448, 550; iii. 37, 466; iv. 510–11,
598, 776, 819–20.
Second Part of the City Shuffler, v.
1308–9.
'Second Part of Mother Shiptons
Prophecies, The,' v. 1365.
Selimus, Part I, iv. 511; vii. 113.
Senilis Amor, v. 1407–8.
'Session of the Poets', iii. 278.
Seven Deadly Sins, ii. 363, 410,
447.
Seven Wise Masters, iii. 49.
Shepherds' Masque, The, v. 1408.
Shorte Treatise against Stage-
Playes (1625), A, iv. 816.
Sight and Search, v. 1419–20.
Simo, v. 1409.
'Singing Cavalier, The', T.L.S.
9 May 1942, v. 1197.
'Sir George Buc, Master of the
Revels' in Thomas Lodge and
Other Elizabethans, ed. C. J.
Sisson (1933), v. 1393.
Sir Giles Goosecap, i. 301; vi. 104.
Sir John Oldcastle, Part I, vii. 61,
75.
Sisigambis, Queen of Syracuse
(fragment), v. 1409.

'Sodayne Burning of the 'Globe', The' (ballad), vi. 179 n. 1.

Solomon and Bersheba, vii. 54.

Solomons Recantation, Entituled Ecclesiastes, Paraphrased (1645), iv. 955, 956.

Sophomorus, v. 1409.

Spanish Contract, The, i. 197; ii. 614; v. 1454.

Spanish Fig, The, iii. 259.

Spanish Lady, The, iv. 825, 827.

Spanish Preferment, iv. 865; v. 1410.

Spanish Puecas, The, v. 1410.

Spanish Purchase, The, v. 1410.

Spanish Tragedy of Petrus Crudelis, A, v. 1411–12.

Spanish Viceroy, The, i. 14, 15 n. 1, 80–81, 101 n. a, 102, 104 and n. 1, 133–4; ii. 375, 377, 448, 501, 532, 533, 547, 552, 557, 565, 569, 570, 593, 611; iv. 790, 791, 792, 826, 827; v. 1412; vi. 20–21.

Sportive Wit, ii. 627.

Stage Acquitted, The (1699) iii. 328.

Stage Condemn'd, The (1698), iv. 589, 844, 847.

Stage Players' Complaint, The (1641), i. 65 n. 2, 317 and n. 1; ii. 398, 399, 400, 540, 541; vi. 117, 170.

Stallion, The (a droll), iii. 324.

'Steps to Parnassus', iii. 42.

Stoicus Vapulans, iii. 11; iv. 527; v. 1232, 1298, 1413–14.

Stonyhurst Pageants, v. 1414–15.

Sucklington Faction or Suckling's Roaring Boys, The, v. 1200.

Supposed Inconstancy, The, v. 1415–16, 1445.

Surfeit to A B C, The (1656), iv. 803.

Surprise, The (droll), iii. 378, 380.

Susanna's Tears, v. 1416.

Swetnam the Woman-Hater Arraigned by Women, i. 174; v. 1416–18.

Syrgiannes, tragoedia, v. 1418.

Tamar Cam, ii. 485, 578; iii. 9; v. 1422.

Telltale, The, v. 1418–19.

Tereus with a Pastoral, iv. 866.

'Thomas Dekker and the Underdog', T.L.S., 31 May 1941, iii. 241.

Thomas Lord Cromwell, vii. 22, 61, 111.

Thomas of Woodstock, or Richard II, ii. 441, 445, 450, 581.

Thracian Wonder, The, v. 1242, 1249, 1445.

Three London Apprentices, The, ii. 690; v. 1346, 1456.

Time's Triumph, iv. 584; v. 1419–20.

Titus and Vespatian, v. 1421.

'To Sr. John Suckling', v. 1202.

Tom Essence, or the Modish Wife, iv. 681; v. 994, 998.

Tom of Bedlam, v. 1372, 1442.

Tooth-Drawer, The, v. 1422–3.

Toy, The, iii. 97; v. 1112, 1423.

Toy to Please Chaste Ladies, A, v. 1423.

Tradeways Tragedy, iv. 866; v. 1423.

Tragedy of Heildebrand, The, v. 1350.

Tragedy of Nero (Piso's Conspiracy), The, v. 1379–82; vii. 57, 62, 88, 125.

Tragedy of the Plantation of Virginia, A, i. 206; v. 1395–96; vi. 137.

Tragedy of Tomerania, The, iv. 866; v. 1421–2.

Tragical History, Admirable Achievements, and Various Events of Guy of Warwick, The, iv. 579; v. 1347–8.

Traytor, or Tragedy of Amidea (adaptation of Shirley's The Traitor), v. 1152.

Trebellius Bulgarorum Rex, v. 1424.

Triumph of Innocence, The, iv. 561, 562, 865; v. 1424.

Troublesome Reign of King John, The, vii. 45.

True narracon of the Confession of 2 murthers [by] John de Paris and John de la Vigne on the person of John de Wely &c., The (1616), iii. 351.

True Tragi-Comedy Formerly Acted at Court . . ., The, v. 1424–5.

Truth's Triumphs, v. 1425–6.

Tunbridge Wells, or a Day's Courtship, v. 994, 998–9.

Turk's Too Good for [Him], A, v. 1426.

Two Merry Milkmaids, The, see I. C.

Two Noble Ladies, The, and the Converted Conjurer, i. 166, 175; ii. 382, 388, 389, 441, 579, 580,

ANONYMOUS (cont.)
581, 590; iii. 8, 42, 45; v.
1426–7; vi. 220.
Two Spanish Gentlemen, The, iv.
866; v. 1427–8.
Two Wise Men and All the Rest
Fools, v. 1428–9; vi. 33.
Tyrannical Government Anato-
mized, or A Discourse Con-
cerning Evil Councellors, Being
the Life and Death of John the
Baptist, v. 1429.
Tyrant, The, see Massinger.
Ultima Linea Savilii (1622), iv.
499.
Unfaithful Wife, The, iv. 866; v.
1429.
Unnamed Play (1636), iv. 634.
Unnamed Play (1642), iv. 635.
'Upon Sir John Suckling's Most
Warlike Preparations for the
Scotish Warre, v. 1199.
Valentinian, or Rape's Revenge, v.
1429.
Valentinianus, v. 1376.
Valiant Scholar, The, i. 185, 197,
205 n. 5; v. 1294, 1430; vi. 59.
Valiant Scot, The, see J. W.
Venetian Comedy, The, iii. 252.
'View of the Cittye of London,
The', vi. 132.
Virgil's Eclogues, v. 1432.
Virtue and Beauty Reconciled, v.
1432.
Vision of Lethe, The, v. 1432.
Vortiger, iv. 885, 887.
Vow and a Good One, A, i. 205,
213, 216; iii. 323; iv. 673; v.
1432–3.
Vox Borealis, or The Northern
Discoverie, By way of Dialogue
between Jamie and Willie (1640),
v. 1234, 1235, 1300, 1301; vi.
167–8.
Wandering Jew, The, iv. 865; v.
1433.
'Warning for Maidens, A', v. 1405.
Wasp, The, ii. 362, 363, 453, 627;
v. 1433–4.
Way to Make a Knave Honest, A,
iv. 866; v. 1435.
Weakest Goeth to the Wall, The, v.
1242; vii. 24, 29, 110, 114.
Welsh Ambassador, The, see
Dekker.
Welsh Traveller, The, i. 167, 175,
205 n. 5; iii. 268; v. 1435–6.
Westminster Drollery, ii. 563.
Whibble, The, v. 1436.

Whimsies of Senor Hidalgo, or The
Masculine Bride, The, v.
1436–7.
Whirligig, The, v. 1437.
Whisperer, or What You Please,
The, v. 1438–9.
White Ethiopian, The, iii. 269; iv.
515.
White Witch of Westminster, or
Love in a Lunacy, The, iv. 865;
v. 1440.
'Whoop Doe Me Noe Harm', v.
1374.
Whore in Grain, The, i. 150, 157;
v. 1440–1, 1442.
Whore New Vamped, The, i. 13 n.
2, 157, 314–15, 323; ii. 400;
iii. 188; iv. 497, 702, 703; v.
1310, 1441–2; vi. 166, 228.
Wild-goose Chase, The (not
Fletcher), iv. 885.
'Wiltshire Tom, An Entertain-
ment at Court', v. 1357.
Wily Beguiled, vii. 51, 71, 76, 101,
102, 113, 115.
Wine, Beer, and Ale [and Tobacco],
v. 1442–4.
Wisdom of Doctor Dodipoll, The,
iv. 805; vii. 16, 111.
Wit and Drollery (1661), v. 1352;
vi. 210 n. 2.
Wit Restored, ii. 563; iii. 318; iv.
887.
Witch of Edmonton, The, see
Dekker.
Witch Traveller, The, v. 1444.
Wits Led By The Nose, or A
Poet's Revenge, iii. 154.
Wits, or Sport upon Sport, The
(1662), v. 1079.
Wits, or, Sport upon Sport, The,
(1673), see Kirkman, Francis.
Wits Recreations, iv. 435, 499,
557, 756, 831, 859; v. 1170,
1202.
Woman Is Too Hard for Him, The,
i. 94, 134; v. 1444–5.
Woman's Law, The, v. 1364, 1445.
Woman's Masterpiece, The, v.
1445, 1446–7.
Woman would wear the Briches,
The (ballad), iii. 60–1.
Woodcock of Our Side, v. 1447.
Work for Cutlers, v. 1443.
World, The, i. 331, 342; v. 1447.
Wronged Widow's Tragedy, The,
iv. 865; v. 1447–8.
Yorkshire Gentleman, The, v.
1448.

Yorkshire Tragedy, A, vii. 75.
'Young Bateman', v. 1045.
Younger Brother, The, or the Male Curtesan, i. 202, 217; ii. 346; iv. 865; v. 1445, 1448; vi. 220.
'Another Globe Theatre', *see* Bernheimer, Richard.
Ansty, Wiltshire, v. 1276.
Anti-Catholicism, v. 1320.
Antick Maske, iv. 667.
Anti-feminist campaign, vii. 35.
Antimasques, iii. 109, 443; iv. 638, 641, 644, 654, 656, 668, 670, 671, 673, 677, 682; v. 1042, 1153, 1231, 1262, 1358, 1375.
Antiphanes, vi. 276 n. 2.
Antipodes, The, see Brome, Richard.
Anti-Puritan, iii. 200.
Antiquarian Repertory, The, ii. 606.
Antiquary, The, see Marmion, Shakerley.
Anti-Scots propaganda, v. 1342.
Anti-Spanish, v. 1329.
Anti-Stratfordians, iii. 306.
Antoninus Bassianus Caracalla, see Anonymous.
Antonio and Mellida, see Marston, John.
Antonio and Vallia, see Massinger.
Antony and Cleopatra, see Shakespeare.
Antrim, Earl of, iii. 443.
Antwerp, ii. 512; iv. 954; v. 1172, 1175.
Antwerp, exile at, iii. 144, 149.
Anything for a Quiet Life, see Middleton.
Apes, vi. 209.
Apethorpe, Northamptonshire, i. 310; ii. 673; iii. 293, 296.
Apollo and Daphne (?), *see* Heywood, Thomas.
Apollo room, v. 979; vii. 54.
Apollo Shroving, see Hawkins, William.
Apology to the Reader, iii. 170.
Apothecaries, v. 1200.
Apothecaries Hall, vi. 74.
Apparel, *see* Costumes.
Apparitions, vi. 294.
Apperley, Elizabeth, ii. 350.
Apperley, John, ii. 349–50.
Apperley, Margaret, ii. 350.
Appian, iv. 936; v. 1370.
Appius and Virginia, or The Roman Virgin, or The Unjust Judge, see Webster, John.
Apples, iii. 103; vi. 171, 210 n., 239.

Appleton, Sir Henry, iv. 566.
Apple-wives, i. 268, 315; vi. 163, 169.
Apprentices, i. 3, 137 n. 6, 161, 163, 166–7, 167, 207, 207 n. 4, 267, 268, 318 n. 1, 335; ii. 366, 443, 463, 475, 484, 491, 496, 499, 517, 532, 544, 546, 550, 553, 559, 563, 572, 584, 599, 601, 604, 688, 690; iii. 193; v. 1220; vi. 54, 56, 57, 82, 161, 162, 163, 220, 239.
Acting, i. 35 n. 2; ii. 692.
Boarding-house, ii. 599.
Cost of, i. 45.
Riot of, i. 161 n. 2.
Apprentices' Prize, The, see Brome, Richard.
Aprons, vi. 236.
'Apron' stage, vi. 277.
Apsley, Sir Allen, ii. 354.
Apuleius, iv. 581, 717.
The Golden Ass, iv. 744.
Aqua Triumphalis, see Tatham, John, v. 1219.
Arabia, scene of play, iv. 727.
Arber, Edward, ed., *The Term catalogues, 1668–1709 A.D.; with a number for Easter term, 1711 A.D. A contemporary bibliography of English literature in the reigns of Charles II, James II, William and Mary, and Anne,* 3 vols. (1903–6), iii. 109; iv. 544.
A Transcript of the Register of the Company of Stationers of London, 1554–1640, iii. 5, 60–61, 81, 82, 351; v. 1045; vi. 179 n. 1.
Arbiter, Petronius, v. 1317.
Arcades, see Milton, John.
Arcadia, The, see Shirley, James.
Arcadia, see Sidney, Philip.
Arcadian Lovers, The, see Moore, Thomas.
Archbishop of Canterbury (William Laud), vi. 26.
Archer, Edward, *The Excellent Comedy, called The Old Law . . . By Phil. Massinger. Tho. Middleton. William Rowley. . . . Together with an exact and perfect Catalogue of all the Playes, with the Authors Names, and what are Comedies, Tragedies, Histories, Pastoralls, Masks, Interludes, more exactly printed than ever before, London,* 1656, iii. 5, 8, 9.
Archer, Robert, ii. 350.
Archer, William, vi. 143–4.

Archer, William (*cont.*)
'Fortune Theatre, 1600, The', *Shakespeare Jahrbuch*, xliv (1908), vi. 139, 143.
'Sad Shepherd, The' [performance], *Study and Stage* (1899), iv. 625.
'Spanish Gypsy, The' [revived], in *Study and Stage* (1899), iv. 892.
Archerie Reviv'd, *see* D'Urfey, Thomas.
Archer's play-list, iii. 283, 378, 397, 424, 457; iv. 500, 501, 502, 729, 828, 951; v. 1043, 1253, 1292, 1293, 1310, 1326, 1336, 1353, 1356, 1370, 1376, 1382, 1384, 1385, 1390, 1402, 1403, 1416, 1432.
Architecture, vi. 291.
Arden of Feversham, *see* Anonymous.
Arena stage, vi. 188, 190.
Argalus and Parthenia, *see* Glapthorne, Henry.
Arguments for plays, iv. 506, 621, 622, 623, 626, 627; v. 1233, 1283, 1284, 1333.
'Argus head' [stage-prop], iv. 574.
Argyll, Earl of, ii. 436.
Argyll, Lady, ii. 436.
Ariosto, Lodovico, *Orlando Furioso*, iii. 363; iv. 500; v. 1388.
Aristippus, or the Jovial Philosopher, *see* Randolph, Thomas.
Aristophanes, iii. 5; iv. 631; vi. 276.
  translation from, iii. 97.
  Ecclesiazusae, iii. 131.
  Plutus, adaptation of, v. 980, 981.
  Thesmophoriazusae, iii. 131.
Aristotle, ii. 538; iv. 624.
Armiger, Edward, i. 272, 275, 281; ii. 350; vi. 164.
Arminianism, iii. 417.
Armour, for dancers, vii. 31.
Arms, vi. 292.
Arms, exhibitions of, vi. 294.
Arms for foot (i.e. use on foot), vi. 293, 294.
Armstead, Edward, *see* Armiger, Edward.
Armstrong, Archibald. *A Choice Banquet of Witty Jest, Rare Fancies and Pleasant Novels* (1660), v. 1137.
Armstrong, Ray Livingstone, ed. *The Poems of James Shirley* (1941), v. 1064, 1069, 1070, 1071.
Armstrong, William A. *The Elizabethan Private Theatres: Facts and*

Problems. Society for Theatre Research, Pamphlet Series, no. 6 (1958), vi. 3, 6, 47.
Army, vi. 40.
Army plot, i. 335; ii. 421; iii. 143, 195; v. 1209; vi. 75, 167, 309.
Armyn, Robert, i. 2, 5 n. 6; vi. 20.
Arnold, James A., *John Milton's Masque. An Historical and Critical Study of Comus.* Unpublished Princeton Thesis (1951), iv. 914.
Arnold, William, ii. 357.
Aronstein, Philipp, *Ben Jonson* (1906), iv. 604.
Aronstein, Philipp, 'Fletcher's *Love's Pilgrimage* und Ben Jonson's *The New Inn*', *Englische Studien*, xliii (1911), iii. 366; iv. 622.
'Thomas Heywood', *Anglia*, xxxvii (1913), iv. 553, 565.
Aristippus, *see* Randolph, Thomas.
Arraignment of Lewd, Idle, Froward, and Unconstant Women, *see* Swetnam, Joseph.
Arraignment of London, The, *see* Daborne, Robert.
Arras, *see* Theatres.
Arrest, players' exemption from, i. 15–16.
Arszch, Robert, *see* Archer, Robert.
Art of Poetry, The, *see* Jonson, Ben.
Artful Husband, The, *see* Taverner, William.
Artice, L', *see* Racan, Seigneur de.
Artillery Garden, Gentlemen of the, vii. 112.
Artillery Ground, vi. 296.
Artois, Prince-Governor of, v. 1450.
Arundel, Lord and Lady, iii. 373.
Arundel, Thomas Earl of, ii. 349; iii. 108, 110; iv. 956; vi. 260, 297, 298, 308, 309.
Arundel, committed to Tower, iv. 549.
Arviragus and Felicia, i and ii, *see* Carlell.
As You Like It, *see* Shakespeare.
Ashborne, Edward, i. 15, 73–89; ii. 350–1.
Ashbourne, Derbyshire, iii. 166, 170.
Ashburnham, Sir John, iv. 637.
Ashbury, Berkshire, v. 1256.
Ashby, Leicestershire, iii. 307.
Ashby-cum-Fenby, Lincolnshire, iv. 554.
Ashchurch, Gloucestershire, iii. 126.
Ashelworth, Gloucestershire, iv. 588.
Ashen, Ed., iv. 731.

Ashley, Sir Anthony, ii. 415; vi. 116, 117.
Ashley, Sir Francis, ii. 416.
Ashley, Sir John, iv. 775.
Ashmole MSS., *see* Oxford, Bodleian Library.
Ashmolean Museum, *see* Oxford.
'Ashton' (actor), iii. 369.
Ashton, Edward, *see* Ashborne, Edward.
Asken, Aaron, ii. 351.
Askewgh, William, ii. 355.
Aspley, William, iii. 440, 451, 454, 456; iv. 565, 583, 742; v. 1030, 1108, 1313.
Asplin, Anne, ii. 650.
'Asse upon Asse', *see* Blunt, Leonard.
Assembly or Parliament of Women, *see* Erasmus.
Assidue, stars of, *see* Arsedine.
Assize Sermon, An, *see* Daborne, Robert.
Astley, Sir John, ii. 471; iii. 119, 121, 610; vii. 43, 48, 54.
Astley, Sir John: list of plays, iii. 313.
Aston, Constance, v. 976.
Aston, Staffordshire, v. 998.
Astraea, *see* Anonymous.
Astrée, *see* D'Urfé, Honoré.
Astrologaster, or the Figure-caster (1620), *see* Melton, John.
Astrologers, vi. 101 n. 1.
Atalanta, *see* Parsons, Philip.
Athenae Oxonienses, *see* Wood, Anthony.
Athens, iv. 508, 509.
Atkins, John, i. 261 and n. 3; ii. 351, 577, 644, 648.
Atkins, John (not actor), vi. 48.
Atkins, Maurice, iii. 1.
Atkins, Richard, ii. 644.
Atkins, Thomas, vi. 174, 175.
Atkinson, Thomas, iii. 3–4; v. 1188, 1190.
    'Andrei Melvini Anti-Tami-Cunicategoria', iii. 4.
    Homo, iii. 4.
    'Melvinus delirans', iii. 4.
Atkinson, William, ii. 631.
Atreus, house of, story of, v. 1394.
Attendants (*see also under* individual companies), i. 332.
Atterley, John, *see* Apperley, John.
Attorney-General, v. 1441; vi. 166, 229, 298, 300.
Attree, John, vi. 217.
Attributions, iii. 258.
Attwell, Hugh, i. 199 and n. 2, 200

and n. 3, 203, 211; ii. 351–3; iv. 881; v. 1016.
Attwell, Hugh, *Attwell's Jig*, ii. 352.
Aubrey, John, *Brief Lives . . . set down by John Aubrey*, ed. Clark, Andrew, 2 vols. (1898), iii. 275, 310; iv. 498, 533, 633, 635, 636, 722, 756, 757, 833, 948, 949, 950; v. 963, 965, 967, 968, 1198, 1199, 1200, 1205, 1207, 1277; vi. 38; vii. 28.
The Natural History and Antiquities of the County of Surrey, 5 vols. (1719), iv. 498.
Auchmouty, John, iv. 670.
Audience, public-theatre, iii. 397.
Audience, size of, iv. 871–2; vi. 11, 183–4, 233, 250, 257, 297.
Audiences, v. 1242; vi. 42–45, 151–2, 171, 186, 238–47.
Audiences, behaviour of, i. 279–80; ii. 690–1.
Audiences, coterie, vi. 4, 12–15, 32–35, 192–3.
Audiences, courtly character of, i. 47 n. 3.
Audiences, cultivation of, v. 990.
Audiences, demands of, iii. 37.
Audiences, fined, vi. 176, 231, 232, 234, 236.
Audiences, middle class, iii. 210; iv. 923–4, 930–1; vi. 69–70, 193–4, 247.
Audiences (royal), vi. 265, 285.
Audiences, women in, v. 1438; vi. 232, 236, 237.
Audley End, Essex, iv. 529.
Audley, Thomas, iv. 497.
Audley, Tobias, iii. 254.
Augustine, William, dedication to, iii. 239.
Augustus (i.e. Charles I), vi. 270.
Aulicus (pseudonym), iv. 589.
Aulus Gellius, iv. 717.
Austen, Richard, of the Boar's Head, vi. 189.
Austen's Rents, Southwark, *see* London, streets and districts of.
Austin, Samuel, *Naps upon Parnassus* (1658), v. 1188.
'Authenticity of Simon Forman's *Bocke of Plaies*, The', *see* Wilson, J. Dover.
Authors as actors, v. 975, 1019, 1237, 1258.
Authors' benefit performances, iii. 53; iv. 848; v. 1438.
Authors' benefit publications, v. 1118, 1119.

Authors, see also Playwrights.
Author-plots, v. 1395.
Autobiography, iii. 292; v. 1267.
Autobiography and Correspondence of Sir Symonds D'Ewes, see D'Ewes, Sir Symonds.
Autobiography of Archbishop Laud, see Laud, William.
Autograph manuscripts, see Plays in MS. autograph.
'Autograph Plan by Wren, An', see Speirs, W. L.
Autographs ('John Fletcher'), iii. 307.
Awnsham, Nicholas, ii. 461, 635, 636.
Axall or Axell, Robert, see Axen, Robert.
Axen, Everelda, ii. 353.
Axen, Robert, i. 142, 220, 223 n. 6, 239, 246, 324, 326 n. 6, 332, 336; ii. 353.
Axen, Symon, ii. 353.
Axen, William, ii. 353.
Axon, Robert, see Axen, Robert.
Aylmer, John, Changes (1890), v. 1094.
Ayloffe, John, ii. 404.
Aynho Manor, Northamptonshire, iv. 736.
Aynhoe, Northamptonshire, v. 1265.
Aynsworth, William, see Ainsworth.
Ayres & Dialogues, see Lawes, Henry.

B., A., Covent Garden Drolleries, ed. Montague Summers (1927), iii. 332, 359, 392.
B., E. (verses by), iii. 153; iv. 928; v. 998.
B., G., Esq., v. 1086.
B., H. (dramatist), iii. 5.
B., H. H., iii. 97.
B., H. H., The World's Idol, or Plutus the God of Wealth, iii. 5.
B., I., iv. 854.
B., J. (verses by), iii. 72; iv. 686.
B., J., iv. 686.
B., T. (dramatist), iii. 5–9, 45; iv. 774; v. 1095, 1096.
B., T., The Rebellion of Naples, or the Tragedy of Massenello, iii. 5, 8–9, 45.
Babb, Lawrence, 'Abnormal Psychology in John Ford's Perkin Warbeck', M.L.N. li (1936), iii. 454.
John Ford and Seventeenth Century Psychology, unpub. diss., Yale (1934), iii. 433.
Baber, Francis, ii. 355.

Babham, Christopher, i. 35; ii. 353–4.
Babington conspiracy, iv. 520.
Baboons, vi. 209.
Babthorpe, Dame Grace, ii. 471.
Babthorpe, Sir Ralph, ii. 471.
Babties, Mr., ii. 486.
Bacchus' Festival, see Jordan, Thomas.
Bachelor, Luce, vi. 204.
Back cloth, iv. 524.
Backdrops, iv. 627; vi. 51.
Backer, Dr., i. 142; ii. 353.
Backstead, William, see Barksted, William.
Bacon, Francis, ii. 347; v. 1090, 1142, 1376, 1377.
Bacon, Francis, Essays, iv. 526.
Historie of the Raigne of King Henry the Seventh (1622), iii. 454–5.
Bacon, Lady Jane, i. 42 n. 3; iv. 548.
Bacon, John, i. 49 n. 2 cont., 73–89; ii. 354; iii. 369.
Bacon, Sir Nathaniel, iv. 548, 715.
Bacon, Roger, iv. 717.
Bacon, Wallace A., 'The Literary Reputation of John Ford', Huntington Library Quarterly, xi (1948), iii. 433.
Bacon Rebellion, iii. 20, 22.
Bad Quarto, iii. 284.
Badby, see Newnham-cum-Badby.
Badger, Sir Thomas, iv. 650; v. 1422.
Badges, v. 994.
Baggont, Anne, ii. 488.
Baggs Seneca, see Anonymous.
Bagnall, Richard, vi. 126.
Bagnall, William, ii. 413; iv. 770, 776–7, 895.
Bagshot Park, ii. 561.
Bagshot, Surrey i. 50.
Bagstare, Richard, see Baxter, Richard.
Bahlsen, Leo, Eine Komödie Fletcher's, ihre spanische Quelle und die Schicksale jenes Cervantesschen Novellenstoffes in der Weltlitteratur (1894), iii. 407.
Baildon, W. P., Records of the Honorable Society of Lincoln's Inn, The, Black Books, 2 vols. (1896), iii. 47, 292; vi. 50 n. 1.
Bailey, John E., ' "Cornelianvm Dolium." By T. R.', N. & Q., Fifth Series, ix (1878), v. 962.
Bailiff, ii. 348, 438; vi. 293.
Baiting of the Jealous Knight, The, see Smith, The Fair Foul One.

Baize, green, vi. 280, 281.
Bajazet the Second, see Goffe, *The Raging Turk.*
Baker, ii. 486.
Baker, Cicely, ii. 605.
Baker, David Erskine, *Biographica Dramatica, or A Companion to the Playhouse,* 2 vols. (1764, 1782, 1812), iii. 22, 43, 149; iv. 838; v. 999, 1008, 1278, 1384.
Baker, G., *The History and Antiquities of the County of Northamptonshire,* 2 vols. (1822), iv. 736.
Baker, George Pierce, iii. 56.
'A New Source of *The Changeling', Journal of Comparative Literature,* i (1903), iv. 861.
Baker, J., v. 1102.
Baker, Sir Richard, *Theatrum Redivivum, or the Theatre vindicated by Sir Richard Baker in Answer to Mr Pryns Histrio-Mastix* (1662), iii. 12.
Baker, Richard, *A Chronicle of the Kings of England* (1660), iii. 127.
Baker, William, vi. 28.
Balaam's Ass Cudgeled, see Chamberlain, Robert.
Balch, Marston Stevens, *The Dramatic Legacy of Thomas Middleton: A Study of the Use of His Plays, from 1627 to 1800.* Unpublished Harvard Thesis (1930), iv. 800, 802, 855, 861, 888, 892, 895.
Bald, R. C. ' "Assembled" Texts', *Library,* 4th Series, xii (1931), iv. 870.
'Arthur Wilson's *The Inconstant Lady', Library,* Fourth Series, xviii (1937–8), v. 1270, 1271, 1272.
Bibliographical Studies in the Beaumont & Fletcher Folio of 1647. Supplement to the Bibliographical Society's Transactions, No. 13 (1938), iii. 305, 313, 317, 323, 327, 331–2, 336, 339, 340, 341, 342, 343, 346, 353, 359, 363, 366, 369, 373, 380, 381, 383, 391, 394, 397, 400, 414, 417, 421, 424, 433.
'Chronology of Middleton's Plays, The', *M.L.R.* xxxii (1937), iv. 855, 860, 869, 889, 905, 906; vi. 147 n. 1.
'Early Version of Middleton's "Game at Chesse", An', *M.L.R.* xxxviii (1943), iv. 870, 879.
'Foul Papers of a Revision, The',

Library, New Series, xxvi (1945), iii. 187, 188.
'Francis Kirkman, Bookseller and Author', *Mod. Phil.* xli (1943), iv. 579, 582.
' "Game at Chesse", A', *T.L.S.* 17 May 1928, iv. 870.
Game at Chesse by Thomas Middleton, A (1929), iv. 630, 858, 870, 871, 873, 874, 875, 876, 877, 878, 879.
Hengist, King of Kent; or The Mayor of Queenborough. By Thomas Middleton (1938), iv. 883, 884, 885, 886, 887; v. 1021, 1296, 1350, 1352, 1421, 1426.
'Middleton's Civic Employments', *Mod. Phil.* xxxi (1933), iv. 855, 879, 897.
'New Manuscript of Middleton's "Game at Chesse", A', *M.L.R.* xxv (1930), iv. 870, 879.
'Revels Office Entry, A', *T.L.S.* 17 March 1927, iii. 92; v. 1315.
'Sources of Middleton's City Comedies, The', *J.E.G.P.* xxxiii (1934), iv. 855.
'Sir William Berkeley's *The Lost Lady', Library,* Fourth Series, xvii (1937), iii. 20, 21, 22, 23, 24, 25.
Baldron, Mathew, ii. 412.
Baldwin, Henry, i. 162; ii. 366.
Baldwin, Katherine, ii. 428.
Baldwin, Thomas Whitfield, iii. 131, 134.
ed., Massinger, *The Duke of Milan* (1918), iv. 775, 776, 819, 820.
Organization and Personnel of the Shakespearean Company, The (1927), iii. 191, 192, 300, 316, 321, 340, 352, 413, 424, 433; iv. 781; v. 1049; vi. 179, 180 n. 1, 181 n. 2.
Baler, Michael, vi. 308.
Ball, John, 'prophet', iii. 339.
Ball, Peter, iii. 152.
Ball, Robert Hamilton, *The Amazing Career of Sir Giles Overreach* (1939), iv. 801, 802, 803.
'Massinger and the House of Pembroke', *M.L.N.* xlvi (1931), iv. 751.
'Sir Giles Mompesson and Sir Giles Overreach', *Parrott Presentation Volume* (1935), iv. 801.
Ball, The, see Shirley, James.

Ballading, iv. 680.
Ballad opera, iii. 84; v. 1365.
Ballads, iii. 60–61, 81, 82, 83, 126, 238, 254, 255, 285, 393, 394; iv. 591–5, 658, 680, 747, 824, 852; v. 1045, 1202, 1219, 1249, 1265, 1365, 1444; vi. 55 n. 1, 133, 135, 136, 162, 179 n. 1, 185 n. 2, 193, 222, 231, 236–7, 240; vii. 35.
Ballads and plays, iii. 82, 83.
Ballads, forged, iv. 571.
Ballads in masques, iv. 646, 658.
Ballads, partners in, iii. 82.
Ballads, popular, iii. 250.
Ballads, Roxburghe collection of, vi. 135.
Ballast-levers, vi. 273.
Balle, Peter, iv. 928.
Balle, William, iv. 928.
Ballet comique (Beaujoyeulx's Circe), v. 1230.
Ballets, i. 30 n. 6 cont.; iv. 646.
Ballmann, Otto, 'Chaucers Einfluß auf das englische Drama', Anglia, Bd. xxv, Neue Folge Bd. xiii (1902), iii. 132, 133.
Balls, Francis, i. 73–89; ii. 354–5; iv. 764, 765.
Balls, Richard, i. 202; ii. 355, 622.
Balsams, ii. 517.
'Bambery hott cockles', game of, v. 1055.
Banbury, Oxfordshire, i. 292 n. 4; ii. 409; iv. 534.
Bancroft, Thomas, Two Bookes of Epigrammes, and Epitaphs (1639), iii. 434; v. 1066.
Band, Thomas, see Bond, Thomas.
Band, Ruff and Cuff, see Anonymous, Exchange Ware.
Bandello, Matteo, Novelle, iii. 358, 373, 386, 439, 470; iv. 810.
Bang, W., 'Dekker-Studien', Englische Studien, xxviii (1900), iii. 241.
    ed., Ben Jonson's Dramen in Neudruck herausgegeben nach der Folio 1616, 2 vols. (1905, 1908), iv. 613.
'Nach der Quarto 1653 Neudruck herausgegeben', Materialien (1906), iii. 457.
    ed., Pleasant Dialogues and Dramma's [Heywood] (1903), iv. 559, 574.
Bang, W., and H. De Vocht, eds., John Fordes Dramatische Werke, Materialien, xxiii (1908) and N.S. i (1927), iii. 438.

Bang, W., and R. Brotanek, eds. The King and Queenes Entertainment at Richmond (1903), v. 1357.
Bangor, Bishop of, v. 1341.
Banished Shepherdess, The, see Manuche, Cosmo.
Bankes, Ralph, ii. 356.
Bankes, Thomas, ii. 356.
Bankes, William, i. 311, 321; ii. 355–6.
Banks, J., vi. 235.
Banks, Theodore Howard, Jr., ed. The Poetical Works of Sir John Denham (1928), iii. 275, 276, 277, 278, 279.
Bankside, see London, streets and districts.
'Bankside Theatres, The: Early Engravings', see Shapiro, I. A.
Banquet entertainment, v. 1303.
Banqueting House, Commission for, vi. 260.
Banqueting House, Whitehall, iii. 107, 108, 199, 207; iv. 652, 655, 669, 880; v. 1088, 1158, 1160, 1228, 1377; vi. 255–9, 259–67, 269, 282, 285, 286, 287; vii. 17, 18, 20, 21, 22, 25, 28, 29, 30, 40, 42, 43, 46, 52, 57, 63, 65, 67, 69, 81.
Banquets, iv. 650, 651, 654, 715, 842, 880; vii. 20, 31, 39, 59.
Baptistes sive Calumnia tragedia, see Buchanan, Geo.
Barbadillo, Salas, El Sagaz Estacio, Marido examinado, iii. 410, 411.
Barbados, vi. 33.
Barbary, vi. 234.
Barber, Lord Doncaster's, vii. 29.
Barber-chirurgion (see also Doctor, Physician, and Surgeon), i. 143; ii. 437, 484.
Barber Surgeon (in Cambridge), v. 972.
Barbican, see London, streets of.
Barbor, Edmond, ii. 356, 682.
Barcelona, iii. 466.
Barclay's Argenis, iv. 719, 720.
Barclay, Will, i. 58.
Barclay, William, see Berkeley, Sir William.
Barefield, Roger, see Barfield, Roger.
Barfield, Anthony, ii. 357.
Barfield, Isabell, ii. 357.
Barfield, Roger, ii. 356–7.
Barfield, Susan, ii. 357.
Barfoote, Roger, see Barfield, Roger.
Barford, Norfolk, iv. 531.

Bargehouse on the Bankside, *see* London, streets of.

Barker, G. F. Russell, and Alan H. Stenning, *Record of Old Westminsters*, 2 vols. (1928), iv. 540, 850, 948; v. 1180, 1188, 1232.

Barker, Thomas, iii. 9, 12, 282, 283.

Barkham, Edward, ii. 416; iv. 882, 896.

Barking, Essex, ii. 497.

Barksted, William, i. 176, 177 and n. 2, 199 and n. 2, 200, 211; ii. 357-8.

Hiren, ii. 357.

Myrrha, ii. 357.

Barlow, Bishop, v. 1179.

Barnabee's Journal, see Brathwait, Richard.

Barnard, John, *Theologo-Historicus, or the True Life of the Most Reverend Divine and Excellent Historian Peter Heylyn* (1683), iv. 550.

Barnavelt, see Fletcher, *Sir John van Olden Barnavelt*.

Barnavelt, Sir John van Olden, execution of, iii. 417.

Barn Elms, iii. 175.

Barnes, Barnaby, iii. 9.

Devil's Charter, The, iii. 9.

Four Books of Office (1606), iii. 437.

Barnes, —, *Madcap, The*, i. 206 n. 3, 214; iii. 9-10.

Barnes, Thomas, i. 190, 192; ii. 358-9; iii. 9.

Barnes, William, iii. 9.

Barnouw, A. J., 'The Cartload in the Gate', *M.L.N.* liii (1938), iii. 415.

Barns, v. 1266; vi. 88, 89, 94.

Barns, converted (into theatres), vi. 90.

Barnstaple, Devonshire, i. 172, 193, 212.

Barnwall, Sir Nicholas, iii. 95.

Baron, Robert, iii. 10-11; v. 1323.

Cyprian Academy, iii. 10.

Deorum Dona, iii. 10.

Mayor of Norwich, iii. 10.

Mirza, a Tragedy, iii. 10, 279.

verses by, iv. 471, 472.

Barratt, Gustavous, ii. 359.

Barrett, John, (actor), i. 285, 286, 287, 288, 289 n. 4 cont., 290, 297; ii. 359.

Barrett, John (playwright), iii. 11; v. 1003, 1414, 1434.

Barrett, Walter, i. 168 n. 1; ii. 359.

Barrett, William, ii. 359.

Barriers, iv. 649; v. 1155; vi. 256, 293, 298, 299; vii. 18, 20.

Barriers, in an entertainment, iv. 649.

Barrington family, iv. 958.

Barrington, Sir Thomas, iv. 956.

Barristers, v. 1155.

Barry, David (Lord), *Ram Alley*, ii. 652; iv. 705; vii. 104.

Barry, Elizabeth, iii. 409.

Bartholomew Fair, iv. 930; vi. 237. *See* Jonson, Ben.

Bartley, *see* Berkeley, Sir William.

Barton, John, carpenter, vi. 272, 274, 275.

Barwell, Leicestershire, iii. 2.

Bas, Dirck, v. 1330.

Basement tiring-house, vi. 189, 191.

Bashford, Mrs., v. 1403.

Bashful Lover, The, see Massinger.

Basildon, Berkshire, v. 1175.

Basing House, ii. 548, 549, 694.

Basins, vi. 167.

Basker, Thomas, iii. 12.

Baskervile family, vii. 11.

Baskervile, Francis, *see* Browne, Francis.

Baskervile, James, i. 158, 159.

Baskervile, Susan, i. 158, 159, 171, 310; ii. 368, 545, 548, 637; vi. 56.

Baskervile papers, i. 207.

Baskervile suit, i. 158-60; vi. 219.

Baskerviles, new agreement with, i. 171.

Baskervill, Charles Read, 'Bandello and *The Broken Heart*', *M.L.N.* xxviii (1913), iii. 439.

'Custom of Sitting on the Elizabethan Stage, The', *M.P.* viii (1911), vi. 7.

Elizabethan Jig and Related Song Drama, The (1929), iii. 140; iv. 681, 770; v. 1049, 1050.

English Elements in Jonson's Early Comedy (1911), iv. 604, 632.

'Some Parallels to *Bartholomew Fair*', *Mod. Phil.* vi (1908), iv. 883, 885, 900, 902.

'Source of the Main Plot of Shirley's *Love Tricks*, The', *M.L.N.* xxiv (1909), v. 1144, 1146-7.

'The Sources of Jonson's *Masque of Christmas* and *Love's Welcome at Welbeck*', *Mod. Phil.* vi (1908), iv. 638, 648, 649.

Basket-maker, ii. 431, 486.

Basle, Thomas Killigrew in, iv. 695, 701, 703, 708.

Basse, Jane, ii. 631.

Basse, Mrs., 'the law-woman', iii. 219.

Basse, Thomas, i. 167, 168 n. 2, 171, 176, 177 and n. 6; ii. 360. Will of, ii. 631.

Basse, Ursula, ii. 631.

Basset, Elizabeth, iii. 142.

Basset, Mrs., 'the great Lace Woman of Cheapside', iii. 219.

Basset, Thomas, the Lancashire Bagpipe, v. 1159.

Bastard, The, see Goffe, Thomas, and Manuche, Cosmo.

Bastwick, John, v. 1194, 1195. *Church of England a True Church, The* (1645), iv. 916–17.

Bate, the Rev. Henry, *see* Dudley, Sir Henry Bate.

Batelier, W., iv. 523.

Bateman, Anthony, v. 1220.

Bates, Katherine Lee, ed. Heywood's *The Fair Maid of the West, Part I*, Belles Lettres Series (1917), iv. 568.

Bath, Marquis of, iv. 536.

Bathurst, Edward, v. 1268.

Battle of the Affections, The, see Anonymous, *Pathomachia.*

Battle of Alcazar, The, see Peele.

Battle of the Vices against the Virtues, see Anonymous.

Battles, vi. 246.

Batty, — (fencer), i. 318; ii. 360.

Baugh, Albert C., 'Some New Facts about Shirley', *M.L.R.* xvii (1922), v. 1064, 1066, 1067.

Baum, Helena Watts, *The Satiric and the Didactic in Ben Jonson's Comedy* (1947), iv. 604.

Bawdy houses, iii. 7, 39, 189, 328; iv. 747; vi. 49, 50, 55, 171, 212, 240, 251.

Bawds, vii. 2.

Baxmann, Emil, *Middletons Lustspiel 'The Widow' und Boccaccios 'Il Decamerone' III, 3 und II, 2.* (1904), iv. 900.

Baxted, William, *see* Barksted, William.

Baxter, Constance, ii. 361.

Baxter, Elizabeth, ii. 362.

Baxter, Jane, ii. 361.

Baxter, Joane, ii. 361.

Baxter, John, ii. 361.

Baxter, John (of Southwark), vi. 202, 203, 204.

Baxter, Michael, ii. 361.

Baxter, Richard, i. 49 and n. 2 cont., 73–89, 166, 167, 168 n. 1, 171; ii. 360–2; iii. 375; iv. 764, 765; vi. 99, 220–1, 239.

Baxter, Robert, ii. 361, 643.

Baxter, Susan, ii. 361.

Baylie, Ann, ii. 392.

Baylie, Dr. Richard, v. 1182, 1183.

Baylie, Simon, iii. 12–14. *Wizard, The,* iii. 12–14.

Bayly, Edward, ii. 362.

Bayne, Ronald, Rev., 'Lesser Jacobean and Caroline Dramatists' (Chapter IX), *C.H.E.L.* vi, iii. 61.

Bays, see Anonymous.

Beaconsfield, Buckinghamshire, iii. 277.

Beadell, Gabriell, iii. 211, 219, 223; iv. 505, 507, 509, 742.

Beadle, Mr., of Banston, v. 1267.

B[eale], J[ohn], iv. 615, 629.

Beale, William, iv. 528, 853; v. 1196, 1237.

Bear, The, see Anonymous, *The Lovers Holiday.*

Bear-baiting, i. 201; ii. 510, 657, 691; vi. 200, 202 n., 203, 209, 211, 298; vii. 10, 14, 18, 27, 35, 36, 40, 43, 44, 45; vii. 47, 48, 65, 67, 70, 79, 87, 93, 101, 110, 116.

days for, vi. 207–8, 214.

fees for, vi. 208 n. 2.

for ambassadors, vi. 211.

for royalty, vi. 211.

'Bear-baiting house', vi. 184, 185 n. 1.

Bear-garden, i. 225, 265, 315; ii. 423, 510, 620; iv. 582; vi. 12 n. 2, 122, 160, 169, 185 n. 1, 200–14, 224 n. 1, 301; vii. 116.

Bear houses at Hope theatre, vi. 202, 203, 204, 205.

Bear-masters, vi. 208.

Bear ward, iv. 658.

Bears, George, vi. 211 n. Harry Hunks, vi. 211 n. Hunks, vi. 210 and n. 2, 211 n. Nan, vi. 211 n. Sakerson, vi. 211 n. Tom Hunks, vi. 211 n. white, vi. 211.

Bears, enumerated, vi. 212–13.

Beard, Thomas, iii. 14. *Evangelical Tragedy, An,* iii. 14. *Theatre of God's Judgments* (1612), iii. 470.

Beaujoyeulx, Baltasar de, *Circe,* v. 1230.

Beaulieu, Hampshire, i. 20; vii. 27, 37.

Beaulieu, Mr., iv. 918; v. 1057.

Beaumont, Elizabeth, v. 1311.

Beaumont, Francis, and Fletcher,
John, i. 2, 22 n. 2, 26, 66, 68,
225; ii. 436, 557, 692; iii. 14,
383, 387, 389; iv. 802, 809, 814,
906; v. 1205, 1274, 1335.
Bonduca, i. 66, 109; ii. 429, 465,
500, 550, 562; iii. 84.
Captain, The, i. 66, 95 n. c, 109–
10; iv. 710.
Coxcomb, The, i. 51, 66, 94, 98,
110; ii. 344, 425, 539.
Cupid's Revenge, i. 186 n. 7, 194,
325, 330–1, 336, 337; iv. 492;
v. 1035; vi. 67; vii. 31, 76, 88,
101, 125.
Dramatick Works of Beaumont
and Fletcher . . . The (1778),
George Colman, the elder, ed.,
iii. 312.
Father's Own Son, see Monsieur
Thomas.
Folio of 1647, i. 69 n. 2, 88–89;
ii. 345; iii. 47, 50, 55, 98,
127, 168, 308, 310, 314, 316,
319, 324, 328, 330, 337, 340,
341, 343, 347, 348, 352, 354,
357, 359, 360, 361, 364, 367,
371, 374, 377, 380, 382, 383,
387, 391, 392, 395, 397, 398,
405, 412, 418, 420, 423, 426,
427, 431, 448, 465; iv. 521,
624, 718–19, 721, 753, 754, 773,
804, 844; v. 1071, 1186, 1252,
1296, 1331; vi. 4, 242.
Folio of 1679, i. 177 n. 3, 6; iii.
310, 315, 316, 320, 325, 330,
334, 337, 341, 345, 349, 352,
355, 357, 360, 362, 364, 367,
372, 375, 378, 379, 382, 385,
388, 389, 392, 393, 395, 399,
403, 407, 409, 413, 419, 423,
424, 427, 431, 432; v. 1099.
Four Plays in One, ii. 435.
Honest Man's Fortune, The, i. 66,
104, 111; ii. 435, 539, 544, 547,
593, 612; iv. 472; v. 1075, 1076.
King and No King, A, i. 28, 51,
96, 98, 111; ii. 343, 541, 597;
iv. 822; v. 1099, 1107; vi. 40,
112, 113, 197; vii. 27, 33, 60,
67, 80, 110, 114, 118.
Knight of the Burning Pestle, The,
i. 236, 248 n. i, 249, 250, 330,
337; ii. 441; iii. 44, 88; vi. 9;
vii. 101.
Maid's Tragedy, The, i. 28, 51, 95
n. c, 96, 98, 113; ii. 505, 693;
v. 1086, 1153; vii. 31, 33, 46,
71, 76, 110, 113, 114, 126.

Philaster, i. 28, 52, 95 n. c, 96, 98,
113; v. 1107, 1118; vi. 197; vii.
34, 38, 46, 67, 69, 110, 114, 118.
Popularity of, at court, i. 29.
Right Woman, A, iv. 827.
Scornful Lady, The, i. 28, 37, 67,
96, 100, 114; ii. 562, 567, 693;
vi. 31, 85, 112, 175, 283; vii. 17,
21, 23, 60, 76, 88, 101, 118, 125.
Tamer Tamed, The, see The
Woman's Prize.
Thierry and Theodoret, i. 114; ii.
435.
Valentinian, i. 66, 115; ii. 465,
500; iv. 865, v. 1036.
Wit at Several Weapons, vi. 242.
Wit without Money, i. 250, 325,
330, 336, 337; ii. 509, 510; iii.
381; v. 1098, 1099, 1129, 1135;
vi. 67, 235.
Woman Hater, The, i. 115.
Woman's Prize, The, i. 37 and n. 2,
38, 66, 86–87, 97, 114, 115; ii.
487, 495, 503, 586; vi. 31, 32.
Works of Mr. Francis Beaumount
and Mr. John Fletcher, The, in
seven volumes (1711), iii. 312.
Works of Mr. Francis Beaumont,
and Mr. John Fletcher . . ., The
(1750), ed. Theobald and
Seward, iii. 312.
Works of Beaumont and Fletcher,
in fourteen volumes . . ., The, ed.
Henry Weber (1812), iii. 312.
Works of Beaumont and Fletcher,
The, ed. George Darley, 2 vols.
(1840), iii. 312.
Works of Beaumont and Fletcher;
the text formed from a new col-
lation of the early editions, The,
ed. Alexander Dyce, 11 vols.
(1843–6), iii. 312.
Works of . . ., The, ed. Dyce
(another edition) (1854), iii.
312.
Works of . . ., The, ed. George
Darley (another edition), 2 vols.
(1866), iii. 312.
Works of Francis Beaumont and
John Fletcher, The, Variorum
Edition; A. H. Bullen, general
ed., 4 vols. (1904–12), iii. 312.
Works of Francis Beaumont and
John Fletcher, The, Arnold
Glover and A. R. Waller, eds.,
10 vols. (1905–12), iii. 312.
Beaumont, Francis, iii. 14, 15, 127,
133, 167, 306, 308, 317, 324,
327, 328, 330, 333, 337, 340,

Beaumont, Francis (*cont.*)
    342, 343, 347, 348, 357, 363,
    364, 365, 371, 377, 380, 382,
    383, 384, 387, 389, 392, 395,
    398, 400, 403, 408, 412, 418,
    423, 426, 431; iv. 499, 502, 523,
    557, 608, 753, 779, 802, 809,
    814, 906; v. 1086, 1212; vi. 9,
    41, 73, 113.
    *Masque of the Inner Temple and
        Grays Inn, The,* vii. 117.
    Metamorphosis of Tobacco, The,
        iii. 15.
    Poems by Francis Beaumont, Gent.
        (1653), iii. 359, 376, 418; vii.
        117.
    Reputation of, iv. 802, 809.
Beaumont, Francis (Sen.), iii. 14.
Beaumont, Sir Henry, iii. 15.
Beaumont, Sir John, iii. 14–16.
    *Bosworth-field; with a taste of the
        variety of other poems, left by
        Sir John Beaumont* (1629), iii.
        15.
    Theatre of Apollo, The, iii. 15–16.
Beaumont, Joseph, iii. 176, 178; iv.
    539; v. 1233.
    Psyche, or Love's Mystery, iv. 539.
Beaumont, Katherine, v. 1311.
Beaumont, Sir Thomas, v. 1311.
Beau's Duel, The, see Centlivre, S.
Beauties, The, see Shirley, James.
Beauty in a Trance, see Ford, John.
Beaver, William, vi. 178.
Beaver, live, vii. 49.
Beccles, Suffolk, iv. 600.
Becher, Sir William, i. 54 n. 2; vi. 27.
Beck, Christoph., *Phil. Massinger,
    The Fatall Dowry. Einleitung zu
    einer neuen Ausgabe* (1906), iv.
    783.
Beck, Edmund, *Robert Barons leben
    und Werke* (1915), iii. 10.
Beckingham, C. F., 'Othello and
    Revenge for Honour', *R.E.S.* xi
    (1935), iv. 489.
Beckland, Ambrose, *see* Beeland,
    Ambrose.
Beddingfield, Anne, vi. 216.
Bedford, Duke of, Library of, iii.
    134, 141.
Bedford, Lord, Francis Russell,
    Earl of Bedford, i. 47; iv. 476; vi.
    34, 476.
Bedford, Lucy, Countess of, iv. 609,
    620, 645, 650; v. 1257, 1258.
Bedingfield, Daniel, i. 46; ii. 376,
    534, 586.
Bedingfield, Nicholas, ii. 350.

Bedowe, Ellis, i. 286, 297; ii. **362**;
    iii. 192.
Bee, William, ii. **362**.
Beech Lane, *see* London, streets of.
Beedome, Francis, iv. 475.
Beedome, Thomas, iii. 16; iv. 475,
    928.
Beedome, Thomas, *Poems Divine
    and Humane* (1641), ii. 509 n. 1;
    iv. 928.
Beeland, Ambrose, i. 15, 72–88; ii.
    362–3.
Beeston, Andrea, ii. 370.
Beeston, Augustine, ii. 364.
Beeston, Christopher (alias Hutchin-
    son), i. 1, 54, 55, 57, 137 n. 3,
    141 n. 6, 158, 159, 160, 162–3,
    163, 165, 169 n. 2, 171, 183 and
    n. 2, 184, 187, 188, 192, 202 and
    n. 6, 203, 204 and n. 4, 205 n. 3,
    211 and n. b, 218, 219 and n. 3,
    222, 223 and n. 6, 224, 225 n. 1,
    228, 229, 230 n. 2, 231, 234, 236,
    237, 241, 246, 247, 248 n. i, 249
    n. e, 324, 325 and n. 4, 326 and
    nn. 2, 6, and 7, 327, 328, 329
    and n. 6, 336 and n. b, 338; ii.
    363–70, 527; iii. 17, 138, 442,
    447; iv. 475, 480, 481, 555, 556,
    581–2, 787, 797, 868; v. 990,
    1016, 1020, 1023, 1024, 1031,
    1033, 1051, 1068, 1070, 1077,
    1078, 1107, 1146, 1312; vi. 12
    n. 1, 37, 48 n. 1, 50, 56, 57, 58,
    59, 60, 61, 63–64, 65, 66, 67, 68,
    69, 70; vi. 73, 103, 138, 219,
    220; vii. 3, 5.
    Companies of, iii. 437, 439, 441,
        556, 754, 755, 768.
    Will of, ii. 631–3.
Beeston, Elizabeth, i. 330, 335; ii.
    370; vi. 70, 72, 75, 77. *See also*
    Kirke, Lady Elizabeth.
Beeston, George, ii. 373.
Beeston, Hugh, iii. 440, 451, 454,
    456.
Beeston, Jane, ii. 345, 364, 365, 366,
    373.
Beeston, John, ii. 369.
Beeston, Mary, ii. 372.
Beeston, Robert, i. 158; ii. 364, **370**.
Beeston, William, i. 35, 36, 62, 242,
    291, 324, 326 nn. 6 and 7, 327,
    330 and n. 3, 331 and n. 4, 332,
    333, 334 n. 1, 335, 336, 338; ii.
    370–4; iii. 53, 54, 56, 64, 65, 71,
    80, 195, 235, 283, 447, 451, 459,
    461, 462, 556, 579, 581–2; iv.
    863, 868, 907, 911; v. 1070,

1129, 1131, 1217, 1246, 1312,
1335, 1446; vi. 48, 52, 68, 70,
71, 73, 74, 75, 76, 77, 90 n. 1,
91, 94, 105, 114, 115, 167, 305,
309.
Beeston, William (no actor), ii. 371.
Beestons, iv. 931.
Beeston's Boys, i. 54, 55, 57, 187,
204 n. 4, 219 n. 3, 283, 324–42;
iii. 54, 57, 64, 65, 67, 71, 72, 73,
80, 195, 203, 228, 232, 235, 282,
308, 329, 385, 446, 451, 460,
461, 462; iv. 476, 479, 480, 482,
483, 495, 579–80, 713, 766, 768,
787, 788, 797, 801, 812, 813,
862, 863, 868, 869, 893, 907,
930, 943; v. 996, 1019, 1030,
1031, 1069, 1089, 1098, 1108,
1114, 1122, 1126, 1129, 1131,
1133, 1135, 1145, 1150, 1163,
1166, 1169, 1217, 1218, 1246,
1247, 1311, 1335, 1340, 1363;
vi. 12, 66–68, 69, 71, 94 n. 2,
165, 166, 309.
    Governorship of, vi. 68, 70, 73, 75,
76, 305.
    Repertory of, i. 337–42; iii. 48, 54.
Beggar plays, iii. 73.
Beggars, The, see Anon., see also
Fletcher, The Beggars' Bush.
Beggars' Bush, see Fletcher, John.
Behel, Jacob, see Pedel, Jacob.
Behn, Aphra, iii. 81; v. 985, 986.
    City Heiress; or, Sir Timothy
Treaty-all, iv. 790, 881–2.
    Debauchee, The: or The Credulous
Cuckold, iii. 80, 81.
    Like Father, like Son, or The
Mistaken Brothers, v. 986.
    Lucky Chance, v. 1127.
    Younger Brother, The, v. 1449.
    The Rover, or the Banished
Cavaliers, iv. 710.
Bel Savage Inn, The, vi. 121, 122,
127.
Beland, Ambrose, see Beeland,
Ambrose.
Belchier, Daubridgcourt, iii. 17–19.
    Hans Beer-Pot, His Invisible
Comedy of See Me and See Me
Not, iii. 18–19.
Belchier, William, iii. 17.
Belgium, pacification of, v. 1292.
Believe as You List, see Massinger.
Believe It is So and 'Tis So, see
Dekker, Thomas.
Bell, C. F., Designs by Inigo Jones for
Masques & Plays at Court, see
Simpson, Percy.

Bell, Hamilton, vi. 274 n. 1.
    'Contributions to the History of
the English Playhouse', Archi-
tectural Record, The, xxxiii
(1913), vi. 267, 274 n. 1, 275–7.
Bell, Jane (printer), iv. 773; v. 1385.
Bell, John, London's Remembrancer,
(1665), ii. 667.
Bell Inn, The, vi. 121, 122, 127.
Bellamira Her Dream, see Killigrew,
Thomas.
Bellamy, Daniel, the elder, The
Young Ladies Miscellany; or,
Youth's Innocent and Rational
Amusement (1726), iii. 180.
Bellamy, Daniel, the younger, The
Perjur'd Devotee; or, The Force of
Love, iii. 182.
Bellamy, Henry, iii. 19–20.
    Iphis, iii. 4, 19–20.
Bellamy, Mrs., Boarding School of,
iii. 180.
Bellamy, Robert, iii. 19.
Bellarmine, St. Robert, Cardinal, ii.
538; vi. 96.
Belleforest, François de, transl.
Histoires tragiques; extraictes des
oeuvres italiënes de Bandel, &
mises en langue françoise . . .
(1580–2), iii. 198, 379, 458; iv. 905.
Bellarmyne, see Bellarmine, Cardinal.
Bellers, Fettiplace, Injured In-
nocence, iii. 222.
Bellinger, John, v. 1034.
Bellingham, Thomas, iv. 816.
Bellman of London, The, see Daborne,
Robert, The Arraignment of Lon-
don.
Bellman of Paris, The, see Dekker,
Thomas.
Bellum Grammaticale, see Spense,
Master.
Belvoir, i. 310; iv. 626, 645, 646.
Benchers, iii. 436; v. 1155.
Benches in theatre, see Theatre.
Benedictine monasteries, v. 1186.
Benedictines, v. 1385.
Benefice, The, see Wild, Robert.
Benefit performances, i. 230, 295 n.
4; iii. 324, 354.
Benefit publications, iii. 426.
Benevolences in 1622, iii. 121.
Benfield, Anne, ii. 376, 634.
Benfield, Bartholomew, ii. 375.
Benfield, Elizabeth, ii. 375.
Benfield, James, ii. 375.
Benfield, Richard, ii. 374, 376, 534,
568, 587, 679; v. 985.
    Will of, ii. 633–5.

Benfield, Robert, i. 4 n. 2, 5 and n. 6
cont., 14, 17, 35 n. 1, 37, 43,
46, 47, 69 n. 2, 72–88, 129, 177
and n. 5, 318; ii. 374–6, 633,
634, 645; iii. 301, 311, 326, 330,
341, 346, 349, 352, 363, 375,
379, 393, 396, 420, 423, 428; iv.
765, 810, 817; v. 1412; vi. 32,
36, 172, 181, 185, 198.
Benfield, William, ii. 633.
Benfield's Rents, *see* London, streets
of.
Benlowes, Edward, *Theophila*, iii.
278.
Bennett, H. S., ed., *The Jew of
Malta and The Massacre at Paris*
(1931), iv. 573.
Bennyfield, Mary, ii. 375.
Bensly, Edward, iii. 318.
'Burton and Fletcher', *N. & Q.*,
Tenth Series, vi (1906); and
Eleventh Series, i (1910), iii. 382.
Benson, John (stationer), iii. 79,
198, 332, 333; iv. 646; v. 1032.
Bent, Robert, vii. 122.
Bentinck, George Cavendish, *see
Calendar of State Papers . . .
Venice.*
Bentley, G. E., ed., *The Development
of English Drama* (1950), iii.
1425.
'James Shirley and a Group of
Unnoted Poems on the
Wedding of Thomas Stanley',
Huntington Library Quarterly,
ii (1939), v. 1064, 1070, 1083,
1185.
'John Cotgrave's *English
Treasury of Wit and Language
. . .*', *S.P.* xl (1943), iii. 402; iv.
859, 886, 929, 1021, 1072, 1091,
1111; v. 1118, 1132, 1244, 1252.
'Lost Dramatic Document, A',
T.L.S. 8 December 1932, iii.
418; v. 1202.
'Players in the Parish of St. Giles
in the Fields', *R.E.S.* vi (1930),
iii. 301; iv. 542, 679, 928; v.
1218.
'Randolph's *Praeludium* and the
Salisbury Court Theatre', in
*Joseph Quincy Adams Memorial
Studies* (1948), iii. 68; v. 964,
967, 986, 987, 989, 990; vi. 86, 97.
'Records of Players in the Parish
of St. Giles, Cripplegate',
P.M.L.A. xliv (1929), iii. 242;
iv. 516.
Review of J. C. Adams, *The Globe*

Playhouse, Mod. Phil. xl (1943),
vi. 187 n. 1.
Review of Wright, ed., *Ghismonda,
J.E.G.P.* xlvi (1947), v. 1340.
'Shakespeare and the Blackfriars
Theatre', *Shakespeare Survey*, i
(1948), iii. 308; iv. 608; vi. 3, 12.
Shakespeare and His Theatre, Lin-
coln, Neb. (1964), vi. 66, 194 n. 1.
Shakespeare and Jonson, 2 vols.
(1945), iii. 310; iv. 526, 604,
608, 612, 647, 658, 681, 756; v.
1086.
'Shakespeare's Fellows', *T.L.S.*
15 November 1928, iv. 555.
Beoley, Worcester, ii. 411.
Bequests to the poor, ii. 635, 637,
639, 641, 644, 645, 650.
Bergen-op-Zoom, iii. 416.
Berkeley Castle, iv. 813.
Berkeley, George Berkeley, eighth
Baron, iv. 728; v. 1169.
Berkeley, John, iii. 21, 22.
Berkeley, Sir Maurice, iii. 20.
Berkeley, Lord, of Stratton, iii. 20.
Berkeley, Sir William, iii. 20–25;
iv. 690; v. 1202; vi. 37, 38.
Cornelia, iii. 22–23.
Lost Lady, The, i. 99, 115; iii.
23–25, 63; vi. 37, 38.
Berkenhead, John, iii. 128.
Berkshire, iii. 25.
Berkshire, Earl of, iv. 721.
Berlin, plays acted in, iv. 479.
Royal Opera House, vi. 275.
'Bermingham, Io' (verses by), iii. 96.
Bermingham, John, verses by, iii.
97.
Bernard, Charles, Serjeant surgeon
to Queen Anne, iii. 26.
Bernard, Samuel, iii. 25–28; iv. 552;
v. 1256.
Andronicus Comnenus, iii. 26–27.
Julius et Gonzaga, iii. 27–28;
v. 1256.
Phocas, iii. 28.
Bernheimer, Richard, 'Another
Globe Theatre', *Shakespeare
Quarterly*, ix (1958), vi. 186 n. 1.
Berry, Herbert, vi. 6.
Bertie, Peregrine, iii. 320.
Bertie, Richard, iii. 285.
Berwick on Tweed, Northumber-
land, i. 147; ii. 682; iv. 586, 702,
732; vi. 74, 157, 168.
Berwick, Treaty of, iii. 22, 147.
Best, John, i. 160; ii. 365; vi. 49, 56.
Best, John, Grocer, vi. 48.
widow of, ii. 368; vi. 64.

Best, Katherine, vi. 49, 72 n. 2.
Best, Richard, v. 1221.
Best Words wear Garlands, The, see C., I. *The Two Merry Milkmaids.*
Bestney, Nicholas, vi. 148.
Bethell, Zachary, vii. 17, 20.
Better Late Than Never, see Wilson Arthur, *The Inconstant Lady.*
Betterton, Ianthe, *see* Saunderson, Ianthe.
Betterton, Thomas, i. 165 n. 8; ii. 506, 546, 597; iii. 175, 371, 374, 377, 409; iv. 767, 768, 770, 817, 862, 864; v. 1248.
Prophetess, The, iii. 349.
revises play, iii. 397.
Betterton, Mrs. (Mrs. Saunderson), v. 1248.
Biddenton, in Kent, v. 1259.
Bidding prayer, English, v. 1349.
Biel, Jacob, *see* Pedel, Jacob.
Bielefeld, Friedrich, *The Witch of Edmonton, by Rowley, Dekker, Ford &c. Eine Quellenuntersuchung* (1904), iii. 270, 271.
Biland, Ambrose, *see* Beeland, Ambrose.
Bilboe's the Best Blade, see S. Rowley, *Hardshift for Husbands.*
Bill, John, stationer, iii. 235; v. 971, 974, 1390.
Billingsley, Captain, iii. 195; v. 1200.
Bills (of advertisement), vi. 206.
Bills of mortality, ii. 667–72; vi. 222.
Bills for Players, vii. 64.
Bills of Adventure, ii. 682; iv. 732, 733.
Bingham, Nottinghamshire, v. 1216, 1221.
Bingley, Sir John, v. 1422.
Binz, Gustav, 'Londoner Theatre und Schauspiele im Jahre 1599', *Anglia,* xxii (1899), vi. 202 n.
Biographia Dramatica, see Baker, David Erskine.
Birch, Elizabeth, ii. 642.
Birch, Ewin, ii. 404.
Birch, George, i. 14, 16, 17, 24, 72–88; ii. 377, 682; iii. 330, 341, 349, 355, 363, 393, 396, 416, 423.
Birch, Thomas, compiler, *The Court and Times of Charles I, see* Williams, R. F.
Birche, Bridget, ii. 377.
Birche, James, vi. 288.
Birchen Lane, *see* London, streets of.
Bird, Anne, ii. 378.
Bird, Christopher, ii. 632.

Bird, Elizabeth, ii. 379, 606.
Bird, Theophilus, i. 56, 57 and n. 2, 64, 69 n. 2, 73–89, 220, 221, 238, 246, 251, 324, 326 nn. 6 and 7, 327, 332, 336; ii. 377–9; iii. 272, 311, 314, 446, 460; v. 1096, 1204, 1216; vi. 68.
Bird (alias Borne), William, i. 135, 136, 138, 139, 140, 143, 147, 155; ii. 379–80; iii. 36; vi. 150, 151.
Bird in a Cage, The, see Shirley.
Birkhead, Henry, iii. 96.
Birredge, Bridget, ii. 452.
Birredge, Elizabeth, ii. 452.
Birredge, Robert, ii. 452.
Birth of Merlin, or The Child Hath Found His Father, The, see Rowley, William.
Bishop, Sir Edward, v. 1057, 1058.
Bishop, Sir Henry Rowley, v. 1104.
Bishop, R., iii. 402.
Bishop, Sir Thomas, v. 1057.
Bishop of London, *see* London, Bishop of.
Bishops, i. 65 n. 2; vi. 167–68; vii. 36, 39.
Bishops' Exclusion Bill, iii. 298; iv. 957; v. 1266.
Bishop's House in Whitefriars, vi. 116.
Bishops Wars, i. 244; iii. 195, 288, 461, 702, 721; v. 1039, 1199, 1200, 1209, 1235; vi. 166–167, 168, 309.
Bishopsgate, *see* London, streets of.
Bishopthorpe, Yorkshire, v. 1047.
Black Batman of the North, see Anonymous.
Black Lady, The, see Anonymous.
Black Lion Inn, London, iv. 850.
Black, Matthew Wilson, *Richard Brathwait. An Account of His Life and Works* (1928), iii. 38, 39, 40; v. 962, 963.
Black, William Henry, *A Descriptive, Analytical and Critical Catalogue of the Manuscripts Bequeathed unto the University of Oxford by Elias Ashmole . . .* 2 vols. (1845–66), v. 1094.
Black-Spread-Eagle in Duck Lane, iv. 691.
Black Wedding, The, see Anonymous, v. 1294.
Blackboy Alley, *see* London, streets of.
Blackbourton, Oxfordshire, v. 1188.
Blackfriars, Elector Palatine at, v. 1287.

Blackfriars district, *see* London, streets and districts.

Blackfriars Gate, *see* London, streets of.

Blackfriars, monastic buildings, vi. 3.

Blackfriars, parish of, vi. 27.
Scrivener in, vi. 178.

Blackfriars, precinct of, *see* London, streets and districts.

'Blackfriars Records', *see* Feuillerat, Albert.

Blackfriars theatre, i. 1–105 *passim*, 149 n. 4, 184, 208, 225 n. 1, 264, 268, 273 n. 1, 319; ii. 638, 692, 694, 696; iii. 8, 22, 24, 51, 52, 54, 62, 63, 75, 77, 78, 79, 82, 84, 85, 86, 87, 112, 113, 115, 116, 118, 120, 121, 123, 124, 135, 144, 146, 147, 149, 150, 163, 167, 169, 194, 195; iii. 201, 204, 206, 210, 211, 212, 220, 221, 223, 224, 230, 276, 277, 278, 300, 308, 320–427 *passim*, 440, 441, 449, 464; iv. 478, 521, 522, 523, 524, 532, 540, 541, 543, 562, 563, 608, 610, 616, 619, 622, 623, 624, 629, 630, 631, 633, 640, 652, 664, 666, 691, 692, 693, 703, 707, 723, 746, 754, 759, 761, 769, 771, 774, 775, 778, 779, 780, 783, 789, 809, 815, 821, 824, 825, 835, 836, 837, 840, 844, 848, 849, 859, 861, 883, 884, 888, 900, 901, 903, 904, 930, 941, 944; v. 996, 1049, 1063, 1064, 1070, 1072, 1082, 1083, 1084, 1085, 1086, 1087, 1097, 1100, 1101, 1105, 1106, 1107, 1109, 1117, 1124, 1125, 1143, 1148, 1202, 1203, 1204, 1206, 1207, 1208, 1210, 1211, 1242, 1252, 1268, 1270, 1271, 1274, 1286, 1288, 1312, 1342, 1425; vi. 3–45, 52, 53, 60, 61, 66, 67, 69, 82, 92, 93, 98, 106, 109, 113, 122, 129, 136, 140, 150, 151, 152, 163, 164, 166, 168, 169, 172, 180 n. 4, 181, 185, 186, 187, 193, 194, 195, 196, 197, 198, 199, 225 n. 1, 226, 235, 237, 242, 266, 283, 306, 307; vii. 4, 7, 9, 26, 28.
Average takings, i. 30 n. 6.
Box at, i. 48; iv. 703.
Children at, iii. 155.
Coaches ordered not to park near, i. 33; vi. 29–30; order rescinded i. 33–34; vi. 30.
Cost of share in, i. 45.
Courtly audience at, i. 47 n. 3.
Favourite theatre of Sir Humphrey Mildmay, i. 48.
Gentlewomen at, i. 33.
Music at, i. 40; vi. 32–33.
Musicians at, ii. 363; vi. 32–33.
Patrons of, i. 38–40; vi. 33–36.
Pit of, vi. 193.
Playing at, stopped by local petition, i. 5.
Popularity of, i. 30 n. 6.
Prestige of, i. 16 n. 6, 30 n. 6, 42, 225 n. 2, 307 and n. 1; vi. 4–15.
Private performance at, ii. 221.
Proposal for removal of, i. 32; vi. 17–20, 21–22, 24–25, 27–28, **39.**
Quarrels in, i. 42, 47, 48; vi. 33–34.
Queen's visits to, i. 39, 48 n. 5; iii. 114, 115, 220, 221; v. 1287; vi. 34–35.
Receipts at, i. 68; vi. 22–23.
Rent of, i. 44.
Shareholder in, ii. 466; vi. 36–37.
Shares in, i. 43–47; vi. 36–37.
Superiority of music at, i. 40.
Time of performance, i. 5.
Total takings, i. 23–24.
Transfer from, to the Globe, i. 3 n. 7; vi. 15–17.
Value of, i. 32 and n. 3; vi. 27–29.
Yearly rent, i. 45.

Blackmore, Edward, iii. 270; iv. 766, 775.

Blacknall, Grace, ii. 565.

Blacksmiths, i. 314; v. 1442; vi. 228.

Blackson, ii. **380**; iv. 885.

Blackwall, Stepney, i. 265, 266; iii. 183; vi. 161.

Blagrave, Dorothy, vi. 64, 67.

Blagrave, Thomas, ii. 380.

Blagrave, William, i. 35, 36, 40, 41, 42, 107, 112, 239 n. 3, 283 n. 7, 284, 291 and n. 6, 292, 299 n. b, 300; ii. **380–1**, 648; iii. 73, 367, 368, 395, 484, 485; iv. 505, **517**, 579, 582, 624, 807, 935, 937; v. 1455; vi. 59, 64, 87, 88, 89, 90, 91, 93–94, 98, 91 n., 100, 103, 162, 164, 194, 212; vii. 3, 4, 6, 11.

Blaiklock, Lawrence, iv. 930.

Blake, John, ii. 381.

Bland, Thomas, Sir, iv. 756, 799.

Blaney, John, i. 167, 168 n. 2, 169, 171, 183 n. 2, 220, 221, 222, 246; ii. **381–2**, 682; iv. 733, 813.

Blatherwick, Northamptonshire, iv. 533; v. 968, 976.

Blaxston, Mr., v. 1298.

Blencowe, John, iii. **28–30**.
Mercurius sive Literarum Lucta, iii. 4, 29–30, 184.
St. Michael's Combat with the Devil, or Moses his Farewell, iii. 29.

Blessing (ship), iv. 922, 923.

Blind Beggar of Alexandria, see Chapman, George.

Blind Beggar of Bethnal Green, The, see Day.

Blind Eats Many a Fly, The, see Heywood, Thomas.

Bliss, Dr., collection of, v. 1409.

Bliss, Mr., v. 1055.

Bliss, Philip, ed., *The Inconstant Lady, A Play. The Author Arthur Wilson, Esq., Sometime of Trinity College* (1814), v. 1267, 1268, 1271.

Bloody Banquet, The, see Thomas Drue.

Bloody Brother, The, see Fletcher, *Rollo, Duke of Normandy*.

Blount, Edward, iii. 461.

Blount, Henry, verses by, iii. 198.

Blount, Thomas, *The Academy of Eloquence* (1656), v. 1118.
De Re Poetica (1694), iv. 832.

Bloxam, John Rouse, ed., *Memorial of Bishop Wayneflete Founder of St. Mary Magdalen, Oxford, By Peter Heylin* (1851), iii. 26, 27; iv. 550, 551, 552, 595; v. 1256.

Blue Boar Tavern, v. 1403.

Blühm, Erich, *Über 'The Knight of Malta' und seine Quellen* (1903), iii. 351.

Blumson, Robert, ii. 640.

Blumson, Thomas, ii. 640.

Blunden, Humphrey, iii. 234.

Blunt, Edward, v. 1008.

Blunt, Henry, iii. 437, 450.

Blunt, Leonard, 'Asse upon Asse' (1661), iii. 153.

Blurt, Master Constable, see Middleton.

Blyth, Nottinghamshire, v. 1232.

Boarne, Thomas, *see* Bourne, Thomas.

Boar's Head Inn, The, i. 158; vi. 121–31, 133, 189.

Boar's Head Inn theatre, vi. 217.

Boar's Head Yard, vi. 122.

Boas, F. S., iii. 184.
Christopher Marlowe: A Biogra-phical and Critical Study (1940), iv. 573.
Diary of Thomas Crosfield, The, (1935), ii. 688–9; iii. 136; iv. 517, 717; v. 1158, 1261, 1263, 1264, 1269.
'Killigrew's *Claracilla*' *T.L.S.* 18 March 1944, iv. 698, 700.
'Lanchinge of the Mary, The', in *Shakespeare & the Universities* (1923), iv. 923.
'Recently recovered manuscripts at St. John's College, Oxford', *M.L.R.* xi (1916), iii. 29, 183–5.
'Seventeenth Century Theatrical Repertoire, A', *Library*, 3rd series, viii (1917), iv. 483, 560, 567; v. 1318, 1332, 1367, 1379, 1419, 1426.
Shakespeare and the Universities (1923), iv. 483, 560, 922, 923.
'Stage Censorship under Charles I: Sir Henry Herbert and Mountfort's Play', in *Shakespeare & the Universities* (1923), iv. 923, 924.
Thomas Heywood (1950), iv. 553, 578.
University Drama in the Tudor Age, v. 1006.
'University Plays', *C.H.E.L.* v. 1390.
'Walter Mountfort, East India Company's Official and Drama-tist', in *Shakespeare & the Universities* (1923), pp. 167–82, iv. 922, 923, 924.
'William Cartwright of the Beau-mont and Fletcher First Folio, The', *M.L.R.* xxv (1930), iii. 126.

Bobarre, Monsieur, ii. 675; v. 1157.

Boccaccio, iii. 336.
Decameron, iii. 103, 142, 228, 386, 431; iv. 603, 617, 797; v. 1097, 1141, 1317, 1341.

Bocke of Plaies, see Forman, Simon.

Bodie, Christopher, ii. 603.

Bodleian Library, *see* Oxford.

Bodymaker, ii. 455.

Boe to a Goose (mock title), v. 1447.

Boger, Jo., ii. 474.

Bohemia, Ambassador of the King of, vii. 36.

Bohemia, King and Queen of, com-pany of, i. 153, 188, 219, **260–9**, 291 and n.1, 308, 309; vi. 160, 162, 163.

Bohemia, King of, company of, *see* Palsgrave's company.

Bohemia, Queen of, *see* Elizabeth.

Boisrobert, François le Metel de *Pyrandre et Lisimène* (1633), iv. 600.
Bold Beauchamps, The, see Heywood, Thomas.
Boleyn, Anne, Catholic commentary on, iii. 125.
Bolland, James, ii. 449.
Bolles, Sir Robert, v. 1124.
Bolley, Rob, v. 1118.
Bolsover Castle, Derbyshire, iii. 143; iv. 612, 649, 653, 654.
Bolte, Johannes. 'Die Oxforder *Tragödie Thibaldus* (1640)', *Shakespeare Jahrbuch*, xxvii (1892), v. 1179.
Bolton, Edmund, iv. 609; vi. 299.
Boncle (Bunkley), John, headmaster of Eton, v. 1176.
Bonarelli della Rovere, Guido Ubaldo, Count, *Filli di Sciro* (1607), v. 970, 1171, 1451.
Bond, R. Warwick, iii. 390.
    'On Six Plays in *Beaumont and Fletcher, 1679', R.E.S.* xi (1935), iii. 329, 331, 363, 365, 366, 376, 384, 387, 390.
    ed., *Custom of the Country*, Variorum Edition (1904–12), iii. 324.
    ed., *The Humorous Lieutenant*, Variorum Edition (1904–12), iii. 343, 346.
    ed., *The Mad Lover*, Variorum Edition (1904–12), iii. 373, 376.
    ed., *Rule a Wife*, Variorum Edition (1904–12), iii. 407, 410.
    'Three Beaumont and Fletcher Plays', *R.E.S.* xii (1936), iii. 363, 387.
Bond, Susan, ii. 636.
Bond, Thomas, i. 168 n. 1, 303, 307, 308, 312, 321; ii. 382–3.
Bond Woman, The, see Anonymous.
Bondman, The, see Massinger, Philip.
Bonds of Peace, The, see Anonymous, *Juno's Pastoral*.
Bonduca, see Fletcher, John.
Bonduca, see Purcell, Henry.
Bonen, William, iii. 30–32, 162.
    The Cra . . . Merchant, or Come to My Country House, i. 185, 194, 206; iii. 30–32; v. 1014, 1294, 1430; vi. 59, 221.
    Two Kings in a Cottage, i. 150, 156; iii. 32, 265; iv. 796.
Bonner, Edmund, iii. 285.
Bonus, John, ii. 390.
'Book in Meeter of Robin Conscience, The', *see* Anonymous.

Book of the play, vi. 31.
Booke of Plaies, see Forman, Simon, *Bocke of Plaies*.
Booker, ii. 545, 581.
Book-keeper, i. 118; ii. 492, 494, 612; iii. 118; iv. 619, 923, 924; v. 1350, 1352.
Book-keeper, of King's Co., ii. 494–5; v. 1296, 1309.
Bookseller, ii. 405, 473, 544, 545; iii. 1, 69, 246, 248.
Bookseller's stock, iv. 561, 563.
Boorne, Thomas, *see* Bourne, Thomas.
Boot and Spur, see Anonymous.
Boote, Ann, v. 1045.
Boothe, Joane, ii. 650.
Bordinat, Philip, 'New Site for the Salisbury Court Theatre, A', *N. & Q.*, n.s. iii, vol. 201 (1956), vi. 86, 89 n. 1.
    'Study of the Salisbury Court Theatre, A', MS. Thesis, University of Birmingham (1952), vi. 86.
Borish, M. Eugene, *John Day*, Harvard MS. Thesis (1931), iii. 238.
    'Second Version of John Day's *Peregrinatio Scholastica*, A', *M.L.N.* lv (1940), iii. 239.
Borlase, Sir John impersonated, iii. 95.
Borne, Mr., i. 139.
Borne, Gilbert, vi. 148.
Borne, Theophilus, *see* Bird, Theophilus.
Borne, William, *see* Bird, William.
Borrose, —, ii. 383.
Boschet, Ambassador, iv. 528, 529.
Bosgrave, George, i. 168 n. 1; ii. 383–4, 384.
Boss carpenter, vi. 262.
Bosseley, Edward, ii. 384.
Boswell, Eleanore, *The Restoration Court Stage* (1932), iii. 216, 409; iv. 524; vi. 52, 267, 270 n. 1, 281, 283 n., 284.
    'Young Mr. Cartwright', *M.L.R.* xxiv (1929), iii. 13–14.
[Boswell, Eleanore, and Chambers, E. K.] 'Dramatic Records: The Lord Chamberlain's Office', *M.S.C.* ii, Pt. 3 (1931), vi. 284.
Boswell, James, ed., *The Plays and Poems of William Shakespeare, with Corrections and Illustrations of Various Commentators: Comprehending a Life of the Poet, and*

*an Enlarged History of the Stage,
by the Late Edmond Malone*, 21
vols. (1821), iii. 17; vi. 10, 59, 159,
164, 165, 225, 226, 229, 244, 283.
Boswell, William, iv. 528; v. 1196,
1237.
*Bosworth Field with . . . Other
Poems . . .*, see Beaumont, Sir
John.
Boteler, Ned, ii. 676; iii. 360.
Boucher, Richard, iv. 736.
Bouchier, Jonathan, 'John Ford:
François Coppée', *N. & Q.*,
Seventh Series, xii (1891), iii. 448.
Boucicault, Dion, *Love in a Maze*, v.
1094.
Boughner, Daniel C., '*The Drinking
Academy* and Contemporary Lon-
don', *Neophilologus*, xix (1934), v.
976.
Boulton, Elizabeth, ii. 650.
Boulton, William, ii. 564.
Bourbon, see Anonymous.
Bourgeois, Baron A. F., v. 1241.
Bourges, iii. 287.
Bourne, Mr., v. 1048.
Bourne, Constance, ii. 385.
Bourne, Edmond, ii. 385.
Bourne, Elizabeth, ii. 384.
Bourne, Francis, ii. 385.
Bourne, Mary, ii. 385.
Bourne, Richard, ii. 385.
Bourne, Susan, ii. 384.
Bourne, Temperance, ii. 385.
Bourne, Theodore, iv. 814.
Bourne, Theophilus, see Bird, Theo-
philus.
Bourne, Thomas, i. 286, 297; ii.
384-5.
Bourne, William, see Bird, William.
Bow Lane, see London, streets of.
Bowen, Alice, ii. 371, 373.
Bowen, Elizabeth, ii. 634, 646.
Bowen, Thomas, ii. 371.
Bowen, William, see Bonen, William.
Bowen, Winifred, ii. 634, 646.
Bower, William, iii. 32.
Bowers, Fredson Thayer, '*Alphon-
sus Emperor of Germany* and
the *Ur-Hamlet*', *M.L.N.* xlvii
(1933), v. 1286.
'Ben Jonson the Actor', *Stud.
Phil.* xxxiv (1937), iv. 604.
'Ben Jonson, Thomas Randolph,
and *The Drinking Academy*',
N. & Q. clxxiii (4 Sept. 1937),
iv. 628; v. 976, 979, 1328, 1329.
'The Date and Composition of
Alphonsus', *Harvard Studies*

and Notes in Philology and Lit.,
xv (1933), v. 1286, 1287, 1288.
'Date of *Revenge for Honour*, The',
M.L.N. lii (1937), iv. 489, 492.
*Elizabethan Revenge Tragedy
1587-1642* (1940), iv. 509; v.
1084, 1087.
ed., *The Fairy Knight, or Oberon
the Second* (1942), v. 1168,
1170, 1328, 1329, 1330.
'Marriot's Two Editions of Ran-
dolph's Aristippus', *Library*,
4th Series, xx (1939), v. 971, 974.
'Middleton's *Fair Quarrel* and the
Duelling Code', *J.E.G.P.* xxxvi
(1937), iv. 867, 869.
'A Possible Randolph Holograph',
Library, 4th Series, xx (1939),
v. 964, 966.
'Problems in Thomas Randolph's
Drinking Academy and Its
Manuscript', *H.L.Q.* i (1938),
v. 966, 976, 977, 978, 979.
'The Stabbing of a Portrait in
Elizabethan Tragedy', *M.L.N.*
xlvii (1932), iii. 257.
'Thomas Randolph's *Salting*',
Mod. Phil. xxxix (1942), v.
991, 992.
Bowers, Fredson T., and Richard B.
Davis, 'George Sandys: a biblio-
graphical catalogue of printed
editions in England to 1700',
*Bulletin of the New York Public
Library*, liv (1950), v. 1047.
Bowers, Jeremiah, ii. 385.
Bowers, John, ii. 385.
Bowers, Mary, ii. 385.
Bowers, Richard, i. 49 n. 2 cont.,
73-89; ii. 385.
Bowers, R. H., 'An Anonymous
Renaissance Pygmalion Play-
let', *M.P.* xlvii (1949-50), v.
1400.
*Byrsa Basilica, seu Regale Ex-
cambium . . . Edited from
Bodleian MS. Tanner 207,
Materials for the Study of the
Old English Drama* (1939), v.
1005, 1006, 1007.
Letter in *T.L.S.* 29 August 1936,
v. 1184.
'The Text of *Grobiana's Nuptials*',
M.L.N. iv (1940), v. 1054, 1056.
Bowles, George, Lord Mayor, iii.
261; iv. 897, 926.
Bowling alleys at Whitehall Palace,
vi. 268.
Bowls, v. 1199.

Bowman, Francis, i. 301; v. 968, 969, 986; vi. 97.

Bowman, John, v. 1098.

Bowrne, Thomas, *see* Bourne, Thomas.

Bowyer, Elizabeth, ii. 635, 636.

Bowyer, Isabell, ii. 386.

Bowyer, Michael, i. 56, 57, 64, 69, 73–89, 220, 221, 231, 232, 239, 246; ii. 385–7; iv. 570, 813.

Bowyer, Michael, dedication to, iii. 225.

Bowyer, Michael, Will of, ii. 635–6.

Bowyer, William, ii. 386; v. 1234.

Box, Edward, vi. 248.

Box for money, *see* Theatre.

Box in theatre, *see* Theatre.

Boxer tumblers, ii. 485.

Boxes at masques, iii. 200.

Boxley Abbey, Kent, v. 1048.

Boy actors, i. 285, 308; ii. 371, 487, 599; iii. 9, 60, 65, 80, 116, 164, 232–3, 300, 371, 385, 413, 428, 482, 484, 495; iv. 570, 580, 596, 597, 639, 670, 678, 686–7, 688, 764–5, 810, 814, 817, 881, 894, 933; v. 978–9, 998, 1003, 1011, 1019, 1049, 1075, 1087, 1093, 1097–8, 1154, 1165, 1172, 1173, 1174, 1175, 1177, 1183, 1187, 1217, 1221, 1256, 1258, 1266, 1283, 1285, 1290, 1292, 1329–30, 1337, 1339, 1344, 1346, 1349, 1359, 1363, 1375, 1383, 1385, 1392, 1394, 1405–6, 1408, 1418, 1424, 1450, 1453; vi. 9, 10, 11, 36, 66 n. 1, 73, 78, 96, 100, 115, 117, 134, 237, 245.

Boarding house for, v. 1049.

Care of, ii. 563.

Comparisons of, with women, ii. 588.

Gloves for, ii. 687; vi. 106, 107.

Impersonations by, ii. 551.

Impressed, iii. 300.

Singing ballads, iii. 255.

Training of, iii. 64.

Wages of, i. 44.

Boy companies, i. 167, 171, 283, 324–5; iii. 54, 57, 60, 155, 308; iv. 857.; vi. 9 n., 33 n., 74, 78–79, 94 n. 2, 103, 107, 115, 122, 178 n. 1.

Children of the Chapel, i. 118, 121 n. 1; ii. 434.

Children of Her Majesty's Revels, i. 122.

Children of the King's Revels, i. 178.

Children of Paul's, i. 115.

Children of the Revels, i. 2, 114, 168, 194, 205 n. 5.

See also Beeston's Boys.

Boys' company, a new, vi. 66.

Boys' company play, iii. 80, 91.

Boyle, Charles, iii. 34.

Boyle, Lewis, Lord Kinalmeaky, iii. 33.

Boyle, R., 'Zur Barnavelt-Frage. Eine Erwiderung auf das Nachwort des Herrn Prof. Delius', *Englische Studien*, ix (1886), iii. 415.

Boyle, Richard, Earl of Cork, iii. 33.

Boyle, Robert, 'On "Massinger and *The Two Noble Kinsmen*"', *New Shakspere Society's Transactions* (1880–6), iv. 819.

Boyle, Roger, Baron Broghill, First Earl of Orrery, iii. 33–35, 266.
  Altemira. A Tragedy . . ., iii. 34.
  The General, iii. 33–35; v. 1112, 1339.
  Mustapha, the Son of Solyman the Magnificent, iv. 866; v. 1379, 1404.

Boyle, William, iii. 35–38.
  Jugurth, King of Numidia, i. 150 and n. 4, 151, 157; ii. 691; iii. 36–38, 103; v. 1456.
  Jugurtha, or the Faithless Cousin German, iii. 36, 37; vi. 171.

Boyse, Joseph, iv. 514.

Brackley, Lord, masquer, iii. 110.

Bradbrook, M. C., *Themes and Conventions of Elizabethan Tragedy* (1935), iv. 861, 905; v. 1191.

Bradby, Northamptonshire, v. 1188.

Bradford, Gamaliel, 'An Unnoted Elizabethan Source', *The Nation*, lxxxvii (1908), iii. 343.
  'The Women of Middleton and Webster', *Sewanee Review*, xxix (1921), iv. 855.

Bradford, Wiltshire, i. 50.

Bradley, E. T. (Miss), iii. 303.

Bradley, Jesse Franklin, 'Robert Baron's Tragedy of *Mirza*', *M.L.N.* xxxiv (1919), iii. 279.

Bradley, J. F., and J. Q. Adams, eds., *The Jonson Allusion-Book* (1922), iii. 451; iv. 604, 606, 619, 623; vi. 26 n. 1.

Bradley, Richard, vi. 148.

Bradshaw, — (fencer), i. 318.

Bradshaw, Alexander, ii. 356.

Bradshaw, John, ii. 350.

Bradshaw, Richard, ii. 387–8.

Bradshaw's Rents, *see* London, streets of.
Bradstreet, John, ii. **388**.
Bradwell, Stephen, v. 1001.
[Braines, W. W.] 'Parish of St. Margaret, Westminster', L.C.C. *Survey of London*, xiv (1931), Pt. 3, vi. 267, 268, 270 n. 1, 284.
'Parish of St. Margaret, Westminster, The', L.C.C. *Survey of London*, xiii, Pt. 2 (1930), 116–20, vi. 255, 259, 260 n. 1.
Site of the Globe Playhouse Southwark, The, Second ed., London: for the London County Council (1924), vi. 179, 180 n. 2, n. 3.
Brainford, iv. 702.
Braintree, Essex, iii. 194.
Bramfield, Bartholomew, *see* Bromefield, Bartholomew.
Bramhall, John, Bishop of Londonderry, iii. 225, 228, 229.
Brande, Thomas, i. 25; vi. 23, 225, 226.
Branded as a felon, iv. 607.
Brandenburg, Elector of, ii. 350, 578.
Brandl, Alois, vi. 189.
Brandon, Charles, iii. 285.
Brandon, Samuel, *The Virtuous Octavia*, iv. 828.
Brasenose College, iii. 99, 161.
Brathwait, Richard, iii. **38–42**; iv. 928, 943; v. 963.
Barnabee's Journal (1638), v. 963.
The English Gentleman (1630), iii. 150.
The Golden Fleece (1611), iii. 39.
Mercurius Britannicus, or The English Intelligencer, iii. **40–42**.
Spiritual Spicerie, A (1638), iii. 39–40.
Tragi-Comoedia . . . Regicidium, iii. **42**.
Whimzies (1631), v. 963.
Wit's Recreations, ii. 605, 606.
Brathwait, Strafford, iii. 39.
Brathwait, Thomas, iii. 38.
Brawles, *see* Dances.
Bray, Antony, i. 286, 297; ii. **388**.
Bray, William, *The Diary and Correspondence of John Evelyn*, 2 vols. (1870), iii. 136; v. 1169, 1190.
Braybrooke, Richard Griffin, Lord, ed., *The Private Correspondence of Lady Jane Cornwallis, 1613–44* (1842), i. 42 n. 3; iv. 548.

Brazen Age, The, *see* Heywood, Thomas.
Bread and drink for workmen, vi. 272.
Breams, Sir Arnold, v. 1092.
Breda, fall of, iv. 802.
Breda, Siege of, v. 982.
Brend, Sir Mathew, i. 30; ii. 647; vi. 186, 200.
Brend, Sir Nicholas, vi. 180.
Brennoralt, *see* Suckling, Sir John.
Brent, Nathaniel, ii. 568; iii. 221; iv. 606, 641, 670, 671; v. 1210, 1216, 1288, 1289, 1377, 1378.
Brent, William, v. 1036.
Brentford, Middlesex, ii. 500, 695.
Brereton, J. LeGay, *Elizabethan Drama, Notes and Studies* (1909), iv. 489, 491.
'Sources of Ford's Perkin Warbeck, The', *Anglia*, xxxiv (1911), iii. 454, 455.
Bretbie, Derbyshire, masque at, iii. 168.
Breton, Robert, iii. 2.
Breton, William, iii. 2, 3, 42.
Brett, Catherine, iii. 468.
Brett, Cyril, ed., of *Little French Lawyer* in B. and F. Variorum Edition, iii. 356, 359.
Brett, William, iii. 468.
Brett-James, Norman G., *Growth of Stuart London* (1935), iii. 91; vi. 298–9.
Breuning, P. S., *see* Hulshof, A.
Brew, Anthony, ii. **388–9**.
Brewer, ii. 482.
Brewer, Anthony, iii. 5, 8, **42–45**; v. 1390.
Lovesick King, The, ii. 388; iii. 8, **42–45**.
Brewer, Thomas, iii. 5, 8, **45–46**; v. 1147.
Knot of Fools, A, or Come Laugh and Spare Not, iii. **45–46**.
The Life and Death of the merry Deuill of Edmonton. With the pleasant prancks of Smug the Smith (1631), iii. 45.
Weeping Lady, The, or London like Niniuie in Sackcloth (1625), iii. 45.
Brewer's servant, ii. 431.
Brice, Ralph, a carpenter, vi. 263.
Brick, vi. 293.
Brick construction, vi. 306.
Brick and stone, construction limited to, vi. 297, 299.

M

Bricklayer, i. 143; ii. 619; iv. 606, 856; vi. 26, 155, 157.

Bricklayers, vi. 260, 280, 281.

Bricklaying, vi. 26.

Bride, The, see Nabbes, Thomas.

Bridegroom and the Madman, The, see Anonymous.

Bride-Oak, Ralph, Commendatory verses, iii. 51; vi. 244.

Bridge, Edward, ii. **389**, 683.

Bridges, Bess, iv. 571.

Bridges, Dr. John, Bishop of Oxford, iv. 588.

Bridges, J., *The History and Antiquities of Northamptonshire*, ed. Peter Whalley (1791), iv. 736.

Bridges, William, iv. 588.

Bridgewater, Countess of, iv. 915.

Bridgewater, John, Earl of, ii. 416.

Bridgewater House, iv. 913.

Bridgewater MS. entitled 'Fortunia', iii. 159.

Bridport, Dorset, i. 213.

Brief Lives, see Aubrey, John.

Briefe Description of the notorious Life of Iohn Lambe, otherwise called Doctor Lambe, A. Together with his Ignominious Death (1628), *see* Anonymous.

'Brieven van Johannes de Wit aan Arend Van Buchel en anderen', *see* Hulshof, A.

Briggs, Robert, ii. **389**; iv. 885.

Briggs, W. D., 'Ben Jonson: Notes on *Underwoods* XXX and on the *New Inn*', *Mod. Phil.* x (1913), iv. 622.

'Birth-Date of Ben Jonson, The', *M.L.N.* xxxiii (1918), iv. 604, 606.

'First Song in *The Beggar's Bush*', *M.L.N.* xxxix (1924), iii. 313.

'Influence of Jonson's Tragedy in the Seventeenth Century, The', *Anglia*, xxxv (1912), iii. 313, 394, 398, 415; iv. 507, 509, 604, 761, 765, 775, 786, 805, 811, 815, 821, 824, 834, 837, 838; v. 1002, 1003, 1379, 1381.

'Source-Material for Jonson's Plays', *M.L.N.* xxxi (1916), iv. 604.

Brigham, Marke, i. 138, 143; vi. 185 n. 2.

Bright, Henry, *Poems from Sir Kenelm Digby's Papers, in the Possession of Henry A. Bright*, Roxburgh Club (1877), iii. 279, 280.

Briley, John, 'Of Stake and Stage', *Shakespeare Survey*, viii (1955), vi. 200, 208 n. 2.

Brill, Oxfordshire, v. 1276.

Brinkley, Roberta Florence, *Nathan Field, the Actor-Playwright*, Yale Studies in English, vol. lxxvii (1928), iii. 299, 300, 301, 302, 351, 352, 353, 398, 400.

Briot, Nicholas, v. 993.

Bristol, i. 92, 151 n. 5, 156, 179, 193, 212, 282; ii. 530, 574; iii. 247; v. 1007.

Bristol, Bishop of, iii. 306.

Bristol, Merchant of, iii. 94.

Bristol, Youths of Her Majesty's Royal Chamber of, ii. 419.

Bristow Merchant, The, see Dekker, Thomas.

Bristowe, Francis, iii. **46–47**.

King Freewill, iii. **46–47**.

Britain's Remembrancer, see Wither, George.

Britannia Triumphans, see Davenant, William.

Britannia's Honour, see Dekker, Thomas.

Britanniae Primitiae, sive S. Albanus protomartyr, see Anonymous.

British Drama, see Nicoll, Allardyce.

British Museum, iii. 229, 264, 269, 282, 293, 295, 297, 313, 315, 317, 332, 333, 344, 371, 378, 385, 403, 415, 416, 419, 466, 467; iv. 527, 536, 638, 639, 648, 653, 687, 690, 696, 728, 729, 730, 731, 732, 744, 762, 765, 767, 801, 812, 834, 835, 852, 863, 864, 868, 870, 873, 874, 876, 879, 900, 913, 917, 923, 924; v. 961, 1036, 1038, 1054, 1119, 1215, 1220, 1223, 1228, 1293, 1322, 1384; vi. 155 n. 1.

Catalogue of the Printed Books in the Library of the British Museum, 58 vols., 1881–1900, iii. 5, 29, 97; iv. 599.

Manuscripts Additional, iii. 12–14, 23, 134, 141, 151; iv. 527, 536, 708, 715, 852, 864, 873, 874, 913; v. 961, 974, 988, 989, 1042, 1102, 1104, 1124, 1171, 1181, 1182, 1184, 1259, 1260, 1262, 1273, 1289, 1315, 1324, 1327, 1330–1, 1336, 1338, 1340, 1349, 1361, 1376, 1378, 1405, 1408, 1430, 1450, 1451; vi. 88, 97.

Manuscripts Egerton, iii. 176, 191; iv. 483, 519, 560, 567, 728, 762, 876, 923, 924; v. 1303, 1304, 1318, 1332, 1367, 1379, 1381, 1419, 1420, 1426, 1427, 1452.

Manuscripts Harleian, iii. 4, 108, 110, 145, 161, 166, 176, 530; iv. 615, 618, 638, 639, 645, 648, 653, 677; v. 1030, 1042, 1174, 1196, 1228, 1277, 1278, 1297, 1390, 1391, 1392, 1393, 1403, 1436, 1439, 1450; vi. 25 n. 1.

Manuscripts Lansdowne, iii. 125; iv. 510, 598, 870, 878; v. 981, 1265; vi. 286.

Manuscripts Royal, iii. 14, 15; iv. 834; v. 1201, 1207.

Manuscripts Sloane, iii. 23, 26; iv. 569, 628, 767, 801, 812, 863, 868, 900, 917; v. 971, 972, 1091, 1124, 1316, 1338, 1352, 1373.

Manuscripts Stowe, iv. 917, 920. Print Room, vi. 132 n. 1.

British Royal Academy, proposals for, iv. 609.

Brittaine, William, vi. 72.

Brittannicus, Mercurius, v. 1443.

Brize Norton, Oxfordshire, iv. 588.

Broadbent, R. J., ed., 'A Masque at Knowsley', *Transactions of the Historic Society of Lancashire and Cheshire*, New Series, xli (1925), v. 1040, 1041.

Broadgate's Hall, iii. 15.

Broadside, iv. 622, 985, 1200; vi. 244.

Broadsides, satirical, vi. 173.

Broadwindsor, Dorset, iv. 512.

Brocke, Marianne, ed. of *The Knight of Malta* (Bryn Mawr MS. Dissertation 1944), iii. 351, 352, 353, 354.

Brodmeier, Cecil, vi. 189.

Brograve, John, iii. 437, 454.

Broken Heart, The, see Ford, John.

Broker, hanged, vi. 259 n. 1.

Brome, Alexander, iii. 47–49, 54, 55, 72.
   Cunning Lovers, The, i. 331, 337; iii. 47, 48–49, 230.
   Songs and Other Poems (1661), iii. 48, 123.

Brome, George, i. 139.

Brome, Henry, i. 116; iii. 86, 87; iv. 922.

Brome, Josias, ii. 357.

Brome, Lucia, ii. 390.

Brome, Richard, i. 63, 188 and n. 4, 192, 227, 241, 292 n. 1, 295 and n. 5, 330 n. 3, 334 n. 1; ii. 389–90, 488; iii. 6, 7, 47, 48, 49–92, 114, 149, 308; iv. 503, 504, 602, 678, 679, 723, 737, 787, 928, 937, 938, 941; v. 967, 974, 1068, 1186, 1199, 1206, 1216, 1217, 1224, 1235, 1311; vi. 38, 62, 70, 71, 72, 98, 102, 105 n. 1, 107, 109.
   Influence of his comedies, v. 1096.
   Jealous of *Aglaura*, i. 58–60.
   Poet for the Cockpit, i. 330.
   Antipodes, The, i. 58–59, 242, 243 n. 2, 250, 283, 338; ii. 372, 390; iii. 51, 54, 55–57, 65, 71, 88, 89, 92, 114, 169; iv. 504; vi. 70, 102.
   City Wit, The, or, The Woman wears the Breeches, iii. 51, 59–61, 65, 66, 192; v. 1123, 1309.
   Court Beggar, The, i. 59–60, 63, 115, 243 n. 2, 324, 334, 337–8; ii. 372–3; iii. 49, 54, 57, 59, 61–65, 71, 88, 89, 114; v. 1123; vi. 71, 75.
   Damoiselle, The, or The New Ordinary, iii. 61, 62, 65–67.
   Dramatic Works of, see Shepherd, R. H. (ed.).
   English Moor, The, or The Mock Marriage, i. 56 n. 1, 241, 250; iii. 54, 67–69, 269; v. 1311, 1386; vi. 102.
   Five New Plays (1653), i. 319; iii. 47, 54, 55, 80, 167; vi. 171 n. 1, 245.
   Five New Plays (1659), iii. 47, 51, 55, 149; v. 1204, 1207.
   Honour of Young Ladies, The, see The Lovesick Maid.
   Jewish Gentleman, The, iii. 70.
   Jovial Crew, A, or The Merry Beggars, i. 324 n. 1 cont., 335, 338; iii. 47, 49, 70–73, 88, 315; v. 1216, 1363.
   Lachrymae Musarum, iii. 54, 55.
   Lovesick Court, The, or The Ambitious Politique, iii. 51, 52, 76–77.
   Lovesick Maid, The, or The Honour of Young Ladies, i. 66, 96, 105, 115; ii. 469; iii. 77–80; iv. 623.
   Mad Couple Well Matched, A, i. 331, 338, 342; iii. 61, 62, 66, 80–81, 85; iv. 487.
   New Academy, The, or The New Exchange, iii. 81.

Brome, Richard (*cont.*)
Northern Lass, The, i. 12, 13, 100,
105, 115–16; iii. 6, 50, 52, 79,
81–84, 88, 437; iv. 571, 877;
vi. 196, 197.
Novella, The, i. 66, 116; iii. 52, 61,
62, 66, **84–85**; iv. 7, 10.
ueen and Concubine, The, i. 295,
300 and n. 1; iii. 54, 85–86; v.
1108; vi. 102.
Queen's Exchange, The [*The Royal
Exchange*], i. 116; iii. 52, 85,
86–87.
Sparagus Garden, The, i. 285, 295,
300 and n. 1, 338; ii. 444, 660;
iii. 53, 54, 56, 64, 65, 80–81, 86,
87–89, 90, 92; iv. 483, 933,
942; v. 1363; vi. 102.
'Upon AGLAURA printed in Folio',
v. 1204, 1207.
*Weeding of Covent Garden, The, or
The Middlesex Justice of Peace,*
iii. 51, 85, 88, 89–92; iv. 483,
932, 933, 942; v. 1169.
Witt in a Madnes, iii. 56, **92**.
Brome, Richard, and Chapman,
George, *Christianetta, or Marriage
and Hanging Go by Destiny,* iii.
58; iv. 865, 866.
Brome, Richard, and Thomas Heywood, *The Apprentice's Prize,*
iii. **58**, 75, 76; iv. 556.
Late Lancashire Witches, The, i.
40, 41, 121; ii. 343, 381; iii. 52,
58, **73–76**, 88, 91; iv. 556, 713,
824, 941; v. 1455; vi. 198, 199.
*The Life and Death of Sir Martin
Skink with the Wars of the Low
Countries,* iii. 58, 75, **76**; iv.
556; v. 1382.
The Wars of the Low Countries,
iii. 76.
Brome, Richard, and Young Jonson,
Fault in Friendship, A, i. 206, 214;
iii. 52, 59, 69–70; iv. 602.
Brome, Robert, ii. 357.
Brome, Sara, ii. 390.
Brome, Stephen, iii. 6, 55, 83; iv. 571.
Bromefield, Bartholomew, ii. 633.
Bromefield, Richard, i. 137; ii. **390**.
Bromfield, Sir Edward, vii. 104.
Bromfield, Mr., the surgeon, *The
Schemers, or, The City-Match,* iv.
850.
Bromham, Bedfordshire, vii. 37.
Brook, Nathaniel, v. 1303, 1322,
1327, 1336, 1351, 1366, 1419, 1422.
Brooke, C. F. Tucker, iv. 573; v.
1241, 1246, 1247.

Brooke, C. F. T., and N. B. Paradise,
eds., *English Drama, 1580–1642*
(1933), iii. 313.
Brooke, Lord, *see* Greville, Fulke.
Brooke, Margaret, iii. 276.
Brooke, Rupert, v. 1249.
'The Authorship of the Later
"Appius and Virginia"', *M.L.R.*
viii (1913), v. 1245.
*John Webster and the Elizabethan
Drama* (1916), iv. 805.
Brooke, Samuel, v. 1371.
Adelphe, v. 1195, 1299.
Melanthe, v. 1195.
Brooke, William, ii. 607.
Brooklyn, N.Y., v. 977.
Brooks, Harold F., Review of
Wright, ed. *Ghismonda, R.E.S.*
xxiii (1947), v. 1340.
Brooks, John Lee, *Alexander Brome:
His Life and Works* (1932), iii. 47,
48.
Brotanek, Rudolf, *Die Englischen
Maskenspiele* (1902), iii. 107,
110; iv. 642, 665, 667, 668, 669,
676, 677; v. 1311, 1357, 1376,
1377, 1378, 1430.
'Ein unerkanntes Werk Sir Wil-
liam Davenant's', *Anglia Bei-
blatt,* xi (1900), 177–81, iii. 207,
208.
Brothels, *see* Bawdy houses.
Brothers, The, see Shirley, James.
Brougham Castle in Westmorland,
vii. 24.
Broughton, Ambrose, ii. **390**, 682.
Broun, Samuell, bookseller, iii. 146.
Brouncker, Lord, v. 1092.
Brown, Carlton, ed., *The Stonyhurst
Pageants, Hesperia* (1920), v.
1414, 1415.
Brown, E. R., 'Jonson's "A Tale of a
Tub"', *T.L.S.* 10 May 1928, iv.
632.
Brown, Horatio F., see *Calendar of
State Papers . . . Venice.*
*Inglesi e Scozzesi all' Università di
Padova, 1618–1765* (1925), iii.
166, 171.
Brown, Ivor, iv. 638.
The Observer (London), 21 July
1935, iv. 638.
'The Witch of Edmonton at the
Old Vic', *The Observer,* 13
December 1936, iii. 270.
Brown, R—, Esq., vi. 61.
Brown, Rawdon, vi. 152.
See *Calendar of State Papers . . .
Venice.*

Brown, Sir Richard, v. 1223.

Brown, Samuel, iii. 403, 408.

Brown, William, i. 159, 169, 303, 307, 308, 310, 312, 321; ii. 391, **391–2**, 645.
Will of, ii. 636–7.

Browne, Anne, ii. 637.

Browne, Christopher, v. 1258.

Browne, Cisley, ii. 548.

Browne, Dr. Edward, iii. 23, 71, 102, 264, 315, 320, 333, 344, 371, 378, 385, 403, 419, 462; iv. 571, 801, 803, 812, 868, 900; v. 1114, 1124, 1135.
'Memorandum Book, 1662', iv. 569, 767, 863; v. 1091.

Browne (*alias* Baskervile), Francis, i. 159; ii. **391**.

Browne, John, ii. 690.

Browne, John, at Cambridge, iv. 601.

Browne, John, stationer, iv. 881.

Browne, Joseph, ii. **391**.

Browne (*alias* Robins), Judith, ii. 406.

Browne, Lucretia, ii. 391.

Browne, Richard, ii. **391**, 683.
Furnishes bail, iv. 737.

Browne, Richard, child actor, v. 1258.

Browne, Robert, ii. **391**, 637; vi. 123, 124, 126–31, 129, 130.

Browne, Robert (haberdasher), ii. 636.

Browne, Samuel, v. 1031.

Browne William, *Britannia's Pastorals*, iv. 531.

Browne v. *Woodliff et al.*, vi. 124.

Bruce, Mrs., i. 16 n. 6.

Bruce, Sir Hervey, MSS. of, vi. 34.

Brumeau, Monsieur, Spanish agent, iv. 643.

Bruno, Giordano, *Spaccio de la Bestia Trionfante* (1584), iii. 110.

Brunswick, Duke of, i. 16 n. 6; vi. 4.

Brus, Mistress, vi. 4.

Brussels, Ambassador, iv. 529.

Bruton, Somerset, iii. 20.

Bryan, Mary, ii. 392–3.

Brydekirk, Dumfriesshire, iii. 111.

Brydges, Sir Samuel Egerton, *Censura Literaria* (1815), v. 1066.

Bryne, Eva A. W., ed., Massinger, *The Maid of Honour* (1927), iv. 791, 796, 798, 799.

Bryne, Muriel St. Clare, ed., Massinger's *A New Way to Pay Old Debts* (1949), iv. 800.

Buc, Sir George, i. 103, 106, 110, 112, 127, 130, 195, 206, 216; ii. 422; iii. 36, 37, **92–94**, 102, 256, 263, 264, 265, 328, 370, 416; iv. 510, 511, 589, 734, 820, 881, 884, 888, 889, 907; v. 1008, 1371, 1393, 1416; vi. 116; vii. 3, 49, 54.
Madness of, vii. 43.
The Ambitious Brother, iii. **93–94**; iv. 866.
The Baron, or Magazin of Honour iii. 93.
Commentary upon the New Roll of Winchester, A, ii. 422; iii. 93, 94.
The History of the Life and Reigne of Richard the Third, iii. 93, 94.
The Third Universitie of England, iii. 93.

Bucephalus, vi. 44.

Buchan, Hannah, ed., *The Poems of Thomas Pestell* (1940), iii. 278; iv. 953.

Buchanan, George, *Baptistes sive Calumnia tragedia*, v. 1429.

Buchel, Arend Van, *see* Van Buchel.

Buck Is a Thief, The, see Anonymous.

Buckden Palace, near Huntingdon, vii. 71, 79.

Buckeridge, John, v. 1056.

Bucket, Rowland, iv. 897.

Buckhurst, Richard Sackville, Lord, v. 1359, 1360.

Buckingham, Bucks., ii. 535; iv. 530, 664.

Buckingham, George Villiers, First Duke of, i. 10 n. 6, 22, 23 and n. 1, 128, 223 and n. 8, 224, 253, 266; ii. 347; iii. 15, 16, 111, 121, 205, 320, 323, 374, 468; iv. 530, 609, 645, 646, 661, 662, 664, 666, 671, 675, 677, 691, 769, 841, 878, 916, 949; v. 965, 1158, 1360; vi. 63, 161, 198, 258; vii. 13, 22, 27, 34, 59, 62, 64, 69.
Assassinated, vii. 68, 69.
Masque of, ii. 518.
Performs in a masque, iv. 647.
Satiric verses on, v. 1353.

Buckingham, Duke of (Second), *The Rehearsal*, ii. 481.
The Chances, iii. 320.

Buckle, Elizabeth, ii. 393.

Buckle, John, i. 275, 281; ii. **393**; vi. 164.

Buckle, Mary, ii. 393.

Buckler Fights, iii. 210; vi. 14.
Bucklers, vi. 168.
Buckley, William Edward, iii. 99.
   ed., *Philosophaster Comoedia, Nunc primum in lucem producta. Poemata, Antehac sparsim edita,* by Robert Burton (1862), iii. 99.
Buckram, vi. 280.
Bucksted, William, *see* Barksted, William.
Budden, John, v. 1276.
Budsdell, Alse, ii. 350.
Buffoonery, v. 1143.
Bugg, Sir Anthony, vi. 49.
Bugge, Andrew, ii. 393.
Bugge, John, i. 190, 192; ii. **393–4,** 634.
Bugge, Mary, ii. 394.
Builder, ii. 348.
Building forbidden, ii. 365–7.
Buklank, Alexander, i. 16 n. 1; ii. **394.**
Bull-baiting, ii. 510; vi. 200, 201, 203, 212, 298; vii. 10, 14, 27, 32, 36, 37, 41, 45, 48, 70, 79, 87, 93, 110.
   advertising for, vi. 213.
Bull, Beare, and Horse, Cut, Curtaile, and Longtaile (1638), *see* Taylor, John.
Bull Head Tavern (London), iv. 757.
Bull house at Hope theatre, vi. 201, 203, 205.
Bull, hunting of, *see* Hunting of the bull.
Bull Inn, The, vi. 122, 127, 131.
Bullard, Alexander, i. 15, 16 n. 1, 73–89; ii. 394.
Bullen, A. H., iii. 100, 312, 321, 390; iv. 489, 521.
   Collection of Old English Plays, A, 6 vols. (1882–7), iii. 145, 147, 148, 230, 234, 257, 415, 416; iv. 476, 483, 484, 489, 560; v. 1060, 1312, 1313, 1318, 1319, 1320, 1332, 1379; vi. 1419.
   'Thomas Dekker' in *Elizabethans* (1924), iii. 241.
   ed., *Works of John Day, The,* 2 vols. (1881), iii. 239, 251, 257, 273; v. 1348.
   ed., *Works of Robert Davenport, now First Collected, The,* in *A Collection of Old English Plays,* New Series (1890), iii. 230, 234.
   ed., *Works of John Marston, The,* 3 vols. (1887), v. 1376, 1378.
   ed., *Works of Thomas Middleton, The,* 8 vols. (1885–6), iv. 857,

858, 859, 860, 879, 882; v. 1073, 1447.
   ed., *Works of Thomas Nabbes, The, Old English Plays,* New Series, 2 vols. (1887), iv. 927, 929, 931, 936; v. 1126.
Bullen, George, 'The Duke of Buckingham and a Play of Shakespeare in 1628', *Athenaeum,* no. 2712 (18 October 1879), i. 22–23 and n. 1.
Buller, Richard, ii. 615.
Bullock, Christopher, v. 1152.
Bullock, Helene B., 'Thomas Middleton and the Fashion in Play-making', *P.M.L.A.* xlii (1927), iv. 855.
Bullocke, Richard, ii. 459.
Bullock's benefit, iv. 887.
Bulls, enumerated, vi. 212–13.
Bulls, Jugler, vi. 211 n.
Bülow, Gottfried, von, assisted by Wilfred Powell, 'Diary of the Journey of Philip Julius, Duke of Stettin-Poemerania, through England in the Year 1602', *Trans. Royal Hist. Soc.,* N.S. vi (1892), vi. 33 n.
   Trans. 'Journey through England and Scotland made by Lupold von Wedel in the Years 1584 and 1585', *Trans. Royal Hist. Soc.,* N.S. ix (1895), vi. 202 n.
Bun Hill, *see* London, streets and districts.
Bunkley, John, *see* Boncle, John.
Bunn, **Alfred,** *Kinsmen of Naples,* iii. 272.
Burbage, Alice (Walker), i. 9; ii. 649.
Burbage, Cuthbert, i. 1, 2, 3, 4 nn. 1 and 2, 9, 30, 32 n. 3, 43, 44, 45, 46; ii. **394–5,** 638, 641, 642, 649, 651; v. 1109; vi. 5, 28, 36, 140, 180, 181.
Burbage, Mrs. Cuthbert, i. 9; ii. 649.
Burbage, Elizabeth (Maxey), i. 9; ii. 649.
Burbage, James, i. 135; ii. 394, 395; vi. 5, 6.
Burbage, Richard, i. 1, 2, 3, 4 n. 2, 5, 6, 7, 30, 43, 72–88, 137 n. 3; ii. **395–7,** 436, 649; iii. 300, 302, 326, 331, 341, 346, 349, 352, 353, 355, 372, 375, 393, 399, 413; iv. 639; v. 1252; vi. 5, 13 n. 1, 140, 180, 181, 206; vii. 2.
   Will of, ii. 638.

Burbage and Shakespeare's Stage, see Stopes, C. C.
Burbage v. Allen, vi. 140.
Burbage, Sara, i. 9; ii. 396, 552, 649.
Burbage, William, i. 32 n. 3, 43, 46; ii. 396, 553, 645; vi. 28.
Burbage, Winifred (Robinson), i. 4 nn. 1 and 2, 46; ii. 396, 638, 639.
Burfeild, Roger, see Barfield, Roger.
Burford, Oxfordshire, iv. 550.
Burges, James Bland, *Riches, or The Wife and Brother*, iv. 774.
Burgess of Edinburgh, iv. 611.
'Burghclere', 'Setting of Precious Stones', *N. & Q.* 10th Series, i (9 January 1904), iv. 614.
Burghe, Nicholas, iv. 541, 542.
Burghley, Lord, iv. 673.
Burght, see Birch, George.
Burials, vi. 20, 24.
Burke, Sister Mary Ransom, Unpublished Fordham dissertation on May's *The Tragedy of Cleopatra*, iv. 835.
Burkhead, Henry, iii. 94–96.
  Cola's Fury, or Lirenda's Misery, iii. 94–95, 96.
  The Female Rebellion, iii. 5, 95–96.
Burlesques, v. 992, 1147.
Burley, Rutlandshire, iv. 645, 646.
Burley-on-the-Hill, iv. 645, 646, 841, 842, 843.
Burnebye, Ann, v. 1311.
Burnebye, Susann, v. 1311.
Burnell, Christopher, iii. 96.
Burnell, Eleonora, verses by, iii. 96.
Burnell, Henry, iii. 96–98; v. 1355, 1423.
  Landgartha, iii. 96, 97–98; v. 1355, 1423.
  World's Idol, The, or Plutus the God of Wealth, iii. 97.
Burneshead Hall, Kendall, Westmorland, iii. 38, 39.
Burney, Charles, *General History of Music*, 4 vols. (1776–89), vi. 32.
Burroughs, —, iii. 98.
  Fatal Friendship, The, i. 116, 117, 123; iii. 98.
Burrows, Montagu, *The register of the visitors of the University of Oxford, from* A.D. *1647 to* A.D. *1658* (1881), iii. 183.
Burstead, Essex, iii. 303.
Burt, Nicholas (see also Nick), i. 69 n. 2, 73–89, 327 n. 3, 336; ii. 397; iii. 314; vi. 237.
Burton, Antony, ii. 397.
Burton, Dorothy, iii. 99.

Burton, Henry, v. 1194, 1195, 1216, 1398.
Burton, Henry, *For God and the King: The Summe of Two Sermons* (1636), v. 1194–5.
Burton, Ralph, iii. 99.
Burton, Robert, iii. 99–100, 384; iv. 931, 1121.
  Anatomy of Melancholy, iii. 99, 450; iv. 818.
  Philosophaster, iii. 99–100; iv. 498, 596; v. 1187.
Burton, Samuel, ii. 411.
Burton, William, iii. 99.
Burtonian melancholy, v. 1034.
Bury St. Edmunds, Suffolk, v. 1404; vii. 35.
Busby, Richard, Headmaster of Westminster School, iii. 137.
Bushell, Sir Edward (Edmund), v. 1167.
Bushell's Rock, Oxfordshire, iv. 679. Presentment of, vii. 103.
Bushey, in Herts., v. 1178.
Busino, Antonio, iv. 263.
Busino, Orazio, iv. 671, 897; vi. 151–2, 256–8, 264.
Buskin (i.e. of tragedy), vi. 246.
Bussy D'Ambois, see George Chapman.
Butchers, ii. 690, 691; vi. 148.
Butler, George, dedication to, iii. 239.
Butler, Joseph, a messenger, i. 279; ii. 545; vi. 168.
Butler, Samuel, iv. 524.
  His commonplace book, v. 1382.
  'Panegyric upon Sir John Denham's Recovery from his Madness, A', iii. 278.
  Satires and Miscellaneous Poetry and Prose, ed. Lamar (1928), iv. 524.
Butler, Dr. William, iv. 890.
Butler, Sir William, iv. 721.
Butter, Nathaniel, iii. 260, 338; iv. 620, 631; v. 1036; vi. 25.
Butts, Dr., Vice-Chancellor of Cambridge, iv. 535, 536; v. 984.
Buxted St. Margaret, Sussex, iii. 26.
Byfield, Pentronill, ii. 350.
Byland, Ambrose, see Beeland, Ambrose.
Byndinge, Richard, carpenter, vi. 272, 274, 275.
Byrd, Theophilus, see Bird, Theophilus.
Byrd, William, vi. 295.
Byron, John, first Lord Byron, iv. 525, 527.

Bysshe, Edward, iv. 691 ; v. 1125.
Bysshe, Margaret Greene, v. 1125.

C., A., Generosus (?Peter Hausted).
    Satyre against Separatists (1642),
    vi. 245.
C., I., iii. 101-4, 186.
    *A Pleasant Comedy called The Two
    Merry Milkmaids, or The Best
    Words Wear the Garland*, i. 166,
    173, 175 ; ii. 417-18, 691 ; iii. 37,
    101-4, 126, 187 ; v. 1019, 1144,
    1401 ; vi. 171, 220, 242.
C., J., verses by, iii. 79.
C., R., iii. 457 ; iv. 689.
C., T., iii. 457.
C., W., a pastor (of Whitechapel,
    London), vi. 222.
    London's Lamentation (1625), vi.
    222-3.
    *The Rape Reveng'd, Or, The
    Spanish Revolution*, v. 1021.
*Cabala, sive Scrinia Sacra: Mysteries
    of State, see* Anonymous.
Cabinet of Mistakes, A, see Chamber-
    lain, Robert, *Jocabella*.
Cademan, Sir Thomas, widow of,
    iii. 196.
Cademan, William, iii. 232 ; iv. 544 ;
    v. 1380.
Caesar, John (of Hyde Hall, Hert-
    fordshire), iii. 8.
Caesar's Fall, or Two Shapes, see
    Middleton.
Caesar and Pompey, see Chapman,
    George.
Caesar's *Commentaries*, iii. 304.
Cain, Andrew, *see* Cane, Andrew.
Calcot, Allin, ii. 345.
Calderon de la Barca, Pedro, *De una
    causa dos efectos*, iii. 336.
    La Dama Duende, iv. 705.
    Magico Prodigioso, v. 1427.
Calendar, Venetian, vi. 257.
*Calendar of State Papers, Domestic
    Series of the Reigns of Edward VI,
    Mary, Elizabeth, and James I
    (1547-1625)*, 12 vols., ed. Robert
    Lemon and M. A. E. Green
    (London, 1856-72), iii. 339, 415 ;
    iv. 606, 641, 670, 671, 873, 874,
    875, 882, 908 ; v. 1288, 1372 ; vii.
    34, 37.
*Calendar of State Papers, Domestic
    Series of the Reign of Charles I
    (1625-49)*, 23 vols., ed. John
    Bruce, W. D. Hamilton, and Mrs.
    S. C. Lomas (London, 1858-97),
    iii. 21, 136, 213-14, 217 ; iv. 540,

548, 549, 637, 737 ; v. 1057, 1158,
    1161, 1176, 1190, 1199, 1227,
    1228, 1229, 1300, 1305, 1404,
    1441, 1442 ; vi. 24, 68, 72 n. 1, 162,
    164, 167, 174, 176, 228, 235, 288,
    307 n. 1, 309 ; vii. 12, 66, 107.
*Calendar of State Papers, Domestic
    Series 1655-6*, ed. Mary Anne
    Everett Green (1882), iv. 728.
*Calendar of State Papers Relating to
    Ireland Preserved in the Public
    Record Office (September 1669-
    December 1670)*, ed. Robert Pent-
    land Mahaffy (1910), iii. 371 ; iv.
    950.
*Calendar of State Papers and
    Manuscripts, Relating to English
    Affairs, Existing in the Archives
    and Collections of Venice, and in
    Other Libraries of Northern Italy
    (1202-1668)*, 35 vols. (in progress),
    ed. Rawdon Brown, G. C. Ben-
    tinck, H. F. Brown, and A. B.
    Hinds (London, 1864-1935), iii.
    107, 217 ; iv. 549, 643, 655, 660,
    661, 664, 666, 673, 674, 842, 874,
    876, 897, 918 ; v. 1155, 1157, 1229,
    1230, 1334 ; vi. 151, 152, 258,
    263, 265 ; vii. 24, 29, 33, 34, 35,
    36, 37, 39, 64, 86, 94.
Calico, vi. 273.
Calico, blue, vi. 273.
Calisto, see Heywood, *The Escapes of
    Jupiter.*
Callidamus et Callanthia, see Stubbe,
    Edmund, *Fraus Honesta.*
Calverley, Sir Richard, vii. 37, 40,
    42, 44, 45, 49.
Calvert, Sir George, vi. 297, 298.
Calvinism, iii. 417.
Camberwell, Surrey, iv. 748, 749.
Cambridge, town of, Cardinals Cap
    Inn, iv. 863.
    Great St. Mary's Church, iv. 533,
    985.
Cambridge University, ii. 491, 537,
    538, 539, 657 n. 4, 688 ; iii. 12,
    25, 38, 105, 131, 160, 183 ; iv.
    498, 528, 529, 539, 551, 554,
    599, 600, 602, 610, 748, 836,
    952, 953, 954, 955 ; v. 961, 963,
    967, 970, 972, 973, 975, 976,
    978, 984, 985, 987, 1007, 1065,
    1066, 1179, 1180, 1181, 1185,
    1190, 1233, 1237, 1259, 1266,
    1267, 1278, 1280, 1298, 1306,
    1329, 1343, 1374, 1388, 1391,
    1407, 1408, 1409, 1443 ; vi. 96,
    295.

Bachelor's Commencement, iii. 11.

Chancellor of, v. 1197.

Colleges, *see under* Christ's College, Clare College, Corpus Christi College, Emmanuel College, Gonville and Caius College, Jesus College, King's College, Magdalen College, Pembroke College, Peterhouse College, Queens' College, St. Catherine's College, St. John's College, Sidney Sussex College, Trinity College.

College saltings, v. 992.

Library, v. 1038, 1039, 1267.

Manuscripts, iv. 600; v. 1173, 1174, 1267, 1269.

M.P. for, v. 1038.

Orator, v. 1197.

Play custom at, iii. 182.

Plays acted at, iii. 159, 160.

Regent House, v. 1197, 1408.

Royal visits to, iii. 159–60, 172, 176–9; iv. 480, 529–30, 532, 535, 954; v. 966–7, 983–5, 1027, 1232, 1238, 1329; vi. 148, 241.

Taxor for, iv. 716; v. 1027.

Tripos, iii. 11.

Vice-Chancellor of, iii. 186; v. 983, 984, 1038.

Cambridge Bibliography of English Literature, 5 vols. (1940–57), iii. 43; iv. 604.

Cambridge History of English Literature, 14 vols. (1907–16), iii. 61; iv. 732; v. 1196, 1297–8.

Cambridge, Parliamentary domination at, iii. 174.

Camby, —, ii. 398.

Camden, William, iv. 606.

Complete History of England, A (1706), vi. 55.

Camels, iv. 894; vi. 212; vii. 48.

Camp (military), vi. 293, 294.

Campaigners, The, see D'Urfey, Thomas.

Campaspe, see John Lyly.

Campbell, James, Lord Mayor, iii. 256.

Campbell, John, *Lives of the Chief Justices of England* (1874), vii. 24.

Campbell, Killis, 'The Source of Davenant's *Albovine*', *J.E.G.P.* iv (1902), iii. 198.

Campbell, Mildred, *The English Yeoman under Elizabeth and the Early Stuarts* (1942), iv. 472, 473.

Campbell, O. J. *Comicall Satyre and Shakespeare's Troilus and Cressida* (1938), iv. 614, 618.

'A Dutch Analogue of *Richard III*', *Shakespeare Studies by Members of the Department of English of the University of Wisconsin* (1916), v. 1014.

Campion, Thomas, ii. 554; v. 1378.

Camps, Goody, iv. 601.

Camus, J. P., *Iphigene*, v. 1209.

Canada, v. 1231.

Canada, Commissioners for, iii. 21.

Canbury, vi. 300, 301.

Cancer, see Anonymous.

Candelabra, vi. 218.

Candia Restaurata, see Fane, Mildmay.

Candlelight, *see* Theatres.

Candlemas, vi. 265.

Candlesticks, v. 1235, 1300; vi. 167.

Candy Restored, see Fane, Mildmay, *Candia Restaurata*.

Cane, Andrew, i. 65 n. 2, 147 and n. 1, 148 and n. 5, 149, 152, 153, 155, 183, 184, 187, 192, 219, 263, 269, 275, 295, 302, 303 n. 1, 307, 308, 309, 311, 312 and n. 7 cont., 314 and n. 4, 315, 317 and n. 2, 321, 323; ii. 398–401, 691; iii. 189; iv. 571; v. 1441, 1442; vi. 59, 98, 117, 158, 170, 171, 172, 227, 228, 232, 240.

Cane, Mary, ii. 399.

Cane, Thomas, ii. 399.

Canopy, iv. 664.

Canterbury, Archbishop of, i. 16 n. 6, 38, 122, 327; ii. 545, 654 n. 2 cont.; iii. 455; iv. 619, 721; v. 1300; vi. 4; vii. 4.

Canterbury Guests, The, see Ravenscroft.

Canterbury His Change of Diet, see Anonymous.

Canterbury, Kent, i. 92, 213, 275, 276; ii. 420; iv. 514, 958; vi. 164.

Mayor of, vi. 164.

Prerogative Court of, iv. 600.

Canvas, vi. 257.

Caparisons, rich, vi. 293.

Capello, Bianca, iv. 907.

Capital investments, vi. 295.

Capon, John, ii. 401.

Caps, iii. 436.

Captain, The, see Beaumont and Fletcher.

Captain Underwit, see Cavendish, William, *The County Captain*.

Captives, or the Lost Recovered, The, see Heywood.

Captives, The, see Manuche, Cosmo.

Capuchins, i. 329; vi. 69.

Cardenio, see Fletcher, John.

Cardiff, Glamorganshire, iv. 757.

Cardiff Public Library, iii. 249, 267; v. 1435.

Cardinal, The, see Shirley, James.

Cardinal's Conspiracy, The, see Anonymous.

Careless Shepherdess, The, see Goffe.

Carew, Sir Matthew, iii. 104, 105.

Carew, Thomas, i. 26, 224, 225, 228; iii. 104–11; iv. 499, 695, 830, 836; v. 1222, 1230.

Coelum Britannicum, ii. 676; iii. 105, 106–10; v. 1158, 1450; vi. 264.

Commendatory verses for Davenant's *Just Italian*, vi. 63, 242.

'Epilogue, The', iii. 111.

'Foure Songs by way of *Chorus* to a play, at an entertainment of the King and Queene, by my Lord Chamberlaine', iii. 110.

'*In answer of an Elegiacall Letter upon the death of the King of Sweden from Aurelian Townsend, inviting me to write on that subject*', iv. 920; v. 1230.

Poems (1640), iii. 106, 110; v. 1076.

'The prologue', iii. 111.

'Rapture', v. 1381.

'*Songs in the Play*', iii. 110.

Unknown Play, iii. 110–11.

Verses by, iii. 205.

Carey, Lucius, Viscount Falkland, iii. 108.

Carey, Patrick, *Trivial Poems and Triolets . . . By Patrick Carey 20th Aug.* (1651), iv. 920.

Carey, Robert, Lord, iv. 658.

Cariclia, see Anonymous.

Carisbrook, Isle of Wight, ii. 673.

Carl H. Pforzheimer Library, iv. 493.

Carlell, Lodowick, ii. 676; iii. 111–24; iv. 887; v. 1314; vi. 38.

Influence of, iv. 492.

Arviragus and Felicia, I and II, i. 48, 51, 98, 99 n. s, 116; iii. 63, 112, 113–15, 118, 121, 123, 212; vi. 35.

Deserving Favourite, The, i. 84–85, 116, 117 n. 1; ii. 375, 477, 479, 480, 502, 552, 569, 571, 575, 585, 594, 600, 692; iii. 112, 115–17, 118, 120, 121, 124; iv. 727, 747, 816; v. 1165.

Fool Would Be a Favourite, The, i. 116, 117, 250; iii. 112, 117–18; 122.

Heraclius, Emperor of the East, iii. 118–19.

Osmond, the Great Turk, or The Noble Servant, i. 103, 116–17, 250; iii. 112, 117, 118, 119–22; iv. 492, 865; v. 1215, 1385.

Passionate Lovers, The, I and II, i. 66, 99, 100, 117; ii. 446, 447; iii. 68, 112, 118, 121, 122–3, 457; vi. 283.

Spartan Ladies, The, i. 39, 117 and n. 1, 123; ii. 676, 681; iii. 98, 112, 117, 118, 121, 124.

Two Fools well met, iii. 118.

Two New Plays, iii. 117.

Carlell, Robert (Laird of Brydekirk), iii. 111.

Carleton, Lady Alice, vi. 182.

Carleton, Sir Dudley, i. 6, 10 nn. 2 and 3, 16 n. 6, 140, 141; ii. 349, 396; iii. 105, 160, 415; iv. 528–9, 549, 591, 641, 643, 645, 646, 647, 650, 655, 656, 658, 660, 661, 669, 670, 671, 673, 674, 677, 841, 842, 873, 874, 875, 894, 922; v. 1288, 1289, 1372, 1377, 1404, 1422; vi. 4, 20, 55, 153, 211, 256, 258, 259, 261.

Carleton, Thomas (alias Medcalf), iii. 125.

Actio . . . de Henrico 8°, iii. 125.

Tragaedia de Emma Angliae Regina ac Matre Hardi-Canuti Regis, iii. 125.

Fatum Vortigerni Seu miserabilis vita et exitus Vortigerni regis Britanniae una complectens aduentum Saxonum siue Anglorum in Britanniam, iii. 125.

Carleton, Bedfordshire, iii. 303.

Carlisle, Dean of (Dr. Comber), v. 985.

Carlisle, Earl of, ii. 349.

Carlisle, James, *The Fortune Hunters, or, Two Fools Well Met*, iii. 118.

Carlisle, Lady, iii. 217.

Carlisle, Thomas, iv. 954.

Carlos, Don, iv. 662.

Carlton by Snaith, Yorkshire, v. 1186.

Carlyle, E. I., v. 1053.

Carlyle, Thomas, *Letters and Speeches of Oliver Cromwell*, ed. S. C. Lomas (1904), vi. 284 n. 1.

Carmathen, Marquis of, iii. 395.

Carmelite monastery, vi. 115, 116.
Carnarvon, Lady, masquer, iii. 213.
Carnarvon, Robert, Earl of, iv. 802;
v. 1190, 1218.
Carnival season, vi. 283.
Carolus Redux (1623), iv. 540, 547.
Caron, Ambassador, iv. 664.
Carpenter, Anne, ii. 402.
Carpenter, Elizabeth, ii. 402.
Carpenter, Francesse, ii. 402.
Carpenter, Robert, ii. 401.
Carpenter, William, i. 176, 203 and
n. 3, 208, 209, 210, 211; ii. 401–2,
682; iv. 881.
Carpenters, i. 143; ii. 358, 482, 499;
iii. 9; vi. 91, 125, 139, 140, 141,
155, 201, 260, 262, 263, 272, 273,
277, 279.
Carpenters, boss of, vi. 262.
Carr, John, i. 298; ii. 384, 402.
Carr, Lord, v. 1360.
Carr, Robert, Earl of Somerset, iv.
902, 1090.
Carrier, ii. 486.
Carrier inns, vi. 122, 124.
Cart, John, iii. 101, 126.
The Cunning Age, iii. 126.
Carter, Albert Howard, ed., *James
Shirley's The Maid's Revenge,
edited from the Quarto of 1639, with
introduction and notes.* Unpub-
lished U. of Chicago Thesis
(1940), v. 1132, 1133, 1134.
Carter, John Stewart, ed., *James
Shirley's The Traitor. Edited from
the Quarto of 1635, with introduc-
tion and notes.* Unpublished U. of
Chicago Thesis (1941), v. 1150,
1152.
Carter Lane, *see* London, streets of.
Carteret, Sir Philip, v. 1130.
Cartis Mundi, see Brewer, *The
Lovesick King.*
Cartwright, Ann, ii. 404.
Cartwright, Jane, ii. 403.
Cartwright, Katherine, ii. 404.
Cartwright, Samuel, v. 1038.
Cartwright, William, Senior, actor,
i. 136, 137, 138, 140, 142, 147, 148,
152, 153, 155, 261 and n. 3, 262
and n. 4, 263 and n. 1, 269, 275,
277, 281, 285, 286, 287, 288, 289
n. 4 cont., 290, 297; ii. 402–4,
682; iii. 13, 14; v. 1003; vi. 150,
158, 164, 165.
Cartwright, William, Junior, actor,
i. 286, 297; ii. 404–5; iii. 314, 409;
iv. 493, 554; v. 1248, 1332, 1367.
Actor's Vindication, The, ii. 405.

Cartwright, William, dramatist, iii.
72, 126–42, 435; iv. 499, 843,
965, 1188.
*Comedies, Tragi-Comedies, With
other Poems, By Mr William
Cartwright,* late Student of
Christ Church in Oxford, and
Proctor of the University . . .
(1651), iii. 47, 72, 127, 131, 134,
135, 278; iv. 844; v. 1186.
'Com O Com I brooke noe
staye', song, iii. 134.
Lady Errant, The, iii. 128–32.
*Ordinary, The, or The City
Cozener,* iii. 132–4; iv. 483.
Persian Slave, The, see *The Royal
Slave.*
Royal Slave, The, i. 51, 52, 53 and
n. 1, 58 n. 3, 98, 99 n. u, 117;
iii. 62, 130, 134–41; iv. 503,
628, 770, 849; v. 1189, 1192,
1195, 1261, 1262, 1263; vi. 38,
281, 306.
Siege, The, or Love's Convert, iii.
127, 128, 141–2.
'Cartwrights Poems and Plays', *see*
Anonymous.
Carver, James, i. 265; ii. 432; vi.
160.
Carver, John Linton, 'The Valiant
Scot, By "J. W."' in Allison
Gaw, *Studies in English Drama,*
First Series (1917), v. 1233, 1234,
1236.
Carver, William, i. 15, 73–89; ii.
405.
Carvers, vi. 271, 272.
Carwidgeon, The, see Anonymous.
Cary, Elizabeth, Lady, *Mariam,* vii.
110, 114.
Cary, Henry, *The Marriage Night,*
iv. 866.
Cary, John, Viscount Rochford, v.
1002, 1003.
Cary, Lucius, *see* Falkland, Viscount.
Case is Altered, The, see Jonson,
Ben.
Cashe, Katherine, alias Nurse,
alias Hutchenson, ii. 365.
Casse, Robert, ii. 406.
Cassington, Oxfordshire, iv. 845.
*Cast over the Water . . . given gratis to
W. Fennor, the Rimer from
London to the King's Bench* (1615),
see Taylor, John.
Castara, see Habington, William, v.
1301.
Castara, or Cruelty without Hate, see
Anonymous.

Castelain, Maurice, *Ben Jonson: l'homme et l'œuvre, 1572–1637* (1907), iv. 604, 614, 618, 622, 636.
Castigo del penséque, El, see Tirso de Molina.
Castile, Don Pedro, King of, v. 1322.
Casting, v. 1252.
Castle, Hester, ii. 405.
Castle, Nicholas, ii. 405.
Castle, Thomas, ii. 405.
Castle Ashby, Northamptonshire, i. 310; iv. 728, 729, 730, 731, 732.
Castle Ashby manuscripts, iv. 728, 729, 730, 731, 732.
Castle Howard Manuscript, iv. 698.
Castleknock, near Dublin, iii. 96.
Castlemaine, Lady, v. 1079.
Castlemartyr, Ireland, iii. 33.
Castleton, John, ii. 522.
Castro, Guillen de, *La Fuerza de la Costumbre,* iii. 366.
Casts, iii. 6, 100, 116, 161, 164, 232–4, 293, 295, 296, 312, 314, 325, 326, 330, 341, 344, 346, 352, 353, 355, 357, 363, 372, 375, 379, 393, 396, 399, 403, 413, 420, 423, 424, 427, 428, 432; iv. 526, 527, 530, 536, 539, 570, 596, 601, 609, 686, 710, 746, 747, 810, 813–14, 816–17, 853, 854, 881, 920, 935, 954, 955; v. 1002, 1003, 1028, 1131, 1141, 1149, 1154, 1165, 1173, 1174, 1197, 1233, 1237, 1238, 1252, 1258, 1261, 1274, 1290, 1298, 1299, 1230.
Casts, double, v. 1252.
Casts, erroneous, iii. 423–4.
Casts in the Beaumont and Fletcher Folio of 1679, iii. 326.
Catalogue of Letters and Other Historical Documents Exhibited at Welbeck, A (1903), *see* Strong, Sandford A.
Catalogue of the Manuscripts and Muniments of Alleyn's College of God's Gift at Dulwich (1881), *see* Warner, George Frederick.
Catchpole, The, see Anonymous, *The Roaring Girl.*
Catherine of Braganza, Queen of Charles II, iii. 320, 344, 395, 403.
Catholic, English, iii. 290.
Catholicism, i. 329; ii. 454; v. 1320.
Catholicism, conversion from, v. 1186.
Catholicism, conversion to, iv. 608, 916; v. 1067–8, 1172; vi. 69.
Catholicism, in theatrical circles, vi. 94.

Catholics, iv. 517, 520, 521, 695, 751, 872, 878; v. 1067, 1068, 1392; vi. 99.
Catholics (Jonson, Ben), iv. 608.
Catilina Triumphans, see Anonymous.
Catiline His Conspiracy, see Jonson, Ben.
Cato, iv. 717.
Catterick, Yorkshire, iii. 39.
Caue, Andrew, *see* Cane, Andrew.
Caulton, Richard, ii. 564.
Caussin, Nicholas, *The Holy Court, or The Christian Institution of Men of Quality,* tr. Sir Thomas Hawkins (1626), iv. 821.
Cavalier Drama (1936), *see* Harbage, Alfred.
Cavalier drama, iii. 23–25, 52, 62, 77, 112–24, 195; iv. 523, 598, 917–21.
Cavalier dramatists, v. 1198.
Cavalier taste, ii. 681.
Cavaliers, iv. 537.
Cavanaugh, Sister M. Jean Carmel (ed.), *Technogamia: or the Marriages of the Arts, a Critical Edition* (1942), iii. 100; iv. 587, 588, 589, 590, 596; vi. 241.
Cave, Lady, v. 1289.
Cavendish, Sir Charles, iii. 142; iv. 640.
Cavendish, Margaret, iii. 142, 144; iv. 654.
Cavendish, William, Earl, Marquis and Duke of Newcastle, ii. 512; iii. 63, 142–51, 196, 454, 455; iv. 485, 612, 615, 640, 645, 648, 649, 653, 654; v. 1070, 1072; vi. 122.
Country Captain, The (Captain Underwit), i. 66, 118; ii. 343, 344; iii. 145–8, 149, 150; iv. 767; v. 1101, 1128.
Dedication to, iii. 88, 89, 226.
French Dancing Master, The, iii. 150, 151.
Humorous Lovers, The, iii. 148.
Humours, The, of M. Galliard, iii. 151.
Pleasant and Merry Humour of a Rogue, A, iii. 148–9.
Triumphant Widow, The, or The Medley of Humours, iii. 149.
Variety, The, i. 118; iii. 55, 146, 149–51; iv. 828.
Cavendish, William, and John Dryden, *Sir Martin Mar-All, or The Feigned Innocence,* iii. 149.
Cawston, Norfolk, iii. 238.

Cayet, P. V. P., *Chronologie Septenaire* (1605), iv. 763.
Cayworth, John, iii. **151–2**.
  Enchiridion Christiados, iii. **151–2**.
Cecil, Diana, daughter of Lord Burghley, iv. 673.
Cecil, Sir Robert, v. 1226.
Cecil, William, 2nd Earl of Salisbury, vii. 48.
Cecil, William, Lord Burghley, iv. 673.
Cecil Papers, *see Hist. MSS. Comm.*
Celestial Publican, The, see Richards Nathanael.
Cenci (the story), iv. 822.
Censored MSS., iii. 416.
Censored plays, *see* Plays, censored.
Censorship, i. 7, 60, 277–8, 332–4; iii. 123, 196–7, 222, 265–6, 327, 415, 416; iv. 769; v. 1272, 1279.
  Evasion of, i. 14.
  Overruled, i. 103, 106–7.
Centlivre, Susanna, *The Beau's Duel; or A Soldier for the Ladies*, iv. 850.
  Stolen Heiress, The, iv. 837.
Cephalus et Procris, see Crowther, Joseph.
Ceremonies of the Church, vi. 167.
Ceriziers, René de, iv. 726.
Certayne tragedie entituled Freewyl, wrytten first in Italian, A, see Cheeke, H.
Certificate of privilege, *see* Tickets of privilege.
Cervantes, Saavedra, Miguel de, iv. 727; v. 1322–33.
  Don Quixote, iii. **228**, 313, 393; iv. 593, 813; v. 1113.
  El Amante liberal, iv. 828.
  'El Caloso Estermeno', iv. 785.
  El Casamiento Engañoso, iii. 410.
  'El Viejo Celoso', iv. 785.
  La Fuerza de la Sangre, iii. 316, 400; iv. 895.
  La Gitanilla, iii. 316; iv. 895.
  La Ilustre Fregona, iii. 339.
  La Senora Cornelia, iii. 321.
  Las dos doncellas, iii. 367.
  Los Baños de Argel, iv. 813.
  Novelas Exemplares (1613), iii. 321, 339, 350, 367, 400, 410; iv. 895.
  Persiles y Sigismunda, iii. 325, 326.
Cespedes y Meneses, Gonzalo de, *Poema trágico del Español Gerardo*, iii. 420.
Chabot, Admiral of France, see Shirley.

Chafin, Francis, Second Butler, v. 1156.
Chain of Golden Poems, A, see Cokayne, Sir Aston.
Challenge at Tilt, A, see Jonson, Ben.
Challenge for Beauty, A, see Heywood.
Challoner, Jacob, iv. 897.
Chalmers, George, iii. 321, 357; iv. 561, 634, 644, 746, 798, 806, 812, 823, 839; v. 1013, 1014, 1074, 1076, 1095, 1138, 1291, 1322, 1325, 1328; vi. 164 n. 1, 173, 196.
  Apology for the Believers in the Shakespeare-Papers, An (1797), iii. 273, 286; iv. 906.
  Supplemental Apology for the Believers in the Shakespeare-Papers, A (1799), iii. 31, 32, 36, 37, 69, 240, 253, 328, 369; iv. 519, 678, 888, 889; v. 1046, 1047, 1075, 1324; vi. **194** and n. 4, 195, 291 n. 1, 308.
Chamber Accounts (Cook & Wilson, eds.), vi. 258, 259.
Chamberlain of the City of London, *see* London, City of, Chamberlain.
Chamberlain, John, The Letters of, 2 vols., ed. Norman Egbert McClure (1939).
Chamberlain, John, i. 3, 6, 10 n. 3, 16 n. 6, 136, 141, 149, 161, 162, 163; ii. 349, 396; iii. 160; iv. 528–9, 530, 549, 591, 641, 643, 645, 646, 647, 650, 655, 656, 657, 658, 660, 661, 663, 669, 670, 671, 673, 674, 675, 676, 677, 841, 842, 843, 875, 894; v. 1247, 1289, 1377, 1404, 1422; vi. 4, 20, 55, 57, 127, 144, 149, 153, 179 n. 1, 181, 182, 183, 211, 256, 258, 259, 260, 261, 269; vii. 216–59 *passim*.
Chamberlain, Lord, *see* Lord Chamberlain.
Chamberlain, Richard, iii. 152.
Chamberlain, Robert, iii. **152–4**; iv. 928, 939; v. 997, 998, 1216.
  'Balaam's Asse Cudgeld', iii. 153.
  Choice Banquet of Witty Jests, A, iii. 224.
  Conceits, Clinches, Flashes and Whimzies Newly Studied (1639), iii. 152, 224; iv. 932.
  Jocabella, or a Cabinet of Mistakes (1640), iii. 152, 153, 224; iv. 932.
  New Book of Mistakes, A (1637), iii. 152.

Chamberlain, Robert (*cont.*)
  Nocturnal Lucubrations (1638), iii.
    152.
  Swaggering Damsel, iii. 153–4; v.
    995.
  Verses by, iii. 55.
  Whimzies (1639), v. 995.
Chamberlaine, William, iii. **154–5**.
  England's Jubilee (1660), iii. 154.
  Love's Victory, iii. **154–5**; v. 1368.
  Pharonnida (1659), iii. 154; iv.
    815.
Chambermaid Turned Quaker, The,
  see B., T., *The County Girl*.
Chambers, Sir Edmund K., iii.
  321; v. 1246; vi. 20.
  *Aurelian Townshend's Poems and
    Masques* (1912), v. 1226, 1227,
    1229.
  'Date of Fletcher's "The
    Chances"', The', *M.L.R.* iv.
    (1909), and v (1910), iii.
    319.
  'Dramatic Records: The Lord
    Chamberlain's Office', see Bos-
    well, Eleanore.
  Ed. of *The Chances Variorum*
    (1904–12), iii. 318, 321.
  Ed. of *Laws of Candy Variorum*
    (1904–12), iii. 354, 355, 356.
  Elizabethan Stage, The, 4 vols.
    (1923), i–v, *passim*; vi. 3, 5, 7,
    9, 12 n. 1, 77, 106, 115, 121, 131,
    132, 133, 139, 140–1, 149,
    179 n. 1, 186, 191, 197, 200 and
    n. 1, 202 n, 205, 214, 217, 247,
    249, 250, 251 n. 1, 252, 255,
    267; vii. 1, 11.
  'Elizabethan Stage Gleanings',
    R.E.S. i (1925), vi. 134 n. 1.
  Review of Frank Marcham, *The
    King's Office of the Revels,
    1610–1623*, *R.E.S.* i (1925), iii.
    340, 352; iv. 867, 883, 890; v.
    1019, 1128, 1296, 1308, 1331,
    1350, 1352, 1406, 1421, 1426.
  *William Shakespeare: A Study of
    the Facts and Problems* 2 vols.
    (1930), iii. 302, 318, 342, 370,
    422; iv. 827; v. 1104, 1421; vi.
    16 n. 1, 180 n. 2; vii. 71, 79.
  and W. W. Greg, eds., *Dramatic
    Records from the Privy Council
    Register* (1911), iii. 382; v.
    1371.
Chambers, William, i. 15, 72–88; ii.
  406.
Chancellor, Ellen, ii. 476.
Chancery Bill, vii. 11.

Chancery, Court of, *see* Court of
  Chancery.
Chancery hand, v. 1267.
Chancery Lane, *see* London, streets
  and districts.
Chancery records, i. 158.
Chancery suit, i. 56, 205 n. 3.
Chancery Town Depositions, vi. 124.
Chances, The, see Fletcher.
Chandler, ii. 479, 564, 565, 615.
Chandler, Frank W., *The Literature
  of Roguery* (1907), iv. 745.
Change, The, see Fane, Mildmay.
Changeling, The, see Middleton.
Changes, or Love in a Maze, see
  Shirley.
Channen, Luke, v. 1103.
Chapel Court, *see* Whitehall Palace.
Chaplain to Queen Elizabeth, iii.
  306.
Chapman, George, ii. 557; iii. 58, 59,
  155–8, 308; iv. 475, 490, 491,
  493, 510, 608, 609, 617, 622,
  634, 865; v. 1018, 1077, 1088–
  90, 1287, 1387, 1428.
  All Fools, iii. 156.
  Alphonsus, Emperor of Germany,
    see Anonymous.
  Ball, The, see Shirley.
  Blind Beggar of Alexandria, iii.
    155, 156.
  Bussy D'Ambois, i. 95 n. c, 97, 99,
    118; ii. 383, 436, 489, 585, 597;
    iii. 156; vii. 126.
  Chabot, Admiral of France, see
    Shirley.
  *Charlemagne, or The Distracted
    Emperor*, iii. 156.
  *Conspiracy and Tragedy of Charles
    Duke of Byron, The*, i. 118; iii.
    156; v. 1420; vii. 60.
  Eastward Ho!, iii. 157.
  *Fatal Love, The, A French
    Tragedy*, iii. 157.
  *Fount of New Fashions, The, or
    The Isle of Women*, iii. 157.
  Gentleman Usher, The, iii. 157.
  Hero and Leander, iv. 818.
  Humorous Day's Mirth, An, iii.
    157.
  May Day, iii. 157.
  *Middle Temple and Lincoln's Inn
    Masque, The*, iii. 157.
  Monsieur D'Olive, iii. 157.
  'Pastoral tragedy, A', iii. 157.
  Revenge for Honour, see Glap-
    thorne.
  Revenge of Bussy D'Ambois, The,
    iii. 157; vii. 46.

Shadow of Night, The, iii. 155.
Sir Giles Goosecap, iii. 157.
Tragedy of a Yorkshire Gentlewoman and Her Son, A, iii. 158.
Wars of Pompey and Caesar, The, i. 118; iii. 158; vii. 79, 80.
Widow's Tears, The, i. 117, 118; iii. 158; iv. 807; v. 1316.
Will of a Woman, The, iii. 158.
Chapman, Henry, i. 317 n. 2.
Thermae Redivivae: the City of Bath Described (1673), ii. 401; vi. 171.
Chapman, Lawrence, stationer, iii. 102.
Chappell, John, iii. 158–60.
Susenbrotus or Fortunia, iii. 37, 159–60.
Chappell, Mr., v. 1298.
Chappell, William, ed., *The Roxburghe Ballads* (1880), v. 1045.
Chapter House, Westminster, vi. 117 n. 1.
'Character of a Common Player', *see* Stephens, John.
Character of a Country Committeeman (1649), *see* Cleveland, John.
Character of an Oxford Incendiary, The, see Anonymous.
Character-writing, iii. 226, 228, 240, 258–9, 273, 304.
Character, change of name, iv. 779.
CHARACTERS, vi. 218; Abbot, iii. 467; Abdomen, iv. 1374; Abner, iii. 95; Abraham, v. 1284; vi. 114; Abstemia, iii. 228; Acanthe, iv. 810; Achmea, v. 1451; Admiral Auria, iv. 486; Adurni, iv. 486; Ægidius, v. 1261; Ægon, iii. 41; Ælius, iv. 817; Aemilia, iv. 744; Æsopus, iv. 817; Ætius, v. 1036; Aga, iv. 814; Agatha, iv. 890; Agnostus, iii. 1; iv, 866; Agrippina, iv. 838; Agurtes, iv. 748; vi. 291; Albertus Monachus, v. 1298; Albion, Lady, iv. 957, 958; Alcidonus, v. 1274; Alcinus, iv. 1195; Alcmena, iv. 567; Ale, v. 1444; Alexis, iv. 759; v. 1283, 1284; Alexius Commenus, iii. 27; Alexius Protosebastus, iii. 27; Alice, iv. 759; v. 1283, 1284; Alinda, iii. 393; Alkin Ethra, iv. 620, 621; Allucius, v. 1400; Almanac, Dr., v. 1042; Almanac-makers, iv. 939; Almanacke, Doctor, iv. 881; Almira, iii. 169; iv. 827; Alonzo, iii. 260; iv. 854; Alphonso, iii. 424; Alumna Pro-

cridus, iii. 184; Alvarez, iv. 894; Amaranta, iii. 420; Ambition, iii. 296; Amboyna, iii. 338; Aminta, iii. 377; Amintas, v. 1284; Amilcar, iv. 764; Amphilucke, v. 1159; Amurath, iv. 506; Ananias, iii. 211; Andrea, iii. 86; Andronicus Commenus, iii. 27; Angelina, iii. 334; Angoleans, iii. 94, 95; Angelo Milanes, iii. 421; Anoetus, iii. 4; Anthony, v. 1284; Antiochus, iv. 764; Antissius, Prince, v. 1139; Antonio, iii. 169; v. 1020, 1133, 1428; Antonio of Ragusa, iv. 760; Antoninus, v. 1291; Apollo, iii. 16; Apothecary, iii. 274; Appius, v. 1248; Apuleius, iv. 581, 582; Archas, iii. 371; Aretina, v. 1127; Argus, iv. 574; Arismena, iv. 502; Aristippus, iv. 515; Armellina, vi. 148, 241; Arminadab, Mr., iv. 803; Armissus, v. 1453; Arterio, v. 1374; Artesio, Dr., iv. 957, 958, 959; Artops, iv. 846; Asambeg, iv. 813; Ascanio, iii. 420; Asdrubal, iv. 764; Asperina, iv. 854; Astolpho, iii. 263; Astrae, iii. 29; Atherball, iii. 38; Atropos, iii. 29; Aubrey, iii. 406; Audax, v. 1193; Aulicus, iii. 160; Aurelio, iv. 741; Aurora, iii. 184; Auster, v. 1452; Author, iv. 743; Autolycus, v. 976; Autumn, iii. 296.

Bacchus, iii. 296; Bagous the Brachman, v. 1345; Balia, v. 1298; Balneola, v. 1452; Baltazar, iii. 260; Barabas, v. 1251; Barber, iii. 443; Bargandell, v. 1345; Bargello, v. 1298; Barnavelt, iii. 301; Bartolus, iii. 420; Bashaw Alcade, iv. 570; Bashaws, v. 1215; Bassanes, iii. 440; Bateman v. 1045; Beaumelle, vi. 10; Beaupré, iii. 358; Beauty, iii. 296; Becanus, Martinus, v. 1401; Beer, v. 1444; Belfare, Sir John, iii. 232; Bellamente, v. 1130; Bellamia, v. 1109; Bellamie, iv. 941; Bellamina, vi. 108; Belleur, iii. 428; Bellows-mender, iv. 667; Belly, v. 1306; Belvidere, iii. 432; Benhadad, v. 1363; Berecinthius, iv. 764; Berinthia, v. 1133; Berosus, iii. 95; Bess, iv. 570; Bettie, iii. 90; Bianca, iii. 452; Bird, v. 987; vi. 95–96; Black Bishop, iv. 878; Black Dog, iii. 270; Black Duke, iv. 878;

CHARACTERS (cont.)
Black Knight, iv. 877, 878;
Black Queen, iv. 878; Blinkes, v.
1284; Bloody-Bones, iv. 741;
Bolt, vi. 110; Bonamico, v. 1354,
1401; Bonus Genius, vi. 108;
Boote, v. 1295; Bornwell, Lady,
v. 1078; Bornwell, Sir Thomas,
v. 1078, 1127; BotiJa, v. 1437;
Bounc-bigge, v. 1343; Bravo, iv.
740; Bread, v. 1306; Bredero,
iii. 301; Bridges, Bess, iii. 6;
British Captain, v. 1359; Brito-
mart, v. 1360; Broker, iii. 274;
Brutus, iv. 741; Bubble, iii. 151;
Buckingham, iv. 769; Bumb-
crack, v. 1343; Burbon, iv. 546;
Busie, iv. 497; Bustopha, iii. 380;
Byad, v. 1159.
    Cacofogo, iii. 409, 411;
Cæcilius, v. 1261; Caenis, iv. 817;
Calibeus, iii. 121; Calista, iii. 362;
Calisto, iv. 567; Calistus, iv. 764;
Callias, iv. 846–7; Callidamus, v.
1195; Calphurnius, iii. 38;
Calumny, iv. 686; Camiola, iv.
791, 797; Cantabrigia, iii. 160;
Capiaga, iv. 814; Captain, iv. 702,
703, 704; Captain Blade, iii. 179,
245; Captain Penniless, iv. 686;
Captain Porpuss, iv. 744; Cap-
tain Whibble, iv. 744; Carazie,
iv. 813; Cardenes, iv. 827;
Cardenio, iv. 827; Cardinal, vi.
167; Careless, iv. 487, 705, 744;
Carionil, iii. 169; Carlo, iii. 260;
Catsbeius, v. 1177; Carolo, v. 1009;
Carpinius, v. 1298; Carrot man,
v. 1159; Carthalo, iv. 764; Case,
v. 1159; Cassius, v. 1153;
Castruccio, iii. 201, 331; iv. 793;
Cataloche, iv. 866; Caunus, v.
988; Cavendish, iii. 296; Cepha-
lon, iii. 95; Cephalus, iii. 184;
Ceres, iii. 296; v. 1266; Cethegus,
v. 1153; Chærinus, v. 1374;
Changeling, iii. 151; iv. 504, 862,
863, 864, 894; vi. 111; Charalois,
vi. 10; Charia, v. 1453; Chariana,
v. 1130; Chariclea, iii. 269; iv.
515; v. 1439; Charilaus, iv. 729;
Charinda, iii. 184; Charitus, iii.
130; Charles, iii. 334; Charon, iii.
29; Chaugh, Mr., iv. 867, 868,
869; Chloris, v. 1453; Chorus, iv.
853; Chorus Catholicorum, v.
1177; Chorus of bards, iii. 304;
Chorus Protestantium, v. 1177;
Chrisea, iv. 486; Christmas, iv.
639; v. 1041; Chronomastix, v.
1341; Chrysalus, iv. 764;
Cicelie, iv. 624; Ciprian v.
1427; Cis, iv. 624; Citizen, iii.
448; Claracilla, iv. 699; Clarange,
iii. 361; Clarindore, iv. 807;
Clarion, iv. 627; Claritia, v. 1298;
Claudiana, v. 1113; Clause, iii.
151, 314; Cleander, iii. 362; iv.
693; Clem, iv. 570; Clemens,
Aretinus, iv. 817; Cleora, iv. 767;
Cleremont. iii. 357, 358, 359; v.
1380; Cleta, v. 1451; Clock-
Keeper, iv. 667; Clod, v. 1271;
Clotho, iii. 29; Clown, iii. 228; iv.
713, 714; Clutch, iv. 686; Cnemon,
v. 1439; Cokes, iii. 300; Cola, iii.
95; Colbrand, v. 1347; Colonel,
iii. 215; Colonel Cutter, iii. 179;
Colonel   Iniquo   Vitruvius,
iv. 654; Colonel Jolly, iii.
179; Columella, v. 1262;
Comastes, v. 1261; Cometa, v.
1452; Commenus, iii. 27; Com-
munis sensus, v. 1374; Comus, iv.
672; Concupiscence, v. 1193;
Confidence, v. 1159; Conscience,
v. 1126; Constant, iv. 702;
Constantia, v. 1298; Constella-
tions, v. 1159; Cook, iii. 404, 662;
v. 1306; Cook, Sir Edward, v.
1425; Coquæus, Leonardus, v.
1401; Coriolanus, iii. 41; Cornari,
v. 1113; Corn-cutter, iv. 667;
Cornego, iii. 260; Cornelia, iv.
764; Corsica, iv. 810; Corydon,
iv. 581; Cosmeta, iii. 130;
Cotys, v. 1451; Count Coell, v.
1452; Country man, v. 1159;
Countrywoman, v. 1363; Court-
wit, iii. 64; Crack, iii. 61;
Crackby, iv. 484; Cranke, v.
1284; Cratander, iii. 137; Creado,
v. 1437; Credit, iv. 686; Critic,
iv. 743; Critus, v. 1284; Crobus
servus, v. 1298; Crow, v. 1159;
Cuddy Banks, iii. 270, 271;
Culinaris, v. 1452; Cupid, iv. 506,
580, 581, 638, 639, 684, 739, 740;
v. 1102, 1369; Cupido, iii. 29;
Curtleax, v. 1402; Cushion, v.
1306; Cutter, iii. 177, 179;
Cymbeline, v. 1144.
    Damalis, iii. 184; Dame Flavia,
iii. 296; Damplay, iv. 620;
vi. 11; Danae, iv. 567;
Dancer, v. 1159; Dancing
Master, v. 1079; Dasher, vi. 53;
Death, v. 1102; DeFlores, iv.

862, 864; De-Gard, iii. 428; Delphia, iii. 397; Demetrius, iii. 346; iv. 764; Democritus, iii. 45, 46; Denmark House, iv. 908; Devil, iii. 344; iv. 695, 713; vi. 152, 171, 243; Devonshire Merchant, v. 1319; Diana, iii. 184; iv. 676; v. 1257, 1258; Diaphanous Silkworm, iv. 620; Dic, v. 1284; Diche, v. 1159; Didimus, v. 1097, 1098; Diego the Sexton, iii. 419; Dinant, iii. 358; Dioclesian, iii. 266, 397; Dionysia, v. 1021; Dissimulation, iii. 296; Ditty, v. 1365; Doctor, iii. 63; Doctor Almanack, vi. 56; Dogrel, iii. 179; Domingilla, v. 1437; Domitia, iv. 817; Domitianus Caesar, iv. 817; Domitilla, iv. 817; Don Henrique, iii. 420; Don John, iii. 169; Don Leon, iii. 409; Don Pedro, King of Spain, iv. 795; Don Quixote, ii. 541; Dondolo, iv. 890; v. 1354, 1400; Donusa, iv. 814; Dora, iii. 95; Dorcas, iii. 90; Dorea, iv. 486; Dorinda, iv. 854; Dorothea, iii. 228; Dorothy, v. 1358; Dotario, iv. 744; Dotterel, iv. 840; v. 1159; Drake, iii. 296; Druid, v. 1359; Duchess, v. 1087, 1452; Duchess of Suffolk, iii. 285; Duke, iii. 383, 452; iv. 740; v. 1418; Duke of Drown'd-land, iv. 615, 616; Duke of Helicon, iv. 551; Duke of Macada, v. 1319; Duke of Mantua, iii. 49; v. 1125; Dulcino, v. 1115; Dumane, iv. 546; Dungworth, vi. 53 n. 1; Durham, Bishop of, iii. 455.

Earine, iv. 626; Edmond, iii. 267; Effre, iv. 471–2; Egyptians, v. 1231; Eldred, iii. 267; v. 1452; Ellaenus, v. 1453; Emperick, iv. 780; Emperor Claudius, v. 1004; Emperor Constans, v. 1406; Encephalus, v. 1374; Enchantress, iv. 620; Epilogus, v. 1295; Erf, v. 1271; Erminia, v. 1298; Estiphania, iii. 409, 410; Ethel, v. 1452; Ethra, Alkin, iv. 620; Etiocles, iv. 511; Eubella, v. 1131; Eubulus, iv. 810; Eucharis, v. 1400; Eumela, iii. 130; Eumetis senex, iii. 184; Eumorphe, iv. 506; Eunomia, v. 1159; Eupathus, iii. 1; iv. 866; Euphormus, v. 1260; Euphyander, iv. 854; Euribates Pseudomagus, iii. 185,

186; Eurick, v. 1271; Eustace, iv. 865; v. 1339.

Facetia, v. 1262; Facundo, iii. 467; Faithfull, iv. 704; Falstaff, iii. 54, 151; Fancy, iv. 677; v. 1159; Fannius, v. 1298; Fantastique, v. 1159; Fantichus, v. 1298; Fasting-day, A, iv. 881; Fat Bishop, iv. 630, 878; Fatuus, v. 1284; Faukius, v. 1177; Featherbrain, Mr., iv. 686; Feli, v. 1271; Felixina, iv. 686; Femina, iv. 686; Fencer, iv. 667; Ferdinand, iii. 63; iv. 810; v. 1252; Ferentes, iii. 452; Fernando, iii. 452; Ferret, Mistress, iv. 931; Fewtricks, iii. 164; Fiametta, v. 1108; Fifth Gentleman, vi. 172; Fiormonda, iii. 452; First Citizen, iii. 424; Fitz-Allen, iv. 869; Fitzavarice, Lord, v. 1109; Fitzdottrell, iii. 322; iv. 616, 617; vi. 10; Fitzdottrel, Mrs., iv. 616, 617; Fitz-herbert, Thomas, v. 1401; Flamen, A., vi. 101; Flash, Sir Petronell, iv. 945; Florelli, v. 1113; Florello, iii. 215; Florenz, iii. 314; Florimel, iii. 377; iv. 784; Florina, iii. 130; Flowerdales, iv. 631; Fly-blow, iv. 731; Fool, iv. 1137; vi. 110, 171, 232; Fop, Sir Gregory, vi. 242; Forobosco, iii. 338; Fortitude, vi. 108; Fortunius adolescens, v. 1298; Four Gossips, vi. 10; Fourth Gentleman, vi. 172; Fowler, v. 1167; Frampole, iv. 865; v. 1339; Francelia, v. 1210; Francisco, iv. 813, 854; Frank, iii. 90; Fredegond, iv. 545; Frederick, iii. 424; Free-wit, iv. 483, 487, 495; Friar Bacon (ghost of), vi. 233; Friswood, iv. 865; v. 1339; Fuga, v. 1195; Fulbanck, Lady, v. 1127; Fulgentio, iv. 798.

Galeas, v. 1333; Galeazzo, iv. 514, 759; Galhispanglo, iv. 854; Gallus, v. 1298; Gayman, v. 1127; Gazet, iv. 813; Genies, v. 1159; Genius, v. 1160, 1162, 1304; Gentili, iii. 274; Gentleman, v. 989; vi. 97; Geraldine, iv. 567; Geta, iii. 397; iv. 764; v. 1291; Ghismonda, v. 1341; Ghost of Captain Coxe, iv. 658, 659; Ghosts, v. 1411; Glausamond, v. 1341; Gleek, v. 1042; God, A, vi. 244; Gondomar

CHARACTERS (*cont.*)
iii. 84; Goodlack, iv. 570; Good-love, iv. 930; vi. 53; Gotharus, iv. 943; Granchio, v. 1298; Gratiana, iii. 232; Great Cham, v. 1345; Gregory, v. 1284; Grimes, iv. 495; Gripeman, iv. 731; Grobiana, v. 1055; Grobianus, v. 1054–6; Grocer, vi. 9; Grocer's Wife, vi. 9; Guiscardo, v. 1341; Guy of Warwick, v. 1347.

Haly, iii. 278; v. 1035; Hannibal, v. 1349; Hanno, iv. 764; Hans, v. 997; Harmonie, iv. 881; Hecate, iv. 904; Hector, v. 1345, 1346; Hedone, iii. 4; Henry Prince of Purpool, v. 1376; Hermenigildus, iv. 731; Hermit, A., vi. 108; Herod the Great, v. 1283; Hesychia, iii. 4; Hibernia, iii. 229; Hidalgo, Señor, v. 1437; Higgin, iii. 318; Higgon, iii. 314; Hilario, iv. 810; Hind, James, v. 1036; Hippolito, iv. 907; v. 1130; 1131, 1132; Hirsutus, iv. 532; Hirtius, iii. 266; Histrio, v. 989; vi. 97; Hoffman, iii. 43; Honoria, iv. 810; Honour, iv. 882, 898; Horatio, v. 1108; Hostess, iii. 151; vi. 93; House-keeper, vi. 238; Hoyden, Tom, iii. 89; Hubert, iii. 314; Hugh, Chan., iv. 941; Hyempsall, iii. 38; Hymen, v. 1262.

Iago, iii. 278; Ieronimo, v. 996; Ignoratio Elenchi, v. 1279; In and In, v. 1042; In-and-In Medlay, iv. 635; Inconstancy, iii. 296; Indamora, iii. 218; Infernal spirits, iv. 638; Influences, v. 1230; Infortunio, v. 1147; Ingenuity, v. 1097; Ingram, v. 1452; Innkeeper, v. 1437; Innocency, iii. 296; Intellectus Agens, v. 1191; Invention, v. 1266; Ipswichus, iv. 601; Irato, v. 1193; Irene, iii. 122; iv. 506; v. 1159, 1215; Isaacius Angelus, iii. 27; Isabella, iv. 907; Iseppo, iv. 814; Ismenia, iii. 377; Ithocles iii. 440.

Jacintha, iii. 420; Jack Pudding, vi. 171 and n. 1, 172 n., 177, 231, 246; Jago, iii. 467; Jane, iv. 869; v. 1164; Jaques, iii. 170; v. 1019, 1020; Jay, v. 1159; Jecorino, v. 1374; Jeerer, iii. 150; Jeffrey, iii. 87; Jerker, Hugh, iv. 933; Jew, iv. 573;

Jews harp, v. 1159; Joannes, Andræas Eudæmon, v. 1401; Jocky, v. 1159; Jocundo, iii. 263; Jogalon, v. 1271; Johannes, iii. 27; Jolly, iv. 703; Jonah, v. 1382; Juanna, iii. 260; Juggler, iv. 667; Jugurtha, iii. 37; Julia, iv. 817; v. 1291; Juliana, iii. 331, 793; Juliet, iii. 358; v. 1251; Julietta, v. 1009; Julio, iii. 188, 190; v. 1009; Julio Baptista, iv. 810; Julius Asper, v. 1291; Junius Rusticus, iv. 817; Juno, iv. 564; v. 1452; Jupiter, iii. 4, 29; iv. 564; v. 1452; Jusculino, iv. 854; Justice, vi. 108; Justice Cockbrain, iii. 90; Justice Eitherside, iv. 617; Justice Greedy, iv. 756, 802, 803; Justice of the Peace, vi. 228; Justina, v. 1427.

Kastril, iii. 211; Kickshaw, Alexander, v. 1127; King, vi. 114; King Beef, v. 1306; King Brawn, v. 1306; King Henry VII, iii. 455; Kite, v. 1159; Knave of Clubs, v. 1343.

La-Castre, iii. 428; Laberio, v. 1009; Lachesis, iii. 29; Lactantio, iv. 890; Lacy, v. 997; Ladislaus, iv. 810; Lady Allworthy, iii. 7; Lady Cressingham, iv. 860; Lady Macbeth, iv. 838; Lamia, iv. 817; Lamira, iii. 358; Lamot, iv. 546; Lamp-man, v. 1159; Lamprias, iii. 400; iv. 851; Lampree, iii. 400; Landlord iv. 504; vi. 110–11, 113; Landrey, iv. 545; Lapardus, iii. 27; Latinus, iv. 817; Latorch, iii. 406; Latrocinio, iv. 902; La Writ, iii. 359; v. 1380, 1381; Leandro, iii. 420; Leidenberch, iii. 301; Le Dirard, iv. 866; Le Fevre, M., vi. 46–47; Lentulus, iv. 764; Leonora, v. 1250, 1251; Lepidus, v. 1261; Lerma, Duke of, his daughter, v. 1063; Leverduce, iii. 430; Libacer, v. 1034; Lickfinger, iv. 630, 631, 877; Lidian, iii. 361; Light, vi. 170; Lillia-Bianca, iii. 428; Lirenda, iii. 95; Lirendans, iii. 94; Lisander, iii. 361, 362; Lodovico, iii. 85; Lopez the Curate, iii. 420; Lord, iii. 432; Lord Mens, iii. 297; Lord Noland, vi. 146; Lord Sauce, v. 1306; Loral, v. 1369; Lorece, iii. 169; vi. 61; Lorenzo, iii. 228; Lorrell, v. 1055; Love, iii. 296; vi. 108, 109; Love-all, iv.

704; Loveall, Mr., iv. 681; Lovewit, vi. 53, 155; Loyola, Ignatius, v. 1401; Lucasia, iii. 128, 130; Lucifer, v. 1401; Lucilius Adolescens, v. 1298; Lucius, v. 1400; Lucora, iii. 169; Lucy, v. 1284; Lugier, iii. 428, 430; Lyncida, v. 1453; Lysa, v. 1298; Lysana, iii. 95; Lysander, v. 1262; Lysandra, iii. 38; Lysippus, v. 1097, 1098.

Machessa, iii. 130; Machiavellus, iv. 530; Macilento, v. 1262; Mad scholar, iii. 393; Madge, iii. 90; v. 1358; Magellan, iii. 296; Mago, v. 1400; Magpie, v. 1159; Mahomet, iii. 122; iv. 506; v. 1215; Malateste, iii. 259; Malevolo, v. 1193, 1195; Malfreda, v. 1452; Malthora, iii. 130; Malus Genius, vi. 108; Man of Canada, A, v. 1231; Manlianus, v. 1298; Manto, iv. 814; Mantua, Duke of, v. 1120; Manuell, iii. 27; Manzoc, v. 1345; Maquarella, iv. 854; Marcellus, iv. 765; Margaretta, iii. 409; v. 1020; Maria Caesarissa, iii. 27; Marian, iv. 621; Mariana, iii. 428; Marius, iii. 38; Mars, iv. 559, 574; Martia, iii. 331; Martino, iv. 902; Master Wild, iv. 703–4; Mathias, iv. 810; Matilda, iii. 233; Maximus, v. 1036; Meager, iii. 223; Medico de Campo v. 972, 973; Meercraft, iv. 616; Melancolico, v. 1193, 1195; Melarchus, v. 1453; Melchoshus, iii. 121; Memor, v. 1193; Memoria, v. 1374; Mendicant, iii. 63; Mercator iii. 227; Mercurius, iii. 29; Mercury, iv. 564, 740; v. 1278; Mercutio, v. 1052; Merry Andrew, vi. 171; Merrythought, iii. 44; Metanoetus, iii. 4; Metullus, A., iv. 764; Midas, iv. 581, 582; Midwife, iv. 640; Mihil, iii. 90, 91; Miles, v. 1045; Milicent, iii. 69; v. 1386; vi. 291; Miller's Son, iii. 380; Minerva, iv. 717; Miniona, iii. 164; Mirabell, iii. 428; Mirmydons, v. 1345, 1346; Mirth, iv. 630; vi. 8; Mirtillus, v. 1033; Mirza, iv. 1035; Mistress Flowerdew, v. 987; vi. 95–96; Mistress Marry Muffe, vi. 241; Modesbargen, iii. 301; Mogibell, iv. 620; Moll Cut-Purse, vi. 146, 148; Money, iv. 686; Monstabales, iii.

37; Moors, v. 1374; Mopsa, iv. 933; v. 1075; Mortimer, iv. 622; Morton, John, the Byad, v. 1159; Mosca, vi. 245 n. 1; Moss, iv. 235; Moth, Robert, iii. 132, 133; Mother Sawyer, iii. 270; Mourner, iv. 880; Mousetrap, v. 1452; Mousetrap Maker, iv. 667; Mufti, iii. 1; iv. 866; Mullisheg, iv. 570; Multecarni, v. 1213; Muly-Sheck, iv. 568; Mumble, v. 1284; Mura, iv. 492; Mustapha, iv. 813; Mustard, v. 1306; Myastis, v. 1451; Mysipsa, iii. 37; Myne [Wynd?] Mill, v. 1159; Mysogynos, v. 1417.

Nabdalsa, iii. 38; Nanthus, v. 1453; Nantolet, iii. 428; Nassuf, iii. 1; iv. 866; Nasus, v. 1374; Nature, vi. 108; Neander, iv. 846–7; Neruus, v. 1374; Newman, iii. 150; New-yeere, iv. 881; Nicetis, v. 1451; Nigella, v. 1262; Novella, iii. 85; Nurse, dry, iv. 640; Nurse, wet, iv. 640; Nymphae, iii. 184.

Occasion, v. 1258; Octavia, iii. 38; Officer, iv. 776; Olanzo, iii. 467; Oldlove, Sir Arthur, iv. 741; Old Lionell, vi. 51, 156; Oldrents, iii. 72; Oldwit, iii. 307; Olivia, iii. 467; Olympa, v. 1262; Olyndus, iii. 130; Onaelia, iii. 259, 260; Onos, iii. 399, 400; Opinion, v. 1159; Orgilus, iii. 440; Oriana, iii. 428; Ormillus, v. 1453; Orpheus, v. 1304; Osirus, iii. 95; Osric, iii. 43; Ossecaster, iv. 854; Oswald, v. 1452; Otho, iv. 854; Otium, iii. 29; Otter, Mistress, iv. 932; Owl, v. 1159; Oxford, iii. 233; Oyestus, v. 1055.

Pacenius, Bartolus, v. 1401; Paeologus, v. 1215; Page, iv. 890; Palabresa, v. 1437; Pallas, iv. 564; Pallatine the Younger, iii. 223; Palphurius Sura, iv. 817; Pamelissa, iv. 854; Pamphagus, v. 1055; Pan, iii. 296; Pandena, iii. 130; Pandolpho, v. 1437; Pantaloons, v. 1231; Pantaloun, v. 1397; Paradox, v. 1377; Paralogismus, v. 1279; Paris, iv. 564, 816, 817; v. 1153; Parma, Duke of, v. 1120; Parson, iv. 702; Parthenia, iv. 479; Parthenius, iv. 817; Paulina, iv. 814; Paulus PP Quintus, v. 1401; Pax, iii. 29; Pazzorello, v. 1169; Peggie, v.

CHARACTERS (cont.)

1236; Penda, iii. 267; Penelope, v. 1167; Penia, iii. 4; Pennyboys, iv. 631; Penurio, iii. 433; Perez, Michael, iii. 409, 410; Perindo, v. 1451; Perseius, v. 1177; Pert, iii. 223; Petella, iii. 428; Petrutio, iv. 739; Phanaticus, iv. 731; Philander, v. 1316; Philargus, iv. 817; Philaritus, iv. 502, 503; Philip III, v. 1063; Philip the Fool, vi. 232; Philosopher, A, vi. 108; Philoxenus, iv. 764; Phorus servus, iii. 184; Phusis, v. 1374; Phylander, iii. 169; Physander, vi. 108; Pickpocketo, iv. 887; Piety, iii. 229; Pimponio, v. 1137; Pinac, iii. 428; Piscinus, v. 1261; Pitho, iii. 95; Plangus, v. 1035; Player, iii. 432; vi. 238; Pleasant, iv. 702; Plenteous, iii. 154; Plot, Lady, v. 1110; Plot, Sir Solitary, v. 1109; 1110; Plotwell, iv. 525; Ploughman, A, vi. 108; Plumporridge, iv. 881; Plutarchus Gilthead, iv. 616; Pluto, v. 1452; Pluvida, v. 1452; Poet, iii. 178; iv. 662; v. 1211; Poland, King of, v. 1209; Policy, iii. 229; Politanus Typographus, v. 1401; Polupragmaticus, iv. 498; Polybrontes, v. 1097, 1098; Polynices, iv. 511; Pompeius, v. 1291; Pompey Doodle, vi. 242; Potluck, Joan, iii. 132; Pretiosa, iv. 894; Pride, iii. 46, 296; v. 1392; Priest, iii. 428; Prig, iii. 314; Primavera, iii. 296; Prince, vi. 244; Prince of Hell, iv. 638; Prince of Orange, iii. 301; Prince Prospero, iii. 49; Prince of Purpool, v. 1377; Princes of Wales, iv. 938; Priscianus Caesariensis, v. 1398; Priscilla, iii. 134; Privatio, v. 1452; Probee, Mr., vi. 11; Procris, iii. 184; Projectors, v. 1159; Prologue, v. 972; Prologus, iii. 4; v. 1295; vi. 110, 111; Prometheus, iii. 4; Promus, v. 1284; Prophet, iv. 667; Prospero, iii. 397; Prudence, iv. 624; vi. 108; Prudentius, v. 1192; Publius Cornelius Scipio, v. 1400; Pug, iii. 322; Pumpie, v. 1295; Punctilla, v. 1437; Pupillus, v. 1052; Puritans, v. 987, 1193; Prusias, iv. 764; Psyche, iv. 581; v. 1374; Pyrachmus, v. 1298;

Quaker, v. 1363; Queen, vi. 245; Queen of the Amazons, v. 1288; Queen of Bithynia, iv. 764; Queen Elizabeth, v. 1044; Queen Mincepy, v. 1306; Quick, vi. 170; Quicksands, Mr., v. 1386.

Ralph, vi. 53 n. 1; Ramires, Don, v. 1084; Rascipolis Arban, v. 1451; Rawbone, v. 1164; Raybright, iii. 460; Redondo, Señor, v. 1437; Reignald, iv, 565; vi. 51, 156; Reuben, iv. 627; Rex Jacobus, v. 1177; Rhodia, iii. 130; Rialto, v. 1006; Ricardo, iv. 810; Richard, v. 1358; Richmond Palace, iv. 908; Roaring Rimer, the, vi. 240; Robert, King of Sicily, v. 1291; Roberto, iv. 798; Rod., v. 1271; Rodericus senex, v. 1298; Roger, v. 1307; Rolande, iv. 797; Romania, King of, v. 1139; Romanus, v. 1403; Romeo, iv. 741; v. 1215; Romelio, v. 1250, 1251; Rosalura, iii. 428; Rosania, iv. 699; Roscius, v. 987; Rosinda, v. 1170; Rossa, v. 1404; Roxina, iii. 125; Roxalana, iv. 767; v. 1404; Roxen, v. 1345; Rufaldo, v. 1147; Russel, iv. 869.

Sabina, iii. 467; Sabroso, v. 1437; St. Chad., v. 1173; St. Ignatius, iv. 871; St. James's Palace, iv. 908; Salmanzar Maurus, iii. 27; Salt, v. 1306; Sancho Panza, iii. 397; Sara, v. 1284; Saturnus, iii. 29; Satyrs, iv. 502, 503; v. 1159; Scarecrow, iii. 211; Scatt, vi. 246 n. 1; Schoolmasters, iii. 60; v. 1397; Scintillulus, v. 1452; Scioppius, Gasper, v. 1401; Sconce, iv. 482; Seaman v. 1159; Search, v. 1420; Sebastiano, v. 997; Second Citizen, iii. 424; Seleucus, iii. 346; Selina, v. 1147, 1274; Semele iv. 567; Sempronius, iv. 764; Sempronius senex, v. 1298; Sensuality, v. 1126; vi. 108; Septimius, iii. 341; Seraphina, iii. 38; Serastus, iv. 854; Shab-Quack, v. 1308; Shamont, iii. 383; Shepherd, A, vi. 108; Shoemaker, v. 1295; Shooe, v. 1295; Shootie, v. 1295; Show, v. 972; Shrove Tuesday, vi. 56; Sight, v. 1420; Signor Calldo, iii. 296; Signor Freddo, iii. 296; Signor No, iii. 260; Silvanus, iii. 296; Simper, v. 1284; Simple, Sir

Gervase, v. 1093; Simpleton, iii. 151; Simplicitas, iii. 29; Simplicity, iv. 909; Singing-boy, iii. 428; Sir Furious Inland, iii. 211; Sir Gervase, vi. 53; Sir Giles Overreach, iv. 802; Sir Pepper, v. 1306; Sir Politic Would-Be, iii. 211; Sir Solemn Trifle, iii. 211; Sir Thomas Long, vi. 146; Sir Timothy, iv. 496; Sir Vinegar, v. 1306; Slipper, v. 1295; Sly, iii. 164; Soarez, Franciscus, v. 1401; Sodom, iv. 731; Soldier, iii. 174, 178; Solyman, iv. 510; Sophia, iv. 810; Sophy of Persia, v. 1345; Soto, iii. 431; Spaniards, v. 1231; Sparke, vi. 110–11; Spartus, v. 1400; Spencer, iv. 570; Spinella, v. 1453; Spiritus, v. 1374; Spongius, iii. 266; Spring, iii. 296; v. 1304; Springlove, iii. 72; Spruce, vi. 110–11; Spurre, v. 1295; Squirrel, vi. 53; Stella, v. 1033, 1283; Stephanos, iv. 817; Stremon, iii. 375; Strevellus, iii. 227; Suckabus, iv. 713; Sulpitia, iv. 1195; Summer, iii. 296; v. 1304; Susan, iv. 933; Susiada, v. 1437; Suzdato, v. 1261; Swash, v. 1417; Switzer, v. 1270; Syringus, v. 1453; Syrus, iv. 764.

T, Sir, v. 1353; Tablecloth, v. 1306; Tabytha, iii. 177; Tailors, v. 995, 996, 997; Tailor-Prophet, iv. 667; Tamburlaine, vi. 245; Tanto, v. 1284; Tantoblin, v. 1055; Tany, v. 1284; Tarentilla, v. 1187; Tarpax, iv. 713, 714; Teazle, Lady, v. 1127; Teazle, Sir Peter, v. 1127; Techne, iii. 4; Temperance, vi. 108; Temple, Lady, iv. 957, 958; Tempus, iii. 4; Tharsalio, iv. 807; Theag, iv. 846; Theagenes, iii. 269; iv. 515; v. 1439; Theo., v. 1271; Theodisius, v. 1406; Theodosius Patriarcha, iii. 27; Theodore, iii. 371; Theophilus, iv. 930, 931; Thetis, v. 1452; Third Citizen, iii. 424; Third Gentleman, vi. 172; Thomas Barber, iv. 630, 877; Thomaso, iv. 710; Thomazo, iv. 945; Thornton, iii. 44; Thoroughgood, iv. 495, 496; Three thieves, v. 1284; Time, iv. 717, 881, 938; Thrift, vi. 110–11; Thrift, a citizen, vi. 166; Thumpa-pace, v. 1343; Thump, Jonny, v.

1093, 1094; Thunder-thwart, v. 1343; Thyrsis, iv. 915; Tickle-Me Quickly, v. 1042; Timeus, iv. 692; Tinder-box Man, iv. 667; Tinker, iv. 667; Tire-woman, iv. 878; Titus, iv. 547, 764; Titus Flaminius, iv. 764; Tobacco, v. 1443; Tom, iv. 681; v. 1358; Tom Hoyden o' Tanton Deane, iii. 88, 89; Tongall, Mrs., iv. 933; Tongs, v. 1159; Tony, iii. 424; Toogood, v. 1452; Tooth-drawer, iv. 667; Tortus, Matthæus, v. 1401; Traitor, iv. 1151; Trash, iii. 154; Treedle, Sir Nicholas, v. 1167; Trencher, v. 1306; Tribulation Wholesome, iii. 211; Trimtram, iv. 867, 868, 869; Trina, iii. 160; Trincalo, vi. 148, 241; Tripes, iv. 688; v. 1401; Tristam, iv. 495; Turner, Mrs., v. 1425; Tyrant, iv. 820; Truman, vi. 53, 155, 237, 245; Tyndarus, v. 985.

Ubaldo, iv. 810; Ungartered, v. 1055; Unjust Judge, The, v. 1248; Ursilia, v. 1298; Ursin, the bearward, v. 1055.

Valentinian, v. 1036; Valentius, iii. 190; Vallia, iv. 760; Vandona, iii. 169; Vandort, iii. 301; Van Dunk, iii. 314; Vanscop, v. 1055; Venatores 3, iii. 184; Venture, v. 1123; Venulus, v. 1374; Venus, iv. 559, 564, 574, 639; v. 1369; Vespatian, iv. 547; Viceroy of Sicily, iv. 827; Vigetto, iii. 467; Villanus, v. 1238; Vintress, v. 1363; Violante, iii. 420; Viraldus, iv. 854; Virginia, v. 1248; Virginius, v. 1248; Virolet, iii. 331; Vitelli, iv. 483, 487, 813; Vitruvius Hoop, iv. 632, 634, 654; Vortigern, iii. 125.

Wallace, v. 1236; Water Nymph, iv. 880; Weatherwise, v. 1134; White Bishop, iv. 878; White Duke, iv. 878; White King, iv. 878; White Knight, iv. 878; White Queen, iv. 878; White Queen's Pawn, iv. 878; Widow, iii. 325; Wife, v. 1418; Wild, iv. 705; Wildman, v. 972; Will-doe, Parson of Gotham, iv. 803; Willie, vi. 168; Wine, v. 1444; Winifred, iii. 272; v. 1250, 1251; Winter, iii. 296; v. 1304; Wittipol, iv. 616, 617; Woolfort, iii. 314; Worm, iii. 179; Would-Be, Sir Politic, v. 1109; Wulfade, v.

CHARACTERS (cont.)
1173; Wulfere, King of Mercia, v.
1172.
  Xamolxis, v. 1451; Xavier, v.
1339.
  Young Bonyface, v. 1284;
Young Factor, iii. 428, 429.
  Zani, v. 1397; Zeale, iii. 211;
vi. 209.
Characters, descriptions of, v. 1138.
Characters (literary type), iii. 39.
Characters, pictures of, iii. 151.
Characters unusually popular, iii.
83, 89.
Charing Cross, see London, streets of.
Chariots, v. 1154, 1158, 1159, 1160.
Charis, see Jonson, Ben.
Charles I, i. 18, 34, 48, 52, 53, 218,
311 n. 1; iii. 3, 15, 22, 95, 381; iv.
548, 551, 637, 642, 643, 644,
652, 661-3, 666, 669, 831, 832,
842, 843, 878, 911; v. 1032,
1048, 1111, 1164, 1224, 1227,
1228, 1230, 1231, 1297, 1305;
vi. 30, 166, 220, 225, 270, 283,
301; vii. 13, 14, 36, 39, 43.
  Arraignment of, v. 1216.
  As censor, i. 61, 106-7; iv. 795.
  At York, v. 1148.
  Chaplain to, iv. 588.
  Cipher correspondence, iii. 276.
  Company of, see King's company.
  Complaint about play, i. 333.
  Coronation at Edinburgh, iii. 288,
289.
  Coronation of, iv. 611, 629, 841,
979; vi. 60.
  Creates a baron, iii. 167.
  Dances in masque, iv. 641, 656,
664, 666, 670, 674.
  Dedications to, iii. 15, 141, 142.
  Entertainment of, iii. 143.
  Execution of, iii. 427; vi. 267.
  Forced loan, v. 975.
  Ford's recommendation to, iii.
455.
  Gift to King's company from, i.
20, 26-27.
  Grants pardon, iii. 195.
  Influence of, iii. 140.
  Investiture of, vii. 18, 19.
  Journey to North, play on, i. 333;
iv. 648, 653; vi. 74.
  Judges of, iii. 42.
  Marriage contract of, iv. 676; vii.
58.
  Offended by play, iii. 121.
  Orders by, vii. 4-5.
  Page at the court of, iv. 694.
  Performances before, iii. 15-16,
24.
  Personal interest in the King's
company, i. 35.
  Presents Masque, vii. 39.
  Proclaimed king, vii. 58.
  Prohibits stools on stage, ii. 687.
  Requests masque, v. 1154.
  Sewer in Ordinary to, iii. 105.
  Suggests plot, iii. 123; v. 1110.
  Visits Phoenix theatre, iv. 740.
Charles, Prince of Wales (later
Charles I), i. 9, 10 n. 6 cont.;
iii. 196; iv. 530, 550, 669, 717,
729; v. 1304, 1305, 1334, 1357;
vi. 58, 59, 257, 258.
  Bedchamber of, vii. 58.
  Company of, see Prince Charles's
(I) company.
  Created Prince of Wales, iii. 105.
  Dances, vii. 29.
  Dancing début of, iv. 641.
  Grooms of the Chamber to, vi.
134.
  Impersonated, iv. 872.
  Journey to Spain, iv. 644.
  Lodging of, vii. 48.
  Prince's pavilion, vii. 36.
  Proposed Spanish marriage, v.
1456.
  Return from Spain, iv. 540.
Charles, Prince of Wales (later
Charles II), ii. 424; iii. 113; iv.
717; vi. 227; vii. 117, 118, 119,
122, 124.
  As masque dancer, v. 1358.
  Born, vii. 74.
  Cambridge entertainment for, iii.
173.
  Company of, see Prince Charles's
(II) company.
  Christened, iv. 891; vii. 74.
  Entertainment for, iii. 172.
  Governor of, iii. 88-89.
  Governess to, v. 1359.
  Play acted before, iii. 176.
  Tutor of, iii. 143.
  Visit to Cambridge, iii. 177, 178.
Charles II, King, vi. 270 n. 1.
  At theatre, iii. 70.
  Commissions William Davenant,
iii. 196.
  Company of (His Majesty's
Servants), iii. 23, 43, 56, 71, 82,
85, 115, 120, 124, 135, 330,
337, 340, 345, 348, 352, 354,
357, 360, 364, 367, 371, 382,
387, 392, 395, 404, 409, 412,
419, 423, 427; iv. 562, 580, 616,

619, 623, 629, 633, 695, 698, 761, 767, 775, 776, 778, 783, 789, 812, 815, 821, 884, 888, 901; v. 1063, 1082, 1085, 1105, 1124, 1148, 1183, 1204, 1208, 1211.

Company, repertory list, iii. 24.

Coronation of, iv. 950, 1223.

Theatre of, iii. 80, 82.

Charles Lewis, Prince of the Palatine, i. 48, 51 and n. 2, 99 n. r, 133; iii. 3, 113, 114, 219; v. 1263, 1286, 1287, 1334; vi. 35; vii. 101.

Entertainment for, iv. 474.

Knighted, iii. 219.

Masque in honour of, iii. 220.

Charles (ship), iv. 923.

Charles, Duke of Bourbon, see Anonymous.

Charles, Duke of Byron, see Chapman, George.

Charley, Alexander, ii. 530.

Charolum (as name of ship), v. 1006.

Charterhouse, i. 142; ii. 353; iv. 721.

Charterhouse, Master of, *see* Garrard, George.

Charterhouse, Hull, iii. 2.

Chartley, Staffordshire, v. 1268.

Chaste Gallant, The, see Massinger, *Alexius*.

Chaste Lover (*Gallant*), *The, see* Massinger, Philip, *Alexius*.

Chaste Maid in Cheapside, A, see Middleton.

Chaste Woman against Her Will, see Anonymous.

Chaste Vestals, The, see Glapthorne *The Vestal*.

Chatsworth, Devonshire, iv. 669.

Chatsworth House, vi. 282.

Chatterton (fencer), i. 318; ii. 406.

Chaucer, Geoffrey, iv. 716.

Influence of, iii. 133.

Boethius, iii. 133.

Book of the Duchess, The, iii. 133.

Canterbury Tales, The, iii. 133.

Legend of Good Women, The, iii. 133.

Troilus and Criseyde, iii. 133.

Wife of Bath's Tale, iii. 431.

Chaundler, Daniel, v. 1236.

Chayne of Golden Poems, see Cokayne, Sir Aston.

Cheam, Surrey, iv. 526.

Cheapside, High Cross, vii. 58.

Cheater and the Clown, The, see Anonymous.

Cheaters Cheated, The, see Jordan, Thomas.

Cheeke, Henry, *A Certayne tragedie entituled Freewyl, wrytten first in Italian*, iii. 47.

Chefinch, Thomas, v. 1358.

Chelli, Maurice, *Étude sur la collaboration de Massinger avec Fletcher et son groupe* (1926), iii. 299, 350, 359, 364, 394, 398, 411, 414, 415, 417, 420; iv. 750, 754, 825.

Le Drame de Massinger (1923), iv. 749, 750, 760, 762, 765, 771, 775, 777, 783, 786, 789, 797, 801, 805, 808, 811, 815, 821.

Chelsea, *see* London, streets and districts.

Cheltenham, Thirlestane House, vi. 177.

Cheltenham, vi. 214 n. 1.

Chenies School, Buckinghamshire, iii. 166.

Cherrington, Will, ii. 406; iv. 686.

Chertsey, Surrey, iii. 175.

Chester, Allan Griffith, *Thomas May: Man of Letters, 1595–1650* (1932), iv. 830, 831, 832, 833, 834, 835, 836, 837, 838, 839, 840; v. 1379, 1381.

Chester Tragedy, or Randal Earl of Chester, The, see Middleton.

Chesterfield, the Countess of, iii. 167.

Chesterfield, Earl of, iii. 166, 168.

Chettle, Henry, iii. 261, 262; iv. 564, 575, 578, 581, 585, 618, 625; v. 1241, 1248, 1254, 1285.

The Tragedy of Hoffman, or Revenge for a Father, iii. 44; v. 1114, 1163; vii. 73, 80, 107.

Chettle, Henry, and Munday, Anthony, *Death of Robert, Earl of Huntington*, iii. 234.

Chettle, Henry, and Dekker, Thomas, *Troilus and Cressida*, ii. 481.

Chettle, Henry, and Thomas Dekker, *King Sebastian of Portugal*, iv. 763.

Chetwood, W. R., *General History of the Stage* (1749), iii. 98.

ed., *A Select Collection of Old Plays* (1750), iii. 42, 43, 213, 214; v. 1144.

Memoirs of the Life and Writings of Ben Jonson, Esq. (1756), iv. 604.

The British Theatre (1752), v. 1035.

Chevreuse, Duchess of, vi. 288; vii. 110.
Chew, Samuel, *The Crescent and the Rose* (1937), iii. 119; iv. 499; v. 509.
'Lycidas and the Play of *Barnavelt'*, *M.L.N.* xxxviii (1923), iii. 415.
Cheynell, Francis, iv. 844.
Chichester, Sussex, ii. 513; iv. 845.
Chicester Cathedral, prebendary of, iii. 186.
Chickley, Thomas, ii. 678.
Chief Justice of the King's Bench, iv. 916.
Child Actors, The, see Hillebrand, Harold Newcomb.
Child Hath Found His Father, The, see Rowley, William, *The Birth of Merlin*.
Child, Francis James, *Popular Songs and Broadside Ballads and the English Drama, 1559–1642* (Harvard MS. Thesis), iii. 61.
The English and Scottish Popular Ballads, 5 vols. (1882–98), iii. 61.
Child, William, vi. 27, 28.
Children, company of, *see* Boy companies.
Children of the Chapel, vi. 32, 268.
Children of the Chapel at Blackfriars, 1597–1603, The (1908), *see* Wallace, Charles W.
Children of Pauls, iii. 243; v. 1241.
Children of the Queen's Revels, iii. 300; vi. 66, 115, 116.
Children of the Revels to the Queen (Anne), iv. 608; vi. 78, 79.
Children of the Revels to the late Queen Anne, company of, vi. 138.
Chilton, Berkshire, iv. 588.
Chimney-boys, i. 315; iii. 189; vi. 169.
'Chimney-Sweeper, The', iii. 189.
Chippenham, Wiltshire, iv. 841.
Chirke Castle, Wales, v. 1304.
Royal visit to, v. 1305.
Chisledon, Wiltshire, v. 1054.
Chiverton, Richard, v. 1221.
Chloridia, see Jonson, Ben.
Choice Banquet of Witty Jests . . . , A, see Armstrong, Archibald.
Choice Poems of Several Sorts, see Cokayne, Sir Aston.
Cholmley, Sir Hugh, *The Memoirs of Sir Hugh Cholmley* (1787), vi. 9.
Cholmley, Sir Richard, v. 1160, 1162; vi. 9.
Choral songs, v. 1363.

Choral summary, iii. 397.
Choreographers, v. 1358, 1360.
Chorister, dry, iii. 173.
Choruses, iii. 397; iv. 620, 621; v. 1343, 1400.
Choruses, male, v. 1125.
Christ Church Cathedral, Oxford, iii. 99, 127.
Prebendary of, v. 1190.
Christ Church, Oxford, i. 52, 117; ii. 470; iii. 17, 46, 99, 100, 126, 128, 133, 135, 136, 137, 140, 141; iv. 498, 505, 506, 507, 508, 509, 512, 540, 588, 589, 590, 595, 596, 690, 844, 845, 847, 848, 849, 850, 851, 852; v. 1187, 1189, 1192, 1262, 1263, 1264, 1374; vi. 135, 241.
Dean of, v. 1189.
Hall of, iii. 135, 137; v. 1191.
Christ, Karl, *Quellenstudien zu den Dramen Thomas Middletons* (1905), iv. 855, 861, 863, 867, 883, 887, 892, 895, 903, 905.
Christenings, vi. 19, 24.
Tables of, ii. 667–72.
Christes Bloodie Sweat, Or the Sonne of God in His Agonie, see Anonymous.
Christian, Mildred Gayler, 'An Autobiographical Note by Thomas Middleton', *N. & Q.* clxxv (1938), iv. 855.
'Middleton's Acquaintance with the *Merrie Conceited Jests of George Peele'*, *P.M.L.A.* 1 (1935), iv. 855.
'A Sidelight on the Family History of Thomas Middleton', *Stud. Phil.* xliv (1947), iv. 855.
Christian Turned Turk, A, see Daborne, Robert.
Christianetta, or Marriage and Hanging Go by Destiny, see Brome, Richard.
Christie's, iii. 294.
Christmas, vi. 265, 283.
Christmas Comes But Once a Year, see Webster, John.
Christmas, Gerard (Gerald, Garrett), iii. 248, 256; iv. 576, 577, 578, 896, 897, 898, 899, 911.
Christmas His Masque, see Jonson, Ben.
Christmas, John, iii. 248; iv. 577, 578.
Christmas, Mathias, iv. 577, 578.
Christmas Messe, A, see Anonymous.
Christmas Ordinary, see Anonymous.

Christmas poems, iii. 151–2.
Christmas Prince, The, see Anonymous.
Christmas, proposed plays for, vi. 59.
Christmas Prince, The, see Sir John Sansbury.
Christmas Tale, A, see Lane, Philip.
Christ's College, Cambridge, iii. 161 ; iv. 537, 538, 912, 953, 955–6; v. 1197, 1232, 1239.
Christ's Passion, see Grotius, Hugo.
Chronicle history plays, iii. 454; v. 1235–6.
Chronicle of the Kings of England, A (1660), see Baker, Sir Richard.
Chronicles (1587), see Holinshed, Raphael.
Chronologer, see London, chronologer to.
Chronologers, v. 1181.
'Chronology of Middleton's Plays, The', see Bald, R. C.
Chrysostom, Dion, iii. 140.
Church, Bartholomew, ii. 633.
Church robe, vii. 9.
Church robes used in a play, i. 294.
Churchill, George B., and Wolfgang Keller, 'Die lateinischen Universitats-Dramen Englands in der Zeit der Königin Elisabeth', '*Shakespeare-Jahrbuch,* xxxiv (1898), iii. 125; v. 1006, 1291, 1387, 1388, 1394.
Churchwardens, ii. 466; vi. 19, 24, 176.
Cibber, Colley, iii. 328.
Caesar in Egypt, iii. 342.
Love Makes a Man, or the Fop's Fortune, iii. 328, 336.
Cicilia and Clorinda, see Killigrew, Thomas.
Cid, The, see Rutter, Joseph.
Part I. See Rowley, William.
Part II. See Rowley, William.
Cigarrales de Toledo, Los, see Tirso de Molina.
Cini, Francesco, iii. 208.
Notes d'Amore, iii. 208; iv. 677.
Cinthio, Gianbattista Giraldi, *Hecatommithi,* iii. 325, 356; iv. 905; v. 1130.
Cirencester, Gloucestershire, Innkeeper at, iii. 126.
Citizens' theatres, ii. 693.
City, The, see Anonymous.
City Bride, or the Merry Cuckold, see Harris, Joseph.

City Cozener, The, see Cartwright, William, *The Ordinary.*
'City Dog in a Saint's Doublet, A', see Anonymous.
City Gallant, The, see Cooke, Jo., *Greene's Tu Quoque.*
City Heiress, The, see Behn, Mrs. Aphra.
City Honest Man, The, see Massinger, Philip.
City Lady, The, see Dilke, Thomas.
City Madam, The, see Massinger.
City-Match, The, see Bromfield, *The Schemers.*
City Match, The, see Mayne, Jasper.
City Nightcap, or Crede Quod Habes & Habes, The, see Davenport, Robert.
City of Bath Described, see Chapman, Henry.
City Poet of London, iv. 680; v. 1218.
'City Show', iii. 244.
City Show, A, see Dekker, Thomas.
City show on the Lord Mayor's day, A, see Dekker, Thomas.
City Shuffler, The, Parts I and II, see Anonymous.
City Wit, The, see Brome, Richard.
Civil War, the, iii. 143; v. 981, 994.
Civitatis Amor, see Middleton Thomas.
Civitas Londini (1600) (map), see Norden, John.
Clampard, Francis, iv. 550.
Clancarty, Earl of, v. 1152.
Clanrickard, Earl of St. Albans, v. 1142.
Clapthorne, Mr., a 'Poore Knight of Windsor', iv. 477.
Clapton, Northamptonshire, iii. 2.
Claracilla, see Killigrew, Thomas.
Clarastella (1650), see Heath, Robert.
Clare College, Cambridge, v. 1028, 1214.
Fellow of, v. 1027.
Clare Market, see London, streets and districts.
Clarendon, Edward Hyde, Earl of, v. 989.
The History of the Rebellion and Civil Wars in England (1712 ed.; first ed., 1702), iv. 648, 652.
Claretus, P., iii. 160–1.
Homo Duplex sive Funestum Corporis et Animae Duellum tragoedia, iii. 160–1.
Clark, Andrew (ed.), '*Brief Lives',* chiefly of Contemporaries, set

Clark, Andrew (*cont.*)
  down by John Aubrey, between
    the Years 1669 & 1696, 2 vols.
    (1898), iii. 194; iv. 948, 949,
    950, 963; vi. 38.
  ed., *The life and times of Anthony
    Wood, antiquary, of Oxford,
    1632–1695, described by him-
    self*, 5 vols. (1891–1900), iii. 59,
    102; iv. 495, 825; v. 1019,
    1163, 1169.
  and Charles William Boase (eds.),
    *Registers of the University of
    Oxford, 1449–1622*, 2 vols.
    (1885–9), iii. 38, 105, 303; iv.
    588.
Clark, Arthur Melville, v. 1247.
  'Authorship of "Appius and
    Virginia", The', *M.L.R.* xvi
    (1921), v. 1245.
  'Bibliography of Thomas Hey-
    wood, A', *Oxford Bibliogra-
    phical Society, Proceedings and
    Papers*, i, Part ii (1924), iv.
    553.
  *Thomas Heywood: Playwright and
    Miscellanist* (1931), iii. 73; iv.
    496, 553–86 *passim*; v. 1022,
    1060, 1061, 1062, 1245, 1318,
    1320.
Clark, Hugh, i. 56, 57, 64, 69 n. 2,
    73–89, 220, 221, 231, 232, 239,
    246; ii. 406–7; iii. 232, 311, 327;
    iv. 570.
Clark, Sill, ii. 407.
Clark, William Smith, II, ed., *The
    Dramatic Works of Roger Boyle,
    Earl of Orrery*, 2 vols. (1937),
    iii. 33, 34.
  'The Relation of Shirley's Prologue
    to Orrery's *The Generall*', *R.E.S.*
    vi (1930), iii. 34, 35.
Clarke, Andrew, stationer, iii. 181.
Clarke, Elizabeth, ii. 407.
Clarke, Ezekiell, ii. 407.
Clarke, H. Butler, ed., 'Middleton
    and Rowley, The Spanish Gypsy',
    in C. M. Gayley, ed., *Representa-
    tive English Comedies*, iii (1914),
    iv. 892, 895.
Clarke, Mary, ii. 431.
Clarke, Robert, i. 15, 72–88; ii. 407.
Clarke, Stephen, coal merchant, iii.
    421.
Clarke, Stephen, *The Kiss; or, the
    Lawyer Outwitted* (1811), iii. 421.
Class appeal, iv. 930.
Claudius Tiberius Nero, see
    Anonymous.

Clavell, John, *Soddered Citizen, The,*
  i. 70, 84–85, 118, 194; ii. 375,
    446, 447, 452, 476, 477, 502,
    516, 532, 534, 562, 563, 566,
    569, 571, 575, 599, 600, 605,
    606, 609; iii. 31, 161–5; iv.
    481, 488, 494, 704, 778, 779,
    780; v. 1314, 1360, 1397.
  *A Recantation of an ill led life.
    Or a discouerie of the High-way
    Law. With vehement dissuasions
    of all (in that kind) Offenders. As
    also many cautelous Admoni-
    tions and full Instructions, how
    to know, shun, and apprehend a
    Theefe* (1628), iii. 161, 162, 163,
    165; iv. 780.
Clay, John, ii. 407.
Clay, Henry, i. 15, 72–88; ii. 407–8.
Clay, Matthew, censor, iii. 108, 114;
    iv. 838, 931; v. 1031, 1202, 1277.
Clay, Nathaniel, i. 298; ii. 408.
Clay, Susanna, ii. 408.
Clayton, Richard, i. 145, 147, 155;
    ii. 408, 682, 683; vi. 157.
Cleander, see Fletcher, *The Lovers'
    Progress.*
Clearke, Hugh, see Clark, Hugh.
Clegorne, James, vi. 283; vii. 84, 86,
    87.
Clement, Elizabeth, ii. 499.
Cleodora, Queen of Aragon, see
    Habington, *The Queen of Aragon.*
Cleopatra, see Anonymous.
Cleopatra, see Daniel, Samuel.
Cleophilus, see Waterhouse, David.
Clergy, vii. 67.
Clergyman dramatists, iii. 2–3, 3–4,
    19–20, 25–30, 125, 126–42, 151–2,
    158–60, 183–5, 185–6, 190, 303–5;
    iv. 498–51, 512–16, 525–30, 530–2,
    532–7, 538, 538–9, 550–3, 587–96,
    600–2, 690–4, 715, 843–50, 852–5,
    947, 952–5; v. 1005, 1066, 1187–95,
    1195–7, 1232, 1236, 1256, 1259,
    1264, 1275.
Clergymen expelled, iii. 21, 28–29.
Clergymen sequestered, iii. 26.
Clerk, Richard, verses by, iii. 198.
Clerk, ii. 350, 504, 644.
Clerk of the Bills, ii. 438.
Clerk of the Ordinance, v. 1054.
Clerk of the Treasury of the Court of
    Common Pleas, iii. 21.
Clerke, Hugh, see Clark, Hugh.
Clerke, Mrs., v. 1100.
Clerkenwell, see London, streets of.
Clerkenwell Close, see London,
    streets of.

Clerkenwell Hill, *see* London, streets of.

Clethrowe, Christopher, iv. 577.

Cleveland, John, iii. 165.
Character of a Country Committeeman (1649), vi. 243.

Cleveland, Sir Thomas Wentworth, 1st Earl of, vi. 72.

Clewett, Master Doctor, ii. 641.

Cley, Henry, *see* Clay, Henry.

Clifford, Lady Anne, i. 112.
Diary of, *see* Sackville-West, V.

Clifford, Lord, ii. 414.

Clifford, Francis, vii. 24.

Clifford family, i. 254; iv. 801.

Clifton, Sir Gervase, i. 42, 126; ii. 552; iv. 792; v. 1288; vi. 33.

Clifton, Henry, iii. 300.

Clifton, Luke, iv. 476.

Clifton, Nottinghamshire, v. 1043.

Clink, liberty of the, *see* London, streets of.

Closet Drama, iii. 8, 41, 45, 94–95, 228–9, 469–70; iv. 697, 710, 945; v. 1035, 1038–9, 1048, 1053, 1054, 1171, 1214, 1219, 1223, 1299, 1315, 1341, 1360, 1371, 1424–5, 1429, 1439.

Cloth, green, vi. 265.

Clothiers, v. 1027.

Clothmaker, ii. 443.

Clothworkers, v. 1220, 1225.

Clothworkers, Company of, iv. 576.

Cloud machines, iii. 109.

Cloudy Queen and the Singing Moor, The, see Anonymous.

Clown-parts, iii. 411, 424; iv. 909.

Clowns, i. 30 n. 6 cont.; iii. 37, 260, 271, 432; iv. 473, 581, 582, 713; v. 1092, 1358; vi. 158, 170, 193, 241, 242, 246 n. 1.

Cloys, Bartholomew, vii. 48.

Club Law, see Ruggle, George.

Clun, Walter, i. 73–89; ii. 408; iii. 71, 314, 344; v. 1087.

Clytophon, see Ainsworth, William.

Co., Ja., iii. 166.

Coach-boot, iv. 594.

Coaches, i. 4, 5 n. 1, 32, 42; iii. 80, 178, 412, 419; iv. 479, 523, 592; v. 1091, 1145, 1191, 1408; vi. 18, 19, 24, 28, 29, 41, 44, 76, 82, 155 n. 1, 176, 230; vii. 12.
Ground for turning in, i. 32 n. 3.
Hackney, i. 4; vi. 18.
Hire of, v. 1243.

Coal-merchant, iii. 421.

Cobb, John, ii. 649.

Cobb, Mary, ii. 649.

Cobb, Peter, ii. 649.

Cobbes, James, iii. 166; v. 1403.

Coborne, Edward, *see* Colborne, Edward.

Cochnower, M. E., 'John Ford' in *Seventeenth Century Studies*, ed. Robert Shafer (1933), iii. 433.

Cock, Sir Robert, ii. 576, 577.

Cockaine, *see also* Cokaine, Cockayne.

Cockaine, Lady Mary, iv. 909.

Cockaine, Sir William, iv. 909.

Cockeram, Henry, *English Dictionary* (1623), iii. 437.

Cockermouth, Cumberland, vi. 177.

Cockfighting, vi. 268, 269, 280 n. 1; vii. 23, 36.

Cockhouses, vi. 48.

Cockpit-in-Court, i. 28 n. 1, 67, 108, 118, 223 n. 8, 234; iii. 82, 113, 122, 203, 220, 319, 324, 438; iv. 524, 573; v. 1202, 1354, 1389; vi. 35, 45, 51–52, 92 n. 1, 256, 266, 267–84; vii. 4, 15, 17, 21, 25, 27, 28, 36, 40, 44, 82, 84, 87.

Cockpit lodgings, vi. 282 n. 1, 283 n.

Cockpit or Phoenix Theatre in Drury Lane, *see* Phoenix.

Cockpits, vi. 48, 49, 50, 268.

'Cockram', iv. 944.

Coelum Britannicum, see Carew, Thomas.

Coffee House, i. 318; vi. 172.

Coffee-House, The, see Tatham, John, *Knavery in All Trades*.

Cohn, Albert, *Shakespeare in Germany in the Sixteenth and Seventeenth Centuries* (1865), iii. 266.

Cohn, Heinrich A., ed. *The Jewes Tragedy von William Hemings nach der Quarto 1662 herausgegeben von Heinrich A. Cohn. Materialien zur Kunde des älteren englischen Dramas*, vol. xl (1913), iv. 546, 547.

Coins, v. 994.

Cokaine, Mary, iv. 880.

Cokaine, Sir William, iv. 880, 899.

Cokayne, Anne, iii. 166, 168.

Cokayne, A. E., ed., *Poems by Sir Aston Cokaine* (1877), iii. 168.

Cokayne, Sir Aston, i. 319; ii. 476; iii. 166–72, 375; iv. 757, 778, 779, 791, 799, 830; v. 988, 1222; vi. 171 n. 1.
'Apology to the Reader' in *A Chain of Golden Poems*, iii. 170.
Chayne of Golden Poems (1658),

Cokayne, Sir Aston (*cont.*)
iii. 166, 167, 168, 170, 309, 310, 376; iv. 753; v. 988.
Dianea, iii. 166.
Masque, A, iii. 168.
Obstinate Lady, The, iii. **168–70**; iv. 828; vi. 61.
'On the Deceased Authour, M^r. John Fletcher, his Plays; and especially, *The Mad Lover*', iii. 375–6.
Præludium for Brome's *Five New Plays* (1653), iii. 167; vi. 245.
Small Poems of Divers Sorts (1658), ii. 478; iii. 167, 168, 170; iv. 597.
Trappolin Supposed a Prince, iii. **170–2**; v. 1336.
The Tragedy of Ovid, iii. 170.
Cokayne, Thomas, iii. 166.
Coke, Lady, ii. 396, 677; iii. 217.
Coke, Sir Edward, ii. 396, 474; iv. 473, 616, 617; vi. 81, 83.
Coke, Lady Frances, vii. 24.
Coke, Sir John (Mr. Secretary), i. 327; ii. 354, 502, 678.
Coke, Sir John the Younger, v. 1155.
Coke, Thomas, v. 1155.
Cola's Fury or Lirenda's Misery, see Burkhead, Henry.
Colborne, Alice, ii. 409.
Colborne, Bartholomew, ii. 409.
Colborne, Edward, i. 136, 139, 155; ii. **408–9**.
Colborne, Elizabeth, ii. 408, 409.
Colborne, John, ii. 409.
Colborne, Margaret, ii. 408.
Colborne, Martha, ii. 409.
Colby [Colebey], John, stationer, iii. 24.
Cole, Francis, iii. 172.
Cole, George, stationer, iv. 766.
Cole, George Watson, 'Bibliographical Ghosts', *Papers of the Bibliographical Society of America*, xiii (1919), iii. 282.
'The Bloody Banquet', *T.L.S.* 25 February 1926, iii. 282.
ed., *The Gypsies Metamorphosed . . . edited from Original and Unexpurgated Sources* (1931), iv. 645, 646.
Cole, Mary, ii. 640.
Cole, Nathaniel, iii. 172.
Cole, Robert, iii. 172.
Cole, Thomas, ii. 403.
Coleman, Charles, v. 1360.
Coleman, Ed., v. 1098.

Cole-Orton, Leicestershire, iv. 953.
Coleoverton, v. 1311.
Colepepper, Sir Thomas, iv. 637.
Coleraine, Lord, *see* Hare, Hugh.
Coleridge, Hartley, ed., *The Dramatic Works of Massinger and Ford* (1840), iii. 438; iv. 758.
Coles, Francis, iv. 569, 922.
Coley, Alice, ii. 555; v. 1009.
Collaborations, iii. 58, 59, 69, 73, 75, 76, 149, 155, 191, 238, 239, 242, 244, 246, 247, 249, 251, 254–5, 258, 265–6, 271, 272, 301–3, 308–9, 317, 327, 331, 335, 342, 351, 353, 358, 365, 378, 396–7, 400, 405, 406, 414, 417, 420, 436, 441, 442, 460; iv. 608, 624, 734, 752, 753, 754, 784, 826, 857, 863, 867–70, 890–1, 895, 901–2, 908–10; v. 1010, 1012, 1015, 1016, 1018, 1054, 1072, 1077–8, 1088–90, 1245, 1249, 1252, 1254.
Collaboration, methods of, iii. 255.
Collars, gold and silver, vi. 294.
Collection box, vi. 150, 166.
Collection of Ancient Documents Respecting the Officer of Master of the Revels, A, and Other Papers Relating to the Early English Theatre, see Halliwell-Phillipps, James O.
Collection of Old English Plays, see Bullen, A. H.
Collection of Sundry Memorable Examples of Gods Judgements upon Sabbath-Breakers, see Anonymous, *A Divine Tragedie Lately Acted*.
Collectors, parish, vi. 19.
College of Augures, The, iv. 657.
College of God's Gift at Dulwich, *see* Dulwich College.
College of Physicians, i. 190; v. 964.
College Plays, see Smith, G. C. Moore.
College plays, i. 52; iv. 534–6, 537, 587, 600–2; *see also under* individual colleges.
Colles, Edmond, v. 1165.
Collewell, Richard, ii. **409**.
Collier (occupation), ii. 508.
Collier, Jeremy, iii. 140; v. 988.
Collier, John Payne, iii. 238, 242, 307, 571; v. 1303, 1304; vi. 27, 86.
Diary of Philip Henslowe, The (1845), iii. 285; iv. 808.
ed., *The First and Second Parts of the Fair Maid of the West; or, A Girl Worth Gold. Two*

Comedies by Thomas Heywood.
The Shakespeare Society, No.
42 (1850), iv. 569.
*History of English Dramatic
Poetry to the Time of Shakespeare: and Annals of the Stage
to the Restoration*, 3 vols. (1831
and 1879), iii. 172, 238; iv. 571;
v. 1157, 1253; vi. 23, 24, 28,
55 n. 1, 213, 226, 300, 301, 304,
307.
*Memoirs of the Principal Actors in
the Plays of Shakespeare* (1846),
iv. 543.
*New Facts Regarding the Life of
Shakespeare in a Letter to
Thomas Amyot, Esq., F.R.S.*
(1835), vi. 116.
Collins, Edward, i. 49 n. 2 cont.,
73–89; ii. **409**, 508.
Collins, Ellen, ii. 404.
Collins, J. C. (ed.), *The Plays and
Poems of Robert Greene*, 2 vols.
(1905), iv. 511.
Collins, Jeffrey, i. 15, 72–88; ii.
409.
Collison, William (sailor), i. 265,
266; vi. 161.
Collop, John, *Poesis Rediviva* (1656),
v. 1126.
'To a Lady of Pleasure', v. 1126.
Colman, Dr., iii. 132.
Colman, Elinor, ii. 507.
Colman, George, the elder, iii. 312.
Colman, G., Intro. to *The Dramatic
Works of Mr. Philip Massinger,
Compleat*, ed. Thomas Coxeter,
Reissued T. Davies, 4 vols.
(1761), iv. 758.
Intro. to *The Dramatick Works of
Philip Massinger*, ed. John
Monck Mason, 4 vols. (1779),
iv. 758.
Colman, G., and Peter Whalley, eds.,
*The Dramatic Works of Ben Jon-
son, and Beaumont and Fletcher*,
4 vols. (1811), iv. 613.
Cologne, ii. 451; iii. 266.
Coloma, Don Carlos, iv. 637, 656,
842, 872, 873.
Colonel, The, see Davenant, William,
The Siege.
Colonies, American, vi. 137.
Colony, Norfolk, iv. 531.
'Colour in the Elizabethan Theatre',
see Southern, Richard.
Columbia University, Dramatic
Museum of, vi. 143.
Columbus, Christopher, iv. 515.

Combat of Caps, The, see Mason,
John, *The School Moderator.*
Combat of Love and Friendship, The,
see Mead, Robert.
Comber, Dr. (Master of Trinity
College, Cambridge, later Vice-
chancellor), iv. 535, 536; v. 983,
985.
Combes, Thomas, v. 1001.
Come laugh and spare not, see
Brewer, Thomas, *A Knot of Fools.*
Come See a Wonder, see Day, John.
Come to my Country House, see
Bonen, William *The Cra . . .
Merchant.*
Comedia Vetus, iv. 615.
Comedians, i. 215, 287; ii. 401, 415,
466, 499, 516, 532, 540, 541, 543,
548, 549, 550, 556, 562–7, 572,
580–1, 605, 612, 693; v. 1015,
1049.
Comedies, vi. 293.
Comedies, cheating, iii. 132–4.
Comedies, French, see French
comedies.
Comedies of London high life, v.
1079.
*Comedies Tragi-Comedies, With other
Poems . . .* (1651), see Cartwright,
William.
Comedy in Disguises, A, see Dekker,
The Welsh Ambassador.
Comedy of Errors, see Shakespeare,
William.
Comedy, facetious, iii. 89.
Comedy of manners, v. 1123, 1127.
Comedy, theory of, iv. 934.
Comedy, unknown, vii. 71.
Comic opera, iii. 71.
Comines, Philippe de, iv. 514.
Commander-in-Chief of the Guard
of the Houses of Parliament, vi.
175.
Commander of the Fleet (Prince
Rupert), v. 982.
Commedia dell' Arte, iii. 171; iv. 780.
Commendatory verses, iii. 6, 9, 10,
11, 16, 47, 50, 51, 54, 55, 72, 79,
83, 88, 89, 95, 96, 97, 126, 127,
141, 149, 153, 165, 167, 198, 204,
205, 245, 278, 300, 308, 310, 311,
359, 363, 375, 376, 427, 435, 437,
438, 443, 450, 451, 452, 454, 457,
460, 462, 464; iv. 471, 472, 475,
498, 499, 507, 512, 515, 518, 521,
523, 531, 537, 555, 571, 609, 678,
679, 686, 689, 715, 718, 731,
737–8, 743, 755, 757, 769–70,
776, 778, 779, 780, 783, 788, 791,

Commendatory verses (*cont.*)
799, 802, 809, 813, 816, 830-2, 836, 844, 845, 850, 894, 895, 906, 927, 928, 932, 937, 938, 939, 943, 950; v. 965, 967, 968, 981, 984, 985, 988, 993, 995, 997, 998, 1000, 1001, 1002, 1003, 1009, 1017, 1018, 1029, 1033, 1040, 1048, 1052, 1054, 1071, 1086, 1103, 1115-18, 1140, 1165, 1171, 1179, 1186, 1202, 1214, 1215, 1216, 1220, 1222, 1241, 1242; vi. 9, 62, 63, 107, 171, 242 n. 1, 244.

Commens, Elizabeth, ii. 627.

'Commentary upon the New Roulle of Winchester', *see* Buc, Sir George.

Commission fraudulently obtained, ii. 618-19.

Commissions of inquiry, vi. 202, 203.

Committee for Religion, iv. 526.

Committee-Man Curried, The, see Sheppard, Samuel.

Committee on Delinquents, v. 1070.

Common Law, vi. 129.

Commonplace books, iii. 162, 250; iv. 591, 595, 717, 854; v. 961, 967, 968, 976, 990, 991, 1040, 1041, 1188, 1295, 1298, 1305, 1343, 1382; vi. 26, 135.

Commonwealth allusions, v. 981.

'Commonwealth Drama, The: Miscellaneous Notes', *see* Rollins, Hyder E.

Commonwealth, play set during, iii. 179.

Commonwealth theatre, vi. 309.

Companies, Breaking of, i. 69 and n. 2, 151-3, 165, 169-70, 177-8, 186-8, 209-10, 236-9, 268-9, 296; ii. 684, 685; vi. 208.

Capital stock of, ii. 647.

Competition between, i. 225 n. 2; vi. 169-70.

Contract with theatre owners, ii. 684.

Financing of, ii. 474.

The four, iii. 30.

French, iii. 452; vi. 23, 45-47, 65; vii. 4, 5, 8, 22, 32, 100.

Governors of, i. 325, 330, 331, 334-5; ii. 684, 685; iii. 64, 195; vi. 104, 305, 306-17, 309.

Powers of, ii. 686.

Leaders of, i. 176, 309.

Licences for, vi. 122.

In London, reduced in number, i. 1.

Managers of, i. 3, 26 n. 5, 36, 54, 135, 137, 148-9, 159, 190, 198, 218, 229, 231, 241, 242, 324 n. 1; ii. 364-5, 369, 390, 454, 465-7, 471-2, 492, 500, 512-13, 529, 537, 544, 560, 574, 590-8, 602-4, 613-15, 615-16, 665, 694.

Patents for, vi. 19-20, 78-79, 103, 217.

Provincial, v. 1396; vi. 137, 138, 208, 215, 225, 251.

Suppressed, i. 178-9.

Recruiting of, vi. 306-7.

Relations with theatre owners, ii. 684.

Repertories of, i. 108-34, 156-7, 174-5, 194-7, 214-17, 250-9, 282, 300-1, 322-3, 337-42; iii. 48, 53, 202, 283, 381, 394; v. 1013, 1023, 1062, 1068, 1069, 1070, 1080, 1082, 1085, 1089, 1098, 1099, 1105, 1108, 1114, 1122, 1124, 1126, 1129, 1132-3, 1135, 1145, 1148, 1150, 1163, 1166, 1169, 1204, 1207, 1208, 1210, 1211, 1246, 1270, 1272, 1273, 1286, 1290, 1293, 1296, 1311, 1327-8, 1335-6, 1357, 1340; vi. 73, 100, 145-6, 158, 196-8, 241-6.

Shares in, ii. 632-3, 637, 651; vi. 100, 129.

Touring, vi. 123, 124.

Touring repertories of, vi. 100.

Unauthorized, iii. 32.

Company treasurer, ii. 503-4.

Company of the Revels, *see* King's Revels company *and* Queen Anne-Revels company.

Compleat History of the Lives and Robberies of the Most Notorious Highwaymen, A, see Smith, Captain Alexander.

Complete History of England, A (1706), *see* Camden, William.

Composers, ii. 432; iii. 1, 109; vi. 295, 296.

Composition, rate of, iii. 242.

Compter, *see* London, streets and districts.

Compton, Sir Henry, i. 283 n. 7.

Compton, James, *see* Northampton, Earl of.

Compton Beauchamp, Berkshire, v. 1256.

Comsbey, Ann, *see* Conisbey, Ann.

Comus, see Milton, John.

Conceited Cuckold, The, see Anonymous, *The Politick Whore.*

Conceited Duke, The, see Anonymous.
Conceited Pedlar, The, see Randolph Thomas.
Conceits, The, see Anonymous.
Conceits, Clinches, Flashes, and Whimzies Newly Studied, see Chamberlain, Robert.
Concerts, vi. 295.
Condell, Elizabeth (Mrs. Henry Condell), i. 4 nn. 1 and 2, 44; ii. 409–10, 413, 650; vi. 36.
Will of, ii. 638–40.
Condell, Henry, i. 1, 2, 4 n. 2, 5, 9, 17, 18, 19, 24, 30, 34 n. 3, 46, 72–88, 184; ii. 410–12, 651; iii. 309, 346, 352, 372, 375, 399; v. 1413; vi. 7, 60, 180.
Will of, ii. 640–2.
Condell, Judith, ii. 413.
Condell, William, ii. 413, 570, 638; v. 1160.
Condover Hall, Shropshire, v. 1160.
Confessor, utinam feliciter nata comœdia, see Sparrow, Thomas.
Coniacke, Madam, singer, v. 1230.
Coningsby, Sir Richard, vi. 268; vii. 28.
Conisbey, Anne, ii. 631.
Conjurer, i. 266.
Conqueror's Custom, or The Fair Prisoner (?), The, see Middleton.
Consistory of London Correction Book, vi. 147.
Conspiracy, The, see Killigrew, Henry.
Conspiracy and Tragedy of Charles Duke of Biron, see Chapman, George.
Constable, Alice, iii. 56, 87, 92; iv. 485, 495, 783.
Constable, Francis, stationer, iii. 56, 87, 92; iv. 485, 495, 783; v. 1066, 1145, 1390.
Constables, i. 266; v. 1156; vi. 19, 24, 29, 161, 293; vii. 79.
Constant Lady, The, or Better Late Than Never, see Wilson, Arthur.
Constant Lovers, The, see Randolph, Thomas.
Constant Maid, The, see Shirley, James.
Constantinople, iv. 778.
Taking of, iii. 122.
Contarini, Piero (Venetian Ambassador), iv. 671.
Contemporary criticism, iii. 23, 107, 136, 320, 426–7.
Contention for Honour and Riches, A, see Shirley, James.

Contention of Ajax and Ulysses for the Armour of Achilles, see Shirley, James.
Contract Broken Justly Revenged, see Dekker, Thomas, *The Noble Soldier.*
Contractor, i. 143.
'Contribution to the History of the English Commonwealth Drama, A', *see* Rollins, Hyder E.
'Contributions to the History of the English Playhouse', *see* Bell, Hamilton.
Controller, vi. 287; vii. 20; *see also* Vane, Sir Henry.
Conventicles, vi. 302.
'Conventual Buildings of Blackfriars, London, and the Playhouses Constructed Therein, The', *see* Adams, J. Q.
Converted Conjurer, The, see Anon. *The Two Noble Ladies.*
Converted Robber, The, see Speed, John.
Converts, The, see Killigrew, Wm., *Pandora.*
Conway, Edward, 2nd Viscount Conway, i. 11, 12, 47 n. 3, 277; iii. 135–6; iv. 873, 874, 875; v. 1190, 1202, 1205, 1206, 1235, 1300; vi. 4, 167, 300, 301.
Conway papers, iv. 808, 882.
Cook, David, and Wilson, Frank P., *Dramatic Records in the Declared Accounts of the Treasurer of the Chamber, 1558–1642,* Malone Society Collections, vi (1961), vi. 255, 256, 267, 268, 269, 270, 271 n. 1.
Cook, Elizabeth, 'The Plays of Richard Brome', *More Books,* xxii (1947), iii. 49.
Cook, Margaret McLaren, and F. P. Wilson, eds., *Demetrius and Enanthe By John Fletcher,* Malone Society Reprints (1951), iii. 343.
Cook, Sarah, iii. 409.
Cooke, Alexander, ii. 429.
Cooke, Elizabeth, ii. 405.
Cooke, John (or Joshua), iii. 101.
Cooke, John, *Greene's Tu Quoque,* i. 185 n. 9, 186 n. 8, 194; ii. 690; iii. 59, 101, 151; iv. 642, 825, 868; v. 1017, 1308; vi. 218, 246; vii. 41, 46, 65, 67.
Cooke, Lady Theophila, v. 1032.
Cooke, Thomas, i. 5 n. 6, 7, 95 n. b; iv. 664.
Cooke, W. H. (ed.), *Students*

Cooke, W. H. (*cont.*)
  *Admitted to the Inner Temple
    1547–1660* (1877), v. 1040.
Cooke, William, i. 308, 311, 321;
  ii. 413; iii. 384, 386; iv. 522, 523;
  v. 1069, 1074, 1077, 1080, 1089,
  1091, 1096, 1097, 1098, 1107,
  1108, 1110, 1120, 1122, 1125,
  1129, 1130, 1132, 1135, 1136,
  1142, 1150, 1156, 1160, 1166,
  1168, 1170.
Cookley, Suffolk, v. 1196.
Cooling, John, ii. 413.
Cooper, ii. 579.
Cooper, Charles Henry, *Annals of
  Cambridge*, 5 vols. (1842–53), iii.
  172, 174, 176, 178; v. 982, 1196,
  1233, 1407.
Cooper, Dru, v. 1140.
Coote, Mr., v. 1298.
Coote, Sir Charles impersonated,
  iii. 95.
*Copy of a Letter Found in the Privy
  Lodgings at Whitehall, see* Suck-
  ling, Sir John.
*Copy of Two Remonstrances . . . by
  the Ghost of Sir John Suckling, see*
  Anonymous.
Copyright, i. 54, 65.
Corantos, English, iv. 631.
Corbet Richard (Dean of Christ
  Church), iv. 591, 595.
Corden, Georg, ii. 414.
Cordova, v. 1405.
Cordwainer, i. 265.
Coriolanus, see Shakespeare.
Cork, Earl of, iv. 695, 703.
Corneille, Pierre, iii. 118, 119; iv.
  726, 727; v. 1031.
  The Cid (Rutter translation), v.
    1028, 1030–2, 1037.
  Heraclius, iii. 28, 112.
Corneille, Thomas, v. 964.
Cornelia, see Berkeley, William.
Cornelianum Dolium, see R., T.
Cornelius the Dutchman, vi. 294.
Cornets, ii. 508; vi. 257, 263.
Cornwall, ii. 617; iv. 720; vi. 240.
Cornwall, Barry [B. W. Procter],
  ed., *The Works of Ben Jonson*,
  1 vol. (1838), iv. 613.
Cornwallis, Sir Francis, v. 1205,
  1207.
Cornwallis, Sir Frederick, iv. 487.
Corona Minervae, see Kynaston, Sir
  Francis.
Coronation Day, vii. 17, 23, 31, 36, 43.
Coronation, The, see Shirley, James.
Corporal, The, see Wilson, Arthur.

Corpus Christi College, Cambridge,
  iii. 17, 306; iv. 474.
Corrantos (dances), iv. 674.
*Correction Book of the Consistory of
  London*, vi. 147.
Correr, Anzolo, iii. 217.
Corseilles, Mr., scenery maker, iii.
  219.
Coryate, Thomas, iii. 399; v. 1392.
  *Coryat's Crudities, Hastily gobled
    up in five months travels . . .*
    (1611), vi. 211 n.
  *Thomas Coriate Traveller for the
    English Wits* (1616), iii. 399.
Cosmography, lectures on, iv. 550,
  551, 553.
Cossart, Anthony, vii. 22.
Costine, John, ii. 414.
Costly Whore, The, see Anonymous.
Costumes, i. 20, 21, 44, 58–60, 120,
  136, 141, 144, 162, 199 n. 2,
  202 n. 1, 204, 228, 234, 242–3
  and notes, 312, 330; ii. 367,
  413, 417, 436, 453, 491, 512,
  534, 555, 562, 564, 576, 591,
  592, 595, 632, 633, 654 n. 2
  cont.; iii. 107, 123, 130, 136,
  137, 138, 139, 147, 206, 217,
  219, 397, 402; iv. 503–4, 522,
  524, 549, 596, 601, 638, 653,
  663, 667, 670, 676, 704, 871,
  875, 887, 913, 938; v. 1055,
  1078, 1145, 1154, 1162, 1190,
  1199, 1202, 1205, 1206, 1210,
  1228, 1230, 1359, 1372, 1389,
  1411; vi. 36, 37–38, 43–44, 54,
  55, 56, 57, 65, 70, 75, 77, 107,
  114, 146, 147, 151, 153, 158,
  171, 174, 207, 208, 219, 231,
  232–3, 235, 236, 280; vii. 5, 9,
  12.
  Described, iii. 298; v. 1229.
  Designs for, v. 1163.
  Gift of, i. 39 and n. 1, 58 and n. 3;
    vii. 5.
  Letter about, i. 211.
  Loan of, i. 52.
  Repair of, ii. 558.
  Sketches for, iv. 653.
Cosulich, Gilbert, 'Revenge for
  Honour and Othello', *M.L.N.* xxix
  (1914), iv. 489.
Cotes, Thomas, v. 1077, 1129.
Cotgrave, John, v. 1072.
  *English Treasury of Wit and
    Language* (1655), iii. 402, 407;
    iv. 859, 886, 887, 929, 1021,
    1091, 1111, 1118, 1127, 1132,
    1244, 1252.

Wit's Interpreter, The English Parnassus (1655), iii. 132, 134; iv. 582.

Cotgrave, Randle, *Dictionary of the French and English tongues* (1611), vi. 192.

Cothelston, near Derby, ii. 618.

Cottam, Nottinghamshire, iv. 732, 733.

Cotterell, Sir Charles, ii. 512.

Cottington, Jack, pickpocket and highwayman, iii. 187–90; iv. 713, 714; v. 1379.

Cotton, Charles, iii. 54, 167, 310, 376; iv. 475, 722, 753.

Cotton, John, ii. 414; vi. 49, 291, 292, 293, 297, 298.

Cotton, Sir Robert Bruce, iv. 717.

Cottrell, James, v. 1443.

Couf, P., iii. 172; v. 1406.

Coules, Francis, iii. 81; v. 1444.

Council Chamber at Greenwich, vii. 20.

Council for Foreign Plantations, iii. 23.

Count Gondomar, *see* Gondomar, Count of.

Counterfeiting, ii. 536.

Counter-Scuffle, The, see Jordan, Thomas.

Countess of Salisbury, vii. 29.

Country Captain, see Cavendish, William.

Country Conversations, see Wright, James.

Country Court, The, see Holles, William.

Country Girl, The, see B., T.

Country Girl, The, see Garrick, David.

Country Innocence, The, see Learned, John.

'Country-life, The', *see* Tatham, John.

Countryman, The, see Anonymous.

Country Wife, The, see Wycherley, William.

Courage of Love, The, see Davenant, *Love and Honour.*

Courageous Turk, The, see Goffe, Thomas.

Coursing of a Hare, The, see Heminges, William.

Court Beggar, The, see Brome, Richard.

Court ladies in plays, iii. 452–3.

Court of Aldermen, vi. 83.

Court of Assistants, iv. 544.
Order from, iii. 232.

Court of Assistants of Dulwich College, vi. 177, 178.

Court of Chancery, iii. 134; vi. 7, 56, 72, 76, 79, 114, 128, 129, 216.
Master in Ordinary of, v. 1038.

Court of Common Council, ii. 400.

Court of Exchequer, vi. 84, 210, 210 n. 1.
Commission appointed by, vi. 202, 203, 204.

Court hand, v. 1267.

Court of High Commission, i. 38, 65 n. 2, 122, 278, 317 n. 1; ii. 440, 442, 561, 568; iv. 619, 620, 747, 919; v. 1235, 1266, 1300; vi. 26, 167; vii. 84.

Court of James I, The, see Goodman, Godfrey.

Court of Probate, i. 314; iv. 497; vi. 228.
Proctors of, v. 1441.

Court of Requests, i. 46; ii. 475; vi. 116, 117 n. 1, 124, 140, 157, 216 and n. 1.

Court of Star Chamber, vi. 240.

Court officials, vi. 280.

Court performances, i. 1, 3, 4, 7, 20, 21, 23, 27–29, 51–52, 57, 60, 62, 64, 94–100, 176, 186, 194, 213, 224, 229, 233, 249, 299, 322, 336; iii. 24, 78, 82, 101, 107, 112, 113, 114, 115, 116, 122, 123, 135, 146, 177, 203–4, 206, 220, 223, 270, 313, 315, 316, 319, 320, 324, 332, 345, 347, 348, 349, 360, 367, 370–1, 373, 374, 377, 384, 391, 392, 395–6, 402–4, 408–10, 418, 422, 425, 427, 438, 445, 461, 465; iv. 474, 479, 482, 485, 486, 501, 505, 522–5, 535, 548–50, 568, 569, 570, 573, 579–82, 590–6, 620, 630, 633, 742, 743, 766, 778, 780, 783, 789, 826, 827, 829, 848–50, 869, 891, 894, 917–21, 941; v. 970–1, 1008, 1017, 1023, 1024, 1031, 1033, 1059, 1092, 1107, 1110, 1111, 1128, 1140, 1141, 1145, 1151, 1168, 1170, 1202, 1204, 1211, 1271, 1272, 1286, 1296, 1297, 1334, 1344, 1350, 1352, 1353, 1370, 1372, 1389, 1399, 1432–3, 1444; vi. 35, 58, 67, 94, 101, 135, 148, 191, 227, 229, 265, 266, 268, 269, 284; vii. 8, 10–126 *passim.*
Admission to, iv. 918.
Bills for, iii. 82, 113, 122, 135, 203,

Court performances (*cont.*)
206, 220, 221, 313, 319, 324, 332, 419; vi. 271, 282; vii. 13.
Cost of, i. 53 n. 1.
Dancers for, iii. 139.
Disturbances at, vii. 20.
Duration of, iv. 918.
Music for, iii. 139.
Preparations for, iii. 139; iv. 522; vi. 17–124 *passim*.
On Sundays, vii. 12–15.
Court Purge, A, see Anonymous.
Court Secret, The, see Shirley, James.
Court of the Star Chamber, vi. 124.
Court and Times of Charles I, The, see Williams, Roger Folkestone.
Courtesans, Venetian, iii. 85.
Courtesy-books, iii. 39.
Courtier playwrights, iii. 20–25, 62–63, 104–11, 112, 111–24, 142–51, 275; iv. 503, 694–710, 720–4; vii. 38.
Courtly Masque, A, see Middleton, *The World Tossed at Tennis.*
Courts of Guard, vi. 288.
Covenant, The, iii. 288.
Covenanter, iii. 63, 288; vi. 167, 168.
Covent Garden, *see* London, streets of.
Covent Garden theatre, iii. 371; iv. 524, 762, 770, 777, 810, 864, 989, 1081.
Covent Garden, see Nabbes, Thomas.
Covent Garden, The, see Brome, Richard, *The Weeding of Covent Garden.*
Covent Garden Weeded, see Brome, Richard, *The Weeding of Covent Garden.*
Coventry, i. 92, 93, 156, 172, 173, 179, 193, 212, 213, 248, 274, 280 n. 2, 282, 298, 299, 322; ii. 344, 419, 420, 421, 452, 458, 484, 514, 530, 600, 613, 617.
Corporation of, iv. 658.
Coventry, Thomas, Baron Coventry, Lord Keeper, vi. 300, 301, 304, 307, 308, 309.
Coverlet, taffeta, vi. 280.
Cow Cross, *see* London, streets of.
Cowes Castle, prisoner in, iii. 196.
Cowle, Michael, v. 1042.
Cowley, Abraham, iii. **172–82**, 691, 852.
    The Cutter of Coleman Street, iii. 175, **176–9**, iv. 789, 790.
    The Four Ages of England, or the Iron Age (1648), iii. 174.

The Guardian, iii. 174, 175, **176–9**; v. 1233; vi. 245.
The Iron Age, iii. 178.
Love's Riddle, ii. 553; iii. 176, **179–80**; v. 1222.
The Mistress, iii. 174.
Naufragium Joculare, iii. 173, 176, **181–2.**
Poems (1656), iii. 173, 174, 175, 178.
Poetical Blossoms (1633), iii. 173; iv. 850.
Poetical Blossoms (1636), 2nd ed., iv. 948.
The Works of Mr. Abraham Cowley (1668), iii. 172, 175–6, 177.
The Second and Third Parts of the Works of Mr. Abraham Cowley (1689), iii. 179, 180, 181.
Cowley, Elizabeth, ii. 377, 414, 642.
Cowley, Richard, i. 2, 3, 5 n. 6 cont.; ii. **414**; vi. 20.
Cowley, Richard, Will of, ii. 642.
Cowper, Thomas de Grey Cowper, Seventh Earl (MSS. of), v. 1155.
Cox, Andrew, ii. 415.
Cox, Beatrice, ii. 415.
Cox, Katherine, ii. 415.
Cox, Robert, i. 327 n. 4, 332, 336; ii. **414–15**; iii. 182–3; vi. 233–4, 235.
    Acteon and Diana (1656), vi. 233.
    John Swabber the Seaman (droll), (published in *Acteon and Diana* . . .), vi. 234.
Coxcombe, The, see Fletcher, John.
Coxe, H. O., *Codicum MSS qui in collegiis oxoniensibus hodie adservantur* (1852), iii. 184.
Coxeter, Thomas, iv. 499, 929.
    ed., *The Dramatic Works of Mr. Philip Massinger, Compleat,* 4 vols. (1759), iv. 758.
'Coy Cælia', *see* Randolph, Thomas.
'Cpl.' 'Museum Minervae', *N. & Q.,* Third Series, vi (1864), 265, iv. 716.
Cra . . . Merchant, or Come to My Country House, The, see Bonen.
Craddell, *see* Gradwell.
Craford, Thomas, v. 1116.
Crafty Merchant, The, see Bonen, William.
Crafty Merchant, or the Souldred Citizen, The, see Clavell, John, *The Soddered Citizen.*
Cranborne House, vii. 48.
Crane, Ralph, i. 127; ii. **415–16**;

iii. 341, 343, 345, 346, 380; iv.
   672, 879, 904.
MS. copied by, iii. 416, 421.
Pilgrim's New Year's Gift, The, ii.
   416.
Works of Mercy, The, ii. 415, 416.
Crane, R. S., 'The Vogue of *Guy of
   Warwick*', *P.M.L.A.* xxx (1915),
   iii. 251; v. 1347, 1348.
Cranfield, Lionel, Lord, iii. 111,
   121; v. 1198.
Crashaw, Richard, iii. 173, 539.
   Delights of the Muses (1646), iii.
   441.
Crate, Christopher, ii. 416.
Crate, Kathe, ii. 416.
Craven, Elisabeth, ii. 370.
Craven, William Lord, iii. 440; iv.
   721.
Craven District, i. 92, 173, 212, 248.
Crawford, Charles, 'Ben Jonson and
   "The Bloody Brother" ', *Shake-
   speare Jahrbuch*, xli. (1905), iii.
   401, 405.
   'John Webster and Sir Philip
   Sidney', in *Collectanea*, First
   Series (1906), v. 1239.
Crawford, Charles, 'Montaigne,
   Webster, and Marston: Donne
   and Webster', in *Collectanea*,
   Second Series (1907), pp. 1–63,
   v. 1239.
   Concordance to Ben Jonson (un-
   published MSS. covering the
   works in the 1616 folio),
   University of Michigan Lib-
   rary, iv. 604.
   ed., *Englands Parnassus. Com-
   piled by Robert Allot, 1600*
   (1913), iv. 579, 581.
Crawford, James, ii. 416–17.
Crawley Arnold & Co., iii. 29, 184.
Crede Quod Habes & Habes, see
   Davenport, Robert, *The City
   Nightcap*.
Credulous Cuckold, The, see Behn,
   Aphra, *The Debauchee*.
Crespin, Jean, *Tragedie du Roy
   Franc-Arbitre*, iii. 46.
Cresswell, Robert, iii. 173, 181.
Creswell, Thomas, ii. 384.
Cribbage, *see* Games.
Criers, vii. 54.
Cripplegate, *see* London, streets of.
Criticism, *see* Plays, criticism of.
Croesus, see Sir William Alexander.
Croftes, Anthony, ii. 676.
Croftes, Cecily, ii. 677; iv. 695.
Croftes, Mr., i. 20.

Crofts, Edward, ii. 355.
Crofts, Sir Herbert, v. 1289.
Crofts, Jack, i. 47.
Crofts, Sir John, v. 1404; vi. 34;
   vii. 42.
   Daughters of, vii. 41.
   House of, vii. 35.
Crofts, Mary, iii. 39.
Crofts, Roger, iii. 39.
Crofts, Will, i. 47; iv. 919; vi. 34.
Croker, T. Crofton, ed. Massinger,
   Believe as You List (1849), iv. 762.
Crome, William, ii. 417, 578.
Cromes, a broker, i. 294; ii. 417; vi.
   101.
Cromwell, Oliver, Lord Protector,
   ii. 487; iii. 174, 317; iv. 521,
   728; v. 1098, 1176, 1277; vi.
   237, 284 n. 1.
   Pardons William Davenant, iii.
   196.
Cromwell, Otelia, *Thomas Heywood,
   A Study in the Elizabethan Drama
   of Everyday Life*, Yale Studies in
   English, vol. lxxviii (1928), iv.
   553, 565, 569.
Crook, John, v. 1102, 1118.
Crooke, Andrew, stationer, iii. 58,
   59, 67, 70, 76, 81, 89, 153, 304,
   384, 385; iv. 527, 629, 656, 674,
   691, 698, 708, 811, 815; v. 972,
   975, 1069, 1073, 1074, 1077, 1089,
   1098, 1107, 1108, 1110, 1122,
   1125, 1129, 1130, 1135, 1136,
   1140, 1168, 1170, 1298, 1413.
Crooke, Edmond, v. 1140.
Crooke, John, stationer, iii. 114, 202,
   402; v. 1140.
Crosfield, Thomas, Diary of, i. 26 n.
   5 cont., 30 n. 6, 231, 246, 274,
   285, 293, 297 and n. b, 309, 310;
   ii. 688–9; iii. 74, 75, 135, 136, 233;
   v. 1158, 1190–1; vi. 12, 94, 99,
   164, 165, 227.
Cross, Robert, ii. 618.
Cross Keys Inn, The, i. 1; ii. 491,
   682; vi. 122, 127, 131.
Crosse, Katherine, ii. 370.
Crosses, vi. 167.
Crossley, James, 'Cornelianvm
   Dolium, Comœdia Lepidissima',
   N. & Q., 2nd Series, xii (1861), v.
   962, 963.
Crouch, Humphrey, *The Welsh
   Traveller, or the unfortunate Welsh-
   man* (1671), v. 1436.
Crouch, John, iv. 579.
Crouse, *see* Cruso.
Crowell, Oxfordshire, iv. 588.

Crown for a Conqueror and Too Late to Call Back Yesterday, A, see Davenport, Robert.

Crown, The, tavern, Oxford, iii. 193.

Crowne, William, A True Relation of All the Remarkable Places and Passages Observed in the Travels of . . . Thomas Lord Howard (1637), iii. 110.

Crowther, Joseph, iii. 183–5.
    Cephalus et Procris, iii. 183–5.

Crowther, Thomas, iii. 183.

Croydon, Surrey, iii. 26.

Crucifixes, v. 1300, 1452; vi. 167.

Cruel Brother, The, see Davenant.

Cruel War, The, see Anonymous.

Cruelty of the Spaniards in Peru, The, see Davenant, William.

Cruelty without Hate, see Anonymous, Castara.

Cruickshank, A. H., 'Massinger's Corrections', Library, 4th Series v. (1924), iv. 750.
    ed., Massinger's A New Way to Pay Old Debts (1926), iv. 800.
    Philip Massinger (1920), iii. 167; iv. 750, 762, 805.

Crundell, H. W. [Reply to W. J. Lawrence], T.L.S. 13 February 1937, iii. 241.

Cruso, Aquila, iii. 185–6.
    Euribates, iii. 186.

Cruso, Francis, iii. 185.

Cruso, John, iii. 185.

Crymes, George, iii. 437, 454.

Cuccheti, Giovanni Donato, La Pazzia, v. 970.

Cuckold's Haven, see Tate, Nahum.

Cuckolds' Masque, The, see Anonymous.

Cuddesdon, Oxfordshire, v. 1264.

Cufaude, Will, iv. 928.

Cuff, P., see Anonymous, Sanguis Sanguinem.

Cuffle, Major, ii. 549.

Culmington, Shropshire, iv. 852.

Cumber, John, i. 165, 167, 168 n. 2, 169, 171, 183 n. 2, 204; ii. 417–18, 682; iii. 101, 102, 126, 186–7; vi. 57, 58.

Cumberland, Earl of, vii. 24.

Cumberland, Richard, iv. 770.
    The Duke of Milan, iv. 777.

Cumberland, iii. 143.

Cunning Age, The, see Cart, John.

Cunning Lovers, The, see Brome, Alexander.

Cunningham, Francis, ed., The Plays of Philip Massinger, from the Text of William Gifford, with the Addition of the Tragedy 'Believe as You List' (1871), iv. 758.
    ed., The Works of Ben Jonson, 3 vols. (1871), iv. 613.

Cunningham, Peter, iv. 678; v. 1304; vi. 88.
    Extracts from the Accounts of the Revels at Court in the Reigns of Queen Elizabeth and King James I, Publications of the Shakespeare Society (1842), iii. 445; v. 1023; vi. 191, 260 n. 1.
    Inigo Jones, see Cunningham and Collier.
    Life of Drummond of Hawthornden, in 1833 ed. of Drummond's Poems, iii. 289.
    'Whitefriars Theatre, The, the Salisbury Court Theatre, and the Duke's Theatre in Dorset Gardens', Shakespeare Society's Papers, iv (1849), vi. 86, 88, 89, 115, 116, 117.

Cunningham, Peter, and J. P. Collier, eds., Inigo Jones, a Life; and Five Court Masques, Publications of the Shakespeare Society (1848), v. 1303, 1304, 1376, 1378.

Cupid, see Middleton, Masque of Cupid.

Cupid and Death, see Shirley, James.

Cupid His Coronation, see Jordan, Thomas.

Cupid's Banishment, see White, R.

Cupid's Festival, see Anonymous.

Cupid's Revenge, see Fletcher, John.

Cupid's Vagaries, see Rowley, Samuel, Hymen's Holidays.

Cupid's Whirligig, see Sharpham, Edward

Cure of Avarice, The, see Massinger, The Roman Actor.

Cure for a Cuckold, A, see Webster, John.

Cure of Pride, The, or Every One in Their Way, see Anonymous.

Curriers' Hall, iv. 639.

Curt, ii. 418.

'Curtain, The', see Hook, Lucyle.

Curtain raisers, v. 989–90, 1353–4.

Curtain rods, vi. 280.

Curtain Theatre, i. 1, 158, 201 n. 2, 205 and n. 3, 206, 207, 208; ii. 370, 531, 555, 558, 651; iv. 491, 555, 868; v. 1011, 1324, 1395; vi. 58, 122, 123, 130, 131–9, 216 n. 2, 217, 221, 238, 241, 250, 251.

Curtains, iii. 467; iv. 692.
Curtains, taffeta, vi. 280.
Curtius, Ernst Robert, *European Literature and the Latin Middle Ages*, New York (1953), English trans. by Willard Trask of *Europäische Literatur und Lateinisches Mittelalter*, Frankfort (1948), vi. 178 n. 1.
Custom House of London, ii. 596.
Custom of the Country, The, see Fletcher, John.
'Custom of Sitting on the Elizabethan Stage, The', *see* Baskervill, C. R.
Cutler, ii. 564.
Cutpurses, vi. 146, 148.
Cuts (in play-texts), iii. 383; iv. 748.
Cutter of Coleman Street, see Cowley, Abraham.
Cutting Dick, see Heywood, Thomas.
Cutts, John P., 'The Masque of Vices', *N. & Q.*, cxcvii (November 1952), 492, v. 988, 1431.
  'Music for Shakespeare's Company, The King's Men' (1956), Unpublished thesis, University of Birmingham, vi. 33.
  Musique de Scène de la Troupe de Shakespeare: The King's Men sous le règne de Jaques Ier (1959), Eds. du Centre National de la Recherche Scientifique, vi. 33 n. 1.
Cycle of plays, v. 1414.
Cymbeline, see Shakespeare.
Cynthia's Revels, see Jonson, Ben.
Cynthio, *see* Cinthio.
Cypher clerk, iii. 174.
Cyprian Academy, The, see Baron, Robert.
Cyprian Conqueror, The, see Anonymous.
Czar of Russia, iii. 396.
  Sees opera, iii. 396.

D., J., iii. 187–90.
  Knave in Grain New Vampt, The, i. 13 n. 2, 282; iii. 187–90; iv. 713, 887; v. 1266, 1356, 1379; vi. 150 n. 1, 151 n.
D., R., v. 1220.
D., T., iii. 9, 190, 281.
  Bloody Banquet, The, see Thomas Drue.
D., W., (trans.), *A tragi-comicall history of our times under the borrowed names of Lisander and Calista* (1627), iii. 363.

Daborne, Robert, i. 176, 177 n. 5, 199 n. 2; ii. 418; iii. 190–3, 353; iv. 752, 790; v. 1385.
  Assize Sermon, An (1618), ii. 418; iii. 190.
  Christian Turned Turk, A, iii. 191.
  Machiavel and the Devil, iii. 191.
  Owl, The, iii. 191; vii. 54, 120.
  Poor Man's Comfort, The, i. 174; ii. 362, 453, 509, 510, 559, 560, 626; iii. 59, 191–2; iv. 785.
  She Saint, The, iii. 193.
Daborne, Robert, and Cyril Tourneur, *The Arraignment of London*, iii. 191.
Daborne, Robert, and Nathan Field, Philip Massinger, and John Fletcher, 'Unnamed Play', iii. 191.
Dahl, Folke, 'Amsterdam—Cradle of English Newspapers', *Library*, Fifth Series, iv (1949), iv. 631.
  The Beginnings of English Journalism (1950), iv. 628.
Dallison, Sir Thomas, ii. 397, 463, 571, 694.
[Dalton, John], ed., *Comus, A Mask: (Now adapted to the Stage) As Alter'd from Milton's Mask At Ludlow-Castle, Which was never represented But on Michaelmas-Day, 1634* (1738), iv. 914, 915.
Dambrooke, Sara, ii. 562, 564, 565.
  Will of, ii. 642.
Damford, John, a carpenter, vi. 273.
Damoiselle, The, see Brome, Richard.
Damport, Edward, ii. 418–19.
Danbury, Essex, ii. 673.
Danby, Thomas Osborne, Earl of, vi. 270.
Dance, Ann, ii. 421.
Dance, James, *The Ladies Frolick*, iii. 73.
Dancer, John, *Nicomede*, ii. 473.
Dancers, i. 53 n. 1; ii. 496, 515, 517–18, 522, 541, 563, 578, 617; iii. 139, 199; vi. 294, 295.
Dancers in Masques, iii. 105, 110, 199, 200; iv. 548, 638, 641, 650, 653, 664, 666, 667–8, 670, 671, 674, 677; v. 1288–99; vi. 257, 264–5.
Dancers on the ropes, ii. 612; v 1050; vi. 194, 195, 209, 248, 296; vii. 5, 6, 8, 17.
Dances, iii. 71, 217; iv. 549, 671, 770, 842; v. 988, 1103, 1155, 1192, 1238, 1257, 1358, 1360, 1376, 1420, 1431, 1444; vi. 9, 14, 108, 109, 146, 234, 258.

Dances (*cont.*)
Aerial, iii. 208.
Antic, iii. 140.
Brawles, iv. 674.
Corrantos, iv. 674.
Country, iv. 674; v. 1211, 1358.
Galliards, iv. 674.
Horn-dance, vi. 234.
Huff Hamukin, iv. 674.
In masques, iv. 909, 910; v. 1228, 1230.
In a pastoral, iv. 549.
In plays, iii. 344, 397, 412; iv. 889, 894, 895; vi. 9.
Soldier's March, The, iv. 674.
Warlike, vii. 31.
Dancing, i. 136–7; ii. 523; iii. 15, 195, 210; iv. 479, 664, 670; v. 1110, 1145, 1157, 1158, 1175, 1210, 1228; vi. 151, 170, 210 n., 256, 265, 293, 297, 305; vii. 14, 24, 35, 94, 107.
Dancing area, vi. 264.
'Dancing-Barne, The Queens', vi. 285.
Dancing Bears tavern, vi. 201.
Dancing-master, ii. 517; iv. 949.
Dancing Master, The, see Cavendish, William, *The French Dancing Master.*
Dancing on the ropes, i. 150; ii. 456, 517, 521, 522, 613, 657, 662, 680; iii. 76; vi. 114, 159, 164, 172 n., 174 n. 1, 175, 177, 231, 233–4, 294, 298; vii. 17, 20, 122, 124.
Dancing, practising for, vii. 38.
Danes, iii. 250.
Danett, Thomas, *The Historie of Philip de Commines* (1596), iii. 331.
Daniel, George, *A Vindication of Poesie*, v. 1029.
Daniel, John, ii. 419–20.
Daniel, P. A., ed., *Beggars Bush*, Variorum edition (1904–12), iii. 312, 317.
Daniel, Samuel, ii. 419; iv. 632.
Cleopatra, v. 1310; vii. 51, 99.
Hymen's Triumph, v. 1033; vi. 51.
Philotas, vii. 51, 99.
Queen's Arcadia, The, vii. 51, 99.
Vision of the Twelve Goddesses, The, vii. 51.
Works, The, (1623), vii. 51, 101.
Daniel, William, i. 298, 299; ii. 420–1, 640.
Daniell, Roger, printer at Cambridge, v. 983.

Danner, John, i. 190 n. 2; ii. 421.
Danton, J. Periam, 'William Cartwright and his *Comedies, Tragi-Comedies, With Other Poems* . . . 1651', *Library Quarterly*, xii (1942), iii. 126.
Danzig, ii. 486.
Dare, Josiah, *Counsellor Manners His Last Legacy to His Son* (1673), iii. 301.
Darius, see Sir William Alexander.
Darley, George, iii. 312, 316.
Darley, Sir Richard, vi. 303.
D'Arsennes, Monsieur, iv. 675.
Dartmouth, fall of, iii. 276.
D'Aubigny, Lord, iv. 609.
D'Audiguier, Vital, iii. 393.
Histoire tragi-comique de nostre temps, sous les noms de Lysandre et de Caliste (1615), iii. 363.
D'Aunay, Josias, *see* Floridor, Josias, and de Soulas, Josias.
Daunce, John, i. 190, 192; ii. 421.
D[auncey], I[ohn], iv. 570.
Dauncey, John, *The English Lovers* (1661–2), iv. 569, 571, 922.
Dausse, Robert, *see* Dawes, Robert.
Davenant, Alexander, iii. 175.
Davenant, Jane Shepherd, iii. 193.
Davenant, John, vintner, iii. 193.
Davenant, Mary, wife of William, iii. 194.
Davenant, Sir William, i. 225, 240 n. 2, 303 n. 1, 324, 334, 335; ii. 421–2; iii. 35, 63, 64, 66, 78, 105, 144, 193–225, 277, 371, 374, 377, 408, 413, 418, 435, 443; iv. 499, 523, 545, 546, 571, 628, 654, 696, 748, 803, 814, 832, 950; v. 990, 1071, 1080, 1114, 1119, 1198, 1200, 1217, 1222, 1363; vi. 14, 47, 74–75, 104 n. 1, 167, 177, 237, 284 n. 1, 304–9.
As poet laureate, v. 1362.
As traveller, v. 1362.
Assistant to, iii. 175.
Projected theatre, iii. 203; iv. 748; vi. 291–309.
Reputation of, vii. 13.
Satirized, iii. 66.
Albovine, King of the Lombards, iii. 194, 197–9, 201; iv. 706; v. 1274.
Britannia Triumphans, iii. 199–200, 208, 214, 221; vi. 166, 252, 266, 286–7, 306.
Courage of Love, The, see Love and Honour.

Cruel Brother, The, i. 104, 118; iii. 194, 198, **201**; iv. 778.

Cruelty of the Spaniards in Peru, The, iii. 202; v. 1362, 1363.

Distresses, The, i. 66, 119; iii. 202, 203.

'Epilogue by Sir Furious', iii. 210.

Fair Favorite, The, i. 66, 99, 100, 108, 119; iii. 203, 204; vi. 38.

First Day's Entertainment at Rutland House, The, iii. 204.

Gondibert, iii. 196.

Hamlet, iii. 197.

History of Sir Francis Drake, The, iii. 204.

Just Italian, The, i. 26, 105, 119, 224, 228; iii. 201, **204–5**; iv. 778; vi. 63, 242 n. 1.

Law against Lovers, The, iii. 197, 205.

Love and Honour, or The Courage of Love, or The Nonpareilles, or The Matchless Maids, i. 40, 51, 66, 98, 107, 119; ii. 676, 681; iii. **205–6**; vi. 5.

Luminalia, or The Festival of Light, iii. **207–9**, 214, 221; vi. 287, 288, 306.

Macbeth, iii. 197, 209.

Madagascar; with Other Poems (1638), iii. 195, 209, 210, 223, 224; iv. 521; v. 1362; vi. 14, 197.

Man's the Master, The, iii. 209.

News from Plymouth, i. 66, 107, 119; ii. 660; iii. **209–11**; vi. 14, 197.

Nonpareilles, or the Matchless Maids, The, see *Love and Honour.*

Platonic Lovers, The, i. 107, 119; ii. 503, 661; iii. 66, **211–12**, 223.

Playhouse to Be Let, The, i. 13; iii. 212; iv. 878; vi. 238.

Preface to Gondibert, iii. 196.

Preparation of the Athenians for the Reception of Phocion, The, iii. 212.

Rivals, The, iii. 197, 213.

Salmacida Spolia, iii. **213–15**; vi. 264, 286, 288.

Satirical Declamations, iii. 215.

Siege of Rhodes, The, I and II, iii. 216; iv. 571; vi. 77.

Siege, The, or The Colonel, iii. **215–16**; v. 1314; vi. 52.

Tempest, The, or The Enchanted Island, iii. 197, 216.

Temple of Love, The, ii. 677; iii. 194, 211, 214, **216–18**; vi. 264, 266, 306.

Triumphs of the Prince D'Amour, The, iii. 218, 220, 221, 444; vi. 264, 306.

Unfortunate Lovers, The, i. 48 n. 5, 66, 99, 107, 119; iii. **220–2**; vi. 35, 38.

Wits, The, i. 39, 61, 97, 106–7, 119; ii. 675, 681; iii. 66, 105, 211, **222–5**; iv. 576; v. 1314, 1338.

Works of Sr William D'avenant Kt (1668), iii. 197.

Works of Sr William D'avenant Kt Consisting of Those which were formerly Printed, And Those which he design'd for the Press, The (1673), iii. 197; iv. 878; vi. 14.

Davenant, William (Jr.), iii. 194.

Davenant's company, iv. 495.

Davenport, Edward, i. 327 n. 4, 332, 336; ii. **422.**

Davenport, John, master carpenter, vi. 279.

Davenport, Rebecca, ii. 422.

Davenport, Robert, iii. 225, 238, 281, 282, 283; v. 975, 997, 998, 1001, 1319, 1320, 1335.

City Nightcap, or Crede Quod Habes & Habes, The, i. 186, 194, 219 n. 4, 251, 331, 338; 225, **227–8**, 235, 246, 265; iv. 726, 796, 866; v. 1118, 1308; vi. 59.

Crown for a Conqueror and Too Late to Call Back Yesterday, A (1639), ii. 387, 553; iii. 225.

'Dialogue between Policy and Piety', iii. 225, 228–9.

Edward the Third, iii. 233.

Fatal Brothers, The, iii. 229–30, 235.

Fool and Her Maidenhead Soon Parted, A, see Anonymous.

Henry II, iii. 231; v. 1049, 1236.

History of Henry the First, The, i. 103, 119–20; iii. 225, 230–1, 235; v. 1049, 1236.

King John and Matilda, i. 221 n. 1, 246, 249, 251, 331, 338; ii. 345, 353, 387, 407, 445, 482, 525, 528, 573, 583, 608, 628, 692; iii. 226, **232–4**, 235; v. 1236.

New Trick to Cheat the Devil, A, i. 331, 338; iii. **234–5.**

Davenport, Robert (*cont.*)
  Pedlar, The, iii. 235–6; v. 971, 973, 975.
  Pirate, The, iii. 236–7.
  Politic Queen, or Murder Will Out, The, iii. 235, 237.
  Woman's Mistaken, The, ii. 427, 428; iii. 235, 237–8. 281, 286.
Davenport, Thomas, ii. 514.
Daventry, Northamptonshire, v. 965.
David and Goliath, story of, vi. 273, 278.
Davies, John, of Hereford, ii. 557; v. 1267.
  A Scourge of Folly (1611), v. 1058.
Davies, Sir John, *Epigrammes and Elegies* (n.d.), vi. 211 n.
Davies, Richard, Oxford bookseller, v. 1188.
Davies, T., Reissue of Coxeter, Thomas, ed., *The Dramatic Works of Mr. Philip Massinger, Compleat*. Intro. by G. Colman, 4 vols. (1761), iv. 758.
  Intro. to *The Dramatick Works of Philip Massinger*, ed. John Monck Mason, 4 vols. (1779), iv. 758.
  ed., *Poems, Songs, and Sonnets: Together with a Masque* (1772), iii. 106.
  Roscius Anglicanus (Waldron ed.), (1789), iv. 817.
Davige, Lawrence, i. 266.
Davis, amateur actor, iii. 296.
Davis, Joe Lee, 'Richard Brome's Neglected Contribution to Comic Theory', *Stud. Phil.* xl (1943), iii. 55.
Davis, Moll (actress), v. 1145.
Davis, Richard, iv. 845, 848.
Davril, R., '*The Broken Heart*, étude critique, texte anglais et traduction française, notes', announced in *Research in Progress, P.M.L.A.* lxiii (1948), Supplement, p. 183, No. 900, iii. 439.
Daw, E. Beatrice, *P.M.L.A.* xxxii (1957), iv. 599.
Dawbridgecourt, George, ii. 561.
Dawe, Jack, *pseud.*, vi. 136, 137, 157.
  Vox Graculi, or Iacke Dawes Prognostication . . . for 1623 (1623), i. 145; vi. 136, 157, 207, 208.
Dawes, Robert, i. 198, 211; ii. 422; iii. 238; v. 1315; vi. 207.

Cupid's Festival, ii. 422.
Dawson, a carrier, iv. 714.
Dawson, Giles Edwin, ed., Massinger's *The Picture*. Unpublished Cornell Thesis (1931), iv. 808.
  'Seven Champions of Christendome, The, by John Kirke', *Western Reserve University Bulletin*, New Series, xxxii, No. 16 (1929), iv. 711, 712, 713.
Dawson, Mr. Eph., stationer, iii. 215.
Day, Cyrus L., 'New Poems by Randolph', *R.E.S.* viii (1932), v. 964.
  'Randolph and Prynne', *Mod. Phil.* xxix (1932), v. 986, 987–8.
  'Thomas Randolph and *The Drinking Academy*', *P.M.L.A.* xliii (1928), 800–9; v. 976, 977, 978, 979, 990, 991, 1239.
  'Thomas Randolph's Part in the Authorship of *Hey for Honesty*', *P.M.L.A.* xli (1926), 325–34, v. 980, 981, 982.
  'Three Notes on Randolph', *M.L.N.* xlvi (1931), v. 965, 969, 971, 986, 989.
Day, Hugh, ii. 479.
Day (Daye, Dey, Deye), John, ii. 426; iii. 238–40, 243, 246, 258–9; iv. 581; v. 1015, 1017, 1026, 1347, 1348.
  collaborator, iii. 251.
  Bellman of Paris, The, see Dekker.
  Blind Beggar of Bethnal Green, The, i. 322; ii. 407; iii. 238.
  Bristow Tragedy, The, iii. 247.
  Come See a Wonder, i. 206; iii. 240, 273, 275; v. 1178.
  Humour Out of Breath, iii. 238; vi. 65, 67.
  Isle of Gulls, The, iii. 238; vi. 90.
  Law Tricks, or Who Would Have Thought It, iii. 238.
  Parliament of Bees, iii. 239, 240, 258–9, 273; vi. 124, 126.
  Peregrinatio Scholastica, iii. 239.
Day, John, Rowley, William, and Wilkins, George, *Travels of The Three English Brothers, The*, iii. 238; v. 1015, 1017, 1026; vi. 132, 133, 216 n. 2.
Day, Thomas, ii. 422–3.
Day's Courtship, A, see Anonymous, *Tunbridge Wells*.
Deal boards, vi. 286.
de Argensola, Bartolome Leonardo,

Conquista de las Islas Malucas
(1609), iii. 350.
Death of the Black Prince, The, see
Anonymous.
'Death of the Red Bull, The', *see*
Van Lennep, William.
*Debauchee, or the Credulous Cuckold,
The, see* Behn, Aphra.
de Beer, E. S., *The Diary of John
Evelyn*, 6 vols. (1955), vii. 108.
de Bellan, *L'Histoire de Ruis Dias,
et de Quixaire, Princesse des
Moluques* (1615), iii. 350.
de' Bonarelli, C. Guidubaldo, *see*
Bonarelli.
DeCaine, Andrew, *see* Cane, Andrew.
Deckar, Tho:, *see* Dekker, Thomas.
Declaration of Sports, 1618, v. 1010.
De Creetes, John, *see* De Critz, John.
De Critz, John, Sergeant painter, vi.
272, 273, 278, 279.
Dedham School, Essex, iii. 159.
Dedications, iii. 4, 5, 8, 14, 15, 18,
19, 20, 39, 45, 49, 54, 67, 71, 72,
83, 88, 95, 97, 98, 113, 116, 120,
123, 141, 152, 153, 154-5, 184,
198, 201, 204, 205, 212, 222,
225, 229, 233, 239, 279, 309,
311, 427, 429, 435, 436, 440,
443, 451, 452, 454, 455, 456,
457, 463, 469; iv. 475, 477, 480,
483, 487, 492, 493, 510, 512,
513, 533, 535, 536, 542, 544,
545, 550, 566, 570, 573, 578,
588, 602, 603, 609, 623, 680,
687, 689, 710, 712, 715, 722,
727, 729, 730, 735, 744, 749,
751, 755, 756, 757, 769, 776,
778, 788, 799, 802, 809, 813,
816, 822, 823, 831, 833, 835,
852, 853, 870, 896, 897, 898,
904, 905, 915, 921, 928, 934,
939, 942, 943; v. 963, 967, 983,
984, 985, 1001, 1002, 1003,
1016, 1017, 1018, 1028, 1029,
1030, 1032, 1040, 1042, 1044,
1048, 1051, 1052, 1061, 1069,
1078, 1083, 1086, 1094,
1096, 1099, 1100, 1113, 1115,
1117, 1123, 1124, 1126, 1131,
1133, 1136, 1138, 1139, 1140,
1142, 1152, 1165, 1167, 1169,
1180, 1185, 1186, 1219-20,
1222, 1223, 1234, 1235, 1240,
1253, 1257, 1258, 1311, 1320,
1358, 1360, 1391; vi. 10, 71, 95,
152, 154, 222, 223.
Alternate, iii. 460.
Blank, iv. 680.

Ironic, v. 1080-1, 1161.
Multiple, iv. 680, 687, 689, 773;
v. 981.
Dedication racket, iv. 773.
Dedicatory epistle, iii. 446, 450,
542, 964; v. 998, 1032.
Dedicatory verse, iii. 421, 689, 690.
*Deep Sigh, A, Breath'd Through the
Lodgings at White-Hall, Deploring
the absence of the Court. And the
Miseries of the Pallace* (1642), *see*
Anonymous.
de Flores, Juan, *La Historia de
Grisel y Mirabella*, iii. 431.
Degrees, building of, vii. 69.
Dekker, Anne, iii. 242.
Dekker, Dorcas, iii. 242.
Dekker, Elizabeth, iii. 242.
Dekker, Thomas, i. 20, 170 n. 1, 184,
208; iii. 6, 55, 83, 84, 239,
241-75, 282, 283, 436, 459, 460;
iv. 499, 564, 575, 581, 585, 625,
754, 760, 808, 857, 861, 879,
891, 892, 926, 936, 938; v. 1241,
1244, 1254, 1255, 1347, 1348;
vi. 146, 147, 221.
Collaboration with Ford, iii. 436.
Bachelor's Banquet, The, iii. 243.
Believe It is So and 'Tis So, iii.
245-6; iv. 866.
Bellman of London, iii. 245, 316-17.
Bellman of Paris, The, i. 206, 209,
214; iii. 243, 246; vi. 221.
Bristow Merchant, The, i. 150,
151, 156; iii. 244, 247-8, 265,
436, 448; iv. 796.
Britannia's Honour, iii. 248.
City Show, A, iii. 248; iv. 865.
*Disguises, or Love in Disguise, A
Petticoat Voyage*, iii. 249; iv.
865, 866.
English   Villainies   (1632),
'Epistle', iii. 242.
Guls Hornbook (1609), iii. 245;
v. 1055; vi. 192.
Gustavus, King of Sweden, iii. 250,
263.
If it be not Good the Devil is in it,
iii. 243, 252; vi. 218.
Jew of Venice, The, iii. 252.
King Sebastian of Portugal, see
Henry Chettle.
Late Murder in Whitechapel, The,
see *The Late Murder of the Son
upon the Mother.*
*Late Murder of the Son upon the
Mother, The, or Keep the Widow
Waking* (with Ford, Rowley,
and Webster), i. 170 n. 1,

Dekker (cont.)
    208 and n. 1, 209, 214; ii.
        380, 402, 556, 557, 560, 626;
        iii. 238, 243, 244, 246, 247,
        252–6, 265, 272, 280, 286, 436;
        iv. 471; v. 1012, 1014, 1016,
        1241, 1243, 1254, 1448; vi. 221,
        222, 240.
    London's Tempe, or The Field of
        Happiness, iii. 248, 256.
    Match Me in London, i. 185 and
        n. 5, 195; iii. 113, 243, 256, 265;
        v. 1314; vi. 59, 225 n. 2; vii. 75,
        81.
    Noble Soldier (The Noble Spanish
        Soldier), or A Contract Broken
        Justly Revenged, The, iii. 257–
        60, 268, 274; v. 1011, 1013.
    Old Fortunatus. iii. 261.
    Owles Almanacke, The, i. 161 n.
        2; vi. 55.
    Patient Grissell, iii. 261.
    Penny-Wise, Pound-Foolish, iii.
        244, 247.
    Phaethon, iii. 242, 460.
    Proposed Pageant (1617), iii. 261.
    Ravens Almanacke, The (1609),
        vi. 147.
    Rod for Run-aways, A (1625), i.
        19; iii. 244.
    Satiromastix, or The Untrussing
        of the Humorous Poet, iii. 242,
        262; iv. 607.
    Shoemakers' Holiday, or The
        Gentle Craft, The, ii. 535; iii.
        262; iv. 588, 589; v. 997; vi.
        54; vii. 29, 57, 81.
    Sun's Darling, The, see Ford.
    Tale of Jocundo and Astolpho,
        The, iii. 250, 262.
    Troia Nova Triumphans, iii. 248,
        363.
    Villainies Discovered by Lanthorn
        and Candlelight, iii. 244.
    Wars, Wars, Wars, iii. 244.
    Welsh Ambassador, or A Comedy
        in Disguises, The, i. 175; iii. 249,
        259, 267–8; iv. 806, 865, 866; v.
        1435.
    White Moor, The, iii. 269; iv.
        865.
    Whore of Babylon, The, iii. 243,
        269.
    Wonder of a Kingdom, The, iii.
        240, 259, 273–5; v. 1020, 1021;
        vii. 102.
    Wonderful Year, The, iii. 243.
    Worke for Armorours (1609), vi.
        211 n.

Dekker, Thomas, and John Ford,
    Fairy Knight, The, i. 206 n. 3,
        214; iii. 243–4, 246, 247, 249–50,
        436; v. 1330.
    Sun's Darling, The, iii. 436; v.
        1216; vi. 50 n. 2, 59; vii. 6, 7, 8.
Dekker, Thomas, and John Ford and
    William Rowley, Witch of Edmon-
        ton, The, i. 202 n. 6, 204 n. 1, 205,
        209, 213, 214, 215, 251–2; ii. 378,
        425, 433, 459–60, 506, 554; iii.
        243, 244, 246, 269, 272, 436, 446;
        iv. 865; v. 1016; vi. 58.
Dekker, Thomas, and Phillip Mas-
    singer, Virgin Martyr, The, i. 166,
        174; iii. 263–6, 397; iv. 735, 754,
        784; v. 1060, 1142; vi. 220.
Dekker, Thomas, and Thomas
    Middleton, Honest Whore, The,
        i. 251; iii. 243, 252; vi. 21, 74,
        77, 101.
    Roaring Girl, The, or Moll
        Cutpurse, i. 136 n. 3; iii. 243,
        261; iv. 568, 857, 892; v. 1401,
        1402; vi. 146; vii. 77.
Dekker, Thomas, and Munday
    Anthony, Jeptha, iv. 794.
Dekker, Thomas, and Henry Chettle
    and John Day, The Golden Ass or
    Cupid and Psyche, iv. 581.
Dekker, Thomas, and John Day,
    The Life and Death of Guy of
    Warwick, i. 228; iii. 251; vii. 28,
        35, 38.
Dekker, Thomas, and John Webster,
    Northward Ho, iii. 81, 243, 261;
        v. 1241.
    Sir Thomas Wyatt, iii. 262; v.
        1241.
    Westward Ho, iii. 243, 268; v.
        1241.
Delattre, Floris, English Fairy
    Poetry (1912), v. 969.
de Lau, Hurfries, see Lau, Hurfries
    de.
Deloney, Thomas, 'The Dutchesse of
    Suffolkes Calamatie' ballad
    (1602), iii. 285.
    Strange Histories (1602), iii. 285.
Demetrius and Enanthe, see Fletcher,
    The Humorous Lieutenant.
Demetrius and Marina [Marsina],
    see Anonymous.
De Naturali, Supernaturali, Praeter-
    naturali et Contranaturali Micro-
    cosmi Historia (1619), see Fludd,
    Robert.
Denbigh, Countess of, attends
    masque in disguise, iii. 219.

Denbigh, Earl of, performs in masque, iv. 647.

Denbigh, alderman of, v. 1040.

Denbigh, burgess of, v. 1040.

Denbigh, common councilman of, v. 1040.

Denbighshire, M.P. for, v. 1040.

Denham, Christopher, v. 1311.

Denham, Sir John, iii. **275-9**.
  Cooper's Hill, iii. 276.
  Horace, iii. 276.
  Poems and Translations, with The Sophy (1668), iii. 277.
  Sophy, The, i. 120; iii. 275, **276-9**; v. 1035, 1149-50.

Denmark House, *see* also Somerset House, i. 201 n. 1 cont., 232; iv. 918; v. 1377; vi. 15, 282, 283; vii. 4, 22, 34, 62, 63, 86.
  Hall at, vii. 60.
  Presence Chamber at, vii. 62.

Denmark, King of, entertainments for, iii. 435.

Denshfield, Katherine, ii. 449.

Dent, Edward Joseph, *Foundations of English Opera* (1928), iii. 220.

Denygten, *see* Downton, Thomas.

Deorum Dona, see Baron, Robert.

Deorum Judicium, see Heywood, Thomas.

Depositions, vi. 202 and n. 2, 210, 219.

De Probatis Sanctorum Historiis, see Anonymous.

Deptford, Kent, v. 1204, 1257, 1258.

Deputy Master of the Revels (William Blagrave), vi. 64.

Derby, iii. 167.

Derby, J. C., iii. 312.

Derby, Dowager Countess of, iv. 913.

Derby House, ii. 401; vi. 170, 232.

Derby, Earl of, dramatic company of, iii. 251; v. 1347; vii. 28.

Derbyshire, iv. 649.

De Re Poetica, see Blount, Thomas.

De Ricci and Wilson, *Census of Medieval and Renaissance MSS in the U.S. and Canada*, v. 1328.

Dering, Sir E., Bt., v. 1368.

Dermiere, Barbara, ii. 456.

Dermiere, John, ii. 456.

De Rojas, Fernando, iv. 727.

De Roode en Witte Roos (Dutch play), v. 1014.

DeRosset, Fr. trans. of Cervantes' *Novelas Exemplares, Les nouvelles de . . . Cervantes* (1613-14), iv. 895.

Description of England, see Harrison, William.

Deserving Favourite, The, see Carlell.

Desiderata Curiosa, see Peck, Rev. Francis.

Designs by Inigo Jones for Masques & Plays at Court, see Simpson, Percy.

Designs for costumes, *see* Costumes.

'Designs for the First Movable Scenery on the English Public Stage', *see* Keith, William Grant.

Desmus, Ralph, *Merlinus Anonymous*, ii. 600.

de Soulas, Josias, *see* Floridor, Josias.

Devereux, Sir Walter, v. 1311.

Devil and St. Dunstan (tavern), vii. 54.

Devil in plays, i. 30 n. 6 cont.

Devil Is an Ass, The, see Jonson, Ben.

Devil of Dowgate, or Usury Put to Use, The, see Fletcher, John.

Devil Tavern, Apollo room, iv. 608.

Devil Turned Ranter, The, see Sheppard, Samuel, *The Jovial Crew*.

Devils Charter, The, see Barnes, Barnaby.

Devil's Law-Case, The, or When Women Go to Law the Devil is Full of Business, see Webster, John.

Devils on stage, vi. 193, 243.

De Vocht, Henry, *The Wizard, A Play by Simon Baylie, Materialen* (1930), iii. 12, 13, 336.

DeVocht, H., and L. Drees, eds., *Thomas Middleton: The Witch, Materials for the Study of Old English Drama*, New Series, xviii (1945), iv. 903.

Devonshire, Countess of, *see* Rich, Penelope.

Devonshire, Duke of, iv. 672.
  MS. collection of, iv. 524, 669; v. 1378.

Devonshire, Earl of, iii. 435; vi. 215.

Devonshire, William Cavendish, Sixth Duke of, v. 1304.

Devonshire, County of, iii. 437.

Dewe, Thomas, iv. 867, 868.

D'Ewes, Richard, v. 1408.

D'Ewes, Sir Simonds, i. 64; iii. 11; iv. 534, 535; v. 991-2, 1042, 1408, 1414; vi. 39.
  The Autobiography and Correspondence of Sir Simonds D'Ewes, ed. J. O. Halliwell (1845), iii. 11; v. 984, 1408, **1414**.

D'Ewes, Sir Simonds (*cont.*)
Journal of Sir Simonds D'Ewes,
    ed. W. H. Coates (1942), vi. 39.
'De Witt Again', *see* Hodges, C.
    Walter.
de Witt, Johannes, vi. 184 n. 2,
    249–50.
Dey, Walter, iii. 238.
Diaconus, Paulus, *De Gestis Lango-
    bardorum*, v. 1274.
Dialect, Scots, v. 1236.
    Yorkshire, iv. 633, 635–6.
Dialects, iv. 635.
Dialogue, iv. 504, 564, 934, 944,
    989; v. 1060, 1074, 1127, 1295,
    1306, 1402; vii. 124.
    Welsh, iv. 642.
Dialogues, German, v. 1287.
'Dialogue between Policy and Piety',
    see Davenport, Robert.
Dialogue of Riches and Honor, A, see
    Shirley, James, *A Contention for
    Honour and Riches.*
Diamond, Hugh W. 'The Prince's
    Masque', *N. & Q.* First Series,
    xii (1855), iv. 666–7.
Diana's Grove, see Anonymous.
Diana's temple, burning of, iii. 399.
Dianea, see Cokayne, Sir Aston.
Diaries, i. 94, 110, 112, 114, 123, 128,
    132, 235, 250, 255, 258; ii. 346–
    9, 373–81, 688–9; iii. 11; vi. 209
    n. 1, 210 n.
*Diaries and Despatches of the Vene-
    tian Embassy at the Court of King
    James I in the Years 1617–18*,
    translated by Rawdon Brown, i.
    136 n. 4.
Diary of John Evelyn, The, see de
    Beer, E. S.
'Diary of the Journey of Philip
    Julius, Duke of Stettin-Pomer-
    ania, through England in the
    Year 1602', *see* von Bülow,
    Gottfried.
Diary of Lady Anne Clifford, see
    Sackville-West, V.
(Diary of Lupold von Wedel)
    Trans. R. Hist. Soc., Second Series,
    ix (1895), vi. 209 n. 1; 210 n.
Diary of Sir Humphrey Mildmay,
    see Mildmay.
Diary of Thomas Crosfield, The, see
    Boas, Frederick S.
Diary or an Exact Journal, A, see
    Newspapers.
Dibden, Charles Isaac Mungo,
    *History and Illustrations of the
    London Theatres* (1826), iv. 777.

Dicconson, Frances, i. 41.
Dick, Hugh G., v. 1225.
    ed., *Albumazar: A Comedy* (1944),
    v. 1225, 1391.
Dick of Devonshire, see Anonymous.
Dickens, Ro., ii. 642, 651.
Dicker, Thomas, *see* Dekker,
    Thomas.
Dickson, M. J., 'William Rowley',
    T.L.S. 28 March 1929, v. 1014,
    1016.
    'William Trevell and the White-
    friars Theatre', *Review of Eng-
    lish Studies*, vi (1930), vi. 115.
Dictionary of American Biography,
    iii. 21, 22; v. 1047, 1048.
*Dictionary of the French and English
    Tongues* (1611), *see* Cotgrave,
    Randle.
Dictionary of National Biography,
    iii. 22, 29, 96, 100, 166, 185, 225,
    279, 290, 303, 468, 469; iv. 498,
    514, 515, 631, 690, 711, 715, 716,
    717, 719, 728, 732, 751, 841, 843,
    844, 851, 916, 951, 954; v. 993,
    994, 999, 1000, 1004, 1027, 1028,
    1029, 1037, 1038, 1039, 1040,
    1042, 1047, 1053, 1054, 1103,
    1164, 1185, 1197, 1224, 1265,
    1277, 1417.
Diekhoff, John S., 'The Text of
    Comus, 1634 to 1645', *P.M.L.A.*
    lii (1937), iv. 914.
Digby, George Lord, iv. 721.
Digby, Sir John, v. 1199; vii. 28.
Digby, Sir Kenelm, i. 42, 47; ii. 416,
    493; iii. 279–80, 343, 346; iv.
    835, 985; v. 1028, 1032, 1033,
    1061, 1164, 1199.
    Dedication to, iv. 710.
    Amyntas, iii. 279.
    Pastor Fido, iii. 280.
    *Private Memoirs of Sir Kenelm
    Digby . . . Written by Himself*
    (1827), v. 1164.
Digby, Mr., vi. 34.
Digby, Lady Venetia, i. 248 n. h;
    v. 1028, 1032, 1033.
Digby, Lord John, vi. 297, 298.
Digby, Lord, Robert Digby, Baron
    Digby, vi. 34, 260.
Digges, Leonard, iii. 379.
    (Transl.) *Gerardo the Unfortunate
    Spaniard* (1622), iii. 366, 420;
    iv. 501, 863.
Dilke, C. W. [ed.] *Old English
    Plays*, 6 vols. (1814–15), iii. 273.
Dilke, Thomas, *The City Lady, or
    Folly Reclaimed*, iv. 774.

Dillon, —, ii. 413.
Dio Cassius, iii. 406.
 Roman History, iv. 817, 834.
Dioclesian, see Anonymous.
Diocletian, v. 1174.
Diodate, John, ii. 639.
Diodorus, iv. 764, 768.
Dionysius of Halicarnassus, v. 1247, 1370.
Dirges, sung, v. 1098.
Disappointed Ladies, The, see Anonymous.
Discontented Colonel, The, see Suckling, Brennoralt.
Discreet Lover, The, see Carlell, Lodowick, The Fool would be a Favourite.
Disguises, iii. 69, 85, 90, 219, 267–8; iv. 472, 549, 630, 740, 894, 934, 944; v. 997, 1063, 1120, 1377.
Disguises, or Love in Disguise. A Petticoat Voyage, The, see Dekker.
Dishley, see Distle.
Disintegrators, iii. 317, 323, 331, 335, 337–8, 342, 347, 350, 353, 355, 358, 363, 365, 369, 375, 379, 383, 386, 390, 394, 396, 400, 405, 414, 420, 424, 433; iv. 754, 826, 859, 901; v. 1018, 1247, 1252.
Disinterested Love, see Hull, Thomas.
Disraeli, Isaac, Curiosities of Literature (1834 ed.), iv. 780.
Distle, —, ii. 423.
Distracted Emperor, The, see Chapman, George, Charlemagne.
Distracted State, The, see Tatham, John, v. 1219.
Distractions, see Jordan, Thomas, Love Hath Found His Eyes.
Distress, The, see Davenant, William.
Distressed Lovers, The, see Theobald, Lewis, Double Falsehood.
Divine Tragedie Lately Acted, A, see Anonymous.
Divorce, The, see Anonymous.
Dixon, Thomas, i. 201 n.; ii. 422, 423; vi. 291, 292, 293, 297, 298, 299, 301, 302, 303, 304.
Doating Lovers, The, see Hamilton, Newburgh.
Dobell, Bertram (ed.), Anon., The Partial Law, London (1908), v. 1388.
 ed., The Poetical Works of William Strode (1907), iii. 384; v. 1187, 1188, 1189, 1192, 1193.
Dobell, Percy, iii. 314.

Dobell, Percy, and Son, Tunbridge Wells, catalogue of, v. 1269.
Dobson, John, i. 220, 246; ii. 423.
Doctor (see also Barber-chirurgion, Physician, and Surgeon), ii. 641; iii. 190.
Doctor in physic, ii. 634.
Doctor Faustus, see Marlowe, Christopher.
Doctor Lamb and the Witches, see Anonymous.
Doctors' Commons, v. 1276; see London, streets of.
 Proctor in, v. 1276.
Doddridge, Richard, v. 988.
Dodds, M. Hope, 'Edmond Ironsides and The Lovesick King', M.L.R. xix (1924), iii. 42, 43, 44.
Dodsley, Robert, A Select Collection of Old Plays, 12 vols. (1744), iii. 24, 304; iv. 522, 701, 739, 741; v. 1401.
 A Select Collection of Old Plays, 12 vols. (1780), iii. 222.
 ed., A Select Collection of Old Plays, 12 vols. (1825–7), iii. 132.
 ed., May's The Old Couple in vol. vii, A Select Collection of Old Plays (1744), iv. 839.
 ed., May's The Heir, vol. vii of A Select Collection of Old Plays (1744), iv. 835.
 ed., Mayne's The City Match in vol. x of A Select Collection of Old Plays (1744), iv. 847.
 ed., Nabbes's Microcosmus, in Select Collection of Old Plays, vol. v (1744), iv. 936.
 Select Collection of Old English Plays, A, ed. W. C. Hazlitt, 15 vols. (1874–6), v. 1034.
Dodson, Daniel, 'Middleton's Livia', Phil. Quart. xxvii (1948), iv. 905.
Doge, letter to, i. 204.
Doge and the Dragon, The, see Anonymous.
Dogs, vi. 210 n., 213.
Dog-yard at Hope Theatre, vi. 203.
Dolben, David, v. 1341.
Dolben, Sir John, v. 1341.
'Doleful ballad of the general overthrowe of the famous theatre on the Bankside, called the "Globe", A', see Parrat, William.
Dominican monastery (at Blackfriars), vi. 4–5.
Don Carlos Caloma, iv. 637
Don Japhet of Armenia, see Lower, Sir William,

Don Juan, v. 1450.
Don Lope de Cardona, see Lope de Vega.
Don Manuel, see Shirley, James, The Court Secret.
Don Pedro, see Anonymous.
Don Phoebo's Triumph, see Fane, Mildmay.
Don Quixote, see Cervantes.
Don Zara del Fogo, see Holland, Samuel, Wit and Fancy in a Maze.
Donato, Antonio, The Venetian Ambassador, vii. 29.
Doncaster, Viscount, i. 6; iv. 666; vii. 39.
House of, vii. 34.
Doncaster, Yorkshire, i. 92, 93, 193, 248, 282; ii. 423, 496.
Donne, Constance, ii. 349; vi. 85.
Donne, George, iii. 437, 450, 454; iv. 788.
Donne, John, ii. 349, 468, 557; iii. 274; vi. 85.
Donne, John (the younger), iv. 844; v. 965.
Donstone, James, i. 135.
Doorkeepers, see Theatres, door-keepers at, vi. 41.
Doors on stage, see Stage doors.
Dorchester, Viscount, i. 302; iv. 637.
Doriela, Dr., ii. 676, 677, 678.
Dorington, Sr., Cambridge actor, v. 1298, 1299.
Dormer, Robert, v. 1223.
Dorney, Margaret, ii. 363.
Dorney, Richard, ii. 363.
Dorothea (martyr), tragedy of, iii. 266.
Dorrell, Thomas, of Lincoln's Inn, v. 1157.
Dorset, Mary, Countess of, ii. 424; v. 1359; vi. 98.
Dorset, Edward Sackville, Fourth Earl of, and Lord Chamberlain to Queen Henrietta-Maria, i. 223, 238, 239 and n. 3, 283 n. 7, 303, 304 and n. 2, 309; ii. 380, 423-4, 684; iv. 517, 891; v. 1028, 1029, 1030, 1034, 1037, 1227, 1359; vi. 67, 87, 88, 89, 90, 91, 98, 103, 162; vii. 31.
Dorset, Edward Sackville, Fifth Earl of, v. 1359; vi. 91.
Dorset, High Sheriff of, v. 1215.
Dorset Garden theatre, iii. 388, 395, 404, 410, 419; iv. 616, 767; v. 985, 998, 999; vi. 116.
Dorset House, vi. 88, 89, 104.

Dort, Synod of, v. 979.
Douai, college for English Catholics, iii. 290; v. 1186.
Douay Bible, v. 1415.
Double Falsehood, The, see Fletcher, Cardenio.
Double Falsehood, The, see Theobald, Lewis.
Double Marriage, The, see Fletcher, John.
Doublet, Breeches, and Shirt, see Heylyn, Peter.
'Doubling', iiii. 297.
Doubtful Heir, The, see Shirley, James.
Douce, Francis, iii. 172; v. 1383.
ed., The Dance of Death (1858), iii. 291.
Doughten or Doughton, Thomas, see Downton, Thomas.
Dounton, Thomas, see Downton, Thomas.
Doutone, Thomas, see Downton, Thomas.
Dove, The, see Zouche, Richard.
Dover, Anthony, i. 286, 288, 290, 297; ii. 425; vi. 100.
Dover, Mary, ii. 650.
Dover, i. 92, 156, 172, 173, 180, 193, 212, 213, 218, 313, 322.
Dowdeswell, Roger, ii. 403.
Dowghton, Thomas, see Downton, Thomas.
Dowgill, Robert, ii. 677; v. 1125.
Dowland, Robert, see Dulandt, Robert.
Dowle, Rowland, i. 49 n. 2 cont., 73–89; ii. 425–6; iii. 321, 369.
Dowling, Harold M., 'Peele and Some Doubtful Plays. I. "Alphonsus, Emperor of Germany"', N. & Q. clxiv (1933), v. 1286.
Dowling, Margaret, 'Further Notes on William Trevell', Review of English Studies, vi (1930), vi. 115.
Downes, John, prompter, iii. 71, 118, 175, 206, 221, 315, 320, 330, 332, 349, 371, 374, 377, 397, 403, 408, 409, 413, 414, 418, 426; iv. 480, 495, 497, 615, 766; v. 1091, 1118, 1167, 1204, 1248; vi. 169.
Downes, John, Roscius Anglicanus (1708), ii. 545; iii. 71, 118, 175, 206, 221, 315, 320, 330, 333, 344, 345, 349, 371, 374, 377, 397, 403, 408, 409, 413, 418, 423, 426; iv. 480, 495, 616, 766, 862, 864; v. 1085, 1091, 1108, 1115, 1135–6, 1145, 1151, 1166, 1204, 1248.

Downes, Thomas, Warden of Stationers Company, v. 1122, 1125, 1168, 1234.

Downey, Nicholas, iv. 531.

Downfall and Death of Robert Earl of Huntingdon, The, see Munday, Anthony.

Downs, the, ship in, v. 1202, 1205.
  Spanish fleet in, iii. 150.
  Naval battle in, iv. 496.

Downton, Anne, ii. 426, 642.

Downton, Ed., ii. 643.

Downton, Jane, ii. 426, 643.

Downton, Thomas, Senior, i. 135, 136, 137, 139, 142, 155; ii. **426**, 623; iii. 239; vi. 149 n. 2.
  Will of, ii. 642–3.

Downton, Thomas, Junior, i. 299; ii. **426–7**.

Dowson, Agnes, ii. 650.

Dowten or Dowton, Thomas, see Downton, Thomas.

Dramatic coach, ii. 371; vii. 83.

Dramatic companies, French, see French dramatic companies.

Dramatic Museum of Columbia University, vi. 143.

Dramatic Records in the Declared Accounts of the Treasurer of the Chamber, 1558–1642, see Cook, David.

'Dramatic Records: The Lord Chamberlain's Office', see Boswell, Eleanore.

'Dramatic References from the Scudamore Papers', see Feil, J. P.

'Dramaticus', 'The Tragedy of "Page of Plymouth" by Ben Jonson and Thomas Dekker', *The Shakespeare Society's Papers*, ii (1845), iv. 625.

Dramatis personae, iii. 4, 20, 27, 37–38, 95, 159, 184, 260, 274, 296, 304, 312, 317, 428, 440; iv. 609, 621, 854, 972; v. 1009, 1197, 1261, 1284, 1295, 1298, 1306, 1317, 1394, 1407, 1451, 1453; vi. 110.

Dramatists, see Playwrights.

Draper, ii. 544, 545, 648.

Draper, Mr., iv. 949.

Draper, William H., ed. of *The Elder Brother* (1915), iii. 332.

Drapers, Ancient and Honorable Society of, ii. 545; iv. 578, 584, 895, 896, 897, 898, 926.

Drapers' Hall, vii. 20.

Drawings, v. 1230.

Drayton, Michael, ii. 557; iv. 818, 861, 936; v. 1240, 1241, 1248.

Dedication to, iii. 15.

England's Heroical Epistles, iii. 233.

Legend of Matilda, iii. 234.

'The Owl', v. 1385.

Poems, iii. 234.

Drayton, Dekker, and Chettle, *The Famous Wars of Henry I and the Prince of Wales*, iii. 231.

Drayton, Michael, Hathway, Munday, and Wilson, *Oldcastle*, i. 28, 96, 99, 120.

Drayton, Staffordshire, v. 1268.

Draytwiche, Worcester, ii. 469.

Drees, L., and H. DeVocht, eds., *Thomas Middleton: The Witch*, *Materials for the Study of Old English Drama*, New Series, xviii (1945), iv. 903.

Dresden, ii. 451.

Drew, John, vi. 134, 135.

Drew, Thomas, see Drue, Thomas, and Drewe, Thomas.

Drewe, Bartholomew, ii. **427**.

Drewe, Elizabeth, ii. 428.

Drewe, Francis, ii. 428.

Drewe, George, ii. 427.

Drewe, Robert, ii. 428.

Drewe, Thomas, i. 163, 169 n. 2, 171, 202; ii. **427–8**.
  Daniel Ben Alexander, the Converted Jew, ii. 428.

Dreydon, Sir John, iii. 442.

Dring, Thomas, stationer, iii. 61, 62, 84; iv. 919.

Drington, Richard, see Errington, Richard.

Drinking Academy, The, see Randolph.

Driwood, Mr., v. 1233.

Drolls, iii. 151, 182–3, 227, 314, 319, 323, 324, 344, 378, 380, 403, 407, 409, 419; iv. 481; v. 1079, 1147, 1314, 1357; vi. 218, 233.

Dromedary, vi. 234.

Drue, Thomas, iii. 237–8, 253, **280–6**.
  Bloody Banquet, The, i. 331, 341; ii. 427; iii. 9, 281, **282–4**; v. 1320.
  Duchess of Suffolk, The, i. 150, 156; ii. 427, 428; iii. 265, 280, **284–6**; vi. 158.
  Unknown Play (1624), iii. 286.

Drue, Thomas, Gentleman Waiter to the King, iii. 281.

Drum, to advertise provincial performances, ii. 608–9, 686.

Drummer, ii. 473.

Drummond, William, of Hawthornden, ii. 436; iii. 238, 243,

Drummond, William (*cont.*)
  287–90, 300, 308; iv. 606, 607,
  610, 611, 616, 621, 627, 733,
  859.
Library of, iii. 288.
*Entertainment of the High and
  Mighty Monarch Charles, King
  of Great Britain, France, and
  Ireland into his Ancient and
  Royal City of Edinburgh, the
  fifteenth of June, 1633* (1633),
  iii. 289–90.
Flowers of Sion (1632), iii. 288.
Forth Feasting (1619), iii. 287.
'*Heads of a Conversation betwixt
  the Famous Poet* Ben Johnson,
  and William Drummond *of
  Hawthornden, January, 1619*'
  (1711), iii. 287; iv. 511.
*History of Scotland from the Year
  1423 until the Year 1542*,
  (1655), iii. 288.
*Mavsolevm or, The Choicest
  Flowers of the Epitaphs, written
  on the Death of the neuer-too-
  much lamented Prince Henrie*,
  Edinburgh (1613), v. 1017.
*Most Elegant And Elabovrate
  Poems Of that Great Court-Wit,
  Mr William Drummond, The*,
  (1659), iii. 288.
Poems, iii. 287.
*Poems, By That most Famous Wit,
  William Drvmmond of Haw-
  thornden* (1656), iii. 288.
*Poems of William Drummond of
  Hawthornden, The* (1790), iii.
  288.
*Poems of William Drummond, of
  Hawthornden, The*, with Life
  by Peter Cunningham (1833),
  iii. 289.
*Poems of William Drummond of
  Hawthornden, The* edited with
  a Memoir and Notes by Wm. C.
  Ward (*Muses' Library*), 2 vols.
  (1894), iii. 289.
*Poems of William Drummond of
  Hawthornden, The* [edited by
  Thomas Maitland and David
  Irving for the Maitland Club]
  (1832), iii. 289.
*Poetical Works of William Drum-
  mond of Hawthornden, The*,
  edited by William B. Turnbull
  (*Library of Old Authors*) (1856),
  iii. 289.
*Poetical Works of William Drum-
  mond of Hawthornden with 'A

Cypresse Grove', The, edited by
  L. E. Kastner, 2 vols. (1913),
  iii. 289.
Tears on the Death of Moeliades
  (1613), iii. 287.
*Works Of William Drummond, Of
  Hawthornden, The* (1711), iii.
  287, 288.
Drums, vi. 242, 246; vii. 54.
Drunken Couple, The, see Anony-
  mous, *Love Lost in the Dark*.
Drury Lane, *see* London, streets and
  districts.
Drury Lane theatre, iii. 71, 222, 317,
  328, 336, 342, 347, 409, 446; iv.
  476, 479, 480, 777, 799, 850,
  862, 864, 895; v. 1108, 1111,
  1127, 1151, 1167, 1170; vi. 49.
Drury, Robert, *Fancied Queen, The*
  (opera), v. 1149.
Drury, William, iii. 290–1.
  Alvredus sive Alfredus, iii. 290.
  *Dramatica Poemata, Avthore D.
  Gvilielmo Drvraeo Nobili Anglo
  . . .* (1628), iii. 290.
  *Dramatica Poemata . . . Editio
  Ultima ab Ipso Auctore Re-
  cognita . . . Antverpiae* (1641),
  iii. 290.
  Mors, iii. 291.
  Reparatus, sive Depositum, iii.
  291.
Dryads, vi. 294.
Dryden, John, iii. 115, 144, 149,
  392, 394, 397, 413, 690, 729.
  Fables Ancient and Modern (1700),
  iii. 328.
  The Indian Emperor, v. 1341.
  King Arthur, iii. 349, 413.
  MacFlecknoe, v. 1072.
  Secret Love, or The Maiden-Queen,
  v. 1094, 1341.
  The Wild Gallant, v. 1207.
Dublin, i. 131; iii. 33, 275; iv. 949,
  950, 956; v. 971, 975, 1069,
  1095, 1096, 1105, 1106, 1107,
  1112, 1113, 1134, 1140; vi. 193.
  Castle, v. 1140, 1141.
  Castle Gate, The, v. 1135, 1136.
  Performances in, iv. 699.
  Plays in, iii. 97, 179.
  Shirley in, iv. 700.
  Trinity College, iv. 752, 756.
  Werburgh Street Theatre, ii. 518;
  iii. 97; iv. 679, 949, 950; v.
  1136, 1138–9, 1140; vi. 193.
Ducarrel, Dr., iv. 741.
Duchess of Fernandina, The, see
  Glapthorne, Henry.

Duchess of Malfi, The, see Webster, John.
Duchess of Suffolk, The, see Drue, Thomas.
Ducie, Robert, v. 998.
Ducket, Thomas, amateur actor, iv. 473.
Ducy, Sir Robert, Lord Mayor, iii. 244.
Ducy, Sheriff of London, iv. 881.
Dudley, Lord, players of, ii. 423.
Dudley, Sir Henry Bate, iv. 810.
Dudlowe, Joane, ii. 536.
Duelling, iii. 357, 406; iv. 869; vii. 58.
Due Sorelle Rivali, Le, see Luchetti, Eusebio.
Duels, iv. 607.
Duets, v. 1002, 1110.
Duff, E. Gordon, *A Catalogue of Books in the John Rylands Library Manchester Printed . . . to . . . 1640* (1895), v. 1225.
Duke, The, see Shirley, James, *The Humorous Courtier.*
Duke and No Duke, A, see Tate, Nahum.
Duke Humphrey, see Anonymous.
Duke of Guise, The, see Shirley, Henry.
Duke of Lerma, The, see Shirley, Henry, *The Spanish Duke of Lerma.*
Duke of Lerma, The, see Howard, Sir Robert, *The Great Favourite.*
Duke of Milan, The, see Massinger, Philip.
Duke of Milan, see Cumberland, Richard.
Duke's Mistress, The, see Shirley, James.
'Duke's Play, The', *see* Anonymous.
'Duke Return'd Againe, The', *see* Anonymous.
Duke, John, i. 1, 158; ii. 428–9; vi. 129, 130.
Duke Humphrey, *see* St. Paul's Cathedral.
Duke of York, birth of, v. 1155.
Dukes company (Restoration), iii. 132, 177, 197, 409; iv. 768, 936; v. 1145, 1183, 1315; vi. 131.
Duke's Theatre in Lincolns Inn Fields, iii. 70, 80, 177, 197; iv. 546, 710; v. 1093, 1100, 1115, 1145–6, 1210, 1245.
Dulandt, Robert, ii. 429.
Dulwich, i. 138, 143; ii. 239, 483.

Mayor of, ii. 346.
Dulwich College, ii. 346, 395, 403, 405, 434, 486, 506, 510, 527, 659, 694; iii. 14, 274, 302; iv. 784; v. 1332, 1367; vi. 85, 149 n. 2, 157, 177, 178.
Court of Assistants of, vi. 177, 178.
Master of, vi. 155.
Masters and Warden of, vi. 141.
Muniments of, v. 1418; vi. 150.
Vs. Tobias Lisle and Thomas Grymes, ii. 568.
Dumb Bawd of Venice, The, see Shirley, Henry.
Dumb Knight, The, see Markham, Gervase.
Dumb show, ii. 579; iii. 397, 400, 692; v. 1175.
Dumfries, James I visits, iii. 112.
Duncombe, Sir S., promoter of sedans, iii. 64.
Dunham, Nottinghamshire, iv. 732, 733.
Dunkel, Wilbur Dwight, 'The Authorship of *Anything for a Quiet Life*', *P.M.L.A.* xliii (1928), iv. 859, 860.
'Did Not Rowley Merely Revise Middleton?' *P.M.L.A.* xlviii (1933), iv. 855; v. 1014.
Dramatic Technique of Thomas Middleton in His Comedies of London Life, The (1925), iv. 855.
Dunkirk, ii. 657 n. 4.
Powder magazines at, iii. 194.
Siege of, iv. 721.
Dunkirkers, iv. 482.
Dunlap, Rhodes, ed., *The Poems of Thomas Carew with His Masque Coelum Britannicum* (1949), iii. 104, 105, 106, 109, 110; iv. 921; v. 1229, 1381.
Dunluce, Lord, iv. 919.
Dunn, Esther Cloudman, *Ben Jonson's Art: Elizabethan Life and Literature as Reflected Therein* (1925), iv. 604.
Dunn, S. G., 'A Jonson Copyright', *T.L.S.* (28 July 1921), iv. 614.
Dunstan, Arthur Cyril. *Examination of Two English Dramas: 'The Tragedy of Mariam' by Elizabeth Carew: and 'The True Tragedy of Herod and Antipater: with the Death of faire Marriam', by Gervase Markham, and William Sampson* (1908), iv. 734.

P

Dunwich, Suffolk, i. 93, 172, 212.
Duport, James, v. 965, 985.
Duppa, Dr. Brian, iv. 844.
Duppa, Brian, ed., *Jonsonus Virbius*
(1638), ii. 662; iii. 51, 133, 437,
844; iv. 521, 612, 626, 738; v.
1029, 1037; vi. 166, 244.
Duquesa de Mantua, La, see Solor-
zano, Castillo,
Durance Masque, see Anonymous.
D'Urfé, Honoré, *Astrée*, v. 1429.
D'Urfey, Thomas, iii. 391.
  Archerie Reviv'd (1676), v. 988.
  Campaigners, The (1698), v. 988.
  Common-Wealth Of Women, A,
  iii. 413, 414.
  *Fool's Preferment, or, The Three
  Dukes of Dunstable, A*, iii. 388.
  *Madam Fickle, or The Witty
  False One*, iv. 741.
  Sir Barnaby Whigg, iv. 744.
Durham, Henry, ii. 558.
Durham, iii. 143.
Durham, Bishop of, iii. 455; v. 1232.
Durham Cathedral, iv. 527.
  Library MS., iii. 12; iv. 527.
Du Rocher, R.-M., *La Melise, ou
les Princes Reconnus*, i. 234; vi.
45, 65.
Du Ryer, Pierre, *Alcimedon*, i. 235
n. 1; vi. 45; vii. 97.
Dutch, iii. 169, 211, 223, 242; iv.
496, 924; v. 1129; vi. 194.
Dutch ambassador, iv. 664, 675.
Dutch, Anti-Dutch sentiments, iv.
482.
Dutch East India Company, agent
of, vi. 145.
Dutch (language), iii. 242.
Dutch, massacre by 1622/3, iii.
338.
Dutch, translation from, iii. 18, 417;
v. 1443.
Dutch vaulter, iv. 781; vii. 6.
Dutch visitors in London, iv. 569;
iii. 387, 409; iv. 569, 801, 803.
Dutch Courtesan, The, see Marston,
John.
*Dutch Painter and the French
Brawle, The, see* Anonymous.
du Tremblay, Henrietta Maria, iii.
196.
Dutton, Henry, ii. 400.
Dutton, Sir Ralph, iv. 744.
Dutton, Sir Thomas, v. 1422.
Dutton, Thomas, ii. 649.
Duty on wines, a new, vi. 228.
Dwarf, iv. 638.
Dwelling houses, vi. 298.

Dwelling houses, erection of pro-
hibited, vi. 306.
Dyce, Alexander, iii. 312, 316, 321;
v. 1447.
  ed., *Demetrius and Enanthe,
  Being The Humorous Lieutenant,
  A Play, By John Fletcher:
  Published from a Manuscript
  Dated 1625* (1830), iii. 343.
  ed., *The Dramatic Works and
  Poems of James Shirley, Now
  First Collected; With Notes by
  the Late William Gifford, Esq.
  And Additional Notes, And
  Some Account of Shirley and
  His Writings*, 6 vols. (1833), v.
  1066, 1072–3, 1087, 1098, 1105,
  1108, 1138, 1149, 1152.
  ed., *The Works of Beaumont and
  Fletcher: the text formed from a
  new collation of the early
  editions*, 11 vols. (1843–6), iii.
  305, 306, 317, 342, 356, 367,
  379, 420.
  ed., *The Works of Thomas
  Middleton*, 5 vols. (1840), iv.
  858, 859, 881, 901, 902.
  ed., *The Works of John Webster*
  4 vols. (1830), v. 1245.
Dyce, Alexander, and William
Gifford, *The Works of John Ford*,
3 vols. (1869 and 1895), iii. 464.
Dyce collection, Victoria and Albert
Museum, iii. 401; iv. 777, 805,
807, 876.
Dyckers, Anne, *see* Dekker, Anne.
Dyckers, Dorcas, *see* Dekker, Dorcas.
Dyckers, Elizabeth, *see* Dekker,
Elizabeth.
Dyer, iv. 471.
Dylke, Joane, ii. 390.
'Dymock' translation of *Il Pastor
Fido*, vii. 88, 90.
Dyos, William, Remembrancer of
the City of London, vi. 83.
Dyot, Richard, ii. 471.
Dysart, Countess of, iv. 951.
Dysart, Earl of, i. 61.
Dyson, Hum., ii. 642, 651.
Dyve, Sir Lewis, iv. 728.

E., G. (printer), iv. 879.
E., W., iii. 427.
Earl Marshal, vi. 186.
Earle, John, i. 316, 321; ii. **429**.
Earle, John, *Micro-cosmographie*
(1628), vii. 2.
'Early London Theatres', *see*
Anonymous.

Earnham, Lincolnshire, iii. 158.

East Allington, Devonshire, iii. 438.

East Anglia, ii. 509 n. 1.

East Bradenham, Norfolk, v. 1188.

East Clandon, Surrey, iv. 498.

East India Company, iv. 922, 924. Dutch, see Dutch East India Company.

East Indies, iv. 670.

East Smithfield, see London, streets of.

Easter, vi. 288.

Eastington, Gloucestershire, iv. 853.

Easton, i. 310.

Easton, Jane, ii. 426.

Easton, Oliver, ii. 426.

Eastward Ho, see Chapman, George.

Eaton, Henry, ii. 624.

Eaton, William, ii. **429**.

Ebblewhite, E. A., 'Ben Jonson's Christmas Masque', *N. & Q.* Sixth Series, xii (1885), iv. 639.

Ebsworth, Joseph Woodfall (ed.), *The Poems and Masque of Thomas Carew* (1893), iii. 106.

'Eccho, or The Infortunate Lovers', see Shirley, James, 'Eccho and Narcissus . . .'.

'Eccho and Narcissus . . .', see Shirley, James.

Eccles, John, v. 971.

Eccles, Mark, 'Arthur Massinger', *T.L.S.* 16 July 1931, iv. 750.

'Jonson's Marriage', *R.E.S.* xii (1936), iii. 69; iv. 604, 607, 678.

'Jonson and the Spies', *R.E.S.* xiii (1937), iv. 604.

'Martin Peerson and the Blackfriars', *Shakespeare Survey*, xi (1958), vi. 3, 7.

'Memorandums of the Immortal Ben', *M.L.N.* li (1936), iv. 604.

'Middleton's Birth and Education', *R.E.S.* vii (1931), iv. 856, 857, 861, 883, 885, 891.

'Sir George Buc, Master of the Revels', in *Thomas Lodge and Other Elizabethans*, ed. Charles J. Sisson (1933), iii. 92; iv. 884.

'Thomas Dekker: Burial-Place', *N. & Q.* clxxvii (1939), iii. 241, 244-5.

Ecclesiastical Court, ii. 641.

Ecclesiazusae, see Aristophanes.

Eccleston, William, i. 5 and n. 6, 9, 16, 72-88, 176; ii. **429-31**, 650; iii. 301, 326, 346, 349, 355, 372, 375, 413, 420.

Eckhardt, Eduard, 'Robert Davenports Lustspiel *A New Trick to Cheat the Devil*', *Anglia*, lix (1935), iii. 234.

Eclogue, or Representation in Four Parts, An, see Jordan, Thomas.

Edgar and Alfrida, Story of, iv. 788.

Edgehill, battle of, iii. 127; iv. 958.

Edinburgh, i. 180 and n. 12; iv. 611, 949; v. 1045; vi. 258.

Charles I's coronation at, iii. 288, 289.

High School, iii. 287.

James's visit to, iii. 287.

Jonson's walking trip to, iv. 610, 665.

Town Council of, iv. 611.

University of, iii. 287, 288.

MSS., v. 974.

Welcomes Charles I, iii. 287.

Edinburgh Magazine and Literary Miscellany; A New Series of the Scots Magazine, ix (July 1821), v. 1036.

Edisbury, Kenrick, ii. 473.

Edition, ghost, iii. 282.

Edmans, John, see Edmonds, John.

Edmondes, Sir Thomas, ii. 349; v. 1227, 1228, 1229; vii. 20.

Edmonds, John, i. 137, 141 and n. 1, 171 and n. b; ii. **431**.

Edmund Ironside, see Anonymous.

Edward II, see Marlowe.

Edward III, see Anonymous.

Edward the Fourth, Parts I and II, see Heywood, Thomas.

Edward VI, vi. 255.

Edwards, John, iii. 291.

Saturnalia, iii. 291.

Egerton, Lady Alice, iv. 915.

Egerton, John, Lord Brackley, iv. 915.

Egerton, John, 1st Earl of Bridgewater, iv. 913, 914, 915.

Egerton, Thomas, iii. 110; iv. 915.

Egglesfield, Francis, stationer, iv. 739; v. 1058, 1073, 1074, 1128, 1129, 1130, 1131, 1208, 1209.

Eglestone, William, see Eccleston, William.

Egypt, v. 1047.

Eisley, Oxfordshire, see Iffley.

Elam, Rev. H. D., iii. 184.

Elder Brother, The, see Fletcher, John.

Elector Palatine (Frederick V), see Palsgrave, The.

Elector Palatine (Charles Lewis), iii. 129; v. 1407, 1408.

Elegie upon the Death of the Renowned Sir John Suckling, see Anonymous.
Elegies, iii. 54.
Elegy, on death of Jonson, v. 1040.
Elegy on Randolph's Finger, see Heminges, William.
Elephants, iii. 399; iv. 894; vi. 291 n. 1; vii. 48.
Elgin, Earl of, iv. 721.
[Eliot, John?] *Poems* (1658), iv. 756.
Eliot, S. A., *The Loathed Lover* (1920), iv. 864.
Eliot, S. A., Jr., *The Duchess of Pavy, Little Theater Classics*, vol. iii (1921), iii. 453.
Eliot, Tom, i. 47; vi. 34.
Eliot, T. S., 'John Ford' in *Elizabethan Essays* (1934), iii. 433, 448.
'Philip Massinger', *Elizabethan Essays* (1934), iv. 750.
'Philip Massinger', *The Sacred Wood* (1920), iv. 750.
'Philip Massinger', *Selected Essays* (1932), iv. 750.
'Thomas Middleton', in *For Lancelot Andrews* (1928), iv. 856, 862.
Elitt, Joane, ii. 361.
Elizabeth I, Queen of England, i. 1, 2; iii. 18, 285; iv. 634, 649, 816, 955; v. 1190, 1290; vi. 255, 292.
Chaplain to, iii. 306.
Company of, ii. 562; v. 1049.
Servant of, ii. 466.
Elizabeth, Lady, Princess of England, Electress Palatine, Queen of Bohemia, i. 48, 267; ii. 657 n. 4; iii. 199; iv. 571, 637, 956; vi. 59, 162, 268.
Birthday of, iii. 82, 220.
Company of, i. 121 n. 1, 137 n. 3, 153, 176–97, 183, 200, 202 n. 6, 203 n. 1, 205, 206, 208, 219, 220, 221, 261, 262 and n. 3, 263, 268, 308; iii. 30, 31, 32, 162, 225, 228, 235, 267, 271, 300, 308, 316, 386, 399; iv. 556, 560, 561, 566, 608, 642, 713, 766, 768, 787, 797, 806, 807, 813, 814, 857, 862, 863, 869, 893, 894; v. 1016, 1019, 1020, 1068, 1146, 1247, 1249, 1294, 1304, 1305, 1315, 1343, 1430, 1456; vi. 12 and n. 1, 58–61, 59, 69, 73, 78, 79, 85, 136, 160, 206–8, 221, 251, 268, 269; vii. 7.

Heywood's epithalamium for, iv. 555.
Letters to, iii. 113, 217.
Marriage of, i. 136, 185 n. 7; vi. 266.
Elizabethan Jig and Related Song Drama, see Baskervill, Charles Read.
Elizabethan Private Theatres: Facts and Problems, The, see Armstrong, William A.
'Elizabethan Stage Gleanings', see Chambers, E. K.
'Elizabethan Theatre, The', see Wilson, F. P.
Ellesmere, Earl of, MSS. of, iv. 913, 915, 916.
Ellice, Robert, iii. 198, 437, 450, 464.
Ellice, Thomas, iii. 198, 437, 464.
Ellis, see Guest, Ellis, and Bedowe, Ellis.
Ellis, Sir Henry, ed., *Original Letters Illustrative of English History*, 2nd Series, 4 vols. (1827), iv. 612, 618 954; vi. 25 n. 1.
Ellis, William, ii. 471.
Ellis-Fermor, U. M. *The Jacobean Drama* (1936), iii. 305; iv. 905.
'John Ford' in *The Jacobean Drama* (1936), iii. 433.
'Thomas Dekker', in *The Jacobean Drama* (1936), iii. 241.
Elsaly, R. C., ed. *Juno in Arcadia*, unpublished thesis, University of Birmingham (1950), v. 1419.
Elsden, Anne, iii. 254, 255, 256; iv. 471.
Elson, John James, ed., *The Wits or Sport upon Sport* (1932), iii. 149, 151, 183, 313, 314, 319, 320, 323, 324, 343, 344, 376, 378, 401, 402, 407, 409, 418, 419, 481; v. 1079, 1135, 1144, 1147, 1337, 1357, 1360; vi. 218 n. 1, 224 n.
Elton, Edward William, iv. 824.
Elton, Richard, ii. 393.
Elvaston, Derbyshire, iii. 166.
Elves (Yelves), Count, iv. 656.
Ely, iii. 238.
Ely episcopal records, v. 1236.
Elys, Edmund, *Dia Poemata* (1655), iii. 438.
Elze, Karl, ed., *George Chapman's Tragedy of Alphonsus, Emperor of Germany* (1867), v. 1285.
Emblems, iv. 925; v. 1191, 1453.
Emery, Jasper, iii. 284.
Emington, Oxfordshire, iv. 588.

Emmanuel College, Cambridge, iii. 2, 151, 185, 292; iv. 527, 554, 600, 601, 853, 854, 855; v. 1005, 1038, 1196, 1197, 1387.
Fellow of, v. 1037.
Library of, iii. 3; v. 1037, 1039.
Master of, iii. 186; v. 1037, 1038.
MSS., iii. 3, 186; iv. 600, 601, 854; v. 1232, 1233, 1387.
Emmerson, Margaret, ii. 433.
Emperor of the East, The, see Massinger.
Emperor Valentinian, The, see Beaumont and Fletcher, *Valentinian*.
Empresses for sheilds, vii. 103.
Enchanted Island, The, see Davenant, William, *The Tempest*.
Enchanted Lovers, The, see Lower, Sir William.
Enchiridion Christiados, see Cayworth, John.
Encroachment, play about, iv. 473.
Encyclopaedia Britannica; a dictionary of arts, sciences, literature and general information, The, 11th ed., 29 vols. (1910-11), iii. 64.
Enders, John F., 'A Note on Jonson's *Staple of News*', *M.L.N.* xl (1925), iv. 628.
Endfield, Middlesex, ii. 428; v. 1372.
'End of Shakespeare's Playhouses, The', see Furnivall, F. J.
Endymion, see Lyly, John.
Englische Comedien und Tragedien (1620), iv. 808.
Engineers, vi. 284, 294.
Engines, vii. 60.
England, Ambassador of to the United Provinces, vi. 153.
England's Comfort and London's Joy, see Taylor, John.
England's First Happiness, or the Life of St. Augustine, see Anonymous.
England's Joy, see Richard Vennar.
England's Jubilee, see Chamberlaine, William.
England's Parnassus (1600), iv. 581.
English actors playing in Germany, v. 1137, 1153.
English Arcadia, The, see Anonymous.
English College (at Douai), iii. 125.
English College at Rome, v. 1172.
Rector of, v. 1172.
English College at St. Omers, v. 1290, 1347.

English Drama and Stage, The, Under the Tudor and Stuart Princes, 1543-1664, see Hazlitt, William Carew.
English Gentleman, The, see Brathwait, Richard.
English Intelligences, The, see Brathwait, Richard, *Mercurius Brittannicus*.
English Moor or the Mock Marriage, The, see Brome, Richard.
English Orator, The, see Richards, William.
English Pageantry, see Withington, Robert.
English Plays to 1700, see Rosenbach.
English Profit (Prophet?), The, see Rowley, Samuel, *Richard III*.
English, translations from, iii. 462.
English Traveller, The, see Heywood.
English Treasury of Wit and Language, see Cotgrave, John.
English Yeoman under Elizabeth and the Early Stuarts, see Campbell, Mildred.
Englishmen for My Money, or A Woman Will Have Her Will, see William Haughton.
Engraved portraits, v. 1004.
Engravers, iv. 949; v. 994.
Engravings of actors, v. 1141.
Enigmaticall Characters (1658), see Flecknoe, Richard.
Entertainer, ii. 578, 617.
Entertainment, The, see Randolph, *The Muses' Looking Glass*.
[Entertainment at Blackfriars], see Jonson, Ben.
Entertainment at Chirke Castle, see Anonymous.
Entertainment at Highgate, see Jonson, Ben.
Entertainment at Sir Thomas Middleton's, see Anonymous, *Entertainment at Chirke Castle*.
Entertainment of King Charles at Edinburgh, The, see Drummond, William.
Entertainment of King James and Queen Anne at Theobalds, An, see Jonson, Ben.
Entertainment of the Queen and Prince at Althorp, see Jonson, Ben.
Entertainment of the Two Kings of Great Britain and Denmark at Theobalds, The, see Jonson, Ben.
Entertainments, iii. 15, 16, 18, 111; iv. 639-40, 882; vi. 291.

Entertainments in manuscript, iv. 882.

Entrepreneurs, vi. 291.

Epichoarnus, vi. 276.

Epicoene, see Jonson, Ben.

Epicurus, vi. 276.

Epigrammes and Elegies (n.d.), *see* Davies, Sir John.

Epigrams, iii. 152; iv. 609; v. 1182; vi. 182.

Collections of, iii. 152.

Epigrams Divine and Moral, see May, Edward.

Epigrams, Theological, Philosophical and Romantic, see Sheppard, Samuel.

Epilogue cloak, iv. 704.

Epilogue, costumes for, iv. 704.

'Epilogue, To a Vacation Play at the Globe', iii. 209, 210.

Epilogues, ii. 440, 691; iii. 3, 4, 26, 29, 34, 50, 52, 53, 54, 57, 62, 64–65, 74, 88, 89, 91, 97, 104, 106, 123, 129–31, 133, 134, 141, 164, 169, 171, 172, 176, 177, 178, 210, 272, 317, 327, 330, 334, 342, 358, 362, 373, 375, 376, 383, 389, 440, 447, 467; iv. 502, 506, 523, 524, 547, 570, 573, 583, 596, 620, 623, 624, 628, 684, 685, 688, 693, 704, 720, 722, 723, 727, 761, 778, 781, 802, 848, 857, 901, 909, 910, 931, 934, 941, 945, 951; v. 973–4, 985, 987, 988, 990, 1006, 1021, 1033, 1056, 1061, 1062, 1068, 1069, 1071, 1084, 1086, 1093, 1107, 1109, 1122, 1140, 1141, 1142, 1144, 1147, 1153, 1182, 1192, 1231, 1233, 1238, 1241, 1251, 1258, 1279, 1295, 1316, 1333, 1339, 1340, 1341, 1342, 1351, 1355, 1365, 1374, 1378, 1388, 1394, 1417, 1428, 1437, 1439, 1440, 1453; vi. 5, 14, 41, 42, 71, 75, 92, 98, 102, 109, 132, 171, 193, 197, 198, 217 n., 270; vii. 117.

Authors of, iii. 53, 327, 334, 362, 388–9; iv. 573, 723–4; v. 1112.

Contract to write, ii. 390.

Duplicate, iii. 389.

Popularity of, iv. 822–3.

Signed, iii. 272, 446–7; v. 1096.

Speakers, v. 1122.

To the reader, v. 1061.

Used again, iii. 389.

Epistle (to London's two sheriffs), iv. 578.

To the Queen, v. 1037.

To the reader, iii. 226, 233, 243, 311; iv. 507, 685, 715, 717–18, 884, 887, 902.

Epistles, iii. 243; iv. 507, 578, 685, 715, 717; v. 985, 1015; vi. 218.

Epistolae Ho-Elianae (1650), *see* Howell, James.

Epitaphs, v. 1182, 1330.

'Equall Match, An' (droll), iii. 409.

Equitation, iii. 142, 144.

Erasmus, Desiderius, iv. 558.

'Assembly or Parliament of Woman, The', iii. 131.

Errington, Richard, i. 271, 281, 299; ii. 431–2.

Ertzer, Robert, *see* Archer, Robert.

Escapes of Jupiter, The, see Heywood, Thomas.

Esdaile, Arundel, ii. 487–8.

Essay for the New Theatre, An, see Davenant, William, *The Preparation of the Athenians for the Reception of Phocion.*

Essays and Characters, see Stephens, John.

Essex, Captain, vi. 6, 7.

Essex, Frances Howard, Countess of, iv. 905; v. 1425; vi. 6, 7.

Essex, Robert Devereux, First Earl of, **v**. 1285.

Essex, Robert Devereux, Second Earl of, v. 976.

Essex, Robert Devereux, Third Earl of, i. 65, 106, 132; ii. 504, 568, 666; iv. 721, 905; v. 1268, 1270, 1311.

Essex, Earl of, servants of, v. 1271.

Essex, County of, iv. 498; v. 1180.

Essex Antic Masque, The, see Anonymous.

Essex House, i. 283 n. 7 cont.; iv. 651; v. 1229; vi. 87.

Essex Review, xiv (1905), v. 965.

Estaines Parva, Essex, iv. 841.

Estate compounded for, iii. 167.

Estoteville, George, *see* Stutville, George.

Estoutevile, George, *see* Stutville, George.

Ethiopia, iii. 269.

Eton, iv. 951, 952; v. 1177.

Fellows of, **v**. 1176.

Headmaster, v. 1176.

Provost of, iii. 468; v. 1176.

Second master of, v. 1176.

Eton College Register, The, see Sterry, Sir Wasey.

Ettington Hall, Warwickshire, v. 1161.
Eumorphus sive Cupido-Adultus, see Wilde, George.
Eunuch, The, see Heminges, William; *see also The Fatal Contract.*
Eunuch, The, see Terence.
Eure, Ralph, iii. 437, 454.
Euribates, see Cruso, Aquila.
Euripides, iv. 499; vi. 276.
    Influence of, iv. 507–9.
Europäische Literatur und Lateinisches Mittelalter, see Curtius, Ernst Robert.
European Culture, Museum of, at the University of Illinois, vi. 143.
European Literature and the Latin Middle Ages, see Curtius, Ernst Robert.
Eutropius, iv. 817.
Evadne, see Sheil, Richard.
Evangelical Tragedy, An, see Beard, Thomas.
Evans, Gouldwais, ii. **432.**
Evans, Gwynne B., *'Comedies, Tragi-Comedies, with Other Poems,* by Mr. William Cartwright (1651), A Bibliographical Study', *Library,* Fourth Series, xxiii (1942), iii. 126.
    The Life and Works of William Cartwright, 3 vols., Harvard MS. thesis (1940), iii. 126, 128, 130, 131, 132, 134, 140, 141, 142.
    'Note on Fletcher and Massinger's *Little French Lawyer', M.L.N.* lii (1937), iii. 356, 359; v. 1379, 1380.
    The Plays and Poems of William Cartwright (1951), iii. 401.
Evans, H. A., *English Masques* (1897), iii. 213.
Evans, Henry, vi. 7, 13 n. 1.
Evans, Thomas, i. 2, 4 n. 2.
Evans, Willa McClung, *Ben Jonson and Elizabethan Music* (1929), iv. 604.
    Henry Lawes, Musician and Friend of Poets (1941), iii. 107, 134, 141; iv. 850, 913, 914, 915; v. 1189, 1192, 1207, 1212, 1231, 1260, 1264.
Evelyn, George, iii. 135, 136; v. 1190.
Evelyn, John, v. 994, 1000.
    Diary of, iv. 900; v. 1190.
    Numismata. A Discourse of Medals, Antient and Modern (1697), v. 994.

Evelyn, John, of Wotton, v. 1257, 1258.
Everard, iv. 601.
Evers, Lord (Ralph Eure, Lord Eure), vi. 80.
Evershott, Dorset, iii. 47.
Every, Alexander, iv. 512.
Every Man in His Humour, see Jonson, Ben.
Every Man Out of His Humour, see Jonson, Ben.
Every One in Their Way, see Massinger, *The City Madam.*
Ewer, Richard, ii. 502.
Ewing, S. Blaine, 'Burton, Ford, and *Andromana', P.M.L.A.* liv (1939), iii. 433; v. 1034, 1035.
    Burtonian Melancholy in the Plays of John Ford (1940), iii. 433, 439, 441, 442, 444, 446, 448, 450, 457, 462.
Example, The, see Shirley, James.
Excellency of Her Sex, The, see Ford, *The Queen.*
'Excellent Actor, An', *see* Webster, John.
Exchange, Royal, vi. 61.
Exchange, the old, vi. 63.
Exchange Ware, see Anonymous.
Exchequer accounts, iv. 667–8.
Exchequer Bills, Public Record Office, vi. 202 n. 2.
Exchequer Office, v. 1267.
Exchequer, Under Treasurer of the, vi. 260.
Exeter, i. 168 n. 1, 180, 193, 212; ii. 485.
Exeter College, Oxford, iii. 152, 153, 435; iv. 530, 531, 532, 927; vii. 108.
Exeter, Earl of, house of, vii. 34.
Exhibitions, vi. 291.
'Explanation of the Plan of Whitehall, An', *see* Speirs, W. L.
Export licences, v. 1313.
Exportation of corn, v. 1313.
Expulsion from Middle Temple, iii. 435.
Extras in plays, i. 318; vi. 243.
Extravagant Shepherd, The, see R., T.
Eydwartt, Johann, ii. **432.**
Eyre, G. E. B., *A Transcript of the Registers of the Worshipful Company of Stationers, 1640–1708,* 3 vols. (1913–14), iii. 5, 118; iv. 682; v. 1261, 1302, 1326, 1387, 1436.

Fabyan, Robert, *The Chronicles of Fabyan . . .* (1559), iv. 887.

Faction of Love and Beauty Re-concill'd, The, see Tatham, John, *Ostella*.

Faenestra in Pectore. Or, Familiar Letters (1660), see Forde, Thomas.

Fair, the, vi. 236.

Fair Anchoress of Pausilippo (or *The Prisoner* ?), see Massinger.

Fair Em, see Anonymous.

Fair Favourite, The, see Davenant.

Fair Foul One or the Baiting of the Jealous Knight, The, see Smith,—.

Fair Maid of Clifton, The, see Sampson, William, *The Vow-Breaker*.

Fair Maid of the Exchange, The, see Heywood.

Fair Maid of the Inn, The, see Fletcher, John.

Fair Maid of the West, The, or A Girl Worth Gold, Parts I and II, see Heywood, Thomas.

Fair Œthiopian, The, see Lisle, William.

Fair Penitent, The, see Rowe, Nicholas.

Fair Prisoner (?), *The*, see Middleton, *The Conqueror's Custom*.

Fair Quarrel, A, see Thomas Middleton and William Rowley.

Fair Star of Antwerp, The, see Anonymous.

Fairfax, Sir Thomas, iv. 851; v. 1186, 1277.

Fairholt, F. W., *Lord Mayors' Pageants: Being Collections towards a History of These Annual Celebrations*, Percy Society (1843–4), iii. 256, 261; iv. 575, 576, 577, 578, 584, 680, 682, 683, 684, 687, 896, 897, 899, 926; v. 1185, 1220.

Poems and Songs Relating to George Villiers, Duke of Buckingham, and His Assassination by John Felton, August 23, 1628 (1850), v. 1353.

Fairy King, The, see Sheppard, Samuel.

Fairy Knight, or Oberon the Second, The, see Anonymous.

Fairy Masque, The, see Anonymous.

Fairy Queen, The, see Anonymous and Settle, Elkanah.

Faithful Couple, The, see Moore, Sir Thomas, *Mangora, King of the Timbusians*.

Faithful Friends, The, see Fletcher, John.

Faithfull Genius, The, see Anonymous, *Diana's Grove*.

Faithful Servant, The, see Shirley, *The Grateful Servant*.

Faithful Shepherd, The, see Sidnam, Jonathan, *Il Pastor Fido*.

Faithful Shepherdess, The, see Fletcher, John.

Faithless Cousin German, The, see Boyle, William, *Jugurth*.

Faithless Raider, The, see Anonymous, *The Cyprian Conqueror*.

Faithorne, William, iii. 197, 696, 709; vi. 224 n. 1.

Faithorne, map by, vi. 274 n. 1.

Falkland, Henry Cary, fourth Viscount. v. 1371.

Falkland, Lucius Cary, Second Viscount, i. 123; iii. 181; iv. 626, 627, 693, 694; v. 1040, 1371.

Fallacy, see Zouche, Richard.

False Friend, The, see Anonymous.

False Friend, The, see Fletcher, *The False One*.

False Friend, The, see Pix, Mrs. Mary.

False Friend, The, see Vanbrugh.

False One, The, see Fletcher, John.

Falstaff, see Shakespeare, *Henry IV, Parts I and II*.

Family of Love, The, see Middleton.

Famous History of Petronius Maximus, The, see S., W.

Famous Tragedy of King Charles I, see Anonymous.

Famous Victories of Henry the Fifth, The, see Anonymous.

Fancied Queen, The, see Robert Drury.

Fancies Chaste and Noble, The, see Ford, John.

Fancies Theatre (1640), see Tatham, John.

Fancy's Festivals, see Jordan, Thomas.

Fane, Francis, first Earl of Westmorland, iii. 292.

Fane, Sir Francis, *Love in the Dark, or The Man of Business*, v. 1153.

Fane, Grace, see Thornhurst, Grace.

Fane, Sir Henry, see Vane, Sir Henry.

Fane, Mildmay, Second Earl of Westmorland, iii. **292–9**; v. 1222, 1420, 1439–40.

Candia Restaurata, or Candy Restored, iii. **293–5**, 298; iv. 959.

Change, The, iii. 295.

Don Phoebo's Triumph, iii. 294, 295–6.

Fugitive Poetry, iii. 293.

Ladrones, or The Robbers' Island, iii. 296.

Otia Sacra, iii. 292, 293.

Φ[Ψ?]yxomaxia id est de pugna animi, iii. 297; v. 1293.

Raguaillo D'Oceano, iii. 296, 297–8.

Time's Trick upon the Cards, iii. 298.

Transl. *Of the Art of Well gouerning A people*, iii. 293.

Virtue's Triumph, iii. 299.

Fanshawe, Sir Richard, iv. 830; v. 1171.

Farce, French, vi. 23.

Farces, iii. 19; iv. 942; vi. 226, 233, 246.

Farley, Henry, *St. Pavles-Church her Bill for the Parliament* (1621), vi. 209, 211, 212.

Farley Church, Surrey, iii. 26.

Farmer, John S., ed., Massinger, *Believe as You List* (1907), iv. 762.

ed., *The Bloody Banquet By T. D.*, Tudor Facsimile Texts (1914), iii. 282.

ed., *The Noble Soldier*, Tudor Facsimile Texts (1913), iii. 257.

ed., *The Two Merry Milke-Maids by J. C.* (1914), iii. 101.

ed., *Two Wise Men and All the Rest Fools*, v. 1428.

Farmer, Richard, *An Essay on the Learning of Shakespeare*, 2nd ed. (1767), v. 1105.

Farnaby, Giles, ii. 432.

Farnaby, Richard, ii. 432.

Farnaby, Thomas, iv. 690; vi. 243.

Farnborough, Warwick, ii. 371.

Farnham Castle, Governor of, iii. 275.

Farnham, Willard, 'Colloquial Contractions in Beaumont, Fletcher, Massinger, and Shakespeare as a Test of Authorship', *P.M.L.A.* xxxi (1916), iv. 750.

Farquhar, George, *The Inconstant, or The Way to Win Him*, iii. 430.

Farrar, J. H., vi. 6.

Fashionable Lover, The, see Anonymous.

Fast and Welcome, see Massinger.

Fasti Ecclesiae Anglicanae, see Le Neve, John.

Fat-clown role, iii. 379.

Fatal Banquet, The, see Anonymous.

Fatal Brothers, The, see Davenport, Robert.

Fatal Contract, The, see Heminges, William.

Fatal Dowry, The, see Massinger.

Fatal Friendship, The, see Burroughes, —.

Fatal Marriage, The, see Anonymous.

Fatal Union, The, see Harding, Samuel, *Sicily and Naples*.

Fate of Disobedience, The, see Pix, Mrs. Mary, *The False Friend*.

Fathers of the Oratory, iv. 916.

Father's Own Son, see Beaumont and Fletcher, *Monsieur Thomas*.

Fatum Vortigerni, see Carleton, Thomas.

Faulcon, Sr., v. 1298.

Faulkner, Thomas, i. 264, 265; ii. 432–3; vi. 160.

Fault in Friendship, A, see Brome, Richard.

Faust, E. K. R., *Richard Brome, Ein Beitrag zur Geschichte der englischen Litteratur* (1887), iii. 49, 55, 59, 61, 70, 73.

Fawne, Catherine, ii. 452.

Fay, Henry, vii. 117.

Fearne, Sir John, ii. 349.

Feast, vii. 29, 59.

Feast, The, see Manuche, Cosmo.

'*Feast' and Welcome, see* Massinger, *Fast and Welcome*.

Featherdressers, vi. 95.

Featherstone, Mr., iv. 562; v. 1002.

Febure, M. le, riding-school of, *see* Le Fevre.

Fee (for revisions), iii. 368.

Fees, iii. 246, 253, 264, 265, 284, 367, 370, 372, 384, 386; iv. 570.

Feigned Innocence, The, see Cavendish, *Sir Martin Mar-All*.

Feil, J. P. 'Dramatic References from the Scudamore Papers', *Shakespeare Survey*, xi (1958), vi. 17, n. 1, 25 n. 1, 26, 265, 282 n. 1, 283 n., 284, 286, 287, 288; vii. 62, 81, 82, 83, 84, 86, 94, 107, 108, 110, 111.

Fellows, E. H., ed., *Songs & Lyrics from the Plays of Beaumont and Fletcher with Contemporary Musical Settings* (1928), iii. 305.

Felsted Church, in Essex, v. 1269.

Felt-makers, vi. 220, 238, 239.

Feltmaker's Apprentice, i. 167.

Felton, John, hanged, vii. 69.

Female Rebellion, The, see Burkhead, Henry.

Fen Drayton, Cambridgeshire, iv. 538.

Fencers, i. 318; ii. 360, 406, 442, 688; v. 1050, 1417; vi. 99, 100, 131, 159, 175, 194, 195, 212, 221 and n. 1, 238, 247, 248, 250, 251, 295.

Fencers' prizes, vi. 221.

Fencing, vii. 6, 8, 23.

Fencing exhibitions, vi. 294, 295, 296, 298.

Fenn, Ezekiel, i. 238, 246, 251, 326 nn. 6 and 7, 327, 332, 336; ii. **433–4**; iii. 272; iv. 474; vi. 68.

Fenn, Lucie, ii. 433.

Fenn, Mauritii, ii. 433.

Fenn, Richard, iv. 577.

Fennor, William, vi. 205–6.

Fennors Defence (1615), *see* Taylor, John.

Fenton, Frank L., 'The Authorship of Acts III and IV of *The Queen of Corinth*,' *M.L.N.* xlii (1927), iii. 398, 400.

Ferdinand II, Emperor, iv. 477.

Ferdinand III, Emperor, ii. 406.

Ferguson, A. S., 'Chapman, "The Tragedy of Chabot", Act III, Sc. ii, ll. 147–68', *M.L.R.* xxiii (1928), v. 1088.

Ferrabosco, Alphonso, iv. 657; vi. 295.

Ferret, James, i. 286, 297; ii. **434**.

Ferriar, John, Essay in *The Plays of Philip Massinger*, ed. William Gifford, 4 vols. (1805), iv. 758.

Ferris, Deavid (?), i. 272, 281; ii. **434.**

Festival of Light, The, see Davenant, William, *Luminalia.*

Fetter Lane, *see* London, streets and districts.

Feuillerat, Albert, vi. 191.
    ed., *Arthur Wilson, the Swisser* (1904), v. 1267, 1268, 1269, 1270, 1273, 1274.
    'Blackfriars Records', *Malone Society Collections*, ii. Pt. i, (1913), vi. 3.

Fiat, Marquess de, French ambassador, iv. 643, 842.

Fickle Shepherdess, The, see Anonymous.

Fiddlers, ii. 363, 469, 621; vi. 133, 237.

Fideli, Signior, ii. 694.

Field, Dorcas, iii. 301.

Field, Henry, i. 286, 297; ii. **434.**

Field, John, ii. 434; iii. 299–300; vi. 80.

Field, Nathan, i. 5 and n. 6 cont., 8, 72–88, 124 n. 2, 176, 177 and n. 3, 203 n. 1; ii. **434–6**, 696; iii. **299–303**, 309, 326, 350, 351, 352, 353, 372, 375, 398, 399, 400, 447; iv. 516, 608, 752, 754, 783, 784, 790; vi. 206.
    Amends for Ladies, i. 176, 198, 201 n. 2; ii. 435, 436; iii. 301, 302; vi. 85; vii. 29, 118.
    Fatal Dowry, The, see Massinger, Philip.
    Four Plays in One, iii. 302.
    Honest Man's Fortune, The, iii. 302.
    Jeweller of Amsterdam, The, see Fletcher.
    Thierry and Theodoret, see Beaumont and Fletcher.
    Woman Is a Weathercock, A, ii. 435; iii. 301, 302; v. 1115, 1145, 1166; vii. 62, 106.

Field, Nathaniel, the printer, ii. 434, 436; iii. 300.

Field, Theophilus, Bishop of Llandaff, ii. 434; iii. 300.

Field of Happiness, The, see Dekker, Thomas, *London's Tempe.*

Fieldinge, Lady Elizabeth, iii. 219.

Fights with halberds, vi. 293.

Fights with partisans, vi. 293.

Fights with pikes, vi. 293.

Filial Piety, see Hill, Aaron, *The Insolvent.*

Filli di Sciro, see Bonarelli, C. Guidubaldo de.

Filli di Sciro, see Sidnam, Jonathan, (translator).

Filmer, Sir Robert, v. 1280, 1298, 1391.

Finch, Edward, v. 1266.

Finch, Elizabeth, ii. 641.

Finch, Harbert, ii. 641.

Finch, Sir Heneage, iii. 34.

Finch, Sir John, v. 1156, 1193.

Finch, Mary, ii. 506.

Finch, Nathaniel, iii. 436, 437, 450.

Finch, Sir Thomas, iv. 735; v. 1253; vi. 49.

Fincham, Francis W. X., 'Notes from the Ecclesiastical Court Records at Somerset House', *Transactions of the Royal Historical Society*, Fourth Series, iv (1921), vi. 147.

Fine Companion, A, see Marmion, Shakerley.

Finett, Sir John, i. 46; ii. 376, 534, 586; iv. 643; v. 1422; vi. 107, 265, 285, 287.

   Finetti Philoxenis, iv. 656, 657, 661–2, 671, 675, 843; vi. 280; vii. 38, 39, 62, 63.

Finetti Philoxenis, see Sir John Finett.

Finney, Gretchen Ludke, '*Comus, Dramma per Musica', Stud. Phil.* xxxvii (1940), iv. 914.

Finsbury Fields, *see* London, streets of.

Fintrye, Robert, ii. **437.**

Fir (wood), vi. 286.

Fire, danger of, vii. 22.

Fire in flax warehouse, v. 1247.

Fires, vi. 24.

Fires in theatres, *see* Theatres burned.

Fireworks, iv. 897; vi. 210 n., 294.

First Antimasque of Mountebanks, The, see Anonymous.

First army plot, v. 1200.

First Bishops' War, v. 1052.

First Blackfriars, *see* Blackfriars theatre.

First Days Entertainment at Rutland House, The, see Davenant, William.

First Fortune, *see* Fortune theatre.

First Globe, *see* Globe theatre.

First Jacobean Banqueting House, *see* Banqueting House.

'First of the Ladyes after the Cuckolds', *see* Anonymous.

First London Theatre, The: Materials for a History, see Wallace, Charles William.

'First of the Lords, The', *see* Anonymous.

First Night of Twelfth Night, The, see Hotson, Leslie.

First Part of the Contention of York and Lancaster (2 Henry VI), The, see Shakespeare, William.

'First witches dance, The,' *see* Anonymous.

Firth, C. H., ed., *The Life of William Cavendish, Duke of New-castle, to which is added the True Relation of My Birth, Breeding, and Life.* By Margaret, Duchess of Newcastle (n.d.), iii. 142, 143, 144, 148; iv. 648, 653.

Fisher, Benjamin, iii. 73, 74, 75.

Fisher, drawings by, vi. 274 n. 1.

Fisher, Edward, vi. 87, 88, 91.

Fisher, Jasper, iii. **303–5.**

   Fuimus Troes, or The True Trojans, iii. **304–5;** v. 1007.

Fisher, John, i. 143, 144; ii. **437,** 545; vi. 157.

Fisher, Margery, 'Notes on the Sources of Some Incidents in Middleton's London Plays', *R.E.S.* xv (1939), iii. 133; iv. 856, 859.

Fisher, Sir Thomas, iv. 483; v. 1131.

Fisher, William, iii. 303.

Fisher play, iv. 620.

'Fishers Folly', iii. 383.

Fishmongers, ii. 576; vii. 104.

Fitche, —, ii. 567.

Fitche, Winifred, ii. 568, 634.

Fitz-Geoffrey, Henry, v. 1243.

   Notes from Blackfriars, see below, *Satyres and Satyricall Epigrams, Satyres and Satyricall Epigrams* (1617), including 'Notes from Blackfriars', v. 1242; vi. 42–56.

Fitzmaurice-Kelly, James, *A History of Spanish Literature* (1926), v. 1211.

Fitzmorris, Robert, ii. 413.

Five New Plays, see Brome, Richard.

Five Plays in One, see Heywood, Thomas.

Flanders, ii. 512, 694; iv. 643.

Flanders, Ambassador from, iv. 643.

Flannel-weavers, vi. 4.

Flatman, Thomas, *Naps upon Parnassus* (1658), v. 1351.

Fleay, Frederick Gard, iii. 272, 444; iv. 678; v. 980, 1241, 1246.

   'Annals of the Careers of James and Henry Shirley', *Anglia,* viii (1885), v. 1056, 1073, 1075, 1096, 1134.

   Biographical Chronicle of the English Drama, 1559–1642, A, 2 vols. (1891), iii. *passim*; iv. *passim*; v. *passim*;

   Chronicle History of the London Stage, 1559–1642, A (1890), iii. 300; v. 1325, 1363, 1441, 1442; vi. 3, 13 and n. 1, 56, 214, 219.

Flecknoe, Richard, iii. 144; iv. 681.

   Enigmaticall Characters (1658), 'Of a Proud one', vi. 245.

   Epigrams of All Sorts (1670), ii. 436.

   Love's Dominion (1654), i. 324; ii. 373–4; vi. 71.

   Love in Its Infancy, v. 1368.

Flecknoe, Richard (*cont.*)
  Love's Kingdom, ii. 436; iii. 118;
    v. 1205, 1368.
  *Miscellania or Poems of all sorts,
    with divers other Pieces* (1653),
    v. 995, 1029; vi. 41.
  *Short Discourse of the English
    Stage, A* (1664), v. 1205.
Fleet Conduit, *see* London, streets
  of.
Fleet prison, the, iii. 39, 183.
Fleet street, *see* London, streets of.
Fleet Street, theatre projected in,
  iii. 64, 195, 216; v. 1267; vi. 74,
  304–9.
Fleir, The, see Edward Sharpham.
Fleming, Sir Daniel, vi. 177.
Fleming MSS., *Historical Manu-
  scripts Commission*, vi. 177.
Fleminge, Mrs., vi. 138.
Flemish Ambassador, vii. 39.
Fletcher, Edward, iii. 306.
Fletcher, Giles, iii. 306–7.
Fletcher, H. F., ed., *John Milton's
  Complete Poetical Works Repro-
  duced in Photographic Facsimile*,
  2 vols. (1943–8), iv. 912, 913, 915.
Fletcher, J. B., 'Précieuses at the
  Court of Charles I', *Journal of
  Comparative Literature*, i (1903),
  iii. 211; iv. 520.
Fletcher, John, *see also* Beaumont
  and Fletcher.
Fletcher, John, iii. 13, 14, 34, 54, 55,
  97, 133, 167, 201, 301, 303,
  305–433, 457; iv. 499, 502, 523,
  557, 608, 752, 753, 754, 755,
  757, 772, 778, 787, 790, 791,
  797, 802, 814, 823, 827, 828,
  837, 891, 900, 901, 902; v.
  1018, 1086, 1088, 1099, 1148,
  1212, 1252; vi. 41, 73, 113, 242.
  Influence of, iii. 201, 318; iv.
    568, 583, 744, 753–4, 822,
    826; v. 1081, 1099, 1107, 1222,
    1274.
  Reputation of, iv. 802, 1086,
    1153.
  Beggar's Bush, The, i. 28, 51, 94,
    96, 98, 100, 109; iii. 73, 140,
    312–18; v. 1293, 1294.
  *Birth of Merlin, or The Child Hath
    Found His Father, The*, iii. 318.
  Bloody Brother, The, see Fletcher
    and Massinger, *Rollo, Duke of
    Normandy, or The Bloody
    Brother.*
  Bonduca, iii. 318, 381.
  Captain, The, iii. 317, 318.

Chances, The, i. 28, 66, 96, 100,
  110; ii. 426, 430; iii. 8, 203,
  318–23, 381; v. 1483.
Coronation, The, see Shirley.
Coxcomb, The, iii. 323, 365, 386.
Cupid's Revenge, iii. 323.
*Demetrius and Enanthe, see The
  Humorous Lieutenant.*
*Devil of Dowgate, or Usury Put to
  Use, The*, i. 103, 110, 127; iii.
  328–9, 386; iv. 888, 889; v.
  1297.
Double Marriage, The, i. 66, 78–79,
  110, 126; ii. 375, 377, 501, 552,
  569, 570, 593, 602, 611; iii.
  329–32; iv. 754, 793, 820, 821.
Elder Brother, The, i. 48, 51, 98,
  110; ii. 660, 677, 681; iii. 13,
  139, 332–6; iv. 754, 804; v.
  1149, 1425.
Fair Maid of the Inn, The, i. 104,
  110; ii. 447, 476, 500, 556; iii.
  336–9; iv. 631; v. 1147.
Faithful Friends, The, iii. 339,
  400, 401.
Faithful Shepherdess, The, i. 39
  and n. 1, 58 n. 3, 97, 110–11,
  133; ii. 592, 595; iii. 107, 300,
  308, 340; iv. 738; v. 970, 1222,
  1389; vi. 9, 283; vii. 69, 72, 95.
False One, The (or *The False
  Friend*), i. 74–75, 111; ii. 375,
  377, 430, 501, 547, 569, 570,
  593, 602, 611; iii. 340–2; iv.
  754; v. 1331.
*Father's Own Son, The, see Mon-
  sieur Thomas or The Father's
  Own Son.*
*Four Plays or Moral Repre-
  sentations in One*, iii. 301, 342.
*Generous Enemies, The, see The
  Humorous Lieutenant.*
*History of Madon, King of
  Britain, The*, iii. 342.
Honest Man's Fortune, The, iii.
  301, 342, 365, 386; iv. 763, 790.
Humorous Lieutenant, The, or *Demetrius and Enanthe*, or *The
  Noble Enemy*, or *Generous
  Enemies*, i. 66, 74–75, 111;
  ii. 374, 411, 416, 430, 475, 500,
  501, 532, 533, 534, 569, 570,
  591, 592, 610; iii. 216, 343–7,
  421; iv. 884, 885; v. 1210.
Island Princess, The, or *The
  Generous Portugal*, i. 66, 74–75,
  94, 111; ii. 374, 377, 430, 500,
  501, 533, 569, 570, 593, 610;
  iii. 347, 391, 425, 827.

Knight of Malta, The, i. 66, 72–73, 95 n. c, 111; ii. 374, 396, 411, 435, 475, 501, 570, 610; iii. 351–4; iv. 754.

Laws of Candy, The, i. 74–75, 111; ii. 377, 430, 501, 533, 570, 592, 599, 602, 610; iii. 354–6; iv. 422, 827.

Lisander and Callista, see Fletcher and Massinger, *The Lovers' Progress.*

Lover's Progress, see Fletcher and Massinger.

Love's Cure, or The Martial Maid, i. 65, 112; ii. 562; iii. 363–6; iv. 754.

Love's Pilgrimage, i. 51, 66, 98, 107, 112; ii. 351, 354, 381, 425, 475, 661; iii. 366–70; iv. 624.

Loyal Subject, The, i. 51, 65, 72–73, 97, 98, 106, 112; ii. 396, 411, 430, 435, 475, 501, 570, 602, 610; iii. 370–3; iv. 634.

Mad Lover, The, i. 28 and n. 1, 62, 66, 72–73, 84–85, 94, 96, 112, 177; ii. 361, 362, 374, 396, 411, 430, 435, 479, 480, 501, 570, 678–9, 681; iii. 373–6; iv. 827; v. 1354.

Martial Maid, The, see Love's Cure.

Masque of the Inner Temple and Gray's Inn, The, iii. 380.

Monsieur Perrolis, iii. 380–1.

Monsieur Thomas, or The Father's Own Son, i. 62, 113, 330, 331, 337; iii. 54, 55, 381; v. 1167, 1235; vi. 114, 118.

Nice Valour or the Passionate Madman, The, i. 133; iii. 381–4; iv. 827; v. 1296.

Night Walker, The, or The Little Thief, i. 226 n. 7 cont., 230, 249, 250, 330, 337; iii. 85, 329, 369, 384–6; v. 1098, 1129, 1135.

Noble Enemy, The, see The Humorous Lieutenant.

Noble Gentleman, The [The New-Made Gentleman], i. 66, 104, 113; iii. 387–91; iv. 827, 829; v. 1096, 1312.

Pilgrim, The, i. 66, 76–77, 94, 113; ii. 375, 377, 479, 501, 593, 600, 602, 611; iii. 347, 391–4, 425.

Prophetess, The, i. 24, 66, 78–79, 103, 113; ii. 375, 377, 475, 501, 562, 565, 570, 593, 602; iii. 341, 413; iv. 754 vi. 197.

Queen, The, iii. 397–8.

Queen of Corinth, The, i. 66, 72–73, 113, 177; ii. 396, 411, 435, 475, 501, 533, 562, 602, 610; iii. 365, 398–400; iv. 754, 800.

Right Woman, A, iv. 400–1, 906.

Rule a Wife and Have a Wife, i. 13, 95, 104, 114; ii. 447, 556, 591; iii. 221, 407–11, 877; v. 1425.

Scornful Lady, The, iii. 421.

Sea Voyage, The, i. 78–79, 103, 114; ii. 430, 475, 501, 593, 602, 611; iii. 131, 331, 411–14, 754; vi. 196.

Spanish Curate, The, i. 65, 78–79, 94, 100, 103, 114; ii. 375, 429, 430, 501, 533, 570, 593, 602; iii. 341, 417–21, 754.

Tamer Tam'd, The, see The Woman's Prize or The Tamer Tam'd.

Triumph of Honour, The, The Triumph of Love, The Triumph of Death, The Triumph of Time (Four Plays in One), iii. 421.

Wandering Lovers, The, see Fletcher and Massinger, *Lover's Progress.*

Widow, The, see Middleton, Thomas.

Wife for a Month, A, i. 52, 66, 80–81, 98, 103, 115; ii. 375, 377, 476, 552, 556, 593, 602, 611; iii. 422–5; v. 1108.

Wild Goose Chase, The, i. 24, 36, 65, 86–87, 94, 115; ii. 376, 430–1, 446, 447, 460, 477, 503, 505, 524, 532, 534, 553, 562–3, 566, 586, 594, 597, 605, 606, 692, 695; iii. 328, 347, 391, 397, 425–30, 465; v. 1301, 1303, 1436, 1444; vi. 22.

Women Pleased, i. 76–77, 115; ii. 374, 430, 475, 501, 562, 570, 593, 602, 610; iii. 357, 431–3; v. 1081, 1417.

Fletcher, John, and Francis Beaumont, *King and No King, A,* iii. 351; iv. 14.

Knight of the Burning Pestle, The, iii. 354, 448; iv. 744.

Maid's Tragedy, The, iii. 201, 380.

Philaster, or Love Lies a Bleeding, iii. 391; iv. 680.

Thierry and Theodoret, iii. 388; iv. 421; vii. 42.

Valentinian, iii. 422; v. 1429.

Fletcher and Beaumont (*cont.*)
Wit at Several Weapons, iii. 329, 430; v. 1297.
Wit without Money, iii. 430; v. 1373; vi. 230; vii. 115, 118.
Woman Hater, The, or The Hungry Courtier, iii. 430.
Woman's Prize, The, or The Tamer Tamed, iii. 221, 386, 430; v. 1373, 1445.
Fletcher, John, and Philip Massinger, *Custom of the Country, The*, i. 24, 27, 66, 74–75, 96, 100, 110; ii. 374, 407, 430, 475, 501, 569, 570, 591, 593, 602, 610; iii. **324–8**, 357, 397, 421, 429, 432; iv. 754, 827; vi. 22.
Little French Lawyer, The, i. 65, 76–77, 111; ii. 374, 430, 475, 501, 570, 591, 593, 602, 611; iii. **356–8**, 421, 432, 754; iv. 784, 807; v. 1380, 1381.
Lovers' Progress, The, or The Wandering Lovers, or Cleander, or Lisander and Calista, i. 66, 80–81, 95, 103, 111–12, 124 n. 1; ii. 375, 377, 476, 501, 533, 562, 570, 591, 593, 600, 611, 676, 681; iii. **359–63**; iv. 754, 774, 804, 805, 827.
Rollo, Duke of Normandy or The Bloody Brother, i. 28, 30, 51, 69 n. 2, 88–89, 96, 98, 99 n. v, 109; ii. 397, 505, 534, 556, 597, 675, 681, 695; iii. **401–7**; iv. 752; v. 1086, 1153; vi. 197, 237.
Sir John van Olden Barnavelt, i. 7, 74–75, 114; ii. 377, 415, 448, 475, 499 and n. 1, 511, 516, 533, 546, 550, 552, 589, 609; iii. 301, 327, 351, **415–17**; iv. 754, 822; vi. 197, 199.
Fletcher, John, and Philip Massinger and Nathan Field, *Jeweller of Amsterdam, The*, ii. 435; iii. 350–1; iv. 754.
Fletcher, John, and William Rowley, *Maid in the Mill, The*, i. 66, 78–79, 95, 103, 112; ii. 375, 476, 500, 501, 533, 556, 557, 593, 600, 611; iii. 341, **376–80**; v. 1016; vi. 196.
Fletcher, John, and William Shakespeare, *Henry VIII*, iii. 342; vi. 172, 198.
Cardenio, or The Double Falsehood, iii. 318, 370; iv. 827; v. 1105.
Two Noble Kinsmen, The, iii. 422.
Fletcher, John, brewer's servant, iii. 308.
Fletcher, John, silkweaver, iii. 308.
Fletcher, John, silkthrostler, iii. 308.
Fletcher, John, waterman, iii. 308.
Fletcher, Jone, ii. 442.
Fletcher, Lawrence, i. 2; vi; 20.
Fletcher, Mr. (publisher), iv. 868.
Fletcher, Mr., Fellow of Gonville and Caius, Cambridge, iii. 238.
Fletcher, Phineas, *Sicelides*, vii. 78, 81.
Fletcher, Richard, iii. 306.
Floating Island, The, see Strode, William.
Flod, William, ii. 564.
Flood, Griffin, v. 1249.
Florence (Italy), iii. 339; v. 1152, 1298.
Grand Duke of, iv. 549.
Thomas Killigrew in, iv. 697, 708.
triumphal tournament at, iii. 218.
Florentine ambassador, iv. 873, 874.
Florentine Friend, The, see Anonymous.
Florentine Ladies, The, see Anonymous.
Florentine nun, the, v. 1391.
Florentine revels, iv. 677.
Flores, Juan de, *Historia da Aurelia y Isabella hija del Rey Escotia* (1556), v. 1416; *see also* Westminster, Matthew of.
Floridor, stage name of Josias de Soulas, i. 235 n. 1; ii. **437**; vi. 45, 46, 65; vii. 100.
Florimene, see Anonymous.
Florus, Publius Annius, *Epitome Rerum Romanarum*, iv. 834.
Flote, John, iv. 954.
Flower, Edmund, ii. 363.
Flower, John, vii. 86.
Flower, Dr. Robin, v. 1342.
Floyd, Giles, *A Critical Edition of Brome's A Jovial Crew, with Introduction, Textual Notes, and Glossary* (MS. Iowa Thesis, 1943), iii. 70.
Fluchère, H., 'Thomas Dekker et le drame bourgeois', *Le Théâtre Élizabéthain, Cahiers du sud*, xx (June–July 1933), iii. 241.
Fludd, Robert, *De Naturali, Supernaturali, Praeternaturali, et Contranaturali Microcosmi Historia*, Oppenheim (1619), vi. 186 n. 1.
Flying Voice, The, see Wood, Ralph.
Foard, John, *see* Ford, John.
Foedera, see Rymer, Thomas.
Folger, Henry Clay, v. 977.
Folger Shakespeare Library, Washington, D.C., ii. 443; iii. 30,

227, 228, 229, 246, 247, 256, 281, 284, 286, 312, 313, 317, 446; iv. 518, 519, 520, 527, 560, 561, 591, 595, 596, 638, 642, 644, 766, 806, 810, 812, 814, 817, 854, 870, 879, 883, 887, 917, 920; v. 994, 1012, 1013, 1014, 1017, 1046, 1050, 1075, 1144, 1238, 1239, 1290, 1291, 1319, 1324, 1328, 1388, 1393, 1396; vi. 135 n. 1, 138 n. 1, 155, 194 n. 3, 200, 202 n. 2, 210 n. 1, 211 n. 1, 212 n. 1, 214, n. 1, 221 n. 1, 231, 241, 250 n. 1, 271; vii. 3.

Manuscripts, iii. 4, 23, 25, 47, 99, 134, 141, 153; iv. 517, 518, 519, 520, 527, 560, 595, 638, 642, 644, 697, 854, 870, 887, 917, 920; v. 1232, 1233, 1260, 1262, 1265, 1266, 1271, 1272, 1273, 1295, 1298, 1299, 1305, 1306, 1321-2, 1343, 1345, 1350, 1395, 1400, 1401, 1404; vi. 42, 54 n. 1, 60 n. 1, 114, 155, 159 n. 1, 173, 177, 200, 208 n. 1.

Publications, i. 27 n. 2.

Folk material, iv. 649.

Foljambe, Francis, Sir, iv. 756, 777, 799.

Follies Anatomie. Or Satyres and Satyricall Epigrams (1619), *see* Hutton, Henry.

Folly Reclaimed, see Dilke, Thomas, *The City Lady*.

Fontenelle, France, v. 1385.

Fool and Her Maidenhead Soon Parted, A, see Anonymous and Davenport, Robert.

Fool without Book, The, see Rowley, William.

Fool Would Be a Favourite, The, see Carlell, Lodowick.

Fools, vi. 113.

Fool's Masque, The, see Anonymous.

Foord, John, *see* Ford, John.

Footes, Thomas (i.e. Sackville), vii. 20, 21, 24, 27, 32.

Footlights, vi. 218.

Footpace, a great, vii. 69.

Force of Love, The, see Bellamy, David the younger, *The Perjured Devotee*.

Forced Lady, The, see Massinger, Philip.

Ford, Elizabeth, iii. 435.

Ford, H. L., *Collation of the Ben Jonson Folios, 1616-31—1640* (1932), iv. 604.

Ford, Henry, iii. 436.

Ford (Foard, Foarde, Foord, Forde), John, i. 184; ii. 488; iii. 6, 55, 78, 83, 244, 247, 249, 252, 262, 265, 268, 269, 270, 280, 286, 337, **433-64**; iv. 787, 788, 816, 830, 938; v. 1018, 1064, 1130, 1165, 1242, 1244, 1252, 1254, 1361; vi. 63, 222.

Bad Beginning Makes a Good Ending, A, see An Ill Beginning has a Good End.

Beauty in a Trance, i. 28, 65, 96, 120; iii. 436, 437, **438-9**, 442.

Bristow Merchant, The, see Dekker, Thomas.

Broken Heart, The, i. 120; iii. 437, 439, **439-42**, 449, 456, 462.

Fairy Knight, The, see Dekker, Thomas.

Fame's Memorial (1606), iii. 435, 463.

Fancies Chaste and Noble, The, i. 252; iii. **442-4**; vi. 66 n. 1.

Honour Triumphant, or The Peers' Challenge (1606), iii. 435.

Ill Beginning Has a Good End, An, iii. 436, 442, **444-6**, 463.

Lady's Trial, The, i. 329, 338; ii. 378; iii. 437, **446-7**, 486; iv. 785.

Late Murder in Whitechapel, The, see Dekker.

London Merchant, The, iii. 436, 442, **447-8**.

Lover's Melancholy, The, i. 82-83, 104, 120; ii. 361, 375, 447, 452, 474, 477, 479, 502, 524, 533, 546, 565, 570, 575, 585, 594, 600, 605, 612; iii. 436, 437, 439, 441, 442, **448-51**, 463, 464, 622, 816.

Love's Sacrifice, i. 252, 331, 338; iii. 442, 449, 456, **451-3**; iv. 743; v. 1161.

Perkin Warbeck, i. 252; iii. 437, 449, **454-6**; v. 1096, 1236.

Queen, or the Excellency of Her Sex, The, ii. 446, 447; iii. 123, 436, 437, **457-8**.

Royal Combat, The, iii. 436, **442**, 458.

Spanish Duke of Lerma, The, iii. 458-9.

Spanish Gipsy, The, iii. 459.

'Tis Pity She's a Whore, i. 252, 331, 338; iii. 442, 449, **462-4**.

Sir Thomas Overburyes Ghost . . . , iii. 435-6.

Witch of Edmonton, The, see Dekker, Thomas.

Ford, John, and Thomas Dekker, *Sun's Darling, The*, i. 185, 195, 331, 336, 338–9; ii. 379, 525; iii. 244, 247, 250, 262, 446, 459–61; iv. 773, 938; v. 1222, 1235.

Ford, John, of Chewford, iii. 437.

Ford, John, of Gray's Inn, ii. 477.

Ford, John (cousin to the dramatist), iii. 435, 437, 451, 454.

Ford, Thomas, of Ilsington, Devonshire, iii. 435.

Forde, Thomas, *Love's Labyrinth, or The Royal Shepherdess* (1660), iv. 514.

Faenestra in Pectore. Or, Familiar Letters (1660), vi. 174.

Foreign princes, vi. 292, 293, 295, 303.

Forewords, v. 1358.

Forgeries, iii. 238, 242, 434, 450, 450–1; iv. 571; v. 1253; vi. 55 n. 1, 86, 116.

Forman, Dr. Simon, iii. 337; iv. 905.

Bocke of Plaies, vi. 16 n. 1.

Formido, Sir Cornelius, iii. 464–8; v. 1361.

Governor, The, i. 52, 98, 120; iii. 465–8.

Forsett, Edward, *Pedantius*, v. 1397; vii. 77.

Forster collection, Victoria and Albert, Museum, i. 132.

Forsythe, Robert Stanley, 'The Bloody Banquet', *T.L.S.* 22 April 1926, iii. 282.

'An Indebtedness of *Nero* to the Third Part of *King Henry VI*', *M.L.N.* xxv (1910), v. 1379, 1381.

The Relations of Shirley's Plays to the Elizabethan Drama (1914), iii. 145, 147; iv. 822; v. 1064, 1073, 1097–1170 *passim*.

Fortesque, George, iii. 15.

Fortunate Isles, The, see Anonymous.

Fortunate Isles and Their Union, The, see Jonson, Ben.

Fortune Inn, i. 137 n. 6.

Fortune (ship), ii. 473.

Fortune theatre, i. 4 n. 3, 25, 135, 136, 137 and n. 6, 138, 138–9, 140, 141, 144, 145, 146, 153, 163, 184, 207, 208, 263, 264, 264–9, 273 n. 1, 274, 275, 276, 280, 289 n. 4 cont., 292, 306 n. 3, 307, 309, 312 and n. 7 cont., 315 and n. 2, 317 and n. 2. 319, 320; ii. 346, 347, 348, 558, 612, 680, 683, 690, 693, 694; iii. 10, 37, 59, 76, 104, 187, 189, 247, 280, 281, 285, 286; iv. 516, 517, 518, 519, 520, 541, 542, 543, 547, 734, 746, 935, 936; v. 995, 996, 1012, 1013, 1014, 1050, 1234, 1235, 1236, 1290, 1300, 1301, 1321, 1327, 1351, 1411, 1456; vi. 11, 12 n. 2, 40, 54, 57, 63, 66, 76, 94, 99, 111–36 *passim*, 139–78, 181 n. 1, 184 n. 2, 185 n. 2, 187, 190, 199, 201, 210, 215, 216 n. 2, 218, 223–50 *passim*, vii. 5, 6, 7, 8.

The First, vi. 139–53.

The Second, vi. 154–78.

Conduct of audiences at, i. 318.

Contractors for, i. 143; vi. 139–43, 154, 306.

Early distinction of, i. 136–7, 140.

Fire at, i. 141 and n. 4; iii. 32, 36–37, 285; v. 1011, 1013, 1441.

Housekeepers at, vi, 93.

Leases, i. 138–9, 143–4.

Manager of, i. 279; ii. 454–8; vii. 5.

Opening of new, i. 144–6 and 144, n. 4.

Players of the, v. 1217; vi. 90 n. 2.

Playwrights for, ii. 690.

Raided, i. 278; vi. 174, 176, 177.

Rebuilding of, i. 142–6; vi. 154–7.

Rent of, i. 138; vi. 157.

Reputation of, i. 268, 280, 315, 319.

Riot at, i. 264–6.

Stock in, i. 144.

Taphouse at, i. 138, 143.

Typical audience at, i. 268.

'Fortune my foe, why dost thou frown on me', *see* Anonymous.

Fortune by Land and Sea, see Heywood, Thomas.

Fortune's Tennis, see Anonymous.

Foscarini, Antonio, Venetian ambassador, vi. 133.

Foss, Hubert J., and E. H. Visiak, eds., Milton's *Comus* (1937), iv. 914.

Foster, Alexander, i. 176, 181, 182, 188, 189 and n. 3, 192; ii. 437–8.

Foster, —, ii. 510.

Foster, Francis, i. 264, 265.

Foster, Francis, a constable, vi. 160.

Foster, Joseph, *Alumni Oxonienses: the members of the University of Oxford, 1500–1714* . . . , 4 vols. (1891–2), iii. 4, 17, 19, 21, 26,

28, 46, 172, 183, 225, 291; iv.
498, 512, 530, 531, 599, 690,
716, 844, 851, 927; v. 1007,
1040, 1047, 1054, 1056, 1178,
1181, 1188, 1225, 1256, 1259,
1265, 1268, 1276, 1277, 1291.
ed., *The Register of Admissions to
Gray's Inn, 1521–1889* . . .
(1889), iii. 39, 47; v. 1069,
1198, 1227, 1291.
Foster, Thomas, i. 199 n. 2; vi. 202.
Foster, William, i. 265.
Fotherbie, Charles, v. 985.
Fouch, Richard, i. 307, 308, 321; ii.
439.
Fount of New Fashion, The, see
Chapman, George.
Fountain of Self-Love, The, see
Jonson *Cynthia's Revels.*
Fountaine, Sir Erasmus de la, iii.
437.
*Four Ages of England, The, or the
Iron Age, see* Cowley, Abraham.
Four companies, the, i. 194, 206,
236; ii. 621, 666 and n. 1; iii. 240,
273.
Four Honourable Loves, The, see
Rowley, William.
Four Plays in One, see Fletcher,
The Triumph of Honour.
Four Prentices of London, The, see
Heywood, Thomas.
Four Sons of Amon, The, see
Anonymous.
Fowler, Adam, ii. 439.
Fowler, Elizabeth, ii. 439.
Fowler, Jane, ii. 439.
Fowler, Richard, i. 138, 139, 147,
148, 152, 153, 155, 261 and n. 3,
262 and n. 4, 263 and n. 1, 269,
303, 307, 308, 318, 319, 321; ii.
439–40, 682, 691; iii. 189; v. 996;
vi. 150, 158, 170, 172, 173, 240.
Fowler, Thomas, ii. 439.
Fowler, Sir Thomas, vi. 202.
Fox, John, v. 1115.
Fox, The, see Jonson, *Volpone.*
Foxe, John (amateur actor), v.
1359.
Foxe, John, *Acts and Monuments* . . .
3 vols. (1641), iii. 285.
Foxley, —, ii. 401.
Fragmenta Aurea, see Suckling, Sir
John.
France, ii. 421; iii. 183, 196; iv. 637,
695, 916, 917, 919; v. 994,
1267; vi. 61; vii. 26.
   Ambassador of, *see* French ambas-
   sador.

Embassy to, iii. 105.
Exile in, iii. 174, 175.
Tour of, iii. 166.
Travel in, iii. 33.
Francelia, see Suckling.
Francis, Michael, vi. 204, 205.
Franke, Robert (sailor), i. 265, 266;
vi. 161.
Frankfort, ii. 451.
Frankfort-am-Main, v. 1407.
Franklin, an innkeeper, i. 293; ii.
689; vi. 100.
Fraud in swearing players, i. 190;
ii. 358–9.
Fraunces, Edward, v. 985.
Fraus Honesta, see Stubbe, Edmund.
Fraus Pia, see Anonymous.
Freake, Thomas, Esq., iv. 773.
Frederick V, *see* Palsgrave, The.
Frederick and Basilea, see Anony-
mous.
Frederick, John, grocer, v. 1221.
Freeman, Elizabeth, ii. 439.
Freeman, Martin, iii. 468.
Freeman, Ralph (Lord Mayor of
London), iii. 468; iv. 576.
Freeman, Sir Ralph, iii. 468–70.
   Imperiale, iii. **469–70.**
   Transl. *Lucius Annaeus Seneca,
   the philosopher: his Booke of the
   Shortnesse of Life* (1663), iii. 469.
Freeman, Vincent, iv. 527.
Freeman, William, iii. 468.
Free-Parliament Quaeres, see
Anonymous.
Freestone, vi. 293.
French, Anne, ii. 634.
French, Rebecca, ii. 634.
French, Sarah, ii. 634.
French, Thomas, ii. 634.
French, iii. 242, 246, 248.
French actors, *see* French players.
French ambassador, i. 6, 283 n. 7
cont.; iii. 200; iv. 641, 643, 650,
656, 661, 664, 670, 673, 674, 675,
872; v. 1197; vi. 87, 287; vii. 26,
31, 38, 39, 56, 62, 116.
French Ambassador's house, vii. 34.
French comedies, i. 25; vi. 45.
French company, *see* Companies,
French.
French farce, *see* Farce.
French forces, v. 1006.
French match, vii. 56.
French pastoral, iii. 453.
French players, i. 25, 207, 233–5,
272–3 and 273 n. 1; ii. 437, 496,
654 n. 2; iii. 453; v. 1334; vi. 23,
45–47, 225–7; vii. 11.

Q

French plays, iv. 549, 1334; vi. 23, 65, 225–7.
French romance, iv. 486.
French, translations from, iii. 46, 112, 118–19, 276, 280, 363, 406; iv. 546, 599–600, 726, 907; v. 964, 1028–32.
French Branke, The, see Anonymous, *The Dutch Painter and the French Branke.*
French Dancing Master, The, see Shirley, James, *The Ball.*
French Dancing Master, The, see Cavendish, William.
French Schoolmaster, The, see Anonymous.
Frere, Daniel, iv. 942, 995, 998; v. 1002.
Friars of Berwick, iii. 234.
Friar Bacon, iv. 717.
Friar Bacon and Friar Bungay, see Greene, Robert.
Frick Gallery, New York, v. 1200.
Frijlinck, Wilhelmina P., ed., *The Tragedy of Sir John Van Olden Barnavelt* (1922), iii. 415, 416, 417.
Frith, Marion, vi. 146, 147, 148.
Frontispieces, vi. 218, 224 n. 1.
Fry, John, *Bibliographical Memoranda in Illustration of Early English Drama* (1816), v. 1397.
Fucus Histriomastix or Fucus sive Histriomastix, see Ward, Robert.
Fuimus Troes, see Fisher, Jasper.
Fulham, Middlesex, i. 19; ii. 412, 638, 639, 641.
Fuller, Thomas, *History of the Holy War* (1639), iv. 512.
Fulsis, Alexander, vi. 239.
Fulwell, Ulpian, *Like Will to Like*, vii. 120.
Funebria Sacra, see Anonymous.
Funeral elegies, v. 1016.
Furies' Masque, see Anonymous.
Furness, H. H., ed., *Macbeth*, New Variorum Edition of Shakespeare (1915), iv. 903, 904.
Furnivall, Frederick J., *see* Harrison, William.
Furnivall, F. J., 'The End of Shakespeare's Playhouses', *Academy*, No. 547, 28 October 1882 (vol. xxii), vi. 42, 200, 208 n. 1, 214 n. 1, 231.
'Further Notes on William Trevell', *see* Dowling, Margaret.
Fynch, Herbert, ii. 638.

G., C., v. 997, 998.
G., C. (of Oxford), verses by, iii. 153; iv. 928, 939.
G., C. [Charles Gerbier ?], verses by, iii. 89.
Gabor, Bethlen, iv. 518.
Gads Hill, iii. 162.
Gainsford, Captain, iii. 338.
Gainsford, Thomas, *The True and Wonderful History of Perkin Warbeck* (1618), iii. 455.
Galathea, see Lyly, John.
Gale, Samuel, iv. 741.
Galfridus's *Monumetensis*, iii. 115, 304.
Galiaso, see Anonymous.
Galinsky, Hans, *Die Familie im Drama von Thomas Heywood* (1936), iv. 553.
Galleries, vi. 258, 268.
Galleries in theatres, *see* Theatres.
Galley-foist, vi. 233.
Galleys, vi. 293.
Galliards, *see* Dances.
Gamblers, v. 1199.
Gambling, iii. 275.
Game at Chess, A, see Middleton.
Games, v. 1020, 1055, 1199, 1268, 1343.
    Cribbage, iii. 150; v. 1199.
    Gleeke, iii. 63.
Game players, ii. 616.
Gamester, The, see Shirley, James.
Gamesters, v. 1198.
Gamesters, The, see Garrick, David.
Gammon, Richard, iii. 232; iv. 544.
Gammon of Westphallia (mock title), v. 1447.
Gannell, *see* Gunnell, Richard.
Gaoler, ii. 354.
Gapp, S. V., 'Notes on John Cleveland', *P.M.L.A.* xlvi (1931), iii. 165.
Gardeners, ii. 352, 564.
Gardens, vi. 88, 178, 180, 224 n. 1.
Gardens at theatres, vi. 186.
Gardiner, Dr. Richard, canon of Christ Church, Oxford, v. 1188.
Gardiner, Robert, iii. 359, 376.
Gardiner, Robert B., *The Admission Registers of St. Paul's School from 1748 to 1876* (1884), iv. 588.
Registers of Wadham College, Oxford (Part I) from 1613 to 1719, The (1889), iv. 736.
Gardiner, Samuel Ralston, *A History of England from the Accession of James I to the*

Outbreak of the Civil War, 1603–1642, 10 vols. (1883–4), iii. 41, 121, 147, 331, 339; iv. 482, 496, 644, 662, 798, 802, 843, 878, 957, 958; v. 975, 982, 988, 1020, 1052, 1148, 1167, 1193, 1194, 1200, 1266, 1300; vii. 58.
'Political Element in Massinger, The', *The New Shakespere Society's Transactions (1875–6)*, iv. 750, 762, 765, 786, 797.
Reports of Cases in the Courts of Star Chamber and High Commission, Camden Society (1886), iv. 747; v. 984.
Gardiner, Stephen, iii. 285.
Garfield, Benjamin, ii. 380; iii. 254, 255; iv. 471–2.
The Unfortunate Fortunate, iv. 471–2.
Garfield, John, *Wandering Whore Continued, The* (1660), vi. 138.
Garland, John, i. 198, 211.
Garlands, vi. 276.
Garman, i. 142.
Garnett, Jasper, iv. 472–3.
Unnamed play, iv. 473.
Garnett, R., 'Ben Jonson's Probable Authorship of Scene 2, Act IV, of Fletcher's "Bloody Brother",' *M.P.* ii (1905), iii. 401.
Garrard, George, letters from i. 33, 39 n. 1, 47, 48, 56 n. 3, 58, 131, 244, 329; ii. 654 n. 2 cont., 660, 662, 665; iii. 22, 24, 107, 108, 135–6, 199, 200, 207, 209, 217, 219, 220; iv. 831, 919; v. 1155, 1156, 1159, 1190, 1202, 1205, 1206; vi. 16, 29, 30, 34, 37, 69, 266, 286, 287; vii. 4.
Garrell, —, ii. 558.
Garrett, John, i. 164 n. 4 cont., 171 and n. b; ii. 440.
Garrett, William, ii. 497.
Garrick, David, book collection of, iii. 14; v. 977.
Country Girl, The, iii. 8.
Gamesters, The, v. 1111–12.
Garrison, vi. 293, 294.
Garrod, H. W., *Genius Loci and Other Essays* (1950), iv. 751.
Profession of Poetry and Other Lectures, The (1929), iv. 750, 775, 777.
Garst, *see* Guest, Ellis.
Garter King of Arms, ii. 469.
Garway, Henry, iv. 578.
Gary, Giles, i. 176.

Gascoigne, Alice, ii. 441.
Gascoigne, Jane, ii. 441.
Gascoigne, William, i. 15, 73–89; ii. 440–1.
Gate House, prison, ii. 568; iv. 721.
Gates, William Bryan, *The Dramatic Works and Translations of Sir William Lower with a Reprint of The Enchanted Lovers* (1932), iv. 725, 726, 727.
Gatherers, *see* Theatres.
Gatherer's box, *see* Theatres, gatherer's box in.
Gaw, Allison, ed., *Studies in English Drama*, First Series (1917), iii. 468, 469; v. 1233.
Gawdy family, the papers of, v. 1231; vii. 102.
Gawthorpe Hall, Lancs., i. 172; ii. 423.
Gayley, Charles Mills, iii. 390; iv. 776.
Beaumont, the Dramatist: a Portrait (1914), iii. 14, 305, 306.
Representative English Comedies, 3 vols. (1914), iii. 55; iv. 892, 895.
Gayton, Edmund, v. 995, 1345, 1456.
Pleasant Notes upon Don Quixote (1654), ii. 690–1; iii. 37, 103, 104, 187, 189; iv. 887; v. 1113, 1345–6, 1356, 1411; vi. 171, 172, 239, 246.
Gee, John, *New Shreds of the Old Snare*, i. 207–8; ii. 396–7.
Gehler, Victor, *Das Verhaeltnis von Fords Perkin Warbeck zu Bacons Henry VII* (1895), iii. 454.
Gell, Robert, i. 129, 253.
Gellius, Gedeon, ii. 441.
Gem engravers, v. 993.
Geminus Alcides, see Anonymous.
Genee, Rudolph, vi. 189.
General, The, see Anonymous.
General, The, see Boyle, Roger, Earl of Orrery.
General Advertiser, iii. 450.
General History of Music, see Burney, Charles.
General History of the Turks, The, see Knolles, Richard.
General Sessions of the Peace, vi. 146, 148.
Generous Enemies, see Fletcher, *The Humorous Lieutenant*.
Generous Portugal, The, see Fletcher, *The Island Princess*.
Genest, John, *Some Account of the*

Genest, John (*cont.*)
  *English Stage from the Restoration
    in 1660 to 1830*, 10 vols. (1832),
    iii. 8, 65, 182, 225, 454; iv. 770,
    817, 887; v. 1081, 1100, 1111,
    1112, 1149, 1152, 1167.
Geneva, iii. 33.
  Thomas Killigrew in, iv. 695,
    703.
Genii, vi. 276.
Genoa, as setting, iv. 486.
Gentillet, Innocent, *Discours sur les
    moyens de bien gouverner*, transla-
    tion of 1602, iii. 406.
Gentle Craft, The, see Dekker,
  Thomas, *The Shoemakers' Holiday.*
Gentle-man of the Bows, iii. 112,
  115.
*Gentleman, No Gentleman, A Meta-
    morphosed Courtier, A, see*
  Anonymous.
Gentleman of the Privy Chamber to
  Prince Charles, v. 1186.
Gentleman Usher, The, see Chapman,
  George.
Gentleman of Venice, The, see
  Massinger, *The Renegado.*
Gentleman of Venice, The, see
  Shirley, James.
*Gentleman's Journal, or the Monthly
    Miscellany*, v. 1152.
Gentlemen of the Artillery Garden,
  vii. 112.
Gentlemen of the King's Bed-
  chamber, iii. 116.
Gentlemen of the Privy Chamber,
  iii. 22, 105.
Gentlemen of the Robes, iii. 108.
Gentry, vi. 54, 292.
George, ii. 441.
George A Greene, see Anonymous.
George Alley in Golding Lane, *see*
  London, streets of.
George Tavern, the, vi. 72, 73.
Gerard, Lord, ii. 496.
Gerber, Friedrich, *The Sources of
    William Cartwright's Comedy, The
    Ordinary* (1909), iii. 132, 133.
Gerdler, Adam, ii. 441.
Gerhardt, Erich, *Massinger's 'The
    Duke of Milan' und seine Quellen*
    (1905), iv. 775.
German customs, v. 1313.
German, dialogue in, v. 1287.
Germany, i. 6; iv. 788; v. 1241.
Germany, Ambassador to, iv. 526.
  English actors in, i. 165; ii. 350,
    351, 388, 391, 406, 429, 432,
    441, 451, 473, 484, 486, 495,
    521, 522, 537, 543, 553, 559,
    561, 578, 579, 599, 613, 615;
    iv. 752; v. 1010, 1137, 1153,
    1288.
  Masque in, iii. 108, 110.
  Wars in, v. 1199.
Gerrard, Edward, ii. 358, 359.
Gerritsen, Johan, 'The Printing of
    the Beaumont and Fletcher Folio
    of 1647', *Library*, Fifth Series, iii
    (1949), iii. 305.
Gerschow, Frederic, diary of, vi.
  32 n. 1.
Gersley, Sir George, i. 239 n. 3, 283
  n. 7 cont., 284.
Gest, Ellis, *see* Guest, Ellis.
Gesta Grayorum, see Anonymous.
Gestures, v. 1317.
Geyst, Ellis, *see* Guest, Ellis.
Ghismonda, see Anonymous.
Ghost, The, see Anonymous.
Ghost edition, iv. 798.
Ghost names, iv. 718, 955.
Ghost titles, iii. 89, 235; iv. 899;
  v. 1301, 1303, 1315, 1321, 1323,
    1326, 1330, 1336, 1338, 1347,
    1349, 1350, 1352, 1353, 1354,
    1356, 1357, 1364, 1373, 1376,
    1384, 1385, 1389, 1398, 1400,
    1402, 1404, 1408, 1409, 1410,
    1416, 1432, 1436, 1437, 1444,
    1447.
Ghost writing, i. 60.
Giant's bone, vi. 209.
Gibb, John, iii. 383.
Gibbens, Margaret, ii. 465.
Gibbes, George, ii. 441.
Gibbons, A., *Ely Episcopal Registers*
    (1891), v. 1236.
Gibbons, Christopher, v. 1103.
Gibbon's Tennis Court, ii. 373; iii.
    22, 23, 24, 56, 71, 82, 147, 149–50,
    197, 221, 264, 314, 319, 333, 344,
    371, 374, 378, 385, 402, 408, 419,
    423, 426; iv. 479, 580, 696, 698,
    699, 706, 708, 767, 812, 900; v.
    1019, 1082, 1085, 1091, 1129,
    1135, 1150, 1151, 1163, 1204,
    1208.
Gibborne, Thomas, *see* Gilbourne,
  Thomas.
Gibbs, Alice, ii. 442.
Gibbs, Mrs. Anne, actress, iii. 104; v.
    1021, 1170.
Gibbs, Anthony, ii. 441–2.
Gibbs, Edward (fencer), i. 285, 287,
    288, 290, 297, 318, 324, 327 n. 1,
    332, 336; ii. 442; vi. 99.
Gibbs, Jone, ii. 442.

Gibbs, Mary, ii. 442.

Gibbs, Richard, organist of Christ Church, Norwich, v. 1188.

Gibbs, Susan, ii. 442.

Gibes, Anthony, see Gibbs, Anthony.

Gibson, —, ii. 442–3.

Gibson, H., i. 323 ; ii. 443.

Gibson, James, vii. 58.

Gibson, Thomas, v. 1067.

Gifford, William, iii. 69, 79, 80, 272 ; iv. 649, 651, 678 ; v. 1049, 1108.
   ed., The Dramatic Works of John Ford, 2 vols. (1827), iii. 437, 438.
   ed., The Works of Ben Jonson, 9 vols. (1816), iv. 613, 623.
   ed., The Works of Ben Jonson, 1 vol. (1846), iv. 613.
   ed., The Works of Ben Jonson, 1 vol. (1853), iv. 613.
   ed., The Works of Ben Jonson, 1 vol. (1858), iv. 613.
   ed., The Works of Ben Jonson, 1 vol. (1869), iv. 613.
   Notes and memoir in Francis Cunningham's ed. The Works of Ben Jonson, 3 vols. (1871), iv. 613.
   Notes and memoir in The Works of Ben Jonson, ed. Francis Cunningham, 9 vols. (1875), iv. 613.
   ed., The Plays of Philip Massinger, essay by John Ferriar, 4 vols. (1805), iv. 758, 761, 770, 773.
   ed., Plays of Philip Massinger, The (1813), iii. 263, 264 ; iv. 785, 806, 807.
   Dramatic Works and Poems of James Shirley; with Notes by the Late William Gifford, . . . (ed.), Alexander Dyce, 6 vols. (1833), v. 1081, 1142, 1149.

Gifford, William, and Alexander Dyce, The Works of John Ford, 3 vols. (1869 and 1895), iii. 270.

Gigantomachia, see Anonymous.

Gilbert, Allan H., The Symbolic Persons in the Masques of Ben Jonson (1948), iv. 604.
   'Thomas Heywood's Debt to Plautus', J.E.G.P. xii (1913), iv. 553, 560, 561, 565.

Gilbert, J. T., iii. 96.

Gilbertson, William, iv. 877 ; v. 1436.

Gilbourne, Thomas, ii. 443.

Gilburne, Samuel, ii. 443.

Gilbye, John, i. 266.

Gilder, —, ii. 642.

Gilding, vi. 265, 285.

Gildon, Charles, vi. 169.
   Miscellaneous Letters and Essays (1695), iv. 681.

Giles, George, i. 189, 192 ; ii. 443–4.

Giles, Gideon, see Gellius, Gedeon.

Giles, Launcelot, ii. 384.

Giles Goosecap, Sir, see Chapman, George.

Gill, Alexander, i. 42, 122, 268 ; ii. 503, 594 ; iv. 474, 538, 606, 619, 620 ; vi. 25, 163.

Gill, John, i. 166 and n. 5 ; ii. 361 ; vi. 9, 99, 220–1, 239.

Gill, Marmaduke, house of, vii. 12 n. 1.

Gillingham, Dorset, iv. 599, 715.

Gilman (Gilmyn), Anthony, stationer, iv. 775.

Gilman, Robert, i. 188, 189, and n. 3, 192 ; ii. 444.

Gilmet, Elizabeth, v. 1067.

Gilmet, Richard, v. 1067.

Gimber, Widow, ii. 641.

Gipsy plays, iii. 73.

Giraldi, Cynthio, iv. 869.

Giraldo, the Constant Lover, see Shirley, Henry.

Girl Worth Gold, A, see Heywood, The Fair Maid of the West.

Gladiators, vi. 294, 295.

Glapthorne, George, iv. 473.

Glapthorne, Henry, ii. 509 n. 1 ; iii. 16 ; iv. 473–97, 721, 1388, 1446.
   Albertus Wallenstein, i. 120 ; iv. 474, 477–9, 490, 492, 824 ; v. 1236 ; vi. 198, 199.
   Argalus and Parthenia, i. 336 and n. d, 339 ; iv. 475, 478, 479–81, 494.
   Duchess of Fernandina, The, iv. 481, 488, 493.
   'Epithalamium', iv. 480.
   His Maiesties Gracious Answer to The Message sent from the Honourable Citie of London, concerning Peace (1643), iv. 474, 477.
   Hollander, The, or Love's Trial, i. 236 and n. 6, 252, 336 and n. f, 339 ; iii. 211 ; iv. 475, 480, 482–3, 487, 495, 497, 747 ; v. 1131 ; vii. 7, 8.
   Lady Mother, The, i. 300 ; ii. 381, 482 ; iv. 483–5, 487, 488, 495, 496, 497 ; v. 1096 ; vi. 117.
   Lady's Privilege, The, i. 336 and n., 339 ; iii. 81, 483, 485–7, 495 ; v. 1094.

Glapthorne, Henry (*cont.*)
'Love', iv. 480.
Love's Trial, see *The Hollander*.
Noble Husbands, The, iv. **487–8,**
866.
Noble Trial, The, v. 1445; iv. 481,
485, **488,** 493.
Poems (1639), ii. 433; iv. 474, 480.
*Revenge for Honour, or The
Parricide*, i. 206 n. 3, 213 n. b,
216, 278; iv. 475, **489–93,** 824;
v. 1387, 1445.
Vestall, The, iv. 481, 488, **493–4.**
Whitehall, A Poem, iv. 476.
Wit in a Constable, i. 339; iv.
485, 494–7, 774.
Glapthorne, Lonelis (Lovelace), iv.
476.
Glapthorne, Mrs. Priscilla, iv. 474,
475, 481.
Glapthorne, Susan, iv. 476.
Glapthorne, Thomas, iv. 473.
'Glapthorne the Porter', iv. 477.
Glascott, the Bailey of Southwark,
v. 1058.
Glasgow, University of, MS., iii. 95,
96.
Globe Alley, *see* London, streets of.
Globe theatre, i. 1, 2, 3 and n. 7,
4 and n. 1, 5, 10 and n. 6 cont.,
17, 30 and n. 6, 40, 43, 44, 101,
103, 129, 141 n. 4, 146, 149 n. 4,
207, 208, 225 n. 1, 264, 307,
319; ii. 612, 638, 651, 658, 675,
694; iii. 74, 75, 82, 84, 209, 210,
396, 397, 402, 412, 416, 429,
441, 449, 475, 477, 478, 532,
540, 541, 543, 554, 562, 563,
699, 747, 778, 780; iv. 809, 821,
824, 861, 876, 878; v. 996, 1049,
1051, 1106, 1107; vi. 4, 11, 12
and n. 2, 13, 14, 15, 16, 17, 20,
21, 22, 23, 37, 39, 63, 69, 114,
122, 123, 127, 129, 135, 136,
139, 140, 141–3, 144, 149, 150,
163, 164, 171 n. 1, 172, 178–200,
212, 215, 216 n. 2, 218, 224 n. 1,
238, 240, 241, 250, 251, 252;
vii. 7, 8, 17.
And Blackfriars, relative im-
portance of, i. 30 n. 6.
Capacity of, iv. 871–2.
Character of audience at, i. 10
n. 6.
Cost of building, i. 45.
Cost of share in, i. 45.
First, i. 146; vi. 201, 202 n. 1.
Garden of, i. 44.
Housekeepers at, iii. 300.

Housekeepers' shares in, vi. 36–37.
Income from shares in, i. 45.
Inferiority of, vi. 193–4.
Intended riot at, i. 21.
Large stage of, i. 30 n. 6 cont.
Lease of, i. 30, 31, 45.
Performance at, i. 22.
Proportion of plays seen at, i. 30
n. 2.
Rent of, i. 44.
Second, i. 146; vi. 155, 178–200.
Shareholder in, ii. 466.
Shares in, i. 43–47.
Taphouse, i. 44.
Tenement, i. 44.
Total takings at, i. 23–24.
Type of plays at, i. 30 n. 6 cont.
Yearly rent, i. 45.
*Globe Playhouse, The: Its Design and
Equipment, see* Adams, John
Cranford.
*Globe Restored, The: A Study of the
Elizabethan Theatre* (1953), *see*
Hodges, C. Walter.
'Globe Theatre, The, 1599–1608',
see Hayward, Wayne Clinton.
Glooston, Leicestershire, iii. 159.
'Glories of our blood and state, The',
see Shirley, James.
Gloucester, i. 299; ii. 411, 421, 613;
v. 1224.
Gloucester, siege of, iii. 196.
Gloucester, Duke of, v. 1220.
Gloucester Hall, Oxford, iv. 721,
724.
Glover, Arnold, iii. 312.
Glover, Jeremy, vi. 205.
Glover, Katherin, vi. 205.
Glover, William, vi. 204, 205.
Gloves for boy actors in new plays,
ii. 687; vi. 106, 107.
Goad, Christopher, i. 220, 223 n. 6,
246, 249 n. f cont., 285, 286,
288, 289 n. 4, 290, 291 n. 2, 297;
ii. **444–5;** iii. 233; vii. 100.
Goad, Constance, ii. 445.
Goad, Elizabeth, ii. 445.
Goad, John, ii. 445.
Goad, Mary, ii. 445.
Goad, Michael, ii. 445.
Goad, Roger, ii. 444.
Goad, Ruth, ii. 445.
Goad, Symon, ii. 445.
Goad, Dr. Thomas, iv. 538.
Goad, Timothy, ii. 445.
Goblins, The, see Suckling, John.
Goborne, John, vi. 140.
Godbid, William, stationer, iii. 168,
169, 170.

Godeau, Anthony, iv. 726.

Godfrey, John T., *William Sampson, A Seventeenth Century Poet and Dramatist* (1894), v. 1042, 1043.

Godfrey, Thomas, Keeper of the Game, vi. 212, 213, 214.

Godfrey, Walter H., vi. 143–4.

'Godly Warning for all Maidens, A', *see* Anonymous.

Godstow, Berkshire, v. 1392.

Godwin, Richard i. 307, 308, 321; ii. 445.

Goffe, Alexander, *see* Gough, Alexander.

Goffe, John, *see* Gough, John.

Goffe, Robert, *see* Gough, Robert.

Goffe (Gouffe, Gough), Thomas, **iv. 498–511**, 547, 814, 816, 843.

  Bajazet the Second, see *The Raging Turk, or Bajazet the Second*.

  Bastard, The, iv. 500–1.

  Careless Shepherdess, The, ii. 540, 541; iii. 41, 58, 304; iv. 499, **501–5**, 589, 863; v. 973–4, 1187, 1222, 1293, 1310, 1370, 1382, 1402; vi. 113, 166, 243.

  Careless Shepherdess, The, Praeludium to, vi. 109–12.

  Courageous Turk, The, or Amurath the First, iii. 100; iv. 502, **505–7**, 508, 509, 510.

  Raging Turk, The, or Bajazet the Second, iv. 508, **509–10**.

  Three Excellent Tragedies (1656), iv. 506, 508, 509.

  Tragedy of Orestes, The, iv. 502, 507–9.

  Unknown Play, iv. 511.

Goffin, R. Cullis, *The Life and Poems of William Cartwright* (1918), iii. 126, 127.

Golden Age, The, *see* Heywood, Thomas.

Golden Age Restored, The, *see* Jonson, Ben.

Golden Fleece, The, *see* Brathwait, Richard.

Golding, —, ii. 445–6.

Golding, Edward, v. 1096.

Golding, S. R., 'The Parliament of Bees', *R.E.S.* iii (1927), iii. 240, 257, 258, 259, 273.

Golding Lane, *see* London, streets of.

Goldsmiths, i. 275; ii. 398, 401, 499; v. 993; vi. 170, 227.

Goldsmiths' Jubilee, The, *see* Jordan, Thomas.

Goldsworthy, W. Lansdown, *Ben Jonson and the First Folio* (1931), iv. 628.

Gollancz, Sir Israel, ii. 412.

  'Ben Jonson's Ode to "The Phoenix and the Turtle"', *T.L.S.* 8 October 1925, v. 1039, 1040, 1041.

  'Contemporary Lines to Heminge and Condell', *T.L.S.* 26 January 1922, v. 1039, 1041.

  Sale of his MSS., v, 1345.

Gomersall, Robert, iv. 512–14.

  Levite's Revenge (1628), iv. 512, 513, 588.

  Poems (1633), v. 513.

  Sermons on St. Peter (1634), iv. 513.

  Tragedy of Lodowick Sforza, Duke of Milan, The, iv. 513–14.

Gomond, Edward, ii. 421.

Gondomar, Sarmiento de Acuña, Count of, i. 12, 140 n. 9; iii. 84, 290; iv. 588, 630, 656, 659, 871, 872, 873, 875, 877, 878; iv. 972, 973, 1413; vi. 153.

Gondomar, *see* Middleton, *A Game at Chess*.

Gonsalvus Sylveira, *see* Anonymous.

Gonville and Caius College, Cambridge, iii. 10, 185, 238; v. 961, 999, 1000, 1001.

Good, Christopher, *see* Goad, Christopher.

Goodale, Edward, ii. 634.

Goodcoale, Henry, *The wonderful Discouery of Eliz[abeth] Sawyer a witch late of Edmonton* (1621), iii. 270, 271.

Goodericke, Mathew, *see* Goodricke, Mathew.

Good-Friday, being meditations on that day (1684), v. 995.

Goodman, Godfrey, *The Court of James the First* [1839], vii. 58.

Goodman, Jo., ii. 490.

Goodman, Nicholas, *Holland's Leaguer: Or, An Historical Discourse . . . of Dona Britanica Hollandia . . .* (1632), iii. 7; iv. 745, 747; vi. 15, 212, 251.

Goodman's Fields theatre, iii. 454.

Goodricke, Mathew, a painter, vi. 272, 273, 277, 278.

Goodwin, Gordon, 'Glapthorne Family', *N. & Q.* Eighth Series, xii (11 December 1897), iv. 473.

  'Robert Gomersall', *N. & Q.*, Ninth Series, i (1898), iv. 512.

Goodwin, William, iv. 498.
Goolfinch, Sr. (amateur actor), v. 1298, 1299.
Gord, Francis, ii. 533.
Gordon, D. J., 'Poet and Architect: The Intellectual Setting of the Quarrel between Ben Jonson and Inigo Jones', *Journal of the Warburg and Courtauld Institutes,* xii (1949), iv. 604, 612, 632, 635, 636, 651; v. 988.
Gore, John, ii. 366; v. 1240, 1254.
Gore, William, ii. 366.
Gorge, Sir Arthur, v. 984.
Gorge, Sir Edward, vi. 78.
Goring, Sir George, Lord Goring, ii. 414; iii. 63, 219; iv. 650, 721, 724; v. 965, 1372, 1422; vii. 81, 94.
Gosnold, John, vii. 23, 32, 36, 37, 38, 39, 40, 41, 46.
Gosse, Sir Edmund, iv. 810, 814, 817.
Gossips' Brawl, The, see Anonymous.
Gosson, Henry, ii. **446**, 682.
Gost, Ellis, *see* Guest, Ellis.
Gouffe, Thomas, *see* Goffe, Thomas.
Gouge, Mrs. Elizabeth, vi. 18 n. 1.
Gouge, William, i. 5; vi. 18, 19, 21, 24; vii. 2.
Gough, Alexander, i. 49, 70, 73–89; ii. **446–7**; iii. 123, 164, 457; iv. 810, 817, 901; vi. 237.
Gough (Goffe), John, iv. 514–16; v. 998.
  Ecclesiae Anglicanae (1661), iv. 515.
  Strange Discovery, iii. 269; iv. 515–16; v. 1440.
Gough, Robert, i. 5, 16, 72–88; ii. **447–8**, 682, 683; iii. 416; iv. 510.
Gough, Stephen, iv. 514.
Gough, Thomas, *see* Goffe, Thomas.
Gough, William, iv. 515.
Goulart, Simon, *Histoires admirables et memorables de nostre temps* (1600), iii. 379, 470; v. 1252.
Gould, Robert, *The Rival Sisters, or The Violence of Love,* v. 1133.
Gourlay, James J., 'Caroline Play, "The Wasp" ', *T.L.S.* 5 June 1943, v. 1433, 1434.
  'Thomas Jordan', *T.L.S.* 17 Aug. 1933, v. 1433, 1434.
Govell, *see* Gunnell, Richard.
Govell, R., *A Mask, see* Gunnell, Richard.
Governor, The, see Formido, Sir Cornelius.
Governor of the company, *see* Company governors.

Gowdy, Framlingham, i. 312.
Gowre, William, v. 1165.
Gowrie conspiracy, iv. 842, 843.
Grace, Charles, ii. 449.
Grace, Elizabeth, ii. 449.
Grace, Francis, i. 136, 138, 140 and n. 1, 147, 149, 155; ii. **448–9**, 682.
Grace, Frank, vi. 150.
Grace, Increase, ii. 449.
Grace, John, ii. 449.
Grace, Margaret, ii. 449.
Grace, Richard, i. 145, 147, 155; ii. **449–50**, 683; vi. 157.
Grace, Sara, ii. 449.
Grace Dieu, Leicestershire, iii. 14.
Gradell, Henry, *see* Gradwell, Henry.
Gradwell, Alice, ii. 450.
Gradwell, Anne, ii. 451.
Gradwell, Elizabeth, ii. 451.
Gradwell, Francys, ii. 450.
Gradwell, Henry, i. 303, 307, 308, 321, 323; ii. **450**.
Gradwell, Jane, ii. 450.
Gradwell, Richard, ii. **450–1**.
Grafton, Richard (historian), iii. 115.
Graham (Grime), Sir James, v. 1276.
Gramercy Wit, see Anonymous.
Granchio, Il, see Salviati, Lionardo.
Grant, R. Patricia, 'Cervantes' *El casamiento engañoso* and Fletcher's *Rule a Wife and Have a Wife',* *Hispanic Review,* xii (1944), iii. 407, 410.
Granville-Barker, Harley, vi. 188 n. 1.
Grateful Servant, The, see Shirley, James.
Gratuities, iii. 78; iv. 796; vi. 59–60, 63, 64, 284.
Graunt, John, *Natural and Political Observations Mentioned in a Following Index and Made upon the Bills of Mortality* (1676), ii. 667.
Graves, desecration of, iv. 833.
Graves, entrances from, vi. 190.
Graves, Elizabeth, ii. 638.
Graves, Thornton Shirley, 'The "Act Time" in Elizabethan Theatres', *S.P.* xii (1915), vi. 9 n.
  'Jonson in the Jest Books', *Manly Anniversary Studies* (1923), iv. 605.
Gravesend, Kent, i. 145.
Gray, Charles H., *Lodowick Carliell, His Life, A Discussion of His Plays, and 'The Deserving Favourite',* *A Tragi-Comedy* (1905), iii. 111, 112, 115, 116, 117, 121.

Gray, H. D., v. 1246, 1247.
'Appius and Virginia: by Webster and Heywood', *Stud. Phil.* xxiv (1927), v. 1245.
' "Cure for a Cuckold, A", by Heywood, Rowley and Webster', *M.L.R.* xxii (1927), v. 1248, 1249.
Gray, J. E., 'The Source of *The Emperour of the East*', *R.E.S.*, N.S., i (1950), iv. 777, 780.
'Still More Massinger Corrections', *Library*, Fifth Series, v (1950), iv. 765, 777, 808, 810, 811, 814, 815, 817.
Gray, Margaret, *see* Grey, Margaret.
Gray, Patrick (sailor), i. 265; vi. 161.
Gray's Inn, ii. 477, 488, 633; iii. 10, 38, 39, 47, 104, 437, 450, 451, 454, 464; iv. 471, 570, 641, 830; v. 1068, 1069, 1158, 1160, 1161, 1180, 1181, 1227, 1291, 1376, 1377, 1378; vii. 96.
Benchers of, iv. 471.
Gray's Inn Lane, *see* London, streets of.
Great Cham, The, see Anonymous.
Great Chamber, *see* Whitehall.
Great Duke, The, see Massinger, *The Great Duke of Florence.*
Great Duke of Florence, The, see Massinger.
Great Dunmow, Essex, iii. 183.
Great Favourite, or The Duke of Lerma, The, see Howard, Sir Robert.
Great Hall, *see* Whitehall.
Great Seal, The, vi. 299, 307.
Great Wardrobe, His Majesty's, vi. 81, 82, 84.
Greece, iv. 567.
Greek lecturer, Cambridge, iii. 185.
Greek, translations from, iii. 5, 97, 142, 155; v. 980–2, 1072, 1103, 1186.
Greeke, Mr., v. 1298.
Greeke, John, v. 1299.
Greeke, Thomas, v. 1299.
Greeks and Trojans, The, see Anonymous.
Green, A. Wigfall, *The Inns of Court and Early English Drama* (1931), v. 1154.
Green, John, *Refutation of the Apology for Actors* (1615), vii. 10.
Greene, Charles, iv. 932, 935, 937, 938, 939, 940.
Greene, John, actor, ii. **451**.

Greene, John, company of, iv. 752.
Greene, John, diarist, i. 110, 114, 123, 128, 132, 235, 250, 255, 258; iii. 332, 408; iv. 692, 862; v. 1125, 1273, 1425; vii. 9, 96, 98.
Greene, Margaret, iv. 691; v. 1125.
Greene, Robert, iv. 511; v. 1314, 1363.
Friar Bacon and Friar Bungay, i. 156; iv. 857, 870; vi. 233; vii. 54, 77, 120.
George a Greene, the Pinner of Wakefield, see Anonymous.
Looking Glass for London and England, A (with Lodge), ii. 542, 543.
Orlando Furioso, iv. 841; vii. 26, 61, 115.
Penelope's Web, iii. 86.
Philomela; the Lady Fitzwater's Nightingale, iii. 228.
Selimus, iv. 511.
Greene, Robert, and Thomas Lodge, *A Looking-Glass for London and England*, v. 1382.
Greene, Robert, saddler, ii. 564.
Greene, Susan Baskervile, ii. 637.
Greene, Thomas, i. 158; ii. 364, **451**, 531, 536; v. 1017; vi. 217, 218, 219, 236 n. 1.
Greene's Tu Quoque, see Cooke, John.
Greenfield, Edward, iii. 437, 443.
Greenwich, iv. 795; v. 1257; vi. 101 n. 1; vii. 17, 18, 19, 27, 79.
Queen's Great Chamber, vii. 19.
Greg, W. W., iii. 43; v. 1296; vii. 16.
'Act-Divisions in Shakespeare', *R.E.S.* iv (1928), vi. 9 n. 1.
'Another Note (on *Believe as You List*)', *Library*, Fourth Series, xii (1931), iv. 762.
'Authorship and Attributions in the Early English Play-Lists', *Edinburgh Bibliographical Society Transactions*, ii, Part 4 (1946), iii. 41, 283, 305, 378, 470; iv. 729; v. 1053, 1150, 1286.
'Authorship of the Songs in Lyly's Plays, The', *M.L.R.* i (1905), 49–51, iii. 459, 461.
'Bakings of Betsy, The', *The Library* (third series), 1911, iii. 30, 31, 124, 204, 230, 250, 262, 438, 439, 445, 448, 458, 465, 466; iv. 481, 488, 493, 518, 543, 598, 684, 720, 758, 759, 760, 763, 765, 782, 785, 786,

Greg, W. W. (*cont.*)
791, 792, 794, 800, 804, 806,
808, 819, 820, 829, 830, 892,
1022, 1023, 1025, 1026, 1046;
v. 1178, 1272, 1273, 1275, 1309,
1317, 1323, 1331, 1367, 1373,
1384, 1410.
*Bibliography of the English Printed
Drama to the Restoration, A,*
4 vols. (1939–59), iii, iv, v,
passim; vi. 14 n., 103 n. 1, 198;
vii. 16.
'Bloodie Banquet, The', *T.L.S.*
24 December 1925, iii. 282.
*Dramatic Documents from the
Elizabethan Playhouses,* 2 vols.
(1931), iii. 12, 13, 93, 141, 145,
192, 267, 332, 335, 343, 346,
401, 415, 416, 484, 510, 560,
561, 567, 568, 585, 598, 762,
805, 806–7, 920, 922, 923, 1076;
v. 1207, 1265, 1316, 1318, 1332,
1333, 1340, 1341, 1367, 1380,
1381, 1382, 1418, 1427, 1433,
1434.
'"Escapes of Jupiter, The". An
Autograph play of Thomas
Heywood's', *Palaestra*, cxlviii
(1925), iv. 562, 567.
ed., *Henslowe's Diary,* 2 vols.
(1904–8), iii. 28, 36, 157, 231,
234, 241, 242, 247, 249, 252,
259, 260, 273, 274, 397, 460,
558, 559, 564, 574, 584; iv.
618, 622, 625, 733, 749, 759,
763–4, 788, 794, 808, 861, 864,
870, 911, 934, 935, 936; v.
1045, 1248, 1337, 1421; vi. 139,
141 n. 1, 145 n. 2, 149 and n. 2,
150, 184 n. 2, 185 n. 1, 200, 201,
203, 207.
Henslowe Papers (1907), iii. 239;
iv. 606, 762; vi. 123, 124, 126,
139, 140, 141–3 and n. 1,
149 n. 2, 150, 155, 157.
ed., Jonson's *The Gypsies Metamorphosed* 'in the Burley,
Belvoir, and Windsor Versions'
(1952), iv. 645.
'Jonson's Masques—Points of
Editorial Principle and Practice', *R.E.S.* xviii (1942), iv.
605, 645, 663, 665.
ed., *Ben Jonson's Sad Shepherd,
with Waldron's Continuation*
(1905), iv. 620, 621, 625, 627.
*List of English Plays, A, Written
before 1643 and Printed before
1700* (1900), v. 981.

*List of Masques, Pageants, &c.,
A* (1902), iii. 397–8; iv. 951; v.
1187, 1253.
'Massinger's Autograph Corrections in "The Duke of Milan",
1623', *Library*, Fourth Series,
iv (1923), iv. 775, 777.
'More Massinger Corrections',
Library,[Fourth Series, v (1924),
iv. 765, 775, 777, 808, 810, 812,
814, 815, 817.
'Nathan Field and the Beaumont
and Fletcher Folio of 1679',
R.E.S. iii (1927), iii. 299.
'Paper-saving in 1639', *The
Library*, Fifth series, ii (1948),
iii. 213.
*Pastoral Poetry and Pastoral
Drama* (1906), iii. 180; iv. 479,
501, 505, 625, 715, 913, 914,
917, 921, 951, 952; v. 969, 970,
971, 999, 1032, 1033, 1034,
1073, 1076, 1144, 1153, 1171,
1181, 1182, 1183, 1184, 1221,
1367, 1368, 1387.
'Perjur'd Nun, The', *T.L.S.* 10
August 1946, iii. 43.
'Printing of Mayne's Plays, The',
*Oxford Bibliographical Society,
Proceedings and Papers*, vol. i,
Part iv (1927), iv. 845, 847.
Review of Bang's edition of
*Pleasant Dialogues and Dram-
ma's von Tho. Heywood, M.L.Q.*
vii (1904), iv. 579.
Review of Dobell, ed., *The
Partial Law, M.L.R.* iv.
(1908–9), v. 1388.
Review of Herford and Simpson's
Ben Jonson, R.E.S. xviii (1942),
iv. 668.
Review of Gertrude Woodward
and J. G. McManaway, *A
Check List of English Plays,
1641–1700, Library*, Fifth
Series, i (1946–7), iii. 43; v.
1213.
'Riddle of Jonson's Chronology,
The', *Library*, Fourth Series,
vi (1926), iv. 605.
*Shakespeare First Folio, The.
Its Bibliographical and Textual
History* (1955), vii. 50.
ed., *The Soddered Citizen, see*
Pafford, J. H. P.
'Some Notes on Ben Jonson's
Works', *R.E.S.* ii (1926), iv.
605, 622, 625, 628, 632, 634,
635.

'Some Notes on Crane's Manuscript of *The Witch*', *Library*, Fourth Series, xxii (1942), iv. 903, 904.

'Some Notes on the Stationers' Registers', *Library*, Fourth Series, vii (1927), iii. 405.

ed., *Theatre of Apollo, The, an entertainment written by Sir John Beaumont in 1625* (1926), iii. 15–16.

'Theatrical Repertories of 1662', *Gentleman's Magazine*, ccci (1906), 69–72, iii. 23, 71, 102, 264, 315, 320, 333, 344, 371, 378, 385, 403, 419, 462; iv. 570, 767, 801, 812, 863, 868, 900; v. 1091, 1114, 1124, 1135.

'*Triumph of Peace, The*: A Bibliographer's Nightmare', *Library*, Fifth Series, i (1946), v. 1154, 1160, 1162.

Variorum edition of *The Elder Brother* in Beaumont and Fletcher, *Works* (1904–12), iii. 335, 336.

Greg, W. W., and F. P. Wilson, eds., *The Witch by Thomas Middleton*, Malone Society Reprints (1950), iv. 903.

Gregg, Kate L., 'Thomas Dekker: A Study in Economic and Social Backgrounds', *University of Washington Publications in Language and Literature*, ii (1924), iii. 241.

Gregory, George M.,'Shirley's Authorship of *The Traytor*', in *Two Studies in James Shirley* (1935), v. 1064, 1150.

Gresham, Thomas, v. 1006.

Gresley, Sir George, iv. 919; v. 1229; vi. 87, 90, 91 n.

Gretton, Northamptonshire, iv. 533.

Greville, Curtis, i. 73–89, 147 and n. 1, 149, 155, 183, 187, 192, 285, 287, 288, 290, 297; ii. 451–2; iv. 493, 764, 817; vi. 59, 100.

Greville, Fulke, First Lord Brook, iii. 194; iv. 917; v. 965, 1038, 1371; vi. 260, 297.
    Influence of, iv. 492.
    Alaham, i. 213 n. b; iv. 492; v. 1244; vii. 90.
    Mustapha, iv. 866; v. 1244, 1404; vii. 90.
    Works, The, vii. 90.

Grew, Obadiah, v. 1042.

Grey, Margaret, ii. 452, 545, 659.

Grey, Robert, Esq., iv. 870; v. 1017, 1018.

Griffin, Benjamin, *Injured Virtue; or, The Virgin Martyr*, iii. 266.

Griffin, Henry, ii. 384.

Griffith, Herbert, 'The Wild-Goose Chase', *The Observer*, London, 26 July 1925 (review of a performance), iii. 425.

Grigg, Michael, ii. 457.

Grime (Graham), Sir James, v. 1276.

Grimes, —, vi. 212.

Grimes, Arthuret, *see* Grymes, Anthony.

Grimes, Thomas, ii. 545.

Grimeston, Edward, *General Inventorie of the Historie of France* (1607) [translation from French], iv. 546.

Grimsby, Lincolnshire, iv. 554.

Grimsthorpe, i. 310.

Grindall, Joan, *see* Tindall, Joan.

Gripsuis and Hegio, or The Passionate Lovers, see Baron, Robert.

Grismond, John, v. 1261, 1364.

Grivell, *see* Greville, Curtis.

Grobiana's Nuptials, see Shipman, Roger.

Grocer, ii. 564, 641, 643; v. 1220, 1221.

Grocers' Company, iii. 244, 261; iv. 897, 898, 926.

Groom of His Majesty's Revels, ii. 620; vii. 57.

Grooms of the Chamber, i. 2, 7, 56, 64, 88–89, 188–9, 189, 190, 191, 271, 303, 309, 311, 315 n. 2, 321, 324 n. 1.

Grooms of His Highness's Bed-Chamber, iv. 870.

Grosart, Alexander B., ed., *The Complete Works in Prose and Verse of Francis Quarles* (Chertsey Worthies' Library), 3 vols. (1880–1), iv. 955, 956, 957.

ed., *The Complete Works in Verses and Prose of Abraham Cowley*, 2 vols. (1881), iii. 176.

ed., *Miscellanies of the Fuller Worthies Library* (1871),'iv. 738.

ed., *The Non-Dramatic Works of Thomas Dekker*, 5 vols. (1884–6), iii. 245.

ed., *The Poems of George Daniel, Esq.* (1878), v. 1029.

ed., *The Poems of Sir John Beaumont* (1869), iii. 14.

ed., *Swetnam the Woman-Hater, arraigned by Women*, 1620 (1880), v. 1416, 1417.

Grotius, Hugo, *Christ's Passion*, v. 1047.
Christ's Passion, G. Sandys's translation, v. 1048.
Groto, Luigi, *Pentimento Amoroso* (1576), v. 970, 1388.
Grove, Sir George, *Dictionary of Music and Musicians*, 5 vols. (1927), iii. 109; v. 1103, 1325.
Grove, Francis, stationer, iii. 82.
Grove, John, iv. 745; v. 1114, 1163, 1164, 1443.
Growth of Stuart London, see Brett-James, N. G.
Grub street, *see* London, streets of.
Grymes, Anthony, ii. 452.
Grymes, John, i. 162; ii. 366.
Grymes, Thomas, ii. 453.
Guards (on playhouses), vi. 174.
Guard-Chamber, iii. 199.
Guardia, C. E., 'Richard Brome as a Follower of Ben Jonson', *Bulletin of the Louisiana State University*, xxxi (1939), iii. 49.
Guardian, The, see Cowley, Abraham.
Guardian, The, see Massinger.
Guarini, Battista. *Il Pastor Fido*, iii. 280; v. 970, 1171, 1187.
Guelphs and Ghibellines, The, see Anonymous.
Guest, Ellis, ii. 453-4; iii. 192.
Guicciardini, Francesco, *L'Historia d'Italia*, iv. 486, 514, 776.
Guido Varvicensis, see Anonymous.
Guildhall, The, iv. 911; v. 1220.
Guildhall Library MSS., vi. 18, nn. 1 and 2, 94 n. 1, 99.
Guilman, Robert, *see* Gilman, Robert.
Guilpin, Edward, *Skialetheia. Or, A shadowe of Truth, in certaine Epigrams and Satyres* (1598), vi. 133.
Guilsborough, Northamptonshire, iii. 17.
Guiney, Louise I. [and Geoffrey Bliss], *Recusant Poets . . . St. Thomas More to Ben Jonson* (1938), iv. 605.
Guise, see Webster, John.
Gull upon Gull, see Anonymous.
Gumm, Charles Clayton, 'Sir Ralph Freeman's *Imperiale*', *Studies in English Drama*, first series, edited by Allison Gaw (1917), iii. 468, 469, 470.
Gumnell, *see* Gunnell, Richard.
Gun firing, iv. 925.

Gunnell, Anne, ii. 455.
Gunnell, Edward, ii. 455, 456.
Gunnell, Elizabeth, ii. 549; vi. 94, 159 n. 1.
Gunnell, Ellenor, ii. 456.
Gunnell, Hellen, ii. 456.
Gunnell, John, ii. 457.
Gunnell, Margaret, ii. 455, 623.
Gunnell, Martyne, ii. 454.
Gunnell, Penelope, ii. 456.
Gunnell, Richard, i. 136, 137, 138, 140 and n. 1, 142, 143, 144, 147, 148, 151, 152, 153, 184, 261 and n. 3, 262 and n. 4, 263 and n. 1, 264, 269 and n. 3, 283 and n. 7, 285, 286-7, 288, 290, 291 n. 6, 295, 297, 308; ii. 454-8; iv. 516-20, 679; v. 1010, 1011; vi. 87, 88, 89, 90, 91, 93-94, 98, 99, 100, 101, 150, 157, 158-9, 160; vi. 162, 165; vii. 5.
Hungarian Lion, The, i. 150, 156; ii. 456; iv. 517, 518.
Masque, The, i. 150 n. 7, 157; ii. 456; iv. 517, 518-19, 642, 644, 796.
Way to Content All Women, or How a Man May Please His Wife, The, i. 150, 156; ii. 456; iii. 265, 517, 519-20, 796.
Gunpowder, iv. 902.
Gunpowder plot, iv. 520, 608; v. 982, 1177, 1392.
Guns, vi. 242.
Gurney, Frances, ii. 642.
Gussoni, Viscenzo, v. 1230.
Gustave Adolph, Count, of Mecklenburg, v. 1023.
Gustavus I (1496-1560), iii. 250.
Gustavus Adolphus (1594-1632), iii. 250; v. 1198.
Gustavus, King of Sweden, see Dekker, Thomas.
Gutteridge, Reverend Barton, iii.20.
Gwalter, William, i. 142, 143, 144; ii. 458; vi. 157.
Gwinne, Matthew, *Nero*, v. 1381; vi. 106, 114, 118.
Gylman, Robert, *see* Gilman, Robert.
Gypsies Metamorphosed, The, see Jonson, Ben.
Gypsy, The, see Anonymous.
Gypsy plays, iii. 73.

H., I., v. 1171.
H., R., *The Arraignement of the Whole Creature* (1631), iii. 460.
H., T., iv. 554.

H., W., verses by, iii. 222.

Haberdasher, ii. 412, 636.

Haberdashers, Company of, iv. 575, 576, 577, 578, 880; v. 1185, 1221.

Haberdasher of small wares, vi. 95.

Habington, Mary, iv. 520.

Habington, Thomas, Sr., iv. 520.

Habington, William, i. 63; ii. 662 n. 5 cont.; iv. 520–5; v. 1117, 1165, 1302; vi. 38.

   Commendatory verses for Shirley's *Grateful Servant*, 1630, vi. 62.

   Verses by, iii. 198, 222.

   Castara, iv. 521, 522; v. 1301.

   Historie of Edward the Fourth, The (1641), iv. 521.

   Observations upon Historie (1641), iv. 521.

   Queen of Aragon, The, or Cleodora, i. 62 and nn. 5 and 6, 120; iii. 62, 63, 147, 216, 278; iv. 521, 522–5, 628, 692; v. 1301; vi. 51–52, 281 and n. 1, 283, 306.

Hach, T., *Über das Drama The Valiant Scot* (1901), v. 1234.

Hacket, Cuthbert, iv. 896.

Hacket, John, iv. 525–30; v. 1237.

   Loyola, iv. 525, 526–30, 854; v. 1196, 1232, 1237, 1238, 1339, 1413.

   Scrinia Reserata (1693), iv. 526.

Hackington, Kent, iv. 514.

Hadham, Hertfordshire, iv. 533.

Hadleigh, Suffolk, iv. 538, 539.

Haeresis Triumphata sive B. Ignatius Societatis Jesu Fundator, see Anonymous.

Hague, The, i. 6, 335; iii. 146, 415, 696, 922; vi. 4, 20, 153, 259, 261.

   Embassy to, iii. 105.

   English actors in, ii. 413, 493–4, 523, 571.

   Exile in, iii. 196.

   Play printed in, iii. 146, 147.

   see Fletcher, *The Jeweller of Amsterdam.*

Haight, Gordon S., 'Francis Quarles', *T.L.S.* 11 April 1935, iv. 955, 956.

   'Francis Quarles in the Civil War', *R.E.S.* xii (1936), iv. 955, 956, 957, 958, 959.

   'Francis Quarles in Ireland', *T.L.S.* 17 October 1935, iv. 955, 956.

   'Sources of Quarles's *Emblems,*

The', *Library,* Fourth Series, xvi (1935), iv. 956.

Haines, Marie, ii. 633.

Halberds, vi. 293, 294, 296.

Haley, Richard, see Hawley, Richard.

'Hall', commendatory verses by, v. 1086.

Hall, Afrika, ii. 459.

Hall, Ann, ii. 459.

Hall, Edward, iv. 532.

Hall, Frances, ii. 459.

Hall, George, ii. **458**.

Hall, Henry, iv. 845, 848.

Hall, Jo., v. 1116.

Hall, Joan, ii. 499.

Hall, John, iii. 51, 55, 72.

Hall, Joseph, Bishop of Exeter, iii. 217.

Hall, Peter, v. 1383.

Hall, Ra., ii. 624.

Hall, S., iv. 532; v. 1202.

Hall, Sarah, ii. 459.

Hall, William, i. 285, 287, 290, 291 n. 1, 297, 303, 308, 321; ii. **458–9**.

Halley, Richard, see Hawley, Richard.

Halliday, Barton, see Holyday, Barton.

Halliwell, J. O., see Halliwell-Phillipps.

Halliwell-Phillipps, James Orchard, i. 23 n. 1; iv. 518, 519, 520; v. 1182; vi. 54, 200, 212 n. 1.

   ed., *The Autobiography and Correspondence of Sir Simonds D'Ewes* (1845), iii. 11; v. 984, 1408, 1414.

   Brief Description of the Ancient & Modern Manuscripts Preserved in the Public Library, Plymouth: To which are added, Some Fragments of Early Literature Hitherto Unpublished, A (1853), iii. 33–34, 155; v. 1368, 1369.

   Collection of Ancient Documents Respecting the Office of Master of the Revels, A, and Other Papers Relating to the Early English Theatre, London (1870), vi. 64, 90 n. 2.

   Dictionary of the Old Actors (MS., Folger Shakespeare Library), iv. 517.

   Dictionary of old English plays, existing either in print or in manuscript, from the earliest times to the close of the seventeenth century; including also

Halliwell-Phillipps, J. O. (*cont.*)
  *notices of Latin plays written by
    English authors during the same
    period, A* (1860), iii. 4, 147; iv.
    744, 838; v. 972, 1181, 1311–12,
    1323, 1326, 1330, 1336, 1338,
    1349, 1351–2, 1404–5, 1408,
    1409, 1444.
  Outlines of the Life of Shakespeare,
    2 vols. (1887), iii. 193; vi. 19,
    211 n. 1.
  Poetry of Witchcraft, The (1853),
    iii. 73, 78.
  Manuscripts of, iii. 30, 32, 33, 34.
  Manuscript Scrap books in Folger
    Shakespeare Library, iii. 30,
    227, 228, 253, 246, 247, 256,
    281, 284, 286; iv. 560, 561, 766,
    806, 812; v. 1012, 1013, 1014,
    1017, 1046, 1050, 1075–6, 1144,
    1146, 1238, 1290, 1291, 1324,
    1328, 1393, 1396; vi. 54 n. 1,
    60 n. 1, 72 n. 1, 138 n. 1, 159 n.
    1, 165 n., 194 nn. 3 and 4, 210
    n. 1, 211 n. 1, 221 and n. 1, 250,
    202 n. 2; vii. 3, 6.
  ed., *The Welsh Traveller or the
    Unfortunate Welshman* (1860),
    v. 1436.
Halls in royal palaces, vi. 282.
Halsey, Bernard, ii. 459.
Halstead, William L., 'Dekker's
  "Phaethon"', *N. & Q.* clxxv
  (1938), iii. 459, 460.
  'Dekker's *Cupid and Psyche* and
    Thomas Heywood', *E.L.H.* xi
    (1944), iv. 579, 581.
Halswell, Major G., v. 1315.
Hamerton, Henry, i. 311, 312, 321;
  ii. 459.
Hamerton, Nicholas, i. 312.
Hamilton, Marquis and Duke of, iii.
  219; v. 1198, 1234; vii. 34.
Hamilton, Newburgh, *The Doating
  Lovers or The Libertine Tamed*, v.
  1167.
Hamlen, Robert, i. 176, 177 and n.
  2, 199 and n. 2, 200 and n. 3, 209,
  210, 211; ii. 459.
Hamlet, see Shakespeare.
Hamlett, Robert, *see* Hamlen,
  Robert.
Hamluc, W., i. 252; ii. 459–60.
Hammersley, Affryca, ii. 459.
Hammersley, Henry, *see* Hamerton,
  Henry.
Hammerton, Mary, ii. 460.
Hammerton, Nicholas, ii. 460.
Hammerton, Richard, ii. 460.

Hammerton, Stephen, i. 35, 36, 64,
  69 n. 2, 73–89, 123, 312; ii. 460–1;
  iii. 311, 428; iv. 704; v. 1107.
Hammon, Thomas, iv. 570, 573.
Hammond, Mary, v. 1000.
Hammond, William, ii. 416; v. 1001.
Hammonds, Captain, ii. 559.
Hamond, Dorothy, ii. 479.
Hamond, John, ii. 361.
Hampden, John, iii. 41, 42.
Hampden House, vi. 270 n. 1.
Hampton Court, i. 27, 28 n. 1, 50,
  52, 53, 97 n. 1†, 117, 133, 249 n. b,
  311; iii. 113, 114, 135, 136, 137,
  138, 139, 140, 206, 220, 313,
  324, 367, 371, 377, 402; iv. 548,
  570, 637, 849; v. 1271, 1286, 1354,
  1399; vi. 35, 258, 266, 271, 283,
  297; vii. 24, 27, 30, 43, 45, 57, 71,
  94.
Hampton Court Masque, iii. 2.
Hanford, James Holly, *Anniversary
  Papers . . . Kittredge* (1913), v.
  1391.
  ed., *Wine, Beer, and Ale, in S.P.*
    xii (1915), v. 1442, 1443, 1444.
Hangings, iii. 467; v. 1411; vi. 51,
  53.
Hanley, Richard, *see* Hawley,
  Richard.
Hannibal, see Anonymous.
Hannibal and Hermes, see Wilson,
  Robert.
Hannibal and Scipio, see Nabbes,
  Thomas.
*Hans Beer-Pot His Invisible Comedy
  of See Me and See Me Not, see*
  Belchier, Daubridgecourt.
Hansley, John, v. 1048.
Hansley, Johannes, v. 1221.
Hanson, Laurence, 'English News-
  books, 1620–41', *Library*, Fourth
  Series, xviii (1938), iii. 260.
Hanson, Nicholas, i. 298; ii. 461.
Hanworth, Middlesex, iii. 20; iv. 690.
Harbage, Alfred, *Annals of English
  drama, 975–1700* . . . (1940), iii.
  4, 97, 230, 235, 237; iv. 839; v.
  1298, 1355, 1423.
  'Authorship of the Dramatic Ar-
    cadia, The', *M.P.* xxxv (1938),
    v. 1058, 1073, 1074, 1128, 1131.
  Cavalier Drama (1936), iii. 21, 76,
    94, 96, 111, 113, 115, 118, 119,
    122, 140, 276, 292, 453, 465; iv.
    501, 522, 523, 531, 548, 598,
    602, 603, 728, 760, 761, 847,
    917, 957; v. 1028, 1030, 1032,
    1197, 1201, 1207, 1210, 1213,

1215, 1314, 1333, 1334, 1357,
1360, 1361, 1365, 1439; vi. 38.
'Census of Anglo-Latin Plays, A',
PMLA, liii (1938), iii. 4.
'Elizabethan Acting', *P.M.L.A.*
(1939), v. 1316, 1317.
'Elizabethan-Restoration Palimp-
sest', *M.L.R.* xxxv (1940), iii.
35, 231, 232, 233, 237, 458; v.
1062, 1064.
'Notes on Manuscript Plays',
T.L.S. 20 June 1936, iii. 465,
466, 468; v. 1332.
*Shakespeare and the Rival Tradi-
tions* (1952), vi. 3, 11.
Shakespeare's Audience, vi. 184
n. 2.
'Shirley's *The Wedding* and the
Marriage of Sir Kenelm Digby',
Phil. Quart. xvi (1937), v. 1082,
1163, 1164.
*Sir William Davenant, Poet
Venturer, 1606–68* (1935), iii.
193, 197, 198, 201, 202, 203,
204, 205, 207, 209, 211, 215,
220, 222, 225.
*Thomas Killigrew, Cavalier
Dramatist, 1612–83* (1930), iii.
20, 23; iv. 690, 694, 695, 696,
697, 698, 700, 701, 704, 705,
706, 707, 708, 709, 710; v. 1137.
'Two Seventeenth Century Plays',
T.L.S. 8 November 1934, iii.
96; iv. 730.
'Unnoted Caroline Dramatist,
An', *Stud. Phil.* xxxi (1934), iii.
292, 294, 295, 297, 298, 299; v.
1419, 1420.
Harding, George, Baron Berkeley,
iv. 813.
Harding, Samuel, iv. 530–2.
*Sicily and Naples, or The Fatal
Union*, iv. 531–2; v. 988, 1186,
1202.
*Hardshift for Husbands, or Bilboe's
the Best Blade, see* Samuel Rowley.
Hare, Hugh, Baron Coleraine, iv.
696.
Harefield, iv. 913.
Harfield, George, ii. 464.
Hargreaves, Mrs., i. 41.
Harington, Henry, ii. 461, 597; iii.
427.
Harison, Toby, ii. 558.
Harlech, Lord, iii. 343.
Harley, Robert, iv. 622.
Harp, v. 1304.
Harpar, Francis, ii. 636.
Harper, Charles, stationer, iii. 181.

Harper, Thomas, iii. 469; iv. 615;
v. 962, 963, 971, 974, 1019.
Harredye, Jone, ii. 459.
Harrier, iii. 112.
Harrington, James, iv. 919.
Harrington, Lord, iv. 645; vi. 268.
Harris, H., iii. 153.
Harris, Henry, actor, v. 1210, 1248.
Harris, John, i. 286, 288, 297; ii.
462.
Harris, Joseph, *The City Bride, or
the Merry Cuckold*, v. 1250.
Harris, Richard, vii. 24, 40, 45,
47–48, 63.
Harris, William, public scrivener,
vi. 143.
Harrison, George Bagshaw, ed.,
Penguin Shakespeare, *As You
Like It* (1937), vi. 178 n. 1.
Harrison, John, stationer, iv. 766,
767, 935, 937.
Harrison, John, Jr., iv. 767.
Harrison, Major, ii. 549.
Harrison, Martha, iv. 767, 877.
Harrison, Richard, i. 163, 169 n. 2,
171; ii. 462.
Harrison, William, *Description of
England*, ed. from his *Description
of Britaine and England* (1577) by
Frederick J. Furnivall, 2 vols.,
London, New Shakespere Society
(1877–8), vi. 152, 214 n. 1.
Harrow in Barbican, ii. 514, 682.
Harruney, Luke, pseud., *see* Walker,
Henry.
Harryson, Mr., iv. 569.
Harsenett, Isaak, ii. 404.
Hart, Anne, ii. 463.
Hart, Charles, ii. 462–3; iii. 115;
v. 1063, 1087, 1092; vi. 237.
Hart, H. C. '"The Captain" in
Fletcher and Ben Jonson',
N. & Q., Tenth Series, ii (1904),
iii. 336, 338; iv. 628, 660; v.
1144.
'Notes on Bullen's Old Plays: Sir
John Barnaveldt', *Academy*,
xxxiv (1888), iii. 415.
'Notes on . . . *The Noble Spanish
Souldier*', *The Academy*, xxxiv
(1888), iii. 257.
Hart, Mary, ii. 464.
Hart, William, i. 49 and n. 2
cont., 69 n. 2, 73–89, 299; ii.
463–4.
Hart, The, in Smithfield, 142; ii.
348.
Hart Hall, Oxford, iv. 550, 599.
Principal of, v. 1291.

Hart Inn, The, vi. 154.
Harte, Sarah, v. 1276.
Harte, Winifred, ii. 464.
Harvard, John, v. 1038.
Harvard College Library, iii. 56; iv. 510, 711; v. 1061, 1094.
Harvard University, Theatre Collection, iii. 13; v. 1141.
Harvey, Richard, vi. 307.
Harvey, Robert, iv. 816; v. 1165.
Harvey, Sir Sebastian, iv. 925.
Harvey, William, ii. 464.
Harwood, Sir Edward, iv. 670.
Haslerigg, Sir Arthur, iv. 500.
Haslewood, Joseph, iii. 267; iv. 596.
    ed., *Barnabae Itinerarium, or Barnabee's Journal.* The seventh edition: to which are prefixed an account of the author, now first discovered (1818), iii. 38.
Hassell, Captain Robert, vi. 292, 303.
Hatcher, O. L., *John Fletcher, A Study in Dramatic Method* (1905), iii. 305, 319, 321, 373.
Hatching, vi. 273.
Hatcliff, Faith, iv. 473.
Hatfield Broad Oak, iv. 956, 958.
Hathaway, Richard, and William Rankins, *Hannibal and Scipio*, iv. 934, 935, 936.
Hatherleigh, Devonshire, iv. 844.
Hathway, Richard, *Oldcastle, see* Drayton.
Hats, iii. 436.
Hatt, John, ii. 639, 640.
Hatton, Sir Christopher, iv. 533; v. 968, 985.
Hatton, Lady, iv. 616; v. 1231; vii. 29, 102.
    Bailiff to, iv. 473.
    House of, vii. 34.
    Masque of, iii. 220.
Hatton House, ii. 695.
Haughten, Sir Gilbert, iv. 670.
Haughton, Hugh, i. 299; ii. 464.
Haughton, Robert, *see* Houghton, Robert.
Haughton, William, iii. 261.
    English Fugitives, The, iii. 285, 286.
    Englishmen for My Money, or A Woman Will Have Her Will, vii. 63, 81.
Hausted (Hawsted), Peter, iv. 532–7; v. 967, 968; v. 1407.
    see Generosus, A. C.
    Ad Populum; or a Lecture to the People (1644), iv. 534.

Hymnus Tabaci (a transl.) (1651), iv. 534.
Rival Friends, iv. 480, 532, **534–6**, 537, 539, 743, 954; v. 966, 970, 982, 983, 984, 985, 1266.
Senile Odium, iv. 532, 536–7; v. 1407.
Haviland, Mr., iv. 590.
Hawkenborough, George, vii. 35.
Hawkesworth, Walter, iv. 538.
    Labyrinthus, iv. 538; vii. 98.
Hawkins, J. S., ed., *Ignoramus,* (1787), v. 1027, 1028.
Hawkins, Sir Thomas, trans., Nicholas Caussin's *The Holy Court, or The Christian Institution of Men of Quality* (1626), iv. 780, 821.
Hawkins, William, iv. 538–9.
    Apollo Shroving, iv. **538–9**; v. 1235.
Hawkwood, Sir John, v. 1255.
Hawle, Richard, *see* Hawley, Richard.
Hawley, Francis, ii. 465.
Hawley, Joanna, ii. 465.
Hawley, Jone, ii. 465.
Hawley, Joyce, ii. 465.
Hawley, Richard, i. 49 and n. 2 cont., 73–89; ii. 465.
Hawley, Roger, ii. 465.
Hawley, Sara, ii. 465.
Hawley, Thomazine, ii. 465.
Hawthornden, Scotland, iii. 287.
    First laird of, iii. 287.
Hay, James, First Earl of Carlisle, ii. 436; iv. 650, 651, 666, 669; v. 1288, 1432.
Hay, Lady, v. 1288, 1289, 1321.
Haydn, Joseph, *Book of Dignities* (1890), iv. 882.
Hayes, Sir Thomas, Lord Mayor, vi. 77.
Hay-house at Hope theatre, vi. 203, 204, 205.
Hayley, William, *Marcella,* iv. 864.
Haymakers' Masque, The, see Anonymous.
Haymarket theatre, iii. 373.
Haynes, —, ii. 474.
Haynes, Joseph, iv. 894.
Haynes, Joseph, epilogue 'written, and spoke, by Mr. Haynes, in the Habit of a Horse Officer, mounted on an Ass', iii. 425.
Haythorn (amateur actor), iii. 296.
Hayward, John, v. 1028.
Hayward, Mabel, ii. 546.
Hayward, Peter, ii. 438.

Hayward *or* Haywood, Thomas, *see* Heywood, Thomas.

Hayward, Wayne Clinton, 'Globe Theatre, The, 1599–1608', MS. Thesis, Shakespeare Institute, Stratford-upon-Avon (1951), vi. 179, 188.

Hazlitt, William Carew, ed., *Barnabae Itinerarium, or Barnabee's Journal* (1876), iii. 38.
Dramatic Works of John Webster, The, 4 vols. (1857), v. 1245, 1253.
English Drama and Stage, The, Under the Tudor and Stuart Princes, 1543–1644, Roxburghe Society (1869), vi. 176.
Handbook to the Popular, Poetical, and Dramatic Literature of Great Britain (1867), iii. 43; v. 1094; vii. 101.
Inedited Poetical Miscellanies (1870), iv. 535.
Manual for the Collector and Amateur of Old English Plays, A (1892), iii. 1, 2, 3, 46, 169, 179, 282, 296, 450; iv. 676, 794, 838, 921, 951; v. 964, 972, 976, 1009, 1012, 1021, 1024, 1033, 1250, 1257, 1270, 1289, 1298, 1302, 1317, 1321, 1369, 1378, 1384, 1397, 1409, 1420, 1427, 1432, 1439, 1448.
Poems, Plays, and Other Remains of Sir John Suckling, The (1874, 1892), v. 1198, 1200, 1201, 1213.
Poetical and Dramatic Works of Thomas Randolph of Trinity College Cambridge . . . 2 vols. (1875), iii. 79; v. 969, 981.
Second Series of Bibliographical Collections and Notes on Early English Literature, 1474–1700 (1882), iii. 351.
ed., *Select Collection of Old English Plays, Originally Published by Robert Dodsley, A*, 12 vols. (1875), v. 1032, 1361, 1364.
Supplements to the Third and Final Series of Bibliographical Collections and Notes 1474–1700 (1889), iv. 879.
ed., 'True Recitall of the Confession of the two Murderers John de Paris, and Iohn de la Vigne: Touching the horrible Murder committed vpon the person of Mr. Iohn de Wely, a Merchant-Ieweller of Amsterdam', *Second Series of Bibliographical Collections and Notes on Early English Literature, 1474–1700* (1882), iii. 351.

Head, Richard, *The English Rogue* (1669), iii. 318.

Headboroughs, vi. 161, 293.

Headmaster of Merchant Taylors' School, iii. 291.

Heads of Roman emperors, vi. 273, 278.

Hearne, John, *see* Herne, John.

Hearne, Richard, iv. 558, 564, 574.

Hearne, Thomas, v. 1400.

Heath, Attorney General, ii. 471.

Heath, Ezechiel, ii. 400.

Heath, Francis, ii. 393.

Heath, John Benjamin, *Some Account of the Worshipful Company of Grocers of the City of London*, 2nd ed. (1854), iii. 261; iv. 926.

Heath, Robert, *Clarastella* (1650), vi. 41 n. 1.

Heather, Edward, a headborough, i. 264, 266; vi. 161.

Heaton, Elizabeth, ii. 472.

Heaton, Hellen, ii. 472.

Hebel, John William, *The Plays of William Heminges*, Cornell MS. Thesis (1920), iv. 542, 543, 545, 546, 547.

Heber, Richard, iii. 466.

Heber collection, iv. 645; v. 1317, 1448.

Heber Sale Catalogue, iii. 14.

Heborne, John, vii. 18, 23, 27, 34, 38.

Hebrew language, v. 1038.

Hebrew, Professor of, ii. 470.

Heckmann, Theodor, *Massinger's 'The Renegado' unds eine spanischen Quellen* (1905), iv. 812, 813.

Hector of Germany, or The Palsgrave, see Smith, W.

Heidelberg, iv. 956.

Heir, The, see May, Thomas.

Heiron, Mr., iii. 221.

Heldt, W., 'Fletcher's *Wild-Goose Chase*, and Farquhar's *Inconstant Neophilologus*', iii (1917), iii. 425, 430.

Heliodorus, iv. 515.
Aethiopian History, iii. 269; iv. 727; v. 1439.

Hellifield, Yorkshire, ii. 460.

Helmdon, Northamptonshire, v. 964, 1004, 1306.

Helme, Anne, iv. 868.

Helme, John, iv. 868.

Helmet Court in the Strand, *see* London, streets of.

Helmingham Hall, Suffolk, iv. 951.

Heminges, Alice, ii. 351.

Heminges, Edward, ii. 470.

Heminges, Elizabeth, ii. 644.

Heminges, George, ii. 469.

Heminges, John, i. 1, 2, 3, 4 nn. 1 and 2, 5, 17, 18, 20 n. 6 cont., 21, 22, 23, 26 and n. 5, 30, 34 n. 3, 35 n. 1, 45, 46, 72–88, 90, 95 nn. a, d, e, f, g, i, and k, 103, 117, 130, 137 n. 3, 142 n. 4, 184, 270, 279, 283; ii. 465–9, 590, 642, 651; iii. 78, 119, 309, 347, 391, 425, 445; iv. 539, 540, 541, 639; v. 990, 1008, 1039, 1050, 1051, 1059, 1413, 1444; vi. 7, 13 n. 1, 37, 60, 96, 180 and n. 2, 182 n. 3, 183 n, 194 n. 4, 225, 265; vii. 3, 4.

Will of, ii. 643–5.

Heminges, Rebecca, ii. 468, 470, 643.

Heminges, Ruth, ii. 470.

Heminges, William, i. 12, 44; ii. 470; iii. 51, 190; iv. 539–47, 756, 844; v. 965; vi. 163.

Coursing of a Hare, or the Madcap, The, i. 293; ii. 470; iii. 10; iv. 541, 542–3, 547; vi. 164; vii. 7, 8.

Elegy on Randolph's Finger, i. 13; ii. 470, 537, 566, 570; iii. 51, 190, 434, 441; iv. 541, 831–2, 877, 967; vi. 96–97.

Eunuch, The, see The Fatal Contract or The Eunuch.

Fatal Contract, The, or The Eunuch, i. 252; ii. 470, 525, 608; iii. 232; iv. 542, 543–6, 547; v. 1235, 1445, 1446.

Jew's Tragedy, The, ii. 470; iv. 540, 546–7.

'On the Time Poets', *see Elegy on Randolph's Finger.*

Henage, Lady, vi. 49.

'Hence all you vaine Delights' (song), iii. 384.

Henderson, Fletcher, 'Camus' "Iphigene" as a Source for Suckling's *Brennoralt', T.L.S.* 4 February 1939, v. 1207, 1209.

Henderson, Robert, *The Arraignement of the Whole Creature* (1631), iii. 245.

Hengist, King of Kent, see Middleton, Thomas, *The Mayor of Quinborough.*

Henrietta Maria, Queen of Charles I, i. 38, 99 n. r; iii. 3, 16, 20, 113, 248, 276, 442, 444, 452; iv. 486, 521, 545, 581–2, 637, 644, 653, 654, 690, 695, 700, 729, 780, 911, 917; v. 1031, 1068–9, 1074, 1080, 1081, 1193, 1212, 1229, 1231, 1261, 1286, 1305, 1358, 1389, 1440; vi. 16, 17, 38, 45, 61, 65, 302, 303; vii. 4, 59, 94, 103.

As actress, iv. 548–9.

At Middle Temple, iii. 219.

At Oxford, ii. 52.

Attends masque in disguise, iii. 219.

Company of, i. 24, 52 n. 2, 55, 56, 64, 121 n. 1, 185 n. 9, 187, 188, 204 n. 4, 218–59, 264, 289 n. 4 cont., 290, 291, 296, 305 n. 3, 326 and n. 4, 327, 331 n. 4; ii. 684–7; iii. 4, 17, 54, 56, 60, 66, 67–68, 75, 80, 90, 91, 92, 117, 118, 120, 138, 192, 228, 232, 233, 235, 244, 271, 272, 275, 308, 327, 329, 369, 384, 385, 386, 442, 443, 447, 453, 454, 456, 462; iv. 480, 482–3, 494, 504, 505, 542, 544, 545, 547, 556, 565, 566, 569, 570, 573, 579, 583, 608, 633, 635, 698, 699, 700, 705, 707, 708, 709, 713, 723, 737, 739, 740, 746, 768, 786, 787, 791, 797, 799, 801, 812, 813, 814, 863, 869, 891, 894, 927, 932, 935, 936, 940, 941, 943; v. 996, 1009, 1019, 1024, 1031, 1032, 1033, 1051, 1060, 1061, 1068, 1070, 1073, 1075, 1077, 1079, 1089, 1095, 1098, 1106, 1107, 1108, 1111, 1112, 1113, 1114, 1115, 1120, 1122, 1126, 1129, 1130, 1131, 1133, 1135, 1136, 1138, 1145, 1146, 1150, 1151, 1163, 1164, 1165, 1166, 1168, 1248, 1251, 1312, 1319, 1426, 1446; vi. 12 and n. 1, 37, 45, 46, 51, 52, 61–67, 69, 70, 71, 73, 103, 104, 112, 165, 242 n. 1, 270, 271, 282, 307; vii. 5, 7.

Court of, iii. 174.

Dances, vii. 63.

Dances in masque, iii. 218; iv. 638, 917–21; v. 1230.

Dances in village, vii. 83.

In disguise, iii. 219.

Lord Chamberlain of, i. 223, 236 n. 8 cont., 239, 304 n. 2; ii. 424, 661 n. 1; v. 1359; vi. 103.

Marriage of, i. 218; vii. 588.
Marriage contract of, iv. 676.
Performs in plays, iv. 548-50, 917-21.
Personal interest in her company, i. 223.
Play MS. prepared for, iii. 24, 25.
Play performed before, iii. 24.
Solicitor General of, iii. 152.
Visit to Blackfriars, i. 39, 99 nn. t and y; iii. 220, 221; iv. 774; v. 1287; vi. 34-35.
Henry II, iv. 831.
Henry II, see Davenport, Robert.
Henry the Second, King of England; with the Death of Rosamond, see Mountfort, Walter.
Henry IV, Part I, see Shakespeare, William.
Henry IV, Part II, see Shakespeare, William.
Henry IV (of France), iv. 548.
Assassination of, v. 1392.
Henry V, see Shakespeare, William.
Henry VI, see Shakespeare, William.
Henry VI, Part II, see Shakespeare.
Henry VI, Part III, see Shakespeare.
Henry VII, v. 1383.
Henry VIII (or All is True), see Shakespeare, William, and John Fletcher.
Henry VIII, vi. 255, 268.
Catholic Commentary on, iii. 125.
Henry E. Huntington Library, *see* Huntington Library.
Henry the minstrel, v. 1236.
Lyfe and Actis of W. Wallace, The, v. 1236.
Henry, Prince of Wales, v. 1255.
Henry, Prince, iii. 155.
Company of, i. 135; iii. 36, 239, 243; v. 1010, 1049; vi. 145, 147.
Death of, i. 136; ii. 655; v. 1241.
Heywood's elegy for, iv. 555.
Household Book of, i. 136.
Verses on the death of, v. 1017.
Henry, Prince, Duke of Gloucester, iv. 917.
Henry the Una . . ., see Anonymous.
Henslowe, Anne or Agnes, ii. 558; vi. 149, 150.
Henslowe, Philip, i. 1, 135, 136, 158, 176, 177 nn. 2 and 3, 198, 199 and n. 2, 200 n. 3, 322; ii. 435, 490, 519, 525, 599, 609; iii. 36, 155, 242, 247, 274, 285, 300, 460; iv. 543, 554, 558, 559, 564, 574, 581, 584, 606, 608, 609, 622, 733, 752, 753, 754, 760,

763, 788, 857, 935, 936; v. 1012, 1014, 1241, 1285, 1333, 1337, 1385, 1421; vi. 79, 80, 130, 139, 140, 141-4, 149, 184, 191, 201, 202, 203, 206, 207, 208, 210, 247, 248; vii. 1.
Diary of, iii. 28, 238, 242, 243, 266; iv. 606, 749, 866, 885, 899; v. 1010, 1014, 1177, 1240, 1253, 1285, 1420, 1440; vii. 11.
Papers of, iii. 231; iv. 606; v. 1010; vi. 177, 178.
Henslowe Papers, see Greg, W. W.
Henslowe, William v. Edward Alleyn (Court of Exchequer), vi. 210 n. 1.
Henslowe's Diary, see Greg, W. W.
Hensman, Bertha, *John Fletcher's The Bloody Brother, or Rollo Duke of Normandy,* Unpublished University of Chicago thesis (1947), iii. 401, 405-6.
Henton, Sir Anthony, vi. 49.
Heptameron, iv. 478.
Heraclius, iii. 28.
Heraclius, see Corneille, Pierre.
Heraclius, Emperor of the East, see Carlell, Lodowick.
Heralds, iv. 856, 858.
Herbert, Lord Charles, iv. 691, 692, 694.
Herbert, Sir Edward, iii. 105; v. 1226.
Herbert, George, iv. 525.
Herbert, Sir Gerard, iv. 641; v. 1288, 1372, 1377, 1378.
Herbert, Henry, 2nd Earl of Pembroke, iv. 750, 751.
Herbert, Sir Henry, i. 10 and n. 6 cont., 11, 12, 14, 15, 21, 22 n. 2, 25, 30 n. 6, 35, 38, 40, 46, 49, 54, 61, 67, 101-8, 147, 151, 165 n. 8, 167, 168 n. 1, 178, 182, 183, 184, 199, 201 n. 2, 207, 222, 228, 229, 233, 234, 236, 240, 285 n. 1, 288, 291, 292, 304, 323 n. 1, 324, 325, 326, 332; ii. 463, 471; iii. *passim*; iv. *passim*; v. *passim*; vi. 15, 21, 22, 23, 31, 32, 43, 60 and n. 1, 64, 65, 67, 70, 74, 89, 90, 91 n., 93, 99, 100, 101, 103 and n. 1, 106, 137, 159, 162, 165, 194 and n. 2, 197, 198, 212, 221, 266, 283, 287; vii. 3, 8, 11, 48.
His censorship, i. 36, 39.
His fees, i. 23, 24, 36; iii. 32, 36, 227, 228.
His interest in Salisbury Court theatre, i. 239 n. 3; vi. 90, 93, 94.

Herbert, Sir Henry (*cont.*)
His office-book, i. 2, 3 n. 7, 29, 183, 218, 270, 279, 293, 305, 329; ii. *passim*; iii. *passim*; iv. *passim*; v. *passim*; vi. 35, 47, 74, 90 n. 2, 97, 136, 164, 165, 173, 194 n. 4, 195, 221 n. 1, 225, 226, 229, 244, 247, 248, 250; vii. 4, 13, 14, 15.
Licenses for publication, *see* Plays allowed for the press.
Licensing practices, iii. 36, 37.
Lodgings for, vii. 65.
Office-book: missing leaf of, iii. 446.
Overruled by King Charles, iii. 222.
Restoration play lists, iii. 22, 24; iv. 698, 706.
Restoration production licence, iii. 134.
Special gifts to, iii. 77, 78.
Herbert, Lucy, iv. 521.
Herbert, Philip, third Earl of Montgomery, *see* Montgomery.
Herbert, Thomas, Deputy Master of the Revels, iii. 332; v. 1122, 1168, 1234; vi. 103 n. 1.
Herbert, Thomas, *A Relation of Some Years Travel Begun Anno 1626, into Afrique and the Greater Asia* (1634 and 1638), iii. 278.
Herbert, William, third Earl of Pembroke, *see* Pembroke.
Herbert, Sir William, vi. 21.
Herberts, family of, iv. 750, 751, 769, 802.
Herbst, Carl, *Cupid's Revenge by Beaumont and Fletcher und Andromana, or the Merchant's Wife in ihrer Beziehung zu einander und zu iher Quelle* (1906), v. 1034, 1035.
Hercules, vi. 178 n. 1.
Hereford, County of, iii. 46.
Herford, C. H., *Studies in the Literary Relations of England and Germany in the Sixteenth Century* (1886), v. 1055.
Herford, C. H., and Percy and Evelyn Simpson, *Ben Jonson*, 11 vols. (1925–53), iii. 79, 143, 239, 243, 260, 287, 300, 366, 368, 401; iv. 511, 606–76 *passim*, 733, 859, 900, 901; v. 1396; vi. 256.
Hermophus, see Anonymous.
Herne, Benjamin, ii. 471.
Herne, John, ii. 471; vi. 88, 89.
Herne, Richard, iv. 476, 477.

Herne, Susanna, ii. 471.
Herne, Kent, iii. 292.
Herod, Henrietta Louise, ed., *James Shirley's Changes, or Love in a Maze*, Unpublished U. of Chicago Thesis (1942), v. 1091, 1093, 1094.
Herod and Antipater, see Markham, Gervase.
Herod and Mariamne, Story of, iv. 776.
Herodian, iii. 406.
Herodotus, iv. 768, 853; vi. 43.
Heroic opera, iii. 140.
Heroic tragedy, iii. 34.
Herrick, Robert, iii. 376; iv. 840.
Hesperides (1648), iv. 840.
Herring, Jone, iii. 307.
Herringe, Robert, i. 265.
Herringman, Henry, stationer, iii. 98, 109, 123, 124, 146, 150, 197, 202, 203, 206, 208, 210, 214, 215, 217, 277, 311, 315, 320, 325, 330, 337, 340, 345, 348, 352, 355, 357, 360, 364, 367, 372, 374, 378, 388, 392, 395, 399, 413, 419, 423, 427, 431; iv. 534, 697, 701, 705, 706, 710, 883, 884, 887, 901; v. 1085, 1105, 1124, 1148, 1270, 1273.
Herris, Ned, ii. 678.
Hershon, Louise, v. 1282.
Hertford, William Seymour, Earl of, iv. 721; v. 1268, 1311.
Hertfordshire, iii. 155.
Hervey, John, theatre share bequeathed to, iii. 175.
Hervey, William, iii. 173.
Herz, Dr. E., *Englische Schauspieler und englisches Schauspiel zur Zeit Shakespeares in Deutschland, Theatergeschichtliche Forschungen*, xviii (1903), v. 1023.
Herzog von Florentz, Der, see Anonymous.
Hesse, Charlotte de, iv. 696.
Hester, a foundling, ii. 399.
Heston, Middlesex, ii. 635.
Heteroclitanomalonomia, see Anonymous.
Heton, Elizabeth, vi. 89, 90, 91 n.
Heton, Richard, i. 237, 238, 239, 240, 241, 295, 296 n. 1, 299 n. c, 303, 304, 309; ii. 471–2; v. 1399; vi. 67, 98, 101, 103–7, 109, 307.
Heton's Papers, ii. 684–7.
Hewitt, Mr., iii. 347.
Hey for Honesty, Down with Knavery see Randolph, Thomas.
Heydon, Drue, ii. 358.

Heyley, Jaspar, i. 327; ii. 663; vi. 68.

Heylyn, Elizabeth, iv. 550.

Heylyn, Henry, iv. 550.

Heylyn, Peter, iii. 4, 27; iv. 550–3, 591; v. 1257; vi. 135, 241.

Doublet, Breeches, and Shirt, iv. 551.

'Heylyn's Own Memoranda', in John R. Bloxham's ed., Memorial of Bishop Waynflete, Founder of St. Mary Magdalen College, Oxford. By Dr. Peter Heylin (1851), iii. 25, 27; iv. 550, 551, 552, 595; v. 1256.

Microcosmus, iv. 550.

'Satyr against Mr Holydayes Technogana or rather Technobigamia, A', iv. 595.

Spurius, iii. 27; iv. 552; v. 1256.

Theomachia, iv. 550, 552–3.

'Whoop Holiday', iv. 591, 595.

Heyrick, Samuel, stationer, iii. 102.

Heywood, Edmund, iv. 566.

Heywood, Reverend Robert, iv. 554.

Heywood (Haywood, Hawood), Thomas, i. 158, 163, 169 n. 2, 171, 183 n. 2, 184; ii. 364, 472–3, 488, 557, 682; iii. 52, 58; iv. 516, 553–86, 679, 733, 737, 941; v. 1022, 1060–1, 1072, 1153; v. 1241, 1247, 1248, 1249, 1254, 1319, 1320; vi. 48, 63, 129, 130, 218, 219; vii. 10.

Influence of, iv. 738, 739, 740.

Ages, The, iv. 557, 559, 574, 580; vi. 218.

'Albe[t]re Galles', iv. 558.

Amphrisa, The Forsaken Shepherdess, or Pelopaea and Alope, iv. 558, 572.

Apollo and Daphne, iv. 558–9, 572, 574.

Apology for Actors (1612), i. 264; ii. 519; iv. 554, 555; v. 1241, 1337.

Appius and Virginia, see Brome, Richard.

Apprentice's Prize, The, see Brome, Richard.

Blind Eats Many a Fly, The, iv. 559.

Bold Beauchamps, The, iv. 560.

Brazen Age, The, iv. 559, 560, 574.

Captives, or the Lost Recovered, The, i. 185, 187 n. 5, 195; ii. 442, 482, 579, 590, 598; iii. 182, 265; iv. 556, 560–2, 567, 573, 574, 796, 861; v. 1424; vi. 59.

Challenge for Beauty, A, i. 120–1; iii. 75; iv. 562–3, 556, 866; vi. 103, 198, 199.

Christmas Comes but Once a Year, iv. 564.

Cupid and Psyche, iv. 581; see Love's Mistress

Cutting Dick, iv. 564.

Deorum Judicium, iv. 564–5, 572.

Edward the Fourth, Parts I and II, iv. 565.

England's Elizabeth (1631), iv. 557.

English Traveller, The, i. 252; iii. 182; iv. 555, 556, 565–7; vi. 51, 156, 219.

Escapes of Jupiter, The, [Calisto], iv. 561, 567–8.

Exemplary Lives and Memorable Acts of Nine the Most Worthy Women of the World (1640), ii. 582; iv. 557.

Fair Maid of the Exchange, The, iv. 568.

Fair Maid of the West, The, or A Girl Worth Gold, I and II, i. 220, 221 n. 1, 246, 249 n. b, 252; ii. 345, 353, 378, 386, 398, 406, 444, 445, 528, 547, 548, 572–3, 583, 608, 619, 692; iii. 6; iv. 556, 568–71, 747, 922.

Five Plays in One, iv. 558, 559, 564, 571–2, 574, 581.

Fortune by Land and Sea (with Rowley), i. 253; iii. 304–5; iv. 572; v. 1015, 1022.

Four Plays in One, iv. 572.

Four Prentices of London, iv. 572, 580; v. 1456; vi. 218, 225 n. 2, 245; vii. 74, 85.

Girl Worth Gold, A, see The Fair Maid of the West.

Golden Age, or The Lives of Jupiter and Saturn, The, iv. 567, 572; vii. 74.

Gunaikeion (1624), iv. 555, 566, 567.

Hierarchie of the Blessed Angels, The (1635), ii. 364, 369, 372; iii. 434; iv. 555, 556, 557, 582, 818; v. 1242.

How a Man May Choose a Good Wife from a Bad, iv. 572.

How to Learn of a Woman to Woo, iv. 572.

If You Know Not Me You Know Nobody, i. 252–3; iv. 572; vii. 51, 85, 116, 118.

Iron Age, The, iv. 559, 573; v. 1346; vii. 85.

Heywood, Thomas (*cont.*)
Jew of Malta, The, iv. 473–4.
Joan as Good as My Lady, iv. 574.
Jupiter and Io, iv. 559, 572, 574.
Lady Jane, Part I, iv. 575, 1241, 1254.
Late Lancashire Witches, The, see Brome, Richard.
Life and Death of Sir Martin Skink, The, see Brome, Richard.
Life and Death of Sir Thomas Gresham, The, see Brome, Richard.
Life of Merlin (1641), iv. 557.
'Lives of all the Poets', iv. 555.
Londini Artium et Scientiarum Scaturigo, or London's Fountain of Arts and Sciences, iv. 575–6.
Londini Emporia, or London's Mercatura, iv. 576.
Londini Sinus Salutis, or London's Harbour of Health and Happiness, iv. 576–7.
Londini Speculum, or London's Mirror, iv. 577.
Londini Status Pacatus, or London's Peaceable Estate, iv. 577–8.
London Florentine, The, iv. 578.
London's Jus Honorarium, iv. 576, 578.
Love's Masterpiece, iv. 579.
Love's Mistress, or The Queen's Masque, i. 232–3, 249, 253, 331, 339; ii. 472; iii. 230; iv. 556, 572, 579–82, 738, 739, 740; v. 1075; vi. 50 n. 1, 63.
Maidenhead Well Lost, A, i. 253; iv. 556, 582–3; v. 1142; vii. 93.
Marshall Osric, iv. 583.
Martyred Soldier, The, see Shirley, Henry.
Misanthropus or The Man Hater, iv. 584.
Miseries of Enforced Marriage, The, iv. 584.
Oenone and Paris (1594), iv. 554.
Pleasant Dialogues and Dramas (1637), i. 28 n. 1, 249 nn. b and d, 252; ii. 400, 540; iv. 557, 558, 559, 564, 570, 572, 574, 581, 584, 737; v. 1224; vi. 270.
Porta Pietatis, iv. 584–5.
Queen Elizabeth's Troubles, see If You Know Not Me You Know Nobody.
Rape of Lucrece, The, i. 22, 174, 223 and n. 8, 253, 331, 339; iii.

230; iv. 585; v. 1169; vi. 63, 218, 225 n. 2.
Royal King and the Loyal Subject, The, i. 253; iii. 373; iv. 585; v. 1061, 1062.
Silver Age, The, iv. 559, 567, 574, 585; vii. 74.
Sir Thomas More, iv. 585.
Sir Thomas Wyatt, iv. 585.
Troia Britannica (1609), iv. 555.
True Description of His Majesties Royal Ship, Built . . . at Wooll-witch, A (1637), iii. 147; iv. 496, 737.
True Relation of the Lives and Deaths of . . . Purser, and Clinton, A (1639), v. 1060–1.
War without Blows and Love without Suit (Strife), iv. 586.
Wars in the Low Countries, The, see Brome, Richard.
Wise Woman of Hogsdon, The, iv. 586; vii. 109, 114.
Woman Killed with Kindness, A, i. 174; iv. 565, 586; v. 1130; vi, 218; vii. 25.
Yorkshire Tragedy, A, iv. 586.
Hickerson, William Howard, The Significance of James Shirley's Realistic Plays in the History of English Comedy unpublished University of Michigan thesis (1932), v. 1064.
Hickes Hall, vi. 62.
Hickes, Mr., v. 1298.
H[ickes], W[illiam], London Drollery or The Wits' Academy (1673), iv. 901.
Hide, Francis, iv. 513.
Hierarchie of the Blessed Angels, see Heywood, Thomas.
Higgins, Richard, iv. 655.
High Commission, Court of, see Court of High Commission.
Highway repairs, see Red Bull, petition about highway repairs.
Highwaymen, iii. 161, 188, 189; v. 1379.
Highways, vi. 215.
Hilary Term, vi. 210.
Hill, Aaron, The Insolvent, or Filial Piety, iv. 785.
Hill, Abraham, his list of plays, i. 216, 217; iii. 1, 58–59, 69, 93, 94, 122, 188, 227, 245, 248, 249, 267, 269, 272; iv. 487, 488, 561, 563, 718, 864, 865–6; v. 1046, 1283, 1285, 1310, 1314, 1324, 1325, 1327, 1331, 1332, 1339, 1365,

1366, 1367, 1371, 1373, 1375,
1378, 1379, 1384, 1386, 1395,
1403, 1410, 1421, 1423, 1424,
1429, 1433, 1435, 1440, 1442,
1446, 1447, 1448.
Hill, Alyce, ii. 473.
Hill, Herbert Wynford, 'Sidney's
Arcadia and the Elizabethan
Drama', University of Nevada
Studies, i (1908), iv. 479, 480.
Hill, John, i. 281; ii. 473.
Hill, Johua, ii. 637.
Hill, Joseph, iv. 550.
Hillebrand, Harold Newcomb, Child
Actors, The, University of
Illinois Studies in Language
and Literature, xi (1926), Nos. 1
and 2, vi. 77, 79, 115.
'Thomas Middleton's The Viper's
Brood', M.L.N. xlii (1927), iv.
858, 899.
Hills, G., iii. 359, 376.
Verses for 1647 Beaumont and
Fletcher folio, iii. 405.
Hinchinbroke, Lord, iv. 900.
Hind (amateur actor), iii. 296.
Hind, Captain James, v. 1035.
Hindlip Hall, iv. 520, 521.
Hinds, Allen B., vi. 152; see Calendar
of State Papers . . . Venice.
Hinksey, Berkshire, v. 1373–4.
Hinman, Charlton, 'Principles
Governing the Use of Variant
Spellings as Evidence of Al-
ternate Settings by Two Com-
positors', Library, Fourth Series,
xxi (1941), iii. 459.
Hint, Robert, i. 272, 281; ii. 473.
Hired men (actors), i. 3, 16, 35 n. 2,
44, 80–81, 187 n. 5, 316, 332; ii.
558, 598, 605, 609, 611; vi. 36.
Hired men, Wages of, i. 44.
His Majesty's Servants, see Charles
II, Company of, and Charles I,
Company of.
His Majesty's theatre, iv. 708.
Historia Regum Britannae, see
Geoffrey of Monmouth.
Hist. Ciceroniana, see Lambin,
Denis.
Historical Manuscripts Commission,
Reports of iii. 113, 134, 213, 294,
320, 349; iv. 505, 522, 536, 549,
871, 918, 951; v. 1155, 1160, 1161,
1202, 1206, 1231, 1396; vi. 34,
35, 64, 177, 215.
Historie of Aurelio and of Isabell,
see de Flores, La Historia de
Grisel y Mirabella.

Histories, vi. 293.
Histories Admirables, see Goulart,
Simon.
Histories Tragiques, see Belleforest,
François.
History and Antiquities of the
County of Leicester, A, see Nichols,
John.
History of Abraham, see Anony-
mous.
History of Cardenio, see Shakespeare,
William, and John Fletcher.
History of Dioclesian, see Fletcher,
The Prophetess.
History of Don Quixote, see Anony-
mous.
History of the Duchess of Suffolk,
The, see Drue, The Duchess of
Suffolk.
History of Dulwich College, The, see
Young, William.
History of English Journalism, A,
see Muddiman, J. G.
History of Eton College, A, see
Maxwell-Lyte, H. C.
History of French Dramatic Litera-
ture, A, see Lancaster, H. C.
History of Great Britain, Being the
Life and Reign of King James the
First, relating what passed from
his first Access to the Crown, till his
Death, The, see Wilson, Arthur.
History of Henry I, The, see Daven-
port, Robert.
History of His Life and Times From
the Year 1602 to 1681 (1715), see
Lilly, William.
History of Italy, The, see Thomas,
William.
History of Joseph, see Salusbury,
Sir Thomas.
History of King Stephen, see
Anonymous.
History of Lewis II, King of France,
see Anonymous.
History of London (1739), see Mait-
land, William.
History of Madon, King of Britain,
The, see Fletcher, John.
History of the Parliament of England,
see May, Thomas.
History of Sir Francis Drake, see
Davenant, William.
History from 1276 to 1956 of the Site
in Blackfriars Consisting of Print-
ing House Square . . . Being the
Freehold Property of the Times
Publishing Company Limited, The,
see Anonymous.

Histriomastix, see Prynne, William.
Hitchens, Francis, ii. 473.
Hitchens, Katherine, ii. 473.
Hobbes, Alice, ii. 474.
Hobbes, Anne, ii. 474.
Hobbes, Thomas (actor), i. 18, 24, 49, 73–89, 198, 199 and n. 2, 200, 209, 211 and n. a; ii. 473–4, 683; iii. 144; iv. 764, 845; v. 1016.
Hobbes, Thomas, *Leviathan*, v. 1103.
Hobby, Sir Thomas, vi. 21.
Hoboyes, vi. 10.
Hobson the Carrier, iv. 714.
Hoby, of Magdalen College School, iii. 27.
Hockington, Cambridgeshire, v. 1236.
Hodder, John, iii. 17.
Hodge, iv. 670.
Hodges, C. Walter, vi. 192.
    'De Witt Again', *Theatre Notebook* (1950–1), 32–34, vi. 249.
    Globe Restored, The: A Study of the Elizabethan Theatre (1953), vi. 143 n. 1, 179, 187.
Hodgeson, Edward, ii. 383, 384.
Hodgson, James, ii. 384.
Hodgson, Jane, ii. 405.
Hoffman, or Revenge for a Father, see Chettle, Henry.
Hog Hath Lost His Pearl, The, see Tailor, Robert.
Hog Lane, see London, streets of.
Holbech, Thomas, iii. 186.
Holbein Gate, see Whitehall.
Holborn, see London, streets of.
Holcomb, Frances, ii. 626.
Holcomb, George, ii. 475.
Holcomb, Thomas, i. 45, 72–88; ii. 475, 626; iii. 326, 352, 396, 399, 416.
Holden, Richard, ii. 474, 575, 594.
Holden, William (actor), iv. 596.
Holdenby, i. 310.
Holdford, Richard, Esquire, iii. 83.
Holdsworth, Richard, Master of Emmanuel College, Cambridge, v. 1038, 1039.
'Hole in St. Martins, The', v. 994.
Holinshed, Raphael, *Chronicles of England, Scotland and Ireland* (1587), iii. 285; iv. 887; v. 1045; vi. 255.
Holland, Aaron, ii. 475, 560, 588; iii. 255; vi. 130, 215, 216, 217, 222.
Holland, Countess of, iii. 219.
Holland, Henry Rich, 1st Earl of, i.

23, 37, 48, 128; iii. 143, 219; iv. 535; v. 1197; vi. 31, 34.
Holland, Mrs., iv. 747.
Holland, Philemon, v. 1247.
Holland, Samuel, iii. 468.
    Don Zara del Fogo. A Mock Romance (1656), iv. 499.
    Wit and Fancy in a Maze [*Don Zara del Fogo*], v. 1244.
Holland, see Netherlands.
Holland House, ii. 695; vi. 237.
Holland's Leaguer, a brothel, iii. 189; vi. 15, 212, 251.
Holland's Leaguer (1632), see Goodman, Nicholas.
Holland's Leaguer, see Marmion, Shakerley.
Hollander, The, or Love's Trial, see Glapthorne, Henry.
Hollar, Wenceslaus, iv. 696, 950.
    Long View of London (1647), vi. 184, 185 n. 1, 202.
Holles, Capt. Francis, iv. 586.
Holles, Gervase, iv. 587.
    Memorials of the Holles Family, 1493–1656, by A. C. Wood (1937), iv. 586.
Holles, William, iv. 586–7.
    Country Court, The, iv. 587.
    Unnamed Latin Comedy, iv. 587.
Hollingbourne, Sussex, iii. 26.
Hollowell Lane, see London, streets and districts.
Hollstein, Ernst, *Verhältnis von Ben Jonson's 'The Devil Is an Ass' und John Wilson's 'Belphegor, or the Marriage of the Devil', zu Machiavelli's Novelle vom Belfagor* (1901), iv. 614, 617.
Holman, Thomas, i. 298; ii. 475.
Holmes, Martin, 'New Theory about the Swan Drawing, A', *Theatre Notebook*, x (1955–6), vi. 249.
Holmes, Thomas, ii. 416; iv. 536, 904.
Holstein, Duke of, vi. 215, 217.
    His company, vi. 217 n. 1.
Holt, James, i. 158, 171; ii. 475–6.
Holy Land, v. 1047.
Holy Week, vi. 194; vii. 5.
Holyday [Halliday], Barton, iv. 512, 587–96, 847; vi. 242.
    Decimus Junius Juvenalis and Aulus Persius Flaccus Translated and Illustrated . . . (1673), iv. 595–6.
    Philosophiae Politobarbarae Specimen (1633), iv. 588.
    Technogamia, or the Marriages of

the Arts, ed. Sister M. Jean Carmel Cavanaugh, Washington, D.C.: Catholic University of America Press (1942), iii. 100; iv. 512, **589–96**; vi. 135 n. 1, 241.

Holyday, Thomas, iv. 587.

Holywell, *see* London, streets and districts.

Homer, translation of, iii. 155.

Homer's *Iliad*, translated, v. 1072.

Homer's *Odyssey*, translated, v. 1072.

Homo, see Atkinson, Thomas.

Homo Duplex sive Funestum Corporis et Animae Duellum tragoedia, see Claretus, P.

Honest Lawyer, The, see Sheppard, Samuel.

Honest Man's Fortune, The, see Beaumont and Fletcher.

Honest Whore, The, see Dekker, Thomas.

Honeyman *or* Honiman, John, *see* Honyman, John.

Honeyman *or* Honiman, Richard, Honyman, *see* Richard.

Honoria and Mammon, see Shirley, James.

Honour in the End, see Anonymous.

Honour of Women, The, see Massinger, Philip, and Anonymous, *The Spanish Viceroy.*

Honour of Young Ladies, The, see Brome, Richard, *The Lovesick Maid.*

Honourable Entertainments, see Middleton, Thomas.

Honyman, Alice, ii. 476.

Honyman, Anthony, ii. 476.

Honyman, Hellin, ii. 478.

Honyman, John, i. 45, 70, 73–89, 316; ii. **476–8**; iii. 164, 167, 428, 429; iv. 596–7, 679, 764, 781, 810, 817.
  Will of, ii. 645.

Honyman, Rachael, ii. 479.

Honyman, Richard, i. 316, 321; ii. **478–9**, 645.

Hoods, vi. 236.

Hook, Lucyle, 'The Curtain', *Shakespeare Quarterly*, xiii (1962), vi. 131, 138.

Hooke, John, a turner, vi. 272.

Hooks, vi. 280.

Hooper, Edith, 'The Authorship of *Luminalia'*, *M.L.R.* viii (1913), iii. 207.

Hooten Pagnel, Yorkshire, iii. 2.

Hope theatre, i. 176, 199 and n. 2, 200 n. 3; ii. 346, 510; iii. 190, 316; iv. 747, 868; vi. 11, 12 n. 1 and n. 2, 15, 112, 122, 129, 131, 144, 199, **200–14**, 215, 216 n. 2, 219, 235, 250, 251.

Hopkins, Will, verses by, iii. 205.

Hopper, Simon, choreographer, v. 1358, 1360.

Hopwood, C. H., ed. *Middle Temple Records* 4 vols. (1904–5), iii. 17, 21, 105; v. 1155, 1156.

Horace, iii. 79, 300; iv. 818; v. 1238.
  Art of Poetry, iv. 646.
  Satires, iv. 817.

Horace, see Denham, John.

Horatius, see Lower, Sir William.

Hore, Henry, ii. 600.

Horne, James, i. 16, 35 n. 1, 72–88; ii. **479**; iii. 393; iv. 817.

Horne, Robert, stationer, iii. 43, 192; v. 1008.

Horne, Thomas, headmaster of Eton, v. 1176.

Horse race, vii. 23.

Horses, iv. 732; vi. 201, 203, 210 n.

Horses and foot, embattling of, vi. 293.

Horses, riding and managing great, vi. 293.

Horses, shows of great, vi. 293, 294, 296.

Horton, Oxfordshire, iv. 912, 913.

Horton, Edward, i. 73–89; ii. **479–80**; iii. 375.

Hosier, ii. 413.

Hosier Lane, *see* London, streets of.

Hosier, Stephen, ii. 607.

Hosley, Richard, 'The Discovery Space in Shakespeare's Globe', *Shakespeare Survey*, xii (1959), vi. 192.
  'Shakespeare's Use of a Gallery over the Stage', *Shakespeare Survey*, x (1957), vi. 192.
  'Was there a Music-Room in Shakespeare's Globe?', *Shakespeare Survey*, xiii (1960), vi. 192.

Hostler, iii. 194.

Hot Anger Soon Cold, see Jonson, Ben.

Hotson, Leslie, vi. 40 n. 1, 48 n. 1, 49 and n. 1, 65 n. 1, 72 n. 1, 75 n. 1, 76, 87, 91 and n. 1, 114, 115.
  'Alleyn's Fortune in the Making', *Shakespeare's Wooden O*, Appendix C (1959), vi. 132 n. 1.
  Commonwealth and Restoration

Hotson, Leslie (cont.)
    Stage, The (1928), iii. 23, 144,
      145, 193, 196, 197, 202, 204;
      iv. 517, 685, 694, 696, 698, 706,
      708, 719, 891; v. 1009, 1111,
      1217, 1235, 1439; vi. 76, 77,
      134, 138, 139, 156, 158 and n. 1.
      171, 173 n. 1, 174, 175, 176,
      177, 199 n. 1, 200, 213, 214,
      215, 216 n. 2, 217, 224, 230;
      vii. 11, 13.
    First Night of Twelfth Night, The,
      (1954), vi. 188.
    I, William Shakespeare, do
      appoint Thomas Russell Esquire
      (1937), v. 1167.
    'Projected Amphitheatre, The',
      Shakespeare Survey, ii (1949),
      24–35; vi. 291, 293, 301, 303.
    'Shakespeare's Arena', Sewanee
      Review, lxi (1953), vi. 188, 259.
    'Shakespeare's Curtain Theatre
      Identified',   Shakespeare's
      Wooden O, Appendix B (1959),
      vi. 132 n. 1.
    Shakespeare's Wooden O (1959),
      vi. 121, 124–31, 132 n. 1, 139,
      145 n. 1, 155 n. 1, 179, 184 n. 2,
      187–92.
Hotspur, The, see Shakespeare,
    Henry IV, Part I.
Hough, Daniel, of Lincoln College,
    Oxford, iii. 193.
Houghton, Edward, ii. 404.
Houghton, Sir Gilbert, vi. 49.
Houghton, Robert, ii. 480.
Houghton, William, Englishmen for
    My Money, or A Woman Will
    Have Her Will, vii. 21.
Houghton Tower in Lancashire, vii.
    24.
Hoult, James, see Holt, James.
Houndsditch, see London, streets
    and districts of.
Hounslow, see London, streets and
    districts of.
House of Commons, i. 64; v. 1265;
    vi. 39, 284 n. 1, 288.
    Journals of, vi. 21, 39, 288.
    Order of, vi. 288.
    Petitioned against playhouses, v.
      1342.
House Is Haunted, The, see
    Anonymous.
House of Lords, iv. 476, 515.
    Examination by, iii. 143.
    Inquiry, iv. 474.
House for white bears at Hope
    theatre, vi. 202, 203, 204, 205.

House for young bears at Hope
    theatre, vi. 202, 203, 204, 205.
Housekeepers, see Theatres, house-
    keepers at.
Houses of prostitution, see Bawdy
    houses.
House-warming, vi. 271.
Hovell, William, ii. 510.
How a Man May Choose a Good Wife
    from a Bad, see Heywood, Thomas.
How a Man May Please His Wife,
    see Gunnell, Richard, The way to
    Content All Women.
How to Learn of a Woman to Woo,
    see Heywood, Thomas.
Howard, Charles, Baron of Effing-
    ham, iv. 880, 909.
Howard, Lord, Company of, i. 135.
Howard, Edward, The Change of
    Crowns, v. 1094.
    Six Days' Adventure, or The New
      Utopia (1671), vi. 246.
    Women's Conquest, The, v. 1086,
      1152.
Howard, Edward, and John Dryden,
    Indian Queen, iv. 729.
Howard, Frances, Countess of
    Somerset, iv. 902; v. 1090.
Howard, H., verses by, iii. 198.
Howard, James, All Mistakes, or
    The Mad Couple, iii. 80.
Howard, Sir Robert, v. 1063.
    Great Favourite, or The Duke of
      Lerma, The, iii. 458–9; v.
      1063.
Howard, Thomas, 2nd Earl of
    Arundel, vi. 153, 308, 309.
Howarth, R. G., 'John Webster',
    T.L.S. 2 November 1933, v.
    1240, 1243.
    'Manuscript of James Shirley's
      Court Secret, A', R.E.S. vii
      (1931), and viii (1932), iii. 148;
      v. 1100, 1101.
    'Shirley's Cupid and Death',
      T.L.S. 15 November 1934, v.
      1102, 1104.
    'Some Unpublished Poems of
      James Shirley', R.E.S. ix
      (1933), 24–29, v. 1064, 1142.
Howe, F. A., 'The Authorship of
    "The Birth of Merlin"', Mod.
    Phil. iv (1906), iv. 883.
Howe, Joseph, verses by, iii. 141.
Howell, James, iii. 220; iv. 599.
    Letter of, i. 184; iii. 218.
    Epistolae Ho-Elianae (1650), i.
      184 n. 4; vi. 61.
    Epistolae Ho-Elianae, ed. Joseph

Jacobs (1892), iii. 217.
Poems (1663), iv. 600.
Howes, Edmund, vi. 154, 212.
  Continuator, *see* Stow, John,
    Annales, 1615 and 1631 eds.
Howes, Oliver, ii. 480.
Howorth, Humphrey, iii. 437, 450.
Howson, Margaret, ii. 371, 372.
Hoyt, Robert, *see* Huyt, Robert.
Huberman, Edward, 'Bibliogra-
  phical Note on James Shirley's
  The Polititian', *Library*, Fourth
  Series, xviii (1937), v. 1112,
  1114, 1137, 1138.
  ed., *James Shirley's The Poli-
    tician.* Unpublished Duke
    University Thesis (1934), v.
    1137, 1139.
Hubert, i. 73–89; ii. 480.
Hudson, Geoffrey, iv. 638.
Hudsone, widow, ii. 490.
Hue and Cry after Cupid, The, *see*
  Jonson, Ben, *Lord Haddington's
  Masque.*
Huff Hamukin, *see* Dances.
Huggins, Sir Constantine, iv. 675.
Hughes-Hughes, Augustus, *Cata-
  logue of manuscript music in the
  British Museum*, 3 vols. (1906–9),
  iii. 2; v. 1324.
Hull, John, ii. 473.
Hull, Thomas, *Disinterested Love*,
  iv. 762.
  Royal Merchant: an Opera, The,
    iii. 317.
Hull, Yorkshire, iii. 2, 143.
  Mayor of, iii. 143.
Hulse, Frances, ii. 642.
Hulshof, A., and Breuning, P. S.,
  'Brieven van Johannes de Wit
  aan Arend Van Buchel en an-
  deren', *Bijdragen en mededeelin-
  gen*, Historisch Genootschap,
  Utrecht, lx (1939), vi. 249.
Humorous Courtier, The, *see* Shirley,
  James.
Humorous Day's Mirth, An, *see*
  Chapman, George.
Humorous Lieutenant, The, *see*
  Fletcher, John.
Humorous Lovers, The, *see* Caven-
  dish, William.
Humour out of Breath, *see* Day, John.
Humour in the End, *see* Anonymous.
Humours of Monsieur Galliard, The,
  see Anonymous.
*Humours of the Patient Man and
  the Longing Wife, The*, *see* Dekker,
  Thomas, *The Honest Whore*.

Humours Reconciled, *see* Jonson,
  Ben, *The Magnetic Lady*.
Humours characters, iv. 934.
Humphrey, Duke, *see* St. Paul's
  Cathedral.
Hungarian Lion, The, *see* Gunnell,
  Richard.
Hungry Courtier, The, *see* Fletcher,
  John, *The Woman Hater*.
'Hungry knave' roles, iii. 433.
Hunneric, v. 1062.
Hunnieman, John, *see* Honyman,
  John.
Hunnyman, John, *see* Honyman,
  John.
Hunsdon, Lord, company of, i. 1.
Hunsdon House, vii. 49.
Hunt, —, i. 140 and n. 6, 155.
Hunt, John, ii. 481.
  ed., *Poems by Robert Wilde, D.D.,
    One of the Ejected Ministers of
    1662* (1870), v. 1264.
Hunt, Mary Leland, *Thomas Dekker.
  A Study* (1911), iii. 241, 242, 243,
  247, 270, 273.
Hunt, R. W., and Wilson, J. Dover,
  'The Authenticity of Simon For-
  man's *Bocke of Plaies*', *R.E.S.*
  xxiii (1947), vi. 16 n. 1.
Hunt, Robert, ii. 481.
Hunt, Thomas, i. 176; ii. 481; iv.
  716.
Hunt, William, ii. 596, 621.
'Hunt Is Up, The', *see* Anonymous.
Hunter, Joseph, *Chorus Vatum
  Anglicanorum*, iii. 229.
Hunter, Susan, ii. 383.
Hunter MS. (Durham Cathedral),
  iv. 527.
Hunting, iv. 953.
Hunting of the bull, vii. 32.
Huntingdon, Archdeacon of, iv.
  600.
Huntingdon, Countess of, iii. 307.
Huntingdon, Henry, Lord Hastings,
  Earl of, iii. 54, 55, 307.
Huntingfield, Suffolk, v. 1196.
Huntington Library, iii. 56, 153,
  155, 239, 293, 295, 304, 307,
  347; iv. 576, 645, 711, 729, 774,
  822, 870, 879; v. 967, 977,
  1007, 1031, 1094, 1228, 1231,
  1353.
  MSS., iv. 645, 870; v. 976–9, 979,
  1102, 1368, 1376.
Huntsman for the King, iii. 112.
Huon of Bordeaux, *see* Anonymous.
Hurd, Edward, ii. 355.
Hurd, Jane, ii. 623.

Hurley, Lord Lovelace of, v. 1126.
Husband's Care, The, see Johnson, Charles, *The Wife's Relief.*
Hussey, Thomas, vi. 48, n. 1, 49, 65 n. 1, 72 n. 2, 75 n. 1, 76.
Hutchinson, Alice, ii. 373.
Hutchinson, Christopher, *see* Beeston, Christopher.
Hutchinson, Elizabeth, *see* Beeston, Elizabeth.
Hutchinson, Jane, ii. 373.
Hutchinson, William, *see* Beeston, William.
Huth, Henry, v. 1119.
  Sale of, v. 1118.
Huts, *see* Theatres.
Hutton, George, iv. 477.
Hutton, Henry, *Follies Anatomie. Or Satyres and Satyricall Epigrams* (1619), vi. 7.
Huyt, Richard, i. 321.
Huyt, Robert, i. 307, 308; ii. 481.
Hyde, Lady Anne, marriage of, iii. 183.
Hyde, Edward, 1st Earl of Clarendon, *The Life of Edward, Earl of Clarendon* (1759), iii. 194; iv. 830, 831; v. 985; vi. 97.
  Verses by, iii. 198.
Hyde Park, *see* London, streets and districts.
Hyde Park, see Shirley, James.
Hymenaei, see Jonson, Ben.
Hymen's Holiday, or Cupid's Vagaries, see Rowley, William.
Hymen's Triumph, see Daniel, Samuel.
Hynoijosa, Marques, iv. 842.
Hypochondriac, The, see Anonymous.
Hythe, M.P. for, v. 1276.

I., T., v. 1140.
I William Shakespeare, see Hotson, Leslie.
'Iacobum' (name of ship), v. 1006.
Ibsen, Henrik, vi. 188 n. 1.
Ice fairs, vii. 39.
If It Be Not Good, the Devil Is in It, see Dekker, Thomas.
If You Know Not Me You Know Nobody, see Heywood, Thomas.
Iffley [Eisley], near Oxford, iv. 588.
Ignoramus, see Ruggle, George.
Iles, Thomas, v. 1291.
Ill Beginning Has a Good End, An, see Ford, John.
Illinois, University of, Museum of European Culture, vi. 143.

Illustrations, in quarto of play, v. 1045.
Ilsington, Devonshire, iii. 435, 438.
Images, v. 1300; vi. 167.
'Impartial Doom, The', *see* Phillips, John.
Impatient Grissell, see Anonymous.
Imperial Impostor and Unhappy Heroine, The, see Anonymous, *Demetrius and Marina.*
Imperiale, see Freeman, Sir Ralph.
Impossible Dowry, The, see Randolph, Thomas, *Amyntas.*
Imposter, The, see Shirley, James, *The Imposture.*
Imprests, Auditorship of, iii. 468.
Imprimatur, iii. 114, 119; v. 1348.
Improvisations, v. 1358.
Inclosure, v. 1313.
Inconstant Lady, The, see Wilson, Arthur.
Indecorum, iv. 693.
Inderwick, F. A., ed., *A Calendar of the Inner Temple Records,* 3 vols. (1896–1901), iii. 357, 385, 409, 419; iv. 814; v. 1082, 1092, 1155, 1158, 1160, 1314.
Indentures, vi. 308.
India, iii. 399; iv. 922, 923, 924.
Indian Emperor, The, see Dryden, John.
In Duc Reducem, see Anonymous.
Induction to the House, An, see Anonymous.
Inductions, i. 28 and n. 1; iii. 448; iv. 630, 908; v. 1101, 1241, 1353–4, 1362, 1363; vi. 8, 112.
Infallible Cure, The, see Manning, Francis, *All for the Better.*
Infanta, reception of the, vii. 47.
Ingleby, C. M., etc., *The Shakespeare Allusion-Book* (1932), i. 121.
Ingram, Sir Arthur, i. 10 n. 1; iv. 871.
'Inigo Jones, Architect and Man of Letters', *see* Wittkower, Rudolph.
Injured Innocence, see Bellers, Fettiplace.
Injured Virtue; or, The Virgin Martyr, see Griffin, Benjamin.
Inner stage, *see* theatres.
Inner Temple, i. 164; iii. 15, 347, 425; iv. 655, 809, 841, 881; v. 1040, 1041, 1155, 1180, 1276; vii. 96.
  General Account Book of, iii. 357; v. 1082.
  Library, i. 166, 167, 182; iii. 270; iv. 830.

MSS., iv. 655; v. 1344, 1370, 1444; vi. 135.
Plays at, iii. 357, 385, 409, 419; v. 1082, 1092, 1344.
Inner Temple Masque, The, see Middleton, Thomas.
Innes, H. McLeod, ed., *Fellows of Trinity College, Cambridge* (1941), iii. 158, 173; iv. 526, 948; v. 1195, 1232.
Innholder, ii. 458.
Innkeeper, ii. 500, 513; vi. 291 n. 1.
Innocentia Purpurata seu Rosa Candida et Rubicunda, see Claretus, P.
Inns, v. 1019.
    Carrier, vi. 122, 124.
    Plays at, i. 293.
    Plays written in, ii. 473.
Inns and Taverns, i. 1, 137, 140, 142, 148, 158, 202 n. 1, 266, 293; ii. 343, 347, 348, 421, 486, 491, 505, 514, 558, 606, 635, 682, 684, 689, 695; iii. 15, 74, 121, 122, 126, 127, 180, 193, 251, 385, 462, 471; iv. 571, 609, 691, 757, 801, 850, 910, 953; v. 1010, 1224, 1322, 1327, 1336, 1347, 1366, 1403, 1422, 1455; vi. 72-73, 80, 82, 95, 100, 121-31, 131, 133, 147, 154, 164, 201, 202, 204, 215, 216, 305, 308; vii. 17, 27, 54, 224, 250.
Inns of Court, iii. 220; iv. 551, 838, 856, 903, 928, 931; v. 1081, 1082, 1092, 1154-62, 1160, 1340; vi. 15, 49, 296; vii. 2, 20, 22, 39, 96.
    Masques, iii. 107, 453; v. 1376-8.
    Men, ii. 654 n. 2; v. 990.
    See under Grays Inn, Inner Temple, Lincolns Inn, Middle Temple, New Inn, Thavies Inn.
Inn yards, vi. 125.
Inojosa, Marquess de la, iv. 661, 662.
Insatiate Countess, The, see Marston, John.
Insolvent, The, see Hill, Aaron.
Instruments, string, vi. 294.
Instruments, wind, vi. 293, 294.
Insurance, plays concerned with, v. 1006.
Intelligence officer, iii. 174.
Interlocutors, v. 1358.
Interludes, ii. 685; iii. 18; v. 1356; vi. 14.
Intermeans, v. 979, 1329, 1334, 1368-9.
Intermedii, vi. 267, 287.

Invention for the Service of the Right Honourable Edward Barkham, Lord Mayor, An, see Middleton, Thomas.
Inventories (Henslowe's), vi. 191.
Investiture, ceremony of, iii. 354.
Invisible Knight, The, see Anonymous.
'Ioconda and Astolso', *see* Dekker, Thomas, *The Tale of Jocunda and Astolpho.*
Iphigene, see Camus, J. P.
Iphis, see Bellamy, Henry.
Iphis and Iantha. See Anonymous.
Ipswich, Suffolk, i. 92, 172, 193, 212; iv. 530.
Ireland, i. 165; ii. 539; iii. 95, 97, 161, 229; iv. 823, 949-50, 956; v. 1068, 1069, 1074, 1078, 1083, 1084, 1096, 1103, 1124, 1130, 1131, 1134, 1136, 1138, 1144, 1356, 1423; vi. 16, 29, 37, 266.
    Chief Baron of the Exchequer, iii. 275.
    Lord Deputy of, i. 47, 56 n. 3, 329; v. 1069, 1100, 1140, 1141, 1155, 1156, 1159; vi. 4.
    Military service in, iii. 469; iv. 728, 733.
    Play about, iii. 94-95.
    Plays acted in, iii. 33, 34, 35, 97.
    Residence in, iii. 225.
    Shirley in, iv. 700; v. 1069-70.
Ireland, Peter, ii. 444.
Irish Rebellion, The, see Anonymous.
Ireland, Richard, bookseller of Cambridge, iv. 525; v. 983.
Ireton, Sir John, iv. 500; v. 1220.
Irish, anti-masque of, iii. 109.
Irish Confederation, iii. 96.
Irish and English footmen, race between, iv. 890.
Irish Gentleman, The, see Anonymous.
Irish Masque, The, see Jonson, Ben.
Irish Rebellion, The, see Anonymous.
Irish Rebellion of 1641, iii. 95.
Irish taste, v. 1143.
Irish theatre, v. 1069.
Irish Wars, iii. 33.
Iron Age, The, see Cowley, Abraham.
Iron Age, The, see Heywood, Thomas.
Ironmonger, ii. 574.
Ironmongers' Company, iii. 256; iv. 577, 925.
Irving, David, ed., *The Poems of William Drummond of Hawthornden* (1832), iii. 289.

Isaacs, J., *Production and Stage-Management at the Blackfriars Theatre*. Shakespeare Association Pamphlet (1933), vi. 3.

Isabella, Princess of Belgium, v. 1292.

Isham, Sir Charles, i. 128.

Isham, Thomas, i. 129.

Island Princess, The, see Fletcher, John.

Isle of Dogs, The, see Jonson, Ben.

Isle of Gulls, The, see Day, John.

Isle of Rhé, v. 975.

Isle of Women, The, see Chapman, George, *The Fount of New Fashion*.

Isley, Ursula, iii. 14.

Islington, iii. 251; v. 1347.

Islip, Oxfordshire, iii. 4.

Islipp, Adam, stationer, i. 143, 144; ii. 481; iii. 82; iv. 534, 629, 797; v. 1091; vi. 157.

Italian actor, ii. 517.

Italian Masque, see Massinger, Philip, *Italian Night-Piece*.

Italian motion, ii. 507.

Italian Night Masque, The, see Massinger, Philip.

Italian Night-Piece, see Massinger, Philip.

Italian pastorals, v. 970.

Italian staging, *see* staging.

Italian, translation from, iii. 46, 171, 279, 280, 293, 373, 431; iv. 999, 1170–1, 1187, 1451.

Italy, iii. 170, 567, 692, 695, 912; iv. 776; v. 1047, 1397; vi. 23.
    Killigrew on embassy in, iv. 706.
    Play from, iii. 170.
    Travels in, iii. 33, 166.

Iter Boreale, see Wild, Robert.

Itinerary, An, see Moryson, Fynes.

Ives, Simon, i. 40; v. 1162, 1163; vi. 32.

Ivieson, Alice, ii. 585.

Ivory, Abraham, ii. 481.

Ivy Lane, *see* London, streets of.

J., B., iv. 597.

J., F., iv. 598; v. 981–2.

Jack, ii. 482.

Jack-an-Apes, vi. 203, 211.

Jack of Oxford, ii. 462.

Jackman, John, iii. 257, 273.

Jackson, —, ii. 482.

Jackson, Edward, i. 143, 144; ii. 482; vi. 157.

Jackson, Gilbert, vi. 72.

Jackson, William A., 'Racan's

L'Artenice, An Addition to the English Canon', *Harvard Library Bulletin*, xiv (1960), vii. 60.

Jacksonne, Henry, ii. 638.

Jacob, P. L., *Bibliothèque Dramatique de Monsieur de Soleinne* (1883–4), iii. 46.

Jacob, Thomas, i. 314; vi. 228, 239.

Jacobi, G. A., 'Zur Quellenfrage von Fletchers "The Sea Voyage"', *Anglia*, xxxiii (1910), iii. 411.

Jacobs, Elizabeth R., *A Critical Edition of Thomas Middleton's Women Beware Women*. Unpublished University of Wisconsin thesis (1941), iv. 905, 906.

Jacobs, Joseph, ed., *James Howell's Epistolae Ho-Elianae* (1892), iii. 217.

Jaggard, Dorothy, vii. 64.

Jaggard, Mr., v. 1416.

James I, iii. 121, 304, 357, 390; iv. 607, 646, 660, 663, 716, 769, 798, 816, 842, 869, 872, 873, 876, 878, 908; v. 1190, 1297, 1298, 1304, 1305, 1401; vi. 21, 22, 135, 148, 222, 255, 259, 261, 286, 299.
    Acts of, vi. 267, 287.
    As Apollo, iii. 16.
    At Newcastle, iii. 44.
    Birthday of, iv. 668.
    Chaplain to, iv. 525.
    Comment at masque, iv. 671.
    Company of, *see* King's company.
    Death of, i. 19, 151, 186; vii. 58.
    Dedication to, iii. 14.
    Disapproves of play, i. 204.
    Exposes demoniacal fraud, iv. 617.
    Funeral of, i. 16, 19, 200, 209.
    Funeral procession of, vii. 59.
    Huntsman of, iii. 111.
    Illness of, vii. 56.
    Letter from, vi. 297.
    Mitigates players' punishment, i. 12.
    Performance for, iii. 15–16.
    Procession of, vii. 36.
    Proclamation of, vii. 10.
    Progress of, vii. 41.
    Progress to Scotland, i. 180–1, 181 nn. 1, 3, and 4.
    Suffering from an infection, vii. 43.
    Visit to Edinburgh, iii. 287.

James II, King of England, *see* York, Duke of.

James, Edward, vii. 54.

James, M. R., iv. 602.
  Descriptive Catalogue of the MSS. of St. John's College, Cambridge, A (1913), v. 1452.
  Western MSS. in the Library of Trinity College, Cambridge, 4 vols. (1900–4), v. 1302.
James, Mrs., ii. 678.
Jaques, Francis, iv. **597–8**.
  The Queen of Corsica, iii. 466; iv. 598; v. 981.
Jaques, Sir Roger, mayor of York, iv. 598.
Jarman, Anthony (carpenter), i. 143, 144; ii. **482**; vi. 155, 157, 185 n. 2.
Jarvice, ii. **482**.
Jay, Tom (actor), ii. **482**; vi. 236.
Jay, Thomas (verse writer), iv. 802, 809.
Jay, Sir Thomas, iv. 816.
Jeaffreson, John Cordy, ed., *Middlesex County Records*, 4 vols. (1886–92), i. 160, 162, 163, 167, 222, 265, 266, 314; ii. 361, 365, 366, 367, 384, 428, 433, 458, 460, 473, 522, 543, 571, 576, 607, 616, 624, 626, 656; iv. 737; vi. 56, 62, 138, 146, 148, 161, 215, 228.
Jealous Husbands, The, see Leanerd, John, *The Rambling Justice.*
Jealous Lovers, The, see Randolph, Thomas.
Jeffere, John, *The Bugbears*, iii. 466.
Jeffes, Anthony, i. 135, 136; ii. **482–3**; iv. 516.
Jeffes, Humphrey, i. 135, 136, 137, 139, 155, 178; ii. **483**.
Jeffes, Richard, ii. 482.
Jeffes, Sara, ii. 483.
Jeffes, William, ii. 482.
Jeffrey, V. M., 'Sources of Daniel's "Queen's Arcadia" and Randolph's "Amyntas"', *Mod. Lang. Rev.* xix (1924), v. 969, 970.
Jeffreys, George, iv. 536.
Jenkins, Henry, i. 22; ii. 469, 570.
Jenkins Love-Course, and Perambulation, see Anonymous.
Jenkins, William, scrivener, vi. 177.
Jenkyn, Pathericke, *Amorea* (1661), v. 1086.
Jephson, Norreys, iii. 427.
Jeptha, see Dekker, Thomas.
Jermyn, Henry, Baron Jermyn, i. 335; ii. 422; iii. 20, 174, 175, 194, 195, 212, 219; iv. 690; v. 1200.
Jerom, John, ii. 545, 581.
Jeronymo, see Kyd, Thomas, *The Spanish Tragedy.*

Jersey, iii. 174, 196.
Jessop, Edmund, iv. 599.
  Discovery of the Errors of the English Anabaptists, A (1623), iv. 599.
Jesuit College for English Boys at St. Omers, iv. 520; v. 1172, 1173, 1174, 1175, 1283, 1285, 1292, 1297, 1337, 1344, 1349, 1375, 1383, 1385, 1392, 1405, 1406, 1418, 1424, 1450.
  Dramatists, iii. 125; v. 1172, 1283, 1285.
  Masques, v. 1292.
  Plays, iii. 125, 160–1; iv. 947, 1172, 1173, 1174, 1175; v. 1283, 1285, 1290, 1297, 1337, 1339, 1344, 1346, 1349, 1375, 1383, 1385, 1392, 1405–6, 1418, 1424, 1450.
Jesuits, ii. 396, 538, 543; iii. 7; iv. 520, 521, 529, 530, 871, 872, 878; v. 1152, 1401, 1415; vi. 171.
  Centenary, v. 1339, 1349.
  English provincial of, v. 1172.
Jesus College, Cambridge, iv. 528, 852, 853; v. 1005, 1006–7.
  Fellow of, v. 1196, 1237.
Jesus College, Oxford, v. 1039.
Jeube, Edward, *see* Juby, Edward.
Jew of Malta, The, see Marlowe, Christopher.
Jew of Venice, The, see Dekker, Thomas.
Jew's Tragedy, The, see Heminges, William.
Jewbe or Jewbey, *see* Juby, Edward.
Jewell, John, i. 189, 192; ii. **483**.
Jewell, Ross, 'Thomas Heywood's *The Fair Maid of the West*', *Studies in English Drama*, First Series, ed. by Allison Gaw (1917), iv. 569.
Jeweller, ii. 554, 587, 695.
Jeweller of Amsterdam, The, see Fletcher, John.
Jewels, vi. 284.
Jewish Gentleman, The, see Brome, Richard.
'Jhon', book-keeper to King's company, iii. 164, 165, 763.
'Jhon', MSS. by, iii. 317.
Jig-dancers, v. 1049; vii. 7.
Jig-makers, ii. 563; v. 1049.
Jigs, i. 103 n. 2; ii. 401, 691; iii. 57, 88; iv. 680, 770, 895; v. 1050, 1137; vi. 111, 113, 146, 148, 152, 166, 171, 210 n., 243; vii. 7.

Jigs (cont.)
  Book of vii. 49.
  Suppression of, vi. 146.
Joan as Good as My Lady, see
  Heywood, Thomas.
Jocabella, see Chamberlain, Robert.
Jocelyn, The Life of the Glorious
  Bishop S. Patrick (1625), v. 1144.
Joco del Cano, vi. 294.
Joco del Tauro, vi. 294.
Jodolet Boxed, see Lower, Sir
  William, The Three Dorothies.
John a Green, see Anonymous.
John-of-all-trades, iv. 601.
John of Salisbury, Policraticus, vi.
  178 n. 1.
John Swabber the Seaman (droll),
  see Cox, Robert.
'John Webb and the Court Theatre
  of Charles II', see Keith, William
  Grant.
Johnson, Charles, iii. 182.
  Country Lasses, or The Custom of
    the Manor, iii. 328.
  Fortune in Her Wits, iii. 182.
  Love and Liberty, iii. 332.
  Masquerade, The, v. 1127.
  Wife's Relief: or, The Husband's
    Care, The, v. 1111, 1112.
Johnson, George, ii. 527.
Johnson, Henry, vi. 140.
Johnson, James, ii. 363.
Johnson, J., ed., Memoirs of the Life
  and Writings of W. Hayley (1823),
  iv. 864.
Johnson, John, iv. 599.
Johnson, Nathaniel, iv. 599-600.
Johnson, Nathaniel, The Morning
  Alarum (1651), iv. 599.
  Pyrander, iv. 600.
Johnson, Richard (actor), i. 285,
  287, 290, 297; ii. 483.
Johnson, Richard, The Most Famous
  History of the Seven Champions of
  Christendom (1596-7), iv. 712.
Johnson, Robert, iv. 647; vi. 295.
Johnson, Roger, iv. 599.
Johnson, Thomas, ii. 400.
Johnson, William (actor), ii. 384,
  483.
Johnson, William, iv. 600-2.
  Valetudinarium, iv. 600-2; v. 1452.
Johnson, William, Sr., iv. 600.
Johnson, William Savage, ed., The
  Devil Is an Ass [Jonson], Yale
  Studies in English, vol. xxix
  (1905), iv. 614, 616, 617.
Johnson, 'Young', iii. 59, 69; iv.
  602.

Johnston, Arthur, Musae Aulicae.
  Interprete F. K. (1635), iv. 716.
Johnston, George Burke, Ben Jon-
  son: Poet (1945), iv. 605.
  'Notes on Jonson's Execration
    upon Vulcan', M.L.N. xlvi
    (1931), iv. 629, 631.
Johnston, Mary, 'Ben Jonson and
  Martial', Classical Weekly, xxviii
  (1934), iv. 626.
Joiners, vi. 260.
Jolly, George, ii. 484, 577; vi. 77.
Jolly, John, ii. 484, 577.
Jolly, Mary, ii. 484.
Joly, A., William Drummond de
  Hawthornden (1934), iii. 287.
Jones, Ann, ii. 485, 486.
Jones, Bartholomew, i. 292 n. 4; ii.
  484-5.
Jones, Edward, ii. 485; v. 1104.
Jones, Elizabeth, ii. 485, 486.
Jones, Sir Francis, iv. 880; v. 1185.
Jones, Fred L., 'Echoes of Shakspere
  in the Later Elizabethan Drama',
  P.M.L.A. xlv (1930), iv. 739, 740;
  v. 995, 997, 998.
Jones, Inigo, i. 53, 117, 229, 233;
  ii. 349, 456; iii. 108, 109, 110,
  123, 136-7, 200, 208, 209, 214,
  215, 216, 217, 276; iv. 521, 524,
  582, 612, 620, 633, 634, 635,
  644, 652, 653, 654, 657, 663,
  670, 672, 673, 674, 676, 740,
  918, 941; v. 988, 1041, 1156,
  1162, 1192, 1228, 1230, 1303,
  1334, 1335; vi. 25, 51, 99, 252,
  260, 261, 263, 264, 265, 274 and
  n. 1, 275-7, 281 and n. 1, 282,
  283, 285, 286, 287; vii. 47.
  Attacks on, iv. 635.
  Court masques of, vi. 107.
  Designs of, iii. 218; v. 1304.
  Monument by, iii. 155.
  Sketches by, iv. 638.
Jones, James, i. 168 n. 1; ii. 485.
Jones, John (actor), ii. 485-6.
Jones, John, iv. 602-3.
  Adrasta, or The Woman's Spleen
    and Love's Conquest, iv. 602,
    603.
Jones, Oliver, i. 189, 192; ii. 486.
Jones, Richard, i. 135; ii. 486-7; v.
  1010.
Jones, Robert, vi. 78, 79, 115.
Jones, Stephen, iv. 838.
Jones, Thomas, iii. 263, 264; v.
  1380.
Jones, William, vi. 89, 90, 91 n.
Jones, William, stationer, iv. 835.

Jones, William, tailor, ii. 571.
Jonson, Ben, i. 2, 7, 26, 59, 66, 68,
  95 n. b, 115, 150 and n. 7, 225;
  ii. 435, 436, 444, 456, 468, 496,
  550, 557, 662 n. 5 cont., 692,
  694; iii. 6, 15, 50, 51, 52, 53,
  60, 66, 69, 77, 78, 79, 80, 88,
  89, 97, 100, 105, 109, 127, 144,
  195, 238, 239, 242, 243, 287,
  300, 308, 309, 310, 334, 337,
  372, 401, 404, 405, 406, 450;
  iv. 472, 474, 499, 502, 511, 526,
  531, 532, 545, 557, 595, 596,
  597, 602, 603–77, 693, 696, 733,
  737, 743, 744, 772, 779, 809,
  818, 830, 831, 858, 877, 900,
  901, 902, 956; v. 967, 968, 972,
  978, 988, 1018, 1029, 1033,
  1040, 1053, 1086, 1117, 1131,
  1140, 1141, 1148, 1161, 1183,
  1213, 1214, 1226, 1228, 1243,
  1245, 1308, 1311, 1337, 1348;
  vi. 41, 146, 206, 244, 258 n. 1,
  304.
Attacks on, iv. 634.
Branded as a felon, iv. 607.
Death of, vi. 166.
Influence of, iii. 50–52, 89, 97,
  113, 198, 211, 279, 296, 308,
  322, 334, 335, 353, 368, 404,
  405, 469; iv. 472, 483, 486,
  507–9, 526, 531–2, 536, 537,
  539, 596, 596, 693, 738, 743,
  761, 830, 834, 838, 885, 902,
  905, 928, 931–2, 933–4, 938,
  940–2, 945; v. 967, 978–9, 988,
  1003–4, 1029, 1033, 1056, 1079,
  1109, 1117, 1131, 1214, 1329,
  1369, 1370, 1381; vi. 244.
Letters of, iii. 143.
Made burgess of Edinburgh, iv.
  611.
Masques and entertainments, iv.
  636–77.
Poems to, vi. 25–26.
Praise of, iii. 97; iv. 609–10.
Reputation of, iv. 808; v. 1086,
  1117, 1131, 1140, 1153, 1245;
  vii. 13.
Satiric characterization, v. 1079.
Sign of, iii. 469.
Sons of, iii. 308; iv. 608, 612, 737,
  744; v. 967, 979, 1029, 1033,
  1040; vii. 54.
Unpublished work, iv. 620–1.
Verses by, iii. 55, 83, 84.
Alchemist, The, i. 24, 62, 94, 121;
  ii. 429, 465, 505, 597, 678, 681,
  693; iii. 100, 133, 328, 441; iv.

483, 608, 613, 803; v. 1169,
  1329, 1330; vi. 22; vii. 74, 98.
Transl. of Horace's Ars Poetica,
  iv. 646; vii. 119.
Bartholomew Fair, i. 117, 121 n. 1;
  iii. 50, 300; iv. 608, 611, 614,
  629, 803, 885, 902; v. 1079,
  1167, 1238; vi. 206; vii. 107.
Induction to, vi. 112, 206.
Case is Altered, The, iii. 44; iv. 614.
Catiline, i. 39, 98, 121; ii. 429,
  465, 676, 681; iii. 198, 199, 279,
  300, 441; iv. 472, 608, 614, 834,
  835, 838; v. 1086, 1152, 1370;
  vii. 98, 100.
'Celebration of Charis, A', v. 1214.
Challenge at Tilt, A, iv. 636.
Chloridia, iv. 611, 636–8; v. 1132.
Christmas His Masque, iv. 638–9.
Cynthia's Revels, or The Fountain
  of Self-Love, or Narcissus, i.
  117, 121 n. 1; ii. 422; iii. 274;
  iv. 539, 607, 614; v. 1056; vii.
  74, 98.
Devil Is an Ass, The, i. 121; ii.
  551; iii. 321, 322, 323, 353; iv.
  483, 610, 611, 614–17, 629, 630,
  704, 901, 1250; vi. 7, 10, 41 n. 1,
  199, 296.
Discoveries, iv. 511.
[Entertainment at Blackfriars], iv.
  639–40.
Entertainment at Highgate (The
  Penates), iv. 640.
Entertainment of King James and
  Queen Anne at Theobalds, An,
  iv. 640.
Entertainment of the Two Kings of
  Great Britain and Denmark at
  Theobalds, The, iv. 640.
Entertainment of the Queen and
  Prince at Althorp [The Satyr],
  iv. 640.
Epicoene, or The Silent Woman,
  i. 51, 95 n. c, 98, 99 n. s, 122; ii.
  344, 505, 523, 597, 692, 693;
  iii. 66, 275; iv. 483, 536, 608,
  617; vii. 38, 46, 74, 98.
'Epigram of Inigo Jones', iv. 635.
Every Man in His Humour, i. 1,
  24, 28, 96, 121; ii. 363, 502, 594;
  iii. 274; iv. 486, 536, 607, 617;
  vi. 22, 48, 132; vii. 26, 61, 98.
Every Man out of His Humour, iv.
  536, 607, 617; vii. 110.
'Execration upon Vulcan, An', iv.
  611, 631; vi. 179 n. 1, 183.
'Expostulation with Inigo Jones,
  An', iv. 635.

Jonson, Ben (*cont.*)

For the Honour of Wales, iv. **641–2**.

Fortunate Isles and Their Union, The, iii. 205, 335; iv. 519, 642–4, 663, 676; v. 1432.

Fox, The, see Volpone.

Golden Age Restored, The, iv. 645.

Gypsies Metamorphosed, The, ii. 691; iii. 73; iv. **645–7**.

'Have you seen but a bright lily grow', iii. 296.

Hot Anger Soon Cold, iv. 607, 618.

Hymenaei, iii. 214, 647.

'*Inviting a Friend to Supper*', iii. 50.

Irish Masque, The, iv. 647.

Isle of Dogs, The, iv. 618.

King's Entertainment at Welbeck, The, iv. **648–9**.

Legales convivales, vii. 54.

London Prodigal, The, iv. 618.

Lord Haddington's Masque (*The Hue and Cry after Cupid*), iv. 608, 649.

Love Freed from Ignorance and Folly, iv. 608, 649.

Love Restored, iv. 608, 649.

Love's Triumph through Callipolis, iv. 611, 637, 638, **651–3**; v. 1132.

Love's Welcome at Bolsover, iv. 635, **653–4**.

Lovers Made Men, iv. **650–1**; vii. 25.

Magnetic Lady, The, or Humours Reconciled, i. 30, 38 and n. 2, 42, 105, 121–2, 268; ii. 495, 503, 594; iii. 294; iv. 537, 611, 612, **618–20**, 627, 635, 743; v. 1169; vi. 11, 25, 26, 32, 163.

Masque of Augurs, The, iv. **655–8**; vi. 262.

Masque of Beauty, iv. 608, 658; vi. 256.

Masque of Blackness, The, iv. 607, 658; vi. 264.

Masque of Christmas, The, ii. 396, 467.

Masque of Gypsies, The, see The Gypsies Metamorphosed.

Masque of Owls, The, iv. **658–9**.

Masque of Queens, The, iii. 214; iv. 608, 659, 905; v. 1329, 1330.

May Lord, The, iv. 620–1, 627.

Mercury Vindicated from the Alchemists at Court, iv. 659.

Mortimer His Fall, iv. **621–2**.

Neptune's Triumph for the Return of Albion, iii. 335, 404, 631, 644, **660–3**, 676; iv. 643.

New Inn, or The Light Heart, The, i. 104, 105, 122; iii. 51, 66, 77, 78, 79, 106, 368; iv. 611, **622–4**, 633, 634, 652, 902; vi. 10.

News from the New World Discovered in the Moon, iii. 338; iv. 631, 663–5.

Oberon, iv. 608, 665.

'*Ode to Himself*', iii. 51, 78, 79, 84; iv. 623.

Ode to the Pretender, Humbly Inscrib'd to Mr. Lesley and Mr. Pope. To which is Added Earl Mortimer's Fall . . ., An (1713), iv. 621.

Page of Plymouth, The, iv. 607, 625.

Pan's Anniversary, or The Shepherds' Holiday, iv. **665–9**.

Panegyre, A, iv. 665.

Part of the King's Entertainment in Passing to His Coronation, iv. 669.

Pleasure Reconciled to Virtue, iv. 641, 642, 669–72; v. 1288, 1396; vi. 256, 263, 264.

Poetaster, or His Arraignment, ii. 422, 610; iii. 97; iv. 607, 625; vii. 64, 68, 76.

Richard Crookback, iv. 607, 625; v. 1014.

Robert the Second, King of Scots, iv. 607, 625.

Rollo, Duke of Normandy, see Fletcher, John.

Sad Shepherd, or A Tale of Robin Hood, The, iv. 505, 621, 625–8, 636; v. 1214, 1369.

Sejanus His Fall, ii. 499; iii. 198, 411, 628; iv. 834, 838; v. 1003, 1004, 1053, 1381; vii. 98.

Silent Women, The, see Epicoene.

Spanish Tragedy, additions to, v. 1014.

Speeches at Prince Henry's Barriers, iv. 672.

Staple of News, The, i. 12, 13, 97 n. h, 122; ii. 557; iii. 260, 294, 339; iv. 610, 611, **628–32**, 665, 704, 778, 877; v. 979, 1016, 1147, 1329; vi. 8, 10.

Staple of News, borrowings from, v. 978.

Tale of a Tub, A, i. 117, 121 n. 1, 229, 230, 249, 253; ii. 496; iv. 608, 611, 627, **632–6**, 654, 940–

1; v. 1079, 1109, 1169, 1310; vi. 63, 91.

Time Vindicated to Himself and to His Honours, iv. 644, 663, 672–6; v. 1341.

'To Inigo, Marquess Would-Be', iv. 635.

Unnamed Play, iv. 636.

Virtue and Beauty Reconciled, iv. 676.

Vision of Delight, The, iv. 676–7.

Volpone, i. 28, 61, 95 and n. c, 96, 99, 122–3; ii. 505, 598, 678, 680, 681, 693; iii. 300; iv. 608, 636, 710; v. 1153; vi. 16 n. 2; 245 n. 1; vii. 98.

Widow, The, see Middleton.

Jonson, Ben, George Chapman, and John Marston, *Eastward Ho!*, iv. 607, 616, 617, 945.

The Workes of Benjamin Jonson (1616), i. 1; iv. 612, 816; vi. 48; vii. 21.

The Workes of Benjamin Jonson. The second Volume (1640), iv. 612, 901.

The Works of Ben Jonson (1692), iv. 613.

The Works of Ben. Jonson in six volumes (1716), iv. 613.

Ben Johnson's Plays, 2 vols., Dublin (1729), iv. 613.

The Works of Ben. Jonson, Peter Whalley, ed., 7 vols. (1756), iv. 613.

The Dramatic Works of Ben Jonson, and Beaumont and Fletcher, P. Whalley and G. Colman, eds., 4 vols. (1811), iv. 613.

The Works of Ben Jonson, William Gifford, ed., 9 vols. (1816), iv. 613.

The Works of Ben Jonson, Barry Cornwall [B. W. Procter], ed., 1 vol. (1838), iv. 613.

The Works of Ben Jonson, William Gifford, ed., 1 vol. (1846), iv. 613.

The Works of Ben Jonson, William Gifford, ed., 1 vol. (1853), iv. 613.

The Works of Ben Jonson, William Gifford, ed., 1 vol. (1858), iv. 613.

The Works of Ben Jonson, William Gifford, ed., 1 vol. (1869), iv. 613.

The Works of Ben Jonson (with Gifford's notes and memoir), Francis Cunningham, ed., 3 vols. (1871), iv. 613.

The Works of Ben Jonson (with Gifford's notes and memoir),

Francis Cunningham, ed., 9 vols. (1875), iv. 613.

The Dramatic Works and Lyrics of Ben Jonson, Selected, J. A. Symonds, ed. (1886), iv. 613.

Masques and Entertainments by Ben Jonson, Henry Morley, ed. (1890), iv. 613.

Ben Jonson's Dramen in Neudruck herausgegeben nach der Folio 1616, W. Bang, ed., 2 vols., Louvain (1905 and 1908), iv. 613.

The Complete Plays of Ben Jonson, E. Rhys, ed., Intro. by F. E. Schelling, Everyman's Library, 2 vols. (1910), iv. 613.

Ben Jonson, C. H. Herford and Percy and Evelyn Simpson, eds., 11 vols. Oxford (1925–53), iv. 613; vi. 163, 179 n. 1, 183, 258 n. 1, 262.

Jonson Allusion-Book, The, see Adams, Joseph Quincy.

'Jonson, Jr., Ben', iv. 678.

Jonsonus Virbius, see Duppa, Bryan.

Jonson, 'Young', *A Fault in Friendship*, see Brome.

Joones, Haris, ii. 486.

Jordan, Anne, ii. 488.

Jordan, Elisabeth, ii. 489.

Jordan, J. C., 'Davenport's *The City Nightcap* and Greene's *Philomela*', *M.L.N.* xxxvi (1921), iii. 227, 228.

Jordan, Richard, ii. 489; iv. 679.

Jordan, Thomas, i. 285, 286, 287, 288, 290, 297; ii. 487–90; iv. 678–90, 928, 998; v. 1001, 1186, 1216, 1333, 1434.

Bacchus' Festival, iv. 680, 681.

Cheaters Cheated, The [a jig], iv. 680, 681.

Counter-Scuffle, The, iv. 682.

Cupid His Coronation, iv. 680, 682, 683, 685.

Diurnal of Dangers, A [pamphlet], iv. 680.

Eclogue or Representation in Four Parts, An, iv. 680, 682.

'*Elegie on his Inestimable friend, Mr. Richard Gunnell, Gent*', in *Poeticall Varieties or Varietie of Fancies, An*, (1637), iv. 518.

'Epitaph on Mr. John Kirke, Merchant, An', iv. 712.

Fancy's Festivals, iv. 677, 680, 682–3, 685.

Goldsmiths' Jubilee, The, iv. 683.

London in Its Splendour, iv. 683.

London in Luster, iv. 683.

Jordan, Thomas (*cont.*)
 London Triumphant: or the City in Jollity and Splendour, iv. 684.
 London's Glory, or The Lord Mayor's Show, iv. 683.
 London's Joy, or The Lord Mayor's Show, iv. 683.
 London's Joyful Gratulation [pamphlet], iv. 680.
 London's Triumphs: Expressed . . ., iv. 684.
 London's Triumphs: Illustrated . . ., iv. 684.
 London's Resurrection to Joy and Triumph, iv. 683.
 London's Royal Triumph for the City's Loyal Magistrate, iv. 683.
 Lord Mayor's Show, The, iv. 684.
 Love Hath Found His Eyes, or Distractions, iv. 680, **684–5**.
 Medicine for the Times . . ., A (pamphlet), iv. 680.
 Money Is an Ass, or Wealth Outwitted, ii. 406, 487, 488, 498, 508, 560, 620; iv. 679, **685–7**.
 Nursery of Novelties, A, in a Variety of Poetry, ii. 487, 488, 489, 493; iv. 712; v. 1333.
 Pictures of Passions (pamphlet), iv. 680.
 Piety and Poesy (1643), ii. 493; iv. 711.
 Poetical Varieties or Variety of Fancies (1637), ii. 457, 477, 488, 509, 510; iii. 55; iv. 518, 678, 679.
 Prologue to the King, iv. 680.
 Royal Arbor of Loyal Poesie (1664), iv. 680, 681, 682; v. 1333.
 Rules to Know a Loyal King from a Disloyal Subject, ii. 489; iv. 680.
 Speech to the People, A (pamphlet), iv. 680.
 'To his faithful ingenuous friend and old acquaintance, JOHN TATHAM, Gent.', v. 1216.
 Tricks of Youth, ii. 487–8, 489.
 Triumphs of London; Performed on Monday . . ., The, iv. 687.
 Triumphs of London; Performed on Tuesday . . ., The, iv. 687.
 Triumphs of London; Performed on Friday, The, iv. 687.
 Walks of Islington and Hogsdon with the Humours of Woodstreet Counter, or Tricks of Youth,

The, i. 13 n. 2; ii. 489; iv. 679, 685, 687, **688–90**; v. 998, 1401, 1402.
 Wit in the Wilderness of Promiscuous Poetry, ii. 489; v. 1216.
Jordan, William (beggar), i. 5 n. 1, vi. 18 n. 2.
Jordan-Smith, Paul, *Bibliographia Burtoniana* (1931), iii. 99.
 ed., *Robert Burton's Philosophaster, with an English Translation of the Same. Together with His Other Minor Writings in Prose and Verse* (1931), iii. 99, 100.
Joseph's Afflictions, see Anonymous.
Josephi Simonis, Tragœdiæ quinque, see Simons, Joseph.
Josephus, Jude von Venedig, see Anonymous.
Josephus Magnus, iii. 98.
Josephus's *History of the Jews*, see Morwyng, Peter, translator.
Joshua, see Rowley, Samuel.
Journal of Nicholas Assheton, The, see Raines, F. R.
Journalist, iv. 718.
Journals of the House of Commons, vi. 175.
Journals of Sir Simonds D'Ewes, see D'Ewes, Sir Simonds.
'Journey through England and Scotland made by Lupold von Wedel in the years 1584 and 1585', see Bülow, Gottfried von.
Jovial Crew, The, see Brome.
Jovial Crew, The, or The Devil Turned Ranter, see Sheppard, Samuel.
Jovial Philosopher, The, see Randolph, Thomas, *Aristippus*.
Jovis et Junonis Nuptiae, see Anonymous.
Juby, Edward, i. 135, 136, 138, 147, 155; iii. **490**, 623; vi. 150.
Juby, Frances, i. 143, 144; ii. **490**; vi. 157.
Juby, Richard, ii. 490.
Juby, Tabitha, ii. 490.
Juby, William, ii. 490.
Judas, see Rowley, Samuel.
Judge, The, see Massinger, Philip.
Judson, A. C., ed., *The Captives; or, The Lost Recovered* (1921), iv. 560, 561.
Jugglers, ii. 612; iv. 673; vi. 165 n., 209.
Jugurth, King of Numidia, see William Boyle.

Jugurtha, *see* Boyle, William.
Julio und Hippolyta, *see* Anonymous.
Julius Caesar (?), *see* May, Thomas.
Julius Caesar, *see* Shakespeare, William.
Julius Caesar, *see* Sir William Alexander, Earl of Stirling.
Julius et Gonzaga, *see* Bernard, Samuel.
Jump, J. D., 'The Anonymous Masque in Egerton 1994', *R.E.S.* xi (1935), v. 1419, 1420.
'*Rollo, Duke of Normandy*: Some Bibliographical Notes on the Seventeenth-Century Editions', *Library*, Fourth series, xviii (1937–8), iii. 401.
Jumping, vi. 294.
Jung, Hugo, *Das Verhältnis Thomas Middleton's zu Shakspere* (1904), iv. 856, 903.
Junge, Otto, *The Fatal Contract, A French Tragedy by William Hemings, Kritische Neuausgabe mit Einleitung und Anmerkungen* (1912), iv. 539, 540, 543, 546.
Juno in Arcadia, *see* Anonymous.
Juno's Pastoral, *see* Anonymous.
Jupe, Edward, ii. 384.
Jupiter and Io (?), *see* Heywood, Thomas.
Jupiter, Mercury, Juno, Pallas, Venus, and Paris, *see* Heywood, *Deorum Judicium*.
Jury of the Sewers, vi. 200.
Just General, The, *see* Manuche, Cosmo.
Just Italian, The, *see* Davenant, William.
Justice of the Common Pleas, iii. 14.
Justices of the Peace, iii. 255; vi. 175, 176, 228, 230, 231, 239, 293, 301.
Justices of the Peace, County of Middlesex, vi. 27.
Justin, iv. 764, 768.
Juvenal, iv. 748; v. 1001, 1003, 1238.
Juxon, William, iii. 20, 184–85.

Kane, Andrew, *see* Cane, Andrew.
Kassel, Germany, vi. 186 n. 1.
Kastner, L. E., ed., *The Poetical Works of William Drummond of Hawthornden with 'A Cypresse Grove'*, 2 vols. (1913), iii. 289; v. 1017.
Katherens, Gilbert, vi. 201, 203, 205.

Katherine of Bologna, iii. 353.
Kay, Arthur, iii. 349.
Kaye, Sir John, dedication to, iii. 229.
Kean, Edmund, iv. 817.
Keast, William R., 'Killigrew's Use of Donne in "The Parson's Wedding" ', *M.L.R.* xlv (1950), iv. 701.
Keep the Widow Waking, *see* Dekker, Thomas, *Late Murder of the Son upon the Mother*.
Keeper of the Bears, vi. 209.
Keeper, Lord, *see* Lord Keeper.
Keeper of the Bears and Mastiffs, vi. 208 n. 2.
Keeper of the Crown land of Hyde Park, v. 1123.
Keeper of St. James's Park, iii. 112.
Keepers of the royal park at Richmond, iii. 112.
Keepers of the Wardrobe, ii. 688.
Keightley, Thomas, 'Fletcher's "Custom of the Country" ', *N. & Q.*, Second Series, xi (1861), iii. 324.
Kein, Andrew, *see* Cane, Andrew.
Keinton, ii. 480, 484, 618.
Keith, William Grant, 'Designs for the First Movable Scenery on the English Public Stage', *Burlington Magazine*, xxv (1914), vi. 285, 286.
'John Webb and the Court Theatre of Charles II', *Architectural Review*, lvii (February 1925), iii. 216; vi. 47, 52, 267, 274 n. 1, 282.
Kellegrew, *see* Killigrew.
Kellock, John, ii. 491.
Kellock, Philadelphia, ii. 491.
Kelly, Philadelphia, ii. 527.
Kelly, Theodore, v. 984.
Kelly, William, *Notices Illustrative of the Drama and Other Popular Amusements* (1865), vi. 124.
Kemble, Fanny, iv. 799.
Kemble, John Philip, ii. 382, 383; iii. 347; iv. 817; v. 1104.
Kemble, Stephen, *The Northern Inn*, iv. 571.
Kemp, Edward, iv. 537.
Kempe, William, i. 1, 4 n. 1; vi. 180.
Kempston, Robert, i. 298; ii. 491.
Kemsall, Faith, ii. 651.
Kendal, Westmorland, iii. 38; iv. 472, 473.
Kendal Castle, play at, iv. 472–3.
Kendall, Joan, ii. 491.

Kendall, Richard, i. 26 n. 5 cont., 30 n. 6, 231–2, 274, 285–8, 289 n. 4, 290, 293, 297 and n. b, 309, 310; ii. 491; vi. 99, 100, 164, 227.

Kendall, Thomas, dedication to, iii. 153.

Kendall, Tomazine, ii. 404.

Kenilworth, iv. 649, 658, 659.

Kent, County of, ii. 421; iii. 14; iv. 515; v. 1178; vi. 248.

Kentisbury, in Devon, v. 999, 1000.

'Kentish Petition, The', iv. 721.

Kerbye, John, i. 266.

Kerke, John, see Kirke, John.

Kermode, J. Frank, 'A Note on the History of Massinger's 'The Fatal Dowry' in the Eighteenth Century', *N. & Q.* cxcii (1947), iv. 783, 785.

Kerr, Mina, *Influence of Ben Jonson on English Comedy 1598–1642* (1912), iv. 482, 483, 605, 739, 742, 745, 931.

Keyes, Ralph, ii. 491, 682, 683.

Keyes, Robert, ii. 492, 683.

Keyne or Keynes, Andrew, see Cane, Andrew.

Keyne, Mary, ii. 400.

Keyser, Robert, vi. 268.

Kidby, John, iv. 539.

Kiddermaster, Worcs., ii. 636.

Kiddermister, Sir John, ii. 576–7.

Kiepert, Willy, *Fletcher's 'Women pleased' und seine Quellen* (1903), iii. 431.

Kildare, Earl of, v. 1140.

Kilian, Eugen, vi. 189.

Kilkenny Castle, ii. 673.

Kilkenny, Ireland, play published at, iii. 94.

Killigrew, Mrs. Anne, iv. 690.

Killigrew, Charles, iv. 696.

Killigrew (Kellegrew), Henry, iv. 690–4.
    Conspiracy, The (Pallantus and Eudora), i. 123; iii. 62; iv. 691–4; v. 1125.

Killigrew, Mary, iv. 690.

Killigrew, Sir Robert, iv. 690, 694.

Killigrew, Thomas, i. 117 and n. 1; ii. 677; iii. 20, 63, 105, 196, 197, 345, 409; iv. 623, 628, 629, 633, 690, 694–710, 803, 824; v. 1229; vi. 38, 90 n. 1, 243.
    Company of, iii. 222, 314, 315, 333, 343, 354, 402, 403; iv. 480, 616, 790, 900; v. 1129, 1149, 1150; vi. 64.
    Plays allotted to, iii. 25.

Bellamira Her Dream, or The Love of Shadows, Parts I and II, iv. 696, 697, 709.

Cicilia and Clorinda, or Love In Arms, Parts I and II, iii. 106, 110; iv. 695, 697–8, 709.

Claracilla, i. 253; iv. 695, 698–700, 705, 707, 709; v. 1106.

Parson's Wedding, The, i. 123; ii. 461, 597; iii. 23; iv. 701–5, 709.

Pilgrim, The, iv. 696, 705–6; v. 1139.

Princess, or Love at First Sight, The, i. 117, 123; iii. 98; iv. 695, 700, 706–8, 709.

Prisoners, The, i. 253; iii. 153; iv. 698, 700, 705, 707, 708–9, 811.
    Revenge, The [?], iv. 709–10.

Thomaso, or the Wanderer, Parts I and II, iv. 696, 709, 710.

Comedies and Tragedies (1664), iii. 106; iv. 696.

Killigrew, Sir William, iv. 690, 694.

Killigrew, William. *Pandora, or The Converts*, v. 1386.

Kimpton, Robert, see Kempston, Robert.

Kinaston (Kynaston), Edward, iii. 371, 377.

Kinde, Dorothy, ii. 525.

King Charles I, see Charles I.

King James, see James I.

King, Edward, iv. 537.

King, John, i. 160; ii. 367, 492.

King of Bohemia, iv. 518.

King of Sweden, iv. 844.

King and Queen of Bohemia, see Bohemia, King and Queen of.

King and Queen's Young Company, see Beeston's Boys.

King and No King, A, see Beaumont and Fletcher.

King and Queen's Entertainment at Richmond, see Anonymous.

King and the Subject, The, see Massinger.

King Arthur, see Dryden, John.

King Freewill, see Bristowe, Francis.

King John and Matilda, see Davenport, Robert.

King of Kent, see Middleton, Thomas, *Hengist, King of Kent*.

King Lear, see Shakespeare.

King Leir, see Anonymous.

King of Numidia, see Boyle, William, *Jugurth*.

King Sebastian of Portugal, see Chettle, Henry.

Kingdom's Weekly Intelligencer, The,
  see Newspapers.
Kingman, Phillip, vi. 78–85, 115.
King's Arms, Oxford, i. 293; ii. 689;
  iii. 74; iv. 801; vi. 100, 164.
King's Arms, Norwich, iii. 385, 462.
King's Bench, i. 42; iii. 161.
Kings Bench, Chief Justice of, iv.
  916.
King's Bench prison, iii. 243, 244;
  vi. 34.
King's Bill, i. 273.
King's College, Cambridge, iv. 946;
  vi. 78.
  Chapel, v. 1408.
  Fellow of, v. 1238.
King's company, i. 1–134, 141 n. 6,
  149, 200, 209, 226, 242, 264,
  270 n. 4, 278, 290, 327, 337; ii.
  494–5; iii. *passim*; iv. *passim*;
  v. *passim*; vi. 4, 11, 69, 73, 85,
  90 n. 2, 105, 113, 122, 136, 137,
  149, 150, 160, 163, 168, 172,
  179–200, 206, 225, 245 n. 1,
  248, 266, 271, 282, 283; vii. 3,
  6, 7, 11, 13.
  Actor lists, i. 70–89.
  Attendance at court, iv. 664, 666.
  Book-keeper, v. 1309.
  Fellows of, vi. 20.
  Plays at Court, i. 94–100; iii. 25.
  Plays at Oxford, iii. 411.
  Plays licensed for, i. 101–8.
  Provincial notices, i. 92–93.
  Repertory of, i. 108–34; iii. 54,
  98.
King's Day, vii. 36, 39, 47.
*King's Entertainment at Welbeck,
  The, see* Jonson.
King's Head, Oxford, ii. 558; iii. 74.
King's Head Yard, *see* London,
  streets of.
King's house, commissioners of the
  iii. 468.
King's Lynn, Norfolk, i. 273.
King's Majesty's Riming Poet, vi.
  205.
King's Mistress, The, see Anony-
  mous.
King's Playhouse in Covent Garden,
  iii. 264, 325, 348, 371, 403, 412,
  426; iv. 893–4; v. 1085, 1092,
  1093, 1100, 1115, 1122, 1130,
  1145, 1204, 1210, 1211.
King's Porter, ii. 500, 591.
King's Revels company, i. 36, 41,
  152, 231, 268, 283–301, 304, 305,
  306 n. 3, 307, 309, 327, 332; iii.
  53, 56, 57, 60, 85, 86, 87, 91, 92,

233, 238, 264, 266; iv. 475, 484,
  485, 505, 543, 679, 687, 746, 835,
  836, 941; v. 966, 967, 969, 971,
  979, 986, 987, 995, 996, 998, 1001,
  1002, 1003, 1009, 1091, 1092,
  1112, 1313, 1344, 1399, 1427,
  1434, 1446, 1455; vi. 12, 87, 94,
  97, 98, 99, 102, 103, 163, 164, 227,
  242.
King's Scholar, Westminster, iii.
  173; iv. 947.
Kingsford, C. L., *Early History of
  Piccadilly, Leicester Square,
  Soho* (1925), v. 1104.
  'Paris Garden and the Bear-
  baiting', *Archaeologia*, Second
  Series, xx (1920), vi. 200 and
  n. 1, 202 n. 2, 211 n.
Kingsmill, Lady Bridget, ii. 442.
Kingston, Earl of, iii. 460.
Kingston, Mr., iii. 257, 273; iv. 622;
  v. 1145.
Kinnaird, Douglas, *The Merchant of
  Bruges: or, The Beggars' Bush,*
  iii. 317.
Kinnersley, Clement, Yeoman of
  the Removing Wardrobe of Beds,
  vi. 265; vii. 65, 66.
Kirby, Ethyn W., *William Prynne,
  A Study in Puritanism* (1931),
  iii. 451; iv. 563.
Kirk, Anne, iv. 476.
Kirk, George, iv. 476.
Kirk, Rudolf, ed., Massinger's *The
  City Madam, Princeton Studies
  in English* (1934), iv. 771, 772,
  773, 774, 847.
Kirkby Lonsdale, ii. 491, 688.
Kirke, Edward, iv. 711.
Kirke, Elizabeth, iii. 493.
Kirke, Lady Elizabeth (formerly
  wife of Christopher Beeston), vi.
  48 n. 1, 65 n. 1, 75 n. 1, 76.
Kirke, George, v. 1228.
Kirke, Henry, v. 1355.
Kirke, John, i. 272, 275, 281, 308,
  311, 312, 321; ii. 492–3; iv.
  710–15; v. 1061, 1062; vi. 164.
  *Seven Champions of Christendom,
  The,* i. 312; ii. 493; iv. 710, 711,
  712–14; v. 1061.
  Untitled Play (1642), iv. 714–15.
Kirke, Sir Lewis, ii. 632; vi. 48 n. 1,
  65 n. 1, 75 n. 1, 76.
Kirke, Marie, ii. 493.
Kirke, Parry, ii. 493.
Kirkham, Edward, vi. 13 n. 1.
Kirkman, Francis, ii. 473; iii. 318,
  324; iv. 579, 582, 859, 955; v.

Kirkman, Francis (*cont.*)
    1249, 1253, 1322, 1356, 1446;
    vi. 233.
Play-list, iii. 5, 8, 283, 469; iv.
    500, 501, 502, 749, 951, 952,
    1390, 1428.
Translator, *Loves and Adventures
    of Clerico and Lozia, The* (1652),
    ii. 373; vi. 71.
*Nicomede, A Tragi-Comedy,
    translated out of the French of
    Monsieur Corneille, by John
    Dancer.* . . . Together with an
    Exact Catalogue of all the
    English Stage-Plays printed,
    till this present Year 1671
    (1671), iii. 5.
*Tom Tyler and his Wife. An
    excellent old Play, as it was
    Printed and Acted about a
    hundred Years ago.* Together,
    with an exact Catalogue of all
    the playes that were ever yet
    printed (1661), iii. 5.
Wits, or Sport upon Sport, The
    (1673), ii. 415; iii. 151, 403,
    481; *see also* Elson, J. J.
Kirtlington, Yorkshire, iii. 39.
Kite, Francis, ii. 494.
Kite, Jeremy, ii. **493–4**.
Kite, William, ii. 494.
Kittredge, G. L., 'Notes on Eliza-
    bethan Plays', *J.E.G.P.* ii
    (1898), iv. 560.
'King James I and *The Devil Is
    an Ass*', *Mod. Phil.* ix (1911),
    iv. 614, 616, 617.
    ed., *William Shakespeare: The
    Complete Works* (1952), iii. 432.
Klein, Emmo, *Fletchers 'The Span-
    ish Curate' und seine Quelle* (1905),
    iii. 418.
Knack to Know a Knave, A, see
    Anonymous.
*Knave in Grain New Vampt, The,
    see* D., J.
*Knave in Print, or One for Another,
    A, see* Rowley, William.
*Knavery in all Trades: Or, The
    Coffee-House* (1664), *see* Tatham,
    John.
Knell, Rebecca, ii. 466.
Knell, William, ii. 466.
Kneller, James, i. 168 n. 1; ii. **494**.
Knepp, *see* Knipp, Mary.
Knevet, Ralph, iv. 715.
*Funeral Elegies Consecrated to the
    Immortal Memory of the Right
    Honorable Lady Katherine*

*Paston, Late Wife to the Truly
    Noble and Heroic William
    Paston of Oxnead, Esquire*
    (1637), iv. 715.
'Gallery to the Temple: Lyricall
    Poemes upon sacred occasions,
    A', iv. 715.
Rhodon and Iris, iv. 715.
*Stratioticon, or A Discourse of
    Military Discipline* (1628), iv.
    715.
Knight, —, i. 37, 121; ii. **494–5**.
Knight, Anthony, i. 15, 73–89; ii.
    495.
Knight, Edward, i. 15, 72–88, 199 n.
    2; ii. **495**, 682.
Knight, I., v. 997, 998.
Knight, Mr., iv. 513, 619.
Knight, Mr. (Bookkeeper of King's
    company), iv. 619; vi. 31, 32.
Knight, Mrs., ii. 622.
Knight, Philip, ii. 384, 495.
Knight Rider, *see* London, streets of.
Knight of the Shire, iii. 292.
*Knight of the Burning Pestle, The,
    see* Beaumont and Fletcher.
Knight and the Cobbler, The, see
    Lane, Philip, *A Christmas Tale.*
Knight of the Ill-Favoured Face, see
    Anonymous, *History of Don
    Quixote.*
Knight of Malta, The, see Fletcher,
    John.
'Knight and the Shepherd's
    Daughter' (ballad), *see* Anony-
    mous.
Knights of the Bath, iv. 841; vii. 20.
Knights of the Garter, vii. 53, 70.
Knights of St. John, ceremony of
    degradation of, iii. 354.
Knights, L. C., *Drama and Society
    in the Age of Jonson* (1937), iv.
    605.
Knipp [Knepp], Mary, actress, iii.
    82, 320, 325, 345, 412, 848; v.
    1092, 1210, 1211.
Knipton, Robert, *see* Kempston,
    Robert.
Knole House, v. 1227, 1359.
Knolles, Richard, *The generall
    historie of the Turkes* (1603), iii.
    122, 354; iv. 486, 492, 506, 509,
    510, 813; v. 1215.
Generall Historie of the Turkes,
    Fifth ed. (1638), iv. 928.
Knot of Fools, A, see Brewer,
    Thomas.
Knot of Knaves, A, see Tatham,
    John.

Knowler, William, ed., *Earl of Strafforde's Letters and Dispatches, with an Essay towards His Life by Sir George Radcliffe*, 2 vols. (1739), iii. 24, 107, 108, 199, 200, 207, 217, 218, 219; iv. 919; v. 1155, 1156, 1159, 1202; vi. 4, 29–30, 34, 37, 69, 266, 286; vii. 4.

Knowlton, Edgar C., 'The Plots of Ben Jonson', *M.L.N.* xliv (1929), iv. 605.

Knowlton, Kent, iii. 25.

Knowsley Hall, ii. 464.

Knowsley, Lancashire, v. 1041.

Knutsford, Cheshire, iv. 505.

Knyvet, Sir Philip, iv. 816.

Knyveton, Sir Gilbert, iii. 167.

Knyveton, Mary, iii. 167.

Koch, J., 'Thomas Nabbes, ein zu wenig beachteter Dichter', *Anglia*, xlvii (1923), iv. 927, 929, 932, 934, 936, 938, 939, 940, 942.

Koeppel, Emil, 'Die Chapman zugeschriebene tragödie "Revenge for Honour"', *Beiblatt zur Anglia*, xviii (1907), iv. 489.

'John Fords "Chronicle History of Perkin Warbeck" und Thomas Gainsfords "History of Warbeck"', *Anglia, Beiblatt*, xxii (1911), iii. 454.

'"Queen and Concubine, The", A Comedie By Richard Brome', *Quellen und Forschungen*, lxxxii (1897), iii. 85, 86.

Quellen-Studien zu den Dramen Ben Jonson's, John Marston's und Beaumont's und Fletcher's (1895), iii. 316–425 *passim*; iv. 562, 563, 605.

Quellen-Studien zu den Dramen George Chapman's, Philip Massinger's, und John Ford's (1897) iii. 263, 266, 270, 433, 439, 442, 446, 448, 451, 454, 459, 462; iv. 750–836 *passim*; v. 1088, 1089, 1286, 1312, 1314.

'Zur Quellenkunde des Stuart-Dramas', *Archiv für das Studium der neueren Sprachen und Litteraturen*, xcvii (1896), iii. 257; iv. 560, 561.

Kostka, St. Stanislaus, v. 1338.

Kostressen, Johan, ii. 495.

Kottas, Karl, *Thomas Randolph: sein Leben und seine Werke* (1909), v. 965.

Krantzius, Albert, iii. 98.

Krzyzanowski, Julius, 'Source of

Suckling's Brennoralt', *T.L.S.* 9 April 1938, v. 1207, 1209.

Kupka, P., *Über den dramatischen Vers Thomas Dekkers* (1893), iii. 241.

Kyd, Thomas, *Spanish Tragedy, The*, ii. 440; iv. 607; v. 996, 1014, 1096, 1179, 1411; vi. 149; vii. 29, 51, 61, 90.

Spanish Tragedy, The, influence of, iv. 509.

Spanish Tragedy, The, Jonson's additions to, iv. 628.

Kynaston, Edward, ii. 545, 546.

Kynaston, Sir Edward, iv. 716.

Kynaston (Kinaston), Sir Francis, iv. 716–17; vi. 49.

(Transl.): *Amorum Troili et Creseidae libri duo priores Anglico-Latini* (1635) [from Chaucer], iv. 716.

Constitutions of the Musaeum Minervae, The (1636), iv. 716.

Corona Minervae, iv. 717.

Leoline and Sydanis (1642), iv. 716.

Musaeum Minervae, iv. 716; vi. 299.

Kynder [Kinder], Philip, iv. 717–18.

Silvia, iv. 717.

Kynder, William, iv. 717.

La Pierre, Sebastian, dancer, iii. 139.

Labourer, ii. 431, 486; vi. 260, 265.

Labyrinthus, see Hawkesworth, Walter.

Lace Woman, iii. 219.

'Lacket, Dr.' (ghost name), iv. 718.

Lackfield, Suffolk, v. 1196.

Lacrymae Cantabrigiensis, see Anonymous.

Lacy, John (actor), i. 327 n. 4, 332, 336; ii. 495–6; iii. 71, 150, 151, 344; iv. 633, 635, 949; v. 1079, 1091, 1092, 1093, 1094.

Lacy, John, *Sir Hercules Buffoon, or The Poetical Squire*, iv. 774, 803; v. 1052.

Ladies, appeal to, iii. 97.

Ladies' Hall, at Deptford, v. 1257.

Ladies Frolick, The, see Dance, James.

Ladies' Masque, see Anonymous, *Masque of Amazons*.

Ladies' Privilege, The, see Glapthorne, Henry.

Ladies, A Second Time, Assembled in Parliament, The, see Anonymous.

Ladrones, see Fane, Mildmay.
Lady Alimony, see Anonymous.
Lady Day (25 March), iii. 72.
Lady Elizabeth, *see* Elizabeth, Princess.
Lady Errant, The, see Cartwright, William.
Lady Hatton's masques, iii. 220.
Lady Jane, Part I, see Heywood, Thomas.
Lady Mother, The, see Glapthorne, Henry.
Lady of Pleasure, The, see Shirley, James.
Lady's Privilege, The, see Glapthorne, Henry.
Lady's Trial, The, see Ford, John.
Laidler, Josephine, 'A History of Pastoral Drama in England until 1700', *Englische Studien*, xxxv (1905), iv. 479, 480, 715; v. 1181, 1184.
Laighton, Ned, i. 142; ii. 349.
Laing, David, 'A Brief Account of the Hawthornden Manuscripts in the possession of the Society of Antiquaries of Scotland; with Extracts containing several unpublished Letters and Poems of William Drummond of Hawthornden', *Transactions of the Society of Antiquaries of Scotland*, iv (1857), iii. 287.
Lake, Sir Thomas, i. 10 n. 6.
Lakin, Daniel, tr., *A Miraculous Cure of the Prussian Swallowknife* (1642), iv. 813.
Lamar, René, ed., *Samuel Butler: Satires and Miscellaneous Poetry and Prose* (1928), iii. 278, 524.
Lamb, Charles, *Specimens of English Dramatic Poets* (1808), iii. 439.
Lambarde volume, Folger Shakespeare Library MS. 1478. 2, i. 132; iii. 227, 312, 313, 317.
Lambe, Dr., John i. 266–8; iii. 339; v. 1266, 1455; vi. 161–2.
Lambert, Lady, vi. 49.
Lambert, Thomas, iv. 735.
Lambeth, *see* London, streets and districts of.
Lambeth Palace MS. v. 1237, 1238; vi. 304.
Lambin, Denis (Lambdinus, Dionysius), *Hist. Ciceroniana*, v. 1370.
Lamport Hall, i. 23 n. 1.
Lancashire, iv. 713.
    Bagpipe, v. 1159.

Schoolmaster in, iv. 472.
Witches, iii. 74; iv. 941; vi. 100.
Lancaster, Anne, ii. 637.
Lancaster, H. C., *A History of French Dramatic Literature in the Seventeenth Century*, 9 vols. (1929–42), iv. 600.
Lancaster, Silvester, i. 316, 321; ii. 496.
Landgartha, see Burnell, Henry.
Landgrave of Hesse-Darmstadt, ii. 432.
Lando, Girolamo, Venetian Ambassador to England, iv. 655, 656; vii. 34, 35.
Lane, Philip, iv. 718, 866.
    Christmas Tale, or The Knight and the Cobbler, A, iv. 718, 865.
Lane, Richard, v. 985.
Laneere, Mr., singer, v. 1230.
Laneham, Robert, iv. 649.
Langbaine, Gerard, *An Account of the English Dramatic Poets* (1691), ii. 182; iii. 8, 43, 49, 98, 103, 115, 122, 134, 137, 142, 144, 169, 182, 206, 228, 275, 303, 315, 321, 325, 329, 347, 367, 368, 379, 385, 404, 406, 407, 409, 410, 420, 424, 458, 470; iv. 492, 500, 501, 511, 514, 532, 536, 603, 617, 624, 729, 730, 731, 732, 741, 744, 748, 780, 828, 833, 839, 858, 869, 881, 901, 936; v. 969, 986, 997, 998, 999, 1020, 1052, 1089, 1093–4, 1097, 1098, 1100, 1103, 1111, 1113, 1115, 1127, 1130, 1133, 1139, 1146, 1153, 1207, 1252, 1323, 1370, 1416, 1428; vi. 97. 233.
    Lives and Characters of the English Dramatick Poets, The (1698), iii. 12, 18.
    Momus Triumphans (1688), v. 998, 999, 1248, 1266.
Langley, Francis, ii. 384; vi. 128, 129, 130, 249.
Langley, Thomas, iii. 251; v. 1347; vi. 240.
Langlies Rents, *see* London, streets and districts of.
L'Anglois, Abraham, v. 1041.
Langton, Dr. William, iv. 550; v. 1256.
Lanham, Henry, vi. 132.
Lanier, Henry, ii. 343.
Lanier, Innocent, vi. 295.
Lanier, John, v. 1159.

Lanier, Nicholas, iv. 651, 657; v. 1304.
Lanier, William, ii. 343.
Lany, Dr., iv. 586.
Larpent Collection, iii. 347.
L'Artenice, see Racan, Seigneur de.
Lasander and Callista, see Fletcher, *The Lovers' Progress.*
Laslett, Peter, ed., *Patriarcha* (1949), v. 1280.
Lasswade, near Hawthornden, iii. 288.
'Last Masque, The', *see* Wedgwood, C. V.
Last Remains of Sir John Suckling, see Suckling.
Last Will and Testament of the Doctors Commons, The (1641), *see* Anonymous.
Late Lancashire Witches, The, see Brome, Richard.
Late Murder of the Son upon the Mother, or Keep the Widow Waking, see Dekker, Thomas.
Late Will and Testament of the Doctors Commons (1641), *see* Anonymous.
Latham, I. (John Tatham?), v. 998.
Latin, iii. 242.
  Mottoes, iii. 62, 181, 227, 229, 256, 273, 274, 274–5, 282, 283, 304, 440, 442, 446, 454; iv. 564, 657; vi. 1021, 1032, 1066, 1318, 1320, 1439.
  Orations, v. 967.
  Plays, *see* Plays, Latin.
  Poems, iv. 478, 499, 538, 540, 550, 691, 716.
  Translations from, iii. 40, 469; iv. 555, 564, 584, 646, 768, 830–1, 844, 946, 962; v. 1047–8, 1054, 1072, 1158, 1247, 1292, 1373, 1415, 1429.
Lau, Hurfries de, ii. 496; vi. 46.
Laud, William, Archbishop of Canterbury, i. 276; iii. 3, 4, 135, 136, 137, 138, 140, 455; iv. 533, 551, 958; v. 1066, 1193, 1194, 1235; vi. 24, 167–8; vii. 12.
  Imprisonment of, v. 1266.
  Autobiography of Dr. William Laud, Archbishop of Canterbury, and martyr, The. Collected from his remains (1839), iii. 3, 136–7; iv. 691; v. 1189–90, 1259, 1262, 1263, 1264.
Launching of the Mary, The, see Mountfort, Walter.
Laureateship, iv. 545.

Lauschke, Johannes, *John Websters Tragodie Appius and Virginia, eine Quellenstudie* (1899), v. 1245.
Lavender, Theophilus, ed., *Travels of Foure English Men and a Preacher into Africa, Asia, Troy . . .* (1612), iv. 813.
Lavenham, Suffolk, v. 1027.
Law courts, iv. 930; vi. 15, 194, 196.
Law, R. A., Review of M. C. Struble's ed. of *Perkin Warbeck*, in *J.E.G.P.* xxvi (1927), iii. 454.
Law against Lovers, The, see Davenant, William.
Law Case, The, see Anonymous.
Lawes brothers, v. 1264.
Lawes, Henry, iii. 109, 134, 141, 219, 220; iv. 536, 912, 915; v. 1159, 1188, 1189, 1192, 1207, 1430.
  Ayres & Dialogues (1653), v. 1431.
  'Health to the nut-brown lass, A', v. 1212.
  Henry Lawes Musician and Friend of Poets (1941), *see* Evans, Willa McClung.
Lawes, William, iii. 110, 141, 219, 220; iv. 850; v. 1162, 1163, 1207.
Lawrence, Sir John, v. 1213, 1221.
Lawrence, William John, iii. 316; iv. 906; vi. 188 n. 1, 223, 224 n. 1; vii. 6.
  'Authorship of "The Careless Shepherdess, The"', *T.L.S.* 24 July 1924, iv. 501, 502; v. 974.
  'Authorship of "The Costlie Whore, The"', *M.L.R.* xvii (1922), v. 1313.
  'Dekker's Theatrical Allusiveness', *T.L.S.* 30 January 1937, iii. 241.
  'Early French Players in England', *Anglia*, xxxii (1909) pp. 60–89, iii. 320.
  'Early Substantive Theatre Masques', *T.L.S.* 8 December 1921, iv. 907, 908, 910.
  Elizabethan Playhouse and Other Studies, The, First Series (1912), iv. 517, 701, 704; vi. 192.
  Elizabethan Playhouse and Other Studies, The, Second Series (1913), vi. 304, 306.
  'Found: a missing Jacobean dramatist', *T.L.S.* 23 March 1922, iii. 101, 186, 187, 237, 280, 281.

Lawrence, William John (*cont.*)
'Goffe's *The Careless Shepherdess*', *M.L.R.* xiv (1919), iv. 501, 503.
'John Honeyman, the Caroline Actor-Dramatist', *R.E.S.* iii (1927), iv. 596.
'John Kirke, the Caroline Actor-Dramatist', *Stud. Phil.* xxi (1924), iv. 711.
'Massinger's Punctuation', *Criterion*, xi (1932), iv. 750.
'Misunderstood Topical Masque Metaphor in Massinger, A', *R.E.S.* vi (1930), iv. 766.
'Mystery of *Macbeth*: A Solution, The', in *Shakespeare's Workshop* (1928), iv. 903, 905.
'New Facts from Sir Henry Herbert's Office Book', *T.L.S.* 29 November 1932. Revised in *Speeding Up Shakespeare* (1937), iii. 119; iv. 482, 839, 862, 893; v. 969, 986, 987; vi. 58, 97.
'New Light on the Elizabethan Theatre', *Fortnightly Review*, xcix, New Series (1916), vi. 139, 156 n. 1, 215.
'Origin of the Substantive Theatre Masque, The', *Pre-Restoration Stage Studies* (1927), iii. 459; iv. 907, 936; vii. 6.
Physical Conditions of the Elizabethan Public Playhouse (1927), vi. 224 n. 1.
Pre-Restoration Stage Studies (1927), iii. 126; iv. 907; v. 1050.
'Problem of Lyly's Songs, The', *T.L.S.* 20 December 1923, iii. 459, 461.
'Renegado, The', *T.L.S.* 24 October 1929, iv. 812.
Shakespeare's Workshop (1928), iv. 903.
Speeding up Shakespeare (1937), iii. 329; iv. 900, 902, 986, 987.
'Thomas Drew the Dramatist', *T.L.S.* 12 July 1923, iii. 440.
Those Nut-Cracking Elizabethans, (1935), iii. 313, 327, 387, 390.
[A review of Edwin Nungezer's *A Dictionary of Actors and of Other Persons Associated with the Public Representation of Plays in England before 1642*.] *M.L.R.* xxv (1930), iii. 192.
Laws of Candy, The, see Fletcher, John.
Lawson, Frances, iii. 39.

Lawson, James (of Nesham), iii. 39.
Lawyers, i. 3 n. 7, 266.
Lawyers as theatre patrons, i. 3 n. 7.
Layton, Mr., ii. 678.
Le Febure, *see* Le Fevre.
Le Fevure, M., *see* Le Fevre, M.
Le Fevre's riding academy, i. 235; ii. 437; vi. 45–47.
Le Grys (Le Greece), Sir Robert, iv. 719–20.
Nothing Impossible to Love, iv. 720.
Le Neve, John, *Fasti Ecclesiae Anglicanae* (1716), iii. 455.
Fasti Ecclesiae Anglicanae, Hardy ed. (1854), iv. 853; v. 1184.
Le Noyer, Charles, vii. 32.
Lea, Kathleen Marguerite, ed., Massinger's *The Parliament of Love*, Malone Society (1928), iii. 356, 358; iv. 805, 806, 807.
'Sir Aston Cokayne and the "Commedia dell' Arte" ', *M.L.R.* xxx iii (1928), iii. 166, 170.
Leach, A. F., v. 1067.
Leadenhall, *see* London, streets of.
Leake, Robert, i. 42; vi. 33.
Leake, William, iv. 515; v. 1114, 1115, 1163.
Leakes, Madame, i. 161 n. 2.
Leanerd, John, iii. 6.
The Country Innocence, or the Chambermaid Turned Quaker, iii. 6, 8.
Rambling Justice, or the Jealous Husbands, The, iv. 890.
Leap staff, tour with, ii. 682.
Lear, see Shakespeare, *King Lear*.
Lecavell, Richard, vii. 17, 22.
Lecherpiere, S., ii. 428.
Leconfield, Lord, iii. 113.
Lectures on cosmography, iv. 551, 553.
Lee, Honoria, iv. 921.
Lee, Sir Humphrey, iv. 716.
Lee, Margaret, iv. 716.
Lee, Mr., Esq., iv. 773.
Lee, Robert, i. 137 n. 3, 158, 165 n. 8, 167, 168 nn. 1, 2, and 3, 171 and n. b, 172 n. 1, 179 n. 2; ii. 496–7, 561, 682; iv. 733.
Lee, Sir Sidney, v. 980, 1246.
Lee, Sophia, *Almeyda: Queen of Granada*, v. 1087.
Lee, William, iv. 767.
Leech, Clifford, 'Francis Jaques, Author of *The Queene of Corsica*', *Durham University Journal*, xxxix, New Series viii

(1947), iv. 597, 598; v. 980, 981–2.

'Jordan's Interregnum Masques', *T.L.S.* 12 April 1934, iv. 682, 683.

ed., Mildmay Fane's *Candy Restored,* in *Materials for the Study of Old English Drama* (1938), iv. 959.

ed., Mildmay Fane's *Raguaillo D'Oceano, 1640, and Candy Restored, 1641. Materials for the Study of the Old English Drama* (1938), iii. 292, 293–4, 295, 297, 298, 299; v. 1419, 1420.

Legales convivales, see Jonson, Ben.

Legatt, John, iii. 304; iv. 629, 815; v. 972, 975, 1048.

Legge, Thomas, v. 1014.

Lehman, Ezra, ed., *The Tragedie of Chabot Admiral of France, Written by George Chapman and James Shirley* (1906), v. 1088, 1089.

Lehuc, Peter, property maker, iii. 139.

Leicester, i. 92, 156, 172, 173, 180, 193, 212, 213, 282, 298, 299, 322; ii. 423, 452, 484, 494, 530, 612, 618; iv. 717; vi. 124, 130.

Leicester, Countess of, iii. 213; v. 1268.

Leicester, Earl of, ii. 414, 661 n. 1; iv. 649.

Leicester, Wyggeston Hospital, iv. 953.

Leicestershire, iv. 617, 953.

Leicester-Warren, John, Esq., MS. of, iv. 505.

'Leigh, Jo.', verses by, iii. 278.

Leigh, Robert, *see* Lee, Robert.

Leinster, iii. 96.

Leipzig, battle of, v. 1199.

Leir, see Anonymous.

Leith, Scotland, v. 1045.

Lely, Peter, iv. 722, 994.

Leman, William, iv. 600.

Lennox, Duchess of, iv. 674.

Lennox, James Stuart, 2nd Duke of, i. 6, 48, 198; iv. 650, 674, 675, 721; vi. 34; vii. 34, 53, 107.

Lennox, Duke of, Steward of the Household, vi. 260.

Lenotius, King of Cyprus, see Manuche, Cosmo.

Lent, i. 5, 22, 186, 275, 276; ii. 654 n. 2; iv. 630; v. 1050, 1051, 1377; vi. 18, 59, 60, 159, 164, 165, 194, 212; vii. 1–9.

Dietary restrictions in, vii. 1 n. 1.

Sermon days in, vi. 45, 65.

Lenten dispensations, vi. 194, 248.

Fees for, vii. 3, 4, 5, 6, 8.

Lenten performances, vii. 1–9.

Fees for, vii. 3, 4, 5, 6.

Lenthall, Sir Edmond, vi. 49.

Lenton, Francis, *The Inns of Court Anagrammatist; or The Masquers Masqued in Anagrammes* (1634), v. 1162.

Young Gallant's Whirligig, The (1629), i. 225 n. 2; ii. 654 n. 2; vi. 8; vii. 2.

Leonhardt, Benno, 'Die Testvarianten von ... *Rule a Wife and Have a Wife'*, *Anglia,* xxiv (1910), iii. 407.

Leopard's Head, ii. 486; v. 1010.

Lepanto, Battle of, v. 1251, 1450.

Leppington, iv. 658.

Lesbiam, & Histrionem, In, see Randolph, Thomas.

Lesley, Robert, ii. 356.

Leslie, Shane, ii. 443.

L'Estrange, Roger, iii. 119, 404; iv. 685, 718–19; v. 1145.

Letters of John Chamberlain, see Chamberlain, John.

Letters and Speeches of Oliver Cromwell, ed. S. C. Lomas (1904), *see* Carlyle, Thomas.

Letters of Mart, v. 1314.

Letters patent, vi. 292.

Theft of, ii. 420.

Letters &c., see Suckling, Sir John.

Levenham Grammar School, v. 1027.

Lewellyn, Peter, iv. 702.

Lewes, Christopher, i. 162; ii. 366.

Lewin, John, *see* Lowin, John.

Lewis, Alice, v. 1133–4.

Lewis, C. S., 'A Note on *Comus*', *R.E.S.* viii (1932), iv. 914, 916.

Lewisham, manor and rectory of, vi. 86.

Lewkner, Mr., a fencer, vi. 221 n. 1.

Lewkner, Sir Lewis, iv. 643, 662; vi. 49.

Ley, William, his list of plays, iv. 500, 501–2, 589, 951; v. 1149, 1187, 1253, 1310, 1326, 1336, 1352, 1369, 1376, 1382, 1384, 1402, 1403, 1416, 1432.

Leyden, Holland, iv. 876.

Liber Eleccionum at St. Albans, v. 1067.

Liberties, *see* London, liberties of.

Libertine Tamed, The, see Hamilton, Newburgh, *The Doating Lovers.*

Licences, i. 5, 19, 49, 50, 181, 188,
    189, 271, 272, 273 and n. 5, 274,
    275, 302, 321; vi. 292–3, 299–
    300, 305.
    Forged, ii. 484–5, 486.
Licences for the press, see Plays
    allowed for the press.
Licenser for the press, iv. 718.
Lichfield Cathedral, iv. 526.
    Library, iii. 67; v. 1311.
Lichfield and Coventry, Bishop of,
    iv. 526.
Lichfield, Dick, v. 972.
Lichfield, Leonard, printer to
    University of Oxford, iii. 301, 402,
    406, 408, 411; v. 968, 969, 986;
    vi. 97.
Liége, v. 1172, 1173, 1174, 1175.
    Theologate at, v. 1172.
Lieutenants of the county of
    Middlesex, i. 163.
Life of Cimon, see Plutarch.
Life and death of Cartis Mundy the
    faire Nunne of Winchester, The,
    iii. 43, see also Brewer, Anthony,
    The Lovesick King.
Life and Death of Guy Warwick, The,
    see Dekker, Thomas.
Life and Death of Mahomet, the
    Conquest of Spaine together with
    the Rysing and Ruine of the
    Sarazen Empire. Written by Sr.
    Walter Raleigh Kt., The (1637),
    iv. 492.
Life and Death of Sir Martin Skink,
    see Brome, Richard.
Life and Death of Purser and
    Clinton, The, see Heywood,
    Thomas, A True Relation. . . .
Life and Death of Sir Thomas
    Gresham, The, see Heywood,
    Thomas.
Life and Letters of Sir Henry
    Wotton, see Smith, L. P.
Life of the Duchess of Suffolk, The,
    see Drue, The Duchess of Suffolk.
Life of Mother Shipton, The, see
    Thompson, Thomas.
Life of St. Augustine, see Anony-
    mous, England's First Happiness.
Life of a Satyricall Puppy called
    Nym (1657), see May, Thomas.
Ligges, see Jigs.
Light Heart, The, see Jonson's The
    New Inn.
Lightcliffe, Yorkshire, iii. 2.
Ligon, Richard, vi. 33.
    True and Exact History of the
    Island of Barbados (1657), vi. 33.

Like Father, like Son or The
    Mistaken Brothers, see Behn,
    Aphra.
Like to Like, see Anonymous.
Like Will to Like, see Fulwell,
    Ulpian.
Lillgrave, George, vi. 72, 73.
Lillie, George, i. 189, 192; ii. **497**.
Lillie, John, i. 188, 192; ii. 438,
    497–8.
Lilly, Mr., iv. 601.
Lilly, Mr. Peter, see Lely, Peter.
Lilly, William, ii. 398; v. 1351.
Lilly, William, an astrologer, vi.
    101 n. 1.
    History of His Life and Times
    From the Year 1602 to 1681
    (1715), vi. 102 n.
Lilypot Lane, see London, streets of.
Limiter, Charles (actor), iv. 596.
Lincoln, iv. 951; vii. 23.
    Bishop of, ii. 622; v. 1180.
    Cathedral, ii. 381.
Lincoln College, Oxford, iv. 587.
'Lincolnes Inne Masque', iii. 2.
Lincoln's Inn, i. 160; iii. 47, 275,
    292; iv. 716, 919, 956; v. 1038,
    1157, 1160; vi. 50, 88, 176.
    Benchers of, v. 1160; vi. 50.
Lincoln's Inn Field, see London,
    streets and districts of.
Lincoln's Inn Fields Theatre, iii. 71,
    115, 118, 154, 175, 179, 197, 225,
    314, 344; v. 971, 1114, 1127, 1149,
    1167; vi. 172.
Lindley Hall, Leicestershire, iii. 99.
Lindsey, Earl of, dedication to, iii.
    233.
Lindsey, Edwin S., 'The Music of
    the Songs in Fletcher's Plays',
    Stud. Phil. xxi (1924), iii. 305.
Lingua, see Tomkis, Thomas.
Linklater, Eric, Ben Jonson and
    King James: Biography and
    Portrait (1931), iv. 605.
Links, vi. 114.
Linthicum, M. Channing, Costume
    in the Drama of Shakespeare and
    his Contemporaries (1936), iv.
    772.
Lionello, Giovanni Battista, vi. 151.
Lirenda's Misery, see, Burkhead,
    Henry Cola's Fury.
Lisander and Calista, see Fletcher,
    The Lovers' Progress.
Lisbon, v. 1029.
Lisle, Lord, impersonated, iii. 95.
Lisle, Tobias, ii. 393, 545.
Lisle, Viscount, iv. 956.

Lisle, William, *The Fair Œthiopian*, v. 1439.
Lisle's Tennis Court, iii. 197.
Lismore Castle, Ireland, iii. 33.
Lismore Papers, Second Series, iv. 695, 703.
List of Masques and Pageants, A, see Greg, W. W.
Lister, J. T., 'A Comparison of Two Works of Cervantes with a Play by Massinger', *Hispania*, v (1922), iv. 783, 785.
Literary reputations, iii. 21–22, 245; see also under individual dramatists.
Lithuania, v. 1209.
Little Britain, see London, streets of.
Little French Lawyer, The, see Fletcher, John.
Little Lincolns Inn-fields, iii. 410.
Little Thief, The, see Fletcher, *The Night Walker*.
Littledale, H., and W. W. Greg, *The Welsh Embassador*, The Malone Society Reprints (1920), iii. 267.
Liverpool, i. 64.
  University Library of, iii. 405.
Livery allowances, i. 1, 3 n. 1, 7, 8, 16, 24, 53, 61, 72–73, 76–77, 80–81, 82–83, 90–91, 164–5, 171, 211, 223 and n. 6, 229, 247–8.
Lives of the Chief Justices of England, see Campbell, John.
Lives of Jupiter and Saturn, The, see Heywood, *The Golden Age*.
Livy, iii. 50, 304; iv. 764, 936, 1247.
Llewenny, Denbighshire, v. 1039.
Lloyd, Bertram, 'The Authorship of *The Welsh Embassador*', *R.E.S.* xxi (1945), iii. 267, 268.
  'Bloody Banquet, The', *T.L.S.* 29 April 1926, iii. 282.
  'Inedited MS. of Ford's *Fames Memoriall, An*', *R.E.S.* i (1925), iii. 434.
  ' "Juggling Captain" in "The Fair Maid of the Inn, The" ', *T.L.S.* 12 January 1928, iii. 336.
  'Minor Source of "The Changeling", A', *M.L.R.* xix (1924), iv. 862, 863.
  '*Noble Soldier* and *The Welsh Embassador, The*', *R.E.S.* iii (1927), iii. 257, 258, 259, 267, 268.
  'Unprinted Poem by John Ford (?), An', *R.E.S.* i (1925), iii. 434, 437.

Loathed Lover, The, see Eliot, S. A.
Lobb, Emmanuel, see Simons, Joseph.
Loch Lomond, iv. 621.
Locke, Matthew, v. 1103, 1104.
Locke, Thomas, iii. 415, 416.
Lockert, Charles Lacy, ed., *The Fatal Dowry. By Philip Massinger and Nathan Field* (1918), iii. 447, 783, 784, 785.
  'Scene in *The Fatal Dowry*, A', *M.L.N.* xxxv (1920), iv. 783, 785.
Lockier, Mr., Provost of Eton, v. 1176.
Lodge, Oliver, 'A Ben Jonson Puzzle', *T.L.S.* 13 September 1947, iv. 622, 624.
Lodge, Thomas, ii. 415; v. 1363.
  Looking Glass for London and England, A (with Greene), ii. 542, 543; vii. 25.
  Scillaes Metamorphosis (1589), ii. 415.
Lodge-keepers at Petersham, iii. 112.
Loffday, Thomas, see Loveday, Thomas.
Loiseau, Jean, *Abraham Cowley, sa vie, son oeuvre* (1931), iii. 172, 173, 180.
Loman, M., iv. 689.
Lomas, S. C., see Carlyle, Thomas, *Letters and Speeches of Oliver Cromwell*.
Lombard, iii. 193.
Lombardy, v. 1274.
LONDON, iii. 33, 35, 47, 248; iv. 496, 512, 575, 576, 617, 695, 733, 747, 757, 793, 801, 803, 824, 838, 840, 849, 857, 871, 872, 894, 896, 897, 898, 899, 911, 912, 916, 917, 918, 919, 925, 926, 927, 933, 943, 950; v. 978, 982, 1001, 1049, 1224, 1275; vi. 20, 86, 230, 231; see also Lord Mayor, Sheriff, Aldermen.
  Aldermen, vi. 78, 222, 228.
  Bishop of, iii. 306, 415, 417, 455.
    Censors play, i. 7.
    Complaints to, i. 32.
  Chamberlain, vi. 83.
  Chronicler of, iv. 832.
  Citizens of, vi. 27.
  City Chronologer, iv. 611, 857–8, 879, 956.
  City poets of, iv. 680.
  Common Council, i. 5.

LONDON (cont.)
Companies, Representative of, ii. 466.
Conduit Heads, the, iv. 880.
Corporation of, i. 5 n. 5; vi. 19.
County Council, vi. 6.
Dutch visitors in, iv. 569.
Fire of 1666, v. 1071.
Heywood in, iv. 554.
Institution, v. 1257.
Killigrew in, iv. 708.
Liberties of, vi. 17, 83.
Lovelace in, iv. 721.
Manuche imprisoned in, iv. 728.
Maps of, vi. 248.
Marshals of, v. 1160.
Mortality tables, ii. 667–72.
Old Exchange, iii. 469.
Place realism, iii. 88, 89.
Prince Charles's return to, iv. 662.
Recorder, vi. 78, 292.
Remembrancer, vi. 83.
Remembrancia, Tabula for, vi. 84.
Remembrancia of the City of London, Analytical Index to, v. 1156; vi. 77.
Sheriffs of, vi. 113, 176, 222.
Streets   and   districts   of:
   Aldermanbury, ii. 587, 641, 682, 695.
   Aldersgate Street, v. 1156.
   Aldgate, ii. 633; vi. 122.
   Asparagus Garden, iii. 88; v. 1363.
   Austen's Rents, Southwark, ii. 448.
   Bankside, i. 200 n. 3, 201; ii. 682, 683; iii. 307; iv. 582, 747; vi. 18, 50, 181, 182, 193, 200, 202, 205, 209, 213, 214, 216 n. 2, 219, 224 n. 1, 249, 252, 301.
   Barbican, ii. 384, 606, 682, 683.
      Nursery in, iv. 492.
   Bargehouse on the Bankside, ii. 520, 682.
   Beech Lane, ii. 652, 682.
   Benfield's Rents, Southwark, ii. 633.
   Birchen Lane, ii. 504.
   Bishopsgate, i. 140; ii. 593, 682; vi. 131.
   Bishopsgate Street, ii. 374.
   Bishopsgate Street Without, ii. 374.
   Blackboy Alley, ii. 467.
   Blackfriars, i. 5, 176; iii. 51; iv. 768; v. 1342; vi. 17, 20, 39, 78, 81, 84, 95 n. 1, 115; vii. 1, 49.
Blackfriars, citizens of, i. 34.
Blackfriars, Inhabitants of, i. 4, 5, 31–32, 64.
Blackfriars Gate, i. 33; vi. 29, 30, 41.
Blackwall, vi. 161.
Boar's Head Yard, vi. 122.
Bow Lane, ii. 455.
Bradshaw's Rents, Southwark, ii. 574.
Bread Street, vi. 248.
Bun Hill, iv. 880.
Cannon Street, vi. 214.
Carter Lane, i. 33; vi. 29.
Chancery Lane, ii. 682; v. 1057.
Charing Cross, ii. 546, 694; vi. 268.
Cheapside, iii. 219.
   High Cross, vii. 58.
Chelsea, iv. 957, 958.
Clare Market, iii. 22, 56, 71, 82; iv. 479, 580, 767, 812, 900.
Clerkenwell, ii. 526, 528, 571, 584, 624, 695; iv. 557; vi. 56, 215, 224 n. 1, 239; vii. 27.
Clerkenwell Close, ii. 561, 682.
Clerkenwell Hill, ii. 473, 682, 683.
Clink, Liberty of the, ii. 635.
Cockpit Alley, vi. 49.
Cockpit Court or Alley, vi. 49.
Compter, i. 267.
Conduit, ii. 688.
Covent Garden, i. 228; ii. 632; iii. 91; iv. 703, 716, 932, 933; vi. 53 n. 1; vii. 12.
   New buildings in, iii. 90.
   Piazzas, iv. 695, 703.
Cow Cross, ii. 384.
Cripplegate, i. 7; ii. 384; iv. 516.
Crown office in the Middle Temple, ii. 682.
Doctors' Commons, ii. 683.
Drury Lane, ii. 675; iv. 766, 768, 786, 797, 801, 812, 813, 863, 868, 893, 895, 930, 932, 935; vi. 45, 46, 49, 50, 54, 55, 72, 114, 219, 226, 231.
East Smithfield, ii. 551.
East Stepney, vi. 247.
Fetter Lane, iv. 476.
Finsbury, vi. 55.
Finsbury Fields, i. 161; vi. 131.
Fleet Conduit, i. 33; vi. 29, 99.
Fleet River, vi. 224 n. 1.
Fleet Street, i. 33, 240; ii. 455,

688; iv. 490, 850, 950; v. 1071; vi. 52, 78, 99, 104 n. 1, 115, 305, 306, 309.
Proposed new playhouse in, ii. 684; vi. 304–9.
Services in, v. 1259.
George Alley in Golding Lane, ii. 495, 521, 523, 598, 682, 683.
Globe Alley, ii. 467.
Golding Lane, i. 138, 143; ii. 384, 408, 448, 449, 452, 536, 564, 612, 682; vi. 18, 141, 148, 152, 153, 154, 155 and n. 1, 156 n., 157, 158, 164, 165, 172 n., 174, 175, 176, 177, 226, 231.
Gracechurch (Gracious) Street, vi. 121, 131.
Gray's Inn Lane, ii. 496, 635, 675; iv. 949.
Great Wild Street, vi. 49.
Grub Street, ii. 384; vi. 148.
Gunpowder Alley, iv. 476.
Haymarket, The, iv. 887.
Helmet Court in the Strand, ii. 640.
High Holborn, vi. 46.
Hog Lane, ii. 370.
Hogsden Fields, iv. 606.
Holborn, i. 314; v. 1403, 1442; vi. 140, 228.
Hollowell Lane, see Holywell Lane.
Holywell, ii. 651; vi. 137.
Holywell Lane, vi. 131, 138.
Hosier Lane, ii. 384, 625.
Houndsditch, ii. 523; vi. 259 n. 1.
Hounslow, ii. 461, 635.
Hyde Park, v. 1122, 1123; vii. 24.
Opening of, v, 1122.
Ivy Lane, ii. 578.
Kensington, ii. 695; vi. 237.
King's Head Yard, ii. 370.
Knight Rider Street, ii. 491, 682.
Lambeth, i. 38; ii. 683; vi. 26.
Langlies' Rents, Southwark, ii. 519.
Leadenhall, ii. 453.
Leadenhall Street, i. 201 n. 2; iv. 910.
Leicester Fields, v. 1104.
Lilypot Lane, ii. 365.
Lincoln's Inn Fields, i. 161, 201 n. 1, 228 n. 1; ii. 369, 620, 632; iv. 812, 863, 900, 921; vi. 55, 297, 299, 301.
Little Britain, iii. 545.

London Bridge, ii. 682; iv. 476; vi. 214.
Long Lane, i. 228, 294; vi. 101.
Lothbury, iv. 694.
Ludgate, i. 4, 33, 64; vi. 18, 24, 29.
Ludgate Hill, vi. 121.
Ludgate Prison, ii. 470; iv. 541, 542; vi. 29.
Maid Lane, vi. 180, 183, 186, 200, 248.
Maiden Lane, ii. 500, 612.
Marshalsea, i. 294, 324, 333; ii. 401, 582, 682; vii. 9.
Moorgate, i. 266, 267; iii. 251; v. 1347; vi. 162.
Moor Lane, ii. 484.
New Exchange, iv. 523.
Newgate, i. 33; iii. 270; v. 1152.
Norman's Rents, Southwark, ii. 574.
Oare's Rents, Southwark, ii. 490.
Old Bailey, ii. 682.
Old Jewry, iv. 856.
Palmer's Rents, Southwark, ii. 448.
Paris Garden, i. 63; ii. 501; iii. 205; vi. 122, 211, 213, 250; vii. 47.
Paul's Churchyard, at the sign of the Greyhound, iii. 402.
Paul's Cross, vii. 47.
Perpoole Lane, ii. 635.
Peterhouse, iv. 722.
Pitt Place, vi. 49.
Playhouse Yard, vi. 178.
Poultry, i. 267.
Princes' Street, vi. 49.
Printing House Square, vi. 5.
Puddle Wharf, vi. 78, 81, 82, 83, 84, 86, 115.
Queen's Street, i. 228 n. 1.
Red Cross Street, ii. 456, 682; vi. 159.
Red Lion Alley, ii. 561.
St. Andrew Undershaft, parish of, vi. 148.
St. Anne's, Blackfriars, parish of, vi. 17.
Parish clerk, vi. 18 n. 1.
St. Bride's Lane, ii. 492, 683.
St. Bride's parish, v. 1342; vi. 39, 87, 91, 305, 306, 307.
St. Dunstan's Church-yard, iv. 490.
St. George's Fields, vii. 58.
St. Giles in the Fields, parish of, vi. 49, 76.

LONDON (cont.)
Streets and districts of (cont.)
St. Giles without Cripplegate,
parish of, vi. 141, 142, 162,
243.
Registers of the parish, vi.
159.
St. James, Clerkenwell, parish
of, vi. 216.
St. James's Park, iii. 112; vi.
268, 270 n. 1.
Keepers of, iii. 112.
St. John's Street, i. 309, 310;
ii. 384, 401, 527, 571, 637,
682, 693; vi. 215, 216, 224
n. 1, 226, 227, 229, 232, 234,
239, 240.
St. Leonard's, Shoreditch,
parish of, vi. 131, 137.
St. Martin's, Ludgate, parish
of, v. 1342; vi. 39.
St. Mary Matfellon, parish of,
vi. 122.
St. Paul's Churchyard, i. 33;
iv. 767, 962, 1036; v. 1255;
vi. 29.
St. Saviour's parish, iv. 554,
555.
Salisbury Court, vi. 87, 88, 89.
Salisbury Square, vi. 89 n. 1.
Shadwell in Stepney, i. 265.
Shoe Lane, ii. 635.
Shoreditch, i. 161 n. 2, 164; ii.
552, 682, 683; vi. 131, 134,
135, 137, 138; vii. 35.
Smithfield, i. 142; iv. 738; vi. 41.
Soare's Rents, Southwark, ii.
519.
South Kensington, iii. 401.
Southwark, i. 1; ii. 633; iv. 753,
757; vi. 208, 209 n. 1, 210,
214.
Bailey of, v. 1058.
Spittle, ii. 593, 682; iv. 681, 682.
Spittlegate, ii. 558.
Spring Garden, v. 1363.
Springs, The, iv. 880.
Stepney, parish of, vi. 247.
Strand, ii. 564, 639, 640; v.
1157; vi. 46, 140, 307 and n. 1.
Temple Bar, vii. 54.
Thames Street, ii. 626.
Three Herring Court, ii. 571.
Toothill Street, ii. 683.
Tower of London, iii. 451, 452;
iv. 549, 655, 944; v. 1090,
1152, 1161, 1200, 1288,
1300.
Prisoners in, iii. 196, 293.

Tower Hill, i. 276.
Turnball Street, vi. 50, 240.
Turnstile Alley, ii. 405.
Tuttle Street, Westminster, ii.
546.
Wapping, i. 161, 265; vi. 54, 55.
Wardrobe, iv. 650.
Water Lane, vi. 88, 89 n. 1,
115.
West Smithfield, vi. 240.
Western suburbs, vi. 139.
Westminster, i. 27, 244; ii. 546,
550, 658; iv. 525, 526, 612,
896, 897, 898, 899, 925; v.
1269, 1280, 1328, 1391; vi.
15, 33, 170, 213, 224 n. 1,
230, 232, 306.
Whitechapel, ii. 621; iii. 238,
254; vi. 124.
Whitechapel Street, vi. 122.
Whitecross street, i. 138, 143;
ii. 384, 452, 484, 536, 577,
580, 600, 635, 682, 683,
693; vi. 141, 148, 154,
156 n., 160, 161, 177, 178.
Liberty of, ii. 635.
Whitefriars, iii. 374, 385, 408,
419; iv. 484, 767; v. 1070;
vi. 76, 94, 95 n. 1, 115, 116,
117.
Liberty of, vi. 17.
Precinct of, vi. 78, 116.
Wood Street, ii. 467.
Woodstreet Compter, iv. 688.
Town Clerk of, v. 1038.
Views of, vi. 248.
Whitechapel, pastor of, vi. 222.
Witches brought to, iii. 74.
London and the Country Carbon-
adoed, see Lupton.
London and the Outbreak of the
Puritan Revolution (1961), see
Pearl, Valerie.
London Chanticleers, The, see
Anonymous.
London Florentine, The, see Hey-
wood, Thomas.
London Frolics in 1638, see Planche,
The Merchant's Wedding.
London in Its Splendour, see Jordan,
Thomas.
London in Luster, see Jordan,
Thomas.
London like Nineva in Sack-cloth,
see Brewer, Thomas.
London Merchant, The, see Ford,
John.
London Prodigal, The, see Jonson,
Ben.

London Triumphant: or the City in Jollity and Splendour, see Jordan, Thomas.

London's Fountain of Arts and Sciences, see Heywood's *Londini Artium et Scientiarum Scaturigo.*

London's Glory, or The Lord Mayor's Show, see Jordan, Thomas.

London's Glory, Represented by Time, Truth, and Fame, see Tatham, John.

London's Harbour of Health and Happiness, see Heywood's *Londini Sinus Salutis.*

London's Joy, or The Lord Mayor's Show, see Jordan, Thomas.

London's Jus Honorarium, see Heywood, Thomas.

London's Lamentable Estate, see Massinger, Philip.

London's Lamentation (1625), *see* C., W.

London's Mercatura, see Heywood's *Londini Emporia.*

London's Mirror, see Heywood's *Londini Speculum.*

'London's New Mermaid Theatre at Puddle Dock', *see* Wagner, Bernard.

London's Peaceable Estate, see Heywood's *Londini Status Pacatus.*

London's Resurrection to Joy and Triumph, see Jordan, Thomas.

London's Royal Triumph for the City's Loyal Magistrate, see Jordan, Thomas.

London's Tempe, see Dekker, Thomas.

London's Triumph for John Fredrick see Tatham, John.

London's Triumphs for John Lawrence, see Tatham, John.

London's Triumph for John Robinson, see Tatham, John.

London's Triumph for Richard Chiverton, see Tatham, John.

London's Triumph for Thomas Allen, see Tatham, John.

London's Triumph, Presented by Industry and Honour, see Tatham, John.

London's Triumph: Illustrated . . ., see Jordan, Thomas.

London's Triumphs: Expressed . . ., see Jordan, Thomas.

London, William, *Catalogue of the Most Vendible Books in England,* v. 1351.

Londonderry, Bishop of, v. 1259.

'Londoner Theater und Schauspiele im Jahre 1599', *see* Binz, Gustav.

Londini Artium et Scientiarum Scaturigo, see Heywood, Thomas.

Londini Emporia, see Heywood, Thomas.

Londini Sinus Salutis, see Heywood, Thomas.

Londini Speculum, see Heywood, Thomas.

Londini Status Pacatus, see Heywood, Thomas.

Londinium Triumphans, see Tatham John.

Long, George, i. 265–6.

Long, Tom, iv. 714.

Long, Mrs., v. 1115.

Long Lane, *see* London, streets of.

Long Meg of Westminster, see Anonymous.

Long Parliament, iii. 294; iv. 526, 695, 846; v. 1084, 1199.

Long View of London (1647) (map), *see* Hollar, Wenceslaus.

Longe, Alice, ii. 392.

Longe, Christopher, i. 162; ii. 366.

Longe, Nicholas, i. 165 n. 8, 176; ii. 498.

Longford, Derbyshire, v. 1196.

Look About You, see Anonymous.

Look to the Lady, see Shirley, James.

Look on Me and Love Me, see Anonymous.

Looking Glass, the Bachelor, or the Hawk, The, see Anonymous, *Mull Sack.*

Looking Glass for London and England, A, see Lodge, Thomas, and Robert Greene.

Loosemore, Mr., and his boy, iv. 601.

Lope de Vega, *Don Lope de Cardona,* v. 1169.

El Peregrino en su Patria, iii. 392–3.

Lord Admiral's company, i. 135–6; iii. 56; iv. 554, 608, 794, 935, 936; vi. 123, 139, 145 and n. 2, 149.

Lord Chamberlain, i. 6, 8, 22, 28 n. 1, 34 and n. 3, 35, 36, 41, 42, 43, 45, 46, 48, 53, 54, 55, 63, 65, 160, 166, 167, 178, 194, 195, 209, 236, 260, 283 n. 2, 324 n. 1, 328, 333, 334; ii. 467, 542, 657 n. 2 cont., 661 n. 1; iii. 106, 111, 119, 120, 136, 138, 139, 309, 380, 408, 409, 425; iv. 524, 635, 655, 691, 752, 756, 831; v. 1062, 1098, 1099, 1105, 1108, 1114, 1122, 1124, 1126, 1129,

Lord Chamberlain (*cont.*)
    1133, 1135, 1145, 1150, 1157,
    1158, 1163, 1166, 1169, 1207,
    1209, 1210, 1232, 1233, 1246,
    1270, 1272, 1286, 1287, 1344,
    1444, 1447, 1455; vi. 12, 21, 22,
    34, 35, 36, 37, 46, 51–52, 69, 73,
    74, 75, 84, 100, 101, 105, 106,
    135, 181, 257, 259, 260, 264,
    265, 279, 280, 281 n. 1, 282 n. 1,
    304; vii. 4, 13.
Box of, iv. 675.
Censors play, iv. 632.
Company of, i. 1, 121; iii. 242; iv.
    607, 608; v. 1049; vi. 48, 123,
    132, 139.
Forbids printing, v. 1082.
His list of King's company plays,
    i. 65–66; v. 1273, 1293, 1296,
    1311, 1312.
His list of King and Queen's
    Young company's plays, i.
    330–1; v. 1335, 1340.
Over rules the Master of the
    Revels, iii. 119.
Petition to, iii. 75.
Play given by, iii. 216.
Protects repertory, i. 65–66, 330–1.
Warrant Books, i. 188, 190, 260
    n. 2, 271, 273, 278, 302, 310;
    ii. 384, 399, 421, 422, 463, 469;
    iii. 107, 135, 139, 199, 207, 213,
    217; iv. 522, 637, 652, 918; v.
    1230, 1232, 1370; vi. 68, 162,
    168, 279.
Warrants of, v. 1399; vi. 285.
Lord Chamberlain to the Queen, i.
    223, 236 n. 8 cont., 239, 304
    n. 2; ii. 424, 661 n. 1; vi. 103.
Lord Chancellor, v. 1376, 1377,
    1407; vii. 4.
Lord Chancellor's Chamber, vi. 258;
    vii. 28.
Lord Haddington's Masque, see
    Jonson, Ben.
Lord Hay's Masque, see Jonson,
    Lovers Made Men.
Lord Keeper, i. 16 n. 6, 201 n. 1,
    327; iv. 528; v. 1154, 1288; vi.
    4, 300, 301, 304, 307, 308, 309.
Chaplain to, iv. 525.
Secretary to, v. 1196, 1237.
Lord Mayor, i. 161, 162 n. 3; iii.
    104, 244, 256, 261, 468; iv.
    575–8, 584, 880, 882, 896, 897,
    898, 899, 925, 926; v. 1040,
    1156, 1158, 1159, 1269; vi. 18,
    29, 39, 54, 77, 78, 80, 81, 82, 83,
    84, 113, 114, 123, 175, 176,

    222, 230, 292; vii. 24, 36, 70,
    74.
Celebration, vii. 122.
Pageants, iii. 244, 248, 256, 261;
    iv. 557, 575–8, 584, 680, 683,
    684, 687, 895–9, 925–6; v. 1097,
    1153, 1185, 1216, 1218, 1220,
    1221, 1223, 1225, 1241, 1254,
    1426; vi. 296.
Pageants described, iv. 897.
Pageants, expenditures for, iii.
    256, 261; iv. 896–8, 926; v. 1255.
Pageants rejected, iv. 926.
Show, see Jordan, Thomas.
Lord Mendall, The, see Anonymous,
    The Peaceable King.
Lord of Arundle tavern, i. 142.
Lord Privy Seal, i. 46, 327.
Lord Protector, vi. 284 n. 1.
Lord Treasurer, i. 327; iv. 916.
    Servant of, vi. 291 n. 1.
Lord's room, see Theatres.
Lorkin, Thomas, ii. 436; vi. 179 n. 1.
Lorraine, v. 1006.
Lorraine, Duke of, iii. 321.
Lorte, Roger, iii. 198.
Lost Lady, The, see Berkeley, William.
Lost Recovered, The, see Heywood,
    The Captives.
Lott, Francis, ii. 389.
Louis the Eleventh, King of France,
    see Anonymous.
Louis XIII, iv. 548.
Love in Arms, see Killigrew, Thomas,
    Cicilia and Clorinda.
Love and Honour, see Davenant,
    William.
Love-and-honour plays, iii. 62–63,
    66, 78; iv. 468, 563.
Love and Liberty, a Tragi-Comedy,
    see Massinger, *The Bondman.*
Love at First Sight, see Killigrew,
    Thomas, *The Princess.*
Love Crowns the End, see Tatham,
    John.
*Love Freed from Ignorance and
    Folly,* see Jonson, Ben.
Love Hath Found His Eyes, see
    Jordan, Thomas.
Love in Disguise, see Dekker, *The
    Disguises.*
Love in a Maze, see Shirley, James,
    The Changes.
Love in Its Ecstasy, see Peaps,
    William.
Love in Its Infancy, see Flecknoe,
    Richard.
Love in the Dark, see Fane, Sir
    Francis.

Love Lies a Bleeding, see Beaumont and Fletcher, *Philaster.*

Love Lost in the Dark, see Anonymous.

Love in a Lunacy, see Anonymous, *The White Witch of Westminster.*

Love Restored, see Jonson, Ben.

Love of Shadows, The, see Killigrew, Thomas, *Bellamira Her Dream.*

Love Tricks, see Shirley, James, *The School of Compliment.*

Love will Find out the Way, see Shirley, James, *The Constant Maid.*

Love Yields to Honour, see Anonymous.

Love, Mr., iv. 553.

Loveday, Thomas, i. 286, 297; ii. **398;** iv. 686.

Lovelace, Richard, iii. 328, 347, 359, 376; iv. 476, 720–4; v. 1186.
  Lucasta (1649), iv. 722, 723; v. 995.
  Scholars, The, iv. 720–1, 722–4.
  Verses, iii. 421, 427.

Lovelace, Captain Richard, iv. 476.

Lovelace, Col. Richard, v. 994.

Lovell, Thomas, i. 286, 297; ii. **498;** iv. 686.

'Lovely Northern Lass, The', (ballad), *see* Anonymous.

Lover's Holiday, The, see Anonymous.

Lovers' Hospital, see Wilde, George, *Love's Hospital.*

Lovers of Ludgate, The, see Anonymous.

Lovers Made Men, see Ben Jonson.

Lover's Melancholy, The, see Ford, John.

Lovers' Progress, The, see Fletcher, John.

Love's Aftergame, see Anonymous, *The Proxy.*

Loves and Adventures of Clerico and Lozia, The (1652), *see* Kirkman, Francis.

Love's Changelings' Change, see Anonymous.

Love's Convert, see Cartwright, William, *The Siege.*

Love's Cruelty, see Shirley, James.

Love's Cure, or the Martial Maid, see Fletcher, John.

Love's Dominion (1654), *see* Flecknoe, Richard.

Love's Graduate, see Webster, John, *A Cure for a Cuckold.*

Love's Hospital, see Wilde, George.

Love's Infancy, see Anonymous.

Love's Kingdom, see Flecknoe, Richard.

Love's Labour's Lost, see Shakespeare.

Love's Loadstone, see Anonymous, *Pathomachia.*

Love's Masterpiece, see Heywood, Thomas.

'Love's Metamorphosis or Apollo and Daphne', *see* Sampson, William.

Love's Mistress, see Heywood, Thomas.

Love's Pilgrimage, The, see Fletcher, John.

Love's Riddle, see Cowley, Abraham.

Love's Sacrifice, see Ford, John.

'Love's Solace, or Sweet is the Lass that Loves Me' (ballad), *see* Anonymous.

Love's Trial, see Glapthorne, *The Hollander.*

Love's Triumph through Callipolis, see Jonson.

Love's Victory, see Anonymous.

Love's Victory, see Chamberlaine, William.

Love's Victory, see Shirley, James, *Doubtful Heir.*

Love's Welcome at Bolsover, see Jonson, Ben.

Love's Welcome at Welbeck, see Jonson's *The King's Entertainment at Welbeck.*

Lovesick King, The, see Brewer, Anthony.

Lovesick Maid, The, see Brome, Richard.

Lovett, George, v. 1255.

Low Countries, vii. 54.
  Jonson's service in, iv. 606.
  Military service in, iii. 242; iv. 736.
  Sir William Lower in, iv. 725.
  Wars, iii. 467.

Lowe, George, i. 10 n. 1; iv. 871.

Lowe, Nicholas, ii. 498–9; iv. 686.

Lowen, G., i. 72–88; ii. 499; iii. 416.

Lowen *or* Lowens, John, *see* Lowin, John.

Lowen, John, clerk, ii. 504.

Lower, Elizabeth, iv. 726.

Lower, Dr. Richard, iv. 725.

Lower, Thomas, iv. 725, 727.

Lower, Sir William, iv. 725–7.
  Amorous Phantasm, The, iv. 726.
  Don Japhet of Armenia, iv. 726.
  Enchanted Lovers, iii. 227; iv. 726.

Lower, Sir William (*cont.*)
Horatius (transl. from Pierre Corneille), iv. 726.
Transl., *The Innocent Lady, or Illustrious Innocence* (1654), (from René de Ceriziers), iv. 726.
Transl. *The Innocent Lord, or The Divine Providence*, 1655 (from René de Ceriziers), iv. 726.
Noble Ingratitude, The (transl. from Philippe Quinault), iv. 726.
Transl. *Paraphrases on the Apostolical Epistles* (from Anthony Godeau), iv. 726.
Phoenix in Her Flames, The, iv. 727; vii. 119.
Transl. *Pleasures of the Ladies, The*, iv. 726.
Polyeuctes, or The Martyr, iv. 727.
Transl. *A Relation in Form of a Journal of the Voyage and Residence [of]* . . . *Charles II*, 1660, iv. 726.
Three Dorothies, or Jodolet Boxed, The (transl. from Paul Scarron), iv. 727.
Transl. *The Triumphant Lady, or The Crowned Innocence*, 1656 (from René de Ceriziers), iv. 726.
Lowin, Elizabeth, ii. 499.
Lowin, Joane, ii. 499, 504.
Lowin, John, i. 4 nn. 1 and 2, 5, 14, 17, 26 n. 5, 34, 35 n. 1, 37, 44, 53, 54, 55, 57, 60, 61, 69 n. 2, 72–88, 90, 97 nn. i, n, and p, 99 nn. u, x, z, and aa, 100 n. bb, 121, 125, 318, 328; ii. 499–506, 647, 651, 666, 683; iii. 212, 301, 311, 326, 330, 341, 346, 349, 352, 355, 363, 372, 375, 379, 393, 396, 399, 413, 420, 424, 426, 427, 428; iv. 519, 764, 781, 794, 810, 817; v. 1016, 1238, 1412; vi. 25, 26, 31, 32, 36, 69, 172, 194 and n. 4, 237; vii. 6.
Lowin, Katherine, ii. 501.
Lowin, Richard, ii. 499.
Lowine *or* Lowing, John, *see* Lowin, John.
Lowndes, W. T., *The Bibliographer's Manual of English Literature*, ed. Henry G. Bohn (1869), iii. 381; iv. 921; v. 1391.
Lownes, Mr., iv. 589.
Lowther, Richard, ii. 455.
Lowyn, John, *see* Lowin, John.
Loyal Lovers, The, see Manuche, Cosmo.

Loyal Subject, The, see Fletcher, John.
Loyola, *see* Hacket, John.
Lucan, iv. 831, 833, 834; v. 1158, 1381.
Pharsalia, iii. 342; iv. 831, 833, 839.
Lucas, F. L., v. 1246.
ed., *The Complete Works of John Webster*, 4 vols. (1927), iii. 336, 337, 338, 356, 358; iv. 805, 807, 859, 860; v. 1240, 1241, 1244, 1245, 1246, 1247, 1248, 1250, 1251, 1252, 1253, 1254.
'Did Dr. Forman Commit Suicide?', *T.L.S.* 7 April 1927, iii. 337.
Euripides and His Influence (1923), iv. 507.
'Unexplained Allusion in Webster and Rowley, An', *T.L.S.* 15 April 1926, v. 1249.
Lucas, Knightly, vi. 72.
Lucas, Margaret, iii. 144.
Lucasta, see Lovelace, *The Scholars*.
Luchetti, Eusebio, *Le due Sorelle Rivali*, v. 1233.
Lucian, iv. 558, 844.
Translations of, iv. 565.
Icaro-Menippus, iv. 665.
Vera Historia, iv. 665.
Lucianus Samosatensis, iv. 584.
Lucinia's Rape, see Rochester, Earl of.
Lucius Cary, Second Viscount Falkland, see Weber, Kurt.
Lucky Chance, see Behn, Aphra.
Lucy, Sir Thomas, ii. 484, 618; iv. 917.
Lucye, Mr., iii. 186.
Ludgate, *see* London, streets and districts of.
Ludlow, Shropshire, i. 172, 271, 282; ii. 432.
Ludlow Castle, iii. 110; iv. 914, 915.
Luminalia, see Davenant, William.
Lumley, E. P., *The Influence of Plautus on the Comedies of Ben Jonson* (1901), iv. 605.
Lumley, Martin, iv. 898, 926.
Lupton, D., *London and the Country Carbonadoed* (1632), i. 146 n. 6 cont.
Lusiuncula, see Anonymous.
Lutanist, ii. 554, 621.
Lute, v. 1002.
Lute, bass, ii. 554.
Luther, Martin, ii. 538; vi. 96.

Lutterworth, Leicestershire, iv. 953.

Lützen, iii. 250.

Lydall, Mrs., i. 121.

Lyfe and Actis of W. Wallace, The, see Henry the minstrel.

Lyly, George, *see* Lillie, George.

Lyly, John, *see also* Lillie, John.
  Alexander and Campaspe, iii. 461; vii. 66.
  Endymion, vii. 66.
  Galathea, vii. 66.
  Midas, vii. 66.
  Mother Bombie, vii. 66.
  Sappho and Phao, vii. 66.
  Six Court Comedies, vii. 75.

Lyme Regis, Dorset, i. 193.

Lynch, Kathleen M., *The Social Mode of Restoration Comedy*, University of Michigan Publications, Language and Literature, vol. iii (1926), v. 1198, 1207, 1210, 1212.
  Review of Byron Gates, *The Dramatic Works and Translations of Sir William Lower*, *M.L.N.* xlix (1934), iv. 727.

Lynching, vi. 161.

Lyng, Norfolk, iv. 715.

Lynge, Nicholas, v. 1385.

Lynn, G., v. 1220.

Lynsey, John (a butcher), vi. 148.

Lysander and Calista, see Fletcher, *The Lovers' Progress*.

Lyson, Daniel, *An Historical Account of Those Parishes in the County of Middlesex Which Are Not Described in the Environs of London* (1800), iii. 20–21; iv. 690.

M., D. L., 'The Witch of Edmonton', *The Nation and Athenaeum*, xxix (1921), 178–80, iii. 270.

M., E., *Wit and Drollery* (1661), v. 1244.

M., J., iv. 544; v. 1446.

M., Sir J. and Ja: S., *Musarum Deliciae* (1655), iv. 757; v. 1199.

M., R., *Micrologia* (1629), iii. 460.

Mabbe, James, iv. 727–8.
  Transl. *The Spanish Bawd . . . or, The Tragicke-Comedy of Calisto and Melibea* (from Fernando de Rojas), iv. 727; vii. 73.

Macaulay, G. C., 'Beaumont and Fletcher', Chapter V, *Cambridge History of English Literature*, vi (1932), iii. 350, 366, 390, 393, 400.

'The Date of "The Chances,"' *M.L.R.* v (1910), 112–13, iii. 319, 321, 322.

Macbeth, see Shakespeare.

McCabe, John, 'A Study of the Blackfriars Theatre, 1608–42'. Unpublished thesis, Shakespeare Institute, Stratford-upon-Avon (1954), vi. 3.

McCabe, William H., 'Fatum Vortigerni', *T.L.S.* 15 August 1935, iii. 125.
  'Notes on the St. Omers College Theatre', *Philological Quarterly*, xvii (1938), iii. 160; iv. 947; v. 1172, 1173, 1174, 1175, 1283, 1285, 1290, 1292, 1297, 1337, 1339, 1344, 1346–7, 1375, 1383, 1385, 1392, 1405, 1406, 1424, 1450.
  'Play-List of the English College of St. Omers, 1592–1762, The', *Revue de Littérature Comparée*, xvii (1937), iii. 160; iv. 947: v. 1172, 1173, 1174, 1175, 1283, 1285, 1290, 1292, 1297, 1337, 1338, 1339, 1344, 1346–7, 1349, 1375, 1376, 1383, 1385, 1392, 1405, 1406, 1424, 1450.

McClure, John Egbert, editor, see Chamberlain, John.

McEuen, Kathryn Anderson, *Classical Influence upon the Tribe of Ben* (1939), iv. 605.

McGinn, Donald Joseph, *Shakespeare's Influence on the Drama of His Age* (1938), iv. 543, 546; v. 1201.

Macham, Margery, iv. 679.

Machiavelli and the Devil, see Daborne, Robert.

Machiavelli, Niccolo, *Belfagor*, iv. 617.
  Florentine Historie, The . . . translated into English by T. B., Esquire (1595), iv. 905.
  Prince, iii. 406.

Machin, Lewis, iv. 734.
  Dumb Knight, The, iii. 458.

Machinery, iv. 643.

Machines, v. 1228.

McIlwraith, A. K., iv. 758.
  'Allusion in Massinger, An', *R.E.S.* vi (1930), iv. 766.
  'Did Massinger Revise *The Emperour of the East ?*' *R.E.S.* v (1929), iv. 778, 779.

McIlwraith, A. K. (*cont.*)
'Further Patron of "The City-Madam," A', *Bodleian Quarterly Record*, viii (1935), iv. 771, 773.
'Marginalia on Press-corrections in Books of the Early Seventeenth Century', *Library*, 5th Series, iv (1950), iv. 766.
'On the Date of "A New Way to Pay Old Debts"', *M.L.R.* xxviii (1933), iv. 801, 802.
'Patrons of "The City-Madam"', *Bodleian Quarterly Record*, v (1928), iv. 771.
'Pen-and-Ink Corrections in Books of the Seventeenth Century', *R.E.S.*, vii (1931), iv. 771.
'Printer's Copy for *The City-Madam*, The', *M.L.N.* i (1935), iv. 771.
'Some Bibliographical Notes on Massinger', *Library*, Fourth Series, xi (1930), iii. 263, 264; iv. 750, 770, 775, 777, 797, 809.
'"The Virgins Character," A New Poem by Philip Massinger' *R.E.S.* iv (1928), 64–68; iv. 750, 770, 777.
Rev. of Telfer's ed. of Massinger's *The Unnatural Combat*, *R.E.S.* ix (1933), iv. 824.
McKeithan, D. M., *The Debt to Shakespeare in the Beaumont-and-Fletcher Plays* (1938), iii. 305, 351, 354.
'Shakespearian Echoes in the Florimel Plot of Fletcher and Rowley's *The Maid in the Mill*', *P.Q.* xvii (1938), iii. 377, 379.
McKerrow, R. B., ed., 'The Spanish Curate', in Variorum Edition of B. and F.'s *Works*, iii. 417, 420, 421.
Macklin, Charles, iii. 450.
Macklin, Mrs., iii. 450.
Maclean, John, ed., *Letters from George Lord Carew to Sir Thomas Roe . . . 1615–17*, Camden Society Publications (1860), iv. 650.
McManaway, James G., 'Latin Title-Page Mottoes as a Clue to Dramatic Authorship', *Library*, Fourth Series, xxvi (1945), iii. 229, 282, 283, 284; v. 1318, 1319, 1320.
'MS. of Davenport's "Policy without Piety"; John Withorn:

Sir John Kaye', *N. & Q.* clxx (1936), 295, iii. 226, 228.
'Philip Massinger and the Restoration Drama', *E.L.H.* i (1934) 276–304, iv. 750, 762, 766, 771, 774, 789, 801, 803, 812, 814, 828.
McManaway, James G., Giles E. Dawson, and Edwin E. Willoughby, eds., *Joseph Quincy Adams Memorial Studies* (1948), iii. 68.
MacMullan, Hugh, 'The Sources of Shirley's St. Patrick for Ireland', *P.M.L.A.* xlviii (1933), 806–14, v. 1143, 1144.
Macray, W. D., *A Register of the Members of St. Mary Magdalen College, Oxford*, 7 vols. (1894–1911), iii. 26, 27, 28.
Mad Couple, The, see Howard, James, *All Mistaken or The Mad Couple*.
Mad Couple Well Matched, A, see Brome, Richard.
Mad Couple Well Met, A, see Brome, Richard, *A Mad Couple Well Matched*.
Mad Lover, The, see Fletcher, John.
Mad Tom, vi. 209.
Mad World, My Masters, A, see Middleton, Thomas.
Madagascar; With Other Poems, see Davenant, Sir William.
Madan, Falconer. *The Early Oxford Press. A Bibliography of Printing and Publishing at Oxford '1468'–1640* (1895), v. 1179.
Summary Catalogue of Western Manuscripts in the Bodleian Library, 7 vols. (1895–1953), iii. 20; iv. 921; v. 1297, 1349, 1374, 1406, 1409.
Madcap, The, see Barnes, —.
Madcap, The, see Heminges, William, *The Coursing of A Hare*.
Maddox, Ronald, ii. 455.
Mad-house scenes, iii. 393.
Madrid, iv. 872, 873, 895; vi. 184.
Killigrew in, iv. 708.
Scene of play, iv. 710.
Maeterlinck, Maurice, transl.: *Annabella* ('*Tis pity she's a whore*). *Drame en cinq actes de John Ford, Traduit et adapté pour le Théâtre de l'Œuvre par Maurice Maeterlinck* (1895), iii. 462.
Magdalen College, Oxford, iii. 25, 304; iv. 514, 550, 551, 552, 591, 592, 595, 711, 727; v. 1256, 1349.

Fellows of, v. 1038, 1256; vi. 135.
President of, iv. 551, 552; v. 1256.
Magdalen Hall, Oxford, iii. 28, 303; v. 1256.
Magdalen School, iii. 25, 26, 27, 28; iv. 552.
Master of, v. 1256.
Maggs catalogue, v. 1322, 1395.
Magicians, vii. 65.
Magico Prodigioso, see Calderon de la Barca.
Magnetic Lady, The, see Jonson.
Mago, William, i. 15, 73–89, 251; ii. 506; iv. 764, 765.
Magoun, F. P., Jr., 'Hermus vs. Hormuz', *P.M.L.A.* xlii (1927), v. 977.
Mahomet-Irene story, the, iv. 506.
Maid, ii. 349, 353, 634.
Maid of Honour, The, see Massinger, Philip.
Maid in the Mill, The, see Fletcher, John.
Maid's Metamorphosis, see Anonymous.
Maid's Revenge, The, see Shirley, James.
Maid's Tragedy, The, see Beaumont and Fletcher.
Maiden Lane, *see* London, streets of.
Maidenhead, sign of the, iii. 251.
Maidenhead Well Lost, A, see Heywood, Thomas.
Maidment, James, ed., R. N., *Sir Thomas Overburies Vision*, Hunterian Club, No. 17 (1873), iv. 902.
Maidment, James, and W. H. Logan, eds., *Dramatic Works of John Tatham* (1879), v. 1218, 1219.
eds., *Dramatic Works of Sir William D'Avenant with Prefatory Memoir and Notes, The*, 5 vols. (1872–4), iii. 197.
eds., *The Dramatic Works of Sir Aston Cokain* (1874), iii. 168.
eds., *The Dramatic Works of Shackerley Marmion* (1875), iv. 738, 747.
Maids of Honor, iii. 320, 395.
Theatre-box for, iii. 403.
Maids of Honour, dance in masque, iii. 216–17.
Maidstone, Kent, Kent Archives Office, vi. 90 n. 1.
Mails, Mrs., vi. 138.
Main, Jasper, *see* Mayne.

Maitland, Thomas, ed., *The Poems of William Drummond of Hawthornden* (1832), iii. 289.
Maitland, William, *History of London* (1739), vi. 178.
Maivrin, i. 286, 297; ii. 506.
Majesties Servants, Their, *see* Beeston's Boys.
Majesty's Theatre, His, *see* Gibbon's Tennis Court.
Makkink, H. J., *Philip Massinger and John Fletcher, A Comparison* (1927), iii. 305; iv. 750.
Malcolm, James Peller, *Londinium Redivivum*, 4 vols., London (1803–7), iii. 256.
Malcolm, King of Scots, see Massey, Charles.
Malcontent, The, see Marston, John.
Malcontent, The, see Webster, John.
Maldon, Essex, iv. 500, 511.
Malespini, Celio, *Ducento Novelle*, iii. 325; v. 1111.
Mallory, Thomas, ii. 552.
Malone, Edmond, iii. 17, 69, 119, 314, 321, 333, 357, 402, 423, 430; iv. 482, 542, 543, 620, 623, 634, 678, 746, 806, 812, 823, 839, 862, 871, 888, 889, 893, 894, 899, 900; v. 970, 986, 987, 988, 1074, 1076, 1084, 1095, 1099, 1104, 1129, 1138, 1146, 1150, 1163, 1322, 1382; vi. 16, 58, 59, 97, 136, 138, 139, 159 n. 1, 163, 164 n. 1, 165, 173, 191, 194, 196, 198; vii. 14.
MS. note by, v. 969.
Variorum, iii. 78, 202, 205–6, 240, 273, 286, 329, 368, 369, 391, 423, 434, 446, 449, 450, 540, 763, 774, 786, 790, 791, 795, 796; iv. 798, 906, 1075, 1350, 1369, 1382; vi. 15, 16, 22, 23, 26, 32, 35, 45, 46, 60 n. 1, 65, 67, 70, 74, 90 and n. 2, 93, 99, 100, 101, 103, 116, 136, 138, 169, 178 n. 1, 195, 198, 247, 248, 250; vii. 3, 4. *See also* Boswell, James.
Malone Society Collections, see under individual titles.
Malone, John, 'The House of Players', v. 1141.
Malone, *Variorum, see* Boswell, James, *The Plays and Poems of William Shakespeare*.
Malta, siege of (1565), iii. 353.
Malvolio, see Shakespeare, *Twelfth Night.*

Man, Thomas, Warden Stationers Company, iii. 6; v. 1038.
Man servant, ii. 349, 353.
Man of Business, The, see Fane, Sir Francis, Love in the Dark.
Man Hater, The, see Heywood Thomas, Misanthropus.
Man in the Moon, The, see Newspapers.
Man in the Moon Drinks Claret, The, see Anonymous.
Manager, see Company manager.
Managers of theatres, Restoration, vi. 105.
Manchester, ii. 414, 507.
Manchester, Henry, Earl of, iv. 476.
Mander, Raymond, and Joe Mitchenson, A Picture History of the British Theatre (1957), vi. 3, 6.
Mandeville, H., ii. 622.
Mandeville, Viscount, ii. 355.
Mandrake, The, see Manuche, Cosmo.
Mangora, King of the Timbusians, see Moore, Sir Thomas.
Manhood and Misrule, see Anonymous.
Mann, Francis Oscar, ed., The Works of Thomas Deloney (1912), iii. 284, 285, 441.
Manneroy, Samuel, see Mannery, Samuel.
Manners, Sir George, iv. 549.
Manners, Henry, iv. 549.
Mannery, Ann, ii. 506.
Mannery, Mary, ii. 506.
Mannery, Samuel, i. 308, 321, 327 n. 2, 332, 336; ii. 506.
Manning, Francis, All for the Better, or The Infallible Cure, iv. 895.
Manningham, John, v. 1226.
Man's the Master, The, see Davenant, William.
Mansfield, Nottinghamshire, iv. 586.
Mansfield, Viscount, see Cavendish, William.
Mansion House, Sherborne, Dorset, iii. 161.
Mansions on stage, vi. 189, 190.
Manson, Dorset, v. 1215.
Manuche, Cosmo, iv. 500, 501, 728-32.
    Agamemnon, iv. 729.
    Bastard, The, iv. 729-30.
    Captives, The, iv. 730.
    Feast, The, iv. 729-30.
    Just General, The, iv. 729, 730.
    Lenotius King of Cyprus, iv. 730.
    Loyal Lovers, The, iv. 729, 731.
    Mandrake, The, iv. 731.

    Mariamne, iv. 731.
    Unnamed Comedy, iv. 731.
    Unnamed Tragedy, iv. 732.
Manuray, Samuel, see Mannery, Samuel.
Manuscript, iii. 165, 226, 227, 228, 229, 239, 258, 264, 267, 269, 270, 279, 281, 283, 284, 286, 292, 293, 295, 297, 298, 299, 307, 315, 332, 333, 335, 341, 343, 344, 346, 347, 349, 371, 378, 380, 385, 403, 419, 425, 462; iv. 500, 511, 523, 533, 536, 541, 542, 543, 549, 569, 595, 615, 634, 647, 700, 708; v. 1091, 1100, 1103-4, 1124, 1139, 1141, 1171, 1177, 1180, 1181, 1189, 1196, 1201, 1205, 1206, 1212, 1227, 1232, 1235, 1237, 1257, 1259, 1260, 1265, 1273, 1277, 1283, 1290, 1291, 1295, 1297, 1298, 1303, 1305, 1311, 1315, 1316, 1317, 1318, 1328, 1332, 1338, 1340, 1343, 1344, 1345, 1349, 1350, 1352, 1361, 1367, 1368, 1373, 1374, 1376, 1379, 1383, 1387, 1390, 1393, 1394, 1400, 1403, 1405, 1406, 1407, 1409, 1414-15, 1418, 1419, 1424, 1426, 1433, 1436, 1439, 1442, 1444, 1449, 1450, 1451, 1452, 1453, 1454; vi. 16 n. 1.
Manuscript borrowed, iii. 426.
Manuscript commonplace books, v. 1040.
Manuscript treatise on anatomy, v. 1181.
Manuscripts, see also Plays in manuscript.
Manuscripts lost, iv. 726, 727, 795, 819, 838, 858; v. 1141.
Manwaring, impeachment of, v. 982.
Maps, iii. 296; vi. 224 n. 1, 255.
Map of London (1746), see Roque, J.
Mapes, Richard, ii. 530.
Marbeck, Maria, see Middleton, Maria.
Marbeck, Thomas, iv. 857.
Marble, vi. 249 n. 1.
Marcella, see Hayley, William.
March, Stuart, Esme, 1st. Duke of Lennox, Earl of, vi. 49.
Marcham, Frank, The King's Office of the Revels, 1610-1622 (1925), iii. 340, 352; iv. 867, 883, 890; v. 1019, 1128, 1296, 1308, 1350, 1351, 1352, 1406, 1421, 1426.
Marcombes, M. Isaac, tutor of young Boyles, iii. 33; iv. 703.
Marcon, Thomas, v. 1455.

Marcus Tullius Cicero, see Anonymous.

Marcy, Charles, *see* Massey, Charles.

Margaret of Navarre, *Heptameron*, v. 1111, 1151.
Novelle, v. 1130.

Margrave, Richard, a sailor, i. 265; vi. 160.

'Mariam' (ship), v. 1006.

Mariam, see Elizabeth, Lady Cary.

Mariamne, see Manuche, Cosmo.

Marian persecutions, iv. 606.

Marine insurance, v. 1006.

Marioni, vii. 33.

Market Bosworth, ii. 484.

Markfield, Leicestershire, iv. 953.

Markham, C. R., *Markham Memorials* (1913), iv. 732.

Markham, Gervase, i. 145, 147; ii. 682; iv. **732–5**; v. 1326; vi. 157.
his suit, ii. 682–3.
Dumb Knight, The, iv. 732, 733, 734.
English Arcadia, The (1607) iii. 239.
Herod and Antipater, i. 166, 174; iv. 732, 733, **734–5**; vi. 220.

Markham, Robert, iv. 732.

Markham, W., v. 1140.

Markward, William B., 'Study of the Phoenix Theatre in Drury Lane, 1617–1638, A'. Unpublished Ph.D. thesis, Shakespeare Institute, Stratford-upon-Avon, (1953), vi. 47, 50–51, 53, 66 n. 1, 69 n. 1.

Marlborough, i. 92, 173, 180, 193, 211.

Marlow, Bucks., ii. 618.

Marlowe, Christopher, iv. 573; v. 1211, 1251; vi. 145.
Influence of, v. 1251.
Doctor Faustus, i. 157, 318, 319; v. 1010; vi. 113, 152, 173; vii. 21, 26, 33, 38, 57, 61, 69, 81.
Edward II, i. 174; vi. 218; vii. 23, 46, 111.
Jew of Malta, The, i. 28 n. 1, 249, 254; ii. 472, 528, 691; iii. 37, 103, 252; iv. 555, 556, 573–4; v. 1251, 1346, 1456; vi. 171; vii. 84, 90.
Massacre at Paris, v. 1059, 1253.
Tamburlaine, ii. 691; iii. 37, 103, 460; iv. 727; v. 1200, 1346, 1456; vi. 171.
Prologue to, iii. 242.

Marmion, Shakerley, i. 110; ii. 595; iii. 7, 30, 31, 162, 445, 458; iv. **736–48**, 928; v. 1397.

Antiquary, The, i. 254; iv. 483, 737, 738, **739–41**; v. 1073.
Cupid and Psyche, iii. 55; iv. 737, 738.
Fine Companion, A, i. 322, 323; iv. 483, 737, **742–5**; vi. 92 n. 1.
Holland's Leaguer, i. 13 n. 2, 152 n. 3, 226, 239 n. 3, 292, 303, 304, 305–7, 308, 311, 321, 323 and n. 1; ii. 383, 392, 398, 399, 423, 439, 445, 450, 458, 481, 506, 509, 560, 577, 579, 617, 620, 625, 627, 692; iii. 7, 88, 89, 189; iv. 483, 737, 742, 743, **745–8**, 933, 942; v. 1114, 1163, 1169; vi. 90, 93, 98, 163, 291.
Soddered Citizen, The, see Clavell, John.

Marovin, —, *see* Maivrin.

Marquesse d'Ancre, The, see Anonymous.

Marrant, Edward, ii. **506**, 545, 659.

Marriage articles, vii. 59.

Marriage contract of Charles and Henrietta Maria, iv. 676.

Marriage in the Dark, see Anonymous, *Look on Me and Love Me*.

Marriage and Hanging Go by Destiny, see Brome, Richard, *Christianetta*.

Marriage of the Farmer's Son, see Anonymous.

Marriage Night, The, see Anonymous.

Marriage Night, The, see Cary, Henry.

Marriage without a Man, A, see Anonymous, *Iphis and Iantha*.

Marriages of the Arts, The, see Holyday, Barton, *Technogamia*.

Marriott, John, iii. 198, 235, 236; iv. 513, 544; v. 971, 973, 974.

Marriott, Richard, stationer, iii. 59, 61, 62, 65, 66, 80, 84, 85, 198, 311; iv. 489, 490, 491, 513, 544, 786, 893; v. 1184, 1187, 1246, 1294, 1301, 1312, 1321, 1333, 1335, 1363, 1364, 1383, 1387, 1395, 1399, 1405, 1415, 1445, 1446, 1448.

Marrow, Lady, iii. 349.

Marrow of the Bible, The, see Ainsworth, William.

Mars (Roman god), vi. 43.

Marsden, J. H., *College Life in the Time of James the First . . .* (1851), v. 991–2.

Marsh, Henry, iv. 922; v. 1338.

Marsh, William, vii. 20.

Marshall, Rebecca, v. 1085, 1122.

Marshall, Charles, i. 137, 178; ii. 507.

Marshall, Humphrey, ii. 643.

Marshall, William, engraver, iii. 311.

Marshall Osric, see Heywood, Thomas.

Marshalsea, *see* London, streets and districts of.

Marston, John, iii. 262; iv. 607, 608, 617; v. 1253, 1378.

Influence of, v. 1003.

Antonio and Mellida, vii. 64, 68, 76, 90.

Antonio's Revenge, iv. 509; vii. 90.

Dutch Courtesan, The, i. 195; iii. 358; v. 1003; vii. 90.

Insatiate Countess, The, ii. 357, 358; vii. 21, 77, 81, 94.

Jack Drum's Entertainment, ii. 690.

Malcontent, The, i. 123; ii. 395; iii. 432; v. 1241, 1254, 1288, 1425.

Parasitaster, or the Fawn, vii. 22, 61, 90, 111.

What You Will, vii. 90.

Wonder of Women, or the Tragedy of Sophonisba, The, iv. 936; vii. 90.

Works, The, vii. 90.

Marston Moor, ii. 398; iii. 144.

Martial, iii. 300; v. 1238.

Martial Court, a, vi. 293.

Martial discipline, vi. 292.

Martial Maid, The, see Fletcher, *Love's Cure.*

Martin, Doctor Edward, iv. 533.

Martin, Elizabeth, ii. 566, 567.

Martin, Henry, iii. 17, 18; iv. 500; v. 1313.

Martin, John, stationer, iii. 98, 123, 124, 146, 147, 150, 202, 203, 204, 206, 210, 311, 315, 320, 325, 330, 337, 340, 341, 345, 348, 349, 352, 355, 357, 360, 364, 367, 372, 374, 375, 378, 388, 392, 395, 399, 413, 419, 423, 427, 431; iv. 534, 706, 707, 884; v. 1085, 1105, 1124, 1148, 1270, 1273.

Martin, L. C., ed., *The Works of Henry Vaughan,* 2 vols. (1914), iii. 301.

Martin, R. G., 'Is *The Late Lancashire Witches* a Revision?' *Mod. Phil.* xiii (1915), iii. 73, 75.

Martin, R. L., vi. 6.

Martin, Sarah, stationer, iii. 98, 202, 204, 206, 315, 325, 330, 345, 349, 355, 357, 364, 367, 372, 375, 378, 382, 388, 392, 395, 399, 413, 419, 423, 427, 431; iv. 534, 707, 884; v. 1085, 1105, 1124, 1148, 1270, 1273.

'Martin Peerson and the Blackfriars', *see* Eccles, Mark.

Martin, widow, iii. 641.

Martyn, Charles, ii. 507.

Martyr, The, see Lower, William, *Polyeuctes.*

Martyred Soldier, The, see Shirley, Henry.

Mary, Lady, iv. 717.

Mary, Princess of Orange, iv. 717.

Mary, Queen of Scots, iv. 634.

Maryland, Lieutenant Governor of, iii. 196.

Masculine Bride, The, see Anonymous, *The Whimsies of Señor Hidalgo.*

Mase, Peter, *see* Mease, Peter.

Masefield, John, and R. Warwick Bond, eds., 'Loyal Subject', *Works of Beaumont and Fletcher,* Variorum Edition, iii. 370, 373.

Maskell, Thomas, ii. 507.

Mason, Bridget, ii. 392.

Mason, John, iv. 748–9.

Princeps Rhetoricus (1648), iv. 749.

School Moderator, or The Combat of Caps, The, iv. 748–9.

Turk, The, iv. 748.

Mason, Michael, iv. 716.

Mason, John Monck, iv. 499.

ed., *The Dramatick Works of Philip Massinger.* Intros. by T. Davies and G. Colman. 4 vols. (1779), iv. 758.

Masons, vi. 260.

Masque, deformed, iii. 297.

Masque sets, iii. 200.

Masque, A, Presented at Bretbie, see Cokayne, Sir Aston.

Masque, A, see Tatham, John.

Masque, The, see Gunnell, Richard.

Masque of Amazons, see Anonymous.

Masque of Augurs, The, see Jonson, Ben.

Masque of Beauty, see Jonson, Ben.

Masque of Blackness, see Jonson, Ben.

Masque of Christmas, The, see Jonson, Ben.

Masque of Cupid, see Middleton, Thomas.

Masque of Disappointed Ladies, see Anonymous.

Masque of the Four Seasons, see Anonymous, *Entertainment at Chirke Castle.*

'Masque at Fryers, A', *see* Anonymous.

Masque of Heroes, see Middleton, Thomas, *The Inner Temple Masque*.

Masque of the Inner Temple and Gray's Inn, The, see Fletcher, John.

Masque at Knowsley, A, see Salusbury, Sir Thomas.

'*Masque of Lethe, The*', *see* Jonson's *Lovers Made Men*.

Masque, A Moral, see Ford, John, and Thomas Dekker *The Sun's Darling*.

Masque of Owls, The, see Jonson, Ben.

Masque of Queens, see Jonson, Ben.

Masque of Vices, The, see Anonymous.

'Masque of Virtues', *see* Randolph, Thomas.

Masque at Witten, The, see Suckling, Sir John.

Masque, religious, vii. 12.

Masquerade, The, see Johnson, Charles.

Masquers, iii. 200, 444.

Masquers, praise of, iii. 107.

Masques, i. 185; ii. 681, 685; iii. 40, 105, 106–10, 168, 207–9, 213–15, 216–20, 297–8, 335, 443, 453; iv. 548–50, 596, 609, 673, 680, 717, 881–2, 882, 907–11, 913–16, 936–8, 939–40, 949; v. 1038–9, 1040–2, 1071, 1096–7, 1102–4, 1153, 1175, 1205, 1212, 1217, 1222, 1227, 1229, 1257, 1262, 1268, 1288, 1292, 1311, 1357, 1372, 1404, 1430–2, 1432; vi. 38, 255, 256, 284, 285–8, 293, 294, 295, 296; vii. 5, 10, 12, 17, 18, 19, 20, 21, 22, 39, 40, 41, 42, 52, 54, 57, 62, 63, 64, 66, 67, 72, 77, 86, 102, 103, 107, 119, 120.

Actors in, v. 1359.

Adaptation of, iv. 881–2, 915.

Allegorical, iv. 579–82.

Allowed for press, iii. 108; iv. 642; v. 1156.

Burlesque, v. 1345.

Censored, iv. 660–3.

Commonwealth, iv. 680, 682–3.

Composition of, v. 1358.

Conduct at, vi. 257–8.

Costumes, iii. 108.

Court, vi. 107.

Dancers in, iii. 199; iv. 664, 666, 667–8; v. 1359.

Dances in, iv. 841; v. 1037.

Dated, v. 1041, 1257, 1292, 1357.

Described, vi. 257.

Designs for, iii. 110, 200, 209, 214, 215, 218.

Expenditures for, iii. 199, 207, 213, 217; iv. 637, 638, 648, 650, 652, 653, 655, 666, 667–8, 670, 672, 676, 677; v. 1155, 1156, 1157, 1158, 1160, 1227–8, 1229; vii. 66.

For dancers (i.e. of the ropes), vi. 159.

Frequency of, iv. 910.

Improvised, v. 1357.

Incidents at, iv. 671, 831; v. 1158.

Incomplete, v. 1231.

Licensed for the press, iv. 200, 881; v. 1096.

Lost, iv. 842–3, 882; v. 1212, 1222, 1231.

Machines, iii. 109.

In MS., iv. 638–40, 645, 648, 653, 669, 672, 677, 682; v. 1102, 1257, 1292, 1311.

In multiple MSS., iv. 638–9, 645, 913, 916; v. 1102.

Masques Anglais, Les, see Reyher, Paul.

'Masques and other Tunes', *see* Anonymous.

Materials for, iii. 199.

Moral, iv. 936–8, 939–40; v. 1096, 1189, 1192.

Music for, iii. 109.

Performers in, iii. 168, 199, 215, 220; iv. 638, 647, 717, 841, 888, 917–21; v. 1041, 1158–60, 1162, 1228, 1229, 1230, 1280, 1311, 1358; vc. 257, 288.

Personal allusions in, iii. 168, 218; iv. 639, 644, 647, 664, 665, 668, 674, 676; v. 1039, 1041.

Political allusions in, iii. 200; iv. 644, 660–3, 842; v. 1039, 1161, 1292.

Popular, v. 1154–63.

Private, iii. 168; v. 1040, 1097, 1102, 1153, 1212, 1222, 1257, 1268, 1311, 1372, 1375.

Processions for, v. 1156–60.

Reception of, iv. 641–2, 646–7, 670, 671, 672.

Rehearsal of, iv. 673; v. 1229, 1289, 1359.

Repeated, v. 1157–9, 1162.

Revision of, iv. 641–2, 643–4, 646–7, 909; v. 1097, 1119.

Revivals of, iv. 638, 645–7, 655–7, 671, 672, 677; v. 1103–4.

Masques (*cont.*)
Running, v. 1404.
School, iv. 682; v. 1071, 1097,
    1153, 1257, 1292.
By schoolgirls, v. 1257.
Short, iv. 939.
Singers in, v. 1230.
Souvenir texts, iv. 644, 651, 657,
    663, 672, 675.
Sylvan, iv. 842, 843.
Time of, iv. 643; vi. 257.
Unacted, iv. 660–3; v. 1096, 1288.
Unknown titles or authors, v.
    1449–54.
Masquing habit, v. 1229.
Masquing Hall, iii. 209.
Masquing House, iii. 199; vi. 266–
    7, 282, 284–88; vii. 108.
Masquing Room, vii. 120.
Massachusetts, v. 1398.
Massam, Phillip, ii. 637.
Massam, P., transcribes MS., iii.
    192.
Massam, Thomas, ii. 412.
Masse, Jan, iv. 876.
Massey, Charles, i. 136, 137 n. 4,
    138, 140, 141 and n. 2, 142, 143,
    144, 147, 148, 152, 153, 155,
    263; ii. 507–8, 564; iv. 749; vi.
    150, 157, 158, 185 n. 2.
    Malcolm, King of Scots, ii. 507;
        iv. 749.
    *Siege of Dunkirk with Alleyn the
        Pirate, The*, ii. 507; iv. 749.
Massey, Elinor, ii. 507, 508.
Massey, George, i. 144; ii. 508; vi.
    157.
Massey, John, ii. 508.
Massey, Margaret, ii. 508.
Massie, Charles, *see* Massey, Charles.
Massinger, Arthur, iv. 750, 751, 769.
Massinger, Philip, i. 63, 184, 218; ii.
    557; iii. 7, 8, 66, 78, 127, 167,
    263, 309, 312, 317, 327, 329,
    331, 332, 335, 337, 338, 340,
    350, 353, 360, 362, 363, 365,
    369, 390, 394, 396, 398, 400,
    405, 406, 411, 414, 415, 417,
    420, 447; iv. 474, 499, 597, 735,
    749–830, 889, 890–1; v. 1018,
    1043, 1070, 1117, 1252, 1273,
    1325, 1335, 1388; vi. 73.
Influence of, v. 1249.
Revision by, iii. 359, 362, 363.
*Alexius, or The Chaste Lover
    (Gallant)*, i. 65, 108, 123; iv.
    758–9, 761, 770; vi. 38.
Antonio and Vallia (?), iv. 759–60.
Bashful Lover, The, i. 66, 107, 108,
    123–4; iv. 597, 758, 759, 760–2,
    770, 828.
Believe as You List, i. 84–85, 101
    n. b, 105, 124; ii. 354, 355, 375,
    397, 418, 425, 441, 452, 474,
    477, 480, 502, 506, 516, 521,
    524, 534, 585, 594, 609, 621;
    iii. 406, 456; iv. 481, 488, 494,
    762–5, 770, 772, 773, 794; v.
    1134, 1169, 1360, 1397.
Bondman, The, i. 185, 186 and n.
    5, 194, 195, 331, 339; iii. 140,
    221; iv. 751, 754, 757, 765–70,
    776, 806, 817, 894, 895; vi. 59.
City Madam, The, i. 30, 66, 105,
    124; ii. 524, 525; iv. 771–4; v.
    1308.
City Honest Man, The (?), iv.
    770–1.
Cleander, i. 39 and n. 2, 97, 107,
    124 and n. 1; iv. 774, 804; vi.
    16, 34–35.
'Copie of a Letter . . .', iii. 307.
Country Girl, The (?), iv. 774.
Duke of Milan, The, i. 124; iv.
    754, 770, 775–7, 822.
Emperor of the East, The, i. 97 n.
    m, 105, 124; iii. 167; iv. 743,
    777–81, 783, 799, 821; vi. 198,
    199; vii. 7, 8.
*Fair Anchoress of Pausilippo,
    The, or The Prisoner*, i. 108, 124;
    iv. 781–2, 800, 810–11; vi. 38.
Fast and Welcome, iv. 780, 782–3.
Forced Lady, The, i. 65, 125; iv.
    785–6, 800.
Great Duke of Florence, The, i.
    218, 223 and n. 4, 254, 331, 339;
    iii. 437; iv. 755, 756, 786–8,
    791; v. 1142.
Guardian, The, i. 66, 97, 106, 125;
    iv. 755, 761, 770, 771, 772, 773,
    789–90, 799, 820, 828.
Honest Man's Fortune, The, see
    Fletcher, John.
Honour of Women, The, see
    Anonymous, *The Spanish
    Viceroy*.
Honour of Women, The, iv. 790–2,
    798; v. 1413.
Italian Night-Piece [*Masque*], *The*
    i. 126; ii. 551, 552; iv. 792–3,
    820, 821.
Jeweller of Amsterdam, The, see
    Fletcher, John.
Judge, The, i. 66, 104, 125; iv.
    765, 770, 784, 785, 787, 788,
    793–4; vi. 196.
King and the Subject, The, i. 60–61,

60 n. 4, 107, 108, 125; ii. 504;
iii. 121; iv. 478, **794–6**, 820;
vi. 166, 197.
London's Lamentable Estate, ii.
416.
Maid of Honour, The, i. 254, 331,
339; iii. 167; iv. 754, 756, 790,
791, **796–9**; v. 1413.
Minerva's Sacrifice, i. 66, 105,
125; iv. 785, 786, **799–800**.
New Way to Pay Old Debts, A, i.
248 n. 2, 254, 331, 339–40; iii.
7, 66; iv. 754, 756, 800–3, 822.
Noble Bondman, The, see *The
Bondman*.
Noble Choice, The, see *The Orator*.
Old Law, The, see Middleton,
Thomas.
Orator, The [*or The Noble Choice*],
i. 107, 125; ii. 660; iii. 336; iv.
803–4.
Painter, The, iii. 361; iv. 804–5.
Parliament of Love, The, i. 186,
195–6; iii. 263, 265, 267, 358;
iv. 754, **805–7**; vi. 59.
Philenzo and Hypollita (?), iv. 808.
Picture, The, i. 82–83, 105, 125; ii.
375, 447, 477, 502, 524, 533,
562, 565, 571, 585, 594, 600,
605, 692; iii. 164; iv. 563, 747,
808–10, 813; vi. 196, 199.
Prisoner(s), The, (?), iv. 810–11.
Prophetess, The, see Fletcher,
John.
*Renegado, The, or The Gentleman
of Venice*, i. 185, 187, 196, 218
n. 3, 219 n. 4, 220–2, 246, 254,
331, 340; ii. 344, 345, 378, 382,
386, 526, 543, 548, 553, 561,
583, 607, 692; iv. 747, 754, 756,
768, 778, 806, 810, **811–15**; v.
1165; vi. 59.
Rollo, Duke of Normandy, see
Fletcher, John.
Roman Actor, The, i. 82–83, 104,
125–6; ii. 375, 447, 452, 476,
479, 502, 521, 533, 546, 552,
570, 575, 585, 593–4, 600, 605,
612, 692; iii. 8, 437; iv. 499,
747, 787, 810, 813, **815–17**; v.
1165.
Secretary, The, iv. 818.
Sir John van Olden Barnavelt, see
Fletcher, John.
Three New Players (1655), iv.
759, 761, 789, 825, 828.
Tyrant, The, iii. 466; iv. 793, 795,
819–20.
Unfortunate Piety, The, i. 105,

126; ii. 552; iii. 331; iv. 772,
773, 792, **820–1**; vi. 196.
Unnatural Combat, The, i. 126;
iv. 754, 784, **821–4**; vi. 198, 199.
*Very Woman, A, or The Prince of
Tarent*, i. 107, 126; iii. 169; iv.
761, 792, **824–8**, 829; vi. 197.
Virgin Martyr, The, see Dekker,
Thomas.
Wandering Lovers, The, see Massinger, *The Painter*.
Woman's Plot, The, i. 66, 94, 126;
iii. 401; iv. 754, 825, 826, **829–
30**.
Massinger, Philip, with Nathan
Field, *Fatal Dowry, The*, i. 28, 96,
124; ii. 435, 436; iii. 447; iv. 754,
783–5, 794, 822; vi. 10.
Masson, David, *Drummond of Haw-
thornden: The story of His Life
and Writings* (1873), iii. 287.
*Life of John Milton: Narrated in
Connexion with the Political,
Ecclesiastical, and Literary His-
tory of His Time, The*, 7 vols.
(1946), iv. 535, 911, 912, 913,
914, 915; v. 973, 982, 984, 1197.
Massy, Charles, *see* Massey, Charles.
Master of the bows, iii. 112.
Master of the Ceremonies, iv. 662;
vi. 257.
Master in Chancery, iii. 104.
Master of the Great Wardrobe, vi.
279.
Master of the Jewel House, ii. 673.
Master of Requests, iii. 468.
Master of the Revels, i. 105, 159,
239, 272; iii. 52, 69, 78, 93, 94,
225, 265, 348, 370, 372, 416,
420; iv. 496–7, 518, 523, 561,
602, 610, 620, 622, 623, 675,
688, 714, 769, 775, 827; v. 1033,
1084, 1252, 1371; vi. 20, 34, 36,
45, 58, 59, 63, 64, 68, 87, 104,
105, 128, 137, 166, 225, 229,
244, 291 n. 1; vii. 1, 3, 4, 54;
see also Herbert, Sir Henry.
Comments by, v. 1168.
Deputy to, iii. 36, 37; iv. 517; vi.
94, 103 n. 1, 162; *see also*
Blagrave, William.
Gifts to, vi. 59–60.
Of Ireland, iii. 97; iv. 949, 950;
v. 1141.
Licences for plays, *see* Herbert,
Sir Henry.
Problems of, v. 1169.
Reversion of office to Jonson, iv.
646.

Masters of the Bench, v. 1156.

Masters of Fence, vi. 296.

Masters, Robert, *History of the College of Corpus Christi* (1753), iii. 306.

Mastership of the Revels, sale of, vii. 48.

Mat-layers, vi. 279.

Match Me in London, see Dekker, Thomas.

Match at Midnight, A, see Middleton, Thomas.

Match or No Match, A, see Rowley, Samuel.

Match Well Made Up, A, see Anonymous, *Like to Like*.

Match without Money, A, see Anonymous.

Matchit, Amb., ii. 508; iv. 686.

Matchless Maids, The, see Davenant, William, *Love and Honour*.

Mathematical and arithmetical readings, vi. 293.

Mathew, Jo., ii. 379.

Mathew, Peter, iv. 546.

Mathews, Augustine, iv. 835; v. 1313, 1380.

Mathews, Ernst G., 'The Murdered Substitute Tale', *Mod. Lang. Quart.* vi (1945), iv. 862.

Mathews, Mr., iii. 264.

'Matron of Ephesus', *see* Anonymous.

Matthew, Sir Tobie, i. 10 n. 6 cont.; vii. 26.

Matthews, Brander, ed., Massinger's *A New Way to Pay Old Debts* in C. M. Gayley, *Representative English Comedies* (1914) (vol. iii.), iv. 800, 801.

Matting, vi. 279, 280.

Maty, Matthew, *Authentic Memoirs of the Life of Richard Mead, M.D.* (1755), v. 1176.

Maund, Mr., ii. 622.

Maundy, vii. 84, 87.

Maurice, Prince, iii. 351; v. 1227.

Maxey, Elizabeth Burbage, ii. 649.

Maxey, Thomas, iv. 493.

Maxwell, Baldwin, iii. 390; vi. 77 n. 1.

   'Date of *Love's Pilgrimage* and its Relation to *The New Inn*, The', *Stud. Phil.* xxviii (1931), iii. 366, 367, 368; iv. 622, 624.

   'Note on the Date of Middleton's *The Family of Love* with a Query on the Porters Hall Theatre.' *Elizabethan Studies and Other Essays in Honor of George F. Reynolds. University of Colorado Studies* (1945), vi. 77.

   'Old Law, The', *Studies in Beaumont, Fletcher, and Massinger* (1930), iv. 889, 890, 891.

   'Source of the Principal Plot of *The Fair Maid of the Inn*, The', *M.L.N.* lix (1944), 122–7, iii. 337, 339.

   Studies in Beaumont, Fletcher, and Massinger (1939), iii. 305, 316, 324, 326, 340, 341, 342, 356, 357, 359, 366, 373, 382, 383, 384, 386, 387, 389, 390, 391, 393, 394, 398, 400, 411, 431, 433; iv. 750, 773, 825, 826, 827, 828, 829, 869, 889.

Maxwell, Helena, ed., *Love's Victory* Unpublished thesis, Stanford U., 1933, v. 1368. 1369.

Maxwell, James, vi. 269; vii. 17, 19, 21, 25, 27, 28, 30.

Maxwell, J. C., 'A Dramatic Echo of an Overburian Character', *N. & Q.* cxcii (1947), iii. 332.

Maxwell, Mr., iv. 637.

Maxwell, Sue, 'A Misprint in Marmion's "Holland's Leaguer"', *Mod. Lang. Rev.* xxxix (1944), iv. 745.

   Shakerly Marmion, Poet and Dramatist. Unpublished Yale thesis (1941), iv. 736, 737, 739, 740, 741, 742, 744, 745, 747, 748.

Maxwell-Lyte, H. C., *A History of Eton College 1440–1875* (1875), v. 1176.

May, Clare, ii. 510.

May, Edward, actor, i. 286, 290, 297, 307, 308, 321, 323; ii. 488, 509–10; iii. 192; iv. 475, 679, 716.

May, Edward, *Epigrams Divine and Moral* (1633), iii. 509 n. 1.

May, Edward, physician, ii. 509 n. 1.

May, Francis, ii. 510.

May, Sir Humphrey, v. 1289.

May, Lady, v. 1289.

May, Mary, ii. 510.

May, Nathan, ii. 510.

May, Thomas, iii. 16, 105, 195, 434, 450; iv. 816, 830–41; v. 1029, 1033, 1158, 1165, 1381; vi. 304.

   Continuation of Lucan's Historical Poem till the Death of Julius Caesar (1630), iv. 831.

   Discourse Concerning the Success

of Former Parliaments, A, (1642), iv. 832.

Heir, The, i. 166, 175; iii. 105; iv. 735, 830, **835–7**, 840; v. 1313, 1381.

Historiae Parliamenti Angliae Breviarium (1650), iv. 833.

History of the Parliament of England Which Began November the Third M.DC.XL, The (1647), iv. 832–3; vii. 12.

Tr., *John Barclay His Argenis* (1628), iv. 831.

Julius Caesar (?), iv. 838–9.

Life of a Satyricall Puppy called Nym (1657), vi. 5, 11.

Tr., *Lucan's Pharsalia or the Civil Wars of Rome,* 10 vols. (1626–7), iv. 830, 832.

Tr., *Mirror of Minds or Barclay's Icon Animorum, The* (1631), iv. 831.

Old Couple, The, iv. 839–40.

Old Wives' Tale, The, iv. 840–1.

Reign of King Henry the Second, The (1633), iv. 831.

Tr., *Selected Epigrams of Martial* (1629), iv. 830.

Tragedy of Antigone, the Theban Princess, The, iv. 833–4, 839.

Tragedy of Cleopatra Queen of Egypt, The, iv. 834–5, 837, 838; v. 1310; vii. 118.

Tragedy of Julia Agrippina, The, iv. 834, 835, 837–8; vii. 118.

Victorious Reign of King Edward the Third, The (1635), iv. 831.

Tr. *Virgil's Georgics* (1628), iv. 1830.

May, Thomas, Sr., iv. 830.

May Day, see Chapman, George.

May Lord, The, see Jonson, Ben.

Mayfield manor, Sussex, iv. 830.

Maynard, Sir Henry, iv. 841.

Maynard, John, iv. 841–3.

Unnamed masque, iv. 842–3.

Mayne, Jasper, iv. 589, **843–50**; vi. 244.

Amorous War, The, iv. 844, **845–7**, 848.

City Match, The, i. 126; iv. 525, 774, 844, 845, 846, 847–50; v. 1308; vi. 166.

Late Printed Sermon against False Prophets, Vindicated by Letter from the Causeless Aspersions of Mr. Francis Cheynell, A (1647), iv. 844.

Maynwaring (rector of St. Giles in the Fields), vi. 60.

Maynwaring, Mary, ii. 510.

Mayor of Quinborough, The, see Middleton, Thomas.

Mead, Jacob, waterman, ii. 510.

Mead, Reverend Joseph, i. 20, 266; ii. 349, 655, 657 n. 4; iii. 161; iv. 529, 610, 646, 647; v. 973, 1197, 1232, 1233; vii. 66.

Mead, Richard, the physician, v. 1176, 1177.

Mead, Robert, iv. 850–2.

Combat of Love and Friendship, The, iv. 486, 851–2.

Mead, Robert, Sr., iv. 850.

Mead, Robert, Warden Stationers' Company, iii. 114.

Meade, Jacob, i. 176, 177 n. 3, 198, 199 and n. 2, 200, 201, 209; ii. 510; iii. 190; vi. 201, 202, 203, 206, 207, 208, 209.

Mease, Peter, iv. 852–3.

Adrastus Parentans sive Vindicta Tragoedia, iv. 852–3.

Measure, William, ii. 463.

Measure for Measure, see Shakespeare.

Medals, v. 994.

Medcalf, *see* Carleton, Thomas.

Medea, see Anonymous.

Medea, see Seneca.

Medici, Marie de, iv. 548.

Medicine, iii. 175.

Medicine show, ii. 517, 537.

Medley of Humours, The, see Cavendish, William, *The Triumphant Widow.*

Medulla Bibliorum, see Ainsworth, William.

Medus, Dr., ii. 349.

Megus, Katherine, ii. 511.

Megus, William, ii. **511**.

Meighen, iii. 211.

Meighen, Mrs. Mercie, iii. 211, 219; iv. 507, 509, 742.

Meighen, Richard, stationer, iii. 161, 219, 223; iv. 505, 507, 508, 509, 742; v. 1416.

Meissner, Johannes, *Die englischen Comoedianten zur Zeit Shakespeares in Oesterreich* (1884), iv. 752.

Melancholy, iii. 384, 434.

'Melancholy Converted', *see* Shirley, James.

Melise, ou les Princes Reconnus, La, see Du Rocher.

Mell, Davies, ii. 363.

Melodrama, v. 995, 1002.

Melpomene, vi. 276.

Melton, John, *Astrologaster* (1620), i. 157; vi. 152.
Melvin, Andrew, iii. 4.
'Melvinus delirans', *see* Atkinson, Thomas.
Membership, 'Mr.' as indication of, i. 287.
Memoirs of Sir Hugh Cholmley, The, *see* Cholmley, Sir Hugh.
Memorial of Bishop Wayneflete, *see* Bloxam, John Rouse.
Memorial reconstructions, v. 1011.
Mendoza, Antonio de, *Querer por solo Querer*, v. 1211.
Mendoza, Don Diego de, iv. 842, 843.
Meneses, Gonzalo de Cespedes y, iv. 500.
Mercer, iv. 893.
Merchants, ii. 486, 493; iii. 94; iv. 670.
Merchant adventurer, ii. 564.
Merchant of Dublin, The, *see* Ogilby, John.
Merchant's Sacrifice, The, *see* Anonymous.
Merchant tailors, i. 143; ii. 508, 555, 578; iii. 12, 19; v. 1223, 1240, 1254.
Merchant Tailors' company, ii. 546; iii. 244.
Merchant Taylor Fellows of St. Johns' College, Oxford, see Simmonds.
Merchant Taylors' Hall, v. 1158, 1159, 1162; vii. 31, 112.
Merchant Taylors' School, ii. 414; iii. 3, 4, 12, 19, 28, 29, 183, 291; v. 1065, 1157, 1178, 1179, 1181, 1259, 1275; vi. 274 n. 1.
Merchant of Venice, The, see Shakespeare.
Merchant's Wedding, The, see Planché.
Merchant's Wife, The, see S. J., *Andromana*.
Mercia seu Pietas Coronata, Tragœdia, see Simons, Joseph.
Mercuruis Britanicus, see Anonymous.
Mercurius Britannicus, see Newspapers.
Mercurius Democritus, see Newspapers.
Mercurius Fumigosus, see Newspapers.
Mercurius Impartialis, see Newspapers.
Mercurius Melancholicus, see Newspapers.

Mercurius Militaris, see Newspapers.
Mercurius Pragmaticus, see Newspapers.
Mercurius Pragmaticus, *The Second Part of Crafty Cromwell* (1648), iv. 499.
Mercurius Publicus, see Newspapers.
Mercurius Rusticans, see Anonymous.
Mercurius sive Literarum Lucta, see Blencowe, John.
Mercurius Vapulans, see Newspapers.
Mercurius Veridicus, see Newspapers.
Mercury Vindicated from the Alchemists at Court, see Jonson.
Mercy, Charles, *see* Massey, Charles.
Merefield, Mrs., ii. 644.
Meres, Francis, iv. 554; v. 985.
Palladis Tamia. Wits Treasury, iv. 607; v. 1017.
Meriden, iii. 419, 484, 618.
Meriell, Jo., v. 995, 998.
Mérimée, Prosper, *The History of Peter the Cruel, King of Castile and Leon*, 2 vols. (1849), v. 1411.
Merle, Alfred, *Massingers 'The Picture' und Painter II*, 28 (1905), iv. 809.
Merlinus Anonymous, see Desmus, Ralph.
Mermaid in Bread street, i. 137; ii. 347; iii. 15; iv. 608.
Mermaid Theatre, vi. 86.
Mermion, Shakerley, *see* Marmion, Shakerley.
Merrell, Anne, ii. 511.
Merrell, Joane, ii. 511.
Merrell, John, ii. 511.
Merricke, Ann, i. 121.
Merry Cuckold, The, see Harris, Joseph, *The City Bride*.
Merry Devil of Edmonton, The, see Anonymous.
'*Merry Milkmaid of Islington*, The', *see* Anonymous.
Merry Wives of Windsor, The, see Shakespeare.
Merton College, Oxford, iii. 21, 104; iv. 514, 750, 777; v. 992.
Mervyn, James, v. 1140.
Merydale, Richard, ii. 637.
Messallina The Roman Emperesse, see Richards, Nathaniel.
Messenger, ii. 448, 683.
Messenger, *see* Massinger, Philip.
Messia, Don Diego de, iv. 842.

Metamorphosis of Princes, The, see
Moore, Thomas, *The Arcadian
Lovers.*
Metamorphosis of Tobacco, The, see
Beaumount, John.
Method, William, iv. 853.
Metrical analyses, v. 1246.
Metz, G. Harold, ed., 'A Critical
Edition of *A Pleasant Comedy of
Two Merry Milkmaids*' (MS.
Pennsylvania thesis), iii. 101.
Mewe, William, iv. 853-5.
　Pseudomagia, iv. 853, **854-5**; v.
　1233, 1387, 1453.
　*Robbing and Spoiling of Jacob
　and Israel . . . 1643, The,* iv.
　853.
Mewe, William, Sr., iv. 853.
Michael, i. 72-88; ii. **511**; iii. 416.
Michaelmas Day, iii. 72.
Michaelmas Term, see Middleton.
Michaelmas term, new plays for, iii.
　420.
Michell, iii. 296.
Michell, Sir Francis, iv. 801-2.
Microcosmographia, see John Earle.
Microcosmus, Island of, iii. 297.
Microcosmus, see Anonymous.
Microcosmus, see Nabbes, Thomas.
Midas, see Lyly, John.
Middle Temple, iii. 17, 21, 93, 105,
　194, 220, 434, 435, 436, 437,
　443, 444, 468; iv. 677, 919, 944;
　v. 1155, 1240, 1276; vi. 32; vii.
　22, 39, 96.
　Masque at, iii. 219.
　Records, iii. 105.
Middle and Inner Templers, iii. 107-
　8, 220.
Middlesex, County of, ii. 428, 458;
　v. 1181; vi. 220, 230, 239.
　Justices of the Peace, vi. 27.
　Lieutenants of, vi. 56, 220.
　Sessions of the Peace, vi. 62.
　Sheriffs of, vi. 176.
　Special Session, i. 162; vi. 56.
Middlesex County Records, see
Jeaffreson, John Cordy, ed.
Middlesex Justice of the Peace, see
Brome, Richard, *The Weeding of
Covent Garden.*
Middlesex, Lionel Cranfield, Earl of,
　iv. 878; v. 1198, 1213.
Middleton, Edward, i. 12; iv. 857,
　858, 876.
Middleton, Lady, v. 1040.
Middleton, Maria, iv. 857.
Middleton, Thomas, i. 6 and n. 7
　cont., 11, 184; ii. 557; iii. 133,

239, 252, 261, 282, 316, 383, 390,
400, 459, 611, **855-911**, 956; v.
1018, 1240, 1241, 1242, 1245,
1248, 1304; vi. 146, 147.
　Influence of, iii. 133; iv. 802.
　Unnamed pageant, iv. 911.
　Unnamed play, iv. 857, 911.
　Annales, iv. 858.
　*Ant and the Nightingale: or
　Father Hubburds Tales, The*
　(1604) (2nd ed.), iv. 856.
　Anything for a Quiet Life, i. 126;
　857, **859-61**; v. 1245.
　Blurt, Master Constable, iv. 710,
　857, 861; v. 1319.
　Caesar's Fall, or Two Shapes, iv.
　857, 861, 899.
　Chaste Maid in Cheapside, A, iii.
　81; iv. 857, 864; vi. 251 n. 1;
　vii. 73, 77.
　Cheater and the Clown, The, iv. 885.
　*Chester Tragedy, or Randal, Earl
　of Chester, The,* iv. 857, 864.
　Civitatis Amor, iv. 864.
　*Conqueror's Custom, or The Fair
　Prisoner, The* (?), iv. **864-6**;
　v. 1410, 1421, 1423, 1424, 1433.
　Family of Love, The, iv. 857, 870;
　v. 1078; vii. 65.
　Game at Chess, A, i. 9-15, 104,
　126-7, 295 n. 6; ii. 416, 556,
　557; iii. 84, 88, 410, 441; iv.
　630, 769, 856, 857, 858, 861,
　870-9, 907; v. 1016, 1412, 1456;
　vi. 21, 128, 183-4, 189, 196,
　197; vii. 7.
　Ghost of Lucrece, The (1600), iv.
　857.
　*Hengist, King of Kent, see The
　Mayor of Quinborough.*
　Honest Whore, The, Part I, iv.
　879, 891.
　Honorable Entertainments [*The
　Cock, The Archer, The Water
　Nymph, Pallas, The Year's
　Funeral, Comus, the Great Sir of
　Feasts, The Triumph of Tem-
　perance, The Seasons, Flora's
　Servants*], iv. **879-81**.
　*Inner Temple Masque, The, or
　Masque of Heroes,* i. 164, 203,
　211; ii. 352, 401-2, 464, 516,
　556, 557, 591, 592; iv. **881-2**,
　939, 940; v. 1016, 1041, 1042;
　vi. 55, 56, 258 n. 1.
　*Invention for the Service of the
　Right Honourable Edward Bark-
　ham, Lord Mayor,* iv. 882.
　Mad World, My Masters, A, i.

Middleton, Thomas (*cont.*)
254; iv. 790, 857, 882; vii. 74,
123.
Masque of Cupid, iv. 882.
Match at Midnight, A, iv. 882.
*Mayor of Quinborough, The, or
Hengist King of Kent*, i. 66,
95 n. c, 127; ii. 380, 389, 579;
iii. 133, 190; iv. 857, 859, 861,
883–7; v. 1301, 1303, 1347, 1354,
1401, 1436, 1437, 1447.
Michaelmas Term, iii. 133; iv.
857, 888; vii. 73, 77.
Micro-Cynicon (1599), iv. 857.
More Dissemblers besides Women,
i. 66, 95, 103, 110, 127; iv. 660,
857, 888–9.
No Wit No Help Like a Woman's,
iii. 61, 65; v. 1069, 1123, 1134.
Phoenix, The, iii. 133; iv. 857,
891; vii. 77.
Puritan, The, iv. 857, 891.
*Puritan Maid, the Modest Wife,
and the Wanton Widow, The*, iv.
892.
*Right Woman, or Women Beware
Women, A*, iv. 829.
Roaring Girl, The, see Dekker,
Thomas.
Running Stream Entertainment,
iv. 857, 892.
'Song in several parts, A', ii. 416.
Sun in Aries, The, iv. 895–6.
Trick to Catch the Old One, A, iii.
8; iv. 802, 857, 896; vii. 21.
*Triumphs of Health and Pros-
perity, The*, iv. 896–7.
Triumph of Honour and Industry,
iii. 261; iv. 897, 926; vii. 25.
*Triumphs of Honour and Virtue,
The*, v. 897–8.
Triumphs of Integrity, The, iv.
898–9, 926.
*Triumphs of Love and Antiquity,
The*, iv. 899.
Triumphs of Truth, The, iv. 899;
v. 1426.
Two New Playes, iii. 117, 119,
124; iv. 888, 906.
Viper and Her Brood, The, iv.
899.
*Wisdom of Solomon Paraphrased,
The* (1597), iv. 857.
Witch, The, i. 127; ii. 416; iv. 857,
Witch of Edmonton, The, see
Dekker, Thomas.
861, 903–5.
Women Beware Women, iv. 858,
905–7; v. 1001, 1002.

Your Five Gallants, iii. 133; iv.
857, 865, 911.
Middleton, Thomas (with Rowley),
Changeling, The, i. 183, 185, 186
n. 6, 187, 194, 196, 219 n. 4,
254–5, 331, 340; ii. 540; iii. 190,
221; iv. 494, 504, 857, 859,
861–4, 894, 906, 910; v. 1016,
1272; vi. 58, 59.
Fair Quarrel, A, i. 213, 215, 331,
340; iii. 133, 323; iv. 857, 867–
70, 908, 910, 911; v. 1016, 1017,
1252, 1296, 1309, 1350, 1353,
1421, 1426, 1433; vii. 25, 65, 67.
Spanish Gypsy, The, i. 185, 186 n.
4, 187, 194, 196, 219 n. 4, 255,
331, 340; iii. 73, 316, 317; iv.
770, 857, 892–5, 906, 910;
v. 1016, 1343; vi. 59.
World Tossed at Tennis, The, i. 201
n. 2, 205, 214, 342; iv. 907–11,
938; v. 1016, 1017; vii. 6.
Middleton, Thomas, with Philip
Massinger and William Rowley,
*The Old Law, or A New Way to
Please You*, iii. 8, 9; iv. 889–91;
v. 1043, 1292, 1326, 1336, 1353,
1370, 1376, 1382, 1384, 1402,
1416, 1432.
Middleton, Thomas (with Fletcher
and Jonson), *Widow, The*, i. 66,
127; ii. 447; iii. 457; iv. 857, 861,
900–3.
Middleton, William, iv. 856.
Middlewich, Chester, ii. 511.
Midgely, Robert, v. 1048.
Midleton, *see* Middleton, Thomas.
Midsummer Night's Dream, A, *see*
Shakespeare.
Milan, scene of play, iv. 705.
Milborne, Robert, iv. 538.
Mildmay, Sir Anthony, ii. 673.
Mildmay, Herbert A. St. John,
*Brief Memoir of the Mildmay
Family, A* (1913), ii. 673.
Mildmay, Sir Henry, ii. 635, 673.
Mildmay, Sir Humphrey, i. 3 n. 7,
30 and nn. 2 and 6, 39, 47, 48,
56 n. 3, 61, 62, 231 and n. 1,
235, 245, 258; ii. 673–81; iii.
362; iv. 695, 835; v. 1125, 1126,
1269, 1389; vi. 16, 174 n. 1, 197.
Records of, ii. 673–81; iii. 107,
124; v. 1110, 1157, 1158; vii. 8.
Buys masque book, iii. 108.
Sees masque, iii. 217, 218.
Sees play, ii. 673–81.
Mildmay, Humphrey St. John, ii.
673.

Mildmay, Nann, ii. 676; iii. 360.
Mildmay, Sir Walter, ii. 673.
Mildmay, Walter, ward for son, iii. 112.
Miles, Bernard, vi. 86.
Miles, Dr. Theodore, iv. 930.
  ed., *James Shirley's Hyde Park edited from the Quarto of 1637.* Unpublished University of Chicago thesis (1940), v. 1121, 1122, 1123.
  'Place-Realism in a Group of Caroline Plays', *R.E.S.* xviii (1942), 428–40; iii. 87, 89; iv. 745, 747, 932, 933, 940, 942; v. 1122.
Military Company, v. 1104.
Military Ground in Leicester Fields, v. 1104.
Military service, iii. 39, 143.
  Playwrights in, iii. 22, 143, 194, 195, 196, 275, 469; iv. 521, 587, 606, 721, 725, 728, 733, 736–8, 850–1; v. 1040, 1070, 1186, 1198–1200, 1218, 1268.
Military show, vii. 112.
Mill, Humphrey, iv. 928.
  Night's Search, A (1640), iii. 55, 153, 245.
Millay, Edna St. Vincent, iv. 788.
Miller, Elizabeth, ii. 631.
Miller, Richard, ii. 527.
Miller, Simon, v. 1364.
Millet, William, vi. 186.
Mills, Laurens J., *One Soul in Bodies Twain: Friendship in Tudor Literature and Stuart Drama* (1937), iii. 113, 117, 359; iv. 485, 532, 533, 534, 535, 536, 537, 852.
  Peter Hausted: Playwright, Poet, and Preacher (1944), v. 965, 966, 967, 983, 984, 985, 1407.
  ed., *Peter Hausted's The Rival Friends* (1951), iv. 534; v. 983.
  ed., *Peter Hausted's Senile Odium* (1949), iv. 537.
Mills, William, iv. 928, 942.
Milton, John, iv. 537, **911–16**; v. 1197, 1222.
  Influence of, iii. 296.
  Arcades, iv. 912–13.
  Comus, iii. 110, 296; iv. 638, 672, 912, **913–16**.
  Il Penseroso, iii. 384.
  Paradise Lost (1667), iv. 912.
  Paradise Regained (1671), iv. 912.
  Poems of Mr. John Milton, Both English and Latin, Compos'd at

Several Times (1645), iv. 912, 914–15.
  Poems, &c. Upon Several Occasions. By Mr. John Milton . . . (1673), iv. 913, 915.
  Poetical Works of Mr. John Milton . . ., The (1695), iv. 913, 915.
  Samson Agonistes (1671), iv. 912.
Milton, John, Sr., iv. 912.
Minerva's Sacrifice, see Massinger, Philip.
Mingay, Anthony, i. 312.
Minion, Samuel, i. 299; ii. **511**.
Minnes, Sir John, iv. 694; vi. 243.
Minshall, Edward, *see* Minshaw, Edward.
Minshaw, Edward, ii. **511**.
Minshaw, Huon, ii. **511**.
Minshaw, Jane, ii. **511**.
Minshaw, John, ii. **511**.
Minshaw, Joyce, ii. **511**.
Minshaw, Julyan, ii. **511**.
Minshaw, Mary, ii. **511**.
Minshaw, Willi, ii. **511**.
Minshew, John, iii. 239, 243.
Mint, the, v. 993.
  Chief Engraver of, v. 994.
  Master worker of, iii. 468.
  Residence at, v. 994.
Miracle plays, v. 1142.
Mirror of the Late Times, The, see Tatham, John, *The Rump.*
Mirza, A Tragedy, see Baron, Robert.
Misanthropus, see Heywood, Thomas.
Miscellania (1653), *see* Flecknoe, Richard.
Miscellany, Being a Collection of Poems by Several Hands (1685), v. 985.
Miseries of Enforced Marriage, The, see Wilkins, George.
Mistaken Brothers, The, see Behn, Aphra, *Like Father, like Son.*
Mistale or Misdale, i. 286, 297; ii. **511**.
'Mr. and Mrs. Browne of the Boar's Head', *see* Sisson, Charles J.
Mistress, The, see Cowley, Abraham.
Mitchell, Francis, vi. 202.
Mitchell, John Arthur, ed., *The Warde by Thomas Neale* (1937), iv. 944, 945.
Mitchenson, Joe, *Picture History of the British Theatre* (1957), *see* Mander, Raymond.

Mitre in Fleet Street, vii. 27.

Mnemotechnics, vi. 186 n. 1.

Mock Marriage, The, see Brome, Richard, The English Moor.

Modern Lucretia, A, see Anonymous, The Fatal Marriage.

Modish Wife, The, see Anonymous, Tom Essence.

Mohun, Lady Catherine, ii. 447; iii. 457.

Mohun, John, Lord, iv. 778.

Mohun (Moone), Michael, i. 327 and n. 4, 332, 336; ii. 511-12; v. 1151, 1217; vi. 68, 74.

Molina, Tirso de, El Castigo del penséque, v. 1136, 1167.
Los cigarrales de Toledo, v. 1167.
Los tres maridos burlados, v. 1167.

Moll Cutpurse, see Dekker, Thomas, The Roaring Girl.

Molle, Henry, v. 1238.

Mompesson, Sir Giles, iii. 468; iv. 616, 801, 802; v. 982; vi. 291 n. 1.

Momus Triumphans, see Langbaine, Gerard.

Monarchic Tragedies, The, see Sir William Alexander.

Monasteries, Carmelite, vi. 115, 116.

Monck, Gerard, George, Duke of Albemarle, ii. 545; iv. 680; vi. 284.

Monday, Anthony, see Munday, Anthony.

Money Is an Ass, see Jordan, Thomas.

Money Works Wonders, see Shirley, James, The Bird in a Cage.

Monke, Samuel, ii. 512.

Monke, William, ii. 512.

Monmouth, Earl of (Robert, Lord Carey), iv. 658.

Monmouth, Geoffrey of Historia Regum Britanniae, iii. 115.

Monologues, v. 974-6, 991.

Monopolers, i. 65 n. 2, 317 n. 1.

Monopolies, suppression of, iv. 492; v. 1266.

Monopoly of London stage, iv. 696.

Monsieur D'Olive, see Chapman, George.

Monsieur Perrolis, see Fletcher, John.

Montacute House, Somersetshire, iv. 918.

Montagu, Edward, 1st Baron Montagu, vi. 72.

Montagu, Sir Henry, 1st Earl of Manchester, iv. 916.

Montagu, Walter, iii. 21; iv. 695, 709, 916-21; vi. 17.
Accomplish'd Woman. Written Originally in French, since Made English, The (1656), iv. 917.
Miscellanea Spiritualia; or, Devout Essaies (1648), iv. 917.
Shepherd's Paradise, iii. 453; iv. 548, 628, 916, 917-21; v. 1074, 1080-1; vi. 283.

Montague, Lady Mary Wortley, iv. 700.

Montague, Thomas, v. 1176.

Monteagle, Baron, iv. 520.

Montgomery, Countess of, iii. 435. Urania, v. 1139.

Montgomery, Philip Herbert, third Earl of, ii. 349; iii. 309; iv. 670, 677, 691, 692, 751, 756-7, 769, 802, 831; vi. 297, 298.

Monuments of Honour, see Webster, John.

Moody, Henry, iv. 802.

Moone, Michael, see Mohun, Michael.

Moor Lane, see London, streets of.

Moor of Venice, The, see Shakespeare, William, Othello.

Moore, Captain Alexander, ii. 438.

Moore, Charlotte, The Dramatic Works of Thomas Nabbes (1918), iv. 927, 929, 932, 934, 936, 938, 939, 940, 942.

Moore, Edward, iv. 737.

Moore, John, i. 64.

Moore, John Robert, 'The Contemporary Significance of Middleton's Game at Chesse', P.M.L.A. 1 (1935), iv. 870.
'The Songs in Lyly's Plays', P.M.L.A. xlii (1927), 623-40, iii. 459, 461.

Moore, Joseph, i. 176, 178, 179, 180 and n. 13, 181, 182, 183, 187, 188, 189 and nn. 3 and 4, 190, 192, 219, 302, 303, 307, 308, 311, 315, 321; ii. 512-15, 682; vi. 59.

Moore, Mr., v. 1375.

Moore, Robert, ii. 438.

Moore, Thomas, iv. 921.
Arcadian Lovers, or the Metamorphosis of Princes, The, iv. 921.
Brief Discourse about Baptism, A (1649), iv. 921.

Moore, Sir Thomas, Mangora, King of the Timbusians, or the Faithful Couple, iv. 921.

Moore Smith, G. C., see Smith, G. C. Moore.

Moorgate, *see* London, streets of.

Moors, iv. 492.

Moor's Masque, The, see Anonymous.

Morality plays, iv. 599, 938; v. 1370.

Morals, ii. 685.

More, H., iv. 921; v. 1390.

More, Roger, *see* Nore, Roger.

More Dissemblers besides Women, see Middleton, Thomas.

More Frightened than Hurt, see Poole, John, *The Wife's Stratagem*

More than Nine Days' Wonder, see Anonymous.

'More Records from the Remembrancia of the City of London', *see* Wilson, F. P.

Moreton, Richard, ii. 564.

Morgan, F., iv. 569, 922.

Morgan, F. C., 'A Deed of Gift (1624) and John Webster', *N. & Q.* cxcii (1947), v. 1240.

Morgan, Fluellen, ii. 515.

Morgan, General, ii. 521.

Morgan, Louise B., 'The Latin University Drama', *Shakespear Jahrbuch*, xlvii (1911), iii. 19, 20, 26, 159; v. 1179, 1260, 1264, 1278, 1383, 1407.

Morgan, Mrs., ii. 646, 647.

Morgan, William, ii. 385.

Morgenroth, Hugo, *Quellenstudien zu William Davenants Albovine* (1911), iii. 197, 198.

Morley, George (actor), iv. 596.

Morley, Henry, ed., *Masques and Entertainments by Ben Jonson* (1890), iv. 613, 637, 639, 641, 642, 645, 650, 651, 655, 658, 660, 663, 665, 669, 672, 676.

Memoirs of Bartholomew Fair (1869), iv. 930.

Morris dancers, vi. 294.

Morris-dances, vi. 209.

Morris, Dr., Oxford Prebendary, v. 1190.

Morris, Edgar Coit, 'The Allegory in Middleton's *A Game at Chesse*', *Englische Studien*, xxxviii (1907), iv. 870, 878.

'On the Date and Composition of *The Old Law*', *P.M.L.A.* xvii (1902), iv. 890, 891; v. 1015.

ed., *The Spanish Gipsie, and All's Lost by Lust, By Thomas Middleton and William Rowley*, Belles-Lettres Series (1908), iv. 892, 895; v. 1018.

Morris, John, ii. 470; iii. 469.

Morris, Matthias, i. 285, 287, 290, 297; ii. 515; v. 1434.

Morrison, Elizabeth Bowyer, ii. 635, 636.

Morrison, Thomas, i. 69 n. 2, 88, 89; ii. 376, 387, 636.

Mors, see Drury, William.

Mors Valentiniani Imperatoris, see Anonymous.

Mortality tables, ii. 667–72.

Mortimer, Mr., ii. 350.

Mortimer His Fall, see Jonson, Ben.

Morton, Sir Albert, i. 10 n. 6.

Morton, Elizabeth, ii. 606.

Morton, Thomas, iii. 455.

Morwyng, Peter, *A Compendious and Most Marvelous History of the Latter Times of the Jew's Commonweal* (1558) (transl. from Josephus), iv. 547, 734, 735, 776.

Moryson, Fynes, *An Itinerary written by Fynes Moryson, Gent* (1617), iii. 85.

Moscovy, *see* Muscovy.

Moseley, Ann, assigns plays, iii. 109, 202, 203, 208, 210, 214, 215, 277, 403, 408, 411; iv. 901.

Moseley, Humphrey, i. 116, 117, 123, 276; iii. 19, 30, 31, 38, 59, 61, 65–66, 76, 78, 80, 82, 84, 85, 98, 109, 115, 117, 119, 122, 124, 128, 131, 132, 141, 145, 146, 149, 162, 198, 201, 202, 203, 206, 208, 210, 214, 215, 217, 221, 230, 231, 237, 250, 252, 262, 277, 310, 311, 314, 324, 330, 333, 337, 340, 343, 346, 348, 350, 352, 354, 357, 360, 364, 367, 370, 371, 374, 377, 380, 381, 382, 387, 388, 392, 395, 398, 400, 412, 418, 422, 423, 426, 427, 431, 438, 439, 445, 447, 448, 458, 464, 465, 466, 467; iv. 481, 488, 490, 493, 494, 513, 615, 626, 633, 684, 706, 707, 720, 753–829 *passim*, 834, 837, 862, 864, 883, 888, 892, 893, 900, 901, 906; v. 979, 990–1, 1004, 1022, 1024, 1025, 1026, 1030, 1046, 1058, 1059, 1060, 1062, 1063, 1066, 1072, 1082, 1083, 1085, 1096, 1100, 1105, 1112, 1124, 1137, 1138, 1147, 1160, 1203, 1208, 1210, 1246, 1270, 1272, 1273, 1277, 1286, 1287, 1306, 1307, 1314, 1323, 1354, 1355, 1360, 1382, 1397, 1412, 1413, 1446.

'Moses his Funeral', *see* Blencowe, John.

Mosley, Margaret, ii. 649.

Mossock, Ann, ii. 515, 598.
Mother Bombie, see Lyly, John.
Mother Rumming, see Anonymous.
Motteux, Peter, v. 1152.
Motteux, Pierre: The Island Princess (opera), iii. 349.
Mount Atlas, vi. 257.
Mountague, Lord, see Montagu, Edward, 1st Baron Montagu.
Mountebanks, foreign, vii. 6.
'Mountebanks Dance at Grayes Inn, The', see Anonymous.
'Mountebankes Receipts, The', see Anonymous.
Mountfort, Walter, iv. 922–4.
    Launching of the Mary, or the Seaman's Honest Wife, The, iv. 853, 923–4.
Mountfort, William, Edward the Third, iii. 237.
    Henry the Second, King of England; with the Death of Rosamond, iii. 231.
Mountney, Richard, iv. 922.
Mountsett, John, ii. 515.
Moxie, James, ii. 394.
Moyle, Walter, v. 1139.
Mucedorus, see Anonymous.
Much Ado about Nothing, see Shakespeare.
Muddiman, J. G. [J. B. Williams], A History of English Journalism . . . (1908), iv. 497.
Mulcaster, Richard, iii. 300.
Mull Sack, see Anonymous.
Mull Sack, alias Jack Cottington, iii. 188, 189.
Mummeries, vi. 294.
Mumming, iv. 639.
Mun, Thomas, A Discourse of Trade, from England unto the East Indies: Answering to divers Objections which are usually made against the same (1621), iv. 924.
Munck, Lewin, ii. 416.
Munda, Constantia (pseud.), v. 1417.
Munday, Anthony, iii. 1, 44, 261; iv. 585, 861, 895, 896, 925–6; v. 1240, 1241, 1243, 1248, 1428.
    Proposed pageant, iv. 926.
    Downfall and Death of Robert Earl of Huntingdon, The, vii. 22, 35, 111.
    Jeptha, see Dekker, Thomas, iv. 794.
    Oldcastle, see Drayton, Michael.
    Siderothriambos, or Steel and Iron Triumphing, iv. 925.

Strangest Adventure . . . containing a discourse concerning the success of the King of Portugal Dom Sebastian, The (1601), iv. 763.
Triumphs of the Golden Fleece, The, iv. 898–9, 926.
Muntford, John, see Mountsett, John.
Murder, v. 1057, 1200.
Murder-plays, iii. 252–6.
Murder Will Out, see Davenport, Robert, The Politic Queen.
Murray, James A. H., ed., A new English dictionary on historical principles; founded mainly on the materials collected by the Philological Society, 10 vols., 1888–1928 [suppl. vol. –1933], iii. 150; v. 1325, 1363.
Murray, John, ii. 385.
Murray, John Tucker, English Dramatic Companies, 1558–1642, 2 vols. (1910), i. passim; iii. 233, 270, 271, 347, 391, 425, 655, 801, 829, 830; v. 1344, 1370, 1444, 1456; vi. 135.
Murray, William, of King's Bed Chamber, i. 60, 61; iv. 477–8, 795; vii. 58.
Murrey, Henry, vi. 303.
Musaeum Minervae, iv. 716, 717; vi. 299.
Musarum Deliciae, see M., Sir J.
Muscovites, iii. 366.
Muscovy, ambassadors, iv. 651, 670; v. 1288.
Muse of New-Market, The (1680), see Anonymous.
Muses' Looking Glass, The, see Randolph, Thomas.
Museum of European Culture, University of Illinois, vi. 143.
Musgrave, Thomas, fencer, vi. 250.
Music, iii. 2, 109, 141, 195, 208, 219, 220, 255; iv. 484, 651, 657, 668, 692, 703, 765, 814, 915; v. 298, 971, 988, 989, 1098, 1102, 1110, 1103, 1104, 1147, 1157, 1159, 1162, 1175, 1183, 1192, 1197, 1228, 1230, 1264, 1289, 1314, 1358, 1360, 1405, 1408, 1430, 1431; vi. 32–33, 53, 108–9, 111, 117, 238, 257, 279, 280, 293, 294, 295, 298, 305; vii. 24, 94.
    At Blackfriars, iv. 703.
    Between acts of a play, iv. 924, 935.
    Instrumental, vi. 151.
    In manuscript, iv. 850, 886.

For Masques, iii. 214, 218, 220; iv. 651, 657.
For plays, iii. 84, 132, 134, 332, 397; iv. 536, 692, 924.
Rooms in theatres, *see* Theatres, music rooms in.
Vocal, vi. 294.
Vocal and instrumental, vi. 284 n. I.
'Music for Shakespeare's Company, The King's Men' (1956), *see* Cutts, John P.
Musical allegory, iv. 882.
Musical Antiquarian Society Publications, v. 1430.
Musical compositions, v. 1188, 1315, 1324, 1327, 1331, 1336.
Short, v. 1338.
Collection of, v. 1349.
Musical entertainments, vi. 305, 306.
Musical farce, v. 1167.
Musical organ, vii. 48.
Musicians, i. 3, 15, 20, 40, 142; ii. 343, 347, 349, 354, 355, 363, 400, 422, 426, 427, 429, 432, 441, 443, 479, 482, 487, 495, 508, 511, 512, 543, 544, 554, 560, 561, 573, 578, 590, 609, 610, 621, 622; iii. 1, 109; iv. 692, 857, 912, 913, 915, 950; v. 1158, 1159, 1162, 1230, 1304; vi. 32–33, 133, 237, 279, 280.
French, vii. 22.
Royal, vi. 296.
'Musicke thou Queene of Soules', *see* Randolph, Thomas.
Musique de Scène de la Troupe de Shakespeare: The King's Men sous le règne de Jaques Ier (1959), *see* Cutts, John P.
Mustapha, *see* Anonymous.
Mustapha, *see* Greville, Fulke.
Mustapha, the Son of Solyman the Magnificent, *see* Boyle, Roger.
Mustard, Wilfred P., 'Notes on the Tragedy of Nero', *P.Q.* i (1922), v. 1380, 1381.
Mutes, vi. 172, 173.
Myers and Company, *Illustrated Catalogue of Rare Books*, ii. 623.
Mylyon, Mr., ii. 622.
Mysteries of Love and Eloquence, *see* Philips, Edward.

N., M., *The Faithful General: A Tragedy*, iii. 373.
N., R., *Sir Thomas Overburies Vision* (1616), ed., James Maid-

ment, Hunterian Club, No. 17 (1873), iv. 902.
Nabbes, Bridgett, iv. 928, 929.
Nabbes, Thomas, ii. 488, 509 n. 1; iii. 16, 39, 55, 66, 76, 90–91, 153; iv. 475, 679, 737, **927–44**; v. 1216; vi. 109.
Bride, The, i. 340; iii. 66, 153; iv. **929–32**, 943; v. 1348; vi. 53, 69–70.
'Continvation of The Tvrkish Historie, From The Yeare Of Ovr Lord 1628, to The End of The Yeare 1637, Collected out of the Dispatches of Sr Peter Wyche Knight, Embassador at Constantinople, and others, A' (1638), iv. 928.
Covent Garden, i. 227, 255; iii. 88, 90, 91; iv. 483, 927, 929, **932–4**, 942; v. 1074, 1169, 1348; vi. 51, 53.
Hannibal and Scipio, i. 221 n. 1, 231, 235, 246, 251, 255; ii. 344, 345, 353, 377, 378, 387, 407, 433, 518, 528, 573, 581, 583, 608, 660, 692; iii. 66; iv. 928, 929, **934–6**, 937; vi. 52, 53, 66 n. 1.
Microcosmus [A Moral Masque], i. 255; iii. 55, 66, 297; iv. 928, 929, **936–8**, 939; v. 1126; vi. 107–9; vii. 6.
Playes, Maskes, Epigrams, Elegies and Epithalamiums. Collected into one Volume. By Thomas Nabbes (1639), iv. 929.
Presentation Intended for the Prince His Highness on His Birthday, A, iv. 927, **938–9**, 940.
Spring's Glory, The, iii. 153; iv. 927, 929, 938, **939–40**; v. 1222.
Tottenham Court, i. 255–6; iii. 66, 76, 88, 90; iv. 483, 929, 933, 938, 939, **940–2**; v. 1417; vi. 92–93.
Unfortunate Mother, The, ii. 444; iii. 39, 66; iv. 927, 928, 940, **942–4**.
Nabbes, William, iv. 928.
Nabes, Joane, ii. 491.
Nabs, Thomas, *see* Nabbes, Thomas.
Nagasaki, v. 1392.
Nagler, Alois M., vi. 192.
Shakespeare's Stage (1958), vi. 179, 187, 191.
Naiads, vi. 294.
Nanteuil, monastery of, iv. 917.

Naples, iii. 9.
  Killigrew in, iv. 707, 708.
  Play written at, iii. 171.
  Scene of play, iv. 706.
Napper family of Oxford, ii. 457, 689; vi. 100.
Naps upon Parnassus, see Austin, Samuel.
Narbona, Dorothea, v. 994.
Narcissus, see Jonson, Ben, *Cynthia's Revels.*
Naseby (ship), iv. 696.
Nashe, Thomas, iii. 18, 440; iv. 618.
  Isle of Dogs, The, i. 1; iv. 607.
  Pierce Penniless, iv. 887.
  Summer's Last Will and Testament, vii. 26, 61.
Nason, Arthur Huntington, *Heralds and Heraldry in Ben Jonson's Plays, Masques and Entertainments* (1907), iv. 605.
  James Shirley Dramatist (1915), v. 1056, 1065–1170 *passim,* 1312, 1318, 1320.
National Portrait Gallery, iv. 696.
Nau, Etienne, dancer, iii. 139.
Naufragium Joculare, see Cowley, Abraham.
Naunton, Sir Robert, v. 1422; vi. 297.
Navarro, John, ii. 515.
Navarro, Juan, vii. 94, 100.
Navy, the, vi. 160, 161.
Naworth Castle, i. 212.
Naylor, Mr. Oliver, tutor, iii. 185–6.
Neale, Anna Sophia, iv. 945.
Neale, Lucy, iv. 945.
Neale, Robert, ii. 637.
Neale, Thomas, iv. 944–5.
  Treatise of Direction how to travel safely and profitably into forraigne countries (1643), iv. 945.
  Warde, The, iv. 945.
Neale, Sir Thomas, iv. 944, 945.
Nearing, Alice Jones, *Cupid and Psyche, by Shakerly Marmion—A Critical Edition: with an Account of Marmion's Life and Works* (1944), iv. 736, 737, 738.
Neck verse, iv. 607.
Needham, Francis, ed., *Welbeck Miscellany No.* 1 (A Pleasante & Merrye Humor off A Roge, by William Cavendish) (1933), iii. 148.
  ed., *Welbeck Miscellany No.* 2 (A Collection of Poems by Several Hands) (1934), iii. 146.
Needlework, v. 1257.

Negri, Francesco (of Bassano), *Tragedia di F. N. B. intitolata, Libero arbitrio,* iii. 46–47.
Neill, J. K., 'Thomas Drue's *Dutches of Suffolke* and the Succession', *M.L.N.* xlviii (1933), iii. 284, 285.
Neilson, William Allan, ed., *The Chief Elizabethan Dramatists* (1911), iii. 425.
Neptune, iii. 393.
Neptune's Address, see Tatham, John.
Neptune's Triumph for the Return of Albion, see Jonson, Ben.
Neri-Bianchi feud, iii. 339.
Nero, see Gwinne, Matthew.
Nethercot, Arthur, 'Abraham Cowley as Dramatist', *R.E.S.* iv. (1928), iii. 172, 176, 180, 181, 182.
  Abraham Cowley, the Muse's Hannibal (1931), iii. 172, 174, 175, 180.
  'Literary Legend of Francis Quarles, The', *Mod. Phil.* xx (1923), iv. 955.
  Sir William D'avenant, Poet Laureate and Playwright-Manager (1938), iii. 192–225 *passim;* iv. 546; v. 1361, 1362.
Netherlands, ii. 578; iii. 351, 467; iv. 696, 721; v. 1176.
  Ambassador from, i. 20.
  Company, iv. 922.
  English actors in, i. 6, 335; ii. 413, 493, 494, 523, 571, 625.
  English Ambassador to, iii. 416.
  Flight to, iii. 188, 194.
  Missions in, iii. 196.
  Six commissioners from, vii. 39.
  Travellers from, iii. 377.
  Troops in, iii. 18.
  Vaulter from, ii. 502.
Nethersole, Sir Francis, i. 10 nn. 2 and 5, 267; iv. 548, 637, 873, 874; vi. 162; vii. 34.
Neville, Robert, iv. 946.
  The Poor Scholar, iv. 946.
New College, Oxford, iii. 29, 139; v. 1276.
  Fellow of, v. 1276.
New College, Winchester, ii. 514.
New England, v. 1193.
New Exchange, the, vi. 307 n. 1.
'New Facts from Sir Henry Herbert's Office Book', *see* Lawrence, William John.
New Facts Regarding the Life of Shakespeare in a Letter to Thomas

Amyot, Esq., F.R.S. (1835), *see* Collier, John Payne.
New Inn, iii. 93.
New Inn, The, see Jonson, Ben.
'New Light on the Elizabethan Theatre', *see* Lawrence, William John.
New Ordinary, The, see Brome, Richard, *The Damoiselle*.
New Prison, the, *see* Prison, the New.
New Shakspere Society, vi. 152.
'New Site for the Salisbury Court Theatre A', *see* Bordinat, Philip.
New Theatre, iii. 82, 120, 124, 135, 146, 150, 325, 330, 333, 337, 340, 344, 345, 348, 352, 354, 357, 360, 364, 367, 371, 382, 387, 392, 395, 398, 403, 409, 413, 419, 423, 427; iv. 616, 619, 623, 629, 633, 761, 775, 778, 783, 789, 812, 815, 821, 888, 900, 901; v. 1085, 1105, 1124, 1148, 1204, 1208.
New Theatre, Dublin, v. 1140, 1141.
New Theatre in Lincoln's Inn Fields, iii. 23; v. 1124.
New theatre proposed, iii. 195; vi. 291-309.
'New Theory about the Swan Drawing, A', *see* Holmes, Martin.
New Trick to Cheat the Devil, A, see Davenport, Robert.
New Way to Pay Old Debts, A, see Massinger, Philip.
New Way to Please You, A, see Middleton, Thomas, *The Old Law*.
New Wonder, a Woman Never Vext, A, see Rowley, William.
New World of English Words, The, see Phillips, E.
New Year's gift to Sir Henry Herbert, iv. 642.
New Year's gifts, iv. 642; vi. 59.
New York, v. 1112.
  Public Library, iv. 850; v. 1212.
Newark upon Trent, iv. 586.
Newbury, Berkshire, v. 1371.
Newcastle coalfields, iii. 468.
Newcastle, Earl, Marquis, and Duke of, *see* Cavendish, William.
Newcastle, King's visit to, ii. 388-9.
Newcome, Sir Henry, Commonplace book (1650-1713), iv. 887.
Newcourt, Richard (his map of London), vi. 224 n. 1.
Newdigate, B. H., v. 967, 976.
  'The Constant Lovers', *T.L.S.* 18 and 25 April 1942, v. 967.
Newgate, *see* London, streets and districts of.

Newgate Prison, *see* Prisons.
Newington Butts, Surrey, iv. 858.
  Theatre, i. 1; vi. 214.
Newman, Dorman, v. 1446.
Newman, Thomas, iv. 946-7.
  Transl. Terence's *Andria* and *The Eunuch* (1627), iv. 946-7.
Newmarket, i. 61; iii. 159, 160, 176, 178, 207; iv. 529, 530, 534, 669, 761, 795, 828, 917, 954; v. 984, 1228, 1238, 1404, 1408; vii. 20, 29, 35, 41, 42, 45, 58, 66.
  Game, iv. 477.
Newnham-cum-Badby, Northamptonshire, v. 965.
Newport, Anne, Countess of, i. 329; vi. 69.
Newport, Earl of, iii. 195.
Newport, Maurice, iv. 947.
  Tragedy, A, iv. 947.
Newport, Mountjoy Blount, Earl of, vi. 69.
News from the New World Discovered in the Moon, see Jonson, Ben.
News from Plymouth, see Davenant, William.
News pamphlets, iii. 338.
Newsletter, i. 223 n. 8; iv. 522; vi. 198.
Newspapers, iv. 589, 631, 832, 847; v. 1011, 1053, 1058, 1443; vi. 40, 76, 230, 232; vii. 12, 13.
  English, iv. 631.
  Satire of, v. 1147.
  Diary or an Exact Journal, A, ii. 549.
  Kingdom's Weekly Intelligencer, The, ii. 481; vi. 76, 113, 114, 172 n., 176, 177, 231.
  Laughing Mercury, The, vi. 233.
  Man in the Moon, The, ii. 462, 531; vi. 213, 232.
  Mercurius Aulicus, iv. 497, 551.
  Mercurius Britannicus, iv. 589, 832; vii. 13.
  Mercurius Democritus, ii. 415; vi. 233-4.
  Mercurius Elencticus, vi. 76.
  Mercurius Fumigosus, ii. 515, 523; vi. 234, 235, 236.
  Mercurius Impartialis, ii. 462.
  Mercurius Melancholicus, vi. 113, 176.
  Mercurius Militaris, ii. 462.
  Mercurius Pragmaticus, ii. 531, 555; v. 1011; vi. 113, 134.
  Mercurius Pragmaticus (for King Charles II), vi. 170, 232.
  Mercurius Publicus, vi. 178.

Newspapers (*cont.*)
Mercurius Vapulans, vi. 40.
Mercurius Veridicus, vi. 175.
Perfect Account of the Daily Intelligence, A, vi. 235.
Perfect Diurnal, A, vi. 230, 231.
Perfect Occurrences, ii. 548; vi. 112, 230.
Perfect Weekly Account, The, vi. 40.
Post-Boy, iii. 395, 396.
Royal Diurnal, ii. 462.
Second Discovery by the Northern Scout, A, i. 13 n. 2.
True Diurnal Occurrences, i. 67.
Vox Borealis, or the Northern Discovery, i. 277, 282.
Weekly Account, The, vi. 155, 174.
Weekly Intelligencer, The, vi. 235, 236.
Newstead Abbey, Nottinghamshire, iv. 527.
News-writers, v. 1235.
Newton, Francis, ii. 384.
Newton, John, i. 137 n. 3, 176, 198, 199 and n. 2, 200 and n. 3, 203 and n. 1, 209, 210, 211; ii. 515–16; iv. 881.
Newton, Lady, iii. 460.
Newton, Peter, vi. 134.
Newton, William, ii. 516.
Niccolls, —, v. 1008.
Nice Valour, or the Passionate Madman, The, see Fletcher, John.
Nicholas, Sir Edward, ii. 473, 512; v. 1176.
Nicholas, John, see Nicols, John.
Nicholls, Ciprian, iv. 947.
Nicholls, William, iv. 947.
Nichols, John, see Nicols, John.
Nichols (Nicholas), John, v. 1419.
Nichols, John, History and Antiquities of the County of Leicester, 4 vols. (1795–1811), iv. 954.
Progresses, Processions, and Magnificent Festivities of King James the First, His Royal Consort, Family, and Court, The, 4 vols. (1828), iii. 101, 159; iv. 530, 590, 596, 658, 659, 896, 897; v. 1185, 1257, 1376; vii. 19, 24, 28, 58.
Nicholson, Brinsley, 'R. Brome's "Queen's Exchange", 1657, and "Royal Exchange", 1661', N. & Q., Seventh Series, vii,i ii. 86.
'Cornelianum Dolium', N. & Q.,

Fifth Series, x (1878), v. 962, 963.
'Date of Northward Ho, A Chaste Maid, and The Northern Lass, The', N. & Q., Fourth Series, xi (1873), iii. 81.
'Henry Glapthorne's "Albertus Wallenstein", Eds. 1639–40', N. & Q., Seventh Series, vii (16 February 1889), iv. 477.
Nicholson, James, i. 276.
Nicholson, John, iii. 187, 188; v. 1302, 1326, 1387.
Nick, actor, ii. 516–17; iv. 764, 765.
Nicolini, Francis, ii. 517; iv. 780, 781.
Nicoll, Allardyce, British Drama (1955), vi. 51.
ed., The Fool would be a Favourit: or The Discreet Lover (1657) by Lodowick Carlell (1926), iii. 117, 118.
History of Restoration Drama, third ed. (1940), iii. 24, 25, 82, 85, 114, 115, 120, 124, 135, 146, 177, 277, 315, 320, 325, 330, 333, 344–431 passim; iv. 616, 619, 623, 629, 633, 719, 761, 776, 778, 783, 789, 815, 822, 848, 884, 888, 901, 936; v. 998, 999, 1063, 1080, 1083, 1085, 1092, 1105, 1122, 1124, 1133, 1145, 1148, 1151, 1204, 1208, 1211.
History of Early Eighteenth Century Drama, A (1925), iii. 84, 328, 332, 336, 342, 397; iv. 921, 932; v. 1021, 1111, 1127.
History of Late Eighteenth Century Drama, A (1937), iii. 72–73; iv. 571, 762, 777, 799, 810; v. 1087.
'Sir Kenelm Digby, Poet, Philosopher, and Pirate of the Restoration', The Johns Hopkins Alumni Magazine, xxi (1933), iii. 279.
Some Account of the Worshipful Company of Ironmongers (1851), iv. 577.
Stuart Masques and the Renaissance Stage (1937), iii. 107, 110, 130, 199, 207, 213, 214, 216, 218; iv. 524, 637, 642, 650, 660, 669, 676, 927; vi. 259, 263; v. 1334, 1335; vi. 259, 263, 268, 282.
ed., Tragedy of Osmond the Great Turk, or the Noble Servant, The (1926), iii. 119.

Nicols, John, ii. 502, 552; iv. 947–8.
Unnamed comedy, iv. 948.
Night performances, iii. 221; vi. 35–36, 164, 284.
Night playing, see Plays at night.
Night Walker, The, see Fletcher, John.
Nightingale, Sir Thomas, v. 1113.
Night-pieces, iv. 792–3.
Nightwalkers, iii. 85.
Nill, John, ii. 517.
Nims, John Frederick, ed., *James Shirley's Love's Cruelty, edited from the Quarto of 1640 with an Introduction and Notes*, Unpublished University of Chicago thesis (1945), v. 1129, 1130, 1131, 1132.
Nineveh's Repentance, see Anonymous.
Ninth Whelp, ship, v. 1136.
Nipping or Snipping of Abuses (1614), *see* Taylor, John.
Nissen, Peter, *James Shirley. Ein Beitrag zur englischen Litteraturgeschichte* (1901), v. 1065, 1142.
Noar *or* Noer, Roger, *see* Nore, Roger.
Nobility, vi. 292; vii. 39, 67.
Noble, — an actor, v. 1434.
Noble Bondman, The, see Massinger, Philip, *The Bondman*.
Noble Choice, The, see Massinger, Philip, *The Orator*.
Noble Enemy, The, see Fletcher John *The Humorous Lieutenant*.
Noble Friend, The, see Anonymous.
Noble Gentleman, The, see Fletcher, John.
Noble Husbands, The, see Glapthorne, Henry.
Noble Ingratitude, The, see Lower, William.
Noble Ravishers, The, see Anonymous.
Noble Servant, The, see Carlell, Lodowick, *Osmond, the Great Turk*.
Noble Soldier (The Noble Spanish Soldier), The, see Dekker, Thomas.
Noble Stranger, The, see Sharpe, Lewis.
Noble Trial, The, see Glapthorne, Henry.
Nobleman, The, see Tourneur, Cyril.
Noblemen as actors, vii. 37.
Nobody in Barbican, ii. 606, 682.
Nocturnal Lucubrations, see Chamberlain, Robert.

Nocturnals, vi. 294.
Noel, Mary, iii. 437.
Nokes, James, iii. 175, 377.
Nonesuch Palace, vii. 65.
Nonesuch, The, see Rowley, William.
Nonpareilles, or the Matchless Maids, The, see Davenant, William, *Love and Honour*.
Norden, John, *Civitas Londini* (1600) (map), vi. 183.
Nore, Amellicoe, ii. 517.
Nore, Elizabeth, ii. 517.
Nore, John, ii. 517.
Nore, Roger, i. 316 and n. 2, 321; ii. 517.
Norfolk, ii. 642; iii. 238, 310.
High Sheriff of, iii. 152.
Norman, Robert, iv. 899.
Norman's Rents, *see* London, streets of.
North, Thomas, Sir, transl., *The Lives of the Noble Grecians and Romans* (1595), iv. 768.
Northampton, Countess of (Isabella Compton), iv. 493, 544, 730.
Northampton, Earl of (James Compton), ii. 525, 608; iv. 493, 534, 544, 728, 729, 730, 731, 732.
Northamptonshire, v. 1341.
Northamptonshire, Lord-Lieutenant of, iii. 293.
Northern Castle, The, see Brome, Richard, *The Northern Lass*.
Northern Discoverie, The, see Anonymous, *Vox Borealis*.
Northern Lass, The, see Brome, Richard.
Northerne Lasse or sweet is the lasse that loues me, The (ballad), *see* Anonymous.
Northumberland, iii. 143; v. 1214.
Northumberland, Duke of, MSS. of, *see* Historical MSS. Commission.
Northumberland, Algernon Percy, tenth Earl of, iii. 213; iv. 650; v. 1159.
Northumberland, Henry Percy, ninth Earl of, v. 1425; vi. 153.
Northumberland, Lady, iii. 217.
Northup, C. S., 'On a School Play of 1648', *Englische Studien*, xlv (1912), iv. 748.
Northward Ho!, see Webster, John.
Northway, iii. 126.
Norton, George, iv. 775.
Norton, Mary, ii. 639.
Norton, Mrs., ii. 639.
Norton, Kent, iv. 515.
Norwich, i. 144 n. 4, 156, 172, 173,

Norwich (*cont.*)
178, 179, 181, 182, 193, 197, 212, 213, 248, 273, 274, 275, 276, 282, 286, 288, 289 and n. 4, 294, 297, 298, 299, 302, 303 and n. 1, 312 and n. 7 cont., 322; ii. 420, 427, 452, 454, 458, 485, 530, 613; iii. 10; iv. 571, 715, 801, 803; v. 1188.
Bishop of, i. 274.
Earl of, *see* Goring, George Lord.
Flemish, family in, iii. 185.
King's Arms, the, iv. 570, 868.
Mayor of, i. 179; iii. 10; v. 1198.
Court at, iv. 687.
Court Books, v. 1456.
St. Stephen, iv. 531.
Nosworthy, J. M., 'William Habington', *T.L.S.* 5 June 1937, iv. 521.
Notary Public, ii. 651.
'Note on the Date of Middleton's *The Family of Love* with a Query on the Porters Hall Theatre, A', *see* Maxwell, Baldwin.
'Note on the Swan Theatre Drawing, A', *see* Anonymous.
Notes from Blackfriars, *see* Fitz-Geoffrey, Henry.
'Notes from the Ecclesiastical Court Records at Somerset House', *see* Fincham, Francis W. X.
Notestein, Wallace, *A History of Witchcraft in England from 1558 to 1718* (1911), iii. 73; v. 1455.
Nothing Impossible to Love, *see* Le Grys, Sir Robert.
Notices Illustrative of the Drama and Other Popular Amusements (1865), *see* Kelly, William.
Nott, Dr., ii. 347.
N[ott], J., ed., *The Gull's Hornbook, Reprinted; with Notes of Illustration by J. N.* (1812), v. 1055.
Notte d'Amore, *see* Cinna, Francisco.
Nottingham, i. 92, 172, 173, 180, 193, 212, 213, 310; ii. 419, 617; v. 1044, 1186.
Castle, underground passages of, v. 1044.
Nottinghamshire, iv. 648, 653, 803.
Nottola, *see* Anonymous.
Novella, The, *see* Brome, Richard.
No Wit No Help like a Womans, *see* Middleton, Thomas.
Noy, William, Attorney-General, iv. 551; v. 1155, 1398.
Noyes, Robert Gale, *Ben Jonson on the English Stage 1660–1776* (1935), iv. 605.

Nuneaton, Warwickshire, iii. 99.
Nungezer, Edwin, *A Dictionary of Actors* (1929), iii. 432.
Nuremberg, ii. 451, 561.
Nursery, The, in Hatton-Garden, iv. 492, 894; v. 1095, 1145.
Nursery of Novelties in a Variety of Poetry, *see* Jordan, Thomas.
Nuts, iii. 103; vi. 171, 293.

O.E.D., *see* Murray, James A. H.
Oakes, Anne, stationer, iii. 25; iv. 565, 583; v. 1060.
Oakes, Edward, iv. 565, 583, 712; v. 1060.
Oakes, John, stationer, iii. 24, 187, 188; iv. 579, 711, 712; v. 1031, 1060, 1061.
Oakes, Nicholas, iv. 565, 582; v. 1061.
Oakham, Rutland, v. 1276.
Oakington, Cambridgeshire, v. 1236.
Oare's Rents, *see* London, streets and districts of.
Oaths, i. 37, 106–7; iii. 222; iv. 923, 924; vi. 25, 26; *see also* Plays, oaths in.
Oatlands, i. 50.
Queen's house at, iv. 695.
Oberon, the Faery Prince, *see* Jonson, Ben.
Oberon the Second, *see* Anonymous, *The Fairy Knight*.
Obituary acrostics, v. 1000.
Oboe, *see* Hoboye.
Observer, The, iv. 638.
Occupations, *see under* Apple wife, Bailiff, Baker, Barber-chirurgion, Basket-maker, Blacksmith, Body-keeper, Body-maker, Bookseller, Box-tumbler, Brewer, Bricklayer, Builder, Butcher, Carpenter, Carrier, Carver, Chandler, Clergyman, Clerk, Clothier, Clothmaker, Clothworker, Coal merchant, Collier, Composer, Conjurer, Constable, Contractor, Cooper, Cordwainer, Cutler, Cutpurse, Dancer, Dancer on the ropes, Dancing master, Doctor in physic, Draper, Drummer, Entertainer, Felt-maker, Fencer, Fiddler, Fishmonger, Flannell weaver, Game player, Gaoler, Gardener, Gatherer, Gem engraver, Goldsmith, Grocer, Haberdasher, Highwayman, Hosier, Huntsman, Inn holder, Inn keeper, Ironmonger, Jeweller,

Jig-maker, Joiner, Juggler, Labourer, Lace woman, Lawyer, Lodge keeper, Lutanist, Maid servant, Man servant, Merchant, Merchant adventurer, Merchant tailor, Messenger, Musician, Organist, Packthread-maker, Painter, Pewterer, Physician, Porter, Preacher, Printer, Property-maker, Puppeteer, Saddler, Sailor, Scene painter, Schoolmaster, Scrivener, Sergeant at Mace, Serving man, Shoemaker, Showman, Sidesman, Silk throstler, Silk-weaver, Smith, Stage keeper, Stationer, Surgeon, Taverner, Tailor, Theatre caretaker, Tight rope walker, Trumpeter, Tumbler, Turner, Undercook, Upholsterer, Vaulter, Victualer, Vintner, Wardrobekeeper, Waterman, Weaver, Workman.

Odell, G. C. D., *Annals of the New York Stage*, 15 vols. (1927–49), v. 1112.

Odoardus Varvici Comes, see Anonymous.

'Of the Passion of Love', *see* Wither, George.

'Of a Proud one', *see* Flecknoe, Richard.

'Of Stake and Stage', *see* Briley, John.

Office of the Works, vi. 271, 275, 277, 281.

Office of the Works Accounts, vi. 283 n.

'Office-Book, 1622–1642, of Sir Henry Herbert, Master of the Revels, The', *see* Adams, Joseph Quincy.

Officers of the Works, vi. 260, 261.

Ogilby, John, ii. 517–18; iv. 948–51; v. 1069, 1072, 1095, 1140, 1141. Dublin theatre of, v. 1339.
Fables of Æsop, Paraphras'd in Verse, The (1651), iv. 950; v. 1103.
The Merchant of Dublin, iv. 950–1.

Ogle, Baron, *see* Cavendish, William.

Ogle, Sir John, iii. 18.

Okes, John, *see* Oakes, John.

Olboston, Master, v. 985.

Old Couple, The, see May, Thomas.

Old Fortunatus, see Dekker, Thomas.

Old Jewry, *see* London, streets and districts.

Old Law, The, see Middleton, Thomas.

Old Style calendar, iv. 781.

Old Vic, iii. 270, 272.

Old Wives' Tale, The, see May, Thomas.

Oldcastle, see Drayton, Michael.

Oldham, John, *Satyrs upon the Jesuits* (1679), iv. 681.

Oldisworth, Michael, iii. 199, 207, 213.

Oldys, William, iii. 303, 858; v. 995, 1098; vi. 177.

Oley, Henry, ii. 518.

Oliphant, E. H. C., 'The Bloodie Banquet', *T.L.S.* 17 December 1925, iii. 282.
The Plays of Beaumont and Fletcher (1927), ii. 677; iii. 299, 303, 305, 313–432 *passim*; iv. 624, 754, 774, 819, 825, 826, 900, 901, 902; v. 1021, 1296.
'Problems of Authorship in Elizabethan Dramatic Literature', *Modern Philology*, viii (1911), iii. 5, 7.
Shakespeare and His Fellow Dramatists (1929), vol. ii, iv. 906.
'Three Beaumont and Fletcher Plays', *R.E.S.* xii (1936), iii. 364, 387.

Olivares, Count-Duke of, iv. 872, 873, 878; v. 972.

Olympiads, exercises of, vi. 293, 294, 295, 303.

Oman, Carola, *Henrietta Maria* (1936), iv. 548.

'On a Lady's Tempting Eye', *see* Rutter, Joseph.

'On that Excellent Cymilist . . . Tho: Rawlins', *see* Flecknoe, Richard.

One for Another, see Rowley, William, *A Knave in Print*.

'One that loved none but deformed Women.' *See* Shirley, James.

Opera, iii. 296, 349, 350, 374, 378, 395, 396, 413.

'Opera house', the projected, vi. 52.

Opera musicale, vi. 306.

Operatic performances, iii. 196.

Operatic style, iv. 651.

Operatic versions of plays, iii. 376.

Ὀφίλος, iii. 450.

Opossum, vii. 111.

Opportunity, The, see Shirley, James.

Orange, Prince of, vi. 35.

Oranges, iii. 103; vi. 171, 239.

Orator, The, see Massinger, Philip.

Orchards, vi. 224 n. 1.

Orchestra at Blackfriars, i. 40.

'Orchestra' in Swan theatre, vi. 192.

Ord, Craven, transcript by, iii. 32, 228, 246, 247, 253, 256, 284, 286; iv. 519, 520, 561, 644, 806, 812; v. 1013, 1014, 1046, 1050, 1075, 1146, 1291, 1321–2, 1324, 1328, 1393, 1396; vi. 60 n. 1, 137, 159 n. 1, 165 n., 173, 194 n. 3, 250.

Order of the Garter, vi. 261.

Ordinance, peal of, vi. 181.

Ordinary, The, see Cartwright, William.

Organist, ii. 422.

Organization and Personnel of the Shakespearean Company, The (1927), *see* Baldwin, Thomas Whitfield.

Oriel College, Oxford, iii. 38; iv. 716.

Oriental languages, v. 1038.

'Origin of the Substantive Theatre Masque, The', *see* Lawrence, W. J.

Original Letters, Second Series, *see* Ellis, Henry.

Orlando Furioso, see Greene, Robert.

Ormond, Earl and Marquis of, ii. 673; iii. 95.

Orpheus, see Anonymous.

Orsini, Napoleone, *Studii sul Rinascimento italiano in Inghilterra* (1937), v. 1340.

Ortenas, see Anonymous, *Ortenus*.

Orton, Mary, ii. 518.

Orton, Thomas, ii. 518.

Osbaldeston, Lambert, iv. 474, 596.

Osbalston, Mrs. Susanna, iv. 474.

Osborne, Alice Lewis, v. 1133–4.

Osborne, Dorothy, ii. 415, 416; iii. 25.

Osborne, Henry, v. 1133.

Osborne, Thomas, ii. 383.

Osborne, Sir Thomas, Earl of Danby, vi. 270 n. 1.

Osgood, Charles Grosvenor, *The Classical Mythology of Milton's English Poems* (1900), iv. 914.

Osman the Turk, see Carlell, Lodowick.

Osman the Turk, or The Ottoman Custom, see Anonymous.

Osmond, the Great Turk, see Carlell, Lodowick.

Ossulston, the Hundred of, Middlesex, ii. 458.

Ost, Gotthardt, *Das Verhältnis von Cibber's Lustspiel 'Love Makes a Man' zu Fletcher's Dramen 'The Elder Brother' und 'The Custom of the Country'* (1897), iii. 328, 336.

Ostella (1650), *see* Tatham, John.

Ostend, the siege of, iii. 467.

Ostler, Thomasina, vi. 180 n. 2.

Ostler, William, i. 5 n. 6 cont.; ii. 374; v. 1252; vi. 180 and n. 2.

Ostrich, iii. 256.

Oteley, Shropshire, iv. 716.

Othello, see Shakespeare.

Ottewell *or* Ottwell, Hugh, *see* Attwell, Hugh.

Ottoman Custom, The, see Anonymous, *Osman, the Turk*.

Otway, Thomas, *The Soldier's Fortune*, iv. 741.

Oukham, Kent, iv. 822.

Oulton, Walley Chamberlayne, *Frightened to Death*, v. 1167.

Oundle, Northamptonshire, iv. 332; v. 1265.

Ounslo, Mr., v. 1257.

Outlawe, Henry, vi. 7.

Outlines of the Life of Shakespeare (1887), *see* Halliwell-Phillipps, J. O.

Ovaa, W. A., 'Dekker and The Virgin Martyr', *English Studies*, iii (1921), iii. 263.

Overbury, Sir Thomas, iv. 620, 902. *Characters*, v. 1241. *Wife, The* (1616), iii. 228, 437; v. 1378.

Overseers of the Poor, vi. 250, 251.

Overton, Richard, iv. 954.

Ovid, iv. 558, 559, 574; v. 1098, 1355; vi. 182 n. 2. Influence of, iv. 558–9. Translation of, v. 962. *Metamorphoses*, iv. 559, 817; v. 1097. Transl. G. Sandys, v. 1048.

Ovo Frisius, see Anonymous.

Owen, Captain Richard, v. 1136.

Owen, C. A., *Thomas Killigrew, A Critical Study*. Unpublished dissertation, New College, Oxford (1938), iv. 694.

Owen, Corbet, iv. 951.

Owen, John, v. 1392.

Owl, The, see Anonymous. *See* Daborne, Robert.

'Owl, The', *see* Drayton, Michael.

Owles Almanacke, The, see Dekker, Thomas.

Owls, vi. 209.

Oxford, City of, i. 2, 19, 50, 52, 92, 172, 212, 293, 309; ii. 565, 688; iii. 31, 104, 127, 135, 138, 139, 141, 172, 196, 502; iv. 498, 502, 503, 505, 506, 508, 511, 516,

525, 551, 586, 591, 610, 717,
718, 722, 725, 770, 827, 836,
843, 844, 845, 846, 847, 850,
857, 944; v. 963, 966, 986, 994,
1007, 1027, 1047, 1055, 1066,
1169, 1170, 1179, 1185, 1186,
1307, 1308, 1357; vi. 97, 227.
All-saints parish, iv. 587.
Archdeacon of, iv. 588.
Bishop of, v. 1264.
Bocardo, iv. 592.
Christ Church Cathedral, Canon
of, iv. 540; v. 1291.
Coach, iv. 592.
Colleges, vi. 189; see also under,
All Souls, Brasenose, Broad-
gates Hall, Christ Church,
Exeter, Gloucester Hall, Hart
Hall, Lincoln, Magdalen, Mer-
ton, New, Oriel, Queen's, St.
Albans Hall, St. John's, St.
Mary Hall, Trinity, University,
Wadham, Worcester.
Custos archivorum, v. 1277.
Divinity Chapel of Christ Church
Cathedral, v. 1188.
Eastgate, v. 1375.
Fall of, v. 1227.
High Street, iv. 592.
King's Arms, The, v. 1019; vi.
164.
Magdalen School, iv. 552.
Mayor of, iii. 193.
Plays printed at, iii. 402, 406, 408,
411.
St. Giles, iii. 19; iv. 592.
St. Thomas, iii. 99.
Scene of play, iv. 723.
Surrender to Fairfax, v. 1277.
Oxford University, v. 1224, 1225,
1265, 1266, 1278, 1374; vi. 295.
Ashmolean Museum, ii. 500; v.
1058.
Bodleian Library, i. 104, 123, 127,
132; iii. 26, 454; iv. 527, 638,
651, 682, 811, 823, 839, 870,
871, 879, 903, 921, 931, 936,
945; v. 1071, 1121, 1353.
Manuscripts, 30, iii. 106; v.
1054.
Manuscripts, Arch. Seld., iii.
134.
Manuscripts, Ashmolean, iv.
541, 542, 717; v. 1094; vi.
26, n. 1, 163.
Manuscripts, Douce, iii. 176,
177; v. 1270, 1283, 1383.
Manuscripts, Eng. misc., iii.
113; v. 1390, 1392.

Manuscripts, Latin misc., iii. 19.
Manuscripts, Malone, iv. 870,
903; v. 1189, 1349.
Manuscripts, Tanner, iii. 95,
165; iv. 533. v. 1005–7; vi.
293–6, 297.
Manuscripts, Rawlinson, iii. 36,
159, 176; iv. 499, 527, 638,
682, 811, 921, 945; v. 1177,
1180, 1237, 1238, 1244, 1270,
1271, 1272, 1291, 1297,
1376, 1394, 1400, 1405, 1406,
1407, 1409.
Manuscripts, Wood, v. 1373,
1374.
Chancellor of, iii. 135; v. 1189,
1263; vi. 100.
Codification of University
statutes, v. 1277.
Convocation for degradation of
Prynne, v. 1193, 1194.
Council of War, iii. 127.
Grants M.D., iii. 175.
Junior proctor, iii. 127.
Matriculation Register, iii. 104.
Music School, iv. 647; v. 1163.
MSS. of, iii. 84; v. 1360.
Performances at, iii. 59, 99–100,
102, 104, 135, 192; v. 1021,
1163, 1170; vi. 99.
Permission to play at, vi. 100.
Proctors of, iii. 3, 141, 291; iv.
513; v. 1188.
Professor of Poetry, iii. 96.
Public expulsion from, v. 1193,
1194.
Public Orator, v. 1188.
Regius Professor of Greek, iii. 183.
Royal visits to, iii. 3, 135; iv. 721,
844, 849; v. 1189–95, 1259,
1261, 1262–4, 1275, 1358.
Royal visits described, v. 1190–2.
Secretary to the Vice-Chancellor
of, vi. 100.
Shows at, iii. 75–76.
Vice-chancellor of, ii. 688; iii. 20.
Oxford, Earl of (Robert Harley), iv.
622.
Company of, vi. 123.
Gives robes to players, iii. 206.
Oxford, Lady Ann, Countess of, ii.
525; iv. 773.
Oxfordshire stone, vi. 262.
Oxnead, iv. 715.

P., A., iv. 545.
P., J., v. 961.
Packington, Leicestershire, iv. 952,
953.

Packthread, vi. 273.

Packthread-maker, ii. 357.

Padua, University of, iii. 166, 171.

Pafford, J. H. P., and W. W. Greg, eds., John Clavell's *The Soddered Citizen* (1936), iii. 161, 162, 163, 164, 165; iv. 737, 780.

Page, Mr., ii. 640.

Page, John, i. 220, 239, 246, 324, 326 n. 6, 332, 336; ii. **518**.

Page, William, ii. 518.
 ed., *The Victoria History of the County of Hertfordshire* (1908), v. 1067–8.

Page, iii. 194; v. 1158.

Page at the court of Charles I, iv. 694.

Page-boys, vi. 45.

Page of the Bedchamber, ii. 438.

Page of Honor, v. 1229.

Page of Plymouth, The, see Jonson, Ben.

Pageant of David, The, see Anonymous.

Pageant of Elias, The, see Anonymous.

Pageant of Gideon, The, see Anonymous.

Pageant of 'Iepthe', see Anonymous.

Pageant of 'Iosue'' see Anonymous.

Pageant of Jacob, The, see Anonymous.

Pageant of Joseph, The, see Anonymous.

Pageant of 'Moyses', see Anonymous.

Pageant of Naaman, The, see Anonymous.

Pageant of Sampson, The, see Anonymous.

Pageant of Saul, The, see Anonymous.

Pageant of Solomon, The, see Anonymous.

Pageant writing, principles of, iv. 925.

Pageants, v. 1415; vi. 294; vii. 47.
 Lord Mayor's, iv. 896–9; v. 1240.

Paget, Justinian, iv. 919; v. 1157.

Paine, Mr., vi. 205.

Painted Lady, The, see Anonymous. *See* Brome, Richard.

Painter, William, *The Palace of Pleasure*, 2 vols. (1566, 67), iii. 353; iv. 797, 810; v. 1130.

Painter, The, see Massinger, Philip.

Painter for the stage, iv. 601.

Painters, i. 48; ii. 395; iii. 139, 147, 373; v. 1255; vi. 272, 273, 277.

Painters' Company, iv. 721; v. 994.

Painting, vii. 103.

Paintings, *see also* Actors, portraits of.

Painton, Edward, vi. 13 n. 1.

Pakeman, Daniel, iv. 475, 479, 480.

Palace Gate, *see* Whitehall Palace.

Palace at Paris, burning of, iii. 399.

Palaces, seasonal, iv. 908.

Palatinate, the, i. 10 n. 6 cont; v. 1268.
 Prince of, *see* Charles Lewis.
 Princes of, v. 1189, 1195, 1262.
 War, iv. 768.

Palatine, Elector, *see* Palsgrave.
 Charles, Prince Elector, *see* Charles Lewis, Prince of the Palatinate.
 Prince Rupert of, v. 1263.

Palavicino, Toby, v. 1027.

Paleography, v. 1267.

Palermo, iii. 85.

Palestine, iv. 567.

Palladio, Andrea, vi. 276.

Pallant, Robert, junior, i. 15, 72–88; ii. **519–20**.

Pallant, Robert, senior, i. 158, 171, 177 and n. 2, 199 and n. 2, 200 and n. 3, 203 n. 1, 211; ii. **518–19**.

Pallantus and Eudora, see Killigrew, Henry, *The Conspiracy*.

Pallas (goddess), vi. 44.

Pallin, John, iv. 951.

Palma, Giovane, painter, vi. 273, 278.

Palme, Per, *Triumph of Peace: A Study of the Whitehall Banqueting House* (1956), vi. 255, 259, 260, 261, 262, 266, 267.

Palmer, Barbara, iii. 70.

Palmer, Joan, iii. 112.

Palmer, John, *Ben Jonson* (1934), iv. 605.

Palmer, Roger, iv. 670.

Palmer, William, iii. 112.

Palmer, Mr., tutor Corpus Christi, Cambridge, iv. 474.

Palmer's Rents, *see* London, streets of.

Palsgrave, the, Frederick V, Elector Palatine, i. 136, 140 n. 2, 185 n. 7; iii. 108; v. 1191, 1231; vi. 59, 269; vii. 102.
 Company of, i. 4 n. 3, **135–57**, 178, 183, 188, 261, 262 and n. 3, 263, 264; iii. 20, 32, 36, 37, 239, 244, 247, 280, 284, 285, 286, 448; iv. 516, 517, 518, 519, 642, 644, 749; v. 1010, 1011, 1014, 1049, 1290, 1327, 1351, 1440; vi. 93,

134, 136, 145, 149, 150, 151, 153, 157, 158, 159–60, 181 n. 1, 185 n. 2.
Pamphleteering, iv. 680.
Pamphlets, iii. 270, 351, 417, 435, 443, 450; iv. 478, 500, 555, 557, 568, 584, 680, 747, 912, 956; v. 1053, 1054, 1061, 1200, 1203, 1224, 1299, 1313, 1319, 1365, 1398, 1401; vi. 171, 283.
    Anti-episcopal, vi. 167.
    Political, ii. 41.
    Satirical, vi. 175.
Panders, vi. 49, 240, 244.
Pandora, see Killigrew, William.
Pandorae Pyxis, see Anonymous.
Panegyre, A, see Jonson, Ben.
Pan's Anniversary, see Jonson, Ben.
Papillon, Philip, iv. 531.
Papist, ii. 549, 688.
Parades, v. 1199.
'Paradoxes, as they were spoken in a Maske, and presented before his Maiesty at White-Hall', see Anonymous.
Parallel passages, iii. 133–4; iv. 740–1, 860.
Paraphrase upon the Psalms of David . . . , see Sandys, George.
Parasitaster, see Marston, John.
Pardon for murder, iii. 194, 195.
Paria, see Vincent, Thomas.
Parigi, Giulio, iii. 208, 218.
    Designs of, v. 1228.
    Triumph of Peace, iii. 208.
Paris, i. 218, 235; iii. 196, 287, 428; iv. 821, 895, 907, 916, 917, 919; v. 1031, 1200; vi. 61; vii. 58.
    English players in, iv. 706.
    Play written at, iii. 171.
    Prisons of, iii. 196.
    Protestants' church-yard, v. 1200.
    Queen Henrietta at, iii. 144.
    Thomas Killigrew in, iv. 695, 705, 708.
    Tragic-Comedy at, A, see Brathwait, Richard, Mercurius Britannicus.
Paris Garden, see London, streets and districts.
'Paris Garden and the Bear-baiting', see Kingsford, C. L.
Parish assessment book, vi. 60.
Parish church, contributions to (by actors), vi. 60.
Parish clerk, vi. 18 n. 1.
Parish Clerks' Hall, ii. 653.
Parish collectors, vi. 19.
Parish, poor of the, vi. 106.

Parish registers, ii. passim; vi. 159.
'Parish of St. Margaret, Westminster, The', see Braines, W. W.
Parish scavangers, vi. 19.
Parker, —, iv. 601.
Parker, Henerie, iv. 755.
Parker, John, iv. 589, 590.
Parker, Philip, vi. 49.
Parkhurst, Robert, v. 1225.
Parkins, Richard, see Perkins, Richard.
Parliament, iii. 143; v. 1220; vi. 173, 175, 213, 224 n. 1, 230–1, 232, 283; vii. 12, 13, 14.
    Guard of the Houses of, vi. 175.
    House, vii. 39.
        Procession to, vii. 67.
    Member of, iii. 93.
    Opened, vii. 52, 67.
    Secretary of, iv. 832.
    Suppresses theatres, ii. 690; iii. 71.
Parliament of Bees, see Day, John.
Parliament of Ladies, The (1647), see Anonymous.
Parliament of Love, The, see Massinger, Philip.
Parliamentary Commission, iv. 953.
Parliamentary Visitors, iii. 21, 29; iv. 845, 851, 948; v. 1259.
Parliamentary Visitors, ejection by, iii. 291.
Parlin, H. T., A Study in Shirley's Comedies of London Life. Bulletin of the U. of Texas, No. 371 (1914), v. 1065, 1077.
Parnassus, vi. 246.
Parnassus Biceps, see Thorn-Drury, G.
    See Wright, Abraham.
Parr, Johnstone, 'A Note on Jonson's The Staple of News', M.L.N. lx (1945), iv. 629.
Parr, Richard, ii. 520.
Parr, Thomas, iii. 443.
Parr, William, i. 136, 137, 138, 140, 147, 155, 178; ii. 520; vi. 150.
Parracide, The, see Anonymous.
Parrat, William, 'Doleful ballad of the generall overthrowe of the famous theater on the Banksyde, called the "Globe", A', vi. 179 n. 1
Parricide, The, see Glapthorne, Henry, Revenge for Honour.
Parroiall of Princes, The, see Anonymous.
Parrott, Henry, Cures for the Itch (1626), ii. 413.
Parrott, Thomas Marc, 'A Note on

Parrott, Thomas Marc (*cont.*)
John Ford', *M.L.N.* lviii (1943)
iii. 444, 445.
ed., *The Plays and Poems of
George Chapman. The Comedies*
(1914), iii. 156; v. 1076, 1077.
ed., *The Plays and Poems of
George Chapman. The Tragedies*
(1910), iii. 156; iv. 489, 490, 491;
v. 1088, 1089, 1090, 1285, 1287.
'Two Late Dramatic Versions of
the Slandered Bride Theme',
Adams Memorial Volume (1948),
v. 1388.
Review of Solve's *Stuart Politics
in Chapman's Tragedy of Chabot*,
J.E.G.P. xxix (1930), v. 1090.
Parry, E. A., ed., *The Letters of
Dorothy Osborne to Sir William
Temple* (1888), iii. 25.
Parry, John J., 'A New Version of
Randolph's Aristippus', *M.L.N.*
xxxii (1917), v. 971, 972.
ed., *The Poems and Amyntas of
Thomas Randolph* (1917), iii.
460; v. 962, 965, 967, 968, 969,
970, 989; vi. 87, 97.
Parson, John, i. 143.
Parsons, A. E., 'Forgotten Poet:
William Chamberlayne and
"Pharonnida", *M.L.R.* xlv (1950),
iii. 154.
Parsons, Philip, iv. 951.
Atalanta, iv. 951.
Parson's Wedding, The, see Killi-
grew, Thomas.
Parsons, Sir William impersonated,
iii. 95.
*Part of the King's Entertainment in
Passing to His Coronation*, see
Jonson, Ben.
Parthenia, see Anonymous.
Partial Law, The, see Anonymous.
Partisans (weapons), vi. 293, 294,
296.
Parton, John, *Some Account of the
Hospital and Parish of St. Giles in
the Fields, Middlesex* (1822), iv.
928–9; vi. 47, 49, 60, 76.
Partridge, A. C., *The Problem of
Henry VIII Reopened* (1949), iii.
342.
Partridge, John, ii. 352.
Partridge, Mary, ii. 352.
Pascal, Thomasin, ii. 559.
Pasquier, Étienne, *Du procés ex-
traordinaire fait, premierement
à Messire Philippe Chabot
Admiral de France, puis à*
*Messire Guillaume Pouyet Chan-
celier* (1611), v. 1090.
Les Recherches de la France (1611),
v. 1089.
Passages of Cosmography, see Zouche
Richard, *The Dove*.
Passages cut, iv. 886.
Passion of Jesus, see Beard, Thomas,
An Evangelical Tragedy.
Passionate Lovers, The, see Baron,
Robert, *Gripsius and Hegio*.
Passionate Lovers, The, see Carlell,
Lodowick.
Passionate Madman, The, see Beau-
mont and Fletcher, *The Nice
Valour*.
Passions Calmed, Prudentius, see
Strode, William, *Floating Island*.
Paston, William, sheriff of Norfolk,
iii. 152.
Paston, Sir William, iv. 715.
Pastor Fido, Il, see Guarini, Battista.
See Digby, Sir Kenelm.
See 'Dymock' translation.
See Sidnam, Jonathan (transla-
tion).
Pastor Stapilton. See Stapleton, Sir
Robert.
Pastoral, The, see Anonymous.
Pastoral eclogues, v. 976.
Pastoral plays, iii. 1, 10, 179–80,
181; iv. 501–5, 548–50, 558,
620, 620–1, 625–8; iv. 715, 717–18,
917–21, 952; v. 969–71, 1033,
1076, 1171, 1181, 1221, 1334,
1367, 1368, 1389, 1451; vi. 17;
vii. 60.
Pastoral poems, iv. 621.
Pastoral Tragedy, A, see Chapman,
George.
'Pastorall Ode, A', see Randolph,
Thomas.
Pastorals, ii. 685.
French, iv. 548.
Patchem, Sussex, v. 1038.
Pate, Edward, ii. 412, 413, 570.
Patent to build a theatre, i. 198.
Patent rolls, iii. 161; vi. 270 n. 1.
Patented member (of company),
iii. 308, 311.
Patents, i. 3 n. 1, 5, 17, 72–73, 80–81,
137, 155, 167–9, 182, 211, 274;
iii. 288; iv. 492, 949; v. 1442;
vi. 20, 61, 228, 304.
Duplicate, condemned, i. 178.
Exemplifications of, i. 178–9.
Proposed, for Queen's company,
ii. 685–6.
Suppression of, iv. 492.

Patericke, S. (transl.): *A Discourse upon the Means of Wel Governing . . . against N. Macchiavell* (1602), iii. 406.

Pathomachia, see Anonymous.

Patient Grissell, see Dekker, Thomas.

Patient Man and the Honest Whore, The, see Middleton, *The Honest Whore.*

Patrick, Margaret, ii. 520.

Patrick, William, i. 15, 49 and n. 2 cont., 72–88; ii. 520–1, 682; iv. 764, 765.

Patronage, iii. 16, 105, 143–5, 155, 167, 194, 224, 307, 463; iv. 487, 550–1, 606, 607, 609, 640, 649, 687, 691, 696, 715, 718, 724, 737, 751, 756, 757, 788, 799, 816, 822, 823, 826, 831, 915, 935, 942, 956; v. 967, 983, 1028, 1029, 1030, 1030–1, 1032–3, 1042, 1044, 1070, 1072, 1083, 1180, 1186, 1226, 1257, 1263, 1268–9; vi. 71.

Patrons, v. 989.

Patten, William, v. 1255.

Pattricke, William, iv. 817.

Paul, H. N., *The Royal Play of Macbeth* (1950), iv. 903, 904.

Paulet, Elizabeth, Lady Essex, v. 1268.

Pauli, Johann, *Schimpf und Ernst,* iii. 142.

Paul's Boys, iv. 857; vi. 66.

Paul's Head Inn, i. 140.

Paulus Diaconus, iii. 198.

Paulus Japonensis, see Anonymous.

Pavier, Thomas, vii. 61.

Payne, Katherine, ii. 647.

Payne, Richard, ii. 486.

Pazzia, La, see Cuccheti, Giovani Donato.

Peaceable King, or the Lord Mendall, The, see Anonymous.

Peacham, Henry, vi. 211 n.

    The Compleat Gentleman (1622), v. 1397, 1398.

Peadle, Abraham, i. 145, 147, 155; ii. 521, 682, 683; vi. 157.

Peadle, Anne, ii. 522.

Peadle, Cornelius, ii. 522.

Peadle, Jacob, ii. 521.

Peadle, Thomas, ii. 522.

Peadle, William, junior, ii. 522–3.

Peadle, William, senior, ii. 522; vii. 17.

Peagott, Richard, ii. 455.

Peaps, William, iv. 951–2.

    Love in Its Ecstasy, iv. 951, 952.

Pearl, Valerie, *London and the Outbreak of the Puritan Revolution* (1961), vi. 17.

Pearn, B. R., ed., *The Tragedie of Lodovick Sforza, Duke of Milan, by Robert Gomersall* (1935), iv. 513, 514.

Pears, vi. 210 n.

Pears, Mr., v. 1298.

Pearsall, Lady, iv. 920.

Pearson, London bookseller, v. 977, 1328.

Pearson, James L., ed., 'Unknown Pageant by Thomas Middleton, the Dramatist', *Shakspere Society Papers,* ii (1845), iv. 897.

Peck, Rev. Francis, *Desiderata Curiosa* (1732), v. 1267.

Peck, Harvey W., ed., *The Magnetic Lady, by Ben Jonson.* Yale Studies in English, vol. xlvii (1914), iv. 618.

Peckham, Kent, v. 1276.

Pedantius, see Forsett, Edward.

Pedel *or* Pedle, *see* Peadle.

Pedlar, The, see Davenport, Robert.

Peeke (Pike), Richard, v. 1319, 1320.

    Three to One: Being, An English-Spanish Combat, Performed by a Western Gentleman, of Tavistock in Devonshire with an English Quarter-Staff, against Three Spanish Rapiers and Poniards, at [Xeres] in Spain, The fifteenth day of November, 1625. In the Presence of Dukes, Condes, Marquesses, and other Great Dons of Spain, being the Council of War (1626), v. 1319.

Peele, George, iii. 133; v. 1287.

    Alphonsus, Emperor of Germany, see Anonymous.

    Battle of Alcazar, The, ii. 481, 578.

Peele, John, v. 1286.

Peers, vii. 36.

Peery, William, 'Nid Field Was Whose Scholar ?', *Shakespeare Association Bulletin,* xxi (1946), iii. 299.

    ed., *The Plays of Nathan Field* (1950), iii. 299, 300, 301, 302, 303.

Peet, Nathan, ii. 523.

Peirce, Theobald, vii. 103, 122, 124.

Peirce, Mr., chaplain to the Earl of Salisbury, vii. 12.

Pelopaea and Alope, see Heywood's *Amphrisa.*

Pelopidarum Secunda, see Anonymous.

Pembroke, Countess of, iii. 435.
Pembroke, William Herbert, third
    Earl of, i. 6, 7, 12, 34 n. 3, 53,
    62, 179; ii. 349; iii. 222, 276,
    307, 309, 435; iv. 521, 523,
    609, 620, 750, 751, 752, 756,
    844, 876; vi. 260, 297, 298, 308.
    Company of, ii. 562; v. 1302;
    vi. 145 n. 2.
Pembroke Hall, Cambridge, iv. 586,
    587, 717, 718; v. 992, 1017.
    Fellow of, v. 1042.
Penates, The, see Jonson, Ben,
    Entertainment at Highgate.
Pendle Forest, i. 41, 294 n. 1.
Penn, Anne, ii. 524.
Penn, John, ii. 524.
Penn, Marie, ii. 523.
Penn, Sibilla, ii. 523.
Penn, William (actor), i. 18, 24, 49,
    73–89, 199 and n. 2, 200, 209, 211;
    ii. 523–4, 682; iii. 428; iv. 764,
    765, 810.
Penn, Sir William, iv. 706; v. 1092,
    1151.
Penneycuick, Andrew, see Penny-
    cuicke, Andrew.
Pennicooke or Pennycooke, Andrew,
    see Pennycuicke, Andrew.
Penniman, J. H., The War of the
    Theatres (1897), iv. 605.
Pennington, Isaac, Alderman, i. 64;
    vi. 39.
Pennycuicke, Andrew, i. 246; ii.
    524–5; iii. 232, 233, 460; iv. 542,
    544, 545, 683, 771, 773; v. 1216.
Pennycuicke, Dorothy, ii. 525.
Pennycuicke, Jacobi, ii. 525.
Pennycuicke, Margaret, ii. 525.
Pennyles Pilgrimage, The, see
    Taylor, John.
Penruddocks, Edward, vi. 308.
Pensions, iv. 609, 646.
Pentimento Amoroso, Il, see Groto,
    Luigi.
Pepys, Mrs., v. 1101.
Pepys, Samuel, iii. 47, 82, 151, 327,
    430, 464; iv. 497, 524, 705, 708,
    768, 850; v. 1094; vi. 238, 243.
    Collection of ballads, see Rollins,
    Hyder E.
    Diary of, iii. 25, 47, 56, 70, 71, 72,
    80, 146, 150, 177, 179, 182, 206,
    222, 264, 314, 315, 319, 320,
    325, 333, 344, 345, 348, 371,
    374, 378, 385, 402, 403, 408,
    412, 419, 426–7, 431, 446; iv.
    479, 495, 523, 580, 694–5, 696,
    701, 702, 706, 707, 767, 768,

    789, 848, 862, 893, 894, 900; v.
    962, 1019, 1079, 1085, 1091,
    1092, 1100, 1115, 1122, 1130,
    1145, 1151, 1204, 1208, 1210,
    1246, 1248.
    Reads play, iii. 324, 374.
Pepys, Thomas, iv. 952.
Pepysian Garland, A, see Rollins,
    Hyder E.
Perckens, Richard, see Perkins,
    Richard.
Percy, Mr., sees a masque, iii. 219.
Percy, Bishop, iv. 729, 730, 731,
    732.
Percy, Christopher, v. 1215.
Percy, Henry, iii. 195; v. 1200.
Percy, Sir Henry, 9th Earl of
    Northumberland, see Northum-
    berland, Earl of.
Percy, Thomas, MS. owner, iii. 20.
Perfect Occurrences, see Newspapers.
Perfect Weekly Account, The, see
    Newspapers.
Perfidus Hetruscus, see Anonymous.
Performances, v. 1266.
    Amateur, v. 1333, 1422; vii. 37.
    Before licensing, v. 987.
    Benefit, iv. 850.
    Commonwealth, iii. 202, 204, 212–
    13, 215, 216; iv. 682, 685, 698;
    v. 1071, 1097, 1102, 1103, 1104,
    1119, 1153, 1217, 1272, 1314,
    1342, 1362; vi. 230–8.
    Complaints about, vi. 164, 225.
    At court, see Court performances.
    Described, iv. 671, 672, 692,
    871–2; v. 1191, 1230, 1398; vi.
    256–8.
    Duration of, iii. 100, 361; iv. 530,
    643, 664, 666, 674, 910, 918,
    944; v. 1191, 1233.
    French, vi. 191.
    Incidents at, v. 984.
    At inns, iii. 74, 251; v. 1347.
    Interrupted, iii. 37.
    Italian, vi. 191.
    In Lent, see Lenten performances.
    Lighting for, v. 1263.
    Preparation for, vi. 127.
    Private, iii. 18, 114, 128–31, 179,
    180, 292–9; iv. 521, 552, 558,
    628, 687, 715, 891, 939; v. 971,
    1040, 1082, 1103, 1154, 1184,
    1256, 1268, 1308, 1347; vi. 109,
    232, 237; vii. 20, 22, 23, 24, 28,
    29.
    Provincial, i. 92–93, 156, 172–3,
    193, 212–13, 248, 282, 298–9,
    322; iv. 801; v. 970, 987, 1019,

1021, 1044, 1163, 1169, 1268–9, 1365, 1455, vi. 164.
Stayed, v. 1309; vi. 99, 100, 101, 225.
Sunday, v. 1228; vii. 10–15.
Surreptitious, vi. 173.
Time of, i. 5; iii. 103, 136; iv. 875; v. 1197, 1264, 1455; vi. 18, 80, 127, 164; vii. 1.
Perfume, vi. 257.
Pericles, see Shakespeare.
Perjured Devotee, The, see Bellamy, Daniel, the younger.
Perjur'd Nun, The, see Brewer, Anthony, *The Lovesick King.*
Perkin Warbeck, see Ford, John.
Perkins, Elizabeth, ii. 527.
Perkins, John, ii. 526.
Perkins, Richard, i. 16, 24, 73–89, 90 n. a, 158, 163, 165, 167, 168 nn. 2 and 3, 169 and n. 2, 171, 204, 220, 221, 222, 231, 237, 238, 244, 245, 246, 247; ii. 525–8, 682; iv. 555, 570, 733; v. 1244, 1251; vi. 57, 58, 67, 103.
Perkins, William, ii. 484.
Perott, Joseph de, 'Über eine Anno 1587 erschienene heute aber gänzlich vergessene Novelle als Quelle von Massingers "A Very Woman"', *Anglia,* xxxix (1916), iv. 825.
Perpoole Lane, *see* London, streets of.
Perrie, William, *see* Perry, William.
Perry, Henry Ten Eyck, *The First Duchess of Newcastle and Her Husband as Figures in Literary History* (1918), iii. 142, 145, 148, 149.
Perry, Jone, ii. 529.
Perry, William, i. 24, 25, 158 n. 1, 178, 271, 272, 273 nn. 3 and 5, 274, 275, 276, 280 n. 2, 281, 282 n. 1, 288; ii. 510, 529–31; vi. 137, 164.
Perryn, Richard, ii. 535.
Persian Slave, The, see Cartwright, William, *The Royal Slave.*
Persius, iv. 744.
Perspectives, i. 52; vi. 293, 294.
Pesaro, Signor, Venetian Ambassador, iv. 643.
Pestell, Thomas, iii. 278; iv. 952–5.
Versipellis, iv. 952, 953, 954–5.
Pestell, Thomas, senior, iv. 952–3.
Petchey, Robert, ii. 564.
Peter, King of Castile, v. 1411.
Peterborough, Northamptonshire,

iv. 538, 600, 853.
Dean of, iii. 306.
Earl of, iii. 437, 463.
Member for, iii. 292.
School, iv. 474.
Peterhouse College, Cambridge, iii. 178; iv. 554.
Peters, Hugh, ii. 401, 531, 548, 549; iv. 731; v. 1011; vi. 40, 134.
Petersham, Lodge-keepers at, iii. 112.
Peterson, J. M., *The Dorothea Legend: Its Earliest Records, . . . and Influence on Massinger's 'Virgin Martyr'* (1910), iii. 263.
Petition, vi. 302–3.
Petitions against playhouses, v. 1342.
Peto, Sir Edward, vi. 49.
Petre, Sir George, i. 10 n. 6 cont.
Petronius Arbiter, iv. 748, 838.
Satyricon, iv. 740.
Pett, John, ii. 384.
Petticoat Voyage, A, see Dekker, *The, Disguises.*
Pettingham, Henry, i. 49 n. 2 cont., 73–89; ii. 531.
Pettington, Henry, ii. 531.
Petworth House MS., iii. 113, 134.
Pewterer, ii. 431, 598, 648.
Pforzheimer Library, *see* Carl H. Pforzheimer Library.
Phaethon, see Dekker, Thomas.
Phaeton, vi. 182 n. 2.
Pharonnida, see Chamberlain, William.
Phelan, James, *On Philip Massinger* (1878), iv. 750.
'Philip Massinger', *Anglia,* ii (1879), iv. 799, 800; v. 1412.
Phelips, Sir Robert, iv. 918.
Phelips's MSS. (Montacute House), iv. 918.
Phialas, P. G., 'Massinger and the *Commedia dell' Arte', M.L.N.* lxv (1950), iv. 777, 780–1.
'Research in Progress', *P.M.L.A.* lxiii (1948), Supplement, p. 184, No. 955, iv. 781.
'The Sources of Massinger's *Emperour of the East', P.M.L.A.* lxv (1950), iv. 778, 780, 821.
Philander, King of Thrace, see Anonymous.
Philaster, see Beaumont and Fletcher.
Philenzo and Hypollita (?), *see* Massinger, Philip.
Philip of Macedon, see Anonymous.

Philip II of Spain, iv. 762.
Philip IV of Spain, iv. 871, 872, 878.
Philipo and Hippolito, see Anonymous.
Philips, John, Esq., iv. 685, 687.
Philips, Mrs. Katherine, iii. 276.
Phillipps collection, iii. 267.
Phillips, Augustine, i. 1, 2, 4 n. 1, 46; ii. 363, 411, 443, 447, 468, 624; vi. 20, 180.
Phillips, Charles J., *History of the Sackville Family* (1930), v. 1359.
Phillips, Edward, iv. 912.
  Mysteries of Love and Eloquence, The (1658), v. 1351.
  New World of English Words, The (1658), v. 1303, 1322, 1327, 1336, 1351, 1366, 1419, 1422.
  Theatrum Poetarum (1675), iii. 18, 47; iv. 507, 511, 745, 840, 841, 851; v. 999, 1242, 1323, 1363, 1371.
Phillips, John, iv. 912, 1207.
  'Impartial Doom, The', in *Sportive Wit*, i. 58 and n. 5; v. 1204.
  Sportive Wit (1656), v. 1204; vi. 38, 237.
Philosophaster, see Burton, Robert.
Philotas, see Daniel, Samuel.
Phiske, Nicholas, iv. 716.
Phocas, see Bernard, Samuel.
Phoebus, vi. 182 n. 2.
Phoenix, The, see Middleton, Thomas.
Phoenix in Her Flames, The, see Lower, Sir William.
Phoenix Society, the, iii. 272.
Phoenix *or* Cockpit theatre, in Drury Lane, i. 3 n. 7, 26, 28 and n. 1, 137 n. 6, 161–3, 164, 165, 174, 178, 182, 183, 184, 185 and n. 9, 187, 188, 194, 195, 196, 201 n. 2, 202 and nn. 1 and 6, 204 and n. 1, 205, 207, 208, 218, 219, 220, 223, 224, 225 and n. 1, 226, 227, 228, 231, 234 and n. 3, 236, 242, 264, 268, 305 n. 3, 307, 319, 325, 327, 329 n. 6, 331, 334; ii. 675, 676, 692, 693, 694, 695; iii. 17, 24, 48, 49, 53, 54, 56, 57, 61, 62, 64, 65, 70, 71, 72, 192, 195, 196, 216, 221, 225, 227, 228, 230, 232, 235, 237, 238, 270, 271, 275, 282, 284, 320, 329, 333, 344, 358, 371, 374, 377, 385, 402, 408, 418, 423, 426, 437, 437–64 *passim*; iv. 475, 479, 480, 482, 483, 485, 495, 542, 556, 565, 579, 580, 583, 633, 635, 679, 691, 698, 699, 700, 705, 707, 708, 709, 712, 713, 737, 739, 740, 741, 746, 754, 755, 766, 768, 769, 786, 787, 788, 797, 801, 802, 806, 812, 813, 836, 862, 863, 868, 869, 881, 893, 894, 895, 907, 910, 927, 928, 930, 931, 932, 935, 936, 938, 940, 941, 942, 944; v. 1016, 1019, 1020, 1024, 1030, 1031, 1033, 1060, 1061, 1062, 1068, 1073, 1075, 1077, 1079, 1080, 1089, 1095, 1096, 1098, 1099, 1106, 1107, 1108, 1111, 1114, 1115, 1120, 1122, 1125, 1126, 1129, 1130, 1131, 1133, 1135, 1136, 1143, 1144, 1145, 1146, 1147, 1150, 1151, 1163, 1164, 1165, 1166, 1167, 1169, 1204, 1217, 1218, 1247, 1311, 1312, 1335, 1340, 1362, 1425, 1426, 1446; vi. 7, 8, 12 n. 1 and n. 2, 37, 40, 41, 45, 46, 46–77, 92, 93, 99, 102, 103, 104, 109, 114, 122, 136, 163, 172 n., 174, 177, 187, 193, 199, 210, 219, 220, 221, 225 n. 1, 231, 237, 238, 242 n. 1, 248, 251, 299, 305, 307; vii. 3, 4, 5, 7, 8, 9.
  Chief actors at, i. 182, 183.
  Early reputation of, i. 164.
  Environs of, i. 228 n. 1.
  King and Queen at, iv. 582.
  Objections to, i. 160.
  Prestige of, i. 184, 226, 234, 307 and n. 1.
  Repertory, i. 337–42; iii. 283, 284.
  Repertory list protected, v. 1079.
  Riot at, i. 161–3; iv. 571.
  Royal visit to, i. 232.
$\Phi[\Psi?]yxomaxia\ id\ est\ de\ pugna\ animi, see$ Fane, Mildmay.
Physician (*see also* Barber-chirurgion, Doctor, and Surgeon), ii. 509 n. 1; iii. 154, 161.
Piazza, see London, streets and districts.
Pickleherring, see Reynolds, Robert.
Pick-pockets, iii. 188; v. 1379; vi. 239, 240.
Picts, antimasque of, iii. 109.
Picture, The, see Massinger, Philip.
Picture History of the British Theatre, A, see Mander, Raymond.
Pictures, iii. 199; vi. 265, 266.
Pierce, Frederick Erastus, *The Collaboration of Webster and Dekker* (1909), iii. 241; v. 1240.

'Collaboration of Dekker and Ford, The', *Anglia*, xxxvi (1912), iii. 241, 270, 272, 434, 459, 460.

Pierce, Mrs., v. 1100, 1210.

Pierre, la, Sebastian, *see* La Pierre.

Pierry, William, *see* Perry, William.

Piety and Poesy, *see* Jordan, Thomas.

'Pigmees Speech, A', *see* Townshend, Aurelian.

Pike, Richard, *see* Peeke.

Pikes, vi. 256, 293, 294, 296.

Pilgrim, The, see Fletcher, John.

Pilgrim, The, see Killigrew, Thomas.

Pilgrim of Castile, The, see Anonymous.

Pilgrim's New Year's Gift, The, see Crane, Ralph.

Pilkingetun, Susann, v. 1311.

Pillars, vi. 272.

Pillement, Georges, transl. *John Ford: Dommage qu'elle soit une prostituée, suivi de Le sacrifice d'amour* (1925), iii. 462.

Pinder, widow, ii. 474.

Pinero, Arthur Wing, vi. 188 n. 1.

Pinnocke, Thomas, a silk-weaver, i. 313; vi. 228, 239.

Pinto, V. de Sola, *Sir Charles Sedley 1639–1701* (1927), iv. 694.

Pirate, The, see Davenport, Robert.

Pirkyns, Richard, *see* Perkins, Richard.

Pisa, scene for play, iv. 740.

Piso's Conspiracy, see Anonymous, *The Tragedy of Nero*.

Pistols, vi. 293, 294.

Pit, *see* Theatre, pit in.

Pity the Maid, see Anonymous.

Pix, Mrs. Mary, *The Conquest of Spain*, v. 1021.
  False Friend, or the Fate of Disobedience, The, v. 1331.

'Place-Realism in a Group of Caroline Plays', *see* Miles, Theodore.

Plagiarism, iii. 10, 65, 208, 258, 258–9, 273–4, 309, 339, 358, 368; iv. 476, 480–1, 483, 485, 487, 490, 495, 497, 503, 514, 546, 624, 631, 649, 744, 802, 807, 851, 924; v. 977–9, 980–1, 1001, 1020, 1053, 1123, 1131, 1170, 1329, 1380, 1420.

Plague, i. 2, 17, 20 and n. 6 cont., 63, 65, 129, 260 n. 3, 262, 270, 271, 296, 313, 316; ii. **652–72**; iii. 67–68, 86, 310, 335; iv. 478, 548, 679, 700, 707, 724, 739, 751, 755, 761, 781, 787, 896,
937, 940; v. 966, 988, 990, 1051, 1069, 1092, 1097, 1101, 1107, 1130, 1133, 1146, 1151, 1194, 1194–5; vi. 21, 23, 24, 37, 38, 39, 61, 63, 66, 68, 69, 97, 103, 107, 112, 123, 160, 162, 165, 170, 176, 207, 211 n. 1, 213, 222, 225, 227, 266; vii. 7, 58, 59, 75, 104.
  Bills, iv. 702; vi. 222.
  Closing regulations violated, i. 56 n. 1.
  Gratuities on raising of restrictions after, ii. 658.
  King's assistance during, i. 53.
  Pamphlets, vi. 222–3.
  Players petition to open after, i. 55–56, 240, 328.
  Precautions against, ii. 656, 658.
  Reason for provincial tours, ii. 686.
  Table of deaths from, ii. 667–72.
  Theatre closed because of, i. 19, 26–27, 29, 49, 186, 222; ii. 652–72; v. 970, 987, 1003, 1031, 1120, 1123.

Plague in Shakespeare's London, The, see Wilson, Frank P.

Planché, J. R., *The Merchant's Wedding; or, London Frolics in 1638*, iv. 524, 850.

Plantation of Virginia, The, see Anonymous.

Plasterers, vi. 260.

Plato, iv. 624, 717.

Platonic-love fad, iii. 211, 212, 216–17, 218; iv. 625, 702; v. 1212, 1363.

Platonic Lovers, The, see Davenant, William.

Platt, John, vii. 79.

Platter, Thomas, vi. 202 n.

Plautus, iv. 730; v. 1238.
  Influence of, iii. 182; iv. 561, 566; v. 1006, 1415.
  Mostellaria, iv. 566.
  Rudens, iv. 561, 566.

Play of the Netherlands, The, see Anonymous.

Playford, Henry, v. 1147.

Playford, John, iii. 110; v. 1147.
  Select Musical Ayres, And Dialogues (1652), iii. 132.

Playbill, i. 197; ii. 541, 604, 614, 686; iii. 37, 169, 362, 456; iv. 684–5, 767, 931; v. 1141, 1455; vi. 30, 41 and n. 1, 112, 171, 230, 238; vii. 4.

Playbooks, i. 162; ii. 534; vi. 54, 55, 219.

'Play doctor', Rowley as, v. 1018.
Players, ii. *343–651*; iv. 503; v.
    1191, 1216, 1241, 1264, 1274,
    1315; vi. 246, 295, 305.
Accidents to, ii. 689.
As dramatists, *see* Actor-drama-
    tists.
Attendance of, on King's pro-
    gress, i. 309 n. 3, 310–11.
Benefits, ii. 507; iii. 354, 426, 427,
    450; iv. 749, 848; v. 1081; vi.
    106.
Benefit publication for, ii. 505.
Betrayed, vi. 232, 234, 235.
Bonds of, i. 148–9, 176, 198, 211,
    263; vi. 158.
Club, New York City, v. 1141.
Manuscript of, v. 1139.
Commits murder, vii. 29.
Contracts of, iv. 554; vi. 208.
With dramatists, iv. 754–5.
Defence of, iv. 816–17; v. 1165.
Dissensions among, vi. 36.
Entertainment by, vi. 153.
Estates of, ii. 396, 412, 502, 535,
    551, 587, 631–51.
Evicted, vi. 57–58, 67–68.
Expenses of, i. 44.
Fined, i. 277; v. 1235, 1300; vi.
    167–8.
Fraudulent activities of, i. 190.
Fraudulent swearing of, i. 190;
    ii. 358–9.
French, *see* French Players.
Hired men, *see under* H.
Imprisoned, i. 332–3, 336; ii. 480,
    484–5, 604, 609, 614; vi. 74,
    166, 167–8.
In Civil War, ii. 694–5.
Incomes of, i. 43, 45; vii. 7, 8.
Mutes, i. 318.
Pass for, i. 86–87.
Petitions against, i. 4–5, 22, 31–33,
    35, 43–47, 64, 190; ii. 351, 355,
    356, 358, 359, 383, 392, 393,
    403, 404, 413, 417, 438, 439,
    440, 456, 457, 459, 463, 469,
    497, 497–8, 514, 531, 570,
    576–7, 577, 578.
Petitions of, i. 55–56, 56 n. 1, 122,
    201 n. 1, 240, 260, 327–8, 328–
    9; ii. 663, 664; iii. 68, 73.
Popularity of, ii. 460; iii. 301.
Portraits of, ii. 382, 395, 403, 405,
    434, 500, 527; iii. 151, 302; iv.
    784; v. 1141; vi. 165, 170.
Profits of, vii. 5.
Punished, i. 11–12; iii. 195; iv.
    619, 874, 875; v. 1077, 1217,
    1300, 1441–2; vi. 113, 114, 230,
    231, 232, 233, 234, 236.
Recruiting of, i. 34.
Reputation of, vi. 49–50, 170,
    206, 246; vii. 29.
Roles of, v. 1149.
Share of profits, division of, i. 44.
Stayed too long at Norwich, i. 274.
Summoned for playing during
    plague, i. 327, 336.
Support of in plague time, ii. 685.
Suppressed, i. 1, 12, 241 and n. 3,
    327, 332–3; iii. 461.
Suspension from stage as punish-
    ment, i. 46.
Theatre duties of, ii. 474.
Training of, ii. 692; iii. 64–65; vi.
    71.
Tributes to, iii. 428; iv. 573,
    767–8, 816, 894; v. 985, 1079,
    1091, 1092, 1118, 1151, 1165,
    1232, 1251; vi. 62; vii. 2.
Warrant to recruit, i. 34, 35 and
    n. 2.
Whipped, vi. 176.
Women, *see* Women actors.
Wounded, vi. 54.
Young, iii. 446.
Playgoers, ii. 673–81.
Playhouse, *see* Theatre.
Playhouse to Be Let, The, see
    Davenant, William.
Playhouse of Pepys, The, see Sum-
    mers, Montague.
Playhouse scrivener, ii. 415–16.
Playing, actor's pleasure in, ii. 505.
At night, i. 180 n. 10, 276, 312.
Days at Amphitheatre, vi. 293,
    298, 299, 301.
Prohibition of, i. 6, 222.
Surreptitious, ii. 362, 695.
Play lists, iii. 41, 61, 78, 80, 82, 84,
    85, 91, 114, 115, 120, 124, 145,
    146, 149, 282, 320, 325, 330, 333,
    337, 340, 343, 345, 348, 352, 354,
    357, 360, 364, 367, 371, 378, 380,
    387, 392, 395, 397, 398, 400, 403,
    409, 413, 419, 423, 424, 426, 433,
    448, 469; iv. 589, 616, 629, 755,
    773, 786, 789, 803, 828, 883, 890,
    903, 910–11, 951. *See also* Pub-
    lishers' play lists.
PLAYS, academic, v. 967.
Acted by candle-light, vi. 54.
Adapted, iii. 6, 8, 180, 197, 266,
    272, 317, 323, 328, 336, 342,
    347, 359, 373, 376, 378, 380,
    391, 403, 409, 421, 430, 453; iv.
    508, 508–9, 524–5, 539, 546,

571, 616, 694, 710, 726, 762, 770, 774, 777, 785, 790, 799, 810, 814, 824, 828, 837, 850, 864, 890, 895, 932, 942; v. 980, 989, 1021, 1023, 1087, 1099, 1104, 1111–12, 1123, 1133, 1137, 1139, 1147, 1149, 1152, 1167, 1170, 1250; vi. 233.

Adding of a scene, iii. 264.

Admission-price, iii. 124, 403.

Advertising in, iv. 487, 630, 703–4, 894, 932–3; v. 1078, 1251, 1402; vi. 147.

Advertising of, iii. 255, 450; iv. 563, 616, 685, 743, 767, 792, 869, 871–9, 886, 931; v. 1079, 1115, 1188, 1278, 1292, 1303, 1310, 1322, 1326, 1327, 1336, 1338, 1351, 1353, 1356, 1367, 1369, 1376, 1382, 1384, 1385, 1390; vi. 13, 41 and n. 1, 42, 222, 230, 233–4, 240.

Allegorical, iii. 94–95, 228–9, 260, 291, 294–5, 297, 298, 299; iv. 589, 589–96, 631–2, 685–7, 715, 729, 870–9, 957–9; v. 987, 1277, 1350, 1390; vii. 7.

Allowed for the Press, iii. 114, 223, 257–8; iv. 513, 519, 534, 734; v. 971, 974, 1008, 1019, 1030, 1031, 1032, 1038, 1048, 1080, 1091, 1114, 1145, 1150, 1166, 1168, 1202, 1221, 1234, 1277, 1313, 1334, 1348, 1380, 1390. See also Plays licensed for the Press.

Altered, iii. 34, 81, 151, 410; iv. 803, 931; v. 1202–7; vi. 26, 99.

Amateur, iii. 3, 4, 15–16, 18, 19–20, 26–27, 40, 99–100, 125, 128–32, 132–4, 134–41, 154–5, 159–60, 160–1, 176–9, 181–2, 187–8, 290–1, 293, 295, 296, 297, 298, 299, 304; iv. 471–2, 473, 506, 534–6, 537, 587, 600–2, 748–9, 952, 954–5; v. 1316.

Performances of, iii. 3, 4, 11, 18, 25, 27, 28, 29, 99, 134, 154, 187, 293–9; iv. 954, 957, 958; v. 1097, 1220, 1221, 1334; vi. 133.

America, On, v. 1396.

And ballads, iii. 60–61.

Anti-Anglican, i. 277–8.

Anti-Catholic, i. 9–15; iv. 5, 26–30, 870–9, 924; v. 1320, 1401.

Anti-Spanish, i. 9–11; iv. 870–9.

Attempt to suppress, i. 67.

At the proposed amphitheatre, vi. 305.

Authors' contract to write, see Playwrights, contract with players.

Author's correction of printed texts, iii. 25.

Autobiographical, iii. 163; iv. 710, 945.

Average number of performances of, i. 135.

Bawdry in, iii. 328.

Beggar, iii. 73.

Burned, iii. 36–37; iv. 714; v. 1356.

Called poems, iii. 363.

Caroline vs. Restoration, ii. 691–2, 693.

Casting of, iv. 763.

Casts for, iv. 764–5.

Censored, i. 7, 36–39, 103, 105, 106, 106–7, 107–8, 115, 121–2, 124, 125, 150, 314; iii. 119, 120–1, 195, 222, 223–4, 284–5, 346, 370, 456; iv. 484, 615, 616, 619, 632, 635, 642, 714, 763, 795, 923–4; v. 1013–14, 1046, 1077, 1078, 1169, 1309, 1310, 1396; vi. 25, 26, 30–32, 63, 99, 101, 137, 166; vii. 51.

Censorship of, iv. 745, 747–8.

Citizens', iv. 847–50, 923–4, 930; vi. 69–70.

Criticism of, i. 31, 58–60, 107, 122, 126, 224, 230; ii. 681; iii. 384.

Collection of, iv. 609.

College, iii. 3, 4, 11, 19–20, 26–27, 27–28, 29–30, 99–100, 132–4, 134–41, 159–60, 165, 176–9, 181–2, 183–5, 186, 304; iv. 498, 502–3, 505–7, 526–30, 531, 532–7, 551–3, 722, 835, 836, 838, 846, 848–50, 851–2, 854–5, 947–8, 954–5; v. 966, 972, 974, 980, 982–6, 987, 1005–7, 1028, 1054, 1179, 1180, 1181, 1189, 1195–7, 1232, 1237, 1239, 1259, 1260, 1266, 1272, 1276, 1277, 1295, 1298, 1305, 1306, 1338, 1343, 1350, 1373, 1374, 1383, 1387, 1390, 1397, 1407, 1409, 1411, 1413, 1419, 1442; vi. 241, 245; vii. 16, 108.

Expenditures for, iii. 26, 177; v. 1189.

Preparations for, v. 1189, 1263.

Commonwealth, iii. 94–96, 170, 212, 216, 292–9; iv. 500–1,

PLAYS (*cont.*)
680, 684–5, 697–8, 705–6, 710, 726–7, 728–32; v. 1215, 1223, 1361–3, 1436, 1438, 1439; vi. 40–41.
Performances, iii. 187, 402.
In competition, iii. 6, 51, 73–75, 78, 81, 83, 88, 90, 131, 253, 281, 286, 444; iv. 483, 503–4, 535–6, 571, 770, 886, 895, 932–3, 938, 943; v. 984–5, 995–6, 1106, 1116–18, 1362–3, 1380, 1417.
Composition of, ii. 473; iii. 178–9.
Conduct at, i. 276.
Confiscated, vi. 74.
Corrupt printing of, i. 54.
At court, *see* Court performances.
By Courtiers, *see* courtier plays.
Cutting of, i. 242; iii. 57, 456; iv. 705, 763, 920, 931; v. 1002, 1077, 1078, 1131, 1152, 1272, 1279, 1310, 1378; vi. 31–32, 70.
Dancing in, vi. 14.
Dated, iii. 84, 97, 99, 159, 177, 181, 416; iv. 601, 715, 838, 935, 940; v. 975, 1134, 1175, 1189, 1196, 1221, 1232–3, 1260, 1261–3, 1290, 1339, 1347, 1375, 1383, 1385, 1392, 1405, 1406, 1418, 1424, 1450; vi. 206, 293–6, 297–9.
Dating of, v. 1251.
Described, iv. 871–2; vi. 42; vii. 33.
At Dublin, iii. 371.
Educational value of, vi. 4.
Elaborate editions of, iii. 427.
Expenditures for, iii. 159; iv. 601, 948; v. 1202, 1204, 1205, 1232, 1263, 1314; vi. 37–38.
Expurgated, ii. 495.
Factions against, iii. 224.
Failure of, vi. 25–26, 163.
Fighting in, vi. 14.
In folio, i. 243 n. 2; iii. 427; v. 1207.
Fragments of, iii. 165; iv. 558, 620–1, 626, 631, 729, 730, 759, 807, 936; v. 1262, 1270, 1283, 1296, 1345, 1349, 1368, 1403, 1407, 1409, 1414, 1439, 1452.
German, iii. 266.
Ghost, iii. 380–1.
As gifts to actors, v. 1206.
Gifts for, iii. 135.
Holiday, v. 1346.
Illegally sold, i. 279.
Illegal use of by King's company, i. 278–9.

Illustrated, v. 1417.
Incomplete, v. 1213, 1270, 1283, 1291, 1297, 1345, 1349, 1352, 1368, 1403, 1409, 1414–15, 1439, 1452.
Inductions to, *see* Inductions.
Inns of Court, iv. 809, 835, 838, 903.
Inscribed, v. 1118.
Jesuit, *see* Jesuit plays.
Juvenile, iii. 180; iv. 685–7, **724**; v. 966, 1214, 1222.
For ladies, iii. 408.
In Latin, iii. 2, 3, 4, 11, 19–20, 26–30, 40–41, 42, 99–100, 125, 159–60, 181–2, 183–5, 186, 290–1; iv. 526, 536–7, 552–3, 587, 717, 717–18, 838, 852–3, 854–5, 866, 936, 954–5, 961, 962; v. 1005–7, 1009, 1027, 1172–5, 1175, 1177, 1179, 1180, 1196, 1232, 1237, 1259, 1283, 1290, 1291, 1297, 1298, 1302, 1322, 1337, 1339, 1344, 1346, 1349, 1369, 1373, 1374, 1375, 1381, 1383, 1385, 1386, 1387, 1392, 1394, 1397, 1400, 1401, 1405–6, 1407, 1409, 1413, 1418, 1424, 1450; vi. 293, 295, 296, 302; vii. 82.
Length of, iii. 246, 255; v. 1396; vi. 70.
Licensed for press, iii. 24, 73, 82, 102, 119, 211, 223, 257, 258, 273, 284, 440, 449, 451, 454, 456–7; iv. 562, 565, 569, 579, 582, 589, 622, 742, 745, 766, 775, 778, 783, 786, 797, 812, 822, 838, 907, 931, 935, 937; v. 1109, 1122, 1196, 1416. *See also* Plays allowed for the Press.
Licensed in Lent, vii. 7.
Licensing fees for, ii. 687; iii. 17, 30, 32, 119, 227, 230, 246, 247, 253, 256, 263–6, 284, 286, 367, 368, 370, 372, 384, 386; iv. 482, 520, 560, 561, 619, 632, 634–5, 701, 704–5, 714, 762, 795–6, 806, 812; v. 1012, 1013, 1023, 1050, 1076, 1144, 1146, 1270, 1271, 1290, 1321, 1322, 1324, 1327, 1355, 1455; vi. 13, 23, 31, 64, 100, 106, 128, 159 n. 1, 165, 173, 221.
Fees analysed, iii. 265.
Fees, standard, v. 1050.
Periods for, vi. 196.
Questioned, vi. 229.

Lists of, i. 65–66, 330–1; iii. 61, 78, 114, 115, 120, 124, 145, 146, 149; iv. 865–6; v. 1105, 1210, 1270, 1272, 1296, 1308.

Losing of, iii. 178; iv. 556.

Lost, iii. 1, 2, 9–10, 17, 22–23, 27, 30, 32, 44, 46–47, 58, 69, 70, 76, 77, 92, 93–94, 96–97, 106, 110, 124, 125, 191, 193, 229, 230, 231, 235, 236–7, 240, 245, 246, 247, 248, 249, 250, 251, 252, 262, 269, 279, 285, 291, 296, 328, 336, 342, 350, 380, 386, 400, 426, 438, 444, 447, 458; iv. 471–2, 473, 481, 487, 488, 493, 517, 519, 542, 543, 548, 552, 564, 574, 575, 578, 579, 583, 586, 587, 600, 602, 611, 618, 620–1, 625, 627, 636, 680, 684–5, 711, 717, 718, 720, 722, 724, 748–9, 755, 758, 759, 763, 770, 780, 781, 782, 785, 790, 792, 793, 794, 803, 804, 808, 810, 818, 819, 820, 826, 827, 829, 838, 861, 864, 887, 892, 899, 911, 935–6, 948, 950, 954; v. 963, 985, 990–1, 1011–14, 1022, 1023, 1025–6, 1027–8, 1036, 1046, 1050, 1058–9, 1060, 1062, 1082, 1105, 1128, 1142, 1175, 1177, 1178, 1187, 1254, 1275, 1276, 1283, 1285, 1288, 1290, 1292, 1293, 1294, 1300, 1301, 1302, 1303, 1308, 1309, 1310, 1311, 1312, 1314, 1315, 1317, 1321, 1322, 1323, 1324, 1326, 1327, 1331, 1332, 1333, 1335, 1337, 1338, 1339, 1344, 1345, 1346, 1349, 1350, 1351, 1352, 1353, 1354, 1355, 1360, 1361, 1363, 1365, 1366, 1367, 1369, 1370, 1371, 1372, 1373, 1375, 1378, 1382, 1383, 1384, 1385, 1386, 1387, 1392, 1393, 1395, 1397, 1399, 1401, 1403, 1405, 1406, 1409, 1410, 1411, 1412, 1415, 1418, 1421, 1422, 1423, 1424, 1425, 1426, 1427, 1429, 1430, 1432, 1433, 1435, 1438, 1440, 1441, 1442, 1444, 1445, 1446, 1447, 1448, 1455.

In manuscript, i. 103, 111, 114, 118, 120, 123, 124, 126–7, 127, 132, 174, 175, 195, 195–6, 216, 216–17, 300, 323; iii. 1, 3, 4, 5, 12–14, 15, 19–20, 22, 23–25, 26, 29, 33–35, 36, 54, 59, 67, 95–96, 99, 103, 113,

125, 145–8, 148–9, 159, 160, 162, 166, 183–5, 185–7, 191, 191–2, 227, 228, 267, 269, 283, 286, 295, 296, 297, 298, 292–9, 312, 313, 317, 332, 343, 346, 375, 376, 380, 381, 415, 416, 454, 456, 465, 466, 467; iv. 483–5, 493–4, 505–7, 510, 526–30, 536–7, 560–2, 567–8, 597–8, 600–2, 697–8, 698–700, 728–32, 759, 760, 761, 805–7, 808, 811, 814, 819, 820, 834–5, 838, 852–3, 864–6, 883, 903, 904, 917, 921, 923, 924, 945, 951; v. 961, 971–3, 974, 976, 989, 1005–7, 1021, 1028, 1054, 1100, 1141, 1172, 1173, 1174, 1177, 1180, 1181, 1189, 1196, 1201, 1232, 1237, 1259, 1265, 1270, 1271, 1273, 1277, 1283, 1290, 1291, 1293, 1295, 1298, 1302, 1303, 1305, 1310, 1316, 1317, 1318, 1328, 1332, 1338, 1340, 1343, 1345, 1349, 1350, 1352, 1367, 1368, 1373, 1374, 1379, 1383, 1386, 1387, 1388, 1390, 1393, 1394, 1400, 1401, 1403, 1405, 1407, 1414–15, 1418, 1419, 1424, 1426, 1433, 1436, 1439, 1442, 1451, 1452.

Autograph, iii. 294, 296, 298; iv. 561, 567, 567–8, 763–5, 777, 856, 879; v. 1272, 1273, 1283, 1291, 1367, 1368, 1427, 1433.

Length of, iii. 119, 246, 255; v. 1013, 1324, 1396; vi. 137, 221.

Licences for, iii. 131–2; iv. 484, 510.

With license, iii. 37.

In multiple MSS., iii. 95–96, 99, 134, 159, 293–5; iv. 526–30, 600–2, 729, 730, 854–5, 870–9, 883, 886, 917, 920; v. 974, 1173, 1174, 1196, 1232, 1237, 1260, 1265, 1270, 1271, 1302, 1310, 1390; vi. 31.

Misattribution of, iii. 5, 8, 9, 10, 18, 19, 31, 34, 41, 48, 257–60, 271, 272, 280, 283, 304, 337–8, 368–9, 397–8, 405, 445, 457, 458, 459; iv. 489–93, 499, 500, 501–2, 510–11, 537, 539, 588, 597, 741, 745, 806–7, 813, 819, 828, 840–1, 850, 851–2, 860, 866, 887, 901–2, 920, 962, 964, 975, 978, 994, 998–9, 1004–5,

PLAYS (cont.)
　　1009, 1013, 1034; v. 1043, 1049,
　　1053, 1058, 1073, 1074, 1077,
　　1098, 1105, 1112, 1128, 1149,
　　1225, 1234, 1245, 1252, 1259,
　　1287, 1306, 1323, 1354–5, 1363,
　　1371, 1378, 1381, 1390, 1407,
　　1428.
Musical, iii. 70.
Music in, iv. 850; v. 1002; vi. 9,
　　10, 53, 111, 117, 147.
In a natural setting, iii. 130.
New, iii. 124; vi. 22, 26, 34, 61,
　　102, 106, 136, 182, 192, 193,
　　195.
　　Annual production of, i. 149
　　　n. 4.
Noises in, vi. 82.
Noisy, iii. 102–3.
Number of, per year, i. 135.
Offensive, ii. 493.
　　At court, i. 204.
Old presented as new, vi. 165.
Old reallowed, i. 103, 104, 106,
　　107, 115, 150, 174–5, 185, 206,
　　229–30, 250, 277, 293–4; iii.
　　36–37, 328, 370; iv. 888, 889;
　　v. 1075, 1337, 1393.
Out of doors, iii. 130–1.
Ownership of, vi. 69, 73.
Parodied, vi. 148.
Pastoral, see Pastoral plays.
Payment for, iii. 36, 66, 357; iv.
　　485, 752, 774, 848, 849, 934–5;
　　v. 1189–90, 1344; vi. 12, 35–36,
　　45, 102, 265, 268, 269.
Performances, time of, see Per-
　　formances, time of.
Performed by court ladies, iv.
　　548, 917; v. 1334.
Periodic prohibitions of, vi. 293,
　　298, 299, 300, 301.
Personal allusions in, i. 228–9,
　　314; iii. 19, 41, 50, 64–65, 74, 95,
　　189, 201, 204, 223, 254, 260,
　　274, 338–9, 341, 351, 386, 399,
　　416–17, 440, 443, 453, 455; iv.
　　473, 497, 545–6, 582, 616–17,
　　620–1, 631, 632, 633, 634,
　　635, 689, 704, 710, 713–14, 719,
　　731, 747, 776, 798, 802, 870–9,
　　890, 902, 905; v. 972, 979, 980,
　　988, 992, 996, 1033–4, 1045,
　　1052, 1056, 1077, 1078, 1079,
　　1081, 1090, 1164, 1182, 1192–5,
　　1213–14, 1223, 1249, 1307–8,
　　1310, 1362, 1379, 1392, 1398,
　　1401, 1417, 1425, 1441, 1454;
　　vi. 99, 228.

Place realism in, iii. 88, 89, 90;
　　iv. 747, 928, 933, 941–2; v.
　　1122.
Poems about, iv. 541–2.
Political allusions in, i. 9–15, 60–
　　61, 333; iii. 41, 63, 68, 94–95,
　　121, 125, 179, 260, 294, 298–9,
　　321, 338–9, 351, 416–17, 455,
　　461, 467, 473; iv. 482, 496, 518,
　　528–30, 563, 581, 629, 685–7,
　　689, 702–5, 729, 731, 761, 763–
　　4, 768–9, 787, 795, 798, 802,
　　823–4, 846–7, 860, 870–9, 924,
　　957–9; v. 975, 980, 980–2, 988,
　　993, 1006, 1020, 1036, 1052,
　　1053, 1090, 1109, 1167, 1177,
　　1192–5, 1209, 1219, 1223, 1234–
　　6, 1251, 1266, 1274, 1279, 1299,
　　1300, 1315, 1319, 1392, 1401,
　　1406, 1413, 1425, 1437, 1443,
　　1441; vi. 74, 166–7.
Popular, i. 10, 13 n. 2, 105; iii. 53,
　　72–73, 77–80, 83, 88, 104,
　　113–14, 155, 187–90, 225, 253–
　　6, 312–18, 318–23, 324–8,
　　332–6, 343–7, 348–50, 373–6,
　　401–7, 407–11, 417–21, 425–
　　30; iv. 571, 742–5, 745–8, 766–
　　8, 803, 862–4, 870–9, 884–6,
　　887, 894; v. 973, 984, 995,
　　1084–7, 1094, 1147, 1150–3,
　　1202, 1208, 1209, 1234, 1356,
　　1441; vi. 102, 171, 189, 199.
　　At court, iii. 113–14, 122–3, 134–
　　　41, 221, 377, 379.
　　Receipts from, i. 10, 295 and
　　　n. 6.
Postdated, v. 1220.
Praised, v. 1033, 1086, 1110, 1125,
　　1126, 1151, 1168, 1169, 1170;
　　vi. 32.
Predated, v. 1121, 1219.
Presentation copies, v. 1180.
Price of, v. 1202.
Printing of prohibited, i. 54,
　　330–1; vi. 69.
Private performances of, i. 6, 39,
　　48 and n. 5, 327–8.
Profits from, see Plays, receipts
　　from.
Prohibited, ii. 652–72; vi. 112,
　　293, 298, 299, 300, 301.
Publishing restrictions for, iii. 53.
Reading of, iv. 523, 893; v. 1204.
Receipts from, iii. 53, 88, 324,
　　327–8, 395, 396, 426, 429; iv.
　　745–6, 759, 873, 876; v. 1023;
　　vi. 13, 22, 38, 65, 100, 102,
　　184 n. 2, 219, 220.

Reception of, iii. 23–24; iv. 504, 522, 532, 534–6, 590–6, 623–4, 632, 633, 708, 767, 768, 772, 778–9, 820, 870–9, 904, 906, 930, 931, 934; v. 984–5, 1115, 1190–2, 1422; vi. 5, 8, 9, 10, 25–26, 70.

Rehearsals of, iv. 792; v. 1210, 1411; vi. 79, 128, 249 n. 2, 282 n. 1; vii. 34.

Rejection of, iii. 53, 119; iv. 603, 943.

Relicensed, *see* Plays, old re-allowed.

Religious satire in, vi. 167.

In repertory, protected, i. 53–54, 65–67, 328, 330–1.

Reputation of, iii. 426; iv. 609, 844, 849–50; v. 983–4, 993, 1152–3, 1194, 1202–7.

Request performances of, i. 23 n. 1.

Revised, i. 41, 149, 174–5, 230, 277, 293–4; iii. 7, 13, 17, 25, 34, 37–38, 43, 53, 58, 65, 73, 75, 81, 100, 121, 131, 142, 149–50, 169, 171, 174, 178–9, 187–90, 199, 200, 210, 215, 222, 224–5, 227, 231, 234, 258, 259–60, 263–6, 264, 268, 277, 294, 298, 317, 320, 331, 346–7, 348, 349, 350, 353, 359, 361–2, 363, 365, 366–9, 372, 377, 384–6, 392, 394, 395, 397, 398, 400, 401, 404, 405, 406, 411, 414, 424, 425, 430, 431, 432, 444, 445, 456, 460, 461; iv. 484, 491, 494–7, 502–5, 528, 562, 567, 573, 590, 595–6, 627, 633, 635, 692–3, 700, 702–5, 709, 710, 714, 754, 760, 762, 763, 774; iv. 779, 788, 793, 794, 795, 796, 807, 824–8, 850, 860, 869, 885–6, 888, 895, 904, 931, 935–6; v. 971, 972, 974, 975, 980–2, 985, 987–8, 1018, 1023, 1031, 1060–1, 1063–4, 1069, 1073, 1078, 1087, 1088–90, 1094, 1095–6, 1101, 1108, 1114, 1115, 1134, 1151, 1152, 1167, 1196, 1202–7, 1248, 1264, 1272, 1279, 1287–8, 1301, 1310, 1329, 1362–3, 1372, 1380, 1402, 1444, 1453, 1455; vi. 63, 100, 102, 165, 168.

Revived, i. 23, 62, 124; ii. 687; iii. 24, 25, 43, 51, 53, 56, 59, 60, 61, 70, 71, 74, 80, 82, 85, 102, 104, 115, 118, 131, 132, 134, 135, 137, 145–8, 150, 171, 177,

192, 206, 221, 222, 224, 256, 264, 272, 275, 314, 315, 321, 322, 325, 327, 328, 330, 333, 344, 345, 347, 354, 365, 367–8, 371, 372, 373, 374, 375, 377, 378, 379, 380, 383, 385, 387, 388, 394, 396, 402–4, 412, 419, 423, 425, 428–9, 430, 431, 432, 446, 450, 454, 456, 462, 464; iv. 478, 479, 495, 497, 522, 573, 580, 589, 589–96, 699, 741, 776, 799, 803, 817, 824, 900–1, 936, 938; v. 1019, 1027, 1035, 1079, 1085, 1091, 1092, 1093–4, 1101, 1122, 1124, 1129, 1130, 1135, 1136–7, 1145, 1148, 1150, 1151, 1152, 1163, 1166, 1169, 1170, 1192, 1197, 1204, 1207, 1208, 1210, 1211, 1234, 1235, 1238, 1246, 1248, 1252, 1273, 1287, 1288, 1300, 1301, 1308, 1340, 1348, 1392, 1393, 1402, 1418; vi. 22, 31, 63, 93, 98, 100, 102, 106, 137, 152, 165, 167, 172, 173, 197, 198.

Rhymed, v. 1368.

Ribaldry in, v. 1377; vi. 31, 32.

Ridiculed, iv. 536, 590–6; vi. 163.

Rights in, i. 330–1.

Rival, iii. 90, 253.

Runs of, i. 13 n. 2, 278, 282, 303; iii. 175, 187; iv. 679, 688–9, 742–3, 873 ff.; v. 995, 1112, 1248, 1441, 1442; vi. 25, 26, 163, 166, 168, 228.

School, v. 1177.

Schoolboy, iii. 27, 180; iv. 538, 538–9, 952; v. 966, 978, 1172–5, 1221, 1256, 1266, 1283, 1285, 1290, 1297, 1337, 1339, 1344, 1346, 1349, 1375, 1383, 1385, 1392, 1393, 1405–6, 1418, 1424, 1450.

Schoolgirl, v. 1257.

Scribal corrections of printed texts, iii. 25.

Selling of, ii. 545.

Short, iii. 15, 29, 148, 160, 184, 284, 293–9, 356, 383; iv. 558–9, 564, 574, 945; v. 961, 976, 1035, 1053, 1054, 1173, 1181–4, 1213, 1221, 1290, 1295, 1299, 1305, 1306, 1343, 1344, 1350, 1364, 1374, 1400, 1405, 1442, 1452.

Shortened, iv. 529–30.

Size of editions, iii. 198.

Songs in, v. 1045.

Souvenir texts of, iii. 24, 141, 313,

PLAYS (cont.)
317; iv. 700; v. 1206-7, 1261, 1272, 1383.
Special productions of, iii. 18, 44, 135-40, 292-9; iv. 524, 582, 686, 691-4, 715; vi. 37-38.
Spectacle in, iv. 739-40.
Statute concerning, vii. 13.
Subsidized, i. 59.
Suppressed, i. 10-15, 36-39, 277-8; iii. 73, 83-84, 195, 415; iv. 535-6, 762, 769, 870-9; v. 972, 1234, 1235, 1300, 1371, 1412-13, 1441, 1456; vi. 74, 166-7, 167-8, 175, 176.
Taste in, ii. 681.
Theatrical cuts in, iii. 317.
Theft of, v. 168-9.
Time of, see Peformance, time of.
Titles altered, i. 107, 107-8, 108, 113, 125, 256-7, 258, 291 and n. 8; iii. 72-73, 81, 86, 147, 154, 159, 170, 176, 182, 202, 205-6, 215, 240, 257-60, 275, 304-5, 341, 343-6, 361-3, 412, 413, 425, 445; iv. 694, 795; v. 988, 1079, 1080, 1084, 1095, 1106, 1114, 1120, 1196, 1246-8, 1260, 1262, 1278.
Misleading, iii. 86, 87.
To order, iii. 212, 254.
Topical, i. 7, 9-15, 40-41, 60-61, 204, 208-9, 228-9, 277-8, 314, 333.
Unacted, iii. 198; v. 1100-1; see also Closet drama.
Unauthorized publication of, iii. 116, 168-9, 174, 178, 220-1, 470; iv. 507, 523, 531, 566-7, 691-2, 850, 946-7.
Unfinished, iii. 37.
University controversy about, iv. 528-9.
With unknown titles and unknown authors, v. 1449-54.
Unlicensed, i. 14, 332-3; v. 1412-13; vi. 20, 74, 221.
Penalty for acting, i. 332-3, 336.
Vacation, iv. 474, 930; vi. 14.
In vogue, iv. 483.
Witches in, i. 40.
Within plays, iv. 817, 885, 887; v. 1080, 1153, 1174, 1301, 1303, 1347.
Playwrights, i. 44; iii. 1-v. 1280.
As actors, see also Actor-dramatists, v. 1019-20, 1258.

Amateur, v. 993, 1051.
Arms of, v. 1000.
Beaten, v. 1199.
Benefit performances for, i. 295 n. 4; ii. 390.
Catholic, iii. 125, 160, 517, 520; iv. 608, 916, 947; v. 1067, 1152, 1172, 1186.
Allegedly, iv. 751.
Charged with treason, v. 1200.
Contracts with players, i. 63, 227, 241, 242, 292 n. 1, 295 and nn. 4 and 5; ii. 390, 538, 555; iii. 52-54, 56, 308; iv. 447, 608, 787; v. 966-7, 1016, 1068, 1070, 1217-18; vi. 36, 62, 71, 98, 102, 105.
Co-operation among, v. 1165.
Descriptions of, v. 1242-3.
Direction of, vi. 71.
Estates of, iii. 167, 244-5, 301, 435; iv. 725, 830, 856, 858; v. 1016, 1027, 1057, 1070, 1071, 1198, 1269.
Fees, iii. 62-63, 361.
Funerals of, iv. 757.
Gratuities to, iv. 749.
Honours for, iii. 195; iv. 609-10.
Imprisoned, iii. 127, 161, 174, 195, 196, 243, 276; iv. 541-2, 607, 608, 695, 722, 728, 752, 916; v. 994.
Murdered, v. 1057-8, 1200.
In orders, see Clergymen dramatists.
Payments to, iii. 53, 261; iv. 858; vi. 102.
Pensions, iv. 757.
Play of, rejected, i. 242 n. 1.
Poems about, iv. 541-2.
Portraits of, iii. 10, 38, 48, 106, 162, 173, 197, 302, 311; iv. 696, 721, 784; v. 1000, 1001-2, 1004, 1071-2, 1138, 1200, 1218.
Prolific, iii. 242-3; iv. 555, 566; vi. 219.
Prosecuted, iii. 39, 161, 194; iv. 607, 737, 872-6, 923; v. 1441-2; vi. 229.
Rate of composition, iii. 18, 53, 97, 173-4, 178; iv. 590, 755, 933; v. 1068, 1070, 1083-4, 1101, 1120, 1151; vi. 102, 166.
Reputations of, iii. 21, 47-48, 49-52 50-51, 55, 106, 127, 144, 310, 318, 434-5, 499, 522; iv. 557, 681, 755-6, 831-5, 858-9; v. 968, 993, 994, 1017, 1072, 1086, 1200, 1244-5; vi. 22, 25, 244, 246.

Speak prologues, iv. 508.
Suicides of, v. 1200.
Wages of, i. 242, 295; ii. 686; iii. 53; vi. 105.
Wills of, v. 1071.
Women, iii. 373; iv. 837, 850; v. 985-6.
Pleasant and Merry Humour of a Rogue, A, see Cavendish, William.
Pleasant Notes on Don Quixote (1654), *see* Gayton, Edmund.
Pleasant Pranks of Smug the Smith, see Brewer, Thomas.
Pleasure Reconciled to Virtue, see Jonson, Ben.
Plenum Reconciled to Kulum, see Anonymous.
Pliny, iv. 838; v. 1001, 1003.
Pliny the Elder, vi. 43.
Naturalis Historia, iv. 834.
Plumbers, vi. 260.
Plume, Archdeacon Thomas, iv. 500, 511, 525, 526, 527; v. 965.
Plumfield, Thomas, i. 303, 308, 321; ii. 531.
Plutarch, iv. 764, 936; v. 1003, 1370.
Life of Cimon, iii. 142.
Life of Timoleon, transl. Sir Thomas North, iv. 768.
Lives, iv. 834.
Plutus the God of Wealth, see B., H., *The World's Idol.*
Plymouth, i. 180, 193, 212.
Public Library, Manuscript in, iii. 33-34.
Pocahontas, iv. 677.
Pocklington, York, ii. 473.
Poems, 1670, *see* Carew, Thomas.
Poems, 1656, *see* Cowley, Abraham.
Poems and Amyntas of Thomas Randolph, The, see Parry, John Jay.
Poems, Latin, *see* Latin poems.
Poems in manuscript, iii. 14, 26, 165, 167; iv. 751, 752, 755, 756, 844.
Lost, iii. 26.
Poems With The Mvses Looking-Glasse: And Amyntas, see Randolph, Thomas.
Poems Sacred and Satyricall (1641), v. 1000, 1001, 1002.
Poesis Rediviva, see Collop, John.
Poetaster, see Jonson, Ben.
Poetical Blossoms, see Cowley, Abraham.
Poetical Varieties, see Jordan, Thomas.

Poeticall Squire, The, see Lacy, John, *Sir Hercules Buffoon.*
Poet laureates, iii. 66, 195; iv. 545, 609, 832; vi. 177.
Poets, *see also* Playwrights.
Poets (i.e. playwrights), vi. 229.
Poet's Revenge, A, see Anonymous, *Wits Led by the Nose.*
Poets satirized, v. 1052.
Poisoning, v. 1200.
Poland, v. 1209.
Policraticus, see John of Salisbury.
Politic Bankrupt, The, see Anonymous.
Politic Queen or Murder Will Out, The, see Davenport, Robert.
Political allegory, v. 1090.
Political plays, iii. 455.
Politician, The, see Shirley, James.
Politick Whore, The, see Anonymous.
Politics in plays, *see* Plays.
Politique Father, The, see Shirley, James *The Brothers.*
Pollard, A. W., and G. R. Redgrave, *A Short Title Catalogue . . . 1475-1640* (1926), iii. 379, 441; iv. 713; v. 1185, 1417.
Pollard, Sir Hugh, v. 1169.
Pollard, Robert, iii. 469.
Pollard, Thomas, i. 4 n. 2, 14, 16, 17, 35 n. 1, 43, 45, 46, 69 and n. 2, 72-88, 318; ii. 532-5; iii. 311, 346, 347, 349, 355, 363, 379, 399, 416, 420, 428; iv. 764, 810, 817; v. 1086, 1412; vi. 36, 172, 181, 185, 237.
Polybius, iv. 936.
Polyeuctes, see Lower, Sir William.
Pomerania, v. 1422.
Pontoise, Abbey of St. Martin, iv. 917.
Poole, John, iv. 955; v. 1287.
Wife's Stratagem: or More Frightened than Hurt, The, v. 1112.
Poole, Joshua, *The English Parnassus: Or a Help to English Poesie* (1657), iv. 818.
Poole, Rachel, *Walpole Society,* xi (1922-3), v. 994.
Pooley, *see* Cowley, Abraham.
Pooley, Jane, vi. 125, 128.
Pooley Hall, iii. 167.
Poor, contributions to, iv. 929; vi. 128, 215, 222, 231, 250-1, 288.
Poor Man's Comfort, The, see Daborne, Robert.
Poor of the parish, vi. 176.
Poor Robin, 1681, An Almanack of the Old and New Fashion, see Anonymous.

Y

Poor Scholar, The, see Neville, Robert.

'Poor Schollers Song, The', *see* Tatham, John.

Pope, the, v. 982; vi. 97.
  Agent to the, iv. 521.

Pope's Bulls, iii. 321.

Pope, Thomas, i. 1, 4 n. 1; ii. 447; vi. 180.

Popham, Lord Chief Justice, iii. 435.

Popular plays, *see* Plays, popular.

Porta Pietatis, see Heywood, Thomas.

Portal, Ethel M., 'The Academ Roial of King James I', *Proceedings of the British Academy* (1915–16), iv. 610.

Porter, Alan, ed., *The Sad Shepherd; the Unfinished Pastoral Comedy of Ben Jonson; now completed by Alan Porter* (1944), iv. 625.

Porter, Charles, v. 1131.

Porter, Endymion, i. 39, 61, 106; iii. 21, 194, 450; iv. 833; v. 1131; vi. 299, 300, 301, 306, 307 and n. 1.
  Complains of censorship, iii. 222.
  Performs in a masque, iv. 647.
  Verses to, iii. 223, 224.

Porter, George, v. 1131.

Porter, Henry, iv. 618.

Porter, Maryan, ii. 565.

Porter, ii. 682.

Porter at the Marshalsea, ii. 682.

Porters' Company, Hall of, vi. 77 n. 1, 78.

Porter's Hall theatre, iii. 192; vi. 12 n. 1, 17–18, 77–86.

Portland, Duke of, ii. 579; v. 1202, 1206.
  MSS. of, iv. 883, 884.

Portman, George, painter, iii. 139.

Portman, Sir William, dedication to, iii. 154.

Portraits, iii. 48, 113, 162, 257, 311; iv. 696, 709, 721; v. 1071–2, 1138, 1218, 1359.
  Of actors, *see* Players, Portraits of.
  Of Dramatists, *see* Playwrights, Portraits of.
  Engraved, v. 1000.

Portsmouth, Hampshire, i. 23 n. 1; v. 1172; vii. 68.
  Scene at, iii. 210.

Portugal, v. 1172.
  Ambassador of, v. 1102.
  Sebastian, King of, i. 105.

Pory, John, iii. 453; iv. 612, 618

619, 652, 917, 918, 954; v. 1228; vi. 6, 17, 25 and n. 1, 26, 282 n. 1; vii. 83.

Post-Boy, The, see Newspapers.

Potter, Russell, 'Three Jacobean Devil Plays', *Stud. Phil.* xxviii (1931), iv. 615.

Pottle, Frederick A., 'Two Notes on Ben Jonson's *Staple of News*', *M.L.N.* xl (1925), iv. 629.

Potts, J. L., ed., *Ben Jonson, The Sad Shepherd, or a Tale of Robin Hood* (1929), iv. 625.

Poulton, Francis, vi. 202.

Poultry, *see* London, streets of.

Powders, ii. 517.

Powell, Edmond, ii. 641.

Powell, Edward, ii. 535.

Powell, George, ii. 535.
  Alphonso, King of Naples, v. 1170.
  Very Good Wife, A, iii. 61, 65; v. 1123.

Powell, Margery, ii. 543.

Powell, Martin, ii. 535.

Powell, Philip, ii. 648.

Powell, Wilfred, *see* von Bülow, Gottfried.

Powell, William C., 'A Note on the Stage History of Beaumont and Fletcher's *Love's Pilgrimage* and *The Chances*', *M.L.N.* lvi (1941), iii. 319, 366.

Power, Esther Melvina, *James Shirley's The Wittie Fair One, a Critical Edition of the 1633 Quarto, with Introduction and Notes*. Unpublished U. of Chicago thesis (1942), v. 1166, 1167.

Powis, Baron, iii. 213; iv. 521.

Poynton, Mr., iv. 586.

Praeludium, see Randolph, Thomas.

Praeludium, v. 972, 973–4; *see also* Goffe, Thomas.

Praeludium for Brome's *Five New Plays*, 1653, *see* Cokayne, Sir Aston.

Praeludium to Thomas Goffe's *The Careless Shepherdess*, vi. 109–12.

Praevaricator, v. 967.

Pragmaticus, Mercurius, *The Second Part of Crafty Cromwell* (1648), v. 1244.

Prague, ii. 451.

Praise of Hemp-seed, The, see John Taylor.

Prat, Angel Valbuena, *Historia de la Literatura Española* (1946), v. 1211.

Prat, Samuel, ii. 535.

Prayer Book, proposed Scottish, vi. 74.

Praying, vii. 12.

Preacher, ii. 435, 649; iv. 471, 512, 587, 844; v. 1188, 1275.

Popular, vi. 17.

Preaching, vii. 12, 36.

Preface to Gondibert, see Davenant, William.

Prefaces, iii. 86–87; iv. 535, 539; v. 964, 981, 984, 1004, 1005, 1306, 1307, 1316, 1317; vi. 266.

Pregion, John, ii. 381.

Preparations, vii. 81.

Preparations of the Athenians . . . , see Davenant, William.

Pre-Restoration Stage Studies, see Lawrence, W. J.

Presbyterians, ii. 587, 695; iii. 63; iv. 841; v. 1265.

Presentation copy, iii. 100, 141, 226, 228.

Presentation Intended for the Prince His Highness on His Birthday, A, see Nabbes, Thomas.

Presenters, v. 1258, 1262, 1304.

Presentment of Bushell's Rock, The, see Anonymous.

Press censors, iii. 417.

Preston, Thomas, impersonated, iii. 95.

Tragedy of Cambyses, v. 1115, 1166.

Price, George R., 'The First Edition of *A Faire Quarrell*', *Library*, Fifth Series, iv (1949), iv. 867.

Price, Henry, ii. 536.

Price, John, v. 1176.

Price, Laurence, 'Newes from Hollands leager', ballad (1632), iv. 747.

Price, Lawrence Marsden, *The Reception of English Literature in Germany* (1932), v. 1137, 1153.

Price, Mary, ii. 536, 537.

Price, Morgan, ii. 536.

Price, Richard, i. 136, 138, 140, 143, 144, 147, 148, 152, 153, 155, 261, 262 and n. 4, 263 and n. 1, 269; ii. 535–7, 683; vi. 150, 157, 158.

Price, Richard, junior, ii. 536, 537.

Price, William, vi. 134, 135.

Pricking of sheriffs, vi. 261.

Pride, Thomas, vi. 214.

'Priest's holes', iv. 520.

Prince, Mr., ii. 675.

Prince Charles, *see* Charles I, Prince and Charles II, Prince.

Prince Charles's (I) company, i. 7,
18 and n. 8, 22 and n. 2, 24, 36, 137 n. 3, 152 n. 3, 164, 165, 176, 177, 178, 183, 193 n. 2, **198–217**, 270 and n. 3; iii. 9, 52, 59, 69, 243, 246, 250, 255–6, 270, 271, 284, 326, 355, 379, 428, 489, 491; iv. 492, 543, 602, 642, 673, 678, 702, 706, 711, 713, 797, 857, 867, 868, 870, 881, 907, 908, 910, 911; v. 1015, 1016, 1017, 1020, 1024, 1046, 1047, 1239, 1247, 1324, 1337, 1370, 1387, 1393, 1396, 1432, 1433, 1446, 1448; vi. 12 n. 1, 57, 73, 78, 79, 85, 124, 134, 135, 136, 137, 158, 208, 219, 221–2, 251, 299, 301; vii. 33, 35.

Prince Charles's (II) company, i. 184, 269, 274, 279–80, 282, 290, 291 n. 1, 292, 293 n. 2, **302–23**, 327; iii. 89, 91, 143, 197; iv. 742, 746, 891, 939, 941; v. 1009, 1093, 1322, 1355, 1360, 1442; vi. 98, 99, 163, 169, 171, 172, 173, 174, 227–9, 244.

Prince Elector, *see* Charles Lewis, Prince of the Palatinate.

Prince of Conceit, A, see Anonymous.

Prince Henry, iii. 287; v. 1304, 1305.

Prince Henry's company, i. 135; iv. 516, 749.

Prince James, v. 1305.

Prince of Orange, iii. 113.

Prince of Prigs' Revels, or The Practices of that Grand Thief Captain James Hind, see S., J.

Prince of Tarent, see Massinger, *A Very Woman*.

Prince's Arms, i. 201 n. 2; iv. 907, 910; vi. 250.

Prince's Arms Bookstall, The, in St. Paul's Churchyard, iii. 146; v. 1072.

Princes, foreign, vi. 292, 293, 295, 303.

Prince's Galleries, iv. 675.

Princes of the Palatinate, iii. 135.

Princes Reconnus, Les, see Du Rocher.

Princess, The, see Killigrew, Thomas.

Princess Elizabeth, *see* Elizabeth, Lady, Princess of England.

Princess Mary, v. 1305.

Printers; ii. 434, 436; vi. 26.

Printers and stationers, company of, i. 53.

Printer's apology, iii. 464.

Printing-house, iv. 950.

Priscianus Vapulans, see Anonymous.

Prisons, King's Bench, vi. 34.
  Ludgate, vi. 29.
  Marshalsea, vi. 74, 101.
  New, the, i. 266; vi. 161.
  Newgate, vi. 29, 56.
Prisoner, The, see Massinger, Philip,
  The Fair Anchoress of Pausilippo.
Prisoners, The, see Killigrew,
  Thomas.
Private Entertainments, v. 1097.
Private House in Drury Lane, see
  Phoenix Theatre.
Private performances, i. 10 n. 6
  cont., 327; iv. 558; vii. 11.
Private theatres, iii. 308.
Private theatres (Apthorpe), iii.
  293.
Privilege, certificates of, see Tickets
  of privilege.
Privy Chamber, iii. 21.
  Gentleman of, v. 1048.
Privy Council, i. 1, 10, 11, 21, 63,
  137, 161, 162 n. 3, 163, 176, 198,
  228 n. 1, 236 n. 7, 296, 324 n. 1,
  327; iii. 21, 68; iv. 497, 875,
  879, 880; v. 1015, 1156, 1371;
  vi. 24–25, 27–30, 38, 39, 54, 56,
  68, 78, 81, 83, 84, 123, 130, 164,
  215, 228, 260, 261, 292; vii. 1,
  4, 28, 57–58.
  President of, i. 12.
Privy Council Register, James I, iv.
  874, 876.
Privy Seal, vi. 297, 304, 307.
  Office, iii. 415.
Prize-fighters, vi. 138, 212, 247, 248,
  250, 251; vii. 5.
Prizes, vi. 238.
Proby, Sir Peter, iv. 882, 898.
Proceedings of the British Academy
  (1927), iv. 536.
Processions, v. 1154–63; vii. 122.
  Described, v. 1158–60, 1161, 1162.
Proclamations, iv. 826; v. 1194,
  1398; vi. 297, 298.
Procter, B. W., see Cornwall, Barry.
Proctor, H., Changes (1876), v.
  1094.
Proctors, vi. 166.
  Of Court of Probate, iv. 497; vi.
  228.
Prodigal Scholar, The, see Randolph,
  Thomas.
Prodromus, Theodorus, Rhodanthes
  et Dosicles Amorum, iii. 140.
Production and Stage-Management
  at the Blackfriars Theatre, see
  Isaacs, J.
Proemes [sic], v. 1139.

Profaneness, see Plays, profaneness
  in.
Profanity, i. 37, 106–7; vii. 84.
Prognosticators, vi. 152.
Progresses of James I, see Nichols,
  John.
Progress, royal, i. 311 n. 1; iv. 646,
  653; vi. 84.
  Players' attendance during, i.
  309 n. 3, 310–11.
  Itinerary of, i. 310.
'Projected Amphitheatre, The', see
  Hotson, Leslie.
Projected theatres, vi. 289–309.
Projector Lately Dead, A, see
  Anonymous.
Projectors, i. 65 n. 2, 314, 317 n. 1;
  iii. 64; iv. 616; vi. 291, 301.
Projects, i. 314; v. 1442; vi. 228.
Prologue actors, iii. 327.
Prologues, i. 228; ii. 440, 691; iii. 4,
  18, 25, 26, 33, 34, 49, 51, 52, 59–
  60, 60, 62, 66, 67–68, 74, 77, 83, 90,
  91, 96, 97, 100, 102, 103, 106, 111,
  112, 114, 115, 116, 118, 128–30,
  130, 133, 134, 141, 147, 148, 152,
  153, 154, 160, 162–3, 164, 170,
  172, 176, 177, 178, 180, 192, 201,
  210, 211–12, 223, 224, 271–2, 275,
  278, 295, 317, 321, 322, 326, 327,
  330, 334, 342, 358, 361, 362, 365,
  369–70, 373, 375, 376, 383, 388,
  389, 392, 394, 397, 410, 411, 413,
  424, 440, 444, 447, 467; iv. 474,
  486, 491, 494, 499, 500, 502, 503,
  504, 505, 506, 508, 509, 515, 523,
  524, 527, 528, 539, 547, 563, 570,
  571, 573, 581, 582, 583, 590, 593,
  595, 596, 627, 628, 630, 699, 720,
  722, 723, 724, 727, 730, 739, 743,
  745, 746, 747, 755, 764, 772–3,
  774, 778, 779, 783, 789, 799, 825,
  826, 848, 849, 857, 877, 887, 901,
  902, 908, 909–10, 924, 930, 931,
  932, 933, 935, 941; v. 961, 964,
  972, 973–4, 979, 986, 987, 990,
  998, 1006, 1020, 1033, 1035, 1041,
  1044, 1045, 1051, 1052, 1055, 1069,
  1071, 1084, 1086, 1093, 1099,
  1106, 1109, 1112, 1124, 1134, 1142,
  1143, 1144, 1146, 1148, 1182,
  1192, 1206, 1212, 1215, 1217,
  1218, 1221, 1223–4, 1233, 1237,
  1238, 1251, 1258, 1278, 1280,
  1307, 1316, 1329, 1333, 1338,
  1339, 1342, 1345, 1350, 1355,
  1362, 1365, 1374, 1394, 1417,
  1428, 1436, 1438, 1439, 1453; vi.
  7, 8, 14, 40, 50, 52–53, 70, 92 n. 1,

93, 98, 111, 163, 169, 171, 172, 193, 197, 198, 199, 229, 242, 270; vii. 117.

'Prologue or Epilogue To The Country Captain', iii. 146.

Prologue, with marigold, v. 1453.

'Prologue to his Majesty At the first Play presented at the Cock-pit in Whitehall, The', see Anonymous.

'Prologue spoken at the Cock-pit, at the coming of the Red Bull Players thither, A', see Tatham, John.

'Prologue spoken at the Red-Bull to a Play called the Whisperer, or what you please', see Tatham, John.

'Prologue spoken upon removing of the late Fortune Players to the Bull, A', see Tatham, John.

Prologues, authors of, iii. 162–3, 322, 327, 334, 361, 373, 383, 388–9, 446; iv. 503, 573, 723–4, 764; v. 1069, 1112, 1134, 1355, 1423, 1438–9.

Confused, iii. 278.

Contract to write, ii. 390.

Costume of, v. 1055.

At court, iv. 778, 779, 780; vi. 198.

Duplicate, iii. 388.

Manner of delivery, v. 1055.

Popularity of, iv. 822–3.

Printed, vi. 284.

Reused, iii. 274–5, 365, 388.

Revised, iii. 365; v. 1020, 1086–7, 1099, 1148.

Signed, iii. 446–7; iv. 593.

Promos and Cassandra, see Whetstone, George.

Prompt books, iii. 25, 59–60, 131, 134, 267–8, 301, 317, 323, 327, 332, 339, 353, 359, 363, 366, 369, 373, 375, 380, 391, 400, 406, 416, 421, 424, 433, 464; iv. 545, 561, 688, 744, 763–5, 773, 868, 874, 885, 886, 922; v. 1141, 1149, 1426, 1433–4; vi. 9 n. 1, 31, 56, 153, 197.

Directions, iii. 327.

Prompter, iii. 118, 267, 321; vii. 8.

Prompter's additions, iii. 397.

Warnings, iii. 60.

Proofreading, iv. 497, 595, 596, 609, 615, 777, 810, 814, 817; v. 1094.

Propaganda, vi. 168.

Plays, iii. 41, 94–95, 200, 228.

Properties, iv. 925; v. 1343; vi. 280.

Ecclesiastical, v. 1235, 1300.

Value of, i. 57.

Property directions, iii. 421.

Makers, i. 53 n. 1; iii. 139; vi. 273, 278.

'Prophecie of Mother Shipton', see Anonymous.

Prophetess, The, see Betterton, Thomas.

See Fletcher, John.

'Proposals for Building an Amphitheatre in London 1620', see A., G. E. P.

Proposed amphitheatre, ii. 423, 620; iv. 748; vi. 291–304.

Costs of, vi. 295, 302.

Proposed pageant, see Munday, Anthony.

Proscenium, design for, iv. 524.

Prosceniums, v. 1190; vi. 51–52, 107, 109.

Prospectus, see Theatre prospectus.

Prostitutes, iii. 90, 254; v. 1126–7.

Prostitution, houses of, see Bawdy houses.

Protectorate, vi. 284 n. 1.

Protestants, vii. 12.

Proude, Searles, ii. 464.

Proverbs, iii. 253; iv. 861, 910.

Provincial audiences, i. 312–13.

Companies suppressed, i. 178–9.

Performances, conduct at, i. 276.

Tours, players' dislike of, i. 146 n. 6.

Visits, i. 92–93, 156, 172–3, 193, 212–13, 248, 282, 298–9, 322.

Length of, i. 274, 275, 276.

Proxy, or Love's Aftergame, The, see Anonymous.

Prudentius, see Strode, William, Floating Island.

Pryce, John, ii. 649.

Prynne, William, i. 25 n. 5, 329; ii. 454, 457; iii. 386, 451, 452, 455; iv. 553, 681, 744; v. 1069, 1193, 1194, 1195, 1213, 1398; vi. 24, 80, 96.

Exhibited in pillory, iv. 563.

Mutilation of his ears, v. 1307.

In prison, v. 1080, 1081.

Satire on, iv. 581, 582; v. 1080–81.

Histrio-Mastix, The Players Scourge, or Actors Tragaedie, (1633), iii. 90, 386, 451, 453; iv. 548, 551, 566, 582, 583, 919–20, 987, 988; v. 1058, 1074, 1160, 1161, 1194, 1307, 1316;

Prynne, William (*cont.*)
  vi. 23, 49, 95, 117, 121, 154, 223, 226; vii. 2, 10, 14.
  Histriomastix controversy, v. 1081.
Pryore, Richard, *see* Price, Richard.
Pseudomasia, see Mewe, William, *Pseudomagia.*
Public houses, v. 1224.
Public Record Office, v. 1269, 1399; vi. 6, 48 n. 1, 49 n. 1, 54, 72 n. 2, 75, 117 n. 1, 124, 158 n. 1, 260, 262, 263, 265, 271 n. 1, 286, 287, 293, 300, 303.
  Exchequer Bills, vi. 202 n. 2.
  Lord Chamberlain's Warrant Books, vi. 46.
  Scudamore Papers, vi. 25 n. 1, 17 n. 1, 282 n. 1.
Public-theatre audience, *see* Audience, public-theatre.
Public works, vi. 299.
Publication, vi. 13.
  Actors opposed to, iii. 53; iv. 566; v. 1018.
  Delay in, iv. 931.
  Surreptitious, iii. 470.
  Unauthorized, iii. 470; iv. 566; v. 1103.
Publisher, iv. 887.
Publishers, dramatists' agreements with, v. 1069, 1136.
Publishers' play lists, v. 1022, 1024, 1025, 1043, 1046, 1058–9, 1060, 1062, 1082, 1085, 1087–8, 1099, 1100, 1105, 1121, 1124, 1134, 1148, 1149, 1184, 1187, 1246, 1253, 1270, 1272, 1273, 1278, 1292, 1293, 1294, 1301, 1303, 1310, 1312, 1314, 1321, 1322, 1323, 1326, 1327, 1333, 1335, 1336, 1338, 1351, 1353, 1354, 1356, 1360, 1361, 1363, 1366, 1369, 1376, 1382, 1383, 1384, 1385, 1390, 1395, 1397, 1399, 1402, 1416, 1419, 1422, 1428, 1432; *see also* Play lists.
Publius Cornelius Scipio Sui Victor, see Anonymous.
Puckering, Sir Thomas, i. 52, 239 n. 3, 283 n. 7 cont., 284; ii. 436; iii. 135, 138, 453; iv. 612, 618, 652, 917, 918, 919, 954; v. 1057, 1228; vi. 25 and n. 1, 87.
Pudding, John, vi. 114.
Puddle Wharf, *see* London, streets and districts.
Puddle Wharf theatre, *see* Rosseter's Puddle Wharf or Blackfriars theatre.

Pudsey, Edward, ii. 537.
Pulpit-place, vi. 258.
Pulpits, vii. 35.
Pulver, Jeffrey, *A Biographical Dictionary of Old English Music* (1927), iii. 109.
Puncteus, John, ii. 537; iv. 780, 781.
Punctuation (of stage-directions), iii. 317.
Punge, Clement, iii. 43; v. 1008.
Puppet play, ii. 480; vi. 209.
Puppet-show, iii. 45, 76.
Puppeteer, ii. 413, 618.
Purbeck, Viscount, performs in a masque, iv. 647.
Purcell, Henry, iii. 397; iv. 647.
  Bonduca, iv. 647; v. 1147, 1163, 1360, 1430.
  Song by, iii. 354.
Purfoote, Mr., stationer, iii. 235, 284; iv. 812; v. 971, 974, 1114.
Puritan, The, see Middleton, Thomas.
Puritan feeling against the players, i. 67.
Puritan Maid, the Modest Wife, and the Wanton Widow, The, see Middleton, Thomas.
Puritan ministers, i. 5.
  Residents in Blackfriars, i. 31.
  Writers, v. 1235.
Puritanism, v. 1408; vi. 17, 82.
Puritans, ii. 537, 538; iii. 95, 200, 299, 467, 473, 514; iv. 529, 530, 551, 556, 592, 844, 847, 850, 877, 916; v. 1028, 1045, 1081, 1119, 1194, 1195, 1198, 1199, 1200, 1308, 1363, 1398; vi. 17, 22, 41, 44, 80, 95 and n. 1, 96, 166–7, 168, 238, 243, 285; vii. 2, 10, 12, 13.
  Anti-Puritan pieces, v. 1218.
  Anti-theatrical activities of, iv. 471.
  Satire of, v. 1238.
Pursevants, v. 1300; vi. 167.
Purslowe, George, iv. 907.
Puttick and Simpson, v. 977.
  Auction, v. 1328.
Pygmalion, see Anonymous.
Pyne, Arthur, *Musarum Deliciae* (1640), ii. 472.
Pyott, Lazarus, *The Orator* (1596), iii. 331, 400.
'Pyramus and Thisbe', in Shakespeare's *M.N.D.,* v. 1153.
Pyrander, see Johnson, Nathaniel.
Pyrandre et Lisimene, see Boisrobert.

Pyrkyns, Richard, *see* Perkins, Richard.
Pyrton, living of, iv. 845.

Quakers, v. 1437.
Quarles, Francis, iv. 955–9.
  Argalus and Parthenia (1629), iv. 480, 956.
  Chronicle of the Citty of London, A. Unpublished, iv. 956.
  Emblems (1635), iv. 956.
  Enchiridion (1640), iv. 956.
  Feast for Worms, A (1620), iv. 956.
  Virgin Widow, The, ii. 294; iv. 956, 957–9.
Quarles, James, iv. 955.
Quarles, Ursula, iv. 956.
  'Short Relation Of The Life and Death of M[r]. *Francis Quarles, by Vrsula Quarles*, his sorrowfull Widow', in *Solomons Recantation, Entituled Ecclesiastes, Paraphrased, A* (1645), iv. 955, 956.
Queen, The, see Dryden.
  See Fletcher, John.
Queen, or the Excellency of Her Sex, The, see Ford, John.
Queen Anne, *see* Anne, Queen of England.
Queen of Aragon, The, see Habington, William.
Queen Camel, Somerset, ii. 673.
Queen and the Concubine, The, see Brome, Richard.
Queen of Corinth, The, see Fletcher, John.
Queen of Corsica, The, see Jaques, Francis.
Queen Elizabeth, *see* Elizabeth, Queen of England.
Queen of Ethiopia, see Anonymous.
Queen Henrietta-Maria, *see* Henrietta-Maria, Queen of England.
Queen's Arcadia, see Daniel, Samuel.
Queens' College, Cambridge, iv. 532, 533, 534, 535, 536, 537, 600, 952, 953, 954; v. 966, 984, 1236, 1238, 1407–8.
  Fellow of, v. 1236.
  Proctor of, v. 1236.
Queen's College, the, Oxford, i. 26 n. 5 cont.; ii. 688; iii. 21, 74, 136; iv. 856; v. 1170, 1175, 1176, 1190–1; vi. 99, 164; vii. 227.
Queen's company, *see* Anne and Henrietta-Maria.
Queen's Exchange, The, see Brome, Richard.

Queen's Masque, The, see Heywood, Thomas, *Love's Mistress.*
'Queen's Play, The', *see* Anonymous.
Queen's street, *see* London, streets of.
Querer por solo Querer, see Mendoza, Antonio de.
Quick, John, iii. 354; v. 1081.
Quiller-Couch, Arthur, and J. Dover Wilson, eds., *All's Well*, iii. 381.
Quinault, Philippe, iv. 726.
Quinborough Oysters (mock title), v. 1447.
Quinne, John, v. 1358.
Quintana, Ricardo, 'Samuel Butler: A Restoration Figure in a Modern Light', *E.L.H.* xviii (1951), v. 1380, 1382.
Quoyten, Bartholomew, ii. 649.

R., Ann, v. 1311.
R., I., v. 1220.
R., M., iii. 153.
R., N., v. 961.
  Tragœdia Miserrima Pyrami et Thisbes fata enuncians, v. 961–2.
R., T., iii. 153; v. 962–4.
  Calanthe, v. 995.
  Cornelianum Dolium, iii. 40; v. 962–4, 976, 1009.
  Extravagant Shepherd, The, v. 962, 964.
R., W., v. 964.
  Master of Arts, v. 1004.
Racan, Seigneur de *L'Artenice*, vii. 60.
'Racan's *L'Artenice*, An Addition to the English Canon', *see* Jackson, William A.
Race, footmen's, vii. 27.
Radcliffe, Sir Alexander, v. 963.
Radtke, Stephen J., *James Shirley: His Catholic Philosophy of Life* (1929), v. 1065, 1068.
Raebel, Karl, *Massinger's Drama 'The Maid of Honour' in seinem Verhältnis zu Painter's 'Palace of Pleasure', Tome II Novelle 32, unter Berücksichtigung der übrigen Quellen* (1901), iv. 797.
Raging Turk, The, see Goffe, Thomas.
Raguaillo D'Oceano, see Fane, Mildmay.
Rainbow, Edward, v. 1038.
Raines, F. R., *The Journal of Nicholas Assheton* (1848), vii. 24.
Rainescrofte, Thomas, *see* Ravenscroft, Thomas.

Raison, Gilbert, *see* Reason, Gilbert.
Raleigh, Sir Edward, ii. 371.
Raleigh, Sir Walter, iii. 341; iv.
    609; vii. 28.
    Book by, vi. 59.
    Execution of, iii. 417.
    History of the World, iv. 764.
Ralph, Philip L., *Sir Humphrey
    Mildmay: Royalist Gentleman*
    (1947), iv. 728; v. 1269, 1390.
Ram Alley, see David, Lord Barry.
'*Rambling Gallants defeated, The*',
    see Anonymous, *The Merry Milk-
    maid of Islington*.
Rambling Justice, The, see Leanerd,
    John.
Ramsey, James, iii. 427.
Ramsey, Mr., iv. 530.
Randal Earl of Chester, see Middle-
    ton, Thomas, *The Chester Tragedy*.
Randolph, Ambrose, i. 42 n. 3.
Randolph, Elizabeth Smith, v. 965.
Randolph, John, v. 965.
Randolph, Robert, v. 963, 985.
Randolph, Thomas, i. 291 n. 8, 292
    n. 1; ii. 416, **537–9**; iii. 68, 174,
    180, 435, 450; iv. 536, 540, 541,
    737, 823, 844, 852, 953; v. 962,
    963, **964–93**, 1009, 1116, 1117,
    1183, 1243, 1328–9.
    Admission to the Tribe of Ben, v.
    979.
    Allusions to, v. 968.
    Reply to Jonson, iii. 51.
    Verses by, iii. 79, 80.
    Amyntas, or *The Impossible
    Dowry,* i. 292, 299 n. a, 300; ii.
    538; iii. 131, 180; v. 966,
    969–71, 974; vi. 98.
    Aristippus, iii. 236, 441; v. 966,
    971–3, 975, 976, 977, 981, 982,
    1343, 1443.
    Conceited Pedlar, The, iii. 236; v.
    966, 971, 973, **974–6**, 982, 1443.
    Constant Lovers, The, v. 967, 976.
    'Coy Cælia', v. 1431.
    Drinking Academy, The, ii. 538;
    iii. 182; v. 966, **976–80**, 991,
    1328–9.
    'Eclogue to Master Jonson', ii.
    538.
    Entertainment, The, see *The Muses'
    Looking Glass*.
    *Hey for Honesty, Down with
    Knavery,* iv. 598; v. 966, 980–2.
    In Lesbiam, & Histrionem, v. 967.
    Jealous Lovers, The, iii. 180; iv.
    532, 535, 916, 954; v. 966, 967,
    977, 979, **982–6**, 1009, 1329.

'Masque of Virtues', v. 1431.
    Muses' Looking Glass, The, or *The
    Entertainment,* i. 291, 292, 301;
    ii. 537, 538; iii. 167; v. 966, 970,
    974, 981, **986–9**, 1431, 1432; vi.
    95–97, 98.
    'Musicke thou Queene of Soules',
    v. 1431.
    Oratio Praevaricatoria, iv. 536,
    537; v. 985.
    'Pastorall Ode, A', v. 1431.
    *Poems With The Mvses Looking-
    Glasse: And Amyntas.* By
    Thomas Randolph Master of
    Arts, and late Fellow of
    Trinity College in *Cambridge.*
    Oxford, Printed by Leonard
    Lichfield Printer to the Vni-
    versity, for Francis Bowman
    (1638, 1640, 1643, 1652, 1664,
    1668, n.d.), v. 968, 981, 983, 986,
    1431; vi. 244.
    *Poetical and Dramatic Works of
    Thomas Randolph of Trinity
    College, Cambridge. Now First
    Collected and Edited from the
    early Copies and from MSS.
    with some Account of the Author
    and Occasional Notes. By W.
    Carew Hazlitt,* 2 vols. (1875), v.
    969.
    Praeludium, iii. 68, 460; iv. 502–
    5; v. 966, **989–90**, 1354; vi.
    97–98.
    '*Praeludium* and the Salisbury
    Court Theatre', *see* Bentley,
    Gerald Eades.
    Prodigal Scholar, The, v. 963, 979,
    990–1.
    'Say Daunce', v. 1431.
    'Thom̃ Randolfs Salting', v.
    966, **991–3**, 1295, 1306, 1307,
    1343.
Randolph, William, v. 965.
Rankins, William, *Hannibal and
    Scipio, see* Hathaway, Richard.
Ranting in theatres, i. 280.
Rape, execution for, ii. 675.
Rape of Lucrece, The, see Heywood,
    Thomas.
Rape's Revenge, see Beaumont and
    Fletcher, *Valentinian*.
Rapiers, vi. 234, 294.
Rapp, Moriz, iii. 397.
'Rapture', *see* Carew, Thomas, v.
    1381.
Ravens Almanacke, The (1609), *see*
    Dekker, Thomas.
Ravenscroft, Thomas, ii. **539, 642**.

The Canterbury Guests, iv. 803.
Ravis, Dr., iv. 588.
Rawley, Dr. (Bacon's chaplain), iv. 526.
Rawlins, Thomas, iii. 153; iv. 722; v. 993–9, 1001, 1216.
Rebellion, The, i. 13 n. 2, 301, 319 n. 1; ii. 440, 444, 446, 489; iii. 153, 226; iv. 515, 679; v. 993, 994, 995, 995–8, 1001, 1216.
Tom Essence or The Modish Wife, see Anonymous.
Raworth, Robert, iv. 562.
Rayer, Alice, ii. 403.
Rayne, Andrew, *see* Cane, Andrew.
Raynton, Nicholas, iv. 575.
Re Vera, or Verily, see Ruggle, George.
Read, of Gray's Inn, v. 1158.
Read, Robert, iii. 213–14.
Reade, Edward, ii. 541.
Reade, Emanuel, i. 171, 177 and n. 6; ii. 539.
Reade, Pennella, ii. 541.
Reade, Robert, v. 1158.
Reade, Thomas, iii. 135, 139, 140.
Reade, Timothy, i. 65 n. 2, 165, 220, 246, 285, 286, 287, 288, 290, 291 and n. 2, 297; ii. 540–1; iv. 504, 864; vi. 99–100, 111, 112, 113, 117, 170.
Reading, i. 92, 172, 189 n. 3, 193, 212, 272, 273, 282, 298; ii. 350, 453, 475, 604.
Reason, Gilbert, i. 178, 198, 209 and n. 2, 210, 211; ii. 541–3.
Rebellion, The, see Rawlins, Thomas.
Rebellion of Naples, The, see B., T.
Rebus, iii. 148.
Recantation of an Ill Led Life, A, see Clavell, John.
Recitatives, vi. 257.
Record of Old Westminsters, see Barker, G. F. Russell.
Record Office, *see* Public Record Office.
Recorder of London, *see* London.
Records of the Honourable Society of Lincoln's Inn, The, see Baildon, W. P.
Recreations, heroic and domestic, vi. 292, 293.
Recreations with the Muses, see Alexander, Sir William, Earl of Stirling.
Recusants, ii. 364, 365, 366, 370, 385, 457, 460, 471, 543, 616; iii. 15, 243, 245; iv. 608.

Red Bull Company, iii. 53, 59; iv. 754.
'Red Bull Company and the Importunate Widow, The', see Sisson, Charles J.
Red Bull theatre, i. 22 n. 2, 25, 26, 137 n. 6, 158, 160, 161, 163, 164, 165, 166, 170 n. 1, 174, 188 n. 4, 190, 194, 201, 202 and n. 1, 203, 206, 207, 208, 220, 224, 225 and n. 1, 228, 270, 272, 273 and n. 1, 274, 275, 279, 280, 309, 310, 312 n. 7, 314, 315, 317 and n. 2, 319, 320; ii. 346, 560, 571, 637, 680, 690, 693, 694, 695; iii. 10, 22, 24, 30, 31, 32, 37, 52, 56, 59, 69, 71, 76, 82, 89, 102, 103, 104, 147, 149, 189, 197, 221, 237, 240, 246, 254, 255, 263, 264, 266, 273, 280, 281, 283, 284, 286, 314, 333, 344, 371, 374, 378, 385, 387, 408, 419, 423, 426; iv. 479, 491, 520, 555, 556, 557, 580, 679, 680, 689, 695, 696, 698, 702, 706, 711, 712, 713, 714, 719, 733, 734, 735, 767, 812, 830, 836, 868, 900; v. 995, 996, 998, 1019, 1050, 1061, 1062, 1082, 1085, 1091, 1129, 1135, 1136, 1137, 1143, 1150–1, 1163, 1177, 1178, 1204, 1208, 1217, 1218, 1223, 1344, 1393, 1396, 1402, 1411, 1416, 1427, 1435, 1438, 1439, 1441, 1442, 1446, 1448, 1449, 1456; vi. 11, 12 n. 1, 40, 54, 56, 57, 63, 66, 76, 99, 102, 111, 113, 114, 122, 129, 130, 133, 136, 137, 146, 148, 154, 163, 164, 166, 169, 170, 172, 173, 174, 177, 187, 188, 191, 199, 200, 214–48, 250; vii. 5, 8, 9, 11.
Chief players at, i. 167, 171.
Conduct of audiences at, i. 316.
Dancing at, ii. 523.
Disturbance at, i. 313–14.
Footways about, i. 169.
Mishap on the stage of, i. 166.
Petition about highway repairs near, i. 171.
Pit, v. 1019.
Playwrights for, ii. 690.
Reputation of, i. 280, 319; vi. 238–47.
Red Bull–King's company, i. 22 and n. 2, 25 n. 3, 171, 270–82, 290, 308, 311, 312, 315; iv. 689; vi. 90 n. 2, 164, 165, 166, 169, 170, 225–7.

Red Bull Revels company, i. 203, 208; v. 1313.

Red Cross street, see London, streets of.

Red Lion Alley, see London, streets of.

Red Lion Inn, vi. 127, 247.

Redman, —, ii. 347.

Reed, Isaac, ed., *Biographia Dramatica* (1782), iv. 829.

Reed, Timothy, see Reade, Timothy.

Reeve, Ralph, vi. 78, 79, 115.

Reformation, The, see Wright, Abraham.

Refutation of the Apology for Actors, see Green, John.

Regent's Park (open-air theatre), iv. 638.

Regicides, iv. 500, 515.

Regius Professor of Civil Law, Oxford, v. 1276.

Rehearsal, The, see Buckingham, Duke of (Second).

Rehearsals, ii. 503, 552; iv. 673; vi. 249 n. 2, 295; vii. 34, 83, 87.

Reignolds, William, i. 220, 221, 222, 246; ii. 543; iv. 813.

Relation of a Journey Begun . . . 1610, see Sandys, George.

Reliquiae Wottonianae, see Wotton, Sir Henry.

Remarks upon E. Settle's Narrative (1683), see Anonymous.

Remembrancer of the City of London, see London, City of, Remembrancer.

Remembrancia of the City of London, see London, City of, Remembrancia.

Removing Wardrobe of Beds, Yeoman of, vi. 265.

Rendle, William, 'The Graves at St. Saviour's, Southwark', *Athenaeum*, 21 August 1886, iii. 310.

Walford's Antiquarian, viii (July–December 1885), vi. 183 n. 1.

Renegado, The, or The Gentleman of Venice, see Massinger, Philip.

Renton (a fencer), vi. 250.

Reparatus, sive Depositum, see Drury, William.

Repertories, see Companies, repertories of.

Reputation (of playwrights), see Playwrights, reputations of.

Reputations, literary, iii. 21, 47–48, 50–51, 55, 106, 127.

Requests, Court of, see Court of Requests.

Resident managers, see Theatres, resident managers of.

Restoration (1660), iii. 33, 144; vi. 38, 47, 53, 75, 77, 122, 171, 214, 230, 238, 246, 274 n. 1, 281, 284.

Restoration Court Stage, The (1660–1702), see Boswell, Eleanore.

Restoration revivals, iii. 146, 192, 206, 222, 264, 313, 314, 315, 320, 333, 347, 354, 373, 419, 421, 464; iv. 481, 492, 571, 580, 581, 628, 744, 817, 862, 864.

Reveling rooms (at court), vi. 284.

Revels, Master of the, see Master of the Revels.

Revels Office, iii. 257, 340; iv. 867, 869, 883, 890; v. 1020, 1074, 1315.

List of plays on waste paper, iii. 352; v. 1018, 1128, 1196, 1308, 1331, 1350, 1352, 1406, 1421, 1426, 1433.

Revels, Players of the, see Queen Anne's Company—Players of the Revels.

Revenge, The, see Killigrew, Thomas.

Revenge of Bussy D'Ambois, The, see Chapman, George.

Revenge for Honour, see Glapthorne, Henry.

Revett, Eldred, v. 1214, 1215.

Poems (1657), iv. 722.

Revivals, see Plays, revived.

Reyher, Paul, *Les Masques anglais* (1909), iii. 107, 108, 110, 199, 207, 213, 216, 443; iv. 647, 651, 655, 660, 669, 676; v. 1154, 1227, 1228, 1229, 1230; vii. 66, 72.

Reynolds, George Fullmer, 'Some Principles of Elizabethan Staging', *Mod. Phil.* iii (1905–6), vi. 191.

Staging of Elizabethan Plays at the Red Bull Theatre, 1605–1625, The (1940), v. 1346, 1416, 1417, 1427; vi. 215.

'Was there a "Tarras" in Shakespeare's Globe?', *Shakespeare Survey*, iv (1951), vi. 179, 186–92.

Review of J. C. Adams, *The Globe Playhouse. Journal Eng. and Ger. Phil.* xlii (1943), vi. 188 n. 1.

Reynolds, Henry (John?), v. 999.

Reynolds, Jane, ii. 543.

Reynolds, John (Henry?), v. 999.

Triumphs of God's Revenge against the Crying and Execrable Sin of Murder (1621), iv. 863; v. 1133.

Reynolds, Margery, ii. 543.

Reynolds, Robert, i. 165, 171; ii. 543.

Reynolds, William, *see* Reignolds, William.

Rheade, Timothy, *see* Reade, Timothy.

Rhé, English expedition to island of, v. 993, 1167.

Rhoads, Howard Garrett, ed., *Wm. Hawkins' Apollo Shroving: An Edition with Notes and an Introduction* (1936), iv. 538–9.

Rhoads, Rebecca G., ed. *The Two Noble Ladies and the Converted Conjurer* (1930) v. 1426, 1427.

Rhodanthes et Dosicles Amorum, see Prodromus, Theodorus.

Rhodes, Ann, ii. 545.

Rhodes, John, i. 15, 73–89, 279; ii. 544–6, 659; iii. 115, 116; vi. 49, 50, 77, 168–9.

Rhodes, John (Restoration manager), Company of, ii. 694; iii. 221, 371, 374, 377, 408, 418, 423, 426; iv. 766, 862; v. 1204, 1262; vi. 53.

Rhodes, Mathew, stationer, iii. 115; iv. 734, 735.

Rhodes, Richard, *Flora's Vagaries*, iii. 409.

Rhodon and Iris, see Knevet, Ralph.

Rhymed tragi-comedy, iii. 35.

Rhys, Ernest, ed., *The Complete Plays of Ben Jonson*. Everyman's Library, 2 vols. (1910), iv. 613.

— ed., *Thomas Dekker*, Mermaid Series (1887), iii. 245.

Ribaldry, *see* Plays, ribaldry in.

Rice, John (actor), i. 8, 14, 17, 24, 72–88, 117, 176; ii. 546–7, 683; iii. 119, 341, 416; iv. 642; v. 1412.

Rice, John, clerk of St. Saviour's, Southwark, ii. 644.

Rice, Warner G., 'The Moroccan Episode in Thomas Heywood's *The Fair Maid of the West*', *P.Q.* ix (1930), iv. 568, 569.

'Sources of Massinger's *The Renegado*, The', *P.Q.* xi (1932), iv. 812, 813, 815.

'Sources of William Cartwright's *The Royall Slave*', *M.L.N.* xlv (1930), iii. 134, 140–1; iv. 766, 770.

Turk, Moor, and Persian in English Literature (Harvard MS.

Thesis, 1926), iii. 119, 122; iv. 489, 506, 510; v. 1215.

Rich, Lady Ann, v. 1269.

Rich, Sir Harry, iv. 650; v. 1289.

Rich, Henry, first Earl of Holland, v. 1123; vi. 31.

Rich, Isabella, v. 1289.

Rich, Sir Nathaniel, vi. 21.

Rich, Penelope, iii. 435, 440.

Rich, Sir Robert, v. 1289.

Richard II, see Shakespeare, **and** Anonymous, *Thomas of Woodstock*.

Richard III, see Shakespeare.

Richard the Third, or the English Profit, see Samuel Rowley.

Richard Crookback, see Jonson, Ben.

Richard, Lewis, composer, iii. 214.

Richards, Gabriel, v. 1001.

Richards, Nathanael, iv. 906; v. 961, 998, **999–1004**.

Celestiall Publican, The, v. 1000, 1001.

Tragedy of Messalina, the Roman Empress, The, i. 285, 286, 287, 288, 289 n. 4, 290, 291 n. 1, 297, 301; ii. 359, 402, 404, 444, **445**, 459, 483, 487, 488, 489, **515**, 549, 550, 600; iii. 226; iv. 678; v. 961, 995, 998, 999, 1000, 1001, **1002–4**; vii. 117.

Truth's Acrostick An Elegie Vpon The most renowned, true, and unparalleld Worthy Knight, Sir Paul Pindar Deceased (1650), v. 1002.

Upon the Declaration of His Majesty King Charles of England the Second (1660), v. 1002.

Richards, Richard, v. 999.

Richards, William, v. 1004–5, 1306. *English Orator, The* (1680), v. 1004.

Wallography, or the Britton Described (1682), v. 1004.

Richards, Capt. William, v. 1001.

Riche his farewell to militarie profession, see Rich, Barnabe.

Riche, Barnabe, *Farewell to Military Profession* (1581), iv. 836; v. 1147.

Riches, see Burges, James Bland.

Richlieu, Cardinal, allusions to, v. 982.

Richmond, Surrey, i. 315; ii. 597, 695; iv. 474, 1357; vi. 229, 283; vii. 117, 118, 119, 121, 122, 124.

Richmond, Duchess of, ii. 420. Page to, iii. 194.

Richmond, Lodowick Stewart, Duke and Earl of, ii. 349; v. 965.
Richmond, Duke of, funeral of, vii. 53.
Richmond and Lennox, Mary, Duchess of, ii. 447; iii. 123.
Richmond palace, vi. 35.
Richmond Park, iii. 112.
Keepers of, iii. 112.
Richmond, plays at, iii. 82, 313, 418; vi. 266.
Rick, G., see Rickner, George.
Rickets, John, v. 1005-7.
Rickner, George, i. 15, 16 n. 1, 72-88; ii. 547.
Rider, John, *Riders dictionarie corrected and enriched. By* F. Holyoke. (Dictionarium etymologicum in hac secunda cura elaborata per F. de Sacra Quercu. *Lat.–Eng.*) (1617), iii. 99.
Rider, William, *The Rider of the White Horse* (1643), v. 1007.
Rider, W., iii. 304; v. 1007-9.
The Twins, iii. 304; v. 1007, 1008-9.
Riding Academy, vi. 45-47.
Riding-schools, vi. 296.
Ridpath, George, *The Stage Condemn'd* (1698), iii. 140, 200.
Right Woman, A, see Fletcher, John.
Riley, Thomas, v. 964, 985, 1009.
Rimbault, Edward F., i. 302; iii. 109; v. 1430.
'Academies of Sir Francis Kynaston and Sir Balthazar Gerbier, The', *N. & Q.*, First Series, iii (1851), iv. 716.
ed., *Bonduca* (*Publications of the Musical Antiquarian Society*, vol. vii, 1842), iii. 84; iv. 536, 647; v. 1147, 1163, 1360.
'Who was "Jack Wilson"?' (1846) ii. 622.
Rimmington, Mr., v. 1298.
Ring, The, see Anonymous.
Rings, copper, vi. 278.
Riots, vi. 54-57.
Ripponden, Yorkshire, iii. 2.
Risley, Derby, v. 1042, 1044.
Rissers, Abraham, ii. 643.
Risus Anglicanus, see Anonymous.
Rites to 'Chloris' and Her Nymphs, see Jonson, Ben, *Chloridia*.
Ritter, Otto, 'Amor und Tod', *Englische Studien*, xxxii (1903), v. 1065, 1102.
Ritual, satire of, i. 277-8.
Rival Friends, see Hausted, Peter.

Rival Nymphs, The, see Anonymous.
Rival plays, see Plays in competition.
Rival Sisters, The, see Gould, Robert.
Rivals, The, see Davenant, William.
Rivers, Mr., v. 1151.
Rivers, the Jesuit, v. 1152.
Roades *or* Roads, see Rhodes, John.
Roades, —, ii. 581.
Roaring Girl, The, see Dekker and Middleton.
Roaring Ranters, v. 1054.
Robb, Dewar M., 'The Canon of William Rowley's Plays', *M.L.R.* xlv (1950), v. 1015.
Robberies, iii. 161.
Robbers' Island, The, see Fane, Mildmay, *Ladrones*.
Robbins, Alice, ii. 548.
Robbins, William, i. 56, 57, 64, 73-89, 167, 168 n. 2, 171, 183 n. 2, 220, 221, 231, 232, 239, 246; ii. 547-9, 693; iv. 570, 733, 813, 863, 864; v. 1164.
Robert the Second, King of Scots, see Jonson, Ben.
Roberts, Benedict, iv. 928.
Roberts, Nicholas, iv. 928.
Robes given players, iii. 206.
Robin Conscience, see Anonymous.
Robin Hood and Little John, see Anonymous.
Robin Hood, Parts I and II, see Anonymous.
Robins, Andria, ii. 405.
Robins, William, see Robbins, William.
Robinson, C. J., *A Register of the Scholars Admitted into Merchant Taylor's School, 1562 to 1874*, 2 vols. (1882-3), iii. 28, 183; v. 1178.
Robinson, Elizabeth, ii. 549.
Robinson, Humphrey, stationer, i. 116, 117, 123; iii. 98, 122, 123, 124, 145, 146, 149, 150, 202, 203, 206, 210, 310, 311, 314, 315, 324, 325, 330, 337, 340, 343, 345, 346, 348, 352, 354, 355, 357, 360, 364, 367, 371, 372, 374, 377, 378, 380, 382, 387, 388, 392, 395, 398, 399, 412, 413, 418, 419, 422, 426, 427, 431; iv. 534, 706, 707, 753, 883, 884; v. 1072, 1082, 1085, 1105, 1124, 1147, 1148, 1270, 1273.
Robinson, Humphrey, Jr., stationer, iii. 202, 203, 206.
Robinson, James, ii. 434, 550.

Robinson, John, i. 285, 286, 288, 290, 297; ii. 457, 549–50; v. 1001, 1220; vi. 100.
Robinson, Margaret, i. 41.
Robinson, Ralph, iv. 874.
Robinson, Mrs. Richard, i. 44, 45 n. 1.
Robinson, Richard, actor, i. 3, 5 and n. 6, 14, 17, 35 n. 1, 45 and n. 1, 69 n. 2, 72–88, 126; ii. 550–3, 637, 650, 682; iii. 311, 416, 423, 428; iv. 642, 764, 792, 793, 817; v. 1087, 1412.
Dedication to, iii. 225.
Robinson, Thomas, ii. 553.
Robinson, Thomas, The Anatomie of the English Nunnerie at Lisbon (1622), iv. 878.
Robinson, William, see Robbins, William.
Robinson, Winifred, i. 43; ii. 553; vi. 36.
Robson, William, see Robbins, William.
Rochford, Viscount, see Cary, John.
Rochester, Bishop of, v. 1341.
Rochester, Wilmot, John, Second Earl of, Lucinia's Rape, v. 1429.
Valentinian, a Tragedy, v. 1429.
Rockets, vi. 210 n.
Rocque, J., Map of London (1746), vi. 49 n. 2.
Rod for Run-aways, A, see Dekker, Thomas.
Rodd, Thomas, i. 302.
Rodes, John, see Rhodes, John.
Rodes, Susan, ii. 565.
Roe, Sir John, iv. 609.
Roe, Sir Thomas, iii. 214, 217, 218; vi. 288.
Roe, William, actor, ii. 553.
Roe, Sir William, iv. 609.
Rogers, Abraham, ii. 384.
Rogers, Edward, i. 220, 221, 246; ii. 553; iv. 814.
Rogers, Hester, ii. 554.
Rogers, Mr., iv. 601.
Rogers, Richard, and Ley, William, List of plays advertised, iii. 41, 304, 469; iv. 500, 501–2, 589, 951; v. 1043, 1149, 1187, 1253, 1293, 1310, 1326, 1336, 1352, 1369, 1376, 1382, 1384, 1402, 1403, 1416, 1432.
Rogers, William, i. 189, 192, 272; ii. 438, 553–4.
Roiston, see Royston, Hertfordshire.
Roiston, Richard, stationer, iii. 24; v. 983.

Rojas, Fernando, de, The Spanish Bawd, see Mabbe, James.
Roles, characteristic, i. 318.
Fat clowns (for Prince Charles's (I) Company and for King's Men), v. 1015–16.
Jaques (All's Lost by Lust), v. 1016.
Plumporridge (Inner Temple Masque), v. 1016.
Simplicity (The World Tossed at Tennis), v. 1016.
Roles in plays, iii. 232–3, 271–2, 301, 321, 344, 346, 347, 369, 371, 377, 379, 400, 405, 411, 413, 416, 424, 428, 433; iv. 487, 491, 498, 503–4, 506, 532, 570, 630, 686, 764–5, 767–8, 781, 810, 813–14, 816–17, 862, 863, 864, 877, 881, 885, 894, 909, 915, 917, 918, 933; v. 1003, 1086, 1091, 1092, 1093, 1094, 1097–8, 1107, 1115, 1149, 1151, 1164, 1165, 1170, 1187, 1193–5, 1195, 1229, 1237, 1251, 1252, 1258, 1274, 1288, 1304, 1360, 1363, 1402; vi. 31, 172.
Rolleston, Robert, vi. 49, 72 n. 2, 75 n. 1, 76, 77.
Rollins, Hyder E., vi. 230, 234.
'Analytical Index to the Ballad-Entries, An', Stud. Phil. xxi (1924), iii. 394; v. 1045.
Cavalier and Puritan (1923), iv. 680.
'Contribution to the History of the English Commonwealth Drama, A', Stud. in Phil., xviii (1921), and xx (1923), iii. 182–3, 188; v. 1314; vi. 87, 112, 113, 139, 173 and n. 1, 174 and n. 2, 175, 176, 199 n. 1, 215, 230, 234, 244.
ed., 'The Drinking Academy, or The Cheaters' Holiday', P.M.L.A. xxxix (1924), v. 976, 977.
ed., Pepys Ballads, The, vi. 240.
Pepysian Garland, A (1927), iv. 745, 747; vi. 162.
'Samuel Sheppard and His Praise of Poets', Stud. Phil. xxiv (1927), v. 1052, 1053, 1245.
'Thomas Randolph, Robert Baron, and The Drinking Academy', P.M.L.A. xlvi (1931), v. 977, 978.
Rollo, Duke of Normandy, see Fletcher, John.

Rolls, Master of the, iii. 468.
Roman Actor, The, see Massinger, Philip.
Roman Catholic priest, vii. 49.
Roman Catholicism, iv. 916; v. 1172; vi. 69.
Roman Empress, The, see Richards, Nathanael, *The Tragedy of Messallina.*
Roman Virgin, The, or The Unjust Judge, see Webster, John, *Appius and Virginia.*
Romanus, see Anonymous.
Rome, English College of the Jesuits in, iv. 695; v. 1172.
   Thomas Killigrew in, iv. 695, 699, 700, 707, 708.
   Play written at, iii. 171.
Romeo and Juliet, see Shakespeare, William.
Romford, Essex, iv. 955.
Ronay, Stephen H., *James Shirley's The Gamester, A Critical Edition of the 1637 Quarto with Introduction and Notes.* Unpublished U. of Chicago thesis (1948), v. 1110, 1111, 1112.
Rondolph, Thomas, *see* Randolph, Thomas.
Roods, John, *see* Rhodes, John.
Rookwood, Edmond, iii. 457.
Rooms, in theatres, *see* Theatres, rooms in.
Root-and-Branch Bill, iv. 957, 959.
Rope dancers, *see* Dancers on the ropes.
Rope-dancing, *see* Dancing on the ropes.
Roper, Abell, iii. 5.
Rosania, see Shirley, James, *The Doubtful Heir.*
Roscians, vi. 235.
Roscio, I. L., *Conclusions upon Dances* (1607), ii. 499.
Roscius Anglicanus, see Downes, John.
Roscommon, Earl of, iii. 96.
Rose, Adam, ii. 384.
Rose, Stephen, iv. 601.
Rose theatre, i. 135, 158, 176; iii. 266; iv. 555, 558, 564, 571, 574; vi. 123, 127, 130, 145 n. 2, 247–8, 250.
Rosee, Mr., ii. 614.
Rosenbach, A. S. W., ii. 443; iii. 350.
   English Plays to 1700 (1940) (catalogue), iii. 141, 464; iv. 727; v. 1079.

Rosenfeld, Sybil, 'Unpublished Stage Documents', *Theatre Notebook*, xi (1956–7), vi. 87, 90 n. 1.
   Theatre Notebook, viii (1953–4), 57–8, vii. 12 n. 1.
Rosicrucians, iv. 644.
Rositer, Sara, ii. 421.
Rosseter, Dudley, ii. 554.
Rosseter, Hugh, ii. 554.
Rosseter, Philip, i. 168 n. 1, 198; ii. 554; vi. 12 n. 1 and n. 2, 17, 77–86, 115.
Rosseter's Blackfriars theatre, *see* Rosseter's Puddle Wharf.
Rosseter's Puddle Wharf or Blackfriars theatre, i. 201 n. 2; ii. 346, 554; vi. 12 n. 2, 77–86.
Rosseter's Queen's Revels, i. 176.
Rossingham, Edmund, i. 52, 277; iii. 135, 138, 139; v. 1235, 1300, 1301; vi. 167.
Rossiter, Philip, *see* Rosseter, Philip.
Rotherby, Leicestershire, iii. 468.
Rothwell, Lincolnshire, iv. 554.
Rothwell, John, Warden Stationers Company, iii. 73; v. 1031.
Rotterdam, ii. 531.
Roulle, William, *see* Rowley, William.
Roundelays, vi. 209.
Round-heads, iii. 95.
Rous, Mr., Provost of Eton, v. 1176.
Rowe, Dorothy, ii. 582.
Rowe, J. Brooking, ed., *Richard Peeke of Tavistock His Three to One, The Commendatory Verses, and the Play of Dick of Devonshire* (1905), v. 1318.
Rowe, Nicholas, *The Fair Penitent*, iv. 785.
Rowe, Sir Thomas, ii. 657 n. 4; iv. 928.
Rowl, *see* Dowle, Rowland.
Rowland, —, actor, i. 252; ii. 554–5; iii. 764, 765.
Rowley, Grace, ii. 558.
Rowley, Samuel, i. 136, 139, 151, 155; ii. 507, 555; iii. 258; v. 1009–14, 1023; vi. 134.
   Bilboe's the Best Blade, see Hardshift for Husbands.
   English Profit, The, see Richard the Third.
   Hardshift for Husbands, or Bilboe's the Best Blade, i. 150, 157; ii. 555; v. 1011–12.

Hymen's Holiday, or Cupid's Vagaries, see William Rowley.

Joshua, v. 1010.

Match or No Match, A, i. 150, 157; ii. 555; iii. 265; iv. 525, 850; v. 1011, 1012–13.

Richard the Third, or the English Profit, i. 149; ii. 555; iii. 265; v. 1011, 1013–14.

When You see Me, You Know Me, v. 1010; vii. 85, 116.

Rowley, Samuel, and Bird, William, *Judas,* v. 1010.

Rowley, Samuel, merchant-tailor, v. 1010.

Rowley, William, i. 14, 17, 18 and n. 8, 72–88, 137 n. 3, 176, 184, 198, 199 and n. 2, 200 and n. 3, 203 and n. 1, 208, 209 and n. 3, 211; ii. 555–8; iii. 244, 252, 265, 269, 270, 271, 280, 309, 316, 337, 377, 378, 379, 383, 390, 400, 411, 424, 459; iv. 516, 572, 630, 770, 806, 807, 857, 861, 862, 863, 867, 868, 870, 877, 881, 889, 890, 892, 893, 894, 895, 907, 908, 909, 910, 938; v. 1010, 1011, 1012, 1014–27, 1043, 1238, 1242, 1244, 1248, 1249, 1254, 1397, 1412; vi. 222.

All's Lost by Lust, i. 187, 196, 215 and n. 1, 219 n. 4, 256, 331, 340; ii. 556, 557; iii. 102, 274, 358; iv. 807, 911; v. 1016, 1018–21. 1296 1309, 1350, 1352, 1421, 1426; vi. 58.

Birth of Merlin, or The Child Hath Found His Father, The, iv. 885–6; v. 1021.

Changeling, The, see Middleton, Thomas.

Cure for a Cuckold, A, see Webster, John.

Fair Quarrel, A, see Middleton, Thomas.

Fool without Book, The, v. 1022.

Fortune by Land and Sea, see Heywood, Thomas.

Four Honourable Loves, The, v. 1022–3.

Guy of Warwick, see Dekker, Thomas.

Hymen's Holiday, or Cupid's Vagaries, i. 230, 249, 256, 331, 340; ii. 368; v. 1016, 1023–4, 1120; vi. 63.

Knave in Print, or One for Another, A, v. 1022, 1024–5.

Late Murder in Whitechapel, or Keep the Widow Waking, The, see Dekker, Thomas.

Match at Midnight, A, v. 1012.

New Wonder, a Woman Never Vext, A, ii. 558; v. 1027; vii. 85.

Nonesuch, The, v. 1022, 1025–6.

Parliament of Love, The, see Massinger, Philip.

Search for Money, A (1609), ii. 473; v. 1016.

Shoemaker a Gentleman, A, iv. 807, 878; v. 997, 1015, 1026, 1060; vi. 218, 225, n. 2; vii. 107, 114.

Spanish Gypsy, The, see Middleton, Thomas.

Travels of Three English Brothers, The, see Day, John.

Witch of Edmonton, The, see Dekker, Thomas.

World Tossed at Tennis, The, see Middleton, Thomas.

Rowling, Kent, v. 1000, 1001.

Rowly, Mr., ii. 486.

Roxana, see Alabaster, William.

Roxburghe collection of ballads, vi. 135.

Roxolana, see Anonymous.

Royal Academy, vi. 299.

Royal Arbor of Loyal Poesie, A, see Jordan, Thomas.

Royal Choice, The, Stapleton, Sir Robert.

Royal Combat, The, see Ford, John.

Royal Diurnal, see Newspapers.

Royal Exchange, v. 1006.

Royal Exchange, The, see Brome, Richard, *The Queen's Exchange.*

Royal Household, comptroller of, v. 1198.

Royal King and the Loyal Subject, The, see Heywood, Thomas.

Royal Master, The, see Shirley, James.

Royal Oak, The, see Tatham, John.

Royal Oak Tavern, London, iii. 47.

Royal Opera House, Berlin, vi. 275.

Royal Shepherdess, The, see Shadwell, Thomas.

Royal Slave, The, see Cartwright, William.

Royalist agent, iii. 174.

Royalists, uprising of the, iii. 196.

Royston, Hertfordshire, i. 50; iii. 159, 160; iv. 954, 1422; vii. 31, 45.

Royston, Richard, iv. 569, 922, 957.

Rubens, Sir Peter Paul, vi. 262. Paintings by in the Banqueting House, iii. 214; vi. 266, 267, 285, 286.

Rudiments of Grammar, The, see Shirley, James.

Rudyard, Sir Benjamin, i. 10 n. 6; iv. 548; vi. 21.

Rudyard, Nicholas, ii. 499.

Rueda, Lope de, *Eufemia*, iv. 563.

Rufin, v. 1173.

Ruffs, vi. 242.

Ruggle, George, v. 1027–8.
  Club Law, v. 1028.
  Ignoramus, iv. 594; v. 1027, 1028, 1279, 1391, 1392; vii. 74, 77, 78.
  Re Vera, or Verily (?), v. 1027–8.

Ruggle, Thomas, a clothier, v. 1027.

Rühl, Ernst, *Grobianus in England, Palaestra*, xxxviii (1904), v. 1054, 1056, 1225.

Rule a Wife and Have a Wife, see Fletcher, John.

Rules to Know a Loyal King from a Disloyal Subject, see Jordan, Thomas.

Rulfs, Donald J., 'Beaumont and Fletcher on the London Stage 1776–1833', *P.M.L.A.* lxiii (1948), iii. 313, 317, 319, 323, 347, 354, 391, 394, 407, 410, 414, 418, 421.

Rump, or The Mirror of the Late Times, The, see Tatham, John.

Runaways' Answer to a Book Called, A Rod for Runaways, The, see Anonymous.

Running, vi. 294.
  At the ring, vi. 293.
  At tilt, vii. 23, 26.
  Masque, v. 1404; vii. 13, 34, 35, 66.

Running Stream Entertainment, see Middleton, Thomas.

Rupert, Prince of the Palatinate, ii. 463, 571, 694; iii. 3, 129, 218, 219, 220; iv. 721; v. 982, 1227.

Russell, Elizabeth, ii. 345.

Russell, H. K., 'Tudor and Stuart Dramatizations of Natural and Moral Philosophy', *Studies in Philology*, xxxi (1934), iv. 459, 589, 595, 936–7; v. 1189, 1390.

Russell, John, i. 138, 143; ii. 558–9; vi. 150.

Rutherford, W. G., 'The Anonymous Play of *Nero*', *Athenaeum*, No. 4123 (November 1906), v. 1380.

Rutland, Countess of, iii. 320; iv. 620, 621.

Rutland, Francis, Earl of, iv. 646; v. 1117.

Rutland House, plays at, iii. 196, 210; vi. 74, 306.

Rutter, Joseph, iv. 830; v. 1028–34, 1029, 1359.
  Cid, The, i. 325 n. 2, 336 and n. c, 340; v. 1030–2.
  'On a Lady's tempting eye', v. 1029.
  Shepherd's Holiday, The, i. 249, 256; v. 1028, 1029, 1030, 1031, 1032–4; vi. 66 n. 1.
  'Thyrsis. A Pastorall Elegie . . . on the Death of . . . the Lady Venetia Digby' (1635), v. 1028.

Rye, Sussex, iii. 306.

Ryece, Robert, v. 1398.

Rylands, John, Library, v. 1225.

Rymer, Thomas, iv. 681.
  Foedera, vi. 305, 306.
  Tragedies of the Last Age Considered, The (1678), iii. 403, 407.

S., F., v. 1214, 1215.

S., J., v. 1034–6.

S., J., *Andromana, or The Merchant's Wife*, v. 1034–5.
  The Prince of Prigs' Revels, v. 1034, 1035–6.

S. S., v. 1053.

S. S., *The Honest Lawyer*, iv. 902; v. 1053; vii. 21.

S.T.C., *see* Pollard, A. W., *A Short Title Catalogue*.

S., W., v. 1036–7.
  The Famous History of Petronius Maximus, v. 1036–7.

Sabbatarianism, iii. 213; vii. 10–15.

Sackton, Alexander H., *Rhetoric as a Dramatic Language in Ben Jonson* (1948), iv. 605.

Sackvile, Mr. Edward, vi. 268.

Sackville, Edward, *see* Dorset, Earl of.

Sackville, Sir Edward, iv. 650; v. 1227.

Sackville, Edward (second son of fourth Earl of Dorset), v. 1037, 1359, 1360.

Sackville, Sir John, i. 283 n. 7.

Sackville, Richard, Lord Buckhurst, v. 1037, 1404.

Sackville, Thomas, ii. 559; vii. 35, 36, 37, 42, 43, 48.

Sackville crest, v. 1031.

Sackville papers (in Kent Archives Office, Maidstone), vi. 90 n. 1.

Sackville-West, V., ed., *The Diary of the Lady Anne Clifford* (1923), i. 112; iii. 373; vi. 16, 17, 258; vii. 21, 30, 31.
Knole and the Sackvilles, v. 1227.
Sad One, The, see Suckling, Sir John.
Sad Shepherd, The, see Jonson, Ben.
Saddler, ii. 564.
Sadler, John, v. 1034, 1037–9.
Masquerade du Ciel, v. 1037.
Sadler, Katherine, ii. 376, 634.
Sadler's Wells, iv. 774.
Saffron Walden, i. 92, 172, 173, 212, 213.
Sage, Jonas, ii. 648.
Sailors, i. 21, 264, 265–6, 267; ii. 431, 690; vi. 160, 161.
Sailors Masque, see Anonymous.
St. Albans, Hertfordshire, v. 1001, 1066, 1067, 1142, 1146; vii. 27.
Corporation Minutes of, v. 1068.
Grammar School, v. 1067.
Mayor of, v. 1067.
St. Alban Hall, Oxford, iv. 751; v. 1185.
Principal of, v. 1276.
St. Alban's School, London, v. 1001.
St. Albans, near Dover, Kent, v. 1000.
St. Aldermary, *see* St. Mary Aldermary.
St. Alphege's Church, Canterbury, iv. 515.
St. Ambrose, v. 1376.
St. Andrew's, Holborn, London, i. 266; ii. 511, 635; iv. 476, 525, 956.
St. Andrew's, Newcastle upon Tyne, Northumberland, v. 1004.
St. Andrews, University of, iv. 599.
St. Andrew's by the Wardrobe, London, ii. 452, 488, 515, 590–1.
St. Andrew's, Whittlesey, Cambridgeshire, iv. 473, 474.
St. Anne's, Blackfriars, London, i. 5 and n. 1, 31; ii. 383, 385, 406, 407, 436, 485, 489, 520, 535, 551, 553, 559, 571, 582, 583, 601, 605, 623; vi. 17, 18 and nn. 1 and 2; vi. 19; vii. 2.
St. Augustine, *see* Anonymous, *England's First Happiness, or The Life of St. Augustine.*
St. Augustine of Canterbury, v. 1326.
St. Bartholomew the Great, London, ii. 426, 428; iv. 738.
St. Bartholmew the Less, London, ii. 457, 578, 589, 610, 611, 622, 651.

St. Bartholomew's Hospital, London, iv. 601, 602.
St. Benedict's Chapel, London, iv. 833.
St. Bodolph's, Aldgate, London, ii. 386, 485, 496, 523, 561, 603, 624; v. 1180.
St. Botolph's, Bishopsgate, London, ii. 439, 476, 478, 479, 499, 517, 533, 592, 593, 606.
St. Bride's, Fleet Street, London, i. 64; ii. 421, 635, 641; iv. 476, 722, 950; vi. 94 and n. 1, 95 and n. 1, 99, 101.
St. Bride's Lane, *see* London, streets of.
St. Catherine's, i. 161.
St. Catherine's College, Cambridge, v. 1066.
St. Clement Dane's, London, ii. 471, 500, 501, 505, 511; iv. 725.
St. Clement's, Eastcheap, London, ii. 536.
S. Damianus Episcopus Ticinensis Turbas Italiæ Divinitus Prædicit, see Simons, Joseph.
St. Dionis Backchurch, London, ii. 442.
St. Dunstan's in the West, London, ii. 421, 511; iii. 105; iv. 851; vi. 305, 306, 308.
St. Edmund Hall, Oxford, iii. 21.
St. Edwards, Cambridge, v. 1232.
St. Faith's, London, iii. 112.
St. Genesius the Comedian, v. 1174.
St. George's Day, vi. 261.
St. George for England, see Smith, Will.
St. Giles without Cripplegate, London, i. 138, 143, 149, 262, 312, 316, 357, 359; ii. 384, 385, 391, 393, 399, 401, 402, 403, 404, 405, 407, 408, 409, 415, 426, 439, 440, 445, 449, 450, 451, 452, 454, 455, 456, 459, 463, 464, 465, 471, 473, 475, 482, 483; ii. 484, 494, 498, 499, 508, 510, 516, 517, 518, 522, 523, 524, 536, 537, 541, 543, 544, 545, 550, 555, 556, 562, 564, 565, 567, 571, 575, 576, 577, 578, 580, 584, 588, 598, 599, 600, 602, 610, 613, 617, 624, 626, 627, 635, 642, 645, 650; iii. 239, 299, 242; iv. 516, 690, 733, 734, 781, 912; v. 1003, 1067, 1068, 1226–7; vi. 178.
St. Giles in the Fields, London, i. 184, 329; ii. 344, 346, 364, 369–70, 371, 372, 378, 379, 403, 405, 421, 436, 441, 445, 465, 472, 485, 489,

St. Giles in the Fields (*cont.*)
496, 506, 509, 511, 522, 525, 526,
559, 568, 572, 573, 582, 606, 608,
616, 631, 632, 635; iii. 155, 301;
iv. 542, 545, 679, 737, 928; v.
1071, 1218.
St. Gregory by St. Paul, London, ii.
390, 421, 449, 507, 585.
St. Helen within Bishopsgate, London, ii. 521.
St. Ives, Huntington, v. 1265.
St. James's, Clerkenwell, London, i.
308, 310, 312; ii. 353, 361, 364,
383, 390, 392, 400, 405, 407, 428,
429, 432, 445, 450, 473, 474, 486,
492, 493, 496, 497, 518, 523, 524,
526, 527, 528, 529, 531, 543, 548,
557, 583, 584, 589, 615, 616, 617,
623, 625, 626, 627, 631, 636, 637;
iii. 194, 280, 244, 245, 343; iv.
524, 557, 711, 734; v. 1016, 1244,
1334, 1399; vi. 49, 148.
St. James's Palace, i. 230, 236, 324,
325; iii. 377, 422, 465; v. 1107,
1168; vi. 15, 32, 67, 220, 266,
288; vii. 74, 93.
  Court at, vi. 134.
St. James's Guard Chamber, iv. 522.
St. James's Park, *see* London,
streets and districts.
St. James's, Westminster, ii. 607.
St. John's College, Cambridge, iii.
11, 46, 142, 165; iv. 601, 711;
v. 992, 1027, 1180, 1181, 1240,
1265, 1408, 1413, 1414.
  Manuscripts of, iv. 600; v. 1173,
1174, 1452.
St. John's College, Oxford, iii. 3, 4,
12, 19, 20, 28, 29, 135, 183, 291;
iv. 592; v. 1054, 1056, 1065,
1178, 1179, 1181, 1182, 1183,
1190, 1225, 1259, 1260, 1261,
1262, 1263, 1264, 1275, 1276,
1308, 1411.
  Fellow of, v. 1184, 1259.
  Library, v. 1181.
  Manuscripts of, iii. 183, 184.
  President of, iii. 182, 185; v. 1056,
1182, 1184.
  Visitors' Register of, iii. 183.
St. Lawrence Jewry, London, iv.
856.
St. Leonard's, Shoreditch, London,
i. 147; ii. 364, 369, 380, 394, 395,
396, 399, 414, 495, 523, 553, 588,
624, 632, 638, 642, 650, 651.
St. Luc, Mlle, iv. 674.
St. Margaret's, Westminster, i. 265;
ii. 460, 576.

St. Martin's, Aldersgate, London
ii. 484.
St. Martin's, Carfax, Oxford, iii. 193.
St. Martin's, Ludgate, London, i. 64.
St. Martin's in the Fields, London,
ii. 433, 496, 525, 545, 632; iii. 112;
v. 1224.
St. Martin Orgar, London, ii. 491.
St. Martin's Outwich, London, iii. 12.
St. Mary's, Aldermanbury, London,
i. 26 n. 5; ii. 343, 410, 411, 412,
413, 418, 455, 466, 467, 468, 469,
470, 501, 585, 587, 588, 643, 644,
648; iv. 540.
St. Mary Overie's, Southwark, iii.
300, 309; iv. 753.
St. Mary's, Romney Marsh, Kent,
iii. 12.
Saint Mary Spittle, London, iv. 880.
St. Mary-le-Strand, Westminster,
ii. 564.
St. Mary Hall, Oxford, iv. 716; v.
1047.
  Principal of, iii. 183.
St. Mary Woolchurch, London, v.
1065.
St. Matthew's, Friday Street, London, v. 1194.
St. Mawes, Castle of, iv. 720.
St. Michael's, Bassishaw, London,
ii. 389, 607.
St. Michael's Combat with the Devil,
see Blencowe, John.
St. Michael's, Crooked Lane, London, ii. 555.
St. Michael's in Bedwardine, London, ii. 486.
St. Michael le Querne, London, ii.
495.
St. Omers, France, Jesuit College at,
iii. 160; v. 1143, 1144, 1283, 1285;
iv. 521, 947.
St. Patrick for Ireland, *see* Shirley,
James.
St. Paul, martyr, v. 1392.
St. Paul's, London, iii. 29; vii. 36.
St. Paul's Cathedral, London, i. 140;
iii. 183; vi. 4, 29, 41, 86.
  Duke Humphrey's Monument, vi.
7.
  Duke Humphrey's Walk, vi. 50.
  prebend of, iv. 600.
*St. Pavles-Chvrch her Bill for the
Parliament* (1621), *see* Farley,
Henry.
St. Paul's Churchyard, *see* London,
streets of.
St. Paul's School, iii. 300; iv. 474,
587, 912, 946.

Headmaster, iv. 474.
Used as theatre, vi. 122.
Usher at, iv. 474.
St. Paul's theatre, vi. 86, 187, 188.
S. Pelagius Martyr, tragoedia, see Anonymous.
St. Peter's, Chester, iii. 2.
St. Peter's, Cornhill, London, ii. 453.
Saint Peter's Day, vi. 179 n. 1.
St. Peter's, Paul's Wharf, London, ii. 616.
St. Saviour's, Southwark, i. 24, 199 n. 2; ii. 391, 418, 426, 427, 431, 432, 447, 448, 467, 472, 473, 490, 491, 500, 501, 504, 510, 511, 512, 519, 520, 522, 547, 560, 562, 564, 573, 574, 575, 578, 590, 592, 593, 596, 610, 611, 612, 623, 634, 635, 644; iii. 307, 310; iv. 757; vi. 186, 211.
Saint-Sorlin, Armand Desmarets de, *Arian* (1632), iv. 700, 707, 709.
St. Stephen (Hackington), Kent, iv. 514.
St. Stephen's, Walbrook, London, iii. 48.
St. Swithin's, London, ii. 479.
St. Thomas's, Salisbury, iv. 751.
St. Werburgh Street theatre, Dublin, v. 1069, 1095, 1136, 1138, 1140, 1339, 1355, 1423.
Sale, Charles, ii. 522.
Sale catalogues, iii. 20, 26.
Salernitano, Masuccio, *Novellino*, iii. 358.
Salerno, Masuccio di, iv. 561.
Salisbury, Sir Robert Cecil, Earl of, iv. 652; v. 1226, 1228.
Salisbury, Wiltshire, i. 50; v. 1182, 1183, 1184; vii. 37.
Cathedral, v. 1183.
Dean of, v. 1182, 1183.
Salisbury Court theatre, i. 26 n. 5 cont., 36, 41, 56, 152 and n. 3, 188 n. 4, 196, 226, 227, 231, 237, 238, 239 and n. 3, 240, 242, 269, 283 and n. 7, 291, 292, 293, 302, 303, 304, 305, 306 n. 3, 307, 308, 309 and n. 3, 319, 330; ii. 379, 537, 538, 623, 680, 684–7, 692, 694; iii. 7, 52, 53, 54, 56, 57, 60, 64, 66, 67, 70, 75, 80, 87, 89, 92, 197, 210, 378, 444; iv. 475, 483, 484, 485, 501, 502, 503, 504, 505, 517, 518, 580, 678, 723, 724, 737, 742, 743, 745, 746, 767, 787, 862, 863, 891, 893, 927, 930, 937, 938, 939,

940, 941, 942, 943; v. 966, 967, 970, 973–4, 979, 987, 988, 989, 990, 996, 1008, 1051, 1068, 1070, 1091, 1092, 1093, 1094, 1112, 1113, 1117, 1126, 1131, 1138, 1223, 1309, 1313, 1342, 1399, 1417, 1418, 1434, 1446, 1445; vi. 7, 8, 12 n. 2, 39, 40, 53, 62, 67, 69, 70, 71, 76, 77, 86–115, 116, 117, 122, 154, 162, 163, 164, 165, 166, 170, 172 n., 173, 175, 177, 187, 193, 199, 210, 223, 225 n. 1, 227, 230, 231, 238, 243, 306, 307; vii. 9.
Company of, v. 1217; vi. 90 n. 2.
Dramatist for, i. 295.
Manager of, i. 241.
Masque at, i. 255.
Opening of, v. 987.
Receipts from, i. 239 n. 3.
Wardrobe keeper at, vi. 94, 99, 100.
Salisbury family, ii. 412.
Salisbury House, London, iv. 890, 891; v. 1157.
Salisbury Plain, iii. 162; v. 1445.
As setting, v. 1184.
Salisbury Plain, see Anonymous.
Sallust, iv. 555, 838.
Salmacida Spolia, see Davenant, William.
Salt Islands, English capture of, v. 993.
Salter, Walter, iv. 716.
Saltings, v. 991, 992.
Saltpetre men, iv. 869.
Salusbury, Henry, first baronet, v. 1039, 1222.
Salusbury, Hester, v. 1040.
Salusbury, Sir Thomas, v. 1039–42.
History of Joseph, v. 1040, 1041.
Masque at Knowsley, A, ii. 464; v. 1040–2.
Salviati, Lionardo, *Il Granchio*, v. 1298.
La Spina, v. 1298.
Sampson, Hanna, v. 1043.
Sampson, Henry, Fellow of Pembroke Hall, v. 1042.
Sampson, M. W., *Thomas Middleton* (1915), iv. 861, 867.
ed., Middleton's *A Fair Quarrel* in *Thomas Midleton* (1915), iv. 867, 869.
ed., Middleton's *The Changeling* in *Thomas Middleton* (1915), iv. 861.
Sampson, William, iv. 732, 734, 735; v. 1036, 1042–7.

Sampson, William (*cont.*)
   Herod and Antipater, see Markham, Gervase.
   'Loues Metamorphosis or Apollo and Daphne', v. 1043.
   Virtus Post Funera Vivit, or Honour Triumphing over Death (1636), v. 1043.
   Vow-Breaker, or The Fair Maid of Clifton, The, v. 1042, 1043–5.
   Widow's Prize, or The Woman Captain, i. 206 n. 3; iv. 642, 865, 866; v. 1046–7, 1442.
Sams, Rev. William, iii. 303.
Samuel, Richard, vi. 125, 126, 128.
Samuel v. *Langley et al.,* vi. 124.
Samwel v. *Woodliff,* vi. 124.
San Germano, Marquis of, vii. 94.
Sancroft, Archbishop, v. 1028, 1037, 1039.
Sanders, Elizabeth, ii. 559.
Sanders, Thomasin, ii. 559.
Sanders, William, i. 15, 72–88; ii. 559.
Sanderson, Georg, ii. 559.
Sanderson, Gregory, i. 171, 174; ii. 384, 559; iii. 192.
Sandidge, William Lee, Jr., ed., Massinger's *The Roman Actor* (1929), iv. 815, 817.
Sands, James, ii. 559–60; iii. 192.
Sands, Lady, iv. 500; v. 1313.
Sands, Thomas, i. 286, 297; ii. 560; iii. 192; iv. 686.
Sandys, Edwin, Archbishop of York, v. 1047.
Sandys, George, iv. 567; v. 1047–8.
   Translation of *Christ's Passion* (1640), v. 1048.
   Paraphrase upon the Psalms of David and upon Hymns Dispersed throughout the Old and New Testaments, A (1636), v. 1048.
   Relation of a Iourney Begun An: Dom: 1010 (1615), iv. 813; v. 1047.
Sanford, Thomas, ii. 651.
Sanguis Sanguinem, tragoedia, see Anonymous.
Sansbury, Sir John, *The Christmas Prince,* iii. 291.
Sappho and Phao, see Lyly, John.
Sardinia, v. 1403.
   Scene of play, iv. 708.
Sargeaunt, M. Joan, *John Ford* (1935), iii. 250, 434, 435, 437, 446, 448, 451, 454, 457, 459, 462, 463.

'John Ford at the Middle Temple', *R.E.S.* viii (1932), iii. 434.
'Writings Ascribed to John Ford by Joseph Hunter in *Chorus Vatum*', *R.E.S.* x (1934), iii. 434, 435.
Sarmiento de Acuña, *see* Gondomar, Count of.
Sarum, *see* Salisbury, Wiltshire.
Satire, political, *see* Plays.
Satire, iii. 45–46, 165, 177–9, 182; iv. 631; v. 1212, 1223, 1228, 1238.
   Semi-dramatic, iii. 45.
Satires, iii. 39.
   Ben Jonson's against Inigo Jones, v. 1228.
Satires and Miscellaneous Poetry and Prose, ed. Lamar, René (1928), iv. 524.
Satirical Declarations, see Davenant, William.
Satiromastix, see Dekker, Thomas.
Saturnalia, see Edwards, John.
Satyr, The, see Jonson, *Entertainment of the Queen and Prince at Althorp.*
Satyre against Separatists (1642), *see* A. C. (?Peter Hausted).
Satyres and Satyricall Epigrams (1617), *see* Fitz-Geoffrey, Henry.
Satyrs, iii. 168.
Saul, Thomas, i. 262; ii. 403, 537.
Saul's Conversion, vi. 273, 278.
Saunders, Francis, v. 1380.
Saunders, Lady (house of), vi. 78, 81.
Saunderson, Ianthe, iv. 767, 768.
Saunderson, Peter, ii. 641.
Saunderson, Thomas, ii. 607.
Savage, James E., 'Beaumont and Fletcher's *Philaster* and Sidney's *Arcadia*', *E.L.H.* xiv (1947), iii. 323.
   'Date of Beaumont and Fletcher's *Cupid's Revenge*, The', *E.L.H.* xv (1948), iii. 323.
Savage, John, ii. 411.
Savage, Ralph, theatre-manager, ii. 560; iii. 18, 254; vi. 222.
Savage, William, iii. 18.
Savile, Sir Henry, iv. 498.
Savill, Arthur, i. 307–8, 308, 321; ii. 560.
Savoian ambassador, i. 23, 128; iv. 664; vii. 23.
Savoy, Duchess of, iii. 353.
Savoy, embassy to, iii. 142.
Savoy, Master of the, iii. 175; iv. 691.

Sawnston, *see* Swanston, Eyllaerdt.
Sawyer, Elizabeth, iii. 270.
Saxham Parva, Suffolk, vii. 35, 41, 42.
Saxo Grammaticus, iii. 98.
'Say Daunce', *see* Randolph, Thomas.
Say, Lord, enters Oxford, iii. 127.
Sayle, R. T. D., *Lord Mayors' Pageants of the Merchant Taylors Company in the 15th, 16th, and 17th Centuries* (1931), iii. 244, 263; iv. 683; v. 1223, 1254, 1255.
Scafe, Ellen, v. 1057.
Scaffolds, iii. 219; iv. 656; vii. 23.
Scantlings, vi. 139, 143.
Scarron, Paul, iv. 726, 727.
  Scarron's Comical Romance; or a Facetious History of a Company of Strowling Stage-players (1676), iii. 278.
  Fruitless Precaution, iii. 358.
Scarves, vi. 236.
Scavengers, parish, vi. 19.
Scenarios, v. 1395.
Scene divisions, iv. 502, 934.
  Painters, i. 53 n. 1.
  Painting, vii. 103.
  Unity of place, iv. 944.
Scenery, i. 52, 53, 58, 59, 117, 120, 233, 243 n. 2; ii. 693–4; iii. 62, 111, 130, 138, 139, 140, 147, 197, 200, 217, 292, 293–4, 296, 298, 397, 461; iv. 506, 522, 524, 549, 582, 596, 636, 627, 630, 638, 643, 651, 657, 663, 673, 692, 693, 814, 872, 928, 934, 935, 938, 944; v. 1102, 1103, 1163, 1183, 1190, 1191–2, 1205, 1206, 1228, 1311, 1334, 1451; vi. 38, 51–53, 66 n. 1, 107–9, 187, 189, 190–1, 238, 257–8, 263, 267 281–2, 283, 286, 287, 295.
  Described, iii. 136; v. 1334.
  Designs for, iv. 524; v. 1355.
  Drawings of, iii. 294.
  Flat revolving wings, iii. 293.
  Flats, iii. 294.
  In masques, iii. 107, 109.
  In plays, iii. 123, 129–30, 136–7, 147; iv. 473.
  Sketches for, iii. 293; vi. 281, 282, 283, 286.
  Traverse, iii. 294.
Scenes, iii. 344; iv. 909; vi. 53, 163, 165, 305, 306.
  Back, vi. 282.
Schadleutner, Sebastian, ii. 561.

Schaep, Gerard of Amsterdam, v. 1330.
Schankes, *or* Schanks, *see* Shank.
Schanks, John, *see* Shank, John.
Schelling, Felix E., *Elizabethan Drama 1558–1642*, 2 vols. (1908), iii. 18, 321; iv. 483, 486, 505, 508, 563, 771–2; v. 1003, 1416.
  Intr. to *The Complete Plays of Ben Jonson*, E. Rhys, ed., Everyman's Library, 2 vols. (1910), iv. 613.
Schemers, The, *see* Bromfield, Mr.
Schenck's Sconce, fortress, fall of, iv. 482.
Scherer, Hans, ed., *A Tale of a Tub nach dem Drucke von 1640* (1913), iv. 632.
Schipper, Jakob, *James Shirley: sein Leben und seine Werke, nebst einer Ubersetzung seines Dramas 'The Royal Master'* (1911), v. 1065, 1089, 1098, 1099, 1100, 1107, 1108, 1110, 1112, 1114, 1120, 1124, 1125, 1129, 1134, 1137, 1139, 1143, 1144, 1147, 1163, 1166, 1168.
  'Shirleys Maskenspiel "The Triumph of Peace"', in *Festschrift Wilhelm Vietor. Die Neueren Sprachen*, Erganzungsband (1910), v. 1154.
Schmid, F. Ernst, ed., *Thomas May's Tragedy of Julia Agrippina Empresse of Rome, nebst einem Anhang, die Tragoedie 'Nero' und Thomas May, Materialien* (1914), iv. 837, 838; v. 1380, 1381.
Schneider, Elizabeth, 'Some Notes on Robert Gomersall', *R.E.S.* ix (1933), iv. 512.
Scholar turned to School Again, The, see Anonymous.
Scholars, The, see Lovelace, Richard.
School of Compliment, The, see Shirley, James.
School Moderator, The, see Mason, John.
School of the Noble and Worthy Science of Defence, see Swetnam, Joseph.
School for Scandal, The, see Sheridan, Richard Brinsley.
Schoolmasters, iii. 25, 26, 126, 193, 291; iv. 472, 474, 538, 552, 586, 690, 748, 946; v. 979, 1066, 1067, 1070, 1119, 1172, 1175–7, 1176, 1177, 1216, 1222, 1256, 1257, 1265, 1266.

Schools, iii. 238.
Schroder, O., *Marlowe und Webster* (1907), v. 1251.
Schumpf und Ernst, see Pauli.
Schwarz, Herbert F., ed., *Alphonsus, Emperor of Germany* (1913), v. 1285.
'One of the Sources of the *Queen of Corinth*', *M.L.N.* xxiv (1909), iii. 398, 400.
Scillae's Metamorphis, see Lodge, Thomas.
Scilly Isles, military service in, iii. 469.
Scollard, Clinton, ed., *The Broken Heart* (1895), iii. 439.
Scornful Lady, The, see Beaumont and Fletcher.
Scot, Reginald, *The Discovery of Witchcraft* (1584), iv. 905.
Scot, Thomas, *The Unhappy Kindness: Or A Fruitless Revenge*, iii. 423, 425.
Scotland, i. 180, 181, 293 n. 2, 311 n. 1; iii. 63, 287, 467; iv. 954; v. 1209, 1224; vii. 23.
Expedition to, iv. 724.
Journey to, John Taylor's, iii. 251; v. 1347.
King's (Charles's) journey to, iv. 649.
Scots, iii. 44, 105, 109; v. 1218.
Invasion of, v. 1266.
King Charles I's expedition against, iv. 737, 738.
Negotiator with, iii. 22.
Scots Figgaries, or A Knot of Knaves, The, see Tatham, John.
Scott, Mr., i. 139; ii. 347.
Scott, Mary Augusta, *Elizabethan translations from the Italian* (1916) iii. 49, 379, 386.
Scott, Robert, stationer, iii. 98, 123, 124, 147, 202, 204, 206, 210, 315, 320, 325, 330, 337, 341, 345, 349, 355, 357, 364, 367, 372, 375, 378, 382, 388, 392, 395, 399, 413, 419, 423, 427, 431; iv. 534, 884; v. 1085, 1105, 1124, 1148, 1270, 1273.
Scott, Thomas, *Vox Populi* (1620), iv. 878.
The Second Part of Vox Populi (1624), iv. 878.
Scott, Sir Walter, *Ancient British Drama* (1810), iii. 132, 222.
ed., *A Collection of Scarce and Valuable Tracts* (Somers Tracts) (1809–15), iii. 40.

Secret History of the Court of James the First (1811), iv. 651.
Scottish, anti-Scottish political satire, v. 1223.
Army, iv. 958.
Payments to, v. 1266.
Scottish Covenant, v. 1052.
Dialect, iii. 304.
Presbyterians, v. 1235.
Scottowe, Norfolk, v. 1195.
Scripture, abuse of, vi. 26.
Scriveners, ii. 351, 415–16, 511, 551, 648, 649; iv. 912; vi. 178.
Scrogge, Alexander, ii. 626.
Scudamore, Viscount, vi. 6, 17, 25, 26, 265, 282 n. 1, 285, 287, 288.
Scudamore Papers, *see* Public Record Office.
Scudéry, Georges de, *Le Trompeur Puni, ou Histoire Septentrionale*, i. 235 n. 1; vi. 45; vii. 97.
Scudéry, Mlle de, *Artamène ou le grand Cyrus*, iv. 698.
Sculcoates, Yorkshire, iii. 2.
Sea captains, v. 1136.
Sea-fights, vi. 293.
Sea-lion, iii. 256.
Sea Voyage, The, see Fletcher, John.
Seabrooke, Thomas, i. 190, 192; ii. 561.
Seale, Ann, iii. 181.
Seale, Mr., v. 1210.
Seals, v. 994.
Seaman, Mrs., ii. 639.
Seaman, Thomas, ii. 638, 639.
Seaman's Honest Wife, The, see Mountfort, Walter, *The Launching of the Mary*.
Seamor, *see* Seymour.
Search for Money, A, see Rowley, William.
Seare, Dorothea, ii. 623.
Searger, Richard, v. 1140.
Searle, W. G., *The History of the Queens' College of St. Margaret and St. Bernard in the University of Cambridge* (1867), v. 1236.
Seasons in theatres, v. 1101; vi. 14–17, 25, 62, 69–70, 194–6.
Seaton, Ethel, '*Comus* and Shakespeare', *Essays and Studies by Members of the English Association*, xxxi (1945), iv. 914.
Literary Relations of England and Scandinavia in the Seventeenth Century (1935), iii. 377, 387, 409; iv. 569, 801; v. 1129.
Sebastian, Don (pretender to Portuguese throne), iv. 762, 763.

Sebeck, Henry, ii. 561.

Seccombe, Thomas, iv. 719.

Second Discovery by the Northern Scout, A, see Newspapers.

Second Maiden's Tragedy, The, see Anonymous.

Second Part of Crafty Cromwell, 1648, Address, The, see Pragmaticus, Mercurius.

'Second Part of Mother Shiptons Prophecies', *see* Anonymous.

Secret service, English in France, iv. 916.

Secretary, The, see Massinger, Philip.

Sedan chairs, iii. 64, 80, 81, 88; iv. 482.

Sedgebrook, Nottinghamshire, iv. 732.

Sedgwick, Obadiah, vi. 76.

Seditious libel, vi. 57.

Sedleian Professor of Natural Philosophy, iii. 291.

See Me and See Me Not, see Belchier, Daubridgecourt, *Hans Beer-Pot.*

Segrave, Leicestershire, iii. 99.

Seile, Henry, stationer, iii. 179, 181, 442; iv. 801.

Seirger, Richard, iv. 656, 661, 667, 674.

Sejanus His Fall, see Jonson, Ben.

Selden, John, iv. 717.

Select Musical Ayres and Dialogues, see Playford, John.

Selimus, Part I, *see* Anonymous.

Sellar, Mr., v. 1374.

Seneca, iv. 499, 833; v. 1002, 1238.
   Agamemnon, iv. 509.
   Medea, v. 1373.
      (Sherburne's transl.), v. 1054.
   Thebais, iii. 406.

Senescu, Frances Frazier, *James Shirley's The Bird in a Cage,* edited from the Quarto of 1633. Unpublished University of Chicago thesis (1948), v. 1080, 1081.

Senile Odium, see Hausted, Peter.

Senob, Alice, ed., Massinger's *The Renegado.* Unpublished thesis, University of Chicago (1939), iv. 811, 813.

Sensabaugh, G. F., 'Burton's Influence on Ford's *The Lover's Melancholy', S.P.* xxxiii (1936), iii. 448.
   'Ford's Tragedy of Love-Melancholy', *Englische Studien,* lxxiii (1939), iii. 448.
   '*Milieu* of *Comus,* The', *Stud. Phil.* xli (1944), iv. 914.

Tragic Muse of John Ford, The (1944), iii. 434, 448, 462.

Sentimental comedy, iii. 66.

Sentliger, Anthony, iv. 822, 823.

Sentliger, Sir Warham, iv. 822.

Sequestration, iii. 39, 183, 293, 469; iv. 512.

Sergeants-at-arms, vi. 291.

Sergeant at mace, ii. 545, 581.

Sergeant Painter, vi. 272, 273.

Sergeants' Inn, vi. 81.

Serger, Richard, stationer, iii. 114, 402.

Serjeant-surgeon, iii. 26.

Sermon Court, *see* Whitehall Palace.

Sermon days (in Lent), vi. 45, 65; vii. 3, 5.

Sermons, iii. 2, 29, 190; iv. 498, 499, 513, 526, 533, 588, 691, 844, 855; v. 1185, 1188, 1194, 1259, 1267, 1341, 1349; vii. 37, 43, 47, 49.
   Arrest for, iv. 533.
   On plays, v. 1194.

Serres, Jean de, *Inventaire général de l'histoire de France,* iv. 546.

Serving man, ii. 449.

Sesostris, story of, iii. 46.

Sessions of the Peace, vi. 239.

'Session of Poets, A', *see* Suckling, Sir John.

Sets, *see* Scenery.

Settings for songs, iv. 647.

Settle, Elkanah, iv. 500.
   The Fairy Queen, iii. 349, 413.
   Love and Revenge, iv. 546.

Seven Champions of Christendom, The, see Kirke, John.

Seven Deadly Sins, see Anonymous.

Seward, Thomas, iii. 312.

Seward, William, iii. 312.

Sewer Commission for Kent and Surrey, vi. 248.

Sewers of Her Majesty's Chamber, ii. 685.

Sewster, Mr., v. 1309, 1310; vi. 99.

'Sexton, or The Mock-Testator, The,' a droll from *The Spanish Curate,* iii. 419.

Seymour, Lady Francis, v. 1311.

Seymour, William Lord, Earl of Hertford Lord Beauchamp, iii. 67; v. 1311.

Seywell, John, the Shalme, v. 1159.

Sforza, Duke of Milan, see Massinger, *The Duke of Milan.*

Shadow of Night, The, see Chapman, George.

Shadwell, Thomas, iii. 144, 146.
Bury-Fair, iii. 307.
Humorists, The, iii. 76.
Royal Shepherdess, The, iii. 118.
True Widow, iv. 803.
Virtuoso, The, ii. 598.
Shaftesbury, Dorset, iii. 154.
Shagbutts, ii. 348, 508.
Shakerley, Edward, i. 220, 221, 222, 246; ii. 561, 682; iv. 813; vi. 59.
Shakespeare, William, i. 1, 2, 4 nn. 1 and 2, 5 n. 6 cont., 22, 46 ,66, 68, 120, 146 n. 6, 177, 270 and nn. 3 and 4; ii. 410, 435, 436, 462, 463, 467, 469, 478, 506, 537, 597, 674, 692, 693; iii. 8, 42, 53, 75, 127, 133, 193, 197, 198, 230, 231, 236, 260, 272, 300, 306, 308, 310, 318, 342, 353, 370, 432, 445, 450; iv. 499, 500, 502, 510, 516, 539, 557, 585, 586, 597, 607, 608, 681, 779, 803, 818, 827, 865, 866; v. 968, 976, 990, 1018, 1048–9, 1086, 1148, 1323, 1354, 1361; vi. 20, 41, 48, 86, 180.
Influence of, iii. 199, 201, 236, 331, 342, 354, 358, 379, 406, 413–14; iv. 478, 492, 497, 509, 546, 547, 597, 697, 740, 761, 833, 837; v. 998, 1003, 1153, 1165, 1200, 1212, 1341, 1372, 1381.
Falstaff plays, v. 1165.
Plays adapted, iii. 197.
Plays of, vi. 225; vii. 64. 107.
Reputation of, v. 968.
The so-called *Collection* of 1619, vii. 33.
Variorum edition, *see* Malone, Edmond.
First folio, i. 8, 22 n. 2, 34 n. 3, 184, 270 n. 4 cont.; ii. 467; iii. 309, 432; iv. 609, 816; v. 1200; vi. 7, 60, 225.
The Second Folio, vii. 85.
All's Well That Ends Well, iii. 260, 281; vii. 50, 75.
Antony and Cleopatra, iii. 342; vii. 50, 75.
As You Like It, i. 137 and n. 7, 157; ii. 347; v. 1222; vi. 178 n. 1; vii. 50, 75.
Comedy of Errors, A, iv. 837; vi. 40; vii. 50, 75.
Coriolanus, vii. 50, 75.
Cymbeline, i. 97, 127; iv. 697; vii. 50, 75.

First Part of the Contention of York and Lancaster (2 Henry VI), vii. 33.
Hamlet, i. 51, 95 n. c, 98, 99 n. v, 127–8; ii. 597, 693; iii. 44, 260, 402; iv. 546, 547, 706; v. 1200; vi. 178 n. 1; vii. 108, 127.
Influence of, iv. 509.
Henry IV, Part I, i. 95, 128; ii. 447, 489, 505, 693 ;v.1145,1200; vii. 46, 85, 119.
Henry IV, Part II, i. 95 n. c, 128–9.
Henry V, vi. 132, 191; vi. 61, 75.
Henry VI, Part III, v. 1381; vi. 50, 75.
Julius Caesar, i. 51, 98, 99, 129; iii. 260, 331; iv. 478, 741; v. 1372; vii. 50, 75.
King Lear, iv. 890; v. 998; vii. 33, 116.
Love's Labour's Lost, ii. 447; v. 1043; vii. 81, 127.
Macbeth, iv. 833, 878, 889, 904; v. 1369; vi. 16 n. 1; vii. 50.
Measure for Measure, iii. 201,406; iv. 837; vii. 50, 75.
Merchant of Venice, The, iii. 252; iv. 680; vii. 32, 33, 108.
Merry Wives of Windsor, The, i. 99, 129; iii. 358; iv. 803; vii. 33, 73, 77.
Midsummer Night's Dream, A, i. 27, 96, 129; ii. 590, 622; v. 998, 1153; vii. 34, 71, 79.
Moor of Venice, The, see Othello.
Much Ado About Nothing, ii. 621, 622; iii. 46, 354; iv. 497, 837; v. 1388, 1165.
Othello, i. 24, 48, 51, 98, 129; ii. 587, 597, 660, 677, 681, 693; iii. 199, 201, 278, 328, 354; iv. 492, 546, 776; v. 1212, 1341; vi. 16, 22, 23, 198; vii. 41, 46, 67, 77, 110, 114.
Pericles, i. 94, 129; ii. 375, 658; iii. 78; vi. 198; vii. 33, 75, 77, 101.
Richard II, i. 1, 24, 129; ii. 566; iii. 328; iv. 546; vi. 16 n. 1, 198; vii. 95.
Richard III, i. 97, 128, 129; ii. 395, 585; iv. 546; v. 1014; vi. 191; vii. 46, 73, 95.
Romeo and Juliet, ii. 347; iii. 353, 354, 379; iv. 741, 833, 837; v. 998, 1274; vi. 132; vii. 108, 127.

Sir John Oldcastle Pt. I, vii. 34.

'Take, oh take those lips away' (*M. for M.*), iii. 406.

Taming of the Shrew, The, i. 97, 129–30; iii. 411, 431, 432; vi. 198; vii. 81, 127.

Tempest, The, iii. 354, 412, 413, 414; v. 1212; vii. 50, 75.

Timon of Athens, vii. 50, 75.

Titus Andronicus, v. 1421; vii. 61, 75.

Troilus and Cressida, v. 972.

True Tragedy of Richard Duke of York, The, v. 1014; vii. 33.

Twelfth Night, i. 94, 130; v. 1118 1149, 1165; vii. 50, 75.

Two Gentlemen of Verona, The, vii. 50, 75.

Two Noble Kinsmen, The, *see* Davenant, William, *The Rivals*.

Venus and Adonis, iv. 741.

Winter's Tale, The, i. 94, 95 and n. c, 97, 103, 130; ii. 468; iii. 265, 372, 379; iv. 889; vi. 16 n. 1; vii. 50, 75.

Yorkshire Tragedy, A, vii. 33.

Shakespeare, William, and John Fletcher, *Henry VIII*, i. 2, 22, 318; ii. 506; vi. 172, 179, 182, 198; vii. 50, 75.

Two Noble Kinsmen, The, i. 82–83, 95 n. c, 114; ii. 418, 452, 606–7; iv. 819; vii. 92, 95.

Shakespeare Memorial Theatre, Stratford-upon-Avon, vi. 6.

Shakespeare First Folio, The, *see* Greg, W. W.

'Shakespeare's Arena', *see* Hotson, Leslie.

'Shakespeare and the Blackfriars Theatre', *see* Bentley, G. E.

'Shakespeare and the Globe', *see* Wallace, Charles W.

Shakespeare and His Theatre (1964), *see* Bentley, Gerald Eades.

Shakespeare and the Rival Traditions, *see* Harbage, Alfred.

Shakespeareana, v. 1141.

Shakespeare's Stage (1958), *see* Nagler, Alois M.

Shakespeare's Wooden O (1959), *see* Hotson, Leslie.

Shalms, v. 1159.

Sham battle, vii. 112.

Shanbrooke, Elizabeth, ii. 562.

Shanbrooke, John, ii. 561–2.

Shanbrooke, Rachel, ii. 562.

Shanbrooke, William, ii. 562.

Shanck, Shancke, Shanckes, *or* Shancks, *see* Shank.

Shandoze, Lord, players of, vii. 12 n. 1.

Shands, H. A., *Massinger's 'The Great Duke of Florence' und seine Quellen* (1902), iv. 786, 788.

Shank, Anne, ii. 565.

Shank, Elizabeth, ii. 564, 566, 567, 568.

Shank, James, ii. 565, 566, 567, 646, 647.

Shank, John, senior, i. 4 nn. 1 and 2, 5 and n. 6, 14, 17, 31, 35 n. 1, 43, 44, 45, 46, 47, 57 n. 2, 72–88, 129, 136, 139, 155, 281, 321; ii. 562–7, 642; iii. 164, 396, 400, 428, 429, 433; iv. 540, 541, 810; v. 1034, 1049–51, 1412; vi. 36–37, 181, 182 n. 3, 198; vii. 6, 7.

Will of, ii. 646–8.

Shank's Ordinary, i. 103 and n. 2, 130; ii. 565; iii. 265; v. 1050–1; vii. 6, 7.

Shank, John, junior, i. 275, 315 n. 2; ii. 567–9.

Shank, Thomas, ii. 565.

Shank, Winifred, i. 46; ii. 564, 565, 566–7, 568, 646, 647.

'Shanks Boy', John', iii. 164.

Shank's Ordinary, *see* Shank, John, senior.

Shanks, William, ii. 565.

Shanucke, John, *see* Shank, John, senior.

Shapiro, I. A., 'Bankside Theatres: The: Early Engravings', *Shakespeare Survey*, i (1948), and ii (1949), vi. 179, 180 n. 2, 183, 185 n. 1, 200, 202 n, 247, 248, 249, 252.

'The "Mermaid Club" ', *M.L.R.* xlv (1950), iv. 608.

'Original Drawing of the Globe Theatre, An', *Shakespeare Survey*, ii (1949), vi. 200, 202 n.

Sharers, in acting companies, i. 310; ii. 688; v. 1010; vi. 36, 129.

Sharers in theatres, vi. 130.

Sharers' Papers (1635), i. 43–47, 86–87; iv. 540; vi. 36–37, 185.

Malone Society Collections, ii (1931), vi. 179, 180.

Shares, vi. 28, 36–37.

Shares, value of, ii. 632–3, 638, 644, 647; vi. 28, 36–37, 70.

Sharlie, James, *see* Shirley, James.

Sharpe, Lewis, iii. 66; v. 1051-2.
Noble Stranger, The, i. 256; iii. 66;
v. 1051-2; vi. 93.
Sharpe, Richard, i. 14, 16, 17, 22,
35 n. 1, 70, 72-88; ii. 569-71; iii.
164, 326, 330, 341, 346, 349, 352,
355, 363, 372, 375, 396; iv. 810,
817; v. 1412.
Sharpe, Robert Boies, 'The Sources
of Richard Brome's *The Novella*',
Stud. Phil. xxx (1933), iii. 84, 85.
Sharpham, Edward, iii. 239, 243.
Cupid's Whirligig. iv. 507; v.
1438; vii. 21, 73, 77.
The Fleir, vii. 81.
Shatterell, Edward, ii. 571.
Shatterell, Robert, i. 327 n. 4, 332,
336; ii. 571-2; iii. 314.
Shaunks, John, *see* Shank, John,
junior.
Shaver, Chester Linn, 'The Date of
Revenge for Honour', *M.L.N.*
liii (1938), iv. 489.
*The Life and Works of Henry
Glapthorne.* Unpublished Har-
vard thesis (1937) iii. 211; iv.
473-96 *passim.*
Shaw, Phillip, 'The Position of
Thomas Dekker in Jacobean
Prison Literature', *P.M.L.A.* lxii
(1947), iii. 241.
Shaw, Robert, i. 135; v. 1337.
Shaw, William Arthur, *The knights
of England; a complete record from
the earliest time to the present day of
the knights of all the orders of
chivalry in England, Scotland, and
Ireland, and of knights bachelors*
(1906), iii. 22; iv. 702, 719; v.
1198.
Shawe, John (a butcher), vi. 148.
She Saint, The, see Daborne, Robert.
Sheapard, Henry, iii. 446.
Sheares, William, v. 1313.
Shearlock, William, *see* Sherlock,
William.
Sheeres, William, iii. 264; v. 1380.
Sheil, Richard, *Evadne, or the
Statue,* v. 1152.
Sheldon, Edward, ii. 411.
Shelton, Thomas, his shorthand, v.
982.
Shelton (transl.), *Don Quixote* (1612),
iii. 390.
Shepard, Mistress, singer, v. 1230.
Shepherd, R. H., ed., *The Comedies
and Tragedies of George Chap-
man,* 3 vols. (1873), iii. 155, 156.
Dramatic Works of Richard Brome

*Containing Fifteen Comedies
Now First Collected in Three
Volumes, The* (1873), iii. 55.
ed., *The Dramatic Works of
Thomas Dekker,* 4 vols. (1873),
iii. 245, 248.
ed., *The Dramatic Works of
Thomas Heywood Now First
Collected with Illustrative Notes
and a Memoir of the Author in
Six Volumes,* 6 vols. (1874), iv.
557.
ed., *The Plays and Poems of
Henry Glapthorne,* 2 vols.
(1874), iv. 474, 477, 483.
Shepherds' Holiday, The, see Jonson,
Ben, *Pan's Anniversary.*
See Rowley, William.
See Rutter, Joseph.
Shepherds' Masque, The, see Anony-
mous.
Shepherd's Paradise, The, see
Montagu, Walter.
Shepley, Mr., iii. 402.
Sheppard, Margaret, ii. 644.
Sheppard, Samuel, iii. 236; iv. 756;
v. 1052-4, 1218.
Committee-Man Curried, The, v.
1053.
*Epigrams Theological, Philosoph-
ical and Romantic* (1651), iii.
199; v. 1219.
Fairy King, The, iv. 499; v.
1244, 1254.
*Jovial Crew, or The Devil Turned
Ranter, The,* v. 1054.
Times Displayed, The (1646), iv.
499, 814, 831, 929; v. 1053.
'To Tatam', v. 1219.
Sheppard, Thomas, ii. 632, 644.
Shepperd, John, ii. 365.
Sheppey, Henry, ii. 682.
Sheppy, Thomas, iii. 371; iv. 862,
864.
Sherborne, Dorset, iii. 161; vii.
28.
Sherburne, Sir Edward, iv. 670; v.
1054; vi. 54, 57.
Transl. of *Medea,* v. 1054.
Sheridan, Richard Brinsley, *The
School for Scandal,* v. 1127.
Sheriffs, vi. 113, 230, 293.
Bailiffs, iv. 473.
Pricking of, vi. 261.
Sherley, James, *see* Shirley, James.
Sherlock, William, i. 163, 183, 187,
192, 219, 220, 221, 222, 231, 232,
237, 238, 246; ii. 572-3; vi. 49,
50, 59, 61, 67, 103.

Sherman, S. P., 'A New Play by John Ford', *M.L.N.* xxiii(1908), iii. 457.

'Stella and the *Broken Heart*', *P.M.L.A.* xxiv (1909), iii. 439, 440.

ed., *'Tis Pity She's a Whore and The Broken Heart*', The Belles-Lettres Series (1915), iii. 435, 439, 462, 463, 464.

Shields, painting and gilding of, vii. 103.

Ship money, iii. 41; v. 1266, 1269.

Shipman, Roger, v. 1054–6, 1225.

Grobiana's Nuptials, v. 1054–6, 1225.

Shipman, William, v. 1054.

Ships, iii. 147; iv. 923–4; v. 1006, 1202, 1205; vi. 293.

'Soveraigne of the Seas', iv. 585.

Spanish, v. 1249.

Shirelock, William, *see* Sherlock, William.

Shirley brothers, of Wiston, Sussex, v. 1057.

Shirley, Lady Anne, wife of the elder Sir Thomas Shirley, v. 1057.

Shirley, Lady Dorothy, v. 967, 976, 1094.

Shirley, Evelyn Philip, v. 1161.

Stemmata Shirleiana (1873), v. 1056, 1057, 1065.

'Who Was Henry Shirley, the Author of "The Martyr'd Soldier"?', *N. & Q.*, xii (1855), v. 1056, 1057, 1058.

Shirley family, v. 1015, 1017.

Shirley, Frances (Vavasour), v. 1057, 1071.

Shirley, Grace, v. 1067.

Shirley, Henry, iii. 458, 459; v. 1056–64.

Duke of Guise, The, v. 1058–9.

Dumb Bawd of Venice, The, i. 96, 130; ii. 469; v. 1059, 1060.

Martyred Soldier, The, i. 256; ii. 493; iv. 711; v. 1060–2, 1064, 1235.

Spanish Duke of Lerma, The, i. 66, 130; v. 1062–4.

Shirley, Sir Henry, v. 976.

Shirley, James, i. 63, 184, 229, 230 n. 2, 231, 305 n. 3, 306 n. 2; ii. 573; iii. 7, 33, 34, 35, 89, 97, 106, 133, 143, 144, 145, 147, 148, 195, 309, 311, 329, 368, 369, 384, 385, 386, 390, 437, 451, 455; iv. 474, 499, 523, 581, 679, 681, 699, 787, 813, 814 823, 830, 860, 950; v. 974, 1024, 1034, 1058, 1064–170, 1186, 1319, 1335, 1339, 1366; vi. 4, 39, 62, 73, 76, 193, 199, 304.

Herbert's commendation of, i. 230.

Influence of, iv. 598; v. 1329.

Plays of, for Queen Henrietta's men, i. 226.

Possible contract of, with Phoenix, i. 227.

Relation of, with Salisbury Court, i. 306 and n. 2.

Verses by, iii. 55, 72.

Arcadia, The, i. 104, 111, 226 n. 7, 227, 256; iii. 106, 110; iv. 933; v. 1073–6, 1129.

Ball, The, i. 226 n. 7, 228–9, 230 n. 2, 250–1; iii. 85, 156; iv. 743; v. 1076–9, 1088, 1108, 1121, 1169, 1310; vi. 63.

Beauties, The, *see The Bird in a Cage*.

Bird in a Cage, The, i. 226 n. 7, 227 n. 2, 256; ii. 573; iii. 452, 453; v. 1069, 1080–1, 1088, 1115, 1121, 1161, 1354, 1400.

Brothers, The (The Politic Father), i. 63, 66, 108, 130–1, 258; v. 1082, 1082–4, 1088, 1138, 1164, 1320.

Cardinal, The, i. 63, 108, 131; ii. 462–3, 534, 692; v. 1074, 1084–8, 1115, 1153; vi. 38.

Changes, or Love in a Maze, i. 227, 285 and n. 1, 301, 304, 305–6, 311, 323; iii. 444; v. 1068, 1088, 1091–4, 1100, 1115, 1121, 1146; vi. 98.

Constant Maid, or Love Will Find out the Way, The, i. 227, 256–7; ii. 378; iv. 485; v. 1074, 1095–6, 1143.

Contention of Ajax and Ulysses for the Armour of Achilles, The, v. 1071, 1097–8, 1119.

Contention for Honour and Riches, A, v. 1096–7, 1119, 1121, 1153, 1160.

Coronation, The, i. 226 n. 7, 257, 331, 337, 340; ii. 660; iv. 598; v. 1088, 1098–9, 1107, 1129, 1135; vi. 50.

Court Secret, The, i. 63, 131; iii. 148; iv. 598; v. 1084, 1093, 1100–2, 1115, 1146.

Cupid and Death, v. 1071, 1102–4.

Shirley, James (cont.)
    Doubtful Heir, The, or Rosania, or
        Love's Victory, i. 30 n. 6, 63, 66,
        108, 131; ii. 461; iv. 598, 699;
        v. 1069, 1084, 1105–7, 1368;
        vi. 14, 193, 196, 197.
    Duke, The, see The Humorous
        Courtier.
    Duke's Mistress, The, i. 226 n. 7,
        236, 248 n. i, 249, 257; v. 1087,
        1107–8, 1121.
    'Eccho and Narcissus the 2
        unfortunate Louers', v. 1066.
    Example, The, i. 226 n. 7, 257, 331,
        340; iv. 483; v. 1079, 1088,
        1108–10, 1121.
    Faithful Servant, The, see The
        Grateful Servant.
    Gamester, The, i. 226 n. 7, 230,
        231, 249, 257; ii. 675; iii. 123;
        v. 1079, 1088, 1108, 1110–2,
        1121.
    Gentleman of Venice, The, i. 244,
        257; v. 1112–14, 1138, 1149.
    'Glories of our blood and state,
        The' (dirge), v. 1098.
    Grateful Servant, The, or The
        Faithful Servant, i. 226 n. 7,
        257, 331, 340–1; iv. 521; v.
        967, 1088, 1093, 1100, 1114–
        18, 1121, 1145, 1146, 1163,
        1165, 1166, 1186; vi. 62.
    'Address to the Reader', vi. 62.
    Honoria and Mammon, v. 1071,
        1072, 1097, 1118–19.
    Humorous Courtier, The (The
        Duke), i. 226 n. 7, 257; v. 1088,
        1120–1, 1130, 1134, 1312.
    Hyde Park, i. 226 n. 7, 257–8, 331,
        341; iii. 61, 65, 88, 89; iv. 933,
        942; v. 1079, 1088, 1108,
        1121–3, 1170.
    Imposter, The, see The Imposture.
    Imposture, The, i. 63, 66, 108, 131;
        ii. 665 n. 7; v. 1084, 1088,
        1123–5; vi. 38.
    Lady of Pleasure, The, i. 226 n. 7,
        231 n. 1, 235, 258, 331, 341;
        ii. 661, 677, 681; iv. 691; v.
        1078, 1079, 1088, 1108, 1121,
        1125–7, 1168, 1170.
    Look to the Lady (?), iii. 147; iv.
        739; v. 1074, 1128.
    Love Tricks with Compliments, see
        The School of Compliment.
    Love Will Find out the Way, see
        The Constant Maid.
    Love's Cruelty, i. 226 n. 7, 258,
        331, 336, 341; ii. 397, 512, 692;

        iii. 384; v. 1073, 1074, 1087,
            1098, 1129–32, 1135.
    Maid's Revenge, The, i. 218 n. 3,
        222, 223 n. 1, 226 n. 7, 258, 331,
        341; v. 1078, 1087, 1121, 1125,
        1132–4, 1164.
    Masque of Peace, see The Triumphs
        of Peace.
    'Melancholy Converted', v. 1110.
    Night Walker, The, see Beaumont
        and Fletcher.
    No Wit No Help Like a Woman's,
        iv. 889.
    'One that loved none but de-
        formed Women', v. 1108.
    Opportunity, The, i. 226 n. 7, 258,
        331, 341; iii. 384; v. 1088, 1098,
        1110, 1121, 1129, 1134–7, 1165.
    Poems &c. (1646), iii. 34, 148; iv.
        503, 699; v. 1069, 1071, 1072,
        1084, 1087, 1094, 1099, 1106,
        1107, 1108, 1110, 1112, 1123,
        1125, 1134, 1142, 1153, 1224,
        1339, 1355, 1423; vi. 194,
        197.
    Politician, The, i. 258; iv. 706,
        943; v. 1113, 1114, 1137–9.
    Politique Father, The, see The
        Brothers.
    Rosania, see The Doubtful Heir.
    Royal Master, iv. 950; v. 1069,
        1088, 1113, 1115, 1121, 1125,
        1139–42.
    Rudiments of Grammar. The Rule
        Composed in English Verse, The
        (1656), v. 1070.
    St. Patrick for Ireland, v. 1069,
        1074, 1088, 1095, 1143–4, 1423.
    School of Compliment, The, or Love
        Tricks, i. 186 and n. 3, 187, 196,
        219 n. 4, 226 n. 7, 258, 331,
        341; iii. 81; iv. 494; v. 978,
        1068, 1076, 1088, 1093, 1100,
        1115, 1121, 1128, 1144–7, 1150,
        1164, 1166; vi. 59, 62.
    Sisters, The, i. 63, 67–68, 108, 131;
        v. 1084, 1086, 1087, 1088,
        1147–9; vi. 38, 40.
    Six New Plays. Viz. The Brothers.
        Sisters. Doubtfull Heir. Im-
        posture. Cardinall. Court Secret
        (1653), v. 1072, 1074, 1079,
        1082, 1083, 1084, 1085, 1086,
        1100, 1101, 1105, 1113, 1124,
        1138, 1148, 1149, 1164, 1320.
    'Song in a Play called Hide-
        Parke, A', v. 1123.
    Tragedy of St. Albans, v. 1133,
        1142.

Traitor, The, i. 226 n. 7, 258, 331, 341; v. 1086, 1087, 1120, 1121, 1130, 1150–3, 1329, 1330.
Triumph of Beauty, The, iv. 503; v. 1071, 1153–4.
Triumph of Peace, The, ii. 573, 675, 676; iii. 107, 453; iv. 677, 831; v. 1069, 1081, 1088, 1096, 1109, 1121, 1154–63, 1360; vi. 264.
'Verses and Poems, by James Shirley', MS., v. 1071.
Via Ad Latinam Linguam Complanata (1656), iv. 950; v. 1070.
Wedding, The, i. 218, 220, 221 and n. 1, 222, 223 and n. 6, 226 n. 7, 231, 246, 259, 331, 341; ii. 345, 386, 406, 423, 518, 528, 540, 548, 553, 572, 583, 608, 619, 628, 692; iii. 232, 437; iv. 485, 521, 747, 816; v. 1088, 1114, 1115, 1121, 1163–5.
Witty Fair One, The, i. 223, 226 n. 7, 259, 331, 341; v. 1088, 1115, 1121, 1145, 1166–7.
Young Admiral, The, i. 226 n. 7, 230, 249, 259, 331, 341; iv. 483; v. 1074, 1110, 1111, 1121, 1126, 1149, 1165, 1168–70, 1329, 1330.
Shirley, James, and Chapman, George, *Chabot, Admiral of France*, i. 226 n. 7, 235, 251, 331, 338; v. 1077, 1087, 1088–91, 1121.
Shirley, Marie, v. 1067.
Shirley, Mathias, v. 1067, 1068.
Shirley, Sir Robert, v. 1428.
Shirley, Sir Thomas, v. 1057.
Shoe Lane, *see* London, streets of.
Shoemaker a Gentleman, A, see Rowley, William.
Shoemakers' Holiday, The, see Dekker, Thomas.
Shoemakers, ii. 690; v. 1265; vi. 175.
Shooters Hill (mock title), v. 1447.
Shopkeepers, vi. 24.
Shoreditch, *see* London, streets and districts of.
Shoreham, Kent, ii. 673.
Short Discourse of the English Stage, see Flecknoe, R.
Short Parliament, vi. 74.
Shorthand, iii. 467.
Shorthand (Thomas Shelton's), v. 982.
Showing Glass, called *The World's Wonder*, vii. 54.

Showmen, ii. 507; vi. 291.
Shows, iii. 76, 248, 287, 289–90, 293, 295–6; iv. 474, 557, 571, 575, 576, 577, 578, 584–5, 607, 629, 639, 640, 646, 648–9, 653–4, 658–9, 683, 684, 687, 857, 858, 865, 879–81, 882, 892, 895–6, 896–9, 907–11, 912–13, 925–6, 936–9; v. 971–3, 974, 991, 1040, 1185, 1192, 1218, 1219, 1220, 1223, 1225, 1243, 1254, 1303, 1305, 1343, 1344, 1353, 1364, 1372, 1376, 1419, 1420, 1442; vi. 267, 287, 291, 293, 295, 296, 298, 301; vii. 37, 47, 111.
Academic, v. 967.
Allegorical, v. 1420.
Christening, iv. 640.
Expenditures for, iv. 577, 653, 897, 898, 911, 926.
Lord Mayor's, *see* Lord Mayor's pageants.
Lost, iv. 911, 1050.
In manuscript, iv. 882, 912–13; v. 991, 1376.
In multiple manuscripts, v. 1376.
Personal allusions in, v. 972.
Political allusions in, iv. 659, 897; v. 973.
Private, v. 1097.
Suppressed, v. 972.
In theatres, iv. 792–3, 907–11, 936–8; v. 1353; vi. 209 and n. 1, 212, 247, 250.
Shrewsbury, Shropshire, i. 212.
Shrove Tuesday, vi. 54, 219, 287, 288.
Riot, i. 161–4; ii. 691.
Shrove-tide, vi. 171; vii. 286, 287, 288.
Performances, iii. 37.
Shurley, James, *see* Shirley, James.
Shurlock, William, *see* Sherlock, William.
Sibley, Gertrude, *The Lost Plays and Masques* (1933), v. 1430.
Sicelides, see Fletcher, Phineas.
Sicilian civil wars, v. 1214.
Sicily, iv. 698, 768.
Scene of play, iv. 699, 706.
Sicily and Naples, see Harding, Samuel.
Siderothriambos, see Munday, Anthony.
Sidesman, ii. 466; vi. 19.
Sidley, Sir John, v. 1220.
Sidley, Sir William, v. 1220.

Sidnam, Jonathan, v. 1034, 1170–1, 1451.
Transl., *Filli di Sciro*, v. 1171.
Transl., *Il Pastor Fido or The Faithful Shepherd*, v. 1171.
Sidney, Mr., iv. 900.
Sidney, Barbara, v. 1289.
Sidney, Lady Dorothy, v. 1289.
Sidney, Sir Philip, iii. 440; v. 1076, 1388.
Arcadia, iii. 440; iv. 480, 860, 921, 933; v. 1035, 1074–5, 1139, 1367; vii. 18, 33, 42, 46, 51, 64, 66, 67, 68, 69, 72, 73, 76, 90, 114.
Entertainment at Wanstead (The Lady of May), The, vii. 18, 33, 51.
Sidney Sussex College, Cambridge, iv. 830, 838, 916.
Siege, vi. 293, 294.
Siege, The, see Cartwright, William.
Siege, The, or The Colonel, see Davenant, William.
Siege of Dunkirk with Alleyn the Pirate, The, see Massey, Charles.
Siege of Rhodes, The, Parts I and II, see Davenant, William.
Siege of Troy, story of, iv. 580.
Sight and Search, see Anonymous.
Sign of the Maidenhead, Inn, v. 1347.
Sign of the ship in St. Paul's Churchyard, v. 1118.
Signet Office Docquet Book, i. 168, 302.
Silbermann, Abraham M., *Untersuchungen über die Quellen des Dramas 'The True Tragedy of Herod and Antipater with the Death of faire Marriam' by Gervase Markham and William Sampson* ⟨1622⟩ (1927), iv. 734, 735.
Silent Woman, The, see Jonson, Ben, *Epicoene*.
Silk-weavers, vi. 228, 239.
Silver Age, The, see Heywood, Thomas.
Silver fleet, iii. 169.
Silver, Thomas, vi. 87, 88, 91.
Silvester, ii. 573.
Silvia, see Kynder, Philip.
Simmonds, Mark John, *Merchant Taylor fellows of St. John's College, Oxford* (1930), iii. 4, 28, 291; v. 1181, 1259, 1275.
Simo, see Anonymous.

Simons, Joseph, v. 1034, 1172–5.
Josephi Simonis, Tragœdiœ quinque (1656, 1657, 1680, 1697), v. 1172.
Mercia seu Pietas Coronata, Tragœdia, v. 1172–3.
S. Damianus Episcopus Ticinensis Turbas Italiœ Divinitus Prœdicit, v. 1173.
Theoctistus sive Constans in Aula Virtus, Tragœdia, v. 1173.
Ultio Divina sive Leo Armenus, Tragœdia, v. 1173–4.
Unnamed Tragedy (Lost), v. 1175.
Vitus sive Christiana Fortitudo, Tragœdia, v. 1174.
Zeno sive Ambitio Infelix, Tragœdia, v. 1174–5.
Simpson, Elizabeth, ii. 554.
Simpson, Evelyn, 'Jonson's Masques: A Rejoinder', *R.E.S.* xviii (1942), iv. 605.
Simpson, Evelyn, and Percy and C. H. Herford, eds., *Ben. Jonson.* 11 vols. (1925–53), *see* Herford.
Simpson, Percy, 'Ben Jonson and the Devil Tavern', *Mod. Lang. Rev.* xxxiv (1939), iv. 742, 744.
'Genuineness of the Drummond Conversations, The', *R.E.S.* ii (1926), iii. 287.
Proof-Reading in the Sixteenth, Seventeenth, and Eighteenth Centuries (1935), iii. 134.
'Thomas Middleton's "Women Beware Women" ', *Mod. Lang. Rev.* xxxiii (1938), iv. 905.
'Two Poems of Philip Massinger', *Athenaeum*, 8 September 1906, iii. 307; iv. 750, 752.
Simpson, Percy, and C. F. Bell, *Designs by Inigo Jones for Masques and Plays at Court* (1924), iii. 107, 110, 122, 199, 200, 207, 209, 213, 216, 218; iv. 522, 524, 637, 638, 642, 652, 653, 655, 660, 663, 669, 672, 917; v. 1154, 1163, 1227, 1228, 1229, 1230, 1334, 1335; vi. 51 n. 1, 281 n. 1, 282 and n.
Simpson, William, ii. 554.
Simson, Edward, *Chronicon Historian Catholicam*, iv. 515.
Sinckler, Elizabeth, ii. 573.
Sinckler, William, ii. 573.
Sincler, John, iii. 432.
Singer, John, i. 135; ii. 612.

Singer, S. W., ed., *Pharonnida; an Heroic Poem in Five Books by William Chamberlayne* (1914), iii. 154.
Singers, v. 1230.
Singing, iv. 479; vi. 151.
  Boy, iii. 61.
  Heroine, iii. 83.
  In a masque, iv. 918.
  In a play, iv. 889.
Singleton, Ralph H., 'Milton's *Comus* and the *Comus* of Erycius Puteanus', *P.M.L.A.* lviii (1943), iv. 914.
Singleton, Thomas, v. 1175-7.
  Of Basildon, Berks., v. 1175.
  Talpae, sive Conjuratis Papistica, v. 1177.
Singleton, William, iii. 437, 450, 778, 779.
Sion College in London, v. 1149.
Sir Charles Sedley, see Pinto, V. de Sola.
Sir Giles Goosecap, see Anonymous.
Sir Gregory Nonsense, see Taylor, John.
Sir Hercules Buffoon, see Lacy, John.
Sir John Oldcastle, see Anonymous.
  Pt. I, *see* Shakespeare, William.
Sir John van Olden Barnavelt, see Fletcher, John.
Sir Martin Mar-All, see Cavendish, William.
Sir Thomas More, see Heywood, Thomas.
Sir Thomas Puckering, iii. 138.
Sir Thomas Wyatt, see Dekker, Thomas.
  See Webster, John.
Sir Timothy Treaty-all, see Behn, Aphra, *City Heiress*.
Sisigambis, Queen of Syracuse, see Anonymous.
Sisson, Charles J., vi. 55.
  ed., Massinger, *Believe as You List* (1927), iv. 762, 763, 764, 765.
  'Keep the Widow Waking: A Lost Play by Dekker', *Library*, Fourth Series, viii (1927-8), iii. 252, 253, 254; iv. 471; v. 1016.
  Lost Plays of Shakespeare's Age (1936), iii. 252, 254; v. 1244.
  ed., *Thomas Lodge and Other Elizabethans* (1933), iv. 884; v. 1393.
  'Mr. and Mrs. Browne of the Boar's Head', *Life and Letters Today*, xv (winter, 1936), vi.

121, 122, 124-31.
'Red Bull Company and the Importunate Widow, The', *Shakespeare Survey*, vii (1954), 57-68; vi. 56, 121, 124-31, 215, 217, 219.
Sisters, The, see Shirley, James.
Site of the Globe Playhouse Southwark, The (1924), *see* Braines, W. W.
Sittingbourne, Kent, iv. 515.
Six Court Comedies, see Lyly, John.
Six Days' Adventure, or The New Utopia, see Howard, Edward.
Skemp, A. R., *Nathaniel Richards' Tragedy of Messallina The Roman Emperesse, Materialien* (1910), v. 961, 999, 1001, 1002, 1003, 1004.
  'Some Characteristics of the English Stage before the Restoration', *Shakespeare Jahrbuch*, xlv (1909), v. 1004.
Sketches, v. 1163, 1230.
  For the costumes, iv. 653.
  By Inigo Jones, v. 1228.
Skialetheia. Or, A shadowe of Truth, in certaine Epigrams and Satyres (1598), *see* Guilpin, Edward.
Skinners, iii 248.
Skinners' Company, iii. 248; iv. 899; v. 1220, 1221.
Skipwith, Sir Henry, iii. 360.
Skooleing, Mary, ii. 421.
Skragg, Mr., ii. 379.
Skrine, H. D., manuscripts of, iv. 549.
Sky borders (of proscenium), iv. 524; vi. 51.
Slagle, Kenneth C., 'Robert Baron, Cavalier Poet', *N. & Q.* clxix (1935), iii. 10.
Slater, Martin, i. 135, 160, 165, 171 and n. b, 172 n. 1, 178; ii. 574-5; iii. 28, 215, 217.
Slater, Thomas, stationer, v. 962.
Slathier, Martin, *see* Slater, Martin.
Slaughter *or* Slauter, *see* Slater, Martin.
Slavery, iv. 768.
Slead, Elizabeth, ii. 625.
Sleepe, Mr., v. 1298.
Sleight of hand, ii. 486.
Slingsby, Sir William, ii. 491, 688.
Sloane MSS., *see* British Museum MSS.
Sloane, Eugene Hulse, *Robert Gould* (1940), v. 1132.
Sly, William, i. 1, 2, 4 n. 2; vi. 20.

Small, R. A., *The Stage-Quarrel between Ben Jonson and the So-Called Poetasters* (1899), iii. 242; iv. 605, 607.

Small Poems of Divers Sorts, see Cokayne, Sir Aston.

Smallpox, vii. 29.

Smart, Jasper, ii. 639.

Smart, Joane, ii. 639.

Smeaton, Oliphant, ed., *The Broken Heart* (1906), iii. 439.

Smectymnians, vi. 245.

Smectymnuus, v. 1338.

Smethwicke, Mr., stationer, iv. 579, 629, 778, 783, 786; v. 1196.

Smith, —, iii. 262.

Smith, playwright, v. 1177–8.
The Fair Foul One, or The Baiting of the Jealous Knight, v. 1177–8.

Smith, Alexander, ed., *The Female Rebellion* . . . (1872), iii. 96.

Smith, Captain Alexander, *A Compleat History of the Lives and Robberies of the Most Notorious Highwaymen* (1719), iii. 187, 189.

Smith, Amye, ii. 543.

Smith, Anthony, i. 18, 24, 35 n. 1, 73–89, 199 and n. 2, 200 and n. 3, 209, 210, 211 and n. a; ii. 575–6, 607; iv. 817; vi. 227.

Smith, Miss C. Fell, v. 1029, 1265.

Smith, Francis, iv. 734, 735.

Smith, G. C. Moore, v. 1236, 1279.
'Aurelian Townsend', *T.L.S.* 23 October 1924, v. 1226, 1227.
'The Authorship of *The Drinking Academy*', *R.E.S.* vii (1932), v. 977, 978, 979.
'The Canon of Randolph's Dramatic Works', *R.E.S.* i (1925), v. 962, 963, 964, 965, 974, 980, 989.
ed., *Club Law* (1907), v. 1028.
College plays performed in the University of Cambridge (1923), iii. 159, 160, 177, 181, 185, 186; iv. 526, 527, 530, 534, 536, 537, 600, 601, 718, 838, 853, 855, 954; v. 1006–7, 1195, 1196, 1197, 1233, 1298, 1299, 1302, 1371, 1374, 1407, 1409; vii. 16.
'*The Drinking Academy* and Its Attribution to Thomas Randolph', *P.M.L.A.* xliv (1929), v. 977, 978, 979.
ed., Robert Ward's *Fucus Histriomastix* (1909), iv. 528; v. 1196, 1237.
'Nathanael Richards, Dramatist',

N. & Q., Tenth Series, xi (1909), v. 999, 1000, 1001.
'Notes on Some English University Plays', *M.L.Q.* iii (1907–8), v. 1338.
Oxford Historical and Literary Studies, v (1915), iii. 318.
Proceedings of the British Academy (1927), iv. 536.
'Randolph's *Epithalamium to George Goring*', *R.E.S.* ii (1926), v. 965.
'Robert Baron, Author of *Mirza a Tragedie*', *N. & Q.*, Eleventh Series, ix (1914), iii. 10; iv. 471.
Thomas Randolph and The Drinking Academy, R.E.S. viii. (1932), v. 978.
'Some unpublished poems of Thomas Randolph (1605–1635)', *Palaestra*, cxlviii (1925), v. 965.
Thomas Randolph, Warton Lecture, *Proceedings of the British Academy* (1927), v. 965, 966, 967, 969, 971, 975, 983, 986.
ed., *William Hemminge's Elegy on Randolph's Finger Containing the Well-Known Lines 'On the Time-Poets'* (1923), iii. 434, 441; iv. 539, 541, 832; v. 1243; vi. 87, 96–97.
Review of Tannenbaum and Rollins's edition of *The Drinking Academy, R.E.S.* vi (1930), 476–83, v. 977.

Smith, G. Gregory, *Ben Jonson* (English Men of Letters Series) [1919], iv. 605.

Smith, Henry, i. 142 n. 6, 143; v. 1042.

Smith, Homer, 'Pastoral Influence in the English Drama', *P.M.L.A.* xii (1897), iv. 501, 505, 715, 917; v. 1032, 1033.

Smith, Humphrey, Alderman of the Ward of Farringdon Within, vi. 28.

Smith, James, 'Innovation of Penelope and Ulysses', *Wit Restor'd* (1658), iv. 757.

Smith, John, i. 160, 161, 202 n. 6, 204 n. 3, 211 n. b; ii. 527, 576; vi. 54, 57.

Smith, John, *vs.* Christopher Beeston, ii. 527.

Smith, Captain John, *A Description of New England* (1616), ii. 455; iv. 518.

Smith, Joyce, ii. 577.

Smith, Judith, ii. 577.
Smith, Lady, i. 10 n. 6.
Smith, Leonard, ii. 576.
Smith, L. P., *The Life and Letters of Sir Henry Wotton*, 2 vols. (1907), iv. 792.
Smith, Margaret, ii. 571; v. 1196.
Smith, Mathew, i. 261 and n. 3, 262, 263 n. 1, 269, 275, 303, 307, 308, 309, 318, 319, 321; ii. 576–7; vi. 170, 172.
Smith, Paul Edward, ed., *Pathomachia*, v. 1390, 1391, 1392.
Smith, Ralph, vii. 23.
Smith, Rebecca, ii. 644.
Smith, Richard, ii. 365.
Smith, Thomas, ii. 651; v. 965.
Smith, Dr. Thomas, of Cockermouth vi. 177.
Smith, Wentworth, iv. 575, 583; v. 1177, 1241, 1254.
  Hector of Germany, The, i. 207 n. 4; v. 1177; vi. 133; vii. 31.
Smith, Will, *St. George for England*, v. 1178.
Smith, William, ii. 503; iii. 409; v. 1177, 1178.
  Fair Foul One, or the Baiting of the Jealous Knight, The, i. 206.
Smith, Captain William, ii. 644.
Smith, Wolfran, v. 1196.
Smithfield, *see* London, streets and districts of.
Smiths, vi. 260.
Smyth, Francis, vi. 143.
Smyth, William, i. 265; iii. 94.
Smythe, Thomas, vi. 140.
Smythson, John, vi. 255–6.
Snell, Florence May, 'The Date of Jonson's *Tale of a Tub*', *M.L.N.* xxx (1915), iv. 632, 634.
Sneller, James, i. 303, 307, 308, 312, 321; ii. 577–8.
Snelling, Thomas, v. 1178–9.
Snelling, Thomas, *Thibaldus sive Vindictæ Ingenium, or Pharamus sive Libido Vindex, Hispanica Tragædia*, v. 1179.
Snelling, William, v. 1178.
Snenton, Notts., iv. 717.
Soame, Thomas, Alderman of London, v. 1001.
Soap, vii. 60.
Soare's Rents, *see* London, streets of.
Society of Florists, iv. 715.
Society of Jesus, *see* Jesuits.
Society of Stationers (Dublin), v. 971, 975.

Sock (i.e. of comedy), vi. 246.
'Sodayne Burning of the 'Globe', The' (Ballad), *see* Anonymous.
Soddered Citizen, The, *see* Clavell, John.
Sodom pie-woman, vi. 234.
Soham, Cambridgeshire, ii. 438.
Soldier, The, *see* Lovelace, Richard.
Soldier for the Ladies, A, *see* Centlivre, S., *The Beau's Duel*.
Soldiers, ii. 438; vi. 177, 214.
'Soldier's Joy', song, iv. 824.
Soldier's March, The, *see* Dances.
Soldiers Marche (dance), *see* Dances.
Soldiers, recruiting of, vii. 54.
Solemn League and Covenant, iv. 958.
Solicitor-General, the, vi. 297.
Solihull, Warwickshire, ii. 419, 484, 618.
Solomon and Bersheba, *see* Anonymous.
Solórzano, Castillo, *La duquesa de Mantua*, iii. 116.
  La Huerta de Valencia (1629), iii. 116.
Solve, Norma Dobie, *Stuart Politics in Chapman's Tragedy of Chabot* (1928), v. 1089, 1090.
Some Account of the Hospital and Parish of St. Giles in the Fields, Middlesex (1822), *see* Parton, John.
'Some Principles of Elizabethan Staging', *see* Reynolds, George Fullmer.
Somerset, Countess of, iv. 620.
Somerset, Edward, Lord Herbert, iii. 95.
Somerset, George, ii. 578.
Somerset, Robert Carr, Earl of, iii. 155, 198; v. 1425.
Somerset Herald, iii. 466.
Somerset House, i. 39, 46, 110, 117, 329; ii. 401; iii. 107, 122; iv. 549, 918, 919; v. 1334; vi. 45, 65, 69, 170, 232, 266; vii. 19, 22, 60, 111, 113.
  Presence Chamber, vii. 19.
  See also Denmark House.
Somner, John, *see* Sumner, John.
'Song in a Play called Hide-Park, A', *see* Shirley, James.
Song, Bawd's, in a play, iv. 867, 868, 869.
Songs, iii. 61, 83, 109, 111, 132, 208, 313, 330, 376; iv. 502, 568, 571, 646, 654, 673, 683, 695, 882, 913; v. 971, 988, 989, 1002,

Songs (*cont.*)

1019, 1076, 1095, 1098, 1123, 1125, 1143, 1175, 1183, 1189, 1192, 1212, 1217, 1219, 1222, 1231, 1233, 1238, 1304, 1374, 1376, 1420, 1422, 1430, 1431; vi. 102, 117, 146, 147, 240; vii. 7, 117.

Contract to write, ii. 390.

In masques, iv. 638, 646, 647, 654, 673, 683, 909, 910, 913.

In plays, iii. 44, 106, 110, 148, 304, 317, 318, 320, 325, 346, 354, 359, 376, 384, 393, 406, 461; iv. 484, 503, 568, 571, 602, 647, 824, 840, 847, 850, 894, 895, 903-4, 920.

Popular, v. 1365.

Settings for, v. 1231.

Song-writer, iii. 47.

Sons of Ben, *see* Jonson, Ben.

Sophia, Princess, ii. 432.

Sophister, The, see Zouche, Richard.

Sophocles, iv. 499, 833; vi. 276 and n. 1, 278.

Sophomorus, see Anonymous.

Sophy, The, see Denham, John.

Sorlings, Islands of, iv. 728.

Sotheby's, ii. 673; iii. 296.

Sotheby's sale, v. 1322, 1412.

Souers, P. W., *The Matchless Orinda* (1931), iii. 276.

'*Souldiers delight, The*', song, iv. 824.

Sources, iii, iv, v, *passim*.

South Africa, v. 1344.

South Kensington, *see* London, streets and districts.

South Kirby, Yorkshire, iii. 2.

South Leverton, Nottinghamshire, v. 1042.

South Warnborough, Hampshire, iii. 3.

Southampton, i. 20, 50, 92, 172, 212, 322; ii. 349.

Southampton, Duchess of, pastoral on death of, v. 1183.

Southampton, Thomas Wriothesley, Earl of, ii. 379, 525; iii. 460, 554.

Earl's (Southampton's) company, the, iv. 554.

Southern, Richard, 'Colour in the Elizabethan Theatre', *Theatre Notebook*, vi (1951-2), vi. 249 and n. 2.

Southlande, —, ii. 676.

Southwark, *see* London, streets and districts of.

Fair, iv. 930.

Southwell, Nottinghamshire, iv. 852.

'Sovereign of the Seas, The' (ship), iv. 496.

Sowerby, E. Millicent, 'Bibliographical Notes: A Pleasant Comedie, called *The Two merry milkmaids*', *Papers of the Bibliographical Society of America*, xxxiv (1940), iii. 101.

Sowerman, Esther (pseudonym), v. 1417.

Soyles, William, ii. 578.

Spaemann, Hermann, ed., *Aston Cokain's Dramen* (1923), iii. 168.

Spain, i. 9; iv. 530, 588, 641, 643, 798, 870-9; v. 1000, 1249; vi. 291 n. 1, 294; vii. 47, 49, 54.

King of, iv. 894; vii. 48.

Play against, i. 15.

Prince Charles's trip to, iv. 662.

Return of Prince Charles from, iv. 540.

Spalatro, Archbishop of, iv. 630, 664, 666, 871, 872, 877, 878; v. 982.

Spaniards, iv. 496; v. 1006; vi. 287, 288.

Spanish ambassador, i. 2, 9, 10, 140; iii. 200, 290; iv. 529, 530, 641, 643, 656, 660, 661, 670, 673, 677, 842, 843, 872; vi. 153, 184, 257, 263; vii. 39, 47, 52.

Steward of, vi. 287.

Spanish Armada, defeat of, iii. 93; v. 1319.

Spanish Bawd, The, see Mabbe, James, translator.

Spanish comedies, iii. 203.

Spanish company, vii. 94, 100.

Spanish Contract, The, see Anonymous.

Spanish Curate, The, see Fletcher, John.

Spanish Duke of Lerma, The, see Shirley, Henry; *see also* Ford, John.

Spanish Fig, The, see Anonymous.

Spanish fleet in the Downs, iii. 150.

Spanish Gypsy, The, see Middleton, Thomas; *see also* Ford, John.

Spanish history, v. 1020.

Spanish Lady, The, see Anonymous.

Spanish Lovers, The, see Davenant, William, *The Distresses*.

Spanish marriage, i. 9; iv. 644, 659, 662; v. 1329.

Spanish match, negotiations for, vi. 85.

Spanish players, ii. 515.
Spanish Preferment, The, see Anonymous.
Spanish Puecas, The, see Anonymous.
Spanish Purchase, The, see Anonymous.
Spanish Tragedy, The, see Kyd, Thomas.
Spanish Tragedy of Petrus Crudelis, A, see Anonymous.
Spanish, translations from, iii. 325, 331, 350, 366, 367, 379, 390, 392-3, 410, 420, 431, 727, 895.
Spanish Viceroy, The, see Anonymous.
Sparagus Garden, The, see Brome, Richard.
[Sparke, Michael], *The Narrative History of King James, for the First Fourteen Years* (1651), iv. 902.
Sparkes, Thomas, i. 143, 144; ii. 578; vi. 157.
Sparrow, Mr., iv. 601.
Sparrow, Thomas, v. 1179-81.
Confessor, utinam feliciter nata comœdia, v. 1180-1.
Spartan Ladies, The, see Carlell, Lodowick.
Speckart, Mr., i. 184; vi. 60.
Spectacles, iii. 109; vi. 298.
Spectators on the stage, i. 166-7, *see also* Stage, sitting on.
Speeches at Prince Henry's Barriers, see Jonson, Ben.
Speed, John, v. 1034, 1181-4.
Converted Robber (Stonehenge?) The, v. 1181-4.
Stonehenge, v. 1405, 1445.
Speed, Samuel, iv. 839.
Speght, Rachel (pseudonym), v. 1417.
Speirs, W. L., 'Autograph Plan by Wren, An', *London Topographical Record*, ii (1903), vi. 268.
'Explanation of the Plan of Whitehall, An', *London Topographical Record*, vii (1912), vi. 268.
Spencer, Benjamin Townley, ed., *The Bondman: An Antient Storie by Philip Massinger* (1932), iv. 765, 768, 769, 770.
'Philip Massinger', *Seventeenth Century Studies*, ed. Robert Shafer (1933), iv. 750.
Spencer, Gabriel, i. 135; iv. 606, 607, 608.

Spencer, Hazleton, 'D'Avenant's Macbeth and Shakespeare's, *P.M.L.A.* xl (1925), iii. 209.
Spencer, John, ii. 578.
Spencer, Mary, i. 41.
Spencer, Nicholas, ii. 578-9.
Spencer, Sir William, ii. 480, 618.
Spender, Constance, 'The Plays of Thomas Dekker', *The Contemporary Review*, cxxx (1926), iii. 241.
Spense, Master, *Bellum Grammaticale*, iii. 258; vii. 92, 100.
Spenser, Benjamin, *Vox Civitatis*, (1625), iii. 460.
Spenser, Edmund, iii. 173; iv. 711; v. 1184, 1211.
Influence of, v. 1184.
Speroni, Sperone, *Canace è Macareo* (1546), iii. 464.
Spidell, John, iv. 716.
Spight, Mr., iii. 238.
Spiller, Lady, v. 1267.
Spiller, Sir Henry, v. 1267; vi. 27, 28.
Spina, La, see Salviati, Lionardo.
Spinola, v. 973.
Spinola, Charles, v. 1392.
Spiritual Spicerie, A, see Brathwait, Richard.
Spittle, *see* London, streets of.
Spittle sermon, iv. 499.
Spittlegate, *see* London, streets and districts of.
Spitty, Susan, v. 1269.
Sportive Wit (1656), *see* Phillips, John.
Sprague, A. C., *Beaumont and Fletcher on the Restoration Stage* (1926), iii. 305, 313, 315, 319, 323, 330, 332, 347, 349, 350, 354, 373, 376, 380, 387, 391, 392, 394, 396, 397, 401, 407, 408, 410, 412, 414, 422, 425, 430.
Sprat, Thomas, 'An Account of the Life and Writings of Mr. Abraham Cowley', in *The Works of Mr. Abraham Cowley* (1668), iii. 172, 174.
Spread Eagle Inn, ii. 635.
Sprigg, Joshua, *Anglia Rediviva* (1647), ii. 549.
Spring-Rice, S. E., v. 1250.
Spring's Glory, The, see Nabbes, Thomas.
Spurius, see Heylyn, Peter.
Squibs, i. 30 n. 6 cont.
Squibs on stage, vi. 193.
Squier, John, ii. 553; v. 1034, 1185.

Squire, John, *Tes Irenes Trophœa, or The Triumphs of Peace*, v. 1185.
Stable at Hope theatre, vi. 201, 203, 205.
Stables, vi. 88, 89, 215, 216.
Royal, vi. 294.
Staffeild *or* Staffield, George, *see* Stutville, George.
Stafford, Alexander, ii. 597.
Stafford, Anthony, v. 985.
Stafford, John, iv. 877.
Stafford, Simon, vi. 179 n. 1.
Stafford, William of Blatherwick, v. 967, 976.
Stafford, Captain William, v. 967.
Stafford, Staffordshire, i. 213; ii. 585.
Staffordshire, iii. 142.
Stage balconies, *see* Theatres.
Stage Condemned, The, see Redpath, George.
Stage directions, iii. 130, 201; iv. 502, 506, 510, 515, 547, 565, 568, 574 693, 697, 727, 931, 934, 939; v. 1002, 1009, 1031, 1183, 1191–2, 1213, 1215, 1262, 1298, 1345, 1382, 1439, 1451; vi. 10, 108, 188.
Anticipatory, iii. 267, 323, 373, 380; iv. 484, 773; v. 1318.
Stage doors, *see* Theatres.
Stage effects, v. 1191–2, 1411.
Stage façade, *see* Theatres.
Stage galleries, *see* Theatres.
Stage houses, *see* Theatres.
Stage-Players' Complaint, The, see Anonymous.
Stagekeepers, *see* Theatres, stage-keepers at.
Stainer, Charles Lewis, *Jonson and Drummond, Their Conversations, A Few Remarks on an 18th Century Forgery* (1925), iv. 605.
Stalbridge, Dorset, iii. 33.
Standish, Lancashire, iii. 152.
Stanhope, Lady Katherine, iv. 776.
Stanhope, Philip, *see* Chesterfield, Earl of.
Stanley, Sir Thomas, i. 335; iii. 49, 71, 72; v. 1000, 1054, 1070, 1083, 1185–6, 1320.
Stanley, Venetia, v. 1164.
Stanly, Isabell, ii. 651.
Stanmer, Sussex, iv. 514.
Stanton, Suffolk, ii. 484.
Staple of News, The, see Jonson, Ben.
Staples, vi. 280.
Stapleton, Harry, iii. 296.
Stapleton, Sir Robert, v. 1186.

Pastor Stapilton, v. 1187.
Royal Choice, The, v. 1187, 1445.
Star Chamber, i. 47, 65 n. 2, 208, 317 n. 1; iii. 300; iv. 472–3, 919; v. 1156, 1266; vi. 6, 34, 260.
Court of the, *see* Court of the Star Chamber.
Starch commission, iii. 468.
Starck, Taylor, 'The German Dialogue in Alphonsus, Emperor of Germany and the Question of Authorship', *Harvard Studies and Notes in Phil. and Lit.*, xv (1933), v. 1286, 1287, 1288.
Starkey, John, stationer, iii. 118.
State (i.e. throne, etc.), vi. 263.
State Papers, see Calendar of State Papers.
States-General, iv. 696.
Stationers, i. 143; ii. 481, 545; iv. 946, 957.
Stationers' Company, i. 65, 328; ii. 504.
Court of, iii. 198.
Wardens of, vi. 69.
Stationers' Hall, iv. 523, 544; vi. 179 n. 1.
Stationers' Register, iii, iv, v, *passim*; vi. 85, 103 n. 1, 133, 135, 152, 169, 213, 216 n. 2, 223.
Statius, iv. 833.
Statue, The, see Sheil, Richard, *Evadne*.
Statuta, of the order of the Knights of St. John, iii. 354.
Staughton, E., ii. 520.
Steadwel, Richard, Esq., iv. 773.
Steel and Iron Triumphing, see Munday, Anthony, *Siderothriambos*.
Steele, Mary Susan, *Plays and Masques at Court during the Regions of Elizabeth, James and Charles* (1926), iv. 909; vii. 66.
Steeling, Thomas, v. 1358.
Steible, Daniel J., *A Critical Edition of William Davenant's The Temple of Love and The Platonic Lovers*. Unpublished thesis, University of Cincinnati (1939), iii. 211, 216.
Stephens, Mr., ii. 479.
Stephens, J., v. 1243.
Stephens, John, vi. 45.
'Character of a Common Player', vii. 2.
Essayes and Characters (1615), vii. 2.

Sterry, Sir Wasey, *The Eton College Register 1441–1698* (1943), iv. 951.

Stettin-Pomerania, Philip Julius, duke of, vi. 32 n. 1.

Stevens, —, ii. 520.

Stevens, David Harrison, 'The Bridgewater Manuscript of *Comus*', *Mod. Phil.* xxiv (1927), iv. 914, 916.

'The Stage Versions of *Comus*', in *Milton Papers* (1927), pp. 21–34, iv. 914.

Milton Papers (1927), iv. 914.

Stevens, William, ii. 438.

Stevenson, Allan H., 'James Shirley and the Actors at the First Irish Theater', *Mod. Phil.* xl (1942), iv. 678, 679, 949, 950; v. 1065, 1069, 1131, 1139, 1140.

'New Uses of Watermarks as Bibliographical Evidence', *Papers of the Bibliographical Society, Univ. of Virginia*, i. (1948), v. 1065.

'Shirley's Dedications and the Date of His Return to England' *M.L.N.* lxi (1946), v. 1065, 1069, 1113, 1132, 1134.

'Shirley's Publishers: The Partnership of Crooke and Cooke', *Library*, Fourth Series, xxv (1944–5), v. 1065, 1069–70, 1074, 1077, 1078, 1135, 1136, 1140, 1170.

'Shirley's Years in Ireland', *R.E.S.* xx (1944), v. 1065, 1069, 1070, 1134.

Stevenson, Mathew, *Occasions Off-Spring, or Poems upon Severall Occasions* (1645), iv. 832.

Stevenson, W. H., of St. John's, Oxford, iii. 29.

Steward, Robert, ii. 453.

Steward of the Household, vi. 260.

Stewards, Essex, iv. 955.

Stewart, Sir Francis, iv. 588.

Stiefel, A. L., 'Die Nachahmung spanischer Komoedien in England unter den ersten Stuarts', *Archiv*, xcix (1897), iii. 364, 366.

'Die Nachahmung spanischer Komödien in England unter den ersten Stuarts', *Romanische Forschungen*, v (1890), v. 1110, 1121, 1168, 1169, 1135, 1139, 1141, 1164.

'Über die Quelle von J. Fletchers' "Island Princess" ', *Archiv*, ciii (1899), 277–308, iii. 347, 350.

Stirling, Earl of, *see* Alexander, William.

Stochholm, Johanne M., ed., Massinger, *The Great Duke of Florence* (1933), iv. 786, 787, 788.

Sttockfish, Hans, ii. 579.

Socks, vii. 14.

Stockwell, 'Carrus', actor, iv. 596.

Stockwell, La Tourette, *Dublin Theatres and Theatre Customs, 1637–1820* (1938), iii. 35, 97; iv. 949, 950; v. 1069, 1143.

Stoddard, Sir Nicholas, i. 140.

Stoicus Vapulans, see Anonymous.

Stoke Hammond, iv. 525.

Stolen Heiress, The, see Centlivre, Susannah.

Stoll, E. E., v. 1246, 1249.

'The Influence of Jonson on Dekker', *M.L.N.* xxi (1906), iii. 241.

'On the Dates of Some of Chapman's Plays', *M.L.N.* xx (1905), iv. 489.

John Webster: The Periods of His Work as Determined by His Relations to the Drama of His Day (1905), iii. 337, 356, 358; iv. 489, 805, 807.

Stone, Mr., v. 1408.

Stone, Phillip, vi. 217.

Stone and brick, construction limited to, vi. 297, 299.

Stone construction, vi. 306.

Stonehenge, see Speed, John, *The Converted Robber.*

Stonehenge, v. 1445.

As setting, v. 1182, 1183.

Stonehouse, Mr., iv. 551.

Stoner, William, ii. 404.

Stonex, A. B., 'The Sources of Jonson's *The Staple of News*', *P.M.L.A.* xxx (1915), iv. 629.

Stonyhurst College, Lancashire, v. 1414.

Manuscripts, iii. 160, 161; v. 1173, 1174, 1290, 1405, 1406, 1414–15.

Stonyhurst Pageants, see Anonymous.

Stopes, C. C., *Burbage and Shakespeare's Stage* (1913), ii. 394, 396; vii. 2.

Stork, Charles Wharton, ed., *William Rowley, His All's Lost by Lust, and A Shoemaker a Gentleman, with an Introduction on Rowley's Place in the Drama* (1910), iii. 356, 358; iv. 807, 883, 890; v. 1015, 1018, 1020.

Storm, The, see Fletcher, *The Sea Voyage.*
Stourbridge Fair, vi. 233.
Stow, John, *Annales,* 1631 (for MS. notes in a copy of this work, *see* Folger Shakespeare Library, MS. 11613), v. 1244; vi. 41–42, 55, 114, 154, 177, 179 n. 1, 181, 182, 183, 200, 208 n.1, 212, 214, 255; vii. 20, 23, 24, 36, 39, 58, 60, 67, 68, 69, 70, 74, 75.
Survey of London (1598), vi. 268.
Stoye, Max, *Das Verhaltnis von Cibbers Tragoedie Caesar in Egypt zu Fletchers The False One* (1897), iii. 340.
'The Whereabouts of Thomas Killigrew 1639–41', *R.E.S.* xxv (1949), iv. 694, 695, 701, 703.
Str—, Robert, ii. **579.**
Strabo, *Geographica,* iv. 834.
Strafford, Thomas Wentworth, first Earl of, i. 58; v. 1141,1200; vi. 4, 16, 34, 37, 69.
beheading of, iv. 685; v. 1266.
Strafford, William Wentworth, second Earl of, v. 1100.
Strafforde's Letters, see Knowler, William, ed., *The Earl of Strafforde's Letters and Dispatches,* 2 vols. (1739).
Strand, *see* London, streets of.
Strange, Lord, v. 1041.
Company of, i. 1, 135; ii. 466, 496, 518; vii. 1.
Strange, William, vi. 189.
Strange company, a, v. 1177–8.
Strange Discovery, The, see Gough, John.
Strangers, Company of, iii. 240, 273.
Strangwick, Sir John, i. 47; vi. 34.
Stratford, Judith, ii. 580.
Stratford, Mary, ii. 580.
Stratford, Robert, i. 307, 308, 321; ii. **579;** iv. 885.
Stratford, William, i. 136, 138, 145, 147, 148, 152, 153, 155, 263; ii. **579–80,** 682, 683; vi. 150, 157, 158.
Stratford, prebendary of, iii. 183.
Stratford-on-Avon, i. 92; ii. 463, 464, 484, 618.
Shakespeare Memorial Theatre, vi. 6.
Stratton, Clarence, 'The Cenci Story in Literature and in Fact', *Studies in English Drama,* ed., Allison Gaw (1917), iv. 821, 822.
Street cleaning, v. 1156; vi. 82.

Street, Andrew, ii. 400.
Streete, Peter, vi. 139, 140, 141–4, 145 n. 2, 190.
Streets, paving of, i. 228 n. 1.
Stretch, John, i. 286, 297; ii. 580.
Strode, William, iii. 384; iv. 843; v. 1036, **1187–95.**
Floating Island (Passions Calmed, Prudentius), The, iii. 135; iv. 849; v. 1189, 1262, 1263; vi. 122.
Stroud, Theodore A., 'Ben Jonson and Father Thomas Wright', *E.L.H.* xiv (1947), iv. 608.
Strowd, Thomas, i. 322.
Strube, Hans, *S. Centlivre's Lustpiel 'The Stolen Heiress' und sein Verhältnis zu 'The Heir' von Thomas May. Nebst Anhang: May und Shakespeare* (1900), iv. 835, 836, 837.
Struble, Mildred Clara, ed., *A Critical Edition of Ford's Perkin Warbeck* (1926), iii. 454, 455.
'The Indebtedness of Ford's "Perkin Warbeck" to Gainsford', *Anglia,* xlix (1925), 80–91, iii. 454, 455.
Structure, peculiar, v. 1362.
Structy, Mr., iv. 601.
Stuart, Arabella, iii. 390.
Stuart Masques and the Renaissance Stage (1938), *see* Nicoll, Allardyce.
Stubbe, Edmund, v. 1195–7.
Fraus Honesta, iv. 528; v. 1195, **1196–7,** 1298.
Stubbe, Francis, v. 1195.
Students Admitted to the Inner Temple, see Cooke, W. H.
Students at Theatres, iii. 39.
'Study of the Blackfriars Theatre, 1608–42, A', *see* McCabe, John.
'Study of the Phoenix Theatre in Drury Lane, 1617–38, A', *see* Markward, William B.
'Study of the Salisbury Court Theatre, A', *see* Bordinat, Philip.
Stukeley, Sir Lewis, iii. 341.
Sturgis, vi. 78.
Stutfield, George, *see* Stutville, George.
Stutville, George, i. 246, 285, 286 and n. 1, 287, 288, 289 and n. 1, 290, 291 n. 1, 297, 303, 308, 321, 323, 324, 326 n. 6, 327 nn. 1, 2, and 4, 332, 333 and n. 1, 336; ii. **580–1;** v. 1217; vii. 74, 100.

Stutville, Sir Martin, i. 20, 129, 253, 266; ii. 657 n. 4; iii. 161; iv. 529, 610, 646, 647; v. 1197, 1232; vii. 66.

Styles, Dorothy, ii. 582, 583.

Styles, John, ii. 583.

Styles, Lanslet, ii. 583.

Styles, William, i. 49 n. 2 cont., 73–89; ii. 582–3.

Styles, William, junior, ii. 582.

Stylo recitativo, iv. 651.

Substantive theatre masque, vii. 6, 7.

Suburbs, western, *see* London, streets and districts.

Suckling, Alfred, *Selections from the Works of Sir John Suckling* (1836), v. 1198, 1199, 1200, 1201.

Suckling, Sir John, i. 42 and n. 3, 58, 243, 335; iii. 21, 22, 24, 25, 35, 62–63, 105, 150, 194, 195, 223, 435; iv. 499, 737, 738, 928, 934; v. 1034, 1197–1214, 1233; vi. 34.

Aglaura, i. 57–58, 58–60, 63, 99 and n. x, 131, 243 nn. 1 and 2; iii. 25, 63, 221, 313, 317; iv. 532, 699, 849, 934; v. 1106, 1199, 1201–7; vi. 37–38.

Brennoralt, or the Discontented Colonel, i. 66, 131; v. 1207–9.

Copy of a Letter Found in the Privy Lodgings at Whitehall, A (1641), v. 1200.

Fragmenta Aurea. A Collection of all The Incomparable Peeces, Written by Sir John Svckling. And published by a Friend to perpetuate his memory. Printed by his owne Copies (1646, 1648, 1658, 1672?), iii. 21; v. 1029, 1200, 1201, 1203, 1208, 1210, 1213; vi. 4.

Francelia, v. 1210.

Goblins, The, i. 66, 131–2; ii. 461; iv. 704, 840; v. 1210–12.

Last Remains of Sr John Suckling. Being a Full Collection of all his Poems and Letters which have been so long expected, and never till now Published. With License and Approbation of his Noble and Dearest Friends, The (1659, 1672?, 1676), v. 1201, 1212, 1213, 1214.

Letter Sent By Sir John Suckling from France, deploring his said Estate and flight, A, v. 1202–3.

Letters, &c. Published by His Friends (from his own Copies) to perpetuate his Memory (1676), v. 1201.

Masque at Witten, The, v. 1212–13.

Roaring Boys, see Anonymous, *The Sucklington Faction*.

Sad One, The, v. 1213–14.

'Sessions of the Poets, A', iii. 21; iv. 920; v. 1029, 1199, 1213–14.

'Upon Sir John Laurence's bringing Water over the hills to my L. Middlesex his House at Witten', v. 1213.

Works of Sir John Suckling, containing All his Poems, Love-Verses, Songs, Letters, and his Tragedies and Comedies. Never before Printed in One Volume, The (1696, 1709, 1719, 1770), v. 1201, 1208, 1211.

Suckling, Sir John, Master of Requests, father of poet, v. 1198.

Suckling, Martha Cranfield, v. 1198.

Sucklington Faction, see Anonymous.

Suell, Thomas, ii. 583.

Suetonius, iv. 717, 838; v. 1001, 1003.

Divus Augustus, iv. 834.

Lives of the Twelve Caesars, The, iv. 817.

Suffield, Norfolk, iii. 151.

Suffolk, Countess of, iv. 620.

Suffolk, Duchess of, iii. 285.

Suffolk, Earl of, iv. 529.

Suffolk, iii. 310.

Sullivan, Frank, ed., *Thomas Middleton's The Witch*. Unpublished Thesis, Yale University (1940), iv. 903, 904, 905.

Sullivan, Mary, *Court Masques of James I* (1913), iv. 660, 669, 670, 671, 675; v. 1288, 1372.

Summer performances, income from i. 24.

Summer and winter theatres, i. 3 n. 7.

Summers, Augustus Montague, ed., *Covent Garden Drollery* (1927), iii. 332, 392.

John Downs's Roscius Anglicanus 1708 (1928), *see* Downes, John.

The Playhouse of Pepys (1935), iii. 8, 118, 119, 170, 171, 175, 193, 197, 201, 202, 203, 205, 209, 220, 222; iv. 514, 694, 942, 946; v. 1170, 1186, 1265, 1266, 1429.

Summers, Augustus (*cont.*)
  Restoration Comedies (1921), iv.
    701, 704, 705.
  'Restoration Prompt-Book, A',
    T.L.S. 24 June 1920, v. 1147,
    1149.
  Restoration Theatre, The (1934),
    v. 986, 1149.
Sumner, Elizabeth, ii. 583.
Sumner, John, i. 220, 221, 231, 237,
  238, 246; ii. 583–4; iv. 813; vi. 67,
  103.
Sumner, Mary, ii. 583.
Sumpner, John, *see* Sumner, John.
Sun in Aries, The, see Middleton,
  Thomas.
Sun's Darling, The, see Ford, John.
Sunday performances, iii. 213; vii.
  10–15.
Suppers, vii. 22, 27, 29, 31, 64, 72,
  102.
Supposed Inconstancy, The, see
  Anonymous.
Suppression of the theatre, petition
  for, i. 31, 64.
Surgeon (*see also* Barber-chirurgion,
  Doctor, and Physician), i. 139,
  265; ii. 453, 617.
Surgeon's bills, vi. 220.
Surrey, County of, i. 21; iv. 856; vi.
  20, 200, 230, 248.
Surrey, Sheriffs of, iii. 275; vi. 176,
  214.
Survey of London, London County
  Council, *see* Braines, W. W.
Survey of London (1598), *see* Stow,
  John.
Surveyor, Royal, iii. 199.
Surveyor of the Works, iii. 276; vi.
  260, 267, 272, 274, 285, 286, 287.
Susanna's Tears, see Anonymous.
Susenbrotus, see Chappell, John.
Sussex, iv. 830.
Sutlin, Sir John, *see* Suckling, Sir
  John.
Sutorians, vi. 234.
Sutors Hill, iii. 162.
Sutton, —, ii. 435.
Sutton, Sussex, iii. 186.
Sutton-Coldfield, Warwickshire, iii.
  99.
Swaen, A. E. H., ed., *Anthony
  Brewer's The Lovesick King*
  (1907), iii. 43.
  'The Date of Brewer's "Love-Sick
    King" ' *M.L.R.* iv (1908), iii.
    43.
  'Robert Daborne's Plays', *Anglia*,
    xxi (1899), iii. 191, 192.

'Two Notes on Jonson's *Tale of a
  Tub*', *Neophilologus*, vii (1922),
  iv. 632.
Swaggering Damsel, see Chamberlain
  Robert.
Swainstone, —, *see* Swanston, Eyl-
  laerdt.
Swallow, Richard, ii. 400.
Swan theatre, i. 176; iv. 747, 910;
  vi. 15, 123, 128, 184 n. 2, 190,
  201, 212, 247, 248, 249–52.
  Drawing of, vi. 192.
'Swan Theatre and the Earl of
  Pembroke's Men, The', *see* Wal-
  lace, Charles W.
Swanstead *or* Swansted *or* Swan-
  strid, *see* Swanston, Eyllaerdt.
Swanston, Alice, ii. 585.
Swanston, Benjamin, ii. 586.
Swanston, Elizabeth, ii. 585, 587,
  648.
Swanston, Eyllaerdt, i. 4 n. 2, 14,
  16, 17, 26 n. 5, 35 n. 1, 37, 43,
  46, 57, 60, 61, 69 n. 2, 73–89, 90,
  97 nn. n and o, 99 nn. u, x, z,
  and aa, 100 n. bb, 183, 187,
  192, 219, 318; ii. 584–8; iii. 301,
  311; iv. 764, 810, 817; v. 1412;
  vi. 32, 36, 59, 172, 181, 185.
  Will of, ii. 648.
Swanston, Francis, ii. 586.
Swanston, Hanna, ii. 586.
Swanston, Hilliard, iii. 428.
Swanston, John, ii. 585.
Swanston, Stephen, ii. 587.
Swantton *or* Swautted, *see* Swan-
  ston, Eyllaerdt.
Swartsenbuk, Count, Ambassador
  from the Emperor, vii. 36.
Swayne, Martin, ii. 536, 588.
Sweden, iv. 851.
Sweete, Robert, vi. 239.
Sweeting, John, stationer, iii. 43,
  191, 192; v. 1008.
Sweetman, Ellen, ii. 477, 645.
Sweetman, John, ii. 476, 477, 645.
Swetherton, Thomas, *see* Swin-
  nerton, Thomas.
Swetnam, Joseph, iv. 498.
  *Arraignment of Lewd, Idle,
    Froward, and Unconstant
    Women* (1615), v. 1417.
  *School of the Noble and Worthy
    Science of Defence* (1617), v.
    1417.
*Swetnam the Woman-Hater Arraigned
  by Women, see* Anonymous.
Swinarton, Abell, i. 189, 192; ii. 588.
Swinburne, A. C., iii. 272.

Contemporaries of Shakespeare (1919), iii. 227, 234; iv. 927.

George Chapman, A Critical Essay (1875), iv. 489.

'James Shirley', *The Fortnightly Review*, N.S. xlvii (1890), v. 1065, 1108.

'Thomas Nabbes', in *Contemporaries of Shakespeare* (1919), iv. 927.

Swinhoe, Gilbert, v. 1214–15.

The Tragedy of the Unhappy Fair Irene, v. 1214–15.

Swinhowe, George, stationer, iii. 18, 102, 263; iv. 734, 907.

Swinnerton, Thomas, i. 158, 160, 165, 171 and n. b, 172 n. 1, 178; ii. 588–9; vi. 130, 216, 217.

Swisser, The, see Wilson, Arthur.

Swords, vi. 168, 242, 256, 293, 294, 296.

Swynerton, Thomas, *see* Swinnerton, Thomas.

Swynnerton, Daniel, ii. 589.

Sydnam, Sir John, vi. 49.

Sykes, H. Dugdale, iii. 400; v. 1010, 1245, 1246, 1247, 1252.

'Authorship of "The Witch of Edmonton", The', *N. & Q.* 151 (18 and 25 December 1926), iii. 270, 272.

'Elizabethan and Jacobean Plays: Suggested Textual Emendations', *N. & Q.*, Twelfth Series, iii (1917), iv. 815.

'Glapthorne's Play: "The Lady Mother" ', *N. & Q.*, Thirteenth Series, i (1923), iv. 484.

'John Ford, the Author of "The Spanish Gipsy" ', *M.L.R.* xix (1924), iii. 459; iv. 893.

'Massinger and Dekker's "The Virgin Martyr" ', *N. & Q.*, Twelfth Series, x (1922), iii. 263, 266.

'Massinger and "The Sea Voyage" ', *N. & Q.*, Twelfth Series, xi (1922), iii. 412.

'Nathaniel Field's Work in the "Beaumont and Fletcher" Plays', *Sidelights on Elizabethan Drama* (1924), iii. 299.

'Peele's Authorship of "Alphonsus Emperor of Germany" ', *N.&Q.*, Twelfth Series, ii. (1916), v. 1286.

' "Revenge for Honour": Glapthorne's Play Attributed to Chapman', *N. & Q.*, Thirteenth Series, i (1916), iv. 489, 490.

Sidelights on Elizabethan Drama (1924), iii. 337, 457; iv. 893; v. 1246.

'Source of Massinger's "Parliament of Love", A', *N. & Q.*, Eleventh Series, x (1914), iv. 805, 807.

'Thomas Middleton's Early Non-Dramatic Work', *N. & Q.* cxlviii (1925), iv. 856.

'Webster–Massinger Play "The Fair Maid of the Inn", A', *N. & Q.*, Eleventh Series, xii (1915), iii. 337.

'Webster–Middleton Play: "Anything for a Quiet Life", A', in *Sidelights on Elizabethan Drama* (1924), iv. 859, 860.

'Webster's Share in "A Cure for a Cuckold" ', *N. & Q.*, Eleventh Series, ix (1914), v. 1249.

Sylveira, v. 1344.

Sylvester, Edward, grammar master, iii. 193.

Symes, —, ii. 504.

Symonds, Mr. and his man, iv. 601.

Symonds, E. M., 'The Diary of John Greene (1635–57)', *English Historical Review*, xliii (1928), i. 110, 114, 123, 128, 132, 235, 250, 255, 258; iii. 332, 408; iv. 691, 862; v. 1125, 1272, 1425; vii. 9, 96, 98.

Symonds, J. A., ed., *The Dramatic Works and Lyrics of Ben Jonson, Selected* (1886), iv. 613.

Synsburye, John, a carpenter, vi. 272, 274, 275.

Syphilis, iii. 194.

Syrgiannes, tragoedia, see Anonymous.

T., A., iv. 545.

T., F., verses by, iii. 83.

T., R., actor, i. 72–88; ii. 589; iii. 416.

T., Walter, v. 1311.

Tableau, iii. 130; v. 1192.

Tabley House, Knutsford, Cheshire, iv. 505.

Tacitus, iii. 50; iv. 817; v. 1001, 1003.

Annales, iv. 838.

Taffeta, vi. 280.

Tailor, Joseph, *see* Taylor, Joseph.

Tailor, Robert (*see also* Taylor), *The Hog Hath Lost His Pearl*, i. 207 n. 4.

Tailors, ii. 413, 446, 455, 486, 491, 688; iii. 194, 310.

Talbert, E. W., 'Current Scholarly Works and the "Erudition" of Jonson's *Masque of Augurs*', *Stud. Phil.* xliv (1947), iv. 655, 657.
Talbot, Sir Gilbert, iv. 728.
Tale of Jocundo and Astolpho, The, see Dekker, Thomas.
Tale of Robin Hood, A, see Jonson's *Sad Shepherd.*
Tale of a Tub, A, see Jonson, Ben.
Tamburlaine, see Marlowe, Christopher.
Tamer Cam, see Anonymous.
Tamer Tamed, The, see Beaumont and Fletcher, *The Woman's Prize.*
Taming of the Shrew, The, see Shakespeare.
Tancred and Ghismonda, see Anonymous, *Ghismonda.*
Tannenbaum, Samuel, A., iv. 604.
Beaumont and Fletcher, A Concise Bibliography (1938), iii. 305.
Ben Jonson, A Concise Bibliography (1938), iv. 605.
'Corrections to the Text of *Believe as You List*', *P.M.L.A.* xlii (1927), iv. 762.
'Hitherto Unpublished John Fletcher Autograph, A', *J.E.G.P.* xxviii (1929), iii. 307.
Thomas Dekker, A Concise Bibliography (1939), iii. 241.
John Ford, A Concise Bibliography (1941), iii. 434.
Thomas Heywood, A Concise Bibliography (1939), iv. 553.
Philip Massinger, A Concise Bibliography (1938), iv. 750.
Thomas Middleton, A Concise Bibliography (1940), iv. 856.
'A Middleton Forgery', *Phil. Quart.* xii (1933), iv. 870, 876.
Tannenbaum, Samuel A., and Dorothy R. Tannenbaum. *Supplement to Beaumont and Fletcher, A Concise Bibliography* (1946), iii. 305.
James Shirley, A Concise Bibliography (1946), v. 1065.
Supplement to a Bibliography of Thomas Dekker (1945), iii. 241.
Supplement to Ben Jonson, A Concise Bibliography (1947), iv. 606.
Thomas Randolph, A Concise Bibliography (1946), v. 965, 966.
Tannenbaum, S. A., and Hyder E.

Rollins, eds., *The Drinking Academy* (1930), v. 976, 977, 978, 979, 991.
Tanner, Mr., vi. 185 n. 2.
Taphouses, vi. 141, 180, 185–6.
Target fighting, i. 30 n. 6 cont. vi. 193.
Targets, vi. 172, 242.
Tarlton, Richard ('Tarltonian mirth'), v. 1035.
Tarras, see Theatres.
Tarring, Sussex, iii. 26.
Tartar, iii. 122.
Tasso, influence of, v. 1033.
Aminta, v. 970.
Translation of, v. 999; vii. 65.
Taste, popular, ii. 541.
Tate, Nahum, iii. 349, 350.
Cuckold's Haven, or, An Alderman No Conjurer, iv. 616.
Duke and No Duke, A, iii. 171.
Tatham, Amy, v. 1218.
Tatham, Dorothy, v. 1215.
Tatham, Joanna, v. 1218.
Tatham, John, iii. 460; iv. 928; v. 998, 1215–24.
Masque, A, v. 1222.
Verses by, iii. 52, 55, 72; v. 1216–17.
Aqua Triumphalis, v. 1219.
Character of the Rump, The (1660), v. 1218.
'Country-life, The (song), v. 1222.
Distracted State, iii. 226; v. 1029, 1218, 1219–20.
Fancies' Theatre, The (1640), i. 279, 315–16; ii. 444; iii. 9, 55, 153, 239; v. 968, 995, 998, 1216, 1221; vi. 169, 229.
Knavery in All Trades, i. 317–19; ii. 360, 376, 388, 406, 439, 440, 442, 505, 535, 576, 577, 588, 598, 627; v. 1220; vi. 172.
Londinium Triumphans, v. 1220.
London's Glory, Represented by Time, Truth, and Fame, v. 1220.
London's Triumph for Thomas Allen, v. 1220.
London's Triumph, Presented by Industry and Honour, v. 1220.
London's Triumphs for Richard Chiverton, v. 1221.
London's Triumphs for John Fredrick, v. 1221.
London's Triumphs for John Lawrence, v. 1221.
London's Triumph for John Robinson, v. 1220.

Love Crowns the End, v. 1216, 1221–2.

Mirrour of Fancies, The (1657), v. 1221.

Neptune's Address, v. 1223.

Ostella, or The Faction of Love and Beauty Reconcill'd (1650), v. 998, 1215, 1216, 1217, 1218, 1222, 1223, 1438.

'Poor Schollers Song, The', v. 1222.

'Prologue spoken at the Cock-pit, at the coming of the Red Bull Players thither, A', v. 1217.

'Prologue spoken at the *Red-Bull* to a Play called the Whisperer, or what you please, A', v. 1217.

'Prologue spoken upon removing of the late Fortune Players to the Bull, A', v. 1216–17.

Royal Oak, The, v. 1223.

Rump, or The Mirror of the Late Times, The, v. 1169, 1218, 1223.

Scots Figgaries, or A Knot of Knaves, The (1652), v. 1218, 1223.

'To my Mother, Mris. Dorothy Tatham . . .', v. 1215.

Whisperer, or What You Please, The, v. 1223–4.

'1 Song: Fortune Descending', v. 1222.

Tatterdell, Hughe, i. 272, 281; ii. 590.

Taubman, Matthew, iv. 680.

Tauerner, Edmund, *see* Taverner, Edmund.

Taurus (constellation), vi. 246.

Tavern scenes, iii. 187, 189.

Taverner, ii. 497.

Taverner, Edmund, iii. 217; iv. 637, 652; v. 1227, 1229; vii. 66.

Taverner, John, Corrector of the press, iii. 18.

Taverner, William, *The Artful Husband*, v. 1127.

Taverns, *see* Inns and taverns. On stage, vi. 53.

Tawier, William, *see* Tawyer, William.

Tawyer, William, i. 15, 73–89; ii. 590.

Taxors (Cambridge), v. 1027.

Taylor, —, ii. 590.

Taylors Revenge (1615), *see* Taylor, John.

Taylors Waterwork (1614), *see* Taylor, John.

Taylor, Ann, ii. 592, 593.

Taylor, Edward, ii. 598, 649.

Taylor, Elizabeth, ii. 592, 593.

Taylor, Hester, ii. 592.

Taylor, Jeremy, iv. 533.

Taylor, John, the Water Poet, iii. 443; iv. 852; v. 1224–5, 1348; vi. 182, 183, 203, 205–6, 207–8, 211, 212–13, 237, 245, 247; vii. 28.

Epigrams by, vi. 182 and n. 2.

All the Workes of Iohn Taylor the Water Poet (1630), iii. 251; iv. 851; v. 1347; vi. 206.

Bull, Beare, and Horse, Cut, Curtaile, and Longtaile (1638), vi. 203, 207, 211 n.

Cast over the Water . . . given gratis to W. Fennor, the Rimer from London to the King's Bench (1615), vi. 206 n. 1.

England's Comfort and London's Joy (1641), v. 1224.

Fennors Defence (1615), vi. 206 n. 1.

Great Britain All in Black (1612), v. 1017.

Nipping or Snipping of Abuses, The (1614), v. 1017; vi. 179 n. 1, 182 n. 2.

Old, Old, Very Old Man, The (1635), iii. 443.

Pennyles Pilgrimage, The (1618), iii. 251.

Pennyles Pilgrimage in *All the Works of John Taylor the Water Poet, The* (1630), v. 1347.

Praise of Hemp Seed (1620), ii. 557; v. 1017.

Sir Gregory Nonsense His News from Noplace (1622), v. 1447.

Taylor's Feast (1638), ii. 612.

Taylors Revenge (1615), vi. 206.

Taylors Waterwork (2nd ed., 1614), vi. 182.

Triumphs of Fame and Honour, The, v. 1224, 1225.

Wit and Mirth (1629), ii. 358, 436.

Taylor, John (not Water Poet), vi. 203.

Taylor, Jone, ii. 592.

Taylor, Joseph, i. 4 nn. 1 and 2, 7, 9, 14, 17, 20, 26 n. 5, 34, 35 n. 1, 37, 44, 53, 54, 55, 57, 60, 61, 69 n. 2, 72–88, 90, 97 nn. i, n, p, 99 nn. u, x, z, and aa, 100 n. bb, 104, 121, 123, 140, 164, 176, 177 and n. 2, 198, 199 and n. 2, 200 and n. 3, 203 and n. 1, 211, 318, 328; ii. 590–8, 621, 650, 682; iii. 311, 326,

Taylor, Joseph (*cont.*)
330, 341, 349, 355, 363, 379, 393, 396, 413, 420, 423, 426, 427, 428; iv. 503–4, 703, 704, 738, 764, 810, 816, 817, 881; v. 1016, 1075, 1076, 1238, 1252, 1412; vi. 17, 25, 26, 31, 32, 36, 69, 172, 194 n. 4, 245 n. 1.
Taylor, Joseph, junior, ii. 593, 596.
Taylor, Margaret, ii. 598.
Taylor, Margerie, ii. 648.
Taylor, Mary, ii. 474.
Taylor, Raphe, ii. 598, 649.
Taylor, Randolph, stationer, iii. 86; iv. 544.
Taylor, Robert (*see also* Tailor), ii. 592, 598.
Taylor, Roger, ii. 599.
Taylor, Samuel, ii. 593.
Taylor, Stage, ii. 598.
Taylor, Thomas, ii. 598–9, 683. Will of, ii. 648–9.
Taylor, William, v. 1054, 1225.
Taylor, Winifred, ii. 593.
Taylor vs. *Heminges*, i. 198.
Technogamia, *see* Holyday, Barton.
Telfer, Robert Stockdale, ed., Massinger's *The Unnatural Combat* (1932), iv. 821, 822, 823, 824.
Telltale, The, *see* Anonymous.
Tempe Restored, *see* Townshend, Aurelian.
Tempest, The, *see* Shakespeare.
Tempest, The, or The Enchanted Island, *see* Davenant, William.
Temple, Lady, v. 1404.
Temple of Love, The, *see* Davenant, William.
Tenison, Thomas, *Baconiana* (1679), iv. 526.
Tennant, George Bremner, ed., *The New Inn* (1908), iii. 79, 80, 366; iv. 622, 623, 624.
Tennant, Thomas, ii. 356.
Tennis courts at Whitehall Palace, *see* Whitehall.
Tent for players' use on progress, i. 310.
Teodor, Jacob, ii. 599.
Terence, v. 1238.
Andria and *The Eunuch*, transl. Thomas Newman (1627), iv. 946–7.
Tereus with a Pastoral, *see* A., M.
Term time, iii. 416; iv. 618, 759, 930–1; vi. 15.
Terra Australis Incognita, iii. 298.
Terry, John, v. 1255.
Terry, William, *see* Perry, William.

Tes Irenes Trophœa, or The Triumphs of Peace, *see* Squire, John.
Tewkesbury, Gloucestershire, iii. 126.
Texas, U. of, Library, v. 1094.
Texts, inaccurate, iii. 103.
Textual variants, iii. 12–13, 410; iv. 506, 545, 657, 672, 693, 698, 700, 702, 703, 709, 798, 810, 822, 869–70, 879, 886, 916, 920, 931; v. 972–3, 975, 1079, 1094, 1095–6, 1101–2, 1134, 1149, 1160, 1162, 1167, 1174, 1207, 1228, 1233, 1237, 1262, 1266, 1272, 1298, 1378, 1380–2, 1392, 1444.
Tey, John, v. 1219.
Tey, Paul, court messenger, ii. 683; vi. 157.
Thala, scene of a play, iii. 38.
Thaler, Alwin, 'Thomas Goffe's Praeludium', *M.L.N.* xxxvi (1921), iv. 501.
'Thomas Heywood, D'Avenant, and *The Siege of Rhodes*', *P.M.L.A.* xxxix (1924), iv. 571.
'Was Richard Brome an Actor?', *M.L.N.* xxxvi (1921), iii. 49.
Thalia, vi. 276.
Thame, Oxfordshire, ii. 484; iv. 736.
Thames, *see* London, streets of.
Thames river, vi. 115, 200, 224 n. 1. Frozen over, vii. 39.
Thavies Inn, iii. 93.
Theatre, The, i. 1, 135; iii. 408; v. 1091, 1208; vi. 129, 131, 135, 140, 250, 252.
Theatre of Apollo, The, *see* Beaumont, Sir John.
Theatre in Lincoln's Inn fields, v. 1091, 1145.
Theatre Royal in Bridges Street, The, iii. 25, 71, 82, 83, 146, 171, 197, 334, 348, 392, 412, 423; iv. 696; v. 1063, 1092, 1100, 1122.
Theatre Royal company, iii. 315; iv. 848.
Theatres, iv. 767; vi. 3–309.
See also Blackfriars, Cockpit in Court, Curtain, Fortune, Globe, Hope, Newington Butts, Phoenix, Red Bull, Rose, Rosseter's Puddle Wharf, Salisbury Court, Swan, Theatre, Whitefriars.
Accidents at, i. 166–7; vi. 99; vii. 9.
Admissions, iii. 462.
Advertising of, iii. 255.

Alterations of, vi. 222–4, 270–82.
Andirons, vi. 280.
Anecdotes about i. 318; ii. 440; iii. 187–8; iv. 693, 694–5; v. 1019, 1137, 1210–11, 1345–6, 1411; vi. 101–2 n., 172–3.
Annual fee for, ii. 370.
Appearance of, ii. 694.
Apse, vi. 276.
Arches, vi. 281 n. 1.
Architraves, vi. 262, 272, 274.
Arras in, iii. 50, 380; vi. 116.
Arsedine (assidue), stars of, vi. 273.
As clubs, vi. 125.
As schools, v. 76.
Attacks on, vi. 17–20, 21–22, 24–25, 27–30, 39, 54–56, 80, 81–82, 83, 84, 113, 167, 228.
Auditoriums, vi. 275.
Baize, green Manchester, vi. 279.
Balconies, side, v. 1246.
Balcony, vi. 275, 277; see also Theatres, galleries.
Bed, property, vi. 280.
Bellows, vi. 280.
Benches in, i. 26, 30 n. 6 cont., 225; ii. 691; iii. 103; vi. 171, 172 n., 193, 239, 246, 257, 275.
Bleachers, vi. 256.
Boxes (for theatre admission moneys), ii. 541, 558; vi. 41, 111, 129, 243.
Boxes in, i. 44, 48, 283 n. 7 cont.; ii. 597; iii. 200, 320, 385, 395, 403, 412; iv. 703, 706; v. 1210; vi. 4, 6, 7, 36, 43, 92, 102 n., 106, 111, 129, 176, 180, 192, 201, 231, 256, 257, 262, 275, 279, 280.
Key to, vi. 34.
Boxes looking down into the Cockpit playhouse, vi. 280, 283 n.
Brackets, vi. 272, 276.
Building of, i. 283 n. 7; iv. 949–50; vi. 5–7, 12 n. 2, 46, 48–54, 79, 89, 125, 139–45, 154–6, 180–4, 201–2, 259–64, 270–5, 285–6.
Estimates for, vi. 295.
Licences for, vi. 292–3, 299–300.
Licence revived, vi. 297–300.
Licence revoked, vi. 297.
Prohibited, vi. 299.
Burned, i. 2, 141; vi. 153, 154–5, 179, 181–2, 258.

Busts, vi. 276.
Calico, blue, vi. 278.
Candelabra, vi. 273, 278, 279.
Candle-light in, ii. 694; vi. 54, 106.
Candles, vi. 106, 279.
Candlesticks, vi. 278, 280.
Iron, vi. 273.
Canopies, vi. 257.
Canopy of crimson velvet, vi. 280, 281.
Capacity of, iv. 871–2.
Capitals, composita, vi. 271, 272, 274.
Corinthian, vi. 271, 274.
Corinth pilaster, vi. 271, 272, 273.
Caretakers of, ii. 432, 462, 485, 506, 544, 572.
Cartouches (cartoozes), vi. 262.
Carving in, vi. 142, 257, 261, 262, 271–3.
Chairs, vi. 273, 278, 280, 281.
Chimneys, vi. 280.
Closed, i. 21, 68.
In Lent, ii. 654 n. 2, vii. 1–9.
By plague, ii. 652–72.
Cloth, gold, vi. 257.
Green, vi. 257, 264.
Cloths, painted, vi. 278.
Clouds in, vi. 273.
Columns in, vi. 249 n. 1, 250, 256, 257, 262, 271, 272, 273, 274.
Columns, Doric, vi. 257.
Ionic, vi. 257.
Competition among, i. 225; vi. 291.
See also Plays in competition.
Concerts at, vi. 33 n.
Conduct at, ii. 693; iii. 37; iv. 719; v. 996; vi. 5–6, 8, 9, 10, 23, 24, 42–45, 169–70, 171, 226, 229.
Contests in, vi. 206, 221.
Contracts for, i. 143; vi. 140–5, 154, 190, 201, 203, 205, 262, 263.
Corbels, vi. 276.
Cornices, vi. 262, 272, 274, 276.
Cost of, i. 283 n. 7 cont.; vi. 143, 177, 182 and n. 3, 260, 286.
Cost of lights in, i. 44; ii. 687.
Couches, vi. 280.
Court theatres, vi. 255–88.
Curtained houses on stage, vi. 189.
Curtains in, vi. 116, 229, 257, 273, 278.
Dancing in, i. 136–7; ii. 523.
Degrees, vi. 256, 263, 272, 279, 280, 285.

Theatres (*cont.*)
    Demonstrations in, i. 25.
    Descents on stage, vi. 108.
    Described, vi. 257-8.
    Destroyed, iv. 881; vi. 41-42, 114,
        140, 171, 176, 177, 200, 208,
        214, 230, 239, 247-8, 252, 255,
        284, 288.
    Dinner at, i. 140.
    Discoveries on stage, vi. 192.
    Districts, vi. 140-1.
    Doorkeepers at, vi. 41, 151.
    Doors in, vi. 272, 274, 277, 279.
    Engines, vi. 284.
    Enlarged, vi. 95, 203-5.
    Entrances, iv. 934; vi. 155, 244.
    Evaluation of, vi. 27-28, 90.
    Exits, iv. 934.
    Expenses, i. 44; vi. 36, 105-6.
    Façades, vi. 276.
    Favourite, ii. 680.
    Fireplaces in, vi. 277, 280, 281.
    Fires in rooms of, ii. 687.
    Fire shovels, vi. 280.
    Flags on, vi. 132, 145, 213, 252.
    Flat below the stage, vi. 279.
    Flowers in, ii. 687; vi. 106.
    Fluting (architectural), vi. 273.
    Friezes, vi. 262, 272, 273.
    Frontispieces (architectural), vi.
        262.
    Fruit sold in, vi. 23, 42.
    Gallery over the stage, vi. 279.
    Gallery, upper, vi. 280, 283 n.
    Galleries, i. 44, 136, 199 n. 2, 202,
        318; iii. 179; vi. 36, 85, 125,
        126-7, 137, 142, 144, 147,
        171, 173, 180, 185, 190, 201,
        202, 208, 215, 216, 219, 230,
        249 n. 2, 256, 262, 263, 272,
        274, 277, 279, 280.
    Galleries, Receipts from, i. 44.
    Gardens by, vi. 216.
    Gates of, vi. 174, 217.
    Gatherers at, ii. 346, 558, 588,
        616, 622, 684; vi. 105, 113, 127,
        129, 150 and n. 1, 216.
    Gatherer's box in, *see* Boxes for
        admission moneys.
    Gatherers' places, ii. 558, 588, 616,
        622, 686.
    Gilding, vi. 262, 273, 278.
    Greek, vi. 270.
    Ground rents for, vi. 292.
    Groundlings, vi. 125.
    Hangings, vi. 280.
    Hatching, cross, vi. 276 n. 2.
    Heat in, vi. 106.
    'Heaven' in, vi. 127, 201.

    Hell, entrances from, vi. 190.
    Holiday audiences at, ii. 690-1.
    Horses in, v. 1122.
    Housekeepers, i. 2, 4, 23, 46, 234;
        ii. 351, 466, 500, 654 n. 2
        cont., 685; iii. 429; vi. 8,
        12 n. 1, 22, 36-37, 65, 93, 98,
        104, 105, 126, 127, 130, 149,
        180, 181, 182; vii. 5.
        Expenses of, i. 44.
        Receipts of, i. 44; ii. 686-7; vii.
            5.
        Shares, vi. 181, 185.
    Houses attached to, vi. 50, 150,
        159, 160, 161, 186, 204.
    Huts in, vi. 132, 185, 224 n.
        1.
    Incidents at, vi. 16, 23, 33-34, 54,
        129, 146, 147, 148, 151, 206,
        211, 220, 227-8, 239; vii. 14.
    Inscriptions, vi. 273, 275, 276 and
        n. 1.
    Ionic columns, vi. 257.
    Iron work, vi. 285.
    Lantern, vi. 280.
    Leases of, i. 30, 138-9, 143-4; vi.
        48-49, 64-65, 78, 87-91, 125-6,
        128-9, 149-50, 154, 156-7,
        179-80, 215, 216-17.
    Legends of the, vi. 113, 121.
    Licences for, vi. 46, 104 n. 1, 115,
        305-6.
        Revoked, vi. 308.
    Lights in, vi. 106, 257, 273, 278,
        279, 286, 287.
        Cost of, i. 44.
    Lobbies, vi. 275.
    Looking glasses, vi. 280.
    Lords' room in, vi. 144, 156 n.,
        191-2.
    Manager, house for, vi. 50, 298.
    Managers of, i. 147, 263-4, 279,
        286, 295; ii. 518; iii. 17, 197,
        254; iv. 516-17, 556, 696, 711;
        v. 1020, 1062, 1077, 1093,
        1355, 1399; vi. 67, 68, 69,
        70-71, 74, 91, 94, 100, 101,
        103-7, 158, 165, 166, 167,
        182 n. 3, 219, 222, 240, 305,
        309; vii. 5.
        Eighteenth-century, vi. 58.
        Restoration, vi. 58.
    Mansions on stage, vi. 191.
    Masques, iii. 459-61; vi. 6, 7.
    Matting, vi. 280 n. 1.
        Under the stage, vi. 280-1.
    Models of, vi. 6, 143-4, 260.
    Money box in, *see* Boxes for
        admission moneys.

Monopoly, iv. 696.
Mortgaged, vi. 75.
Mouldings, vi. 272, 274.
Music in, i. 136–7; vi. 36, 53.
  Cost of, i. 44.
Music rooms in, v. 1019; vi. 106, 144, 244.
Niches, vi. 272, 274, 276, 278.
Non-dramatic entertainment at, vii. 5, 6.
Northamptonshire stone, vi. 262.
Opening of, v. 987, 990, 1140, 1353–4; vi. 54, 68, 205, 270–2.
Order closing, ii. 690.
Outer doors of theatre, receipts from, i. 44 and n. 3.
Outhouses for, vi. 293.
Painting of, vi. 142, 144, 145 n. 2, 249 n. 1, 250, 262, 272, 273, 277–8.
Paintings in, vi. 266, 267, 273, 274, 278, 284, 285, 286, 287.
  Cost of, vi. 285.
Palladian style, vi. 276.
Pan, iron, vi. 280.
Patents for, ii. 421; iii. 195; vi. 19–20, 78–79, 81–82.
Patrons of, ii. 674; vi. 4, 12–17, 30.
Pediments, vi. 276.
Pendants, vi. 272, 274.
Petitioned against, i. 31–33; v. 1342.
Pictures of, v. 1004; vi. 186, 190, 202, 218, 224 n. 1, 249–50, 252.
Pilasters, vi. 262.
Pillars, see Columns.
Pit in, i. 30 n. 6 cont.; ii. 694; iv. 479, 503, 767, 943; v. 1145, 1211; vi. 54, 137, 156, 190, 224, 275, 276, 277, 279.
Pits, entrances from, vi. 190.
Plans for, vi. 255–6, 263, 272, 274, 275–7.
Plaster of Paris, vi. 272, 275.
Private, vi. 1–117, 238.
  Houses attached to, iv. 517; vi. 91, 92, 94.
Proclamations concerning, vii. 10.
Profits from, i. 43, 330; vi. 7, 36, 76, 93; vii. 11.
Projected, vi. 289–309.
Proscenium, vi. 274 and n. 1, 275, 276, 277, 278, 280.
  Arch, vi. 281 n. 1.
  Arched, vi. 281 n. 1.
  Flat, vi. 281 n. 1.
  Opening, vi. 282 n.
Prospectus, vi. 293–6.
Public, v. 1106–7; vi. 9 n., 121–252.

Pulleys, vi. 284.
Purbeck stone, vi. 262.
Quilts, vi. 280.
Raided, i. 278; ii. 695; iii. 402; iv. 698; vi. 76, 112–14, 129, 172 n., 174, 175, 176, 177, 230–8.
Railings, vi. 276.
Ranting in, ii. 690.
Receipts, iii. 324, 327–8, 395, 396, 426, 429; vi. 180 n. 4.
Remodelled, vi. 95, 125, 154–7.
Rent for, i. 138; vi. 28, 36, 48, 76, 88, 130, 157, 180, 183, 185–6.
Repairs of, ii. 686; vi. 91, 105.
Reputations of, ii. 693; v. 1442; vi. 4, 12–17, 39, 47, 59–61, 146–9, 238–47.
Resident managers of, vi. 50.
Rings, copper, vi. 273.
Riots at, vi. 160, 161–2, 219.
Roman, vi. 270.
Rooms in, ii. 686, 687; iv. 930, 941; vi. 92–93, 105, 110, 127, 142–3, 144.
Rooms, retiring, vi. 305.
Rooms, viewing, i. 283 n. 7 cont.
Royal visits to, iv. 582, 774; vi. 34–35.
Scaffolds, vi. 256.
Scenery in, see Scenery.
Sconces, vi. 279.
Seats in, vi. 176.
Sets, vi. 281 n. 1.
Shadow (i.e. cover) over stage, vi. 142, 144.
Shape of, iii. 60; vi. 50, 132, 141, 144, 155–6, 178, 185, 188, 190, 201 and n. 1, 202–3, 215, 216, 224 n. 1, 249, 252, 270, 277.
Shares in, i. 1, 2, 3–4, 303, 329–30; ii. 638, 644, 647, 651; iii. 175; iv. 540–1; v. 1049; vi. 64, 90, 130, 157, 158, 165, 179, 181, 217, 295; vii. 11.
  Prices of, iv. 540–1.
  Value of, vi. 70.
Signs, vi. 156, 178 n. 1, 250.
Size of, iv. 941; vi. 6, 53, 92–93, 141–2, 144, 183, 218, 250, 255–6, 260, 262, 275–7, 285–6, 306.
Smoking in, vi. 43, 44.
Stables, vi. 293, 298.
Stage, accidents on, i. 166–7; v. 1204.
  And scene erected, vii. 72.
  Attendants, vi. 150, 152.
  Balconies, vi. 51.

Theatres (*cont.*)
  Stage (*cont.*)
    Bason on, i. 277–8.
    Candlesticks on, i. 277–8.
    Covering of, vi. 279.
    Dimensions of, vi. 264.
    Doors, vi. 51, 144.
    Engraving of, v. 1004.
    Façades, vi. 156.
    Galleries, vi. 156 n., 176.
    Hangings, ii. 534; vi. 280.
    Houses, vi. 191.
    Inner, vi. 187, 192.
    Keeper, ii. 579, 686; iv. 935; vi. 105.
    Machines, iii. 397.
    Making a, vii. 81.
    Movable, vi. 201, 208, 214.
    Pictures, v. 1417.
    Raked, vi. 280.
    Rushes on, ii. 687; vi. 106.
    Shadow (i.e. cover) over, vi. 142, 144.
    Sitting on, i. 225 n. 2; vi. 5, 6, 7–9, 44–45, 106, 110–11, 220, 239.
      Abolished, ii. 687; vi. 8, 106.
    Size of, vi. 142, 201.
    Stools on, ii. 687.
    Tents on, vi. 191, 257.
    Traps, iv. 506; vi. 51, 190, 281.
    Windows, vi. 51.
    Wings (i.e. stage sets), vi. 51.
      Designs for, iv. 524.
  Stages, vi. 125, 126–7, 190, 201, 230, 264, 273, 275, 279.
    Described, v. 1191.
    Upper, i. 283 n. 7; vi. 187, 192.
  Staging, Italian, iii. 293.
  Staircases in, vi. 5–6, 132, 142, 144, 145, 201, 271, 275, 276, 277, 279.
  Stands, vi. 280, 281.
  Stars of assidue, vi. 273.
  State in, vi. 275, 280, 281, 287.
    Crimson velvet canopy for, vi. 280, 281.
  Statues, vi. 271, 272, 273, 275, 276.
  Stools, vi. 257, 280, 281.
  Sunday closing of, vii. 10–12.
  Suppression of, i. 68–69; vi. 19, 74, 78, 83.
  Sweepers of, ii. 686; vi. 105.
  Tables, vi. 280, 281.
  Tapestry, vi. 262.
  Tarras, vi. 188 n. 1, 258.
  Taverns near, i. 44, 138, 143; vi. 72–73, 141, 180, 185 n. 2.
  Teachers at, vi. 76.

Threatened, vi. 220.
Thrones, vi. 257, 273, 278.
Tiles in, ii. 691.
Time of performance at, *see* Performances, time of.
Tiring-house, i. 44 and n. 3, 318; ii. 440; iii. 362; v. 1211; vi. 44, 106, 126–7, 142, 144, 152, 172, 190, 201, 236, 258, 305.
  In basement, vi. 189, 191.
  Door, vi. 180.
Tiring-room, lower, vi. 281.
  Upper, vi. 280, 281.
Tongs, vi. 280.
Turndoor, vi. 287.
'Twelve-penny room', vi. 192.
Wages in, vi. 70.
Wardrobe, vi. 281, 295.
Weather-boarding, vi. 286.
Windows in, vi. 271, 275, 277, 278.
Yard, iii. 103; v. 1346; vi. 156, 224 n. 1.
Theatre of God's Judgments, The, see Beard, Thomas.
Theatro Olympico, Vicenza, vi. 274 n. 1, 276, 278.
Theatrum Orbi (picture of theatre), vi. 186 n. 1.
Theban Princess, The, see May, Thomas, *The Tragedy of Antigone.*
Theft, iii. 238.
Thelwall, Simon, i. 165 n. 8.
Theobald, Lewis, iii. 312.
  Double Falsehood, or the Distressed Lovers, v. 1104–5.
Theobalds, Hertfordshire, Palace at, i. 50, 178; iv. 655, 716, 954; v. 1198, 1372, 1422; vi. 260; vii. 23, 43, 45, 57 .
Theoctistus sive Constans in Aula Virtus, Tragœdia, see Simons, Joseph.
Theodosius, iv. 780.
Theologate at Liége, rector, of, v. 1172.
Theomachia, see Heylyn, Peter.
Thermae Redivivae: the City of Bath Described (1673), *see* Chapman, Henry.
Thesmophoriazusae, see Aristophanes.
Thespian Magazine and Literary Repository, The (1793), v. 1134.
Thespis, vi. 276.
Thetford, Norfolk, ii. 453, 604.
Thibaldus sive Vindictæ Ingenium, or Pharamus sive Libido Vindex, Hispanica Tragœdia, see Snelling, Thomas.

Thicknis, Mr., i. 142.
Thierry and Theodoret, see Beaumont and Fletcher.
Thime, Margarete, *Marlowes 'Jew of Malta' Stil- und Echtheitsfragen* (1921), iv. 573.
'Third Booke of Humours: Intituled Notes from Black-Fryers', see Fitzgeffrey, Henry.
Thirlestane House, Cheltenham, vi. 177, 200, 208 n. 1, 214 n. 1.
Thirty Years War, iii. 250; iv. 518.
'This Wooden O', see Hotson, Leslie.
'Thom Randolfs Salting', see Randolph, Thomas.
Thomas, D. L., 'Authorship of *Revenge for Honour*', *M.P.* v (1908), iv. 489, 490.
'Concerning Glapthorne's Wit in a Constable', *J.E.G.P.* xiv (1915), iv. 494.
Thomas, John, ii. 476.
Thomas, William, junior, ii. 411.
Thomas, William, senior, ii. 411.
Thomas, William, *The History of Italy* (1549), v. 1274.
Thomas Lord Cromwell, see Anonymous.
Thomas of Woodstock, or Richard II, see Anonymous.
Thomaso, see Killigrew, Thomas.
Thomason, George, Collection in the British Museum, v. 1036, 1039, 1053, 1054, 1103, 1119, 1200, 1215, 1220, 1223, 1287; vi. 283, 284.
His copy of *Masquerade du Ciel*, v. 1038.
Thompson, A. Hamilton, ed., *The Works of Sir John Suckling* (1910), v. 1198, 1201, 1211, 1212, 1213.
Thompson, Anne, ii. 600.
Thompson, John, i. 45, 72–88; ii. 455, **599–600**; iii. 164, 363, 379, 393; iv. 781.
Thompson, Lettice, ii. 600.
Thompson, Richard, ii. **600**.
Thompson, Samuel, i. 285, 288, 290, 297; ii. **600–1**; vi. 100.
Thompson, Thomas, *The Life of Mother Shipton*, iv. 774.
Thorncombe, Devonshire, iv. 512.
Thorndike, Ashley, iii. 321.
Thorn-Drury, G., iii. 141.
Little Ark, A (1921), iii. 226, 292; iv. 755, 917, 920; v. 983, 986.
ed., *Parnassus Biceps* (1927), iii. 132; v. 1275, 1276.

ed., *The Poems of Thomas Randolph* (1929), v. 965, 968.
T[horn]–D[rury], G., 'Jordan's *Money Is An Asse*, 1668', *R.E.S.* i (1925), iv. 685, 687; vi. 284.
Thornhurst, Grace, iii. 292.
Thornhurst, Sir William, iii. 292.
Thorpe, Mr., v. 1156.
Thorpe, Elizabeth, ii. 613.
Thorpe, Thomas, bookseller, iii. 14; v. 1293.
Thorrells Hall, Essex, iv. 788.
Thrale, Benjamin, stationer (warden of Sta. Co.), iii. 56, 88, 92; iv. 486, 495, 784, 922.
Thrale, Dorothy, iii. 56, 87, 92; iv. 486, 495, 783–4.
Thrale, Richard, stationer, iii. 56, 92; iv. 485, 486, 495, 783, 784; v. 1196.
Three Dorothies, The, see Lower, Sir William.
Three Herring Court, see London, streets of.
Three Kings Ordinary in Fleet Street, ii. 421, 684 n. 1; iii. 195; vi. 305, 307 n. 1, 308.
Three London Apprentices, The, see Anonymous.
Three London Theatres of Shakespeare's Time, see Wallace, Charles W.
'Three Merry Boyes, The' (droll from *The Bloody Brother*), iii. 403, 407.
Three New Playes (1655), see Massinger, Philip.
Three Pigeons at London, The, book stall, iii. 146; v. 1072.
Three Pigeons at Brentford, Inn, ii. 505, 695.
Three Wise Men (feast of the), vi. 257.
Thurles, Lord, vi. 6, 7.
'Thyrsis. A Pastoral Elegy', see Rutter, Joseph.
Tiballs, see Theobalds.
Tichbourne, Sir Richard, iv. 510.
Tickets, iii. 108; vi. 284.
Tickets of privilege, i. 15, 49 n. 2, 80–81, 86–87, 260, 262 n. 6, 316, 321, 332, 336; ii. 379, 561, 570.
Tieck, L., ed., *'Die Hexen in Lancashire'* (1823), iii. 73.
Tight-rope dancers, see Dancers on the ropes.
Tight-rope walkers, see Dancers on the ropes.
Tiling, vi. 280.

Tilley, Morris Palmer, *A Dictionary of the Proverbs in England in the Sixteenth and Seventeenth Centuries* (1950), iv. 861.

Tillieres, Count de, iv. 646, 656.

Tillotson, Geoffrey, '*Othello* and *The Alchemist* at Oxford in 1610', *T.L.S.* 20 July 1933, iii. 100.

Tillotson, Kathleen, 'William Sampson's "Vow-Breaker" (1636) and the Lost Henslowe Play "Black Batman of the North" ', *M.L.R.* xxxv (1940), v. 1043, 1045.

Tilly, Johann Tzerclaes, Count of, v. 1109.

Tillyard, E. M. W., 'The Action of Comus', *Essays and Studies by Members of the English Association*, xxviii (1942), iv. 914.

Tilney, Edward, iii. 264.

Tilting, iv. 655, 666; v. 1376; vi. 293, 298, 299; vii. 20, 31, 36, 38, 39, 44.
    Postponed, vii. 43.

Tiltyard, *see* Whitehall Palace.

Timber, strong, vi. 293.

Time Vindicated to Himself and to His Honours, *see* Jonson, Ben.

Times, The (London), vi. 5, 145 n. 1.

Times Displayed, The, *see* Sheppard, Samuel.

Time's Trick upon the Cards, *see* Fane, Mildmay.

Time's Triumph, *see* Anonymous.

Timon of Athens, v. 1055.

Timon of Athens, *see* Shakespeare.

Tindall, Joan, iii. 238.

Tindall (or Grindall), Joan, murder of, iii. 254.

Tindall (or Grindall), Nathaniel, iii. 254, 256.

Tipling house, v. 972.

Tipsley, Francis, v. 1185.

Tire men, vi. 237.

Tiring-house, *see* Theatres, tiring-houses in.

Tirlemont, sack of, iv. 482.

Tirringham, Sir Thomas, v. 1422.

'Tis Pity She's a Whore, *see* Ford, John.

Tischner, Friederich, *Die Verfasserchaft der Webster-Rowley Dramen* (1907), v. 1015.

Titian, heads of Roman emperors by vi. 273, 278.

Title-pages, iii. 87; vi. 13, 85, 97, 109, 146, 196, 197, 198, 225, 251 n. 1, 286, 287.
    Cuts, v. 1417.
    Misleading, iii. 61, 117, 120; v. 1093.
    Mottoes, *see* Latin mottoes.
    Titles altered, iii. 87; iv. 692; v. 1443.

Ghost, v. 1289, 1293, 1297–8, 1301, 1303, 1315, 1321, 1323, 1326, 1330, 1336, 1338, 1347, 1349, 1350, 1353, 1354, 1356, 1357, 1364, 1373, 1376, 1384, 1385, 1389, 1398, 1400, 1402, 1404, 1408, 1409, 1410, 1416, 1423, 1436, 1437, 1444, 1447.
    Identical, v. 1330, 1406, 1449.
    Misleading, iii. 343; iv. 709, 884; v. 1082, 1187, 1277, 1343, 1356.
    Multiple, iii. 343, 359, 421; v. 1013, 1189, 1245, 1303, 1390, 1419.

Titus Andronicus, *see* Shakespeare.

Titus and Vespatian, *see* Anonymous.

'To his beloved friend Maister Thomas Heywood', *see* Webster, John.

To Dr. R. (*festschrift*), i.e. Dr. A. S. W. Rosenbach, vi. 250 n. 1.

'To his faithful ingenuous friend and old acquaintance, JOHN TATHAM, Gent.', *see* Jordan, Thomas.

'To a Lady of Pleasure', *see* Collop, John.

'To my Mother, Mrs. Dorothy Tatham . . .', *see* Tatham, John.

'To Sr. John Suckling', *see* Anonymous.

'To Tatam', *see* Sheppard, Samuel.

Tobacco, iii. 165; v. 1345, 1443–4.
    Pipes, i. 318; vi. 173.
    Shops, vi. 147.

Tobye, Edward, i. 168 n. 1; ii. 601.

Todd, Henry John, ed., Milton's *Comus* (1798), iv. 914.

Todd, Mary, ii. 428.

Token books, ii. 448, 467, 486, 490, 500, 510, 519, 546, 560, 564, 574, 575, 592, 633; iv. 554.

Tokens, v. 994.
    Town, v. 994.
    Tradesmen's, v. 994.

Tollemache, John, iv. 951.

Tolman, Albert H., vi. 189.

Tom of Bedlam, *see* Anonymous.

Tom Essence, or the Modish Wife, *see* Anonymous.

'*Tom Hoyden o' Tanton Deane*', *see* Brome, Richard, *The Sparagus Garden*.

Tomeland, in Norwich, v. 1454.

Tomkis, Thomas, v. 1225–6, 1390.
   Albumazar, iii. 13; v. 1225, 1391, 1392; vi. 148–9, 241; vii. 74, 95.
   Albumazar, ed. Hugh G. Dick (1944), vi. 149 n. 1.
   Lingua, v. 1391, 1392, 1443; vii. 25, 46, 85, 99.

Tomlinson, Warren E., 'Der Herodes–Charakter im englischen Drama', *Palaestra*, cxcv (1934), iv. 734.

Tompson, Peter, vi. 204.

Tomson, John, iv. 810, 817.

Tooley, Isabell, ii. 556; v. 1016.

Tooley, Nicholas, i. 5, 9, 16, 72–88; ii. 556, 601–2, 638; iii. 301, 326, 330, 331, 341, 355, 372, 393, 396, 399, 413, 420, 423; v. 1016, 1238.
   Will of, ii. 649–51.

Tooth-Drawer, The, see Anonymous.

Topp, Henry, schoolmaster, iii. 126.

Torches, vi. 114, 265, 284, 285.

Torgau, ii. 451.

Torpley, Nathaniel, ii. 642.

Torrington, Devonshire, v. 999, 1001.

Tosedall, Roger, i. 286, 297; ii. 602.

Totnell, James, ii. 635.

Tottenham Court, see Nabbes, Thomas.

Tounesend, Aurelian, *see* Townshend, Aurelian.

Tour, Baron de, iv. 650; v. 1432.

Touring companies, i. 146 n. 6, 178, 228.
   Fees of, paid, i. 293; ii. 689.
   Precautions about audiences of, i. 312.
   Quarrelling between, i. 294.
   Repertory of, i. 293; ii. 689.
   Size of, i. 288–9, 298.

Tournaments, *see* Tourneys.

Tourneur, Cyril, iii. 191; v. 1226.
   Influence of, iv. 509; v. 1372.
   Great Man, The, i. 132.
   Nobleman, The, i. 66, 132; iii. 389; v. 1226.
   Revenger's Tragedy, v. 1372.

Tourneys, vi. 293, 298, 299.

Tower Hill, *see* London, streets of.

Tower of London, *see* London, streets and districts.

Towers, W., verses by, iii. 141.

Towne, Thomas, i. 135, 136; iv. 516.

Townsend, Freda L., *Apologie for Bartholmew Fayre: The Art of Jonson's Comedies* (1947), iv. 606.

'Ben Jonson's "Censure" of Rutter's *Shepheards* Holy-Day', *Mod. Phil.* xliv (1947), v. 1032, 1033.

Townsend, George Alfred, *The Life, Crime and Capture of John Wilkes Booth,* v. 1141.

Townsend, John, actor, i. 176, 180 and n. 13, 181, 182, 189 and n. 3, 192, 299; ii. 602–4.

Townshend, Aurelian, iv. 620, 652, 654, 920; v. 1222, 1226–31.
   Albion's Triumph, v. 1227–8, 1230.
   'Pigmees Speech, A', v. 1231.
   Tempe Restored, iii. 208; iv. 921; v. 1229–30.
   Unknown Masque (?), v. 1231.

Townshend, John, v. 1226.

Towyer *or* Toyer, William, *see* Tawyer, William.

Toy, The, see Anonymous.

Toy to Please Chaste Ladies, A, see Anonymous.

Tradeways Tragedy, see Anonymous.

Traffic, i. 4–5, 33; vi. 24, 25, 27, 29–30.

Tragedia de Emma Angliae Regina, see Carleton, Thomas.

Tragedia di F. N. B., see Negri, Francesco.

Tragedie du Roy Franc-Arbitre, see Crespin, Jean.

Tragedies, vi. 293.
   Changed to tragi-comedies, v. 1202–7.

Tragedy, A, see Newport, Maurice.

Tragedy of Amidea, or The Traytor, see Shirley, James.

Tragedy of Andromana or the fatall & deserved end of Disloyalty and Ambition, see J. S., *Andromana.*

Tragedy of Antigone, The, see May, Thomas.

Tragedy of Cleander, The, see Massinger, Philip.

Tragedy of Cleopatra Queen of Egypt, The, see May, Thomas.

'Tragedy of Doctor *Lambe,* The' (Ballad), i. 267–8; vi. 162.

'Tragedy of the Golden Fleece', play-within-play Shirley's *Triumph of Beauty,* v. 1153.

Tragedy of Heildebrand, see Anonymous.

Tragedy of Julia Agrippina, see May, Thomas.

Tragedy of Lodovick Sforza, Duke of Milan, The, see Gomersall, Robert.

Tragedy of Massenello, see B., T., *The Rebellion of Naples.*

Tragedy of Messallina, the Roman Empress, The, see Richards, Nathanael.

Tragœdia Miserrima Pyrami et Thisbes fata enuncians, see R., N.

Tragedy of Nero (Piso's Conspiracy), The, see Anonymous.

Tragedy of Orestes, The, see Goffe, Thomas.

Tragedy of Ovid, The, see Cokayne, Sir Aston.

Tragedy of the Plantation of Virginia, see Anonymous.

Tragedy of St. Albans, The, see Shirley, James.

Tragedy of Sophonisba, The, see Marston, John, *The Wonder of Women.*

Tragedy of Thierry, King of France, and His Brother Theodoret, The, see Fletcher, John.

Tragedy of Tomerania, The, see Anonymous.

Tragedy of the Unhappy Fair Irene, The, see Swinhoe, Gilbert.

Tragedy of a Yorkshire Gentlewoman, and her Son, see Chapman, George.

Tragedy, costumes for, iii. 37.
Definition of, iii. 18.
Theory of, iv. 833, 943–4.

Tragi-comedy, iii. 97.

Tragi-Comoedia . . . Regicidium, see Brathwait, Richard.

Tragical History, Admirable Achievements, and Various Events of Guy of Warwick, see Anonymous.

Tragoedia Andronicus Commenius, see Bernard, Samuel, *Andronicus Comnenus.*

Trained-bands, iii. 39; vi. 175.

Traitor, The, see Shirley, James.

Translations, iii. 5, 41, 46, 97, 142, 275, 276, 279, 280, 293, 321, 322, 325, 326, 331, 350, 363, 366, 367, 379, 410, 469; v. 963, 964, 980, 981, 999, 1030–2, 1047–8, 1072, 1170, 1171, 1186, 1187, 1247, 1292, 1341, 1373, 1381; vi. 71.

Translators, iii. 46, 97, 118, 155; v. 962, 964, 999, 1028, 1047, 1054, 1170, 1171, 1186–7.

Transome, Nicholas, ii. 357.

Trappolin creduto Principe, see Cokayne, Sir Aston.

Trask, Willard R., translator, see Curtius, Ernst Robert.

Travels of Three English Brothers, The, see Rowley, William.

Travis, Edward, ii. 346.

Treason, Suckling charged with, v. 1200.

Treasurer of the Chamber, vi. 267, 268, 269.

Treasury, the, vi. 131.

Treasury warrants, vi. 138.

Trebellius Bulgarorum Rex, see Anonymous.

Tremere, St. Tudy, Cornwall, iv. 725.

Tremyll, —, v. 1157.

Trent (river), iv. 626.
Petition that it be made navigable, v. 1044.

Tres maridos burlados, Los, see Tirso de Molina.

Tresham, Sir Lewis, vi. 49.

Trevell, William, see Trevill, William.

Trevill, William, vi. 116, 117.

Trevill *vs.* Woodford, ii. 625.

Tribe of Ben, see Jonson, Ben, Sons of.

Trick to Catch the Old One, A, see Middleton, Thomas.

Trick to Cheat the Devil, A, see Davenport, Robert, *A New Trick to Cheat the Devil.*

Tricks of Youth, see Jordan, Thomas, *The Walks of Islington and Hogsdon with the Humours of Woodstreet Counter.*

Triennial Parliament Bill, iii. 41.

Trigg, Elizabeth, ii. 606.

Trigg, Mathew, ii. 606.

Trigg, Thomas, ii. 606.

Trigg, William, i. 49, 73–89, 327 n. 3, 332, 336; ii. 604–6, 647; iii. 428, 429; iv. 810, 817.

Trinity College, Cambridge, iii. 158, 159, 160, 166, 172, 174, 176, 177, 178, 180, 181, 182; iv. 525, 526, 527, 529, 530, 532, 534, 535, 536, 716, 854, 870, 878, 947, 948, 953; v. 964, 966, 982, 983, 984, 991, 1009, 1027, 1195, 1198, 1232, 1237, 1299, 1387, 1391, 1392, 1397, 1408, 1419; vi. 148, 149, 241, 245; vii. 16.
Butler of, v. 972.
Fellow of, v. 1195, 1196, 1232.
Library of, iv. 535.
Master of, v. 966, 967, 983.
Master and fellows of, iii. 173.
Manuscripts of, iv. 526, 526–7, 854, 912, 913, 916; v. 1196, 1197, 1302, 1374, 1449, 1452.
Senior Bursar's Accounts, iii. 159, 160, 177.

Trinity College, Dublin, iii. 33, 307.
Trinity College, Oxford, iii. 275; v. 964, 1004, 1268, 1272, 1306.
Fellow of, v. 1004, 1306.
Triplex Memoriae, see Ainsworth, William.
Triumph, ship, v. 1202, 1205.
Triumph of Beauty, The, see Shirley, James.
Triumph of Death, The, see Fletcher, John, *The Triumph of Honour.*
Triumph of Honour, The, see Fletcher, John.
Triumph of Innocence, The, see Anonymous.
Triumph of Love, The, see Fletcher, John, *The Triumph of Honour.*
Triumph of Peace, The, see Shirley, James.
Triumph of Peace: A Study of the Whitehall Banqueting House, see Palme, Per.
Triumph of Time, The, see Fletcher, John, *The Triumph of Honour.*
Triumphant Widow, The, see Cavendish, William.
Triumphs of Fame and Honour, The, see Taylor, John.
Triumphs of God's Revenge against Murder, The, see Reynolds, John.
Triumphs of the Golden Fleece, The, see Munday, Anthony.
Triumphs of Health and Prosperity, The, see Middleton, Thomas.
Triumphs of Honour and Industry, The, see Middleton, Thomas.
Triumphs of Honour and Virtue, The, see Middleton, Thomas.
Triumphs of Integrity, The, see Middleton, Thomas.
Triumphs of London; Performed on Monday . . ., The, see Jordan, Thomas.
Triumphs of London; Performed on Friday . . ., The, see Jordan, Thomas.
Triumphs of London; Performed on Tuesday . . ., The, see Jordan, Thomas.
Triumphs of Love and Antiquity, The, see Middleton, Thomas.
Triumphs of Peace, The, see Squire, John, *Tes Irenes Trophœa.*
Triumphs of the Prince D'Amour, see Davenant, William.
Triumphs of Truth, The, see Middleton, Thomas.
'Triumvirate' (Shakespeare, Jonson, Beaumont and Fletcher), iii. 310.

Troia Nova Triumphans, see Dekker, Thomas.
Troilus and Cressida, see Chettle, Henry.
Troilus and Cressida, see Shakespeare, William.
Trompeur Puni, Le, ou Histoire Septentrionale, see Scudéri, Georges de.
Troop of carabineers, v. 1199.
Troop of 100 horse, v. 1199.
Troops, English, starvation of, on the Continent, v. 1247.
Troubles of Great Hermenia, see Zouche, Richard, *Fallacy.*
Troublesome Reign of King John, The, see Anonymous.
Troy, Siege of, iv. 580.
Troyte-Bullock, Lieutenant-Colonel E. G., iii. 162.
True Diurnal Occurrences, see Newspapers.
True and Exact History of the Island of Barbados (1657), *see* Ligon, Richard.
True Hungarian History, A, see Massinger, Philip, *The Picture.*
True Relation of All the Remarkable Places and Passages Observed in the Travels of . . . Thomas Lord Howard, see Crowne, William.
True Tragedy of Richard Duke of York (3 Henry VI), The, see Shakespeare, William.
True Tragi-Comedy Formerly Acted at Court, see Anonymous.
True Trojans, The, see Fisher, Jasper, *Fuimus Troes.*
True Widow, see Shadwell, Thomas.
Trumbull, Sir William, ii. 436.
Trumpeters, ii. 357, 483, 609; iii. 256; v. 1159.
Trumpets, vi. 242, 246, 257, 263.
Trumpets, to advertise provincial performances, ii. 686.
Before performances, vi. 42.
Trundle, John, actor, ii. **606**, 682, 683.
Trundle, John, stationer, iii. 251; iv. 868, 907; v. 1319, 1347.
Trunks, vi. 54.
Truth's Acrostick . . ., see Richards, Nathanael.
Truth's Triumphs, see Anonymous.
Tu Quoque, see Cooke, John, *Greene's Tu Quoque.*
Tubbe, Henry, 'On the Dominical Nose of O[liver] C[romwell]', iii. 317.

Tuchborne, —, ii. 347.

Tucke, T., see Tuckfield, Thomas.

Tuckfield, Thomas, i. 15, 72–88; ii. 606–7.

Tufton, Sir Humphrey, vii. 58.

Tumblers, ii. 459, 486, 522, 657; iv. 673; vi. 209, 296; vii. 5.

Tumbling, vi. 294, 298.

Tunbridge Wells, or a Day's Courtship, see Anonymous.

Tunes, v. 1361, 1378.

Tunstall, Sir John, vii. 20, 62.

Tupper, James W., ed., *Love and Honour and The Siege of Rhodes by Sir William D'Avenant* (1909), iii. 205.

Turin, Thomas Killigrew in, iv. 697, 708.

Turkey, iv. 567; v. 1047.

Turkey colours (i.e. blue), vi. 43.

Turks, iv. 486; v. 1450.

Turk's Too Good for Him, A, see Anonymous.

Turmoil of Love, The, see Anonymous, *The Hypochondriac*.

Turnbull, William B., ed., *The Poetical Works of William Drummond of Hawthornden* (*Library of Old Authors*) (1856), iii. 289.

Turner, —, ii. 682.

Turner, Anthony, i. 183, 187, 192, 219, 220, 221, 222, 231, 237, 238, 244, and n. 2, 245, 246, 247, 248 n. j; ii. 607–8; iv. 542, 545, 570; vi. 59, 61, 67, 103.

Turner, Celeste, *Anthony Mundy: An Elizabethan Man of Letters* (1928), iv. 925; v. 1429.

Turner, Dorothy, ii. 607.

Turner, Drew or True, ii. 608–9.

Turner, Henry, i. 244 n. 2, 248 n. j; ii. 608, 609.

Turner, Jane, ii. 608.

Turner, Jone, ii. 608.

Turner, Mary, ii. 608.

Turner, Mrs. (of Overbury trial), iv. 902, 905.

Turner, R. S., v. 1257.

Turner, W., *Dish of Lenten Stuff, A*, ii. 563.

Turner, W. J., ' "A New Way to Pay Old Debts" . . . at the "Old Vic" ', *Spectator*, cxxix (1922), iv. 801.

Turners, vi. 272.

Turney, Edmund, ii. 444.

Turning, vi. 272.

Turnstile Alley, see London, streets of.

Tuscan Resident to the Grand Duke of Florence, iv. 549.

Tutbury, i. 310.

Tutor's accounts, v. 992.

Tuttells, Richard, ii. 637.

Tuttle, Westminster, see London, streets of.

Tweed, River, v. 1200.

Twelfth day (i.e. 6 January), vi. 256.

Twelfth Night, see Shakespeare, William.

Twelfth Night, vi. 258, 283.

Twelfthtide, vi. 286.

Twelves, —, iv. 601.

Twickenham, Middlesex, iii. 22; v. 1198, 1213.

Twiford, Henry, v. 1208.

Two Bookes of Epigrammes, and Epitaphs, see Bancroft, Thomas.

Two Constant Women, see Anonymous, *More than Nine Days' Wonder*.

Two Fools Well Met, see Carllel, Lodowick.

Two Fools Well Met, see Carlisle, James, *The Fortune Hunters*.

Two Gentlemen of Verona, The, see Shakespeare, William.

Two Harpies, see Middleton, Thomas, *Caesar's Fall*.

Two Kings in a Cottage, see Bonen, William.

Two Merry Milkmaids, or the Best Words Wear Garlands, The, see C., I.

Two New Plays, see Carllel, Lodowick.

Two Noble Kinsmen, The, see Fletcher, John.

Two Noble Ladies, The, see Anonymous.

Two Noble Ladies, The, and the Converted Conjurer, see Anonymous.

Two Shapes, see Middleton, Thomas, *Caesar's Fall*.

Two Spanish Gentlemen, The, see Anonymous.

Two Wise Men and All the Rest Fools, see Anonymous.

Twynnes tragedye, The, see Rider, W., *The Twins*.

Tyburn, vii. 69.

Tychebourne, Leonell, i. 139.

Tyldesley, Thomas, ii. 471.

Tyler, Zachary, a carver, vi. 271.

Tyn, Jacob, vii. 35.

Tyrannical Government Anatomized, or A Discourse Concerning Evil

Councellors, Being the Life and Death of John the Baptist, see Anonymous.

Tyrant, The, see Massinger, Philip, *The King and the Subject.*

Tyrant King of Crete, The, see Sedley, Charles.

Udall, Edward, ii. 564.
Udall, Henry, ii. 564.
Ulrich, Otto, *Die pseudohistorischen Dramen Beaumonts und Fletchers 'Thierry and Theodoret', 'Valentinian', 'The Prophetess' und 'The False One' und ihre Quellen* (1913), iii. 340, 394.
Undercook, ii. 546.
Underell, Thomas, *see* Underhill, Thomas.
Underhill, Alphonso, ii. 610.
Underhill, Nicholas, i. 15, 72–88; ii. **609**; iii. 416.
Underhill, Samuel, ii. 384, 625.
Underhill, Thomas, ii. **609**–10.
Underwood, Burbage, ii. 651.
Underwood, Elizabeth, ii. 651.
Underwood, Henry, i. 144.
Underwood, Isabella, ii. 639, 651.
Underwood, John, i. 5, 9, 16, 44 and n. 6, 72–88; ii. 584, **610–11**, 641, 650, 696; iii. 301, 326, 330, 341, 352, 355, 363, 372, 379, 393, 399, 413, 423; vi. 36, 137, 180 and n. 1.
   Will of, ii. 651.
Underwood, John, junior, ii. 651.
Underwood, Mr., house of, vi. 154.
Underwood, Thomas, ii. 651.
Undrill, Thomas, *see* Underhill, Thomas.
Unfaithful Wife, The, see Anonymous.
Unfortunate Fortunate, The, see Garfield, Benjamin.
Unfortunate Lovers, The, see Davenant, William.
Unfortunate Lovers, see The Fortunate, the Deceived and the Unfortunate Lovers.
Unfortunate Mother, The, see Nabbes, Thomas.
Unfortunate Piety, The, see Massinger, Philip.
Unfortunate Welshman, The, see Crouch, Humphrey, *The Welsh Traveller.*
Unger, E. V., and W. A. Jackson, *Carl H. Pforzheimer Library:*

English Literature 1475–1700 (1940), iv. 493; v. 1162.
Uniformity, Act of, v. 1265.
Uniforms, v. 1199.
'Union of the two companies', iii. 403, 409.
United Companies, iii. 315, 320, 330, 349, 403, 419.
Unity of time, iv. 934.
University College, Oxford, iv. 495; v. 1163.
University of Chicago Library, v. 1149.
University of Edinburgh Manuscripts, v. 1442, 1443.
University of Illinois, v. 1134.
University plays, iii. 304, 443.
Unjust Judge, The, or The Roman Virgin, see Webster, John, *Appius and Virginia.*
Unknown Masque, see Townshend, Aurelian.
Unknown play, see Drue, Thomas.
   see Carew, Thomas.
Unnamed comedy, see Nicols, John.
Unnamed Masque, see Maynard, John.
Unnamed pageant, see Middleton, Thomas.
Unnamed Pastoral and Masque, see Henrietta Maria, Queen.
Unnamed Play, see Beeston, Christopher.
   See Daborne, Robert.
   See Middleton, Thomas.
Unnamed tragedy, iii. 280.
Unnatural Combat, The, see Massinger, Philip.
'Unpublished Stage Documents', *see* Rosenfeld, Sybil.
Untrussing of the Humorous Poet, The, see Dekker, Thomas, *Satiromastix.*
Upcott, William, v. 1257.
Upham, A. H., *The French Influence in English Literature* (1908), v. 1209.
Upholsterers, vi. 280.
'Upon Aglaura printed in Folio', *see* Brome, Richard.
Upon the Declaration of His Majesty King Charles of England the Second, see Richards, Nathanael.
'Upon Sir John Laurence's bringing Water over the hills to my L. Middlesex his House at Witten', *see* Suckling, Sir John.
'Upon Sir John Suckling's Most Warlike Preparations for the Scotish Warre', *see* Anonymous.

Upper parliament House, vii. 36.
Upper stage, see Theatres.
Uppingham, Rutlandshire, iv. 533.
Upton on Severn, ii. 486.
Urania, see Montgomery, Countess of.
Urson, John, iv. 658.
Ursuline nuns, 'miracles' of, iv. 695.
Urswick, —, a tailor, iii. 194.
Usher of the Revels, vi. 284.
Ussher, James, Archbishop of Armagh, iv. 956; vi. 176.
Usurers, v. 1329.
Usury Put to Use, see Fletcher, John, *The Devil of Dowgate.*
Utrecht, iii. 18, 19; v. 1176.
    University of, vi. 132.
Utter Barristers, v. 1155.
Uvedale, Lucy, *see* Neale, Lucy.
Uvedale, Sir William, iv. 945.

Valencia, iv. 656.
Valency, Maurice J., *The Tragedies of Herod and Mariamne* (1940), iv. 734.
Valentinian, see Anonymous.
    See Fletcher, John.
Valentinian, or Rape's Revenge, see Anonymous.
Valentinian, a Tragedy, see Rochester, Earl of.
Valentinian II, v. 1376.
Valeresso, Signor, Venetian ambassador, iv. 643.
Valet of the Chamber to the Queen, v. 1069, 1081.
Valetudinarium, see Johnson, William.
Valiant Scholar, The, see Anonymous.
Valiant Scot, The, see W., J.
Van Buchel, Arend, vi. 249.
Van Dam, B. A. P., 'Robert Greene's "Alphonsus",' *English Studies*, xiii (1931), v. 1286.
Van Dyke, Sir Anthony, i. 48; iii. 106, 113; vi. 35, 136.
    portrait of Suckling, v. 1200.
Van Lennep, William, iii. 13; iv. 719; v. 1141.
    'Death of the Red Bull, The', *Theatre Notebook*, xvi (1961–2), vi. 215, 224 n. 1, 238.
    'The New-Made Nobleman', *T.L.S.* 29 June 1936, p. 523, iii. 387.
    'Thomas Killigrew Prepares His Plays for Production', *Joseph*

Quincy Adams Memorial Studies (1948), iv. 694, 697, 698, 701, 705, 710.
Van Mal, Monsieur, iv. 643.
Van Trumpe, Admiral, iii. 150.
Van Wely, John, murder of, iii. 351.
Vanbrugh, Sir John, iii. 392, 394.
    False Friend, The, v. 1331.
Vandal persecutions, v. 1062.
Vane, Sir Henry, i. 64; iii. 214; v. 1157, 1159, 1199, 1227, 1228, 1229; vi. 39, 287, 288.
Vanham, William, ii. 356.
Varieties, see Cavendish, William Duke of Newcastle.
Variety, The, see Cavendish, William.
Variety shows, vi. 212.
Variorum, see Boswell, James, *The Plays and Poems of William Shakespeare.*
Varnishing, vi. 273.
Vasely, Elizabeth, ii. 587, 648.
Vaughan, Henry, iii. 301.
    Olor Iscanus (1651), iii. 301.
Vaughan, John, iii. 31.
Vaughan, Mrs., iv. 601.
Vaughan, Richard, (actor), iv. 596.
Vaughan, Thomas, ii. 632.
Vaulters, ii. 486, 502, 522, 613; vi. 194–5, 296.
Vaulting, vi. 159, 294; vii. 8.
Vaux, Sir Ambrose, v. 1058.
Vavasour, Mary, iii. 82.
Vavasour, Nicholas, stationer, iii. 81, 82, 257, 258, 273.
Velte, Mowbray, *The Bourgeois Elements in the Dramas of Thomas Heywood* (1922), iv. 553, 562, 565, 566, 569, 579, 582; v. 1318, 1320.
Velvet, crimson, vi. 280.
Vendosme, Duke de, v. 1227, 1229.
Venetian Comedy, The, see Anonymous.
Venice, v. 1388.
    Ambassador of, i. 20, 204; iv. 492, 643, 655, 656, 660, 661, 664, 670, 673, 674, 675, 842, 843, 874, 876, 908–9, 918; v. 1155, 1157, 1229, 1334; vi. 58, 133, 257, 263; vii. 23, 111.
    Embassy in London, vi. 151, 152, 256–8.
    Embassy to, iii. 105.
    Epistle from, iii. 166.
    Killigrew in, iv. 697, 706, 708.
    Play performed in, iii. 170.
    Scene for play, iv. 740.
Venn, John, *Biographical history of Gonville and Caius college, 1349–*

1897 . . ., 4 vols. (1897–1912), iii. 185, 186, 238; v. 1000, 1001.

Venn, John, and J. A. Venn, *Alumni Cantabrigienses: a biographical list of all Known students, graduates and holders of office at the University of Cambridge, from the earliest times to 1900.* Part I (to 1751), 4 vols. Part II (1752–1900), 6 vols. (1922–1954), iii. 2, 11, 105, 142, 151, 159, 166, 172, 173, 225, 292, 306; iv. 525, 527, 532, 586, 600, 716, 947, 948, 953, 956; v. 966, 1005, 1027, 1037, 1038, 1180, 1195, 1196, 1198, 1214, 1232, 1236, 1239, 1240, 1265.

Venner, Richard, '*England's Joy*', v. 1212.

Vere Street Theatre, iii. 71.

Vere, Thomas, stationer, iii. 25; iv. 479, 565, 583, 712; v. 1060.

Verhasselt, Elaine, 'A Biography of Nathan Field, Dramatist and Actor', *Revue belge de philologie et d'histoire*, xxv (1946–7), iii. 299.

Verily, see Ruggle, George, *Re Vera*.

Verity, A. W., ed., Milton's *Arcades, with Introduction, Notes, and Indexes* (1906), iv. 913.

Verity, A. W., ed., Milton's *Comus* (1921), iv. 914.

Vernon, Anne, ii. 612.

Vernon, Elizabeth, ii. 612.

Vernon, George, i. 15, 16, 35 n. 1, 72–88; ii. 611–12; iv. 817.
    The Life of the Learned and Reverend Dr. Peter Heylyn . . . (1682), iv. 550.

Verrier, George, iv. 596.

Versipellis, see Pestell, Thomas.

Vertue, map, by, vi. 274 n. 1.

Very Good Wife, A, see Powell, George.

Very Woman, A, see Massinger, Philip.

Vestal, The, see Glapthorne, Henry.

Vestments used in a play, i. 294.

Via Ad Latinam Linguam Complanata, see Shirley, James.

Vicars, Helen, v. 1042.

Vice-Chamberlain, vi. 260.

Vicenza, Theatro Olympico, vi. 274 n. 1, 276, 278.

Victoria and Albert Museum, i. 132; iv. 805.
    Dyce collection, v. 1348.
    Manuscripts, v. 1270, 1271, 1311.

Victoria Theatre, iv. 824.

Victualler, ii. 564.

Vienna, iii. 108; v. 1338.

Vienne, France, v. 1376.

View of London (1616), see Visscher, J. C.

Village, Royal dancing in, vii. 83.

Villarejo, Oscar M., 'Lope de Vega's comedia *El Gran duque de Moscovia* as the main source of Fletcher's *The Loyal Subject* and the partial source of Heywood's *The Royall King and the Loyall Subject* and Fletcher's *The Humorous Lieutenant*', Research in Progress, *P.M.L.A.* lxiii (1948), iii. 370, 373.

Villiers, Lord Francis, v. 1360.

Villiers, George, see Buckingham, Duke of.

Villiers, Sir John, vii. 24.

Villiers, Lady Mary, iv. 691, 692, 694; vii. 107.

Vincent, Arthur, ed., *The Poems of Thomas Carew* (1899), iii. 104, 106.

Vincent, James, ii. 613.

Vincent, Margaret, ii. 613.

Vincent, Thomas, prompter, ii. 612.

Vincent, Thomas, v. 985, 1232–3.
    Paria, iv. 527, 854; v. 1232–3, 1387, 1413, 1453.

Vincent, William, rope dancer, ii. 612–13; vi. 164, 165 n.; vii. 6, 65.

Vindication of Poesie, A, see Daniel, George.

Vindicta Tragoedia, see Mease, Peter, *Adrastus Parentans*.

Vintners, i. 314; ii. 426, 642; iii. 193; v. 1329, 1442; vi. 228.

Violence of Love, The, see Gould, Robert, *The Rival Sisters*.

Violin, treble, v. 1002.

Violins, vi. 264.

Viper and Her Brood, The, see Middleton, Thomas.

Virgil, iii. 50; iv. 838; v. 1238.
    Translated, v. 1072.
    Polydore, iii. 115.

Virgil's Eclogues, see Anonymous.

Virgin Martyr, The, see Dekker, Thomas.

Virgin Widow, The, see Quarles, Francis.

Virginia, v. 1047, 1374.
    Governor of, iii. 20, 21, 22, 23.
    State of, iv. 677.
    Treasurer of, iii. 196.

Virtue and Beauty Reconciled, see Anonymous.

Virtue and Beauty Reconciled, see Jonson, Ben.

Virtue's Triumph, see Fane, Mildmay.

Virtuoso, The, see Shadwell, Thomas.

Virtuous Octavia, The, see Brandon, Samuel.

Virtus Post Funera Vivit, or Honour Triumphing Over Death, see Sampson, William.

Visiak, E. H., and Hubert J. Foss, eds., Milton's *Comus* (1937), iv. 914.

Vision of Delight, The, see Jonson, Ben.

Vision of Lethe, The, see Anonymous.

Vision of the Twelve Goddesses, The, see Daniel, Samuel.

Visions, vi. 294.

Visitations of Essex, The, ii. 673.

Visscher, J. C., *View of London* (1616), vi. 185 n. 1.

Vitus sive Christiana Fortitudo, see Simons, Joseph.

Vizards, v. 1377.

Vocht, Henry de, iv. 609.

Vogt, George McGill, '*The Wife of Bath's Tale, Women Pleased,* and *La Fée Urgele*: A Study in the Transformation of Folk-Lore Themes in Drama', *M.L.N.* xxxvii (1922), iii. 431.

Volpone, see Jonson, Ben.

Vortiger, see Anonymous.

Vow and a Good One, A, see Anonymous.

Vow-Breaker, The, see Sampson, William.

Vox Borealis, see Newspapers.

Vox Borealis, or The Northern Discoverie, By way of Dialogue between Jamie and Willie (1640), *see* Anonymous.

Vox Graculi, or Iacke Dawes Prognostication . . . for 1623 (1623), *see* Dawe, Jack, pseud.

Vulcan, vi. 44, 183.

Vulgate Bible, v. 1415.

W., E., iv. 539.

W., J., *Valiant Scot, The,* i. 13 n. 2, 278, 282; v. 1233–6; vi. 168.

W., R., iii. 88; iv. 928, 943; v. 997, 998, 1258.

W., T., v. 1102, 1118.

Wabes, —, ii. 413.

Wadd, Thomas, ii. 384.

Wadham College, Oxford, iv. 736.
  Fellow-Commoner at, v. 1276.

Wadsworth, James, *The English Spanish Pilgrim* (1629), iv. 521.

Wagers, vi. 269.

Wagner, Bernard M., 'A Jonson Allusion, and Others', *P.Q.* vii (1928), v. 1424, 1425.
  'London's New Mermaid Theatre at Puddle Dock', *Shakespeare Quarterly,* x (1959), vi. 77.
  'Manuscript Plays of the Seventeenth Century', *T.L.S.* 4 October 1934, iii. 67, 113; iv. 728, 729, 730, 731, 834; v. 974, 1267, 1270, 1272, 1386, 1443.
  'New Verses by John Webster', *M.L.N.* xlvi (1931), v. 1240.
  'Thomas Randolph's *The Conceited Pedlar*', *T.L.S.* 9 April 1931, v. 974, 975.

Waide, Johann, ii. 613.

Waight, Richard, ii. 643.

Waintworth, John, vi. 216.

Waite, John, dedication to, iv. 712.

Waith, Eugene M., 'The Sources of *The Double Marriage* by Fletcher and Massinger', *M.L.N.* lxiv (1949), iii. 329, 331, 398, 400.
  'Tragicomedy of Humors: Fletcher's *The Loyal Subject*, A', *M.L.Q.* vi (1945), iii. 370.

Wakefield, Mr., v. 1455.

Walbanke, Elizabeth, iii. 102.

Walbanke, Mathew, stationer, iii. 102.

Walbancke, Matthew, *Annalia Dubriensia* (1636), iv. 737.

Walcott, Mackenzie E. C., ed., *An Account of the Life and Death of the Right Reverend Father in God John Hacket.* Published by Thomas Plume, D.D. (1865), iv. 525, 526, 527.

Walden, Richard, v. 1170, 1180, 1181.
  Io Ruminans (1662), iii. 104; v. 1021, 1170.

Waldron, Francis Godolphin, iv. 807.
  ed., *The Sad Shepherd . . .* (1783), iv. 625.

Wales, v. 1305; vi. 4.
  National Library of, ii. 412; v. 1040.

Walesby, Nottinghamshire, iii. 99.

Walker, Alice Burbage, i. 9; ii. 649.

Walker, Andrew Jackson, *Popular Songs and Broadside Ballads in the English Drama 1559–1642.* Harvard manuscript thesis (1934), iii. 61; v. 1364, 1365.

Walker, Henry, alias 'Luke Harruney', vi. 176.

Walker, John, property-maker, vi. 273, 278.

Walker, John, *Sufferings of the Clergy* (1714), iv. 948.

Walker, Thomas, a petticoat-maker, vi. 214.

Walkley, Thomas, stationer, iii. 108, 109, 208, 214, 217, 276, 277; iv. 615, 619, 626, 633, 809, 834, 837, 901; v. 1030, 1202, 1203.

Walks of Islington and Hogsdon with the Humours of Woodstreet Counter The, see Jordan, Thomas.

Wallace, Charles William, iii. 52, 53, 64, 86.
  Children of the Chapel at Blackfriars, 1597–1603 The (1908), vi. 3, 6, 7, 11.
  First London Theatre, The: Materials for a History (1913), vi. 140 n. 1.
  'Gervase Markham, Dramatist', *Shakespeare Jahrbuch,* xlvi (1910), ii. 682–3; iv. 732.
  Globe Theatrical Apparel (1909), v. 1015.
  'Shakspere and the Blackfriars', *Century Magazine,* lxxx (1910), iii. 52, 64, 88.
  'Shakespeare and the Globe', *The Times,* London, 30 April 1914, vi. 247, 248.
  Shakespeare and his London Associates (1910), iii. 300; vii. 31.
  'Swan Theatre and the Earl of Pembroke's Servants, The', *Englische Studien,* xliii (1910–11), vi. 249, 250.
  Three London Theatres of Shakespeare's Time (1909), vi. 47, 54, 57, 215, 216 n. 1, 219.

Wallace, Sir William, v. 1236.

Wallenstein, assassination of, iv. 761; v. 1109.

Wallenstein, Albert, iv. 474.

Waller, A. R., and Arnold Glover, eds., *The Works of Francis Beaumont and John Fletcher,* 10 vols. (1905–12), iii. 312.

Waller (amateur actor), iii. 296.

Waller, Edmund, iii. 277.

Waller, William, iii. 21.

Wallerstein, Ruth, 'Cowley as a Man of Letters' *Transactions of the Wisconsin Academy of Sciences, Arts, and Letters,* xxvii (1932), iii. 173.

'Suckling's Imitation of Shakespeare', *R.E.S.* iii (1926), v. 1210, 1212.

Walley, Harold Reinoehl, and John Harold Wilson, eds., *Early Seventeenth-Century Plays 1600–1642* (1930), iii. 205, 425.

Wallinger, Ben, iii. 676, 678.

Wallingford, Berkshire, iv. 725.

Wallis, John, v. 1277.

Wallis, Lawrence B., *Fletcher, Beaumont, & Company. Entertainers to the Jacobean Gentry* (1947), iii. 305.

Wallography, or the Britton Described, see Richards, William.

Wallrath, Hans, *William Sampson's Vow-Breaker, Materialien zur Kunde des alteren Englischen Dramas* (1914), v. 1042, 1043, 1045.

Walpole, Mr., amateur actor, v. 1298.

Walpole, Francis, i. 165, 171; ii. 613.

Walpole, Horace, *Anecdotes of Painting in England . . .,* 5 vols. (1826–8), v. 993, 994.

Walter, J. H., 'Henry Glapthorne', *T.L.S.* 19 September 1936, iv. 473, 474, 476–7, 480.
  ed., Mountfort's *The Launching of the Mary,* Malone Society Reprints (1933), iv. 923, 924.
  Plays and Poems of Henry Glapthorne, The, London MS. thesis (1935), iv. 473, 475, 476, 477, 490, 492.
  'Revenge for Honour: Date, Authorship and Sources', *R.E.S.* xiii (1937), iii. 278; iv. 478, 479, 480, 483, 489, 490, 491–2.
  '"Wit in a Constable": Censorship and Revision', *M.L.R.* xxxiv (1939), iv. 494, 495, 496, 497.

Walton, Izaak, *The Lives,* ed. 1807, v. 1098.

Wamus, Francis, *see* Wambus, Francis.

Wambus, Francis, i. 176, 181, 182, 189, 192, 197; ii. 613–15; v. 1456.

The Wanderer, see Killigrew, Thomas, *Thomaso.*

Wandering Jew, The, see Anonymous.

Wandering Lovers, The, see Fletcher, John, *The Lovers' Progress.*

Wandering Whore Continued, The (1660), *see* Garfield, John.

Wanibus, Francis, *see* Wambus, Francis.

Wapping, *see* London, streets and districts.

Warbeck, Perkin, v. 1096, 1383.

Warboys, Huntingdonshire, iv. 600.

Warburton, Ann Benfield, ii. 376.

Warburton, —, apothecary, ii. 376.

Warburton, John, iv. 510; v. 1177.
His list of MS. plays, i. 60 n. 4, 108, 120, 123, 125, 132, 134; iii. 30, 31, 204, 230, 250, 262, 438, 445, 448, 458, 465; iv. 481, 488, 493, 518, 543, 598, 684, 720, 758, 759, 760, 763, 765, 782, 785, 786, 791, 793, 794, 795, 800, 804, 806, 808, 819, 820, 829, 830, 892; v. 1022, 1025, 1026, 1046, 1178, 1272, 1273, 1275, 1309, 1317, 1331, 1366, 1373, 1384.

War of the Theatres, iii. 242; iv. 607.

War Without Blows and Love without Suit (Strife), see Heywood, Thomas.

Ward, A. W., *A History of English Dramatic Literature to the Death of Queen Anne* (1899), iii. 216, 272, 313, 316, 359, 415, 434, 460, 463; iv. 744; v. 980, 1113, 1114, 1164, 1372.

Ward, Henry, amateur actor, iv. 473.

Ward, Mr., iv. 601.

Ward, Robert, v. **1236–9**.
Fucus Histriomastix or Fucus sive Histriomastix, iv. 530, 532, 853; v. 1016, 1196, **1237–9**.
Fucus Histriomastix, ed., G. C. Moore Smith (1909), iv. 528.

Ward, William C., ed., *The Poems of William Drummond of Hawthornden (Muses' Library)*, 2 vols. (1894), iii. 289.

Warde, Ja:, ii. 675.

Warde, The, see Neale, Thomas.

Wardrobe, great, ii. 505.
His Majesty's, vi. 80.
Keeper, i. 26 n. 5 cont.; ii. 491, 546; iv. 517; vi. 164, 169, 227.

Officer of the, vi. 291 n. 1.

Wardrobes, iv. 650; v. 1229, 1288, 1432.
Theatrical, *see* Costumes.

Warner, Bartholomew, v. 1181.

Warner, George F., iii. 279.
'Autograph Play of Philip Massinger, An', *Athenaeum*, 19 January 1901, iv. 762.
Catalogue of the MSS. and Muniments of Alleyn's College of God's Gift at Dulwich, v. 1332, 1367, 1419; vi. 79, 86, 139, 150.

Warnford, Hampshire, iv. 944, 945.

'Warning for Maidens, A', *see* Anonymous.

Warren, Robert, v. 1239.

Warren, Thomas, iii. 194, 195, 204.

Wars of the Low Countries, The, see Brome, Richard, and Heywood, Thomas.

Wars of Pompey and Caesar, The, see Chapman, George.

Wharton, Thomas, *Poems upon Several Occasions . . . by John Milton* (1785), v. 1276.

Warwick, ii. 484; iv. 658, 659; vii. 40.

Warwick Castle, i. 60; iii. 221; v. 1005.
Players' bill at, i, 60 and n. 3; iii. 221.

Warwick, Earl of, iv. 842; v. 1197, 1268, 1269, 1383.
House of, vii. 34.

Warwickshire, iv. 649.

'Was there a "Tarras" in Shakespeare's Globe?', *see* Reynolds, George F.

Washbourne, William, ii. 411.

Washington, William, iv. 868.

Washington, D.C., Folger Shakespeare Library, *see* Folger Shakespeare Library.

Wasp, The, see Anonymous.

Water pageants, iv. 576, 577, 578, 584–5, 898–9, 926; v. 1185, 1223, 1225, 1254.

Water Poet (John Taylor), *see* Taylor, John.

Waterhouse, David, v. 1239.
Cleophilus, v. 1239.

Watermen, ii. 486, 510, 690; iv. 852; v. 1224; vi. 175.

Waterson, John, stationer, iii. 201, 204, 352; iv. 629, 778, 797, 798, 809, 812, 821; v. 1234.

Waterston, Francis, iv. 745.

Waterworks, vi. 294.
On stage, vi. 233.

Watkins-Jones, A., 'Seventeenth-Century Plays', *T.L.S.* 15 November 1934, iv. 728.
Watkinson, amateur actor, iii. 296.
Watson, R., iii. 186.
Watson, Thomas, v. 1388.
Way to Content All Women, The, see Gunnell, Richard.
Way to Make a Knave Honest, A, see Anonymous.
Waymus, Francis, *see* Wambus, Francis.
Weakest Goeth to the Wall, see Anonymous.
Wealth Outwitted, see Jordan, Thomas, *Money Is an Ass.*
Weaver, Edmund, stationer, iii. 449; v. 1019, 1049, 1080, 1156.
Weavers, ii. 464, 564, 566, 646.
Webb, John, architect, iv. 524; v. 1335; vi. 274 n. 1, 286.
Weber, Henry, ed., *The Works of Beaumont and Fletcher* . . . 14 vols. (1812), iii. 316, 321, 325, 329, 336, 356, 379, 393, 401.
ed., *The Dramatic Works of John Ford,* 2 vols. (1811), iii. 438.
Weber, Kurt, *Lucius Cary, Second Viscount Falkland* (1940), iii. 108, 181.
Webster, John, English actor in Germany, v. 1241.
Webster, John, ii. 526; iii. 244, 252, 261, 262, 265, 268, 272, 280, 286, 337, 436; iv. 499, 575, 860, 861; v. 964, 997, 1018, 1234, 1239-56; vi. 44, 222.
Influence of, iii. 201; v. 1087.
Brother of, v. 1243.
Appius and Virginia or The Roman Virgin or The Unjust Judge, i. 331, 341; v. 1120, 1241, 1245-8, 1254.
Devil's Law-Case, or When Women Go to Law the Devil is Full of Business, The, i. 174; v. 1241, 1250-2, 1253, 1254, 1364; vi. 218; vii. 51.
Duchess of Malfi, The, i. 28, 76-77, 96, 132; ii. 374, 375, 395, 410, 465, 501, 519, 520, 533, 547, 552, 569, 570, 593, 600, 601, 602, 610, 611, 692; iii. 201, 437, 441; iv. 813, 816; v. 1017, 1087, 1241, 1242, 1243, 1244, 1252, 1253, 1371; vi. 14, 198; vii. 51, 123.

'Excellent Actor, An', v. 1243.
Fair Maid of the Inn, The, v. 1252-3.
Guise, v. 1059, 1253-4.
Late Murder in Whitechapel, or Keep the Widow Waking, The, see Dekker Thomas.
Love's Graduate, see A Cure for a Cuckold.
Malcontent, The, see Marston, John.
Monumental Column, A, v. 1241, 1255.
Monuments of Honour, v. 1240, 1241, 1243, 1254-5; vii. 57.
Roman Virgin Or Unjust Judge, The, see Appius and Virginia.
Thracian Wonder, The, v. 1256.
'To his beloved friend Maister Thomas Heywood', v. 1241.
White Devil, The, i. 259; ii. 526; v. 1241, 1243, 1244, 1251, 1253; vi. 218; vii. 77, 81, 90.
Caesar's Fall, or The Two Shapes, with Dekker, Drayton, Middleton, and Munday, v. 1240, 1241, 1248.
Christmas Comes But Once A Year, with Chettle, Dekker, and Heywood, v. 1248.
Cure for a Cuckold, A, with William Rowley, v. 1248-50; iii. 358; iv. 807; v. 1248-50.
Lady Jane, with Chettle, Dekker, Heywood, and Wentworth Smith, v. 1254.
Late Murder of the Son upon the Mother, or Keep the Widow Waking, with Dekker, Ford, and Rowley, *see* Dekker, Thomas.
Northward Ho!, with Thomas Dekker, v. 1255.
Sir Thomas Wyatt, with Thomas Dekker, v. 1255.
Westward Ho!, with Thomas Dekker, v. 1256.
Webster, John (not the playwright), *The Displaying of Supposed Witchcraft,* 1677, i. 41 n. 3.
Weckherlin, George Rudolph, v. 1288.
Wedding, The, see Shirley, James.
Wedel, Lupold von, vi. 201, 209 n. 1.
Wedgwood, C. V., 'Last Masque, The'. *Truth and Opinion: Historical Essays* (1960), vi. 285, 288.
Wedwer, William, ii. 615.
Weeding of Covent Garden, see Brome, Richard.

Weekes, Mr., stationer, v. 1108, 1109.
Weekly Account, The, see Newspapers.
Weeks, Ann, ii. 616.
Weeks, Joan, ii. 616.
Weeks, Richard, i. 189, 192, 272, 273, 275, 276, 281, 282 n. 1; ii. 615–16; vi. 164.
Weeping Lady, The, see Brewer, Thomas.
Welbeck Abbey, Nottinghamshire, i. 310; iii. 142, 143, 148; iv. 612, 648, 653, 654; v. 1202.
Manuscripts at, iii. 146; iv. 883.
Welbeck Miscellany (1934), iii. 146.
Welby, Henry, iv. 928.
   The Phoenix of These Late Times (1637), iv. 738.
Welcome from the Isle of Rhe, A, see Anonymous, *In Duc Reducem.*
Welcome songs, iv. 649.
Weldon, Anthony, *The Court and Character of King James* (1651), i. 181; iv. 651.
Wellek, Rene, 'Bohemia in Early English Literature', *Slavonic and Eastern European Review*, xxi (1943), v. 1286.
Wells, William, iii. 390.
   'Alphonsus, Emperor of Germany', *N. & Q.* clxxix (1940), v. 1286.
   'Birth of Merlin. 1608, *The',* M.L.R. xvi (1921), v. 1021.
   'Bloody Brother, The', *N. & Q.* cliv (1928), iii. 401.
Welsford, Enid, *The Court Masque* (1927), iii. 199, 200, 207, 208, 213, 216, 218; iv. 637, 669, 672, 676, 677, 907, 909, 937, 938, 939, 940; v. 1102, 1154, 1227, 1228, 1229, 1290.
Welsh, iv. 642; v. 1219, 1304.
   Speeches, iv. 641, 642.
Welsh Ambassador, or A Comedy in Disguises, The, see Dekker, Thomas.
Welsh Traveller, The, see Anonymous.
Welsh Traveller, or the unfortunate Welshman, The, see Crouch, Humphrey.
Welshmen, iv. 671; v. 1147.
Welsted, Leonard, v. 1341.
Wentworth, Sir John, i. 47 n. 3; ii. 368, 371, 660, 676.
Wentworth, Thomas, first Earl of Strafford, iii. 22, 24, 41, 199, 200, 207, 217, 218, 219; iv. 831, 949; vi. 29, 266, 286, 287.

Earl of Strafforde's Letters and Dispatches, The, see Knowler, William.
Werburgh Street Theatre, Dublin, iv. 679; v. 1069; vi. 193.
Werner, Alexander, *Thomas May als Lustspieldichter* (1894), iv. 830.
Wesley, Samuel, Maggots, or Poems on Several Subjects (1685), iv. 681.
West, Mistress, v. 1289.
West, Edward Sackville, 'The Significance of *The Witch of Edmonton', Criterion*, xvii (1937), iii. 270.
West, Richard, v. 965.
West, Sibilla, ii. 523.
West, Thomas, third Lord Delawarr, v. 1289.
West Dereham, Norfolk, v. 1226.
West Harling, Norfolk, i. 312.
West Milton, Dorset, iii. 47.
West Wickham, Kent, iii. 104.
Westerman, John, v. 1067, 1068.
Westminster, *see* London, streets and districts.
   Abbey, iii. 15, 144, 175, 197, 443; iv. 551, 600, 612, 696, 832, 833; v. 1140; vii. 60.
   Organist of, iii. 422.
   Assembly, iv. 853.
   Boys, v. 978, 1329.
   Canon of, iv. 690–1.
   Chapter House, vi. 117 n. 1.
   Hall, i. 145; v. 1377; vi. 157, 232.
   Matthew of, *Flores Historiarum*, iii. 115.
   Palace yard, v. 1299.
   School, ii. 470; iii. 126, 173, 174, 179, 180, 181, 182; iv. 525, 526, 844, 850, 852, 947, 948, 952; v. 965, 966, 1180, 1181, 1187, 1195, 1198, 1222, 1232.
      Headmaster of, iii. 137.
      Jonson at, iv. 606.
      King's Scholar at, iv. 498, 540.
   Sheriffs of, vi. 176.
Westmorland, iii. 38, 39, 143; v. 1236.
Westmorland, Mildmay Fane, second Earl of, *see* Fane, Mildmay.
Weston, Lord, dedication to, iii. 201.
Weston, Thomas, ii. 551.
Westward Ho! see Webster, John.
Westwood, Jonas, vi. 48.
Whaddon, Wiltshire, v. 1054.
Whalebone, vi. 273, 278.
Whalley, Peter, ed., *The Works of Ben Jonson*, 7 vols. (1756), iv. 613.

Whalley, Peter, and G. Colman, eds., *The Dramatic Works of Ben Jonson, and Beaumont and Fletcher*, 4 vols. (1811), iv. 613.

Wharton, Rachel, ii. 478.

What You Please, see Anonymous, *The Whisperer.*

What You Will, see Marston, John.

Wheatley, Andrew, ii. 643.

Wheaton, Elizabeth, ii. 616–17, 639.

Wheeler, C. F., *Classical Mythology in the Plays, Masques, and Poems of Ben Jonson* (1938), iv. 606.

When Women Go to Law the Devil is Full of Business, see Webster, John, *The Devil's Law-Case.*

When You See Me, You Know Me, see Rowley, Samuel.

Whethampstead, Hertfordshire, iv. 691.

Rector of, iv. 691.

Whetstone, George, *Promos and Cassandra*, iv. 902.

Whetstone, Roger, ii. 617.

Whetstone, Thomas, ii. 617.

Whibble, The, see Anonymous.

Which Is the Best Girl, see Anonymous, *Politic Bankrupt.*

Whimsies of Senor Hidalgo, The, see Anonymous.

'*Whimzey written from beyond Seas, see* Flecknoe, Richard, *Miscellania.*

Whimzies, see Brathwait, Richard. See Chamberlain, Robert.

Whirligig, The, see Anonymous.

Whisperer, The, see Anonymous.

Whitaker, Lawrence, Alderman, vi. 27, 28.

Whitaker, Richard, v. 1095, 1143.

Whitaker, Thomas, bookseller, iii. 47.

Whitbee, William, ii. 457.

Whitby, Mr., vi. 21.

Whitchurch, Denbighshire, v. 1040.

White, Edward, v. 1385; vi. 179 n. 1.

White, Francis, iii. 27; iv. 552; v. 1256–7.

White, Josias, ii. 617.

White, Mary, ii. 617.

White, Robert, actor, ii. 617.

White, Robert, v. 1257–8, 1436. *Cupid's Banishment*, v. 1257–8.

White, W. A., of Brooklyn, v. 977. Library, iii. 99, 100.

White Devil, The, see Webster, John.

White Ethiopian, The, see Anonymous.

White Moor, The, see Dekker, Thomas.

White Hart in the Old Bailey, ii. 343, 682.

White Horse, Norwich, v. 1455.

White Witch of Westminster, The, see Anonymous.

Whitebakers, vi. 126.

Whitechapel, *see* London, streets and districts.

Whitecross street, *see* London, streets of.

Liberty of, *see* London, streets of.

Whitefriars, precinct of, *see* London, streets and districts.

Whitefriars theatre, i. 176; ii. 540, 554, 574; iv. 722, 723, 862; vi. 12 n. 1, 78; vi. 115–17, 122.

'Whitefriars Theatre, The, the Salisbury Court Theatre, and the Duke's Theatre in Dorset Gardens', *see* Cunningham, Peter.

Whitehall, Banqueting House, *see* Banqueting House, Whitehall.

Whitehall palace and environs, i. 28 n. 1, 34, 39 n. 1, 49, 104, 133, 178, 222, 223, 230, 234, 244, 284, 311, 333; ii. 695; iii. 107, 115, 129, 199, 200, 204, 214, 219, 313, 315, 320, 330, 345, 349, 360, 370, 404, 408, 420, 460, 461; iv. 485, 505, 522, 523, 524, 573, 615, 642, 660, 664, 673, 691, 720, 738, 742, 743, 766, 848, 849, 862, 888, 893; v. 969, 970, 971, 974, 1023, 1032, 1110, 1156, 1157, 1158, 1199, 1230, 1269, 1297, 1334; vi. 15, 45, 49, 62, 65, 92 n. 1, 114, 170, 232, 255, 261, 266, 282, 284 n. 1, 285, 286, 288, 296; vii. 19, 23, 26, 29, 30, 35, 39, 57, 58, 63, 66, 67, 70, 77, 81, 82, 107, 108, 110, 120.

Whitehall Palace. Bowling alleys, vi. 268.

Chapel Court, vi. 255.

Cockpit area, vi. 270, n. 1.

Cockpits in, vi. 268, 269, 270, 271, 272, 273, 280 n. 1.

First Court, vi. 286.

Garden, vi. 268.

Great Chamber, vi. 256, 270, 285; vii. 25, 28, 34, 38, 63, 64, 69.

On the Queen's side, vii. 38, 42, 45.

Great Hall, vi. 256, 263, 264, 267, 269, 270, 277, 281 n. 1, 283; vii. 25, 39, 65, 84, 87.

Great Room, vii. 59.

Guard at, vi. 237.

Whitehall Palace (*cont.*)
  Guard Chamber, vi. 286.
  Hall, iii. 111; vi. 52; vii. 21, 28, 30, 38, 42, 45, 63, 64, 69, 87.
  Holbein Gate, vi. 255.
  Long gallery, v. 1157.
  Masque at, iii. 106, 108, 208.
  Masquing Room, vii. 119.
  New Year's Gift Chamber, vii. 87.
  Orchard, vi. 268.
  Palace Gate, vi. 255.
  Play at, iii. 377.
  Preaching place, vi. 286.
  Presence Chamber, vii. 119.
  Privy Chamber on the Queen's side, vii. 38.
  Sermon Court, vi. 255.
  Tennis courts, vi. 268, 270 n. 1.
  Terrace at, vi. 285.
  Tiltyard, vi. 1157; vi. 255, 268, 296; vii. 27, 36, 48.
  Whitehall 'Square', vi. 255.
Whitehead, Christopher, ii. 617.
Whitelock, Bulstrode, vi. 32.
  Memorials of the English Affairs (1732), v. 1154, 1160, 1161, 1162.
  Whitelocke's Coranto, i. 40; vi. 32.
Whitford, David, iv. 950.
Whiting, Edward, ii. 617–18.
Whiting, Edward, surgeon, ii. 617.
Whiting, Richard, ii. 618–19.
Whitlock, Richard, *Zootomia* (1654), iv. 845.
Whitmore, George, iv. 578.
Whitney, Lieutenant, ii. 568.
Whitton, Middlesex, v. 1213.
'Whoop Doe Me Noe Harm', *see* Anonymous.
Whore of Babylon, The, see Dekker, Thomas.
Whore in Grain, The, see Anonymous.
Whore New Vamped, The, see Anonymous.
Whores (in London), iii. 416.
Wich, Worcestershire, iv. 927.
Wickes, Henry, Paymaster, vi. 271, 272, 273.
Wicks, Richard, *see* Weeks, Richard.
Widow, The, see Middleton, Thomas.
Widow Captain, The, see Anonymous.
Widow's Prize, The, see Sampson, William.
Widow's Tears, The, see Chapman, George.
Wife and Brother, The, see Burges, James Bland, *Riches*.

Wife for a Month, A, see Fletcher, John.
Wife's Relief, The, see Johnson, Charles.
Wife's Stratagem, The, see Poole, John.
Wiggett, Thomas, *see* Wigpitt, Thomas.
Wiggin [Leonard], Pauline G., *An Inquiry into the Authorship of the Middleton–Rowley Plays.* Radcliffe College Monographs, No. 9 (1897), iv. 856, 862, 863, 867, 870, 893, 909; v. 1015, 1018.
Wight, Isle of, ii. 657 n. 4.
Wignor-bridge, vii. 41.
Wigpitt, Thomas, bricklayer, i. 142, 143, 144; ii. 545, 619; vi. 155, 157.
Wilborowe, Thomas, ii. 631.
Wilbraham, Avice, ii. 619.
Wilbraham, William, i. 220, 246, 286, 290, 297; ii. 619; vi. 75.
Wild, Dr. George, v. 994.
Wild, Robert, v. 1264–6.
  'Alas! poor scholar, whither wilt thou go?', v. 1265.
  Benefice, The, iii. 466; iv. 598; v. 1265–6.
  Iter Boreale, v. 1265.
Wild beast fights, vi. 294, 298.
Wild Gallant, see Dryden, John.
Wild-goose Chase, The, see Anonymous.
Wild Goose Chase, The, see Fletcher, John.
Wilde, George, v. 1182, 1259–64.
  Eumorphus sive Cupido-Adultus, v. 1182, 1183, 1259–60, 1350, 1357.
  Love's Hospital (Lovers' Hospital), iii. 135, 136; iv. 849; v. 1182, 1183, 1189, 1195, 1260–4, 1275, 1411.
Wilde, Henry, iv. 897; v. 1259.
Wildman, Martha, v. 1057.
Wilkes, Marie, ii. 633.
Wilkins, George, v. 1015, 1017, 1026.
  Miseries of Enforced Marriage, The, iv. 584; vii. 73, 106, 108.
Wilkinson, Charles, ii. 601.
Wilkinson, C. H., 'A Note on Thomas May', *R.E.S.* xi (1935), iv. 830, 832.
  ed., *The Poems of Richard Lovelace*, 2 vols. (1925), iv. 720, 721, 724.
Wilkinson, John, ii. 384.
Wilkinson, Nicholas, *see* Tooley, Nicholas.

Wilkinson, R., *Londina Illustrata* (ed. 1819–25), iv. 747.

Will of a Woman, The, see Chapman, George.

Willans, George, *see* Williams, George.

William Hemminge's Elegy on Randolph's Finger Containing the Well-Known Lines 'On the Time-Poets', see Smith, G. C. Moore.

William of Malmesbury, iv. 788.

'William Trevell and the Whitefriars Theatre', *see* Dickson, M. J.

William of Wickam, v. 1394.

Williams, Bishop, Lord Keeper, iv. 526, 551; v. 965, 1180.

Williams, Edmond, ii. 357.

Williams, Sir Edmund, v. 1051, 1052.

Williams, Elizabeth, ii. 620.

Williams, George, i. 272, 281, 286, 290, 297; ii. **619–20.**

Williams, Hugh, v. 1341.

Williams, J. D. E., *Sir William Davenant's Relation to Shakespeare* (1905), iii. 198.

Williams, John, Bishop of Lincoln, vii. 71, 79.

Williams, John, Dean of Westminster, iv. 525.

Williams, John, i. 201 n. 1; ii. **620;** iv. 739, 748; v. 1073, 1074, 1128, 1129, 1130, 1131; vi. 291, 292, 293, 297, 298, 299, 301, 302, 303, 304.

Williams, Roger Folkestone, ed., *Court and Times of Charles I, The,* 2 vols. (1848) (from records compiled by Thomas Birch), iii. 139, 453; iv. 528, 530, 610, 646, 652, 917, 918, 919; v. 973, 1197, 1229, 1232; vi. 87, 179 n. 1; vii. 62, 63, 64, 66, 71, 72.

Williams (sister of Lady Alice Carleton), vi. 182.

Williams, Walter, i. 286, 297; ii. **620;** iv. 686.

Williamson, Joseph, vi. 235.

Willington, Thomas, ii. 442.

Willis, —, v. 1157, 1158.

Willis, Mr., iii. 177.

Willis, Richard, ii. **620.**

Willobie, Fulke Greville, 5th Lord, v. 1311.

Willoughby, Anne, v. 1042, 1044.

Willoughby, Elizabeth, v. 1042.

Willoughby, Sir Henry, i. 42; v. 1042, 1044, 1199.

Willowby's players, vii. 12 n. 1.

Wills, ii. 631–51; iii. 4, 47, 113, 167,
175, 306, 435; v. 1027, 1042, 1049, 1057, 1071, 1269; vi. 70.

Wilson, Arthur, v. 1266–74.

His autobiography, v. 1274.

Corporal, The, i. 66, 102 n. a, 105–6, 132; v. 1268, **1270–3,** 1273.

History of Great Britain, Being the Life and Reign of King James the First, relating what passed from his first Access to the Crown, till his Death, The (1653), v. 1269, 1274.

Inconstant Lady, or Better Late Than Never, The, i. 27 and n. 2, 66, 96, 132; iii. 381; iv. 862; v. 1268, 1270, **1271–3,** 1314, 1360, 1397.

'Observations of God's Providence, in the Tract of my Life', in Francis Peck, ed., *Desiderata Curiosa* (1732), Lib. xii, No. v (1779), i. 106; v. 1267.

Swisser, The, i. 66, 71, 84–85, 132; ii. 375, 446, 447, 451, 452, 502, 524, 532, 534, 571, 576, 586, 594, 600, 605, 606; v. 1268, 1273.

Wilson, Captain, ii. 568.

Wilson, Edward M., 'Did John Fletcher Read Spanish?' *P.Q.* xxvii (1948), iii. 319, 321, 350.

'Rule a Wife and Have a Wife and *El Sagaz Estacio*', *R.E.S.* xxiv (1948), iii. 408, 410.

Wilson, Edward M., and Olga Turner, 'The Spanish Protest against *A Game at Chess*', *M.L.R.* xliv (1949), iv. 872, 873; vi. 184 n. 1.

Wilson, Professor Frank Percy, vi. 271 n. 1.

'More Records from the Remembrancia of the City of London', *Malone Soc. Collections,* iv (1956), vi. 77.

Plague in Shakespeare's London, The, Oxford (1927), vi. 162.

'Three Notes on Thomas Dekker', *M.L.R.* xv (1920), iii. 241, 242, 245.

Wilson, Frank P., *see* Cook, David, and 'Elizabethan Theatre, The', *Neophilologus,* xxxix (1955), vi. 259, 263.

Wilson, F. P., and W. W. Greg, eds., *The Witch by Thomas Middleton,* Malone Society Reprints, 1948 (1950), iv. 903.

Wilson, George, i. 236; ii. 597, **620–1**, 661 n. 1; vi. 99; vii. 57.

Wilson, Henry, i. 15, 72–88; ii. **621**; iv. 765.

Wilson, John Dover, i. 11 n. 6 cont.
ed., *Macbeth* (1947), iv. 903, 905.
(Review of R. C. Bald's ed. of Middleton's *A Game at Chess*), *Library*, 4th Series, xi (1930), iv. 870.

Wilson, John Dover, and R. W. Hunt, 'The Authenticity of Simon Forman's *Bocke of Plaies*', *R.E.S.* xxiii (1947), vi. 16 n. 1.

Wilson, John, actor, ii. 355, 578, **621–2**.

Wilson, Dr. John, iii. 84.

Wilson, John, father of Arthur, v. 1267.

Wilson, John Harold, *The Influence of Beaumont and Fletcher on Restoration Drama* (1928), iii. 306, 328.

Wilson, Jone, ii. 622.

Wilson, Joseph, ii. 587, 648.

Wilson, Joseph, junior, ii. 587.

Wilson, Robert, iv. 936.
Hannibal and Hermes, or Worse Afeared than Hurt, iv. 936.
Oldcastle, see Drayton, Samuel.

Wilson, Sarah, ii. 587, 648.

Wilson, Sr., college actor, v. 1298.

Wilson, Susan, v. 1267.

Wilson, Thomas, iv. 682, 688.

Wilson, the widow, iv. 482.

Wilson, William, ii. **622–3**.

Wilson, William, stationer, iii. 403, 408.

Wilton House, iii. 276; iv. 751.

Wiltshire, ii. 382; v. 1358.
Dialect, v. 1358.

Wily Beguiled, see Anonymous.

Wimberley, William, iv. 689.

Winchelsea, M.P. for, iii. 468.

Winchester, i. 92, 156, 180, 193, 212, 213; ii. 349; iv. 853; v. 1276.
Bishop of, vi. 202 and n. 2, 203, 204, 205.
School, v. 1183, 1394.

Windebank, Sir Francis, Secretary of State, iii. 135, 139, 140; iv. 637; v. 1266, 1404; vi. 27, 39, 72, 300, 304.

Windebank, Thomas, iii. 214; v. 1158.

Winden, Elizabeth, ii. 534.

Windmill Tavern in Lothbury, i. 266.

Windsor, i. 93; iv. 645, 646, 696; vii. 53.

Castle Library, iii. 381.
Royal collection at, iii. 106.

Wine, Beer, and Ale [and Tobacco], see Anonymous.

Wines, duty on, v. 1442.

Wines, new duty on, i. 314; vi. 228.

Wing, Donald, *Short-Title Catalogue* . . . 1641–1700, 3 vols. (1945), iv. 680; v. 1038.

Winsor-Bull, The, vi. 213.

Winstanley, William, *The Lives of the Most Famous English Poets* (1687), iii. 18, 47–48, 84; iv. 507, 841, 994, 995; v. 1242, 1323, 1371.

Winter and summer theatres, i. 3 n. 7.

Winter, De, ed., *The Staple of News by Ben Jonson* (1905), iv. 618, 628, 631, 632.

Winter performances, income from, i. 24.

Wintersall, *or* Winterscale, William, *see* Wintershall, William.

Wintershall, Jane, ii. 623.

Wintershall, Margaret, ii. 400; vi. 158.

Wintershall, William, ii. 400, 623–4; v. 1092; vi. 89, 90, 91 n., 158.

Wintershall, William, junior, ii. 623.

Winter's Tale, The, see Shakespeare.

Winthrop, John, v. 1398.

Winthrop Papers, ed., Allyn Bailey Forbes, Massachusetts Historical Society, 5 vols., Boston (1929–47), v. 1398.

Wire, vi. 273, 278.

Wisdom of Doctor Dodipoll, The, see Anonymous.

Wise Woman of Hogsdon, The, see Heywood, Thomas.

Wiseman, Robert, Sir, iv. 756, 788.

Wiston, Sussex, v. 1057.

Wit and Drollery, see Anonymous.

Wit and Fancy in a Maze [Don Zara del Fogo], see Holland, Samuel.

Wit at Several Weapons, see Fletcher, John.

Wit in a Constable, see Glapthorne, Henry.

Wit in a Madness, see Brome, Richard.

Wit in a Wildernesse of Promiscuous Poesie, see Jordan, Thomas.

Wit in Necessity, see Anonymous, *The Fashionable Lover*.

Wit Without Money, see Fletcher, John.

Witch, The, see Middleton, Thomas.

Witch of Edmonton, The, see Dekker, Thomas.
Witch Traveller, The, see Anonymous, *The Welsh Traveller.*
Witchcraft, iii. 13, 73–76.
Witches, iii. 73–76, 270.
Lancashire, vi. 100.
Witches in plays, i. 40–41.
Witham, Essex, iv. 947.
Wither, George, ii. 557; iv. 674, 676; v. 1341.
Impersonated, iii. 201.
Abuses Stript and Whipt (1613), iii. 201; vi. 133.
'Of the Passion of Love', vi. 241.
Britain's Remembrancer (1628), vii. 12.
Withington, Robert, *English Pageantry*, 2 vols. (1918), iv. 911; vii. 112.
'Lord Mayor's Show for 1623, The', *P.M.L.A.* xxx (1915), iv. 896, 898, 926.
Withorn, John, of Broomhead, iii. 229.
Withrington, Mr., iv. 615.
Wits, The, see Anonymous.
Wits, The, see Davenant, William.
Wits Interpreter, The, see Cotgrave, John.
Wits Led by the Nose, see Anonymous.
Wits Recreations, see Anonymous.
Wits or Sport upon Sport, see Kirkman, Francis.
Witt, Johannes de, *see* de Witt.
Wittenberg, v. 1055.
Witter, John, ii. 411, 468, **624**.
Witter *vs.* Heminges and Condell, ii. 468, 624; vi. 182 n. 3.
Wittkower, Rudolph, 'Inigo Jones, Architect and Man of Letters', *Journal of the Royal Institute of British Architects*, Third Series, lx (1952–3), vi. 259, 261.
Witty Fair One, The, see Shirley, James.
Wives' Prize, The, see Anonymous, *A Match without Money.*
Wizard, The, see Baylie, Thomas.
Woking, Surrey, i. 20; vii. 37.
Wold, Northamptonshire, iv. 533.
Wolf, Heinrich, *Thomas May's Tragedy of Cleopatra Queen of Egypt* (1914), iv. 834.
Wolgast, Duke of, ii. 429.
Wolvercot, Oxfordshire, iv. 592.
Wolverhampton, Staffordshire, v. 1391.

Woman Captain, The, see Sampson, William, *The Widow's Prize.*
Woman Hater, The, see Beaumont and Fletcher.
Woman is a Weathercock, A, see Field, Nathan.
Woman Is Too Hard for Him, The, see Anonymous.
Woman Killed with Kindness, A, see Heywood, Thomas.
Woman Wears the Breeches, The, see Brome, Richard, *The City Wit.*
Woman will have her will, A, see Houghton, William, *Englishmen for My Money.*
Woman's Law, The, see Anonymous.
Woman's Masterpiece, The, see Anonymous.
Woman's Mistaken, The, see Davenport, Robert.
Woman's Plot, The, see Massinger, Philip.
Woman's Prize, The, see Fletcher, John.
Woman's Spleen and Love's Conquest, The, see Jones, John, *Adrasta.*
Wombwell, William, ii. 355.
Women actors, i. 25; iii. 82, 104, 128, 128–30, 197, 314, 320, 325, 345, 412, 450, 452, 453; iv. 479, 548, 701, 702, 767–8, 799, 848, 900, 917; v. 1021, 1085, 1092, 1115, 1122, 1145, 1170, 1210, 1211, 1257, 1258, 1334, 1362; vi. 23, 66, 225, 280.
Condemnation of, iv. 919–20; vi. 23.
Female cast, iv. 701–2, 705.
In men's roles, iv. 479–80, 549; v. 971, 1115.
Women Beware Women, see Middleton, Thomas.
Women dramatists, v. 1021.
Women Pleased, see Fletcher, John.
Women Wear the Breeches, The, see Anonymous, *The Gossips' Brawl.*
Women's Conquest, The, see Howard, Edward.
Wonder of a Kingdom, The, see Dekker, Thomas.
Wonder of Women, The, see Marston, John.
Wood, Abraham, ii. 624.
Wood, A. C., ed. *Memorials of the Holles Family, 1493–1656, By Gervase Holles.* Camden Society, Third Series, vol. lv (1937), iv. 586.

Wood, Alice, ii. 624.

Wood, Anthony, ii. 624; iv. 515, 827; v. 992, 1065, 1066, 1070, 1179, 1191; vi. 76.

His accounts, v. 1169.

Athenae Oxonienses. An Exact History of all the Writers and Bishops who have had their Education in The University of Oxford from 1500 to 1690, 2 vols. (1691–2), iii. 21, 38, 39, 41, 94, 126, 127, 136, 137, 138, 143, 145, 152, 167, 275, 277, 303; iv. 498, 499, 500, 511, 512, 514, 520, 521, 523, 530, 531, 552, 587, 588, 590, 591, 595, 690, 691, 721, 722, 724, 725, 736, 737, 738, 751, 757, 844, 845, 851, 949, 950; v. 1040, 1066, 1067, 1068, 1070, 1071, 1072, 1178, 1181, 1182, 1188; v. 1259, 1275, 1276, 1277, 1411.

Fasti oxonienses, or Annals of the University of Oxford [1500–1691] . . . ed. Philip Bliss (1820), iii. 18, 20, 29, 183; iv. 514, 527, 532, 533, 534; v. 1039.

History and Antiquities of the University of Oxford, 4 vols. (1786–96), iii. 136–7, 137–8; iv. 849; v. 1191, 1192, 1193, 1262, 1264.

Wood, Ralph, v. 1275.

Flying Voice, The, v. 1275.

Wood, Randall, ii. 347.

Wood, William, ii. **624**.

Wood street, *see* London, streets of.

Woodbridge, Elisabeth, *Studies in Jonson's Comedy* Yale Studies in English, vol. v (1898), iv. 606.

Woodcock of Our Side, see Anonymous.

Woode, John, ii. 624, **625**, 682.

Wooden, Katherine, ii. 501.

Woodford, Elizabeth, ii. 625.

Woodford v. Holland, vi. 130.

Woodford, Robert, ii. 634.

Woodford, Thomas, ii. 384, **624–5**; vi. 216; vii. 11.

Woodgate, Ursula, *see* Quarles, Ursula.

Woodhouse, A. S. P., 'The Argument of Milton's *Comus*', *University of Toronto Quarterly*, xi (1941), iv. 914.

Woodliff v. Browne et Jurdaine, vi. 124.

Woodliffe, Oliver, vi. 125, 126, 128, 129.

Woodliffe, Susan, vi. 125, 129.

Woodruff, Joan, ii. 533.

Woodstock, i. 20; iv. 550, 590, 591, 592, 595, 596, 845; vi. 241; vii. 19.

Hall, vii. 40.

Palace, vi. 135.

Woodward, Gertrude, and James G. McManaway, *A check list of English plays, 1641–1700* (1945), iii. 41.

Woodward, Rowland, iv. 637; v. 1404.

Woolfall, Richard, v. 1052.

Woolwich, Kent, iv. 721.

Worcester, i. 92, 282; iv. 520, 927.

Battle of, v. 1036.

Bishop of, iii. 306.

John Gauden, Bishop of, v. 1269.

Siege of, iv. 521.

Worcester College, Oxford, iv. 705, 721, 730; v. 1101.

Library, vi. 274, 275, 276 n. 1.

Manuscripts, iii. 33, 148; v. 1100, 1102.

Worcester, Earl of, iv. 869.

Company of, i. 158; ii. 363, 469, 486, 499, 518, 525, 609; iv. 555; vi. 123.

Queen Anne's company, vi. 48.

Worcestershire, ii. 635.

Work for Cutlers, see Anonymous.

Work for Jupiter, see Anonymous, *Gigantomachia*.

Worke for Armorours (1609), *see* Dekker, Thomas.

Workmen, ii. 348.

Works of Mercy, The, see Crane, Ralph.

Works, Office of, Declared accounts, vii. 16–124 *passim*.

Worksop Manor, iv. 648.

World, The, see Anonymous.

World Tossed at Tennis, The, see Middleton, Thomas.

World's Idol, or Plutus the God of Wealth, see B., H. H.

World's Wonder, The, see Showing Glass.

'World's wonder', ii. 600.

Worral, Walter, 'The Authorship of "The Costelie Whore"', *M.L.R.* xvii (1922), 411; iv. 500; v. 1313.

Worse Afeared than Hurt, see Wilson, Robert, *Hannibal and Hermes*.

Worsley, Thomas, ii. 471.

Worth v. *Baskervile*, vi. 219.
Worth, Elizabeth, iii. 626.
Worth, Elizeus, ii. 627.
Worth, Ellis, actor, i. 163, 165, 166, 167, 168 n. 2, 169 and n. 2, 170 n. 1, 171, 174, 183 n. 2, 204, 208, 275, 302, 303, 307, 308, 309, 311, 318, 319, 321; ii. **625-7**; iii. 192; v. 1344; vi. 57, 58, 170, 172, 227.
Worth, Marie, ii. 627.
Wortham, John, ii. 356.
Wortley, Sir Francis, ii. 674, 678.
Wotton, Sir Henry, i. 10 n. 6, 126; ii. 551, 552; iii. 142; iv. 792, 793.
  Reliquiae Wottonianae (1672), vi. 179 n. 1.
Wotton, Surrey, v. 1257.
Wrath, John, Esq., iv. 773.
Wren, Christopher, v. 1056.
Wrestlers, vi. 296.
Wrestling, vi. 298; vii. 40.
  In oiled skins, vi. 293, 294.
Wright, Abraham, v. 1275-6.
  Parnassus Biceps, *see* Thorn-Drury, ed.
  The Reformation, v. 1275.
Wright, Aldis, v. 1371.
Wright, Sir Edmund, grocer, vii. 122.
Wright, Herbert G., 'The Date and Authorship of *Ghismonda*', *R.E.S.* xxiii (1947), v. 1340, 1341.
  ed., *Ghismonda*, *A Seventeenth Century Tragedy* (1944), v. 1340, 1341.
Wright, James, v. 1345.
  Country Conversations (1694), v. 1244.
  Historia Histrionica (1699), ii. **691-6**; iii. 402, 407; v. 1087; vi. 15, 53, 93, 155, 156 n., 237, 247.
Wright, John, actor, i. 307, 308, 321, 327 n. 2, 332, 336; ii. **627-8**; vi. 236.
Wright, John, stationer, iii. 25, 82; iv. 565, 583, 590, 712, 893; v. 1060; vi. 236.
Wright, Louis B., i. 11 n. 6 cont.
  'Extraneous Song in Elizabethan Drama after the Advent of Shakespeare', *Stud. Phil.* xxiv (1927), v. 1143, 1365.
  'Game at Chess, A', *T.L.S.* 16 February 1928, iv. 871.
  Middle-Class Culture in Elizabethan England (1935), iv. 553.

'Notes on Thomas Heywood's Later Reputation', *R.E.S.* iv (1928), iv. 554, 557.
Wriothesley, Thomas, Earl of Southampton, *see* Southampton, Earl of.
Wronged Widow's Tragedy, The, *see* Anonymous.
Wroth, Ellis, *see* Worth, Ellis.
Wroth, Lady, iv. 620.
  Impersonated, iv. 620.
Wroth, Sir Robert, iv. 609.
Wroth, Warwick, v. 993, 994.
Wrotham, Kent, iv. 550.
Wyburd manuscript, Bodleian Library, iii. 106, 111.
Wycherley, William, *The Country Wife*, iii. 8.
Wykes, Dr. Thomas, corrector of the press, iii. 6, 24; iv. 822; v. 995, 1002, 1030, 1048.
Wylde, Robert, *see* Wild, Robert.
Wylmington Hayes, Honiton, Devonshire, v. 1315.
Wine Beer and Ale, *see* Anonymous.
Wyngaerde's sketch, vi. 268.
Wyrley, John, iii. 437, 446.
Wyrley, Mary, iii. 446.
Wythies, Anne, v. 1226.

Xantippe, iv. 498.
Xiphilinus, Joannes, Epitome of Dio Cassius's *Roman History*, iv. 838.

Yard of Ale (mock title), v. 1447.
Yarmouth, Norfolk, v. 1267.
Yaxeley, Sir Robert, v. 1422.
Yeoman of the Removing Wardrobe of Beds, vi. 265.
Yeoman of the Revels, ii. 591, 596, 621.
  Remuneration of, ii. 596.
Yeomen, vi. 148.
Yonge, Robert, ii. 642.
York, Duchess of, at theatre, iii. 70.
York, Duke of, later Prince Charles, i. 198; v. 1024.
York, Duke of, Prince Charles's (I) company, *see* Prince Charles.
York, Duke of (James II), i. 129, 191; ii. 424; iii. 276, 374, 377, 378, 412, 446; iv. 690, 717; v. 1220.
  Birthday of, iv. 474, 522, 524; vii. 117.
  Chaplain to, iii. 183.

York (*cont.*)
Company of, iii. 431; iv. 863; v. 1015, 1023, 1080.
Gives robes to players, iii. 206.
House, play at, iii. 431.
Mistress of, iii. 276.
York, i. 67, 271, 273 and n. 3; ii. 471, 473, 529; iii. 2, 173, 178; v. 1087, 1148, 1233; vii. 23.
Archbishop of, v. 1180, 1341.
Corporation Minute Books, vii. 12 n. 1.
Dean of, iii. 144.
Deputy-auditor for, iii. 303.
His Majesty's servants for the city of, i. 24.
Marmion sick at, iv. 738.
Mayor of, iv. 598.
Philip Kynder at, iv. 717.
York House, iv. 691, 692, 693, 842, 843; vii. 13, 59, 64, 107.
Yorkshire, ii. 496.
Yorkshire dialect, iv. 633, 635–6.
Yorkshire Gentleman, The, see Anonymous.
Yorkshire Tragedy,A see Anonymous.
Yorkshire Tragedy, A, see Heywood, Thomas.
Young Admiral, The, see Shirley, James.
'Young Bateman', *see* Anonymous.
Young, Dr., ii. 531.
Young Gallants Whirligig, The (1629), *see* Lenton, Francis.
Young, James, iii. 74.
Young, John, i. 220, 246, 249 n. f cont., 285, 286, 287, 288, 290, 291 n. 2, 297; ii. 628; iii. 233; vi. 99.
Young Ladies Miscellany, see Bellamy, Daniel, the elder.
Young, Mary, vi. 89.
Young, Percy, iii. 109, 110.

Young, Sir Richard, vi. 303.
Young, Robert, iii. 74.
Young, William, *History of Dulwich College, The,* 2 vols. (1889), iv. 749; v. 1448; vi. 139, 153, 154, 220; vii. 44.
Younger Brother, The, see Anonymous.
See Behn, Aphra.
Your Five Gallants, see Middleton, Thomas.
Youth's Innocent and Rational Amusement, see Bellamy, Daniel, the Elder, *The Young Ladies' Miscellany.*

Zany on tumbling (mock title), v. 1447.
Zeals House, Mere, Wiltshire, iii. 162.
Zeno of Byzantium, v. 1175.
Zeno sive Ambitio Infelix, see Simons, Joseph.
Ziszan, Sir Alexander, iv. 736.
Zouch, Edward, Lord, v. 965.
Zouch, Sir Edward, v. 1422; vii. 37.
Zouche, Dr., iv. 851.
Zouche, Francis, v. 1276.
Zouche, Richard, v. 1098, **1276–80.**
The Dove: or Passages of Cosmography (1613) v. 1277.
Fallacy, or the Troubles of Great Hermenia, see *The Sophister.*
Sophister, The, or *The Fallacy, or The Troubles of Great Hermenia,* v. 1277–80, 1392.
Zwartkruis, Theodore, *Habington.* Nijmegen Dissertation, announced in *Research in Progress, P.M.L.A.* lxiii (1948), Supplement, iv. 520.
Zwickert, Max, *Henry Glapthorne* (1881), iv. 473.

PRINTED IN GREAT BRITAIN
AT THE UNIVERSITY PRESS, OXFORD
BY VIVIAN RIDLER
PRINTER TO THE UNIVERSITY